CCNP Cisco LAN Switch

Configuration Study Guide

(Exam 640-404)

CISCO CERTIFIED NETWORK PROFESSIONAL

CCNP Cisco LAN Switch Configuration Study Guide

(Exam 640-404)

Syngress Media, Inc.

Osborne/McGraw-Hill

Berkeley New York St. Louis San Francisco Auckland Bogotá Hamburg London Madrid Mexico City
Milan Montreal New Delhi Panama City Paris São Paulo Singapore Sydney Tokyo Toronto

Osborne/**McGraw-Hill**
2600 Tenth Street
Berkeley, California 94710
U.S.A.

For information on translations or book distributors outside the U.S.A.,
or to arrange bulk purchase discounts for sales promotions, premiums, or
fund-raisers, please contact Osborne/**McGraw-Hill** at the above address.

CCNP Cisco LAN Switch Configuration Study Guide (Exam 640-404)

1234567890 AGM AGM 90198765432109

ISBN 0-07-211906-3

Publisher Brandon A. Nordin	**Project Editor** Jody McKenzie	**Indexer** Karin Arrigoni
Associate Publisher and Editor-in-Chief Scott Rogers	**Editorial Assistant** Tara Davis	**Computer Designers** Gary Corrigan Liz Pauw Roberta Steele Jani Beckwith
Senior Acquisitions Editor Gareth Hancock	**Technical Editors** Neil Lovering Richard Hornbaker	
Editorial Management Syngress Media, Inc.	**Copy Editor** Kathleen Faughnan	**Illustrators** Beth Young Brian Wells
Series Editor Mark Buchmann	**Proofreader** Carol Burbo	**Series Design** Roberta Steele Arlette Crosland

This book was composed with Corel VENTURA.

From Global Knowledge

At Global Knowledge we strive to support the multiplicity of learning styles required by our students to achieve success as technical professionals. In this series of books, it is our intention to offer the reader a valuable tool for successful completion of the CCNP Certification Exam.

As the world's largest IT training company, Global Knowledge is uniquely positioned to offer these books. The expertise gained each year from providing instructor-led training to hundreds of thousands of students worldwide has been captured in book form to enhance your learning experience. We hope that the quality of these books demonstrates our commitment to your lifelong learning success. Whether you choose to learn through the written word, computer-based training, Web delivery, or instructor-led training, Global Knowledge is committed to providing you the very best in each of those categories. For those of you who know Global Knowledge, or those of you who have just found us for the first time, our goal is to be your lifelong competency partner.

Thank you for the opportunity to serve you. We look forward to serving your needs again in the future.

Warmest regards,

Duncan Anderson
President and Chief Executive Officer, Global Knowledge

The Global Knowledge Advantage

Global Knowledge has a global delivery system for its products and services. The company has 28 subsidiaries, and offers its programs through a total of 60+ locations. No other vendor can provide consistent services across a geographic area this large. Global Knowledge is the largest independent information technology education provider, offering programs on a variety of platforms. This enables our multi-platform and multi-national customers to obtain all of their programs from a single vendor. The company has developed the unique CompetusTM Framework software tool and methodology which can quickly reconfigure courseware to the proficiency level of a student on an interactive basis. Combined with self-paced and on-line programs, this technology can reduce the time required for training by prescribing content in only the deficient skills areas. The company has fully automated every aspect of the education process, from registration and follow-up, to "just-in-time" production of courseware. Global Knowledge, through its Enterprise Services Consultancy, can customize programs and products to suit the needs of an individual customer.

Global Knowledge Classroom Education Programs

The backbone of our delivery options is classroom-based education. Our modern, well-equipped facilities staffed with the finest instructors offer programs in a wide variety of information technology topics, many of which lead to professional certifications.

Custom Learning Solutions

This delivery option has been created for companies and governments that value customized learning solutions. For them, our consultancy-based approach of developing targeted education solutions is most effective at helping them meet specific objectives.

Self-Paced and Multimedia Products

This delivery option offers self-paced program titles in interactive CD-ROM, videotape and audio tape programs. In addition, we offer custom development of interactive multimedia courseware to customers and partners. Call us at 1 (888) 427-4228.

Electronic Delivery of Training

Our network-based training service delivers efficient competency-based, interactive training via the World Wide Web and organizational intranets. This leading-edge delivery option provides a custom learning path and "just-in-time" training for maximum convenience to students.

ARG

American Research Group (ARG), a wholly-owned subsidiary of Global Knowledge, one of the largest worldwide training partners of Cisco Systems, offers a wide range of internetworking, LAN/WAN, Bay Networks, FORE Systems, IBM, and UNIX courses. ARG offers hands on network training in both instructor-led classes and self-paced PC-based training.

Global Knowledge Courses Available

Network Fundamentals
- Understanding Computer Networks
- Telecommunications Fundamentals I
- Telecommunications Fundamentals II
- Understanding Networking Fundamentals
- Implementing Computer Telephony Integration
- Introduction to Voice Over IP
- Introduction to Wide Area Networking
- Cabling Voice and Data Networks
- Introduction to LAN/WAN protocols
- Virtual Private Networks
- ATM Essentials

Network Security & Management
- Troubleshooting TCP/IP Networks
- Network Management
- Network Troubleshooting
- IP Address Management
- Network Security Administration
- Web Security
- Implementing UNIX Security
- Managing Cisco Network Security
- Windows NT 4.0 Security

IT Professional Skills
- Project Management for IT Professionals
- Advanced Project Management for IT Professionals
- Survival Skills for the New IT Manager
- Making IT Teams Work

LAN/WAN Internetworking
- Frame Relay Internetworking
- Implementing T1/T3 Services
- Understanding Digital Subscriber Line (xDSL)
- Internetworking with Routers and Switches
- Advanced Routing and Switching
- Multi-Layer Switching and Wire-Speed Routing
- Internetworking with TCP/IP
- ATM Internetworking
- OSPF Design and Configuration
- Border Gateway Protocol (BGP) Configuration

Authorized Vendor Training

Cisco Systems
- Introduction to Cisco Router Configuration
- Advanced Cisco Router Configuration
- Installation and Maintenance of Cisco Routers
- Cisco Internetwork Troubleshooting
- Cisco Internetwork Design
- Cisco Routers and LAN Switches
- Catalyst 5000 Series Configuration
- Cisco LAN Switch Configuration
- Managing Cisco Switched Internetworks
- Configuring, Monitoring, and Troubleshooting Dial-Up Services
- Cisco AS5200 Installation and Configuration
- Cisco Campus ATM Solutions

Bay Networks
- Bay Networks Accelerated Router Configuration
- Bay Networks Advanced IP Routing
- Bay Networks Hub Connectivity
- Bay Networks Accelar 1xxx Installation and Basic Configuration
- Bay Networks Centillion Switching

FORE Systems
- FORE ATM Enterprise Core Products
- FORE ATM Enterprise Edge Products
- FORE ATM Theory
- FORE LAN Certification

Operating Systems & Programming

Microsoft
- Introduction to Windows NT
- Microsoft Networking Essentials
- Windows NT 4.0 Workstation
- Windows NT 4.0 Server
- Advanced Windows NT 4.0 Server
- Windows NT Networking with TCP/IP
- Introduction to Microsoft Web Tools
- Windows NT Troubleshooting
- Windows Registry Configuration

UNIX
- UNIX Level I
- UNIX Level II
- Essentials of UNIX and NT Integration

Programming
- Introduction to JavaScript
- Java Programming
- PERL Programming
- Advanced PERL with CGI for the Web

Web Site Management & Development
- Building a Web Site
- Web Site Management and Performance
- Web Development Fundamentals

High Speed Networking
- Essentials of Wide Area Networking
- Integrating ISDN
- Fiber Optic Network Design
- Fiber Optic Network Installation
- Migrating to High Performance Ethernet

DIGITAL UNIX
- UNIX Utilities and Commands
- DIGITAL UNIX v4.0 System Administration
- DIGITAL UNIX v4.0 (TCP/IP) Network Management
- AdvFS, LSM, and RAID Configuration and Management
- DIGITAL UNIX TruCluster Software Configuration and Management
- UNIX Shell Programming Featuring Kornshell
- DIGITAL UNIX v4.0 Security Management
- DIGITAL UNIX v4.0 Performance Management
- DIGITAL UNIX v4.0 Intervals Overview

DIGITAL OpenVMS
- OpenVMS Skills for Users
- OpenVMS System and Network Node Management I
- OpenVMS System and Network Node Management II
- OpenVMS System and Network Node Management III
- OpenVMS System and Network Node Operations
- OpenVMS for Programmers
- OpenVMS System Troubleshooting for Systems Managers
- Configuring and Managing Complex VMScluster Systems
- Utilizing OpenVMS Features from C
- OpenVMS Performance Management
- Managing DEC TCP/IP Services for OpenVMS
- Programming in C

Hardware Courses
- AlphaServer 1000/1000A Installation, Configuration and Maintenance
- AlphaServer 2100 Server Maintenance
- AlphaServer 4100, Troubleshooting Techniques and Problem Solving

About Syngress Media

Syngress Media creates books and software for Information Technology professionals seeking skill enhancement and career advancement. Its products are designed to comply with vendor and industry standard course curricula and are optimized for certification exam preparation. You can contact Syngress via the Web at http://www.syngress.com.

About the Contributors

Ryan Russell (CCNA, CCNP) has been employed in the networking field for more than 10 years, including more than five years working with Cisco equipment. He has held IT positions ranging from help desk support to network design, providing him with a good perspective on the challenges that face a network manager. Recently, Ryan has been doing mostly information security work involving network security and firewalls. He has completed his CCNP and holds a Bachelors of Science degree in Computer Science

Tony Costa (CCIE #4140, MCSE, CNE) started his career in networking in 1979 working extensively with IBM SNA and TCP/IP networks. He teaches the CLSC course to Cisco employees and the public through Chesapeake Computer Consultants, Inc. He also develops new courses for Cisco, recently contributing to the Interconnecting Cisco Network Devices (ICND) and the IP/TV 3.0 course. Tony lives near the "Silicon Mesa" in New Mexico with his wife Karen, their five children, and a rapidly growing number of pets. You can contact him at tcosta@msn.com.

Glenn Lepore is a Senior Network Engineer with Niche Networks, LLC a network services and training firm in Herndon, Virginia. He has more than 13 years of experience in LAN and WAN design, installation, and troubleshooting. His background includes Frame Relay, X.25, TCP/IP, IPX, and SNA. His experience includes Novell and Unix administration,

Web page design, and Internet Service Provider (ISP) network operations. He is working toward CCIE certification as well as MCSE.

John Dyer (CCIE) is a partner at Niche Networks, LLC, an Internetwork Consulting and Training firm in Herndon, Virginia. He has13 years of experience in systems integration and networking in the information technology industry, including design and installation of LAN/WAN infrastructures, network management and network security platforms. John is a Cisco Certified Instructor teaching Introduction to Cisco Router Configuration, Advanced Cisco Router Configuration, CiscoWorks, and Managing Cisco Switched Internetworks.

Stace Cunningham (CCNA, MCSE, CLSE, COS/2E, CLSI, COS/2I, CLSA, MCPS, A+) is a systems engineer with SDC Consulting in Biloxi, Mississippi. SDC Consulting specializes in the design, engineering, and installation of networks. Stace received his MCSE in October 1996, and is also certified as an IBM Certified LAN Server Engineer, IBM Certified OS/2 Engineer, IBM Certified LAN Server Administrator, Microsoft Certified Product Specialist, IBM Certified LAN Server Instructor, and IBM Certified OS/2 Instructor.

Stace has participated as a Technical Contributor for the IIS 3.0 exam, SMS 1.2 exam, Proxy Server 1.0 exam, Exchange Server 5.0 exam, Exchange Server 5.5 exam, Proxy Server 2.0 exam, IIS 4.0 exam, IEAK exam, and the revised Windows 95 exam. He recently was an instrumental force in the design and engineering of a 1,700-node Windows NT network that is located in more than 20 buildings at Keesler Air Force Base in Mississippi. Among his current projects is assisting in the design and implementation of a 10,000-node Windows NT network, also located at Keesler Air Force Base.

His wife Martha and daughter Marissa are very supportive of the time he spends on the computers located throughout his house.

About the Series Editor

Mark Buchmann (CCIE #3556, CCSI #95062) is a Cisco Certified Internetworking Expert and has been a Certified Cisco Systems Instructor since 1995. He is the owner of MAB Enterprises, Inc, a company providing consulting, network support, training, and various other services. Mark is also a co-owner of www.CertaNet.com, a company providing online certification assistance for a variety of network career paths including all the various Cisco certifications. In his free time he enjoys spending time with his family and boating. He currently lives in Raleigh, North Carolina. Mark is Series Editor for Syngress Cisco books.

Technical Review and From the Classroom Sidebars by:

Neil Lovering (CCIE #1772, CCSI #95010) is a CCIE-certified network consultant and Cisco-certified instructor. He has helped with many large and small network design and optimization projects throughout the United States and Canada, specializing in OSPF configuration and migration. Neil has taught thousands of students over the last few years how to configure Cisco routers and switches, how to design and troubleshoot complex networks, and how to earn various Cisco network certifications. Neil has also authored the first in a series of Cisco-based computer-based training courses offered through Global Knowledge. He is currently working on some Web-based educational sites.

Technical Review by:

Richard D. Hornbaker (CCIE #3355, MCSE, MCNE) is a consultant with the Forté Consulting Group, based in Phoenix, Arizona. He specializes in large-scale routing and switching projects for Fortune 500 companies. Recent projects include a 12,000-node campus network using a combination of routing, switching, and ATM. Richard is currently designing the network for a major corporate merger.

Richard has more than 10 years of internetworking experience and holds several certifications. His skills are diverse, ranging from operating systems and software to telephony systems and data networks. Protocol analysis and troubleshooting are among his strong suits.

ACKNOWLEDGMENTS

We would like to thank the following people:

- Richard Kristof of Global Knowledge for championing the series and providing us access to some great people and information. And to Shelley Everett and Chuck Terrien for all their cooperation.

- Imran Qureshi and Tina Dupart at Cisco for their time and insight.

- To all the incredibly hard-working folks at Osborne/McGraw-Hill: Brandon Nordin, Scott Rogers, Gareth Hancock, Tara Davis, and Jody McKenzie for their help in launching a great series and being solid team players.

CONTENTS AT A GLANCE

CONTENTS

8   Managing the Catalyst 5000 Series Switches ... 281

9   Troubleshooting the Catalyst 5000 311

This book's primary objective is to help you prepare for and pass the required CLSC exam so you can begin to reap the career benefits of CCNP certification. We believe that the only way to do this is to help you increase your knowledge and build your skills. After completing this book, you should feel confident that you have thoroughly reviewed all of the objectives that Cisco has established for the exam.

In This Book

This book is organized around the topics covered within the Cisco exam administered at Sylvan Testing Centers. Cisco has specific objectives for the CLSC exam: we've followed their list carefully, so you can be assured you're not missing anything.

In Every Chapter

We've created a set of chapter components that call your attention to important items, reinforce important points, and provide helpful exam-taking hints. Take a look at what you'll find in every chapter:

- Each chapter begins with the **Certification Objectives**—what you need to know in order to pass the section on the exam dealing with the chapter topic. The Certification Objective headings identify the objectives within the chapter, so you'll always know an objective when you see it!

EXERCISE

- **Certification Exercises** are interspersed throughout the chapters. These are step-by-step exercises that mirror vendor-recommended labs. They help you master skills that are likely to be an area of focus on the exam. Don't just read through the exercises; they are hands-on practice that you should be comfortable completing. Learning by doing is an effective way to increase your competency with a product.

■ **From the Classroom** sidebars describe the issues that come up most often in the training classroom setting. These sidebars give you a valuable perspective into certification- and product-related topics. They point out common mistakes and address questions that have arisen from classroom discussions.

■ **Q & A** sections lay out problems and solutions in a quick-read format:

QUESTIONS AND ANSWERS

My network is growing rapidly and I would like to segment the network at Layer 2 of the OSI model…	Segment the network using a bridge. Bridges function at Layer 2 of the OSI model.
When I configure my RSM with a new subinterface, I often find that I can't ping it right away. The #SHOW INTERFACE display says that it is up and up. What's up?	You are experiencing an interaction between the Catalyst CAM table learning function and the RSM software. The fastest way to clear this condition is to ping the Catalyst SC0 IP client address from the RSM. This forces the RSM's MAC address into the CAM table, resolving the problem.

■ The **Certification Summary** is a succinct review of the chapter and a re-statement of salient points regarding the exam.

■ The **Two-Minute Drill** at the end of every chapter is a checklist of the main points of the chapter. It can be used for last-minute review.

■ **Tables** are liberally sprinkled throughout the chapters. You'll find that these provide an easy way to look up information and show material you may find worthy of memorization:

Protocol	Familiar Name	Port
Trivial File Transfer Protocol	TFTP	69
Domain Name System	DNS	53
Time Service	-	37
NetBIOS Name Server	-	137
NetBIOS Datagram Server	-	138
Boot Protocol (Client and Server)	BOOTP	67 and 68
TACACS	TACACS	49

■ The **Self Test** offers questions similar to those found on the certification exams. The answers to these questions, as well as explanations of the answers, can be found in Appendix A. By taking the Self Test after completing each chapter, you'll reinforce what you've learned from that chapter, while becoming familiar with the structure of the exam questions.

Some Pointers

Once you've finished reading this book, set aside some time to do a thorough review. You might want to return to the book several times and make use of all the methods it offers for reviewing the material:

1. Re-read all the Two-Minute Drills, or have someone quiz you. You also can use the drills as a way to do a quick cram before the exam.

2. *Review all the Q & A scenarios* for quick problem solving.

3. *Re-take the Self Tests.* Taking the tests right after you've read the chapter is a good idea, because it helps reinforce what you've just learned. However, it's an even better idea to go back later and do all the questions in the book in one sitting. Pretend you're taking the exam. (For this reason, you should mark your answers on a separate piece of paper when you go through the questions the first time.)

4. Complete the exercises. Did you do the exercises when you read through each chapter? If not, do them! These exercises are designed to cover exam topics, and there's no better way to get to know this material than by practicing.

5. *Check out the Web site.* Global Knowledge invites you to become an active member of the Access Global Web site. This site is an online mall and an information repository that you'll find invaluable. You can access many types of products to assist you in your preparation for the exams, and you'll be able to participate in forums, online discussions, and threaded discussions. No other book brings you unlimited access to such a resource. You'll find more information about this site in Appendix C.

How to Take a Cisco Certification Examination

By Richard D. Hornbaker (CCIE #3355, CNX, MCSE, MCNE), Forté Consulting Group

This chapter covers the importance of your CCNP certification and prepares you for taking the actual examination. It gives you a few pointers on methods of preparing for the exam, including how to study, register, what to expect, and what to do on exam day.

Catch the Wave!

Congratulations on your pursuit of Cisco certification! In this fast-paced world of networking, few certifications compare to the value of Cisco's program.

The networking industry has virtually exploded in recent years, accelerated by non-stop innovation and the Internet's popularity. Cisco has stayed at the forefront of this tidal wave, maintaining a dominant role in the industry.

Since the networking industry is highly competitive, and evolving technology only increases in its complexity, the rapid growth of the networking industry has created a vacuum of qualified people. There simply aren't enough skilled networking people to meet the demand. Even the most experienced professionals must keep current with the latest technology in order to provide the skills that the industry demands. That's where Cisco certification programs can help networking professionals succeed as they pursue their career.

Cisco started its certification program many years ago, offering only the designation of Cisco Certified Internetwork Expert, or CCIE. Through the CCIE program, Cisco provided a means to meet the growing demand for experts in the field of networking. However, the CCIE tests are brutal, with a failure rate over 80 percent. (Fewer than five percent of candidates pass on their first attempt.) As you might imagine, very few people ever attain CCIE status.

In early 1998, Cisco recognized the need for intermediate certifications, and several new programs were created. Four intermediate certifications were added: CCNA (Cisco Certified Network Associate), CCNP (Cisco Certified Network Professional), CCDA (Cisco Certified Design Associate), and CCDP (Cisco Certified Design Professional). Two specialties were also created for the CCIE program: WAN Switching and ISP Dial-up.

CCNP @dvice

I would encourage you to take beta tests when they are available. Not only are the beta exams less than the cost of the final exams (some are even free!), but also, if you pass the beta, you will receive credit for passing the exam. If you don't pass the beta, you will have seen every question in the pool of available questions, and can use this information when preparing to take the exam for the second time. Remember to jot down important information immediately after the exam, if you didn't pass. You will have to do this after leaving the exam area, since materials written during the exam are retained by the testing center. This information can be helpful when you need to determine which areas of the exam were most challenging for you as you study for the subsequent test.

Why Vendor Certification?

Over the years, vendors have created their own certification programs because of industry demand. This demand arises when the marketplace needs skilled professionals and an easy way to identify them. Vendors benefit because it promotes people skilled in their product. Professionals benefit because it boosts their career. Employers benefit because it helps them identify qualified people.

In the networking industry, technology changes too often and too quickly to rely on traditional means of certification, such as universities and trade associations. Because of the investment and effort required to keep network certification programs current, vendors are the only organizations suited to keep pace with the changes. In general, such vendor certification programs are excellent, with most of them requiring a solid foundation in the essentials, as well as their particular product line.

Corporate America has come to appreciate these vendor certification programs and the value they provide. Employers recognize that certifications, like university degrees, do not guarantee a level of knowledge, experience or performance; rather, they establish a baseline for comparison. By seeking to hire vendor-certified employees, a company can assure itself that, not only has it found a person skilled in networking, but it has also hired a person skilled in the specific products the company uses.

Technical professionals have also begun to realize the value of certification and the impact it can have on their careers. By completing a certification program, professionals gain an endorsement of their skills from a major industry source. This endorsement can boost their current position, and it makes finding the next job even easier. Often, a certification determines whether a first interview is even granted.

Today, a certification may place you ahead of the pack. Tomorrow, it will be a necessity to keep from being left in the dust.

CCNP 🖐 **advice** *Signing up for an exam has become more effortless with the new Web-based test registration system. To sign up for any of CCNP exams, access http://www.2test.com, and register for the Cisco Career Certification path. You will need to get an Internet account and password, if you do not already have one for 2test.com. Just select the option for first time registration, and the Web site will walk you through that process. The registration wizard even provides maps to the testing centers, something that is not available when calling Sylvan Prometric on the telephone.*

Cisco's Certification Program

As previously mentioned, Cisco now has six certifications for the Routing and Switching career track, and four certifications for the WAN Switching career track. While Cisco recommends a series of courses for each of these certifications, they are not required. Ultimately, certification is dependent upon a candidate passing a series of exams. With the right experience and study materials, each of these exams can be passed without taking the associated class. Table i-1 shows the various Cisco certifications and tracks.

Figure i-1 shows Cisco's Routing and Switching track, with both the Network Design and Network Support paths. The CCNA is the foundation of the Routing and Switching track, after which candidates can pursue either the Network Design path to CCDA and CCDP, or the Network Support path to CCNP and CCIE.

TABLE i-1   Cisco Certifications

Track	Certification	Acronym
Routing and Switching: Network Support	Cisco Certified Network Associate	CCNA
Routing and Switching: Network Support	Cisco Certified Network Professional	CCNP
Routing and Switching: Network Support	Cisco Certified Internetwork Expert (Routing and Switching)	CCIE-R/S
Routing and Switching: Network Support	Cisco Certified Internetwork Expert (ISP Dial Technology)	CCIE-ISP Dial
Routing and Switching: Network Design	Cisco Certified Design Associate	CCDA
Routing and Switching: Network Design	Cisco Certified Design Professional	CCDP
WAN Switching: Network Support	Cisco Certified Network Associate—WAN switching	CCNA-WAN Switching
WAN Switching: Network Support	Cisco Certified Network Professional—WAN switching	CCNP-WAN Switching
WAN Switching: Network Support	Cisco Certified Internetwork Expert—WAN Switching	CCIE-WAN Switching
WAN Switching: Network Design	Cisco Certified Design Professional—WAN Switching	CCDP-WAN Switching

FIGURE i-1

Cisco's Routing and
Switching certification track

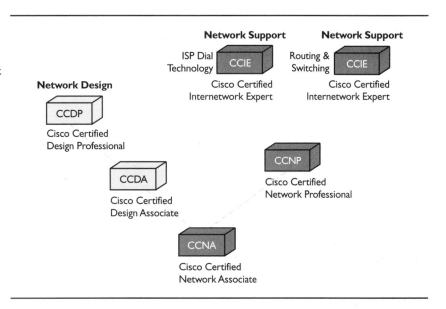

*In addition to finding the technical objectives that are being tested
for each exam, you will find much more useful information on Cisco's
Web site at http://www.cisco.com/warp/public/10/wwtraining/certprog.
You will find information on becoming certified, exam-specific
information, sample test questions, and the latest news on Cisco
certification. This is the most important site you will find on your
journey to becoming Cisco certified.*

Table i-2 shows a matrix of the exams required for each Cisco certification.
Note that candidates have the choice of taking either the single Foundation
R/S exam, or the set of three ACRC, CLSC, and CMTD exams—all four
exams are not required.

You may hear veterans refer to this CCIE R/S Qualifying Exam as the
"Cisco Drake test." This is a carryover from the early days, when Sylvan
Prometric's name was Drake Testing Centers and Cisco only had the
one exam.

TABLE i-2						

Exam Name	Exam #	CCNA	CCDA	CCNP	CCDP	CCIE
CCNA 1.0	640-407	x	x	x	x	
CDS 1.0	9E0-004		x		x	
Foundation Routing and Switching	640-409			x	x	
ACRC	640-403			x	x	
CLSC	640-404			x	x	
CMTD	640-405			x	x	
CIT 3.0	640-406 (or exam 640-440)			x		
CIT 4.0	640-440			x		
CID	640-025				x	
CCIE R/S Qualifying						x
CCIE Lab						x

Examinations Required for Cisco Certifications

CCNP advice

When I find myself stumped answering multiple-choice questions, I use my scratch paper to write down the two or three answers I consider the strongest, and then underlining the answer I feel is most likely correct. Here is an example of what my scratch paper looks like when I've gone through the test once:

21. B or C

33. A or C

This is extremely helpful when you mark the question and continue on. You can then return to the question and immediately pick up your thought process where you left off. Use this technique to avoid having to re-read and re-think questions.

You will also need to use your scratch paper during complex, text-based scenario questions to create visual images to better understand the question. For example, during the CCNP exam you will need to draw multiple networks and the connections between them. By drawing the layout while you are interpreting the answer, you may find a hint that you would not have found without your own visual aid. This technique is especially helpful if you are a visual learner.

Computer-Based Testing

In a perfect world, you would be assessed for your true knowledge of a subject, not simply how you respond to a series of test questions. But life isn't perfect, and it just isn't practical to evaluate everyone's knowledge on a one-to-one basis. (Cisco actually does have a one-to-one evaluation, but it's reserved for the CCIE Laboratory exam, and the waiting list is quite long.)

For the majority of its certifications, Cisco evaluates candidates using a computer-based testing service operated by Sylvan Prometric. This service is quite popular in the industry, and it is used for a number of vendor certification programs, including Novell's CNE and Microsoft's MCSE. Thanks to Sylvan Prometric's large number of facilities, exams can be administered worldwide, generally in the same town as a prospective candidate.

For the most part, Sylvan Prometric exams work similarly from vendor to vendor. However, there is an important fact to know about Cisco's exams: they use the traditional Sylvan Prometric test format, not the newer adaptive format. This gives the candidate an advantage, since the traditional format allows answers to be reviewed and revised during the test. (The adaptive format does not.)

CCNP Advice *Many experienced test takers do not go back and change answers unless they have a good reason to do so. Only change an answer when you feel you may have misread or misinterpreted the question the first time. Nervousness may make you second-guess every answer and talk yourself out of a correct one.*

To discourage simple memorization, Cisco exams present a different set of questions every time the exam is administered. In the development of the exam, hundreds of questions are compiled and refined using beta testers. From this large collection, a random sampling is drawn for each test.

Each Cisco exam has a specific number of questions and test duration. Testing time is typically generous, and the time remaining is always displayed in the corner of the testing screen, along with the number of remaining questions. If time expires during an exam, the test terminates, and incomplete answers are counted as incorrect.

CCNP Advice

I have found it extremely helpful to put a check next to each objective as I find it is satisfied by the proposed solution. If the proposed solution does not satisfy an objective, you do not need to continue with the rest of the objectives. Once you have determined which objectives are fulfilled you can count your check marks and answer the question appropriately. This is a very effective testing technique!

At the end of the exam, your test is immediately graded, and the results are displayed on the screen. Scores for each subject area are also provided, but the system will not indicate which specific questions were missed. A report is automatically printed at the proctor's desk for your files. The test score is electronically transmitted back to Cisco.

In the end, this computer-based system of evaluation is reasonably fair. You might feel that one or two questions were poorly worded; this can certainly happen, but you shouldn't worry too much. Ultimately, it's all factored into the required passing score.

Question Types

Cisco exams pose questions in a variety of formats, most of which are discussed here. As candidates progress toward the more advanced certifications, the difficulty of the exams is intensified, both through the subject matter as well as the question formats.

CCNP Online

In order to pass these challenging exams, you may want to talk with other test takers to determine what is being tested, and what to expect in terms of difficulty. The most helpful way to communicate with other CCNP hopefuls is the Cisco mailing list. With this mailing list, you will receive e-mail every day from other members discussing everything imaginable concerning Cisco networking equipment and certification. Access http://www.cisco.com/warp/public/84/1.html to learn how to subscribe to this wealth of information.

True/False

The classic true/false question format is not used in the Cisco exams, for the obvious reason that a simple guess has a 50 percent chance of being correct.

Instead, true/false questions are posed in multiple-choice format, requiring the candidate to identify the true or false statement from a group of selections.

Multiple Choice

Multiple choice is the primary format for questions in Cisco exams. These questions may be posed in a variety of ways.

"SELECT THE CORRECT ANSWER."   This is the classic multiple-choice question, where the candidate selects a single answer from a list of about four choices. In addition to the question's wording, the choices are presented in a Windows "radio button" format, where only one answer can be selected at a time.

"SELECT THE 3 CORRECT ANSWERS."   The multiple-answer version is similar to the single-choice version, but multiple answers must be provided. This is an "all-or-nothing" format; all the correct answers must be selected, or the entire question is incorrect. In this format, the question specifies exactly how many answers must be selected. Choices are presented in a check box format, allowing more than one answer to be selected. In addition, the testing software prevents too many answers from being selected.

"SELECT ALL THAT APPLY."   The open-ended version is the most difficult multiple-choice format, since the candidate does not know how many answers should be selected. As with the multiple-answer version, all the correct answers must be selected to gain credit for the question. If too many answers are selected, no credit is given. This format presents choices in check box format, but the testing software does not advise the candidates whether they've selected the correct number of answers.

CCNP Online

Make it easy on yourself and find some "braindumps." These are notes about the exam from test takers, which indicate the most difficult concepts tested, what to look out for, and sometimes even what not to bother studying. Several of these can be found at http://www.dejanews.com. Simply do a search for CCNP and browse the recent postings. Another good resource is at http://www.groupstudy.com.

Freeform Response

Freeform responses are prevalent in Cisco's advanced exams, particularly where the subject focuses on router configuration and commands. In the freeform format, no choices are provided. Instead, the test prompts for user input and the candidate must type the correct answer. This format is similar to an essay question, except the response must be very specific, allowing the computer to evaluate the answer.

For example, the question

Type the command for viewing routes learned via the EIGRP protocol.

requires the answer

```
show ip route eigrp
```

For safety's sake, you should completely spell out router commands, rather than using abbreviations. In the above example, the abbreviated command SH IP ROU EI works on a real router, but might be counted wrong by the testing software. The freeform response questions are almost always commands used in the Cisco IOS.

Fill in the Blank

Fill-in-the-blank questions are less common in Cisco exams. They may be presented in multiple-choice or freeform response format.

Exhibits

Exhibits accompany many exam questions, usually showing a network diagram or a router configuration. These exhibits are displayed in a separate window, which is opened by clicking the Exhibit button at the bottom of the screen. In some cases, the testing center may provide exhibits in printed format at the start of the exam.

Scenarios

While the normal line of questioning tests a candidate's "book knowledge," scenarios add a level of complexity. Rather than just ask technical questions, they apply the candidate's knowledge to real-world situations.

Scenarios generally consist of one or two paragraphs and an exhibit that describe a company's needs or network configuration. This description is followed by a series of questions and problems that challenge the candidate's ability to address the situation. Scenario-based questions are commonly found in exams relating to network design, but they appear to some degree in each of the Cisco exams.

CCNP advice

You will know you are coming up on a series of scenario questions, because they are preceded with a blue screen, indicating that the following questions will have the same scenario, but different solutions. You must remember the scenario will be the same during the series of questions, which means you do not have to spend time reading the scenario again.

Exam Objectives for CLSC

Cisco has a clear set of objectives for the CLSC exam, upon which the exam questions are based. The following list gives a good summary, by topic, of the things a candidate must know how to do for this exam:

Overall CLSC Course Objectives

1. Describe the major features of the Catalyst switches.
2. Describe the architecture and functions of the major components of the Catalyst switches.
3. Place Catalyst series switches in a network for optimal performance benefit.
4. Use the command-line menu or menu-driven interface to configure the Catalyst series switches and their switching modules.
5. Use the command-line menu or menu-driven interface to configure trunks, virtual LANs, and ATM LAN Emulation.
6. Maintain Catalyst series switches and perform basic troubleshooting.

Introduction to Switching Concepts

7. Describe the advantages of LAN segmentation.
8. Describe LAN segmentation using bridges.
9. Describe LAN segmentation routers.
10. Describe LAN segmentation using switches.

11. Name and describe two switching methods.

12. Describe full- and half-duplex Ethernet operations.

13. Describe Token Ring switching concepts.

Virtual LANs

14. Define VLANs.

15. Name seven reasons to create VLANs.

16. Describe the role switches play in the creation of VLANs.

17. Describe VLAN frame filtering and VLAN frame tagging.

18. Describe how switches can be used with hubs.

19. Name the five components of VLAN implementations.

20. Describe static and dynamic VLANs.

21. Describe the VLAN technologies.

22. Describe Token Ring VLANs.

23. Describe Cisco's VLAN architecture.

Placing Catalyst 5000 Series Switches in Your Network

24. Describe demand nodes and resource nodes.

25. Describe configuration rules for demand nodes and resource nodes.

26. Describe local resources and remote resources.

27. Describe configuration rules for local resources and remote resources.

28. Name five applications for Catalyst 5000 series switches.

Catalyst 5000 Series Switch

29. Describe Catalyst 5000 series switch product evolution.

30. Describe Catalyst 5000 product features.

31. Describe Catalyst 5002 product features.

32. Describe Catalyst 5500 product features.

Catalyst 5000 Series Switch Product Architecture

33. Describe the architecture and function of major components of the Catalyst 5000 series switch:

   ■ Processors : NMP, MCP, and LCP

   ■ Logic Units : LTL, CBL, Arbiter, and EARL

   ■ ASICs : SAINT, SAGE, SAMBA, and Phoenix

34. Trace a frame's progress through a Catalyst 5000 series switch.

Catalyst 5000 Series Switch Hardware

35. Describe the hardware features, functions, and benefits of Catalyst 5000 series switches.

36. Describe the hardware features and functions of the Supervisor engine.

37. Describe the hardware features and functions of the modules in the Catalyst 5000 series switches.

Configuring Catalyst 5000 Series Switches

38. Prepare network connections.

39. Establish a serial connection.

40. Use the Catalyst 5000 switch CLI to:

   ■ Enter privileged mode.

   ■ Set system information.

   ■ Configure interface types.

Managing the Catalyst 5000 Series Switch Family

41. Upon completion of this module, you will be able to describe the different ways of managing the Catalyst 5000 series switch, including:

   ■ Out-of-band management (console port)

   ■ In-band management (network connection using SNMP)

   ■ RMON

- SPAN
- CWSI

Troubleshooting the Catalyst 5000 Series Switches

42. Upon completion of this module, you will be able to:

- Describe the approach for troubleshooting Catalyst
- Describe the physical-layer problem areas
- Use the *show* commands to troubleshoot problems
- Describe the switch hardware status
- Describe network test equipment

Catalyst 5000 Series Switch FDDI Module

43. Describe the major features and functions of the Catalyst 5000 FDDI/CDDI Module.

44. Describe IEEE 802.10 VLANs.

45. Configure the Catalyst 5000 FDDI/CDDI Module.

Introduction to ATM LAN Emulation

46. Define LAN emulation.

47. Describe the LAN Emulation components.

48. Describe the start-up procedure of a LAN Emulation Client.

49. Describe how one LEC establishes communication with another LEC.

50. Discuss how internetworking is achieved in a LANE environment.

Catalyst 5000 Series Switch ATM LANE Module

51. List the features of the Catalyst 5000 LANE module.

52. Outline the performance ratings for the ATM bus and the switching bus.

53. Describe how to access the CLI for the LANE module.

54. Describe the Simple Server Redundancy Protocol (SSRP).

Configuring the Catalyst 5000 Series Switch ATM LANE Module

55. Explain ATM address structure.

56. Describe how ATM addresses are automatically assigned.

57. Describe the rules for assigning ATM components to interfaces.

58. Configure LANE components on a Catalyst 5000 switch.

Catalyst 1900 and Catalyst 2820 Hardware

59. Describe the major features and benefits of the Catalyst 1900 and Catalyst 2820 switches.

60. Describe the hardware components and their functions of the Catalyst 1900 and Catalyst 2820 switches.

61. Describe the architecture.

Catalyst 1900 and Catalyst 2820 Features

62. Describe the following key features and applications of the Catalyst 1900 and Catalyst 2820 switches:

   - Switching modes.
   - Virtual LANs.
   - Multicast packet filtering and registration.
   - Broadcast storm control.
   - Management support, CDP, and CGMP.

63. Trace a frame's progress through a Catalyst 1900 or a Catalyst 2820 switch.

Configuring Catalyst 1900 and Catalyst 2820 Switches

64. Use the Catalyst 1900 and Catalyst 2820 switch menus for configuration.

65. Configure IP addresses and ports on the Catalyst 1900 and Catalyst 2820 switches.

66. Configure VLANs on the Catalyst 1900 and Catalyst 2820 switches.

67. View the Catalyst 1900 and Catalyst 2820 switch reports and summaries.

68. Configure the ATM LANE module on the Catalyst 2820 switch.

Catalyst 3000 Series Switches

69. Describe Catalyst 3000 series LAN switch products.

70. Describe Catalyst 3000 series LAN switch product differences.

71. Describe the Catalyst Stack System.

Configuring the Catalyst 3000 Series Switches

72. Perform initial setup of a Catalyst 3000 series switch.

73. Configure the switch for management.

74. Configure port parameters.

75. Configure VLANs and trunk links.

76. Configure the ATM LANE module.

77. Perform basic router module configuration.

Maintaining the Catalyst 1900 and Catalyst 2820 Switches

78. Describe the POST and diagnostic messages on the Catalyst 1900 Catalyst 2820 switches.

79. Describe the cabling guidelines for the Catalyst 1900 Catalyst 2820 switches.

80. Use the statistics and reports to maintain the Catalyst 1900 Catalyst 2820 switches.

81. Describe the firmware upgrade procedures for the Catalyst 1900 Catalyst 2820 switches.

Troubleshooting the Catalyst 3000 Series Switches

82. Troubleshooting the Catalyst 3000 series switch subsystems.

83. Troubleshooting network interfaces and connections.

84. Use the switch LEDs to isolate problems.

85. Isolate network segment problems.

Studying Techniques

First and foremost, give yourself plenty of time to study. Networking is a complex field, and you can't expect to cram what you need to know into a single study session. It is a field best learned over time, by studying a subject and then applying your knowledge. Build yourself a study schedule and stick to it, but be reasonable about the pressure you put on yourself, especially if you're studying in addition to your regular duties at work.

CCNP Advice

One easy technique to use in studying for certification exams is the 15-minutes per day effort. Simply study for a minimum of 15 minutes every day. It is a small, but significant commitment. If you have a day where you just can't focus, then give up at 15 minutes. If you have a day where it flows completely for you, study longer. As long as you have more of the "flow days," your chances of succeeding are extremely high.

Second, practice and experiment. In networking, you need more than knowledge; you need understanding, too. You can't just memorize facts to be effective; you need to understand why events happen, how things work, and (most importantly) how they break.

The best way to gain deep understanding is to take your book knowledge to the lab. Try it out. Make it work. Change it a little. Break it. Fix it. Snoop around "under the hood." If you have access to a network analyzer, like Network Associate's Sniffer, put it to use. You can gain amazing insight to the inner workings of a network by watching devices communicate with each other.

Unless you have a very understanding boss, don't experiment with router commands on a production router. A seemingly innocuous command can have a nasty side effect. If you don't have a lab, your local Cisco office or Cisco users group may be able to help. Many training centers also allow students access to their lab equipment during off-hours.

Another excellent way to study is through case studies. Case studies are articles or interactive discussions that offer real-world examples of how technology is applied to meet a need. These examples can serve to cement your understanding of a technique or technology by seeing it put to use. Interactive discussions offer added value because you can also pose questions of your own. User groups are an excellent source of examples, since the purpose of these groups is to share information and learn from each other's experiences.

And not to be missed is the Cisco Networkers conference. Although renowned for its wild party and crazy antics, this conference offers a wealth of information. Held every year in cities around the world, it includes three days of technical seminars and presentations on a variety of subjects. As you might imagine, it's very popular. You have to register early to get the classes you want.

Then, of course, there is the Cisco Web site. This little gem is loaded with collections of technical documents and white papers. As you progress to more advanced subjects, you will find great value in the large number of examples and reference materials available. But be warned: You need to do a lot of digging to find the really good stuff. Often, your only option is to browse every document returned by the search engine to find exactly the one you need. This effort pays off. Most CCIEs I know have compiled six to ten binders of reference material from Cisco's site alone.

Scheduling Your Exam

The Cisco exams are scheduled by calling Sylvan Prometric directly at (800) 204-3926. For locations outside the United States, your local number can be found on Sylvan's Web site at http://www.prometric.com. Sylvan representatives can schedule your exam, but they don't have information about the certification programs. Questions about certifications should be directed to Cisco's training department.

The aforementioned Sylvan telephone number is specific to Cisco exams, and it goes directly to the Cisco representatives inside Sylvan. These representatives are familiar enough with the exams to find them by name, but it's best if you have the specific exam number handy when you call. After all, you wouldn't want to be scheduled and charged for the wrong exam (for example, the instructor's version, which is significantly harder).

Exams can be scheduled up to a year in advance, although it's really not necessary. Generally, scheduling a week or two ahead is sufficient to reserve the day and time you prefer. When scheduling, operators will search for testing centers in your area. For convenience, they can also tell which testing centers you've used before.

Sylvan accepts a variety of payment methods, with credit cards being the most convenient. When paying by credit card, you can even take tests the same day you call—provided, of course, that the testing center has room. (Quick scheduling can be handy, especially if you want to re-take an exam immediately.) Sylvan will mail you a receipt and confirmation of your testing date, although this generally arrives after the test has been taken. If you need to cancel or reschedule an exam, remember to call at least one day before your exam, or you'll lose your test fee.

When registering for the exam, you will be asked for your ID number. This number is used to track your exam results back to Cisco. It's important that you use the same ID number each time you register, so that Cisco can follow your progress. Address information provided when you first register is also used by Cisco to ship certificates and other related material. In the United States, your Social Security Number is commonly used as your ID number. However, Sylvan can assign you a unique ID number if you prefer not to use your Social Security Number.

Table i-3 shows the available Cisco exams and the number of questions and duration of each. This information is subject to change as Cisco revises the exams, so it's a good idea to verify the details when registering for an exam.

In addition to the regular Sylvan Prometric testing sites, Cisco also offers facilities for taking exams free of charge at each Networkers conference in the USA. As you might imagine, this option is quite popular, so reserve your exam time as soon as you arrive at the conference.

| TABLE i-3 | Cisco Exam Lengths and Question Counts |

Exam Title	Exam Number	Number of Questions	Duration (minutes)	Exam Fee (US$)
Cisco Design Specialist (CDS)	9E0-004	80	180	$100
Cisco Internetwork Design (CID)	640-025	100	120	$100
Advanced Cisco Router Configuration (ACRC)	640-403	72	90	$100
Cisco LAN Switch Configuration (CLSC)	640-404	70	60	$100
Configuring, Monitoring, and Troubleshooting Dialup Services (CMTD)	640-405	64	90	$100
Cisco Internetwork Troubleshooting (CIT)*	640-440	77	105	$100
Cisco Certified Network Associate (CCNA)	640-407	70	90	$100
Foundation Routing & Switching	640-409	132	165	$100
CCIE Routing & Switching Qualification	350-001	100	120	$200
CCIE Certification Laboratory	N/A	N/A	2 days	$1000

*As of this writing, Cisco is still offering the CIT, exam 640-406, which has 69 questions and runs 60 minutes. The exam will likely retire once the new exam is established.

Arriving at the Exam

As with any test, you'll be tempted to cram the night before. Resist that temptation. You should know the material by this point, and if you're too groggy in the morning, you won't remember what you studied anyway. Instead, get a good night's sleep.

Arrive early for your exam; it gives you time to relax and review key facts. Take the opportunity to review your notes. If you get burned out on studying, you can usually start your exam a few minutes early. On the other hand, I don't recommend arriving late. Your test could be cancelled, or you may not be left with enough time to complete the exam.

When you arrive at the testing center, you'll need to sign in with the exam administrator. In order to sign in, you need to provide two forms of identification. Acceptable forms include government-issued IDs (for example, passport or driver's license), credit cards, and company ID badge. One form of ID must include a photograph.

Aside from a brain full of facts, you don't need to bring anything else to the exam. In fact, your brain is about all you're allowed to take into the exam. All the tests are "closed book", meaning you don't get to bring any reference materials with you. You're also not allowed to take any notes out of the exam room. The test administrator will provide you with paper and a pencil. Some testing centers may provide a small marker board instead.

Calculators are not allowed, so be prepared to do any necessary math (such as hex-binary-decimal conversions or subnet masks) in your head or on paper. Additional paper is available if you need it.

Leave your pager and telephone in the car, or turn them off. They only add stress to the situation, since they are not allowed in the exam room, and can sometimes still be heard if they ring outside of the room. Purses, books, and other materials must be left with the administrator before entering the exam. While in the exam room, it's important that you don't disturb other candidates; talking is not allowed during the exam.

Once in the testing room, the exam administrator logs onto your exam, and you have to verify that your ID number and the exam number are correct. If this is the first time you've taken a Cisco test, you can select a brief tutorial for the exam software. Before the test begins, you will be provided with facts about the exam, including the duration, the number of questions, and the score required for passing. Then the clock starts ticking and the fun begins.

The testing software is Windows-based, but you won't have access to the main desktop or any of the accessories. The exam is presented in full screen, with a single question per screen. Navigation buttons allow you to move forward and backward between questions. In the upper-right corner of the screen, counters show the number of questions and time remaining. Most importantly, there is a 'Mark' checkbox in the upper-left corner of the screen—this will prove to be a critical tool in your testing technique.

Test-Taking Techniques

One of the most frequent excuses I hear for failing a Cisco exam is "poor time management." Without a plan of attack, candidates are overwhelmed by the exam or become sidetracked and run out of time. For the most part, if you are comfortable with the material, the allotted time is more than enough to complete the exam. The trick is to keep the time from slipping away during any one particular problem.

The obvious goal of an exam is to answer the questions effectively, although other aspects of the exam can distract from this goal. After taking a fair number of computer-based exams, I've naturally developed a technique for tackling the problem, which I share with you here. Of course, you still need to learn the material. These steps just help you take the exam more efficiently.

Size Up the Challenge

First, take a quick pass through all the questions in the exam. "Cherry-pick" the easy questions, answering them on the spot. Briefly read each question, noticing the type of question and the subject. As a guideline, try to spend less than 25 percent of your testing time in this pass.

This step lets you assess the scope and complexity of the exam, and it helps you determine how to pace your time. It also gives you an idea of where to find potential answers to some of the questions. Often, the answer to one question is shown in the exhibit of another. Sometimes the wording of one question might lend clues or jog your thoughts for another question.

Imagine that the following questions are posed in this order:

Question 1: "Review the router configurations and network diagram in exhibit XYZ (not shown here). Which devices should be able to ping each other?"

Question 2: "If RIP routing were added to exhibit XYZ, which devices would be able to ping each other?"

The first question seems straightforward. Exhibit XYZ probably includes a diagram and a couple of router configurations. Everything looks normal, so you decide that all devices can ping each other.

Now, consider the hint left by the Question 2. When you answered Question 1, did you notice that the configurations were missing the routing protocol? Oops! Being alert to such clues can help you catch your own mistakes.

If you're not entirely confident with your answer to a question, answer it anyway, but check the Mark box to flag it for later review. In the event that you run out of time, at least you've provided a "first guess" answer, rather than leaving it blank.

Take on the Scenario Questions

Second, go back through the entire test, using the insight you gained from the first go-through. For example, if the entire test looks difficult, you'll know better than to spend more than a minute or so on each question. Break down the pacing into small milestones; for example, "I need to answer 10 questions every 15 minutes."

At this stage, it's probably a good idea to skip past the time-consuming questions, marking them for the next pass. Try to finish this phase before you're 50 – 60 percent through the testing time.

By now, you probably have a good idea where the scenario questions are found. A single scenario tends to have several questions associated with it, but they aren't necessarily grouped together in the exam. Rather than re-reading the scenario every time you encounter a related question, save some time and answer the questions as a group.

Tackle the Complex Problems

Third, go back through all the questions you marked for review, using the Review Marked button in the question review screen. This step includes taking a second look at all the questions you were unsure of in previous passes, as well as tackling the time-consuming ones you deferred until now. Chisel away at this group of questions until you've answered them all.

If you're more comfortable with a previously marked question, unmark it now. Otherwise, leave it marked. Work your way through the time-consuming questions now, especially those requiring manual calculations. Unmark them when you're satisfied with the answer.

By the end of this step, you've answered every question in the test, despite having reservations about some of your answers. If you run out of time in the next step, at least you won't lose points for lack of an answer. You're in great shape if you still have 10–20 percent of your time remaining.

Review Your Answers

Now you're cruising! You've answered all the questions, and you're ready to do a quality check. Take yet another pass (yes, one more) through the entire test, briefly re-reading each question and your answer. Be cautious about revising answers at this point unless you're sure a change is warranted. If there's a doubt about changing the answer, I always trust my first instinct and leave the original answer intact.

Rarely are "trick" questions asked, so don't read too much into the questions. Again, if the wording of the question confuses you, leave the answer intact. Your first impression was probably right.

Be alert for last-minute clues. You're pretty familiar with nearly every question at this point, and you may find a few clues that you missed before.

The Grand Finale

When you're confident with all your answers, finish the exam by submitting it for grading. After what will seem like the longest 10 seconds of your life, the testing software will respond with your score. This is usually displayed as a bar graph, showing the minimum passing score, your score, and a PASS/FAIL indicator.

If you're curious, you can review the statistics of your score at this time. Answers to specific questions are not presented; rather, questions are lumped into categories, and results are tallied for each category. This detail is also printed on a report that has been automatically printed at the exam administrator's desk.

As you leave the exam, you'll need to leave your scratch paper behind or return it to the administrator. (Some testing centers track the number of sheets you've been given, so be sure to return them all.) In exchange, you'll receive a copy of the test report.

This report will be embossed with the testing center's seal, and you should keep it in a safe place. Normally, the results are automatically transmitted to Cisco, but occasionally you might need the paper report to prove that you passed the exam. Your personnel file is probably a good place to keep this report; the file tends to follow you everywhere, and it doesn't hurt to have favorable exam results turn up during a performance review.

Re-Testing

If you don't pass the exam, don't be discouraged—networking is complex stuff. Try to have a good attitude about the experience, and get ready to try again. Consider yourself a little more educated. You know the format of the test a little better, and the report shows which areas you need to strengthen.

If you bounce back quickly, you'll probably remember several of the questions you might have missed. This will help you focus your study efforts in the right area. Serious go-getters will re-schedule the exam for a couple days after the previous attempt, while the study material is still fresh in their mind.

Ultimately, remember that Cisco certifications are valuable because they're hard to get. After all, if anyone could get one, what value would it have? In the end, it takes a good attitude and a lot of studying, but you can do it!

CISCO CERTIFIED NETWORK PROFESSIONAL

1

Introduction to Switching Concepts

CERTIFICATION OBJECTIVES

A s businesses grow, so do the networks they use to share information. As the networks grow, bandwidth becomes an issue. Simply put, you can only squeeze so much data through a pipe before it becomes overloaded. When you try to send more data than it can handle, slowdowns and bottlenecks occur for everyone. This chapter discusses collisions and broadcast domains and how they affect the traffic on the network. In the second section, LAN segmentation using a variety of equipment is covered. The third section discusses two methods of switching, cut-through and store and forward. The fourth section discusses LAN switching, and the final section discusses Token Ring switching.

Collisions and Broadcast Domains

Two items that can affect the performance of the network significantly are collisions and broadcast domains. Let's look at how both of these items slow down the network.

Collisions

Imagine trying to pull out on the freeway, and each time you tried, another vehicle blocked your entry. If you pulled out, a collision would occur. This is similar to what happens on an Ethernet network using carrier sense multiple access with collision detection (CSMA/CD). The Institute of Electrical and Electronics Engineers (IEEE) defines a CSMA/CD Ethernet network as the 802.3 standard that is widely used throughout the networking industry. The Media Access Control (MAC) sublayer of Layer 2 of the Open Systems Interconnect (OSI) model uses CSMA/CD for access to the physical medium.

All nodes on the network are free to transmit whenever they need to, and a CSMA/CD network attempts to ensure that no one else is transmitting on the wire before allowing another node the opportunity to transmit. However, it is possible for two nodes to see the wire as clear and transmit at the same time, as shown by Node 1 and Node 4 in Figure 1-1. When this occurs, a collision results. To continue our driving analogy, this is equivalent to pulling out onto the freeway because you do not see any other vehicles blocking your path. Just as you pull out, another vehicle, going 100 miles per hour, crashes into you, causing a collision.

However, unlike with the vehicles on the freeway, which may not be able to recover from a collision, the nodes on the network continue to listen as they transmit. If one of the devices detects a collision, then it stops transmitting and alerts the other nodes on the network about the collision that just occurred. At that point, all nodes that are transmitting stop, wait a random period of time, and then attempt transmit again. Collisions are going to happen on Ethernet networks. The only concern is when the collisions occur frequently enough to impact the performance of the network.

FIGURE 1-1

Two nodes transmitting at the same time on an Ethernet network

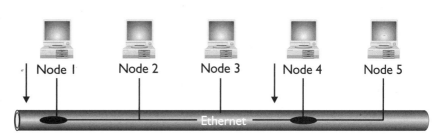

on the

Job

Use the LED indicators on the front of your Ethernet hubs to help you detect when network segments are saturated with collisions. Even though there are several tools available to detect network slowdowns and bottlenecks, I have found using the LEDs on the hubs to be very quick and painless. I had one segment where the collision LED was lit almost constantly. Surprisingly enough, in this particular situation I never heard any of the users on that segment complain about the network. I know that may be hard to believe, but it is true!

Broadcast Domains

Before broadcast domains are discussed, you first must understand what a broadcast is. A broadcast consists of data that is sent to all nodes on a network segment and not just to a single node or group of nodes. A broadcasting node sends the data to the MAC address 0xFFFFFFFFFFFF. A broadcast domain, therefore, consists of a set of nodes that receive broadcast traffic from all other nodes located within the same group. Normally, a broadcast domain consists of all nodes out one port of a router, as shown in Figure 1-2.

All sixteen nodes make up the broadcast domain for this particular network. Node 2 on Hub 3 not only broadcasts to the other nodes on Hub 3, but also to all nodes on Hub 1, Hub 2, and Hub 4. Likewise, any node on any of the other hubs broadcasts to all other nodes in this network. As the size of networks grow, so does the amount of broadcast traffic encountered in the broadcast domains. All of this broadcast traffic does affect the performance of your network, and it even has the possibility of bringing your network down, if not managed properly!

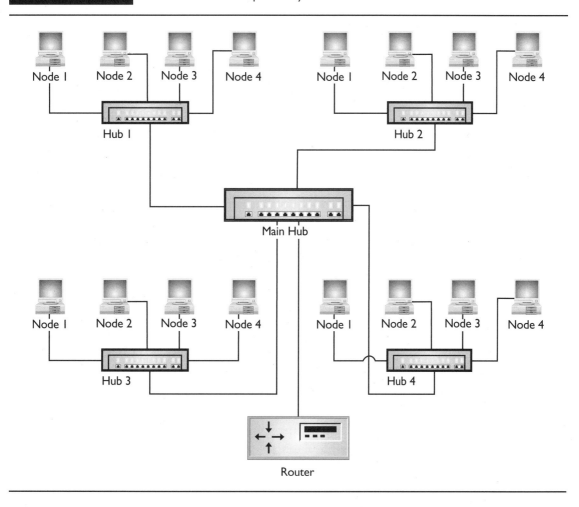

FIGURE 1-2   Broadcast domain separated by a router

LAN Segmentation

Two problems commonly affecting Ethernet performance are high collision rates and overwhelming broadcast traffic. Each of these problems can be resolved by splitting the network into smaller pieces through a process called "segmentation."

Bridges, switches, and routers reduce collisions by segmenting collision domains into smaller pieces and reducing the competition for bandwidth. Routers have the added benefit of also controlling broadcast traffic, thus segmenting broadcast domains into smaller domains. For reference, "subnet" and "VLAN" are more common terms for broadcast domains, and a subnet may contain several collision domains.

LAN Segmentation Using a Router

A router can be used to segment broadcast domains because it does not pass any broadcast traffic. Routers work at Layer 3 (network) of the OSI model; since they do not pass broadcasts, they are an easy way to reduce the size of your broadcast domains, as shown in Figure 1-3.

Figure 1-3 illustrates the same network depicted in Figure 1-2, except that the "Main Hub" has been replaced with a router. Each of the four networks coming off of the router is its own broadcast domain. Node 2 on Hub 3 broadcasts to all other nodes located on Hub 3, and Node 4 on Hub 1 broadcasts to all other nodes located on Hub 1. The same is true for the nodes on the other two hubs, also. However, the broadcasts do not cross over to any of the other hubs, because routers do not forward broadcast traffic. The amount of collisions is also reduced by minimizing the traffic on each network segment. In this example, it is very likely that neither the broadcast traffic nor collisions will be a cause of network slowdown.

LAN Segmentation Using a Bridge

A bridge can be used to segment collision domains for better performance, but if it is placed at the wrong spot in your network, it can then cause the

FIGURE 1-3   Four broadcast domains separated by a router

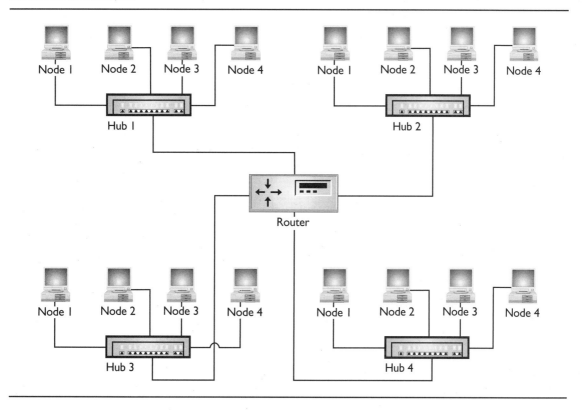

network to perform worse instead of better. Unlike routers, bridges operate at the MAC sublayer of Layer 2 (data link) of the OSI model. Not only do they create separate physical segments, but they also create separate logical segments. Bridges build a table of all known MAC addresses that pass through them, as well as which segment the MAC address is located on. When the bridge examines the destination MAC address for a packet of data, it determines the proper segment to forward the data to, if forwarding is necessary. However, if the bridge does not know the location of the destination MAC address, then it floods the data to all of the segments attached to it. For example, in Figure 1-4, if the bridge does not know the destination for data sent from Node 2, then it sends the data to all three of

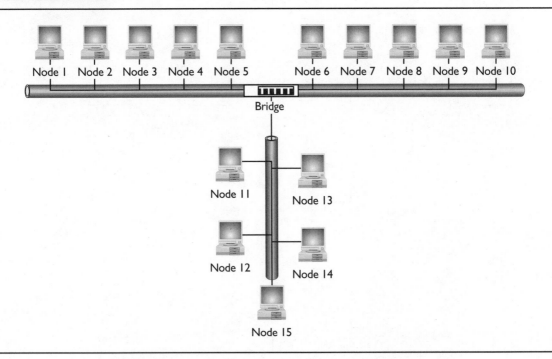

FIGURE 1-4   Bridge with 15 nodes on three segments

its attached segments. The bridge does not forward the data to the originating node.

Unlike routers, bridges do pass broadcasts to their attached segments. As you can see, this feature is a disadvantage to using a bridge to segment your LAN because of the broadcast storms that may occur. Bridges can be an acceptable solution to segmenting your LAN if you're not worried about broadcast storms.

LAN Segmentation Using a Switch

A switch can be used to segment your LAN to improve the performance for your end users. A switch is really nothing more than a multiport bridge that performs its operations in hardware using application-specific integrated circuits (ASICs) instead of software, used by bridges. Like bridges, switches also use the destination MAC address to make sure data is forwarded to the correct port. For example, Figure 1-5 shows a network segmented by a switch. Bandwidth is increased, since each segment operates on its own dedicated port of the switch, and only traffic destined for other segments passes through the source port on the switch to the destination port. No other port receives traffic not destined for it.

There is one caveat to this scenario, though. Since a switch is, in essence, a multiport bridge that uses ASICs, it also passes all broadcast traffic. However, most switches can be configured to have a broadcast threshold set in them. After the threshold is reached, all broadcast packets above the threshold limit are discarded. It is possible to set this threshold so that the only time broadcasts are discarded is in the event of a broadcast storm.

FIGURE 1-5   Switch used to segment a LAN

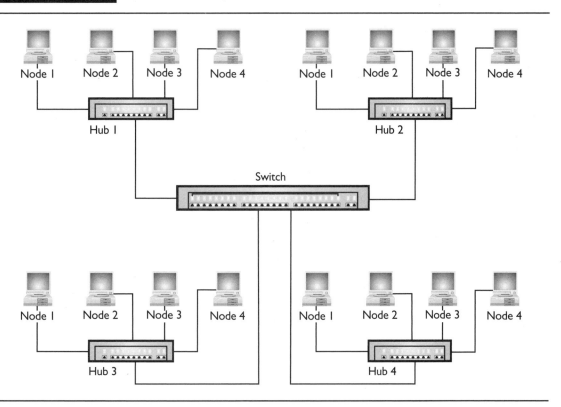

QUESTIONS AND ANSWERS	
The performance on my LAN is slowing to a crawl due to the amount of broadcasts traversing the wire...	Segment the network using a router. Using a router reduces the size of your broadcast domains.
My network is growing rapidly and I would like to segment the network at Layer 2 of the OSI model...	Segment the network using a bridge. Bridges function at Layer 2 of the OSI model.
My network uses Ethernet and I would like to increase the bandwidth available to each of my end users...	Replace the hubs with switches. Plug the Ethernet cable of each end user's system into one of the available ports on the switches. This gives each user his or her own 10/100Mbps of bandwidth.

exam
ⓦatch *It is important to remember the different results that each of these hardware items (routers, bridges, and switches) presents when used to segment local-area networks.*

CERTIFICATION OBJECTIVE 1.03

LAN Switching

Now that the various methods of segmenting LANs have been covered, it is time for a closer look at switching technologies in local-area networks. This book concentrates on the traditional Layer 2 switches, even though Layer 3 switches are available today. The difference with Layer 3 switches is that they forward packets based on network layer destination addresses, not on the MAC addresses used by Layer 2 switches.

In the not-so-distant past, it was acceptable to have LANs with 10Base2 coaxial cable or 10BaseT utilizing one or two hubs. The majority of traffic did not use much bandwidth, so there was plenty of bandwidth for everyone to share. However, in today's environment of network connectivity to every employee's desk and applications such as video and audio teleconferencing, bandwidth is a precious commodity. Before the use of switches in networks today is examined, let's look briefly at the history of switching technology.

In the early 1990s, several vendors decided to develop an alternative to routers. This was because routers were expensive to build and often difficult to configure. Even though the early switches were much cheaper than routers, they still were not cheap. Switches were initially limited to specific applications as well as to providing an alternative to the more costly routers. In comparison to the complexity of routers, switches are very simple to configure. In reality, switches are plug-and-play devices.

Over the years, the price of switches has dramatically decreased. Early switches could easily cost more than $1000 per port, whereas some switches today cost around $100 per port. The MAC address table could hold a maximum of 500 entries. (These prices are to illustrate that switching costs have decreased over the last few years. They should not be used to calculate how much it will cost you to build a Cisco switched network.)

Switches have become so cheap that they are replacing hubs on a number of networks. For example, earlier in the chapter, in Figure 1-2, we saw a local-area network that consisted of multiple nodes on five hubs. All sixteen nodes share the 10 Mbps that is theoretically available on the Ethernet network. Imagine trying to feed video to a couple of the nodes on that network. In today's network environment, the hubs could be replaced by switches, as shown in Figure 1-6.

Utilizing switches in this manner is called *microsegmentation.* Microsegmentation segments the local-area network to smaller segments, thereby increasing the available bandwidth to each user. Eventually, microsegmentation can conclude with each end user having his or her own

Sixteen-node switched network

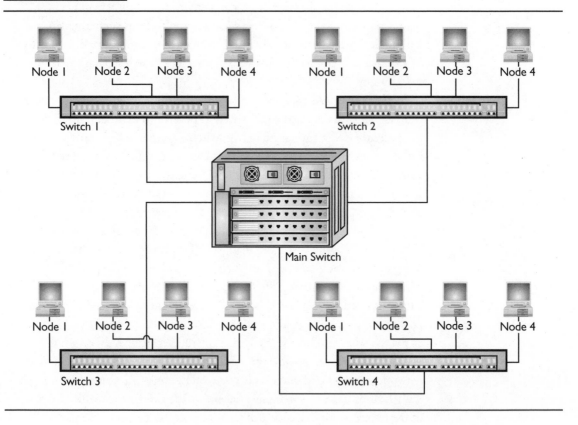

dedicated LAN segment, as shown in Figure 1-7. As you can see, microsegmentation is a collision domain with one station. On a standard Ethernet network, each user shown in Figure 1-7 has his own 10-Mbps segment.

Switches monitor traffic and compile a MAC address table so they can forward frames directly to the destination port of the switch. For example, assume that Node 2 transmits data to Node 16. Figure 1-8 shows the path the data flows within the switch. As you can see, both Node 8 and Node 20 are not aware of the transfer of data, since the data is not sent to those ports.

As switches replace hubs in the LAN, they can also provide access to high-speed backbones such as Asynchronous Transfer Mode (ATM) and

Dedicated 10-Mbps
segment for each end user

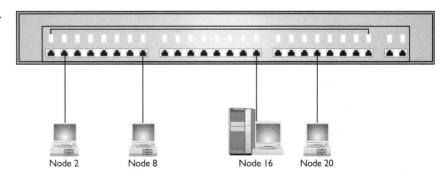

Gigabit Ethernet. This helps to provide the bandwidth necessary for
applications such as real-time video or digitized audio.

The use of switches is beneficial to making the most of the bandwidth
available on your network, especially if there is multimedia in the network.
Other benefits of switches are shown in Table 1-1.

Data flow from Node 2 to
Node 16 on a switch

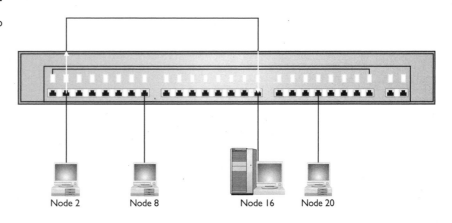

TABLE 1-1	Benefits of a Switch Compared to Hubs or Repeaters

Function	Benefit
Multiple data streams pass simultaneously	Allows more traffic to flow at the same time, thus increasing the amount of traffic moving on the network at any given time. Hubs and repeaters cannot perform this function.
Virtual local-area networks (VLANs)	VLANs increase the flexibility of networks and decrease costs by removing the cost associated with physically moving nodes.
Upgrade path to other high-performance switching solutions	Switches allow access to high-speed backbones but they also offer an upgrade path to these faster technologies.
Superior management over standard hubs	Switches are capable of preventing runt frames and other malformed frames from entering the network. Switches also provide much more information on activities occurring on each port over standard hubs. Examples of information that can be obtained from a switch include the flow of traffic in and out of a particular port and the number of alarm thresholds that have been exceeded.
Superior security over standard hubs	Because data is destined for a particular port and not the entire switch, it is impossible to eavesdrop on a switch just by plugging into an available port. Conversely, using standard hubs it is possible to monitor all traffic on the network segment simply by plugging into any available port and using sniffing software to collect login and password information as well as other sensitive data.

Translational Switching

Some switches offer the capability of *translational switching*. This type of switching allows the translation of one frame type to another frame type. For example, from Ethernet MAC to Fiber Distributed Data Interface (FDDI) SubNetwork Access Protocol (SNAP). This is useful so that the backbone of your network does not have to use the same protocol as other systems on other segments of the network. For example, FDDI operates at 100 Mbps but standard Ethernet operates at 10 Mbps. Can you imagine if the backbone for this network had to be 10 Mbps?

Another benefit of translational switching is that it allows systems that utilize different protocols to communicate with each other. For example, some portions of the network may use Token Ring and other portions may use Ethernet. Translational switching allows systems on these different protocols to communicate with each other. However, translational switching does have to account for a couple of differences in order for the process to work smoothly: differences in the size of the frames and differences in MAC headers.

Differences in Frame Sizes

Different protocols use frames of different sizes. This can cause problems when translating from one protocol to another. For example, Ethernet and Fast Ethernet use frames that are a maximum of 1526 bytes, but FDDI uses frames that are a maximum of 4500 bytes, as shown in Figure 1-9. Token Ring supports a maximum of 4472 bytes when operating at 4 Mbps, and 17,800 bytes when running at 16 Mbps. The switch has to consider this difference when it is converting from one protocol to another.

Differences in MAC Headers

Just as different protocols use different frame sizes, they also use different structures within the MAC header. An example of the differences is in the way addresses are transmitted in the frames. Ethernet and Fast Ethernet transmit the least significant bit (LSB) first, whereas FDDI and Token Ring transmit the most significant bit (MSB) first. For proper MAC addressing, translational bridging reverses the bit sequence in the MAC addresses when

FIGURE 1-9

Differences in frame sizes for various protocols

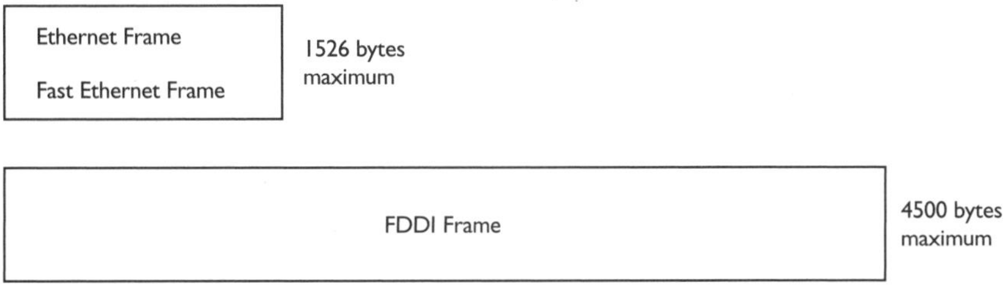

| Ethernet Frame / Fast Ethernet Frame | 1526 bytes maximum |

| FDDI Frame | 4500 bytes maximum |

forwarding between LSB and MSB topologies, as shown in Figure 1-10. These two types of formats are called canonical and non-canonical, respectively.

This address translation may appear trivial, but it has a painful effect on higher-layer protocols. While MAC addresses are properly translated within the header, they are not translated inside the data packet. When these MAC addresses are extracted from the data packet and used to form a new MAC header, the MAC address is invalid and the communication fails. This problem is specifically addressed for common protocols like ARP and IPX SAP, but it is the Achilles heel of translational bridging, rendering many software products inoperable.

A more subtle concern for translational bridging is also a difference in multicast MAC addresses. They are called "group" addresses in Ethernet and "functional" addresses in Token Ring. Translating these addresses poses an additional challenge, since Ethernet has 256 group addresses and Token Ring provides only 16 functional addresses.

The first bit transmitted by various LAN protocols

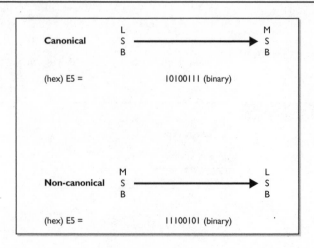

Cut-Through vs. Store and Forward Switching

Switch vendors normally use either *cut-through* or *store and forward* as the method of forwarding frames out of their switches. Other vendors use the *modified cut-through* method. Cut-through and store and forward each have their strengths and weaknesses. Let's discuss the cut-through method first.

The cut-through method forwards a frame as soon as the switch determines the destination MAC address and the correct port to send the frame out of. Normally, the forwarding begins after approximately 14 bytes of the frame's header has been received, as shown in Figure 1-11. This allows the cut-through method to have a lower port-to-port latency than the store and forward method, since it forwards the frame as quickly as possible. One problem with the cut-through method is that it can forward runt frames or frames that are malformed in some other manner. The second problem is that it forces all ports on the switch to operate at the same speed. In other words, if you are using a 10-Mbps Ethernet switch, then you

FIGURE 1-11

Example of an IEEE 802.3 frame and the approximate point at which it would be forwarded using the cut-through method

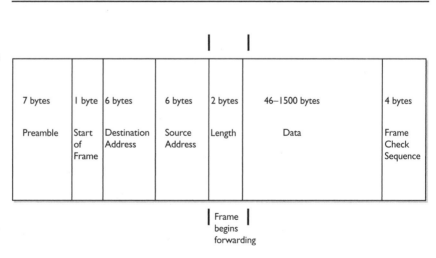

cannot have a Fast Ethernet or FDDI uplink, if you use the cut-through method. The reason for this is that there cannot be any gaps in the transmission of the frame. Anytime you switch from a low-speed rate to a high-speed rate there will be a gap, unless some type of buffering is taking place.

exam
ⓦatch

Cisco uses two varieties of the cut-through method, FastForward and FragmentFree. FastForward immediately forwards a frame after receiving the destination address. FragmentFree determines that the frame is not a collision fragment before it is forwarded. Collision fragments are normally less than 64 bytes. If the frame is over 64 bytes, then the FragmentFree mode considers the frame valid.

Using the store and forward method, the switch receives the entire frame and processes it before it is sent out the destination port. When this method is used, the switch receives the entire frame, performs a cyclic redundancy check (CRC), and determines the destination address. It also stores the entire frame in memory buffers until the resources are available to send it on its way to the final destination. An advantage to using the store and forward method is that it discards any runt frames as well as any other damaged frames so they are not placed back on the network. A disadvantage to this method is that it incurs latency, since the entire frame must be received and processed prior to being forwarded.

Table 1-2 summarizes the cut-through and store and forward methods of forwarding used in switches.

exam
ⓦatch

The Catalyst 5000 and Catalyst 5500 switches use the store and forward method of switching.

TABLE 1-2	Comparing Methods for Forwarding Frames from Switches

Method	Strengths	Weaknesses
Cut-through	Lower latency than store and forward switches	Forwards malformed frames to the network. All ports must operate at the same speed.
Store and forward	Only complete frames are forwarded to the network. Malformed frames are discarded.	Higher latency than cut-through.

FROM THE CLASSROOM

Switching Methods

The different switching methods introduce a level of confusion in most classes. Some people walk into the course thinking that switches switch and routers route. Although there is some truth to that statement, it does not explain the true details of either transaction.

Switching is simply the action of moving one packet (or frame) from one port to another. How that decision is made defines whether a switch or router is involved. If OSI Layer 2 is used, then a switch or a bridge has been involved. OSI Layer 3 represents the routers.

How fast this decision and forwarding process occurs is another topic, although closely related. Since routers work at Layer 3, they must perform store and forward operations. This gives the router an additional opportunity to introduce latency into the forwarding process. But switches have the opportunity to forward a packet before the entire frame has been received and verified.

Cut-through and modified cut-through switching methods have fixed delays in the forwarding process. Cut-through starts forwarding once the destination MAC address has been received; this MAC address and source VLAN are compared to the forwarding table. Modified cut-through is also fixed, only this time the actual packet exit does not occur until at least 64 bytes have arrived in the switch. This prevents runt frames (collision leftovers) from being propagated.

The next question is, which switches can perform which switching methods? Some switches automatically toggle between the modes based on user-defined thresholds. Others require administrator intervention, either for a software setting or a DIP switch adjustment. In the CLSC course, the answer is simple. The Catalyst 5000 series only supports store and forward operations. Thus, this is one configuration option that cannot be incorrectly set.

—*Neil Lovering, CCIE, CCSI*

Token Ring Switching

So far, only Ethernet switching has been discussed. Now it is time to look at Token Ring switching and how it is used in today's network environment. It is important to note that currently there is not a defined standard for the functions of Token Ring in a switched environment.

Ethernet switches are replacing Ethernet hubs on networks and Token Ring switches are replacing Token Ring hubs, albeit not as fast as Ethernet. Token Ring switches can also substitute for bridges in Token Ring networks that use bridges to pass a nonroutable protocol such as System Network Architecture (SNA), or other protocols such as IPX or IP.

Connecting a Token Ring switch to a Token Ring hub can be done using two different methods. The first method connects the switch to the hub using the ring in/ring out ports (RI/RO). In this method, the switch pretends to be the next hub in the ring. For example, the Cisco Catalyst 3900 uses port 19 or 20 to attach to the main ring path coming from a multistation access unit (MSAU or MAU) or controlled access unit (CAU). Ports 19 and 20 have a loopback function, so if either port is disabled or the switch has power removed, there will not be a break in the main ring attached to the switch. Only one of the ports is necessary. For example, a cable from a MAU RI port has to only be attached to port 19, as shown in Figure 1-12. This joins the primary and backup rings in a MAU/CAU main ring system. If you connect the other end of the main ring to port 20, then you have created redundant paths, since both ports 19 and 20 of the switch are connected to the same segment.

The second method of integrating a Token Ring switch into a Token Ring network is by having the switch pretend to be a device and connecting it to an MAU on one of its ports, as shown in Figure 1-13.

FIGURE 1-12

MAU ring is cabled to port 19 of a Catalyst 3900 Token Ring switch

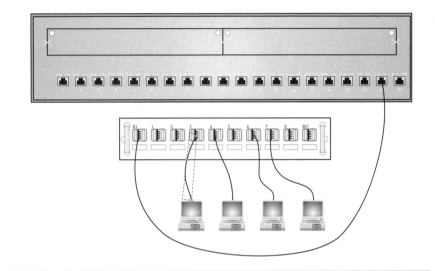

Using the switch in this fashion, the MAU can recognize when a cable breaks between the MAU and switch. The ring within the MAU remains functional, as shown in Figure 1-14.

FIGURE 1-13

Catalyst 3900 switch connected as a device to a multistation access unit

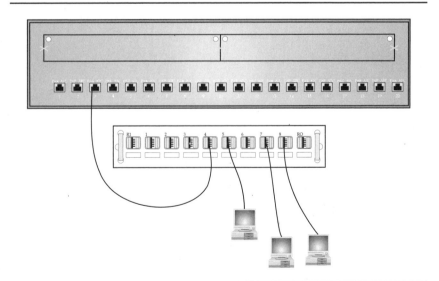

FIGURE 1-14

Cable break between a switch and hub affects connectivity, but the devices continue to function

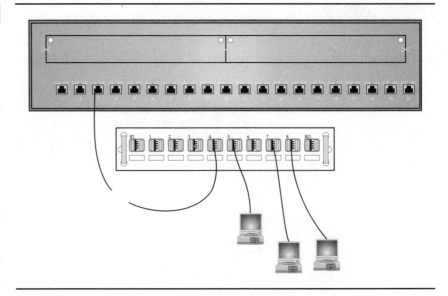

Bridging Methods

The three bridging methods supported by Token Ring switches are source-route bridging, source-route transparent bridging, and source-route switching.

■ **Source-route bridging** This bridging method is the earliest method used to connect Token Ring segments. It makes all forwarding decisions by looking at the data located in the Routing Information Field (RIF). MAC addresses are not examined in source-route bridging, so if there is no RIF, the frame is not forwarded.

■ **Source-route transparent bridging** This bridging method combines source routing and transparent routing into an IEEE standard that uses the IEEE Spanning-Tree Protocol. This method forwards frames that have a RIF, based upon the data in the RIF. If the frames do not have a RIF, then they are forwarded based upon the MAC address, similar to Ethernet bridging.

- **Source-route switching**   This bridging method uses dual frame-forwarding technology. It forwards frames based upon the MAC address unless you have source-route bridges on your network. In that case, it forwards frames based upon the RIF. One of the benefits of source-route switching is that it allows an existing Token Ring to be partitioned into several segments without requiring changes to the source-route bridges or the existing Token Ring numbers.

CERTIFICATION SUMMARY

Collisions and broadcast domains affect the performance of networks. Collisions occur when two Ethernet nodes try to transmit frames at the same time. Broadcast domains affect network performance when the quantity of broadcasts interferes with the flow of normal network traffic.

Segmenting local-area networks helps to control collisions and the amount of broadcast traffic. LAN segmentation can be accomplished using routers, bridges, and switches. The demands on your network dictate which of these hardware items is most beneficial for segmenting the network.

LAN switches improve the performance available on a network, which is extremely important with the advent of video teleconferencing and other bandwidth-intensive applications. In recent years, as switches have come down in price, they have increasingly replaced hubs. In comparison to routers, switches are easy to configure.

Frames are normally forwarded using either the cut-through or store and forward methods. Each method has its own strengths and weaknesses. A strength of the cut-through method is its low latency. A strength of the store and forward method is that it does not forward any malformed frames onto the network.

Token Ring switches can be placed into a Token Ring network using two different methods. The first method consists of connecting the switch to the ring in/ring out ports of an MAU so that it is seen as just another hub in the ring. The second method consists of connecting the switch to a port on the MAU so that it is seen as a device on the network.

✓ TWO-MINUTE DRILL

❑ Two items that can affect the performance of the network significantly are collisions and broadcast traffic.

❑ Collisions are going to happen on Ethernet networks. The only concern is when the collisions occur frequently enough to impact the performance of the network.

❑ A broadcast domain consists of a set of nodes that receive broadcast traffic from all other nodes located within the same group.

❑ As the size of networks grow, so does the amount of broadcast traffic encountered in the broadcast domains.

❑ Collisions and broadcast domains can be brought into control by segmenting your local-area network (LAN).

❑ A router can be used to segment broadcast domains because it does not pass any broadcast traffic.

❑ A bridge can be used to segment collision domains for better performance but if it is placed in your network at the wrong spot, then it can cause the network to perform worse instead of better.

❑ A switch can be used to segment your LAN to improve the performance for your end users.

❑ It is important to remember the different results that each of these hardware items (routers, bridges, and switches) presents when used to segment local-area networks.

❑ Switches have become so cheap that they are replacing hubs on a number of networks.

❑ Microsegmentation reduces/splits the local-area network to smaller segments, thereby increasing the available bandwidth to each user.

❑ Translational switching allows the translation of one frame type to another frame type. (For example: Ethernet to FDDI or Token Ring.)

❑ Translational switching also allows systems that utilize different protocols to communicate with each other.

❑ Switch vendors normally use either *cut-through* or *store and forward* as the method of forwarding frames through their switches.

❑ The cut-through method forwards a frame as soon as the switch determines the destination MAC address and the correct port to send the frame out of.

❑ Cisco uses two varieties of the cut-through method, FastForward and FragmentFree. FastForward immediately forwards a frame after receiving the destination address. FragmentFree determines that the frame is not a collision fragment before it is forwarded. Collision fragments are normally less than 64 bytes. If the frame is over 64 bytes, then the FragmentFree mode considers the frame valid.

❑ Using the store and forward method, the switch receives the entire frame and processes it before it is sent out to the destination port.

❑ The Catalyst 5000 and Catalyst 5500 switches use the store and forward method of switching.

❑ It is important to note that currently there is not a defined standard for the functions of Token Ring in a switched environment.

❑ Connecting a Token Ring switch to a Token Ring hub can be done using two different methods.

   ❑ In ring in/ring out ports (RI/RO) the switch pretends to be the next hub in the ring.

   ❑ The second method of integrating a Token Ring switch into a Token Ring network is by having the switch pretend to be a device and connecting it to an MAU on one of its ports

❑ The three bridging methods supported by Token Ring switches are source-route bridging, source-route transparent bridging, and source-route switching.

SELF TEST

The following Self Test questions will help you measure your understanding of the material presented in this chapter. Read all the choices carefully, as there may be more than one correct answer. Choose all correct answers for each question.

1. Which bridging method checks for the RIF and discards the frame if it is not present?

   A. Source-route bridging

   B. Source-route transparent bridging

   C. Source-route switching

   D. Source-route transparent switching

2. What is a benefit of using a router to segment networks?

   A. It reduces the number of routes on the network

   B. It increases the number of replications on the network

   C. It increases the number of protocols on the network

   D. It reduces the number of broadcasts on the network

3. Which forwarding method has a low latency rate?

   A. Store and forward

   B. Cut-and-store

   C. Cut-through

   D. Store-and-cut

4. What port(s) on a Cisco Catalyst 3900 switch are used to connect to the ring in/ring out ports of a media access unit?

   A. 1

   B. 2

   C. 19

   D. 20

5. What type of network uses carrier sense multiple access with collision detection?

   A. Ethernet

   B. T1

   C. Token Ring

   D. OC-3

6. What type(s) of hardware can be utilized to segment local-area networks?

   A. Routers

   B. Switches

   C. Media altering unit

   D. Bridges

7. What type of forwarding does the Catalyst 5500 use?

   A. Cut-through

   B. Store and forward

   C. FragmentFree

   D. FastForward

8. What happens to a Token Ring network if the cable connecting the switch to a port on the multistation access unit breaks?

   A. The network no longer functions

   B. The network continues to function, but the switch or MSAU cannot communicate

C. The network continues to function at a lower speed

D. The network continues to function except for nodes on the switch

9. Which item(s) can negatively affect the performance on your network?

A. FDDI

B. Collisions

C. ATM

D. Broadcast domains

10. Which forwarding method performs a cyclic redundancy check on each frame?

A. Store-and-cut

B. Cut-through

C. Store and forward

D. Cut-and-forward

11. Why did vendors decide to invent the switch?

A. As a replacement for repeaters

B. As a replacement for ASIC

C. As a replacement for SNA

D. As a replacement for routers

12. Which of the following is another term for a switch?

A. A multi-port repeater

B. A multi-port bridge

C. A multi-port router

D. A multi-port segmentor

13. What is the purpose of microsegmentation?

A. It provides a decrease in available bandwidth to the end users

B. It provides an increase in available ports to the end users

C. It provides an increase in available bandwidth to the end users

D. It provides a decrease in available ports to the end users

14. How does a switch know which port to forward a frame to?

A. It reads the source MAC address

B. It uses a MAC address table

C. It reads the source ARP address

D. It uses an ARP address table

15. How can a switch transfer an Ethernet frame to an FDDI backbone?

A. Translational switching

B. Transmedial switching

C. Transferral switching

D. Transcrossial switching

16. Which bridging method uses the IEEE Spanning-Tree Protocol?

A. Source-route bridging

B. Source-route transferral bridging

C. Source-route switching

D. Source-route transparent bridging

17. Which forwarding method uses the most memory during normal operation?

    A. Cut-through

    B. FragmentFree

    C. FastForward

    D. Store and Forward

18. What item(s) does translational switching have to account for in networks?

    A. Differences in frame sizes

    B. Differences in redundancy

    C. Differences in the BRI rate

    D. Differences in MAC headers

19. What function makes switches superior to standard hubs?

    A. Increased driver availability

    B. Increased security

    C. Increased port availability

    D. Increased prioritization

20. What is the maximum frame size for FDDI?

    A. 1526 bytes

    B. 5400 bytes

    C. 2615 bytes

    D. 4500 bytes

CISCO CERTIFIED NETWORK PROFESSIONAL

2

VLANs

C hapter 1 introduced the concepts of bridging and switching. In this chapter, those concepts (bridged local-area networks) are extended into virtual local-area networks, or VLANs. The different aspects of VLANs are examined in detail. This includes ways of assigning clients to VLANs, tracking them between switches, standards for VLANs, and interoperating with traditional backbone networks.

As much as possible, this chapter covers VLANs in the general sense, without being tied to a particular product. Obviously, within the Cisco product line, the product-specific discussion of VLANs involves Cisco routers and Cisco Catalyst switches. Those products are covered more thoroughly in later chapters of this book. By beginning the discussion of VLANs in a general sense, this chapter examines why Cisco made some of its product decisions, and explores some alternate ways of implementing VLANs.

In general, switches mentioned in this chapter are from the Cisco Catalyst 5000 family. However, on the CLSC exam, you will be tested on both general VLAN concepts and Catalyst-specific VLAN information. Therefore, even if you have some experience with the Catalyst products, you'll want to read this chapter for general VLAN questions that will appear on the test.

CERTIFICATION OBJECTIVE 2.01

Broadcast Domains

Chapter 1 explored how unicasts, multicasts, and broadcasts traverse a bridged network. Most LAN protocols rely on broadcasts for many functions.

In Chapter 1, the LAN consisted of all the nodes bridged and repeated together. The defining characteristic of a LAN segment is that all the nodes can communicate directly with each other, without having to pass through some Layer 3 or higher device such as a router. In most cases, these direct communications are set up by the nodes sending broadcasts for physical addresses, and then using unicast LAN addresses to perform the communication.

With traditional LANs, if a node is attached to a particular piece of network equipment (a hub, repeater, or bridge) then it is on the same LAN as other nodes attached to the same piece of equipment. In Figure 2-1 Node A is attached to Hub A. Likewise, any other Layer 1 or Layer 2 devices that are attached to Hub A become part of the same LAN, and nodes attached to that device (the Repeater, Bridge, Hub B, and Node B) are on the same LAN as devices attached to Hub A.

Logically speaking, as long as the specifications are maintained, hubs, repeaters, and bridges can be added or removed, and the LAN still exists. Abstracted a bit further, a LAN is really the group of nodes that can send broadcasts to each other. A group of nodes that can reach each other by broadcast are said to be in the same *broadcast domain*. To state the same thing in a different order for emphasis, a broadcast domain is a group of nodes that can send broadcasts to each other. A broadcast domain is logically equivalent to a LAN segment. Broadcast domains are commonly connected to each other by routers, and usually Layer 2 broadcast packets do not cross routers.

A broadcast domain is the central concept behind VLANs. In the interest of oversimplifying (for now) a VLAN is a broadcast domain. There are some extra complications for Token Ring, which are discussed in the Token Ring section of this chapter.

FIGURE 2-1   Two nodes connected by hubs, a bridge, and a repeater

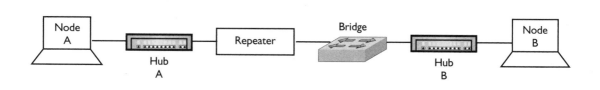

VLAN Characteristics

A VLAN is roughly equivalent to a broadcast domain, but that is also the definition of a LAN, or traditional bridged and repeated network. The difference is really very simple: traditional switches contain one broadcast domain per physical box, and VLAN switches can have more than one.

Despite all the hype surrounding VLANs, it is really as simple as that. The main difference between a plain switch and a VLAN switch is the capacity to maintain separate broadcast domains in the same box. The other factor is the capacity to maintain separate broadcast domains between boxes, but that is covered later in the section on trunking.

CERTIFICATION OBJECTIVE 2.02

Dynamic Versus Static VLANs

It is worthwhile discussing how a box might be divided into different broadcast domains. There are two main categories of VLAN assignment: static and dynamic. Static VLANs are easiest to understand, so those are covered first. Static VLANs are defined by some characteristic of the box they exist in, usually slots, ports, or groups of ports. For example, in a modular chassis that has eight slots for networking ports, slots 1–4 may be VLAN 1, while slots 5–8 may be VLAN 2.

Dynamic VLANs are usually defined by some characteristic of the node attached to the box. This might be the Media Access Control (MAC) address of the node, the protocol that it is sending, or perhaps even some authentication information, such as a name and password. An example would be a switch deciding which VLAN to place a node in by watching for the MAC address of the node. You may find these statements somewhat vague. The reason for this is that the terms VLAN and switch are somewhat artificial; they are vendor-created. The end result is that those terms, while not without meaning, are not completely agreed upon by all vendors. The definitions used here closely match Cisco's definitions.

Cisco supports both dynamic and static VLANs. Cisco dynamic VLANs are based on the node MAC address. Cisco static VLANs are *port-assigned*. The term port-assigned implies that VLANs can be assigned on an individual port basis, which is more or less true. The exception is the Cisco 48-port group switched cards for the Catalyst 5000 family that have ports switched in groups of 12. These 12 ports are equivalent to a hub, and all the ports in a group share the same VLAN assignment. These cards have been declared end-of-life, and replaced with 48 individually switched port cards. For more details on how to assign VLANs in Cisco switches, consult the chapters for the various Cisco Catalyst products later in this book.

It should be noted that VLAN switches were not the first pieces of equipment to do segmentation within the same box or chassis. There are chassis-based repeated solutions, some of which included a few bridge segments on the backplane. A card could be placed on a particular bridge segment or be isolated from the backplane entirely, providing some of the features of a VLAN. The difference is that most VLAN switches have the capability to do this completely within software, while the repeater chassis may or may not be separable via software. Another difference is that most VLAN switches are much more granular, usually allowing VLAN assignment on a per-port basis, and allowing for many more VLANs.

How can VLANs help solve practical networking problems? VLANs exist to help with cost and flexibility. To explain each of these advantages, let's look at some examples.

VLANs Reduce Costs

One of the items that VLANs help with is cost. Imagine a network of eight LANs, or more specifically, eight broadcast domains. There are many reasons to implement multiple broadcast domains, such as broadcast control, security, and resource grouping. With traditional networking technologies, implementing eight broadcast domains requires at least eight sets of networking equipment, as shown in Figure 2-2.

A router connecting
eight LANs using
traditional equipment

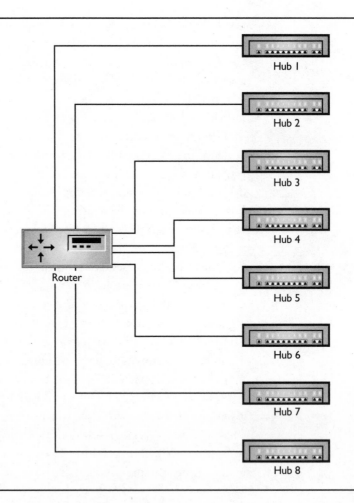

The word "hub" in the figure and in the following discussion is meant to
be generic. It may actually be a hub, which is a common term for a large,
multiport repeater, or it may be a full switch. For this chapter, it represents
the whole set of networking equipment required for each LAN.

If designed well, the nodes that make up each LAN are grouped in such a
way as to minimize the number of hubs needed. One way this might be
done is to divide the groups by geography. For example, each group could
represent a building, or perhaps one floor of a building.

If not designed well, groups are spread out, which means the LANs will be in physically separated locations, requiring more hubs. Imagine if the LANs are divided by department, and if most departments are spread among multiple buildings. Potentially, this could require that a hub for each LAN be in each building, as shown in Figure 2-3.

FIGURE 2-3   Eight LANs in two buildings using traditional equipment

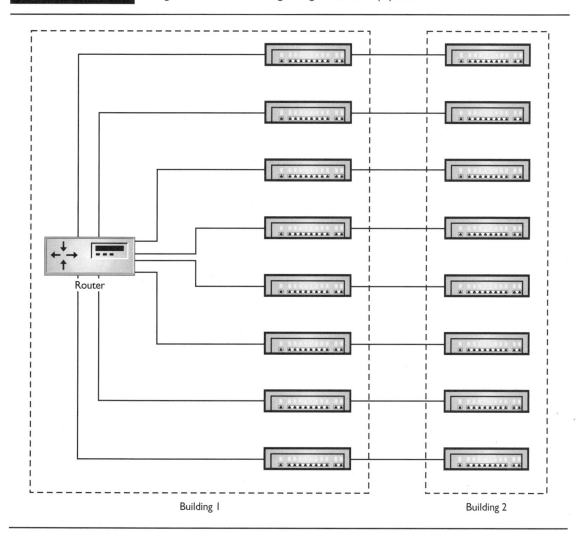

In the simplest arrangement of eight LANs, each LAN would represent a floor of an eight-story building, with one hub for each floor. Only eight hubs would be required (see Figure 2-2). Now, consider the case of eight LANs in two buildings. Now we're up to 16 hubs, and eight LAN connections between buildings (see Figure 2-3).

Now imagine a more complicated arrangement of eight LANs. Each LAN relates to a department. The campus consists of five buildings. There is someone from each department in each building. This arrangement requires at least 40 hubs, possibly more if one hub per department per building is not enough to connect all of the nodes for that LAN in that building. What really makes this an expensive arrangement is not the hub costs, but the amount of cabling required between buildings. Most campuses do not have quite this much cable or fiber in the ground.

The number of hubs will grow as it becomes necessary to separate LANs. You must also consider interconnections between the equipment. It may not be possible to have sufficient physical connections between buildings.

This is where the concept of being able to divide a box into VLANs starts to look really attractive. As long as the VLAN-capable switch has ample ports, a separate hub is not needed for each traditional LAN.

VLANs Increase Flexibility

At this point, it may already be apparent why VLANs increase flexibility. With VLANs, where a node is located can be independent of which LAN it is connected to. If you consider this in the context of the preceding example (with LANs mapping to departments), you can see that this could be a big time-saver. When employees change departments, the network administrator can simply change which VLAN the employee's node is assigned to.

Dynamic VLANs offer another example of increased flexibility. Again, using the example where LANs are mapped to departments, if employees roam or change locations often, the network administrator can implement dynamic VLANs; wherever the employees connect their nodes, they are on the correct LAN.

Network Security

VLANs can be used to help increase network security. Networks can be segmented into VLANs so that nodes on different VLANs must cross a router or perhaps even a firewall in order to communicate with each other. Additionally, some VLAN switches include the capability to control which nodes can attach to a particular port, to prevent someone from bypassing security mechanisms by switching ports with other nodes.

If each VLAN is a broadcast domain, then a router is needed to connect the different VLANs. In this case, access lists can be configured on the routers to prevent traffic from flowing between VLANs. This is similar to using access lists on a router to prevent traffic from flowing from one interface to another. Since traffic cannot simply flow between VLANs within a switch, security is a definite plus.

Frame Filtering Versus Frame Tagging

Consider how a traditional (non-VLAN) switch keeps track of which frames are destined for which ports. When a frame enters a switch, the switch has to determine where to send it. Traditional switches simply examine the destination of the frame, consult their bridge tables, and forward it to the appropriate port, regardless of where the frame came from. If the destination is unknown, or the destination is a broadcast, then the frame is flooded to all ports except the one it came from.

Things are a bit more complicated in a VLAN switch. In addition to the forwarding decisions that need to be made based on the destination address, the source of the frame also has to be considered, because that often affects which VLAN it belongs to, and hence which ports it may be forwarded to.

There are at least two obvious ways that the source of a frame can be tracked. The first is to track what VLAN the port it came in belongs to. This is called frame tagging, also known as explicit tagging. Note that this process takes place internally in a switch. The frame itself may not be modified, but other information about the frame may be tracked separately. The other way to track the source of a frame is to keep a list of MAC addresses for each VLAN (which the switches must do anyway). After the destination has been determined, a determination is made as to whether the frame passes. This is called frame filtering, also known as implicit tagging. Theoretically, frame filtering could also be done with other criteria, such as Layer 3 information.

The major difference between the two methods concerns when the VLAN decision is made. With frame tagging, the decision is made as the frame enters the VLAN. With frame filtering, the decision is made when the frame needs to be forwarded, and not necessarily as soon as the frame enters the switch.

Most of the discussion of how switches make decisions about VLAN membership internally is academic. Really, it doesn't matter how a switch tracks VLANs internally, as long as correct forwarding decisions are made. The theoretical discussion is necessary on a conceptual basis, and because Cisco tests on it. How VLANs are identified only becomes an issue when frames need to be forwarded between switches. Part of this discussion is slightly premature, as it is more relevant to trunking, but we need to consider VLANs between switches to complete the implicit vs. explicit discussion.

The advantage to frame tagging is that the VLAN is identified immediately, and no further VLAN membership decisions need to be made on that frame. Tagging is usually done by adding a field to the frame that contains a VLAN number. (The Cisco documentation sometimes also refers to this as VLAN *coloring*.) The disadvantage to this approach is that most non-VLAN-aware equipment will consider such frames invalid, since they don't follow the standard formats. Also, there are a number of incompatible implementations of frame tagging, so use of frame tagging will often limit the choice of equipment to one vendor. The IEEE 802.1Q standard is intended to address this issue by defining a standard frame tagging mechanism.

The advantage to frame filtering is that it does not modify the frames, so there is no problem passing the frames across standard networks. The disadvantage is that all VLAN devices must be capable of making the identical

VLAN determination about each frame. In practice, this means that if filtering is being done by source MAC address, then all VLAN switches must have a table containing that MAC address and the VLAN to which it belongs. The same goes for other methods, such as filtering by Layer 3 address, though that may be easier if the VLAN is a direct function of the Layer 3 address. (For example, if IP subnet 10 is equal to VLAN 10.) For this type of arrangement to be manageable and scalable would require a protocol for VLAN switches to communicate this information amongst themselves.

For the tests, Cisco wants you to be aware of the difference between the two methods. In reality, frame tagging has more or less "won." All the major switch vendors favor tagging in their implementations, the IEEE standard is for tagging, legacy backbones (FDDI) support a flavor of tagging, and Cisco supports two additional flavors of tagging. The one exception may be ATM LANE, which resembles frame filtering more closely than tagging.

CERTIFICATION OBJECTIVE 2.05

VLAN Trunks

Until now, trunks have not been covered in detail, though they've been hinted at. The discussion in the preceding section regarding frame tagging and frame filtering will start to make more sense when those ideas are used between switches rather than within a switch.

The main characteristic of VLAN switches is their capability to maintain separate VLANs within a switch, and also between switches. The time has come to discuss how to extend VLANs between switches.

For VLAN switches, a trunk is an interconnect between two switches that carries traffic for more than one VLAN. This is different from a link between two regular bridges, because each switch has to identify which VLAN a frame belongs to when it is received. This adds some complexity, but also gives us a good deal of flexibility.

Consider the example from earlier in the chapter of the VLANs defined by department, in a multibuilding campus. Even though the number of boxes in each building was drastically reduced by combining all the LANs in each building into one box, a separate network link for each LAN between buildings was still needed. With trunking, as long as there is sufficient bandwidth, that can be reduced to one link to each building, as illustrated in Figure 2-4.

FIGURE 2-4   Single link for each VLAN now replaced by larger trunk link

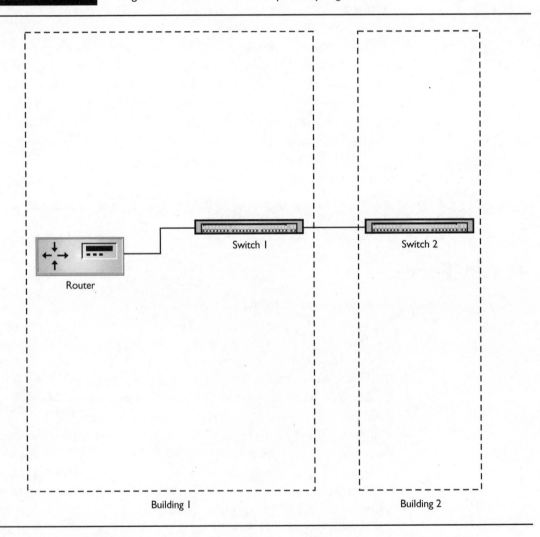

Router   Switch 1   Switch 2

Building 1   Building 2

For this type of arrangement, how to handle frames within a VLAN becomes much more important. A switch handling frames internally has a lot more flexibility in how it makes VLAN decisions, as it typically has all the information it needs to handle VLANs in a variety of ways. Once a frame leaves the control of the processor of a switch and goes onto a piece of dumb wire, VLANs become a bit more complicated.

In order to decide whether to mark a frame or not, a switch has to know what is on the other end of the wire onto which it is placing the frame. The easiest case is an end node, such as a PC or a server. Typically, end nodes do not know anything about VLANs. Although it is possible to run VLAN-aware software on some operating systems. This is usually done to multihome a server. In the case of an end-node, the switch simply has to restore the frame to its original state (or close to it, in the case of a translational or source-routing bridge).

If the frame is placed on a network segment that contains both end nodes and switches, then care must be taken when considering whether to use frame tagging, since some stations may consider such packets illegal. This may still be okay, as some nodes may simply ignore the frames, or report errors if they track network statistics.

If the frame is being sent just to another switch, the sending switch has to know what type of tagging formats the receiving switch can handle. This is nontrivial, and there are at least three ways to handle this, as follows:

- **Static Trunk Configuration**   This type of trunk configuration is easiest to understand. Simply put, each switch on a trunk is programmed to send and receive frames of a particular trunking protocol only. In this setup, the port is normally dedicated to trunking, and cannot be used for end node attachment, at least for end nodes that don't speak a trunking protocol. Static configuration is often useful when automatic negotiation is not working properly or not available. The disadvantage is that static trunk configuration must be maintained manually.

- **Trunk Capability Advertisement**   It is possible for switches to send periodic announcement frames to indicate that they are capable of performing a particular trunking function. For example, a switch could advertise that it is capable of performing a particular type of frame tagging VLAN, so it is legal to send it tagged frames in that format. A switch could also potentially go beyond that, and advertise which VLANs it is willing to trunk for. This type of trunk setup might be useful for a network segment that is a mixed end-node and trunk.

■ **Trunk Auto-Negotiation**   Trunks can also be set up automatically via a negotiation process. In this scenario, switches will periodically send frames that indicate that they wish to switch to trunking mode. If the switch at the other end receives these frames, recognizes them (and is capable of the requested function), and is configured to trunk automatically, the two switches will put those ports into trunking mode. This type of automatic negotiation normally depends on the existence of a point-to-point link between two switches (one that is all on that network segment). The port attached to this link is dedicated to trunking, much as with a static trunk setup.

Cisco Switch Trunk Capabilities

Without getting into too many hardware specifics or exact trunking protocols (which are covered in the next section), let's briefly look at which trunk setup methods Cisco switches are capable of.

Like almost any VLAN switch, Cisco switches can be programmed with a static trunking setup. Cisco switches do not use advertisement to decide when to send trunk frames, but once the trunk is up by some other means, they do use advertisement to indicate which VLANs are available, and to maintain information about those VLANs. This feature is called the Virtual Trunking Protocol (VTP) and is covered later in the book. Cisco switches do support auto-negotiation. The default configuration has this feature semidisabled, so that every connection between switches does not automatically become a trunk. With the default configuration, if one of the two switches is manually configured to trunk, the other will automatically switch to trunking mode. This means that only one end of a link needs to be configured to get trunking going.

FROM THE CLASSROOM

Trunk Confusion

The term *trunk* often creates confusion. Keep in mind that this is a Cisco-centric book, so our point of view for this discussion is that of a Cisco switch. First you learn that any port of a switch can only be a part of one VLAN. It really does not make any sense to have one port part of two different broadcast domains. Then you read about trunking, and now a port can have multiple VLANs. Which is right?

Well, the simple answer is both. A port can only have one VLAN assigned to it. When a trunk is configured, the port loses its individual VLAN identity, and adopts all VLANs in the switch. The actual VLANs allowed to traverse the port can be manually configured.

The thing to remember is, in order for this trunk to operate, the frame that is sent across it must be modified somewhat. The reason is simple. On an average switch port, a VLAN is assigned. (There is no such thing as a switch port without a VLAN assignment.) Whenever a frame arrives on any port, the switch knows that the frame belongs to VLAN *X*. This is because the port is configured in VLAN *X*. The end station out there somewhere has no idea about this VLAN identity. The original frame carried no such VLAN information.

The VLAN identity is important to the switch when it comes to determining where the frame goes next. It cannot cross into another VLAN without first visiting the local router.

Now, if this same frame arrived on a trunk port, which VLAN does it belong to? The switch must know the VLAN in order to send it out the correct destination port. But without the port-based VLAN identity, the switch is stumped. Thus, for all trunk links, something in the frame indicates the VLAN identity. LANE is an exception, since it used a different virtual circuit for each VLAN.

A trunk port must understand whatever tagging mechanism is used to identify the frame as part of VLAN *X*. When a frame exits a trunk port, it is tagged with the same VLAN that the frame was determined to be in when it arrived. Thus, the scope of the VLAN is extended between multiple switches, and possibly even multiple buildings.

Although trunk ports allow for multiple VLANs, the frames are not blindly dumped out the ports, as they are for end stations or single-VLAN ports. The tag modification is necessary to inform the next switch of the true VLAN identity of the frame enclosed in the tag.

—Neil Lovering, CCIE, CCSI

ISL, 802.10, 802.1Q, and LANE

Let's look at some trunking protocols in detail. Cisco's Catalyst family of switches support four trunking protocols: Inter-Switch Link (ISL), 802.10, 802.1Q, and LAN Emulation (LANE). Not all trunking protocols are available on every model of Catalyst switch. For example, LANE, being an ATM protocol, is not available on the lower-end switches that do not support ATM. Consult the hardware-specific chapters later in the book for more information on which switches support which trunking protocols. Some protocols, for example 802.1Q, are only available in the latest versions of software.

ISL and 802.10 are frame tagging VLAN protocols. LANE is not quite either frame tagging or frame filtering, as you will see shortly.

ISL

Inter-Switch Link (ISL) is a Cisco-created, proprietary trunking protocol. Proprietary in this case means that it was not created or approved by an independent standards body. It does not necessarily mean that it is not seen in non-Cisco products. There are a few NIC cards and drivers that will do ISL to virtually multihome servers, and there is a free Linux driver for DEC Tulip-based Fast Ethernet cards. Other switch vendors are starting to support ISL on their switch products as well.

Cisco implements ISL on Fast Ethernet ports in its routers and Catalyst switch products. In the current software, ISL can be used to trunk VLAN traffic for Ethernet, FDDI, and Token Ring LANs. When a frame from one of the supported LAN types needs to be placed on an ISL trunk, an additional frame header is placed at the beginning of the frame, called an ISL header. We will discuss the frame header in a moment, but for now, accept that part of it is 10 bits that represent the VLAN number. 10 bits allow for a possible 1024 VLANs, numbered 0 through 1023. A number of these are reserved, so some of the Cisco documentation states that there are 1000 VLANs that can be used. The earliest versions of the software only allowed for 256 VLANs. Consult Chapter 7 for more information on software versions.

ISL can carry a wide range of frame sizes. The ISL headers take up 26 bytes, so those 26 bytes are added onto the size of the frame being trunked. There is also a new CRC added to the end, which is four bytes. The smallest allowed frame of the protocols trunked is from FDDI, which allows frames as small as 17 bytes. The largest is Token Ring, which allows packets as large as 17,800 bytes. So frames may range in size from 47 bytes to 17,830 bytes, although the protocol allows for smaller and larger. This process of adding a new header and checksum is known as *encapsulation*. ISL encapsulates the entire frame, without doing any sort of fragmentation.

Obviously, ISL frames at the maximum size are well beyond Ethernet's maximum of 1,518 bytes (not counting the preamble). Some of you may be curious as to why ISL only runs over Fast Ethernet (and Gigabit Ethernet). There's no technical reasons why ISL couldn't be done at 10-Mbps Ethernet, or over FDDI, or Token Ring. This choice is more for business reasons than anything else. Token Ring and 10-Mbps Ethernet really are just too slow to be useful for trunking. FDDI is fast enough, but Cisco likely doesn't want to put a great deal of development time into what is quickly becoming a legacy networking technology. On the Catalyst equipment, a single-port FDDI card costs about the same as a 12-port Fast Ethernet card. FDDI rings also tend to have legacy equipment connected to them, which probably would not be compatible with the nonstandard frames. Remember that, like Token Ring, FDDI is a logical ring, and each station gets each frame and has to pass it. Should a station decide a frame is illegal, it might drop it. Similar problems would happen on a Fast Ethernet link if you tried to run ISL over a link with stations on it, so you should use point-to-point links for ISL. You could theoretically use point-to-point links with FDDI too, but it would be too expensive.

There is another reason why ISL does not work over 10-Mbps Ethernet. The chipset that Cisco used for 10-Mbps Ethernet was hard-wired for a maximum frame size of 1518 bytes. They were not going to start over designing a new 10-Mbps chipset. The conclusion one can draw from this, and other evidence, is that the Fast Ethernet hardware is more flexible in terms of what frame sizes it can accept. This looks good for forward compatibility through software upgrades. This would be useful if, for example, the proposal to allow larger frame sizes on Fast Ethernet to boost throughput is passed.

Let's take a look at the ISL header format. Table 2-1 shows the contents of the 26-byte ISL header.

TABLE 2-1 Fields of the ISL Header	**Field**	**Bits**	**Function**
	DA	40	Destination Address. Cisco uses 01:00:0C:00:00. Note that the first three bytes are Cisco's manufacturer ID for MAC addresses, with the multicast bit on.
	TYPE	4	A four-bit field to indicate the type of frame being carried.
	USER	4	User-defined field. May be used to define priority. Note that the DA, TYPE, and USER fields total 48 bits, which would be a normal MAC address size.
	SA	48	Source address. MAC addresses of the switch port sending the frame.
	LEN	16	Length (in bytes) of the frame, minus parts of the header (18 bytes worth).
	(fixed)	24	This field is fixed, and always equals 0xAAAA03
	HAS	24	This is equal to the first three bytes of the SA field. Currently must be 0x00000C, which is Cisco's manufacturer ID.
	VLAN	15	15 bits to identify the VLAN number.
	BPDU	1	A one-bit flag to indicate if the encapsulated packet is a BPDU packet.
	INDX	16	Cisco's documentation says this is the port index of the device that sent the frame. This implies that it's set to the number that the sending switch uses to identify the sending port internally. Cisco's documentation says the receiver can safely ignore it, and that it's used for diagnostic purposes only.
	RES	16	All 0s for Ethernet. May contain AC and FC fields if carrying a Token Ring frame, or FC if a FDDI frame.

A few interesting things to note: Cisco has encoded part of the information into what would otherwise appear to be a multicast destination address. The LEN field would seem to allow 64KB frames. Of particular interest is the VLAN field, which is 15 bits long, not 10 as implied. Cisco is currently using only 10 bits, which allows for 1024 VLANs. This field would seem to imply that it's possible to define up to 32,768 VLANs if all 15 bits were used in future versions of the software. Many of Cisco's documents for their Catalyst switches say they have "hardware support for up to 1024 VLANs," so it's not clear if there is a limitation in the hardware, even though the protocol might allow for more.

As you can see, ISL is pretty simple as far as networking protocols go. It just takes the existing frame, throws a (relatively) simple header on the front, and a checksum at the end, and sends it along. In order to keep this trunking protocol simple, the tradeoffs that Cisco makes are that it breaks the Ethernet standard, and requires you to dedicate ports to that purpose. Overall, it is a very reasonable tradeoff in all-Cisco equipment, or another vendor who has decided to adopt Cisco's protocol.

Note: There is a different ISL header that has been added for Token Ring, and that one is discussed below in the section "Token Ring VLANs."

802.10

The next trunking protocol is less simple, but more interoperable, and it works across a wider variety of links. (Cisco's implementation works across FDDI and HDLC serial links.) Conceptually, it is similar to ISL, in that there is an encapsulation of sorts, and a VLAN identifier is part of the new header, but the details are more involved. Cisco takes advantage of an exiting IEEE standard, 802.10, which was designed to allow differentiation of LANs across a shared backbone—in other words, a trunking protocol. The 802.10 standard includes a four-byte Security Association Identifier (SAID) which is used to identify which LAN the traffic belongs to. Theoretically, this allows for over four billion different VLANs. In practice, Cisco software maps the SAID to one of the 1024 VLAN numbers, so the effective limit is still 1024.

Although Cisco makes it fairly easy to configure, the details underlying 802.10 VLANs are somewhat involved. The 802.10 encapsulation is based on the 802.2 standard, which includes a distinct Logical Link Control (LLC) layer.

First, a quick review: The IEEE has divided the OSI Layer 2 into two parts, the Media Access Control layer, and the Logical Link Control layer. The MAC portion is responsible for things like preamble bits and collision handling. The LLC layer is responsible for frame formats and providing a MAC-independent method of accessing Layer 2. The IEEE defines two LLC types, 1 and 2, which are connectionless and connection-oriented, respectively. LLC type 1 (which is used in 802.10) includes service access points (SAPs) which identify what the function of the frame is. SAPs are akin to Ethertypes, or port numbers compared to TCP/IP transport protocols.

802.10 uses a fixed link service access point (LSAP) of 0x0A0A03. A LSAP is a combination of the three bytes that make up the destination SAP (DSAP), source SAP (SSAP), and control byte. This identifies the frame as an 802.10 frame, and tells other stations what additional fields to expect in that frame.

Let's look at an example. To keep things simple, let's start with a generic 802.3 packet as shown in Figure 2-5.

This is how the frame appears before it is placed on the trunk, viewed as a simple block format. Figure 2-6 illustrates what the frame looks like on the trunk.

Table 2-2 explains these new fields.

Naturally, the process is reversed when the frame leaves the trunk.

Cisco's 802.10 VLAN implementation is slightly different from the official 802.10 spec, so some consider Cisco's implementation to be another proprietary extension. I've seen a presentation from a competing vendor that went so far as to call Cisco's use of 802.10 "illegal," because it violates the standard. That statement is a bit too strong, but keep in mind that

FIGURE 2-5   Simple representation of an 802.3 packet before trunking

Destination	Source	Length	802.2 Header	Data

FIGURE 2-6 802.3 packet while on a trunk link using 802.10 trunking

Destination	Source	Length +16	0A0A03	SAID	Station ID	Frag flag	Original 802.2 header	Data

Cisco has made some proprietary enhancements if you plan to use 802.10 to mix vendors.

802.1Q

Cisco's latest addition to the trunking protocols is 802.1Q, the first industry-standard trunking protocol. Since it's an industry standard, you should be able to use it to trunk VLANs between switches created by different vendors, once the implementations mature. Like many of the IEEE standards, it's very feature-rich, which also means it's not as simple as other protocols.

802.1Q has a few options that are not available in ISL or 802.10. For example, the IEEE spec claims that tagged frames will work over shared 802 networks as well as point-to-point. The 802.1Q is also a more ambitious

TABLE 2-2

The Fields of an 802.3 Packet Using 802.10 Trunking

Field	Bits	Function
Length	16	This existed before, but now it's been increased by 16 bytes, because we've added 16 bytes of additional header.
LSAP	24	This is the LSAP field, fixed at 0x0A0A03 to identify it as an 802.10 frame.
SAID	32	The SAID field, which holds the VLAN number.
Station ID	64	Contains the 6 bytes for the source address of the original frame.
Frag	16	Two bytes to handle fragmentation information. Not supported by Cisco, so they are set to 0.
Original Header		This is the original 802.2 LLC header.

standard in that it covers more possible configuration options. Therefore, a direct comparison is not really possible. If you are curious, the 802.1Q tagged frames (without additional options) resemble 802.10 tagged frames. This is perhaps not surprising, since they're both IEEE standards.

Cisco supports 802.1Q in the latest available IOS version (12.0T) as of this writing. Cisco added support for 802.1Q in version 4.1 of the Catalyst software.

Like ISL, 802.1Q allows priority information to be added to each trunked frame. 802.1Q uses three bits for priority information, yielding eight possible priority levels. 802.1Q uses 12 bits for the VLAN ID (VID), allowing for 4096 possible VLANs, a couple of which are reserved. VID 0 is a nontrunked VLAN, and is used to indicate only that priority bits are used, allowing for priority without trunking. VLAN 1 is the default VLAN, similar to the Catalyst default. VLAN 4096 (FFF hex) is reserved.

Like 802.10, the headers vary depending on the type of frame being carried, and the type of network it's being carried over. 802.1Q allows for source-route bridge information in the header.

Cisco has not yet documented which features of 802.1Q they support. As of this writing, Cisco does not test on 802.1Q in the CLSC exam. It's likely that over time, Cisco will add support for any 802.1Q features they do not currently support. It's also worth noting that the 802.1Q standard hasn't passed every phase of the approval process yet, although it doesn't seem likely the specification will change. Normally, the IEEE charges for copies of their standards, but since the standard is still technically a draft, it's available free of charge on the Web.

LANE

Asynchronous Transfer Mode (ATM) was designed to be a network protocol for many purposes, including acting as a trunk for both LAN and WAN connections. It's not just for data traffic either, since it is just as capable of carrying voice and video traffic, if you have the right ATM equipment. For now, our interest is in data networking, and specifically in using ATM as a VLAN trunking mechanism.

LAN Emulation (LANE) is covered in detail in Chapter 11, and some ATM hardware specifics can be found in the various hardware chapters of this book. For those who are somewhat familiar with ATM, we'll be doing a short review. If you're very familiar with ATM, and have worked with it before, then you probably already know that ATM trunking is just a by-product of how LANE works.

For the purposes of discussing LAN Emulation, ATM is used as a backbone network designed to carry large amounts of traffic. It is primarily of interest for carrying mixed traffic types, such as video and voice, in addition to data, or if a lot of bandwidth is needed. ATM comes in various speeds, including OC-3 (155 Mbps) and OC-12 (622 Mbps). These speeds existed before Fast Ethernet and Gigabit Ethernet products were available, so some early adopters who needed a lot of bandwidth may have deployed ATM backbones some time ago.

exam
ⓦatch

There are many acronyms associated with ATM, and you will need to memorize what they stand for and what functions they represent. They are covered fairly quickly here, so be sure to read Chapter 11 carefully and work on learning the new terms.

Originally, when ATM was created, the assumption seemed to be that it would replace all legacy LAN and WAN links, and everyone would have an ATM NIC in their desktop computers and servers. That did not happen, and it never will happen. Still, ATM has a lot of nice characteristics and many people wanted to use it for specific functions, such as a backbone trunk. So the standards bodies behind ATM created a new set of standards called LANE, which allows traditional LANs to use ATM as a backbone trunk.

Here are the new terms. The device that does most of the work in a LANE environment is called a LAN Emulation Client (LEC). A LEC is the software running on a device that has both traditional networking ports (Ethernet, Token Ring) as well as at least one ATM port. Be clear on this point: The LEC is typically not the desktop computer attached to the switch; it is the switch itself, or rather the VLAN function of the switch. In the Cisco world, a Catalyst (or possibly LightStream) switch with ATM hardware is the device that has a LEC. Each separate Emulated LAN

(ELAN) that is trunked over ATM has at least one LEC. If there are five VLANs defined, then that switch has at least five LECs. Each LEC is associated with one VLAN. It is possible for a client PC to be a LEC if it has an ATM card, and is attached to the ATM fabric that way, though for the purposes of our LANE discussion, that case isn't important. We're concerned about the Catalyst as a LEC.

ATM uses the term ELAN instead of VLAN. Conceptually, they perform the same function, which is to allow multiple, distinct LANs to exist in the same box. They have different names, though, because of the fundamental difference in how they are created. VLANs work by controlling broadcast forwarding. ELANs control broadcasts (and unicasts) in a different way. VLANs work because the underlying technology is broadcast-based. Since ATM is connection-oriented, there is no underlying broadcast mechanism, and the broadcast function must be added to support LAN stations that expect to be able to use broadcasts. To do so, LANE has broadcast servers that create the copies of broadcast frames that are needed. In short, VLANs work by *limiting* broadcasts, ELANs work by *enabling* broadcasts. The end result looks the same, but the processes are very different.

The term LEC implies that there is a server. Indeed, there is a LAN Emulation Server (LES). The basic job of the LES is to provide LANE information to the LEC. The types of services that the LES provides to LECs includes MAC address mappings, MAC registration services, and addresses of other LANE components. When an LEC adds a new Ethernet station to an ELAN, it registers that station's MAC address with the LES. We'll call this station A. When a new station (let's call it station B) wants to communicate with station A, the LEC to which station B is attached queries the LES for the ATM address of the LEC that has station A. Station B's LEC then creates an ATM connection to the LEC that has station A, and forwards the frame.

You may have spotted a problem with the scenario just mentioned, which is, what to do if the desired MAC address has not been registered with the LES, or if a broadcast frame is to be sent? To solve this problem, a *broadcast and unknown server* (BUS) is added. As the name implies, a BUS is involved in forwarding frames that are broadcast (or multicast) frames, for which the location is unknown. The simplified version of how a BUS is used is that when a LEC queries the LES for the LEC that has a broadcast or unknown MAC address, it is given the ATM address of the BUS instead. The LEC forwards the frame to the BUS. The BUS then creates a copy of the frame for each LEC in the ELAN, and forwards it to them. Those LECs are then responsible for sending a copy of the frame to each port in that VLAN. In the Cisco implementation, the LES and BUS devices are the same, and there is only one active per ELAN. Cisco puts this function on their routers and switches. For performance reasons, you'll almost always want this function to live on a Catalyst switch.

The final LANE-related device is the LAN Emulation Configuration Server (LECS.) When a LEC first joins an emulated LAN, it consults the LECS for certain information, such as the address of the LES for that ELAN. The LECS also contains ATM naming information. One LECS is required per ATM cloud, which is to say all of your interconnected ATM devices.

That's how ATM trunking works. Using ATM to trunk VLANs is really just a by-product of how ATM handles LANE. Since LANE is able to deal with more than one emulated LAN across an ATM switch fabric, the trunking capability is automatically there. The various LANE components take care of checking which ports and stations are allowed on which VLANs. There's not a lot to say about trunking on ATM as a separate function, because it's not separate. If you develop an understanding of LANE, you will see how the trunking portion works.

Other Options

There's one last "trunking" option I want to mention, and that is not to trunk. A set of examples was given at the beginning of the chapter describing the advantages of trunking. The main reason is to save resources—specifically, ports and cabling. However, given sufficient resources, you don't have to use new features just because they're there. That's important to remember, especially if the software isn't very mature.

on the
Job

At the company where I work, we've been using Catalyst switches for some time—since just before the Catalyst 5500 family was released. This means that we started with early 2.x software. We're very fortunate that in our headquarters campus, which consists of several buildings, we own our underground fiber. In each building, we have at least 24 pairs of fiber, and in most cases, much more than that. In order to keep things as simple as possible, and make our cutovers from the older equipment easy, we kept one link per VLAN per switch in place. This means that we were essentially using Spanning Tree instead of a trunking protocol. About the same time, our Cisco sales engineer had another customer who was trying to use just about every feature in the Catalyst. They had many problems and kept the SE quite busy. We had no such problems.

CERTIFICATION OBJECTIVE 2.07

Token Ring VLANs

Why a separate section on Token Ring? As discussed in Chapter 1, Token Ring bridging is a little different from Ethernet bridging. The main difference is that Token Ring can use source-route bridging (SRB) as well as transparent bridging, while Ethernet uses strictly transparent bridging. This makes Token Ring considerably more complicated than Ethernet, but also gives it some extra capabilities, and Cisco wants to maintain those capabilities in their Token Ring implementation. Because of the SRB capability, Token Ring stations can be aware of the logical structure of any interconnected rings. Token Ring includes the concept of a local-ring-only broadcast, and an all-rings broadcast, which is under the control of the station sending the broadcast. A number of protocols implemented on top of Token Ring use that capability.

This type of broadcast arrangement is different from Ethernet. An Ethernet LAN has one broadcast domain, and indeed the LAN is defined by that broadcast domain. On Token Ring, there is a possibility for more than one broadcast domain, but still only one LAN (no router needed to cross rings). This allows for a certain amount of hierarchy in the broadcast structure.

In traditional Token Ring, all stations on the same MAU (also sometimes called a concentrator) or interconnected MAUs are on the same ring, and have the same ring number. If there is more than one ring, they may be connected by a bridge or a router. If connected by a bridge, each ring has a different number.

Cisco Catalyst switches have the capability to define a ring number on a per-port basis for Token Ring. You can define different ring numbers, and have the Catalyst act as an SRB, or you can define ports to have the same ring number, and have the Catalyst switch act like a logical MAU.

When a Catalyst is acting like a logical MAU, and forming a (single) logical ring, it's said to be performing a Token Ring Concentrator Relay Function (TrCRF). When the Catalyst is configured with ports in different logical rings, it's said to be performing a Token Ring Bridge Relay Function (TrBRF). You can, of course, mix the two functions within a single switch.

exam
ⓦatch

You probably will see questions on the test involving Token Ring bridging functions. It's likely that you will only be given the abbreviations (TrCRF, TrBRF) and be expected to answer based on their meaning. Be sure that you know what they stand for and how they interrelate. If you are clear on what a concentrator is and what a bridge is, you should be able to distinguish the two, but you must memorize what the acronyms stand for. Be especially aware of how many of something can be used (one TrBRF per TrCRF).

TrCRFs (with a couple of exceptions) can only exist within a single switch. For this purpose, a Catalyst 3900 stack is considered a single switch. Each TrCRF can have a single TrBRF associated with it. Stations on different rings (TrCRFs) can communicate with each other at Layer 2 via the TrBRF, assuming the TrCRFs share the same parent TrBRF.

Here are the exceptions. There is a default TrCRF that exists in all Token Ring Catalyst switches as VLAN 1003. It's called, plainly enough, the default TrCRF. Its TrBRF is called the default TrBRF, which is VLAN 1005. To take advantage of the default TrCRF, the switches must be connected via ISL. The default TrBRF can only have the default TrCRF associated with it. The default TrBRF doesn't perform any bridging functions; it doesn't need to, as it only has the one TrCRF.

The other exception is the backup TrCRF. It's possible to define a single port on multiple switches with the same TrCRF number, if that TrCRF is marked as backup. You can have one backup TrCRF defined per TrBRF shared between switches. The purpose of the backup TrCRF is to provide another network path if the ISL link between switches, which is providing a path for the TrBRF, goes down. Normally, all but one of the ports in a backup TrCRF is down. When the ISL link goes down, those ports become active, thereby providing an interconnecting ring across which stations can communicate.

DRiP

Since Cisco does not allow the use of the same TrCRF in different switches (except for the exceptions noted) they have created the Duplicate Ring Protocol (DRiP). Switches use DRiP to inform each other about which TrCRFs they have active. This information can be used to prevent the definition of duplicate TrCRFs on different switches. DRiP is also used for the following purposes:

- **All-routes explorer (ARE) filtering**   If the switch knows which TrCRFs are attached to a TrBRF, it can correctly drop AREs that have already been to an attached ring

- **Detection and shutdown of duplicate TrCRFs**   If two switches determine that they have the same TrCRF in use, the switch with the higher MAC address will shut down its ports in that TrCRF

- **ISL link failure detection**   This is related to the backup TrCRF. DRiP will advertise when ISL links go up and down, so backup links can be activated and de-activated.

Cisco provides an excellent set of documents regarding their Token Ring switching products. I highly recommend them for further study, particularly the one titled *Token Ring VLANs and Related Protocols*, which can be found at:

http://www.cisco.com/univercd/cc/td/doc/product/lan/trsrb/

QUESTIONS AND ANSWERS

How do I decide which trunking protocol to use?	This will depend on your needs and your infrastructure. If you need to interoperate with another switch vendor, you'll have to find a common protocol. If you have an ATM backbone, you'll have to use LANE. If you have a Cisco FDDI backbone, you'll want to use 802.10. If you're building from scratch using all Cisco gear and Fast Ethernet links, ISL is easy to use.
How do I start using LANE?	This chapter only covers ATM lightly. To get started, a good place to look is Chapter 11, which covers LANE in detail.
Which is better, frame tagging or frame filtering?	It's a bit of a moot point, unless you're using LANE. It seems pretty clear that frame tagging is the preferred method.
What's the best way to get started setting up a VLAN infrastructure?	You'll want to check out Cisco's VTP protocol, and design with that in mind from the beginning. If you're using Fast Ethernet for trunks, try to build a short tree, without too many three-way links. If you decide to use some of the advanced redundancy features, you'll be much happier with that type of layout.

CERTIFICATION SUMMARY

VLANs expand on the concepts of bridging and switching by allowing the creation of multiple, logical LANs within a single switch chassis. Further, this concept is extended to trunk links, which allow those logical groups to be kept separate while passing between switches.

There are two main types of trunking mechanisms, frame tagging and frame filtering, also called explicit tagging and implicit tagging. Frame tagging is also sometimes called coloring a frame. Frame tagging modifies frames as they leave a switch to somehow mark which VLAN they belong to, to make it easy for other switches to make forwarding decisions. The modification is removed when the frame leaves the last switch on its way to the original intended recipient. Frame filtering makes forwarding decisions based on some information contained within the frame, without modifying it. The information filtered on may include MAC address, Layer 3 address, or some other information that can be inferred from each frame. For frame filtering to be effective, there has to be a protocol to share VLAN mapping information among switches.

Cisco provides several trunking protocols in their switch and router products. These include ISL, 802.10, LANE, and in newer versions of the software, 802.1Q. With the exception of LANE, these are all frame tagging trunking protocols. LANE works a little bit differently, and is closer to frame filtering than frame tagging. LANE can trunk VLAN connections because it inherently includes the concept of multiple LANs being emulated across an ATM switch fabric.

ATM LANE includes a number of pieces that are required for LANE to function. These include the LAN Emulation Server (LES), LAN Emulation Client (LEC), broadcast and unknown server (BUS), and the LAN Emulation Configuration Server (LECS). Each of these pieces has a critical function in determining ELAN membership or delivering frames to the intended recipients.

Token Ring VLANs are a bit more complicated than Ethernet VLANs, because Token Ring includes more bridging options. Cisco divides the two types of Token Ring broadcast domains into Token Ring Concentrator Relay Function (TrCRF) and Token Ring Bridge Relay Function (TrBRF). With a couple of exceptions, TrCRFs can only live within a single switch. These are joined, possibly across switches, by TrBRFs. Cisco also provides the DRiP to help prevent duplicate TrCRFs between switches, and also to help enable some redundancy features.

TWO-MINUTE DRILL

- ❑ The defining characteristic of a LAN segment is that all the nodes can communicate directly with each other, without having to pass through some Layer 3 or higher device such as a router.

- ❑ A group of nodes that can reach each other by broadcast are said to be in the same *broadcast domain*.

❑ Cisco static VLANs are *port-assigned*. The term port-assigned implies that VLANs can be assigned on an individual port basis.

❑ VLANs can be used to help increase network security.

❑ There are at least two obvious ways that the source of a frame can be tracked: The first is to track what VLAN the port it came in belongs to and is called *frame tagging,* also known as *explicit tagging.*

❑ The second way to track the source of a frame is to keep a list of MAC addresses for each VLAN (which the switches must do anyway). After the destination has been determined, a determination is made as to whether the frame passes. This is called *frame filtering,* also known *as implicit tagging.*

❑ The advantage to frame tagging is that the VLAN is identified immediately, and no further VLAN membership decisions need to be made on that frame.

❑ The main characteristic of VLAN switches is their capability to maintain separate VLANs within a box, and also between boxes.

❑ Cisco implements ISL on Fast Ethernet ports in its routers and Catalyst switch products.

❑ The device that does most of the work in a LANE environment is called a LAN Emulation Client (LEC).

❑ ATM uses the term ELAN instead of VLAN. Conceptually, they perform the same function, which is to allow multiple, distinct LANs to exist in the same switch.

❑ VLANs work by *limiting* broadcasts, ELANs work by *enabling* broadcasts.

❑ Token Ring bridging is a little different from Ethernet bridging. The main difference is that Token Ring can use source-route bridging (SRB) as well as transparent bridging, while Ethernet uses strictly transparent bridging.

SELF TEST

The following Self Test questions will help you measure your understanding of the material presented in this chapter. Read all the choices carefully, as there may be more than one correct answer. Choose all correct answers for each question.

1. A VLAN is roughly equivalent to:

    A. A collision domain

    B. A broadcast domain

    C. A VTP domain

    D. A DNS domain

2. What is the difference between a regular switch and a VLAN switch?

    A. VLAN switches can do SNMP

    B. VLAN switches have RMON

    C. VLAN switches can do multiple Layer 3 protocols

    D. VLAN switches can maintain separate broadcast domains

3. Static VLAN assignment is usually based on:

    A. Port

    B. MAC address

    C. IP address

    D. VLAN ID

4. Which of the following are potential dynamic VLAN criteria? (Select two.)

    A. MAC address

    B. Slot number

    C. Port number

    D. IP address

5. Cisco supports which type of VLANs in their switches?

    A. Static

    B. Dynamic

    C. Both static and dynamic

    D. Neither static nor dynamic

6. VLANs can help with which of the following? ·

    A. Decreased costs

    B. Reducing latency

    C. Increased flexibility

    D. Consolidate WAN links

7. How do VLANs increase security?

    A. By bridging between segments

    B. By providing RMON capabilities

    C. By isolating traffic to specific broadcast domains

    D. By providing a firewall feature

8. Frame tagging is also known as: (Select two.)

    A. Frame filtering

    B. Trunking

    C. Explicit tagging

    D. Coloring

9. What is a trunk?

   A. A VLAN tagging mechanism

   B. A way of passing more than one VLAN over a link

   C. An SRB to link TrCRFs

   D. A way to bridge between VLANs

10. Cisco switches support which kinds of trunk setup? (Select two.)

    A. Static

    B. Advertisement

    C. Auto-negotiation

    D. ISL

11. Which trunking protocols does Cisco support? (Choose all that apply.)

    A. ISL

    B. LANE

    C. 802.10

    D. STP

12. Who created ISL?

    A. IEEE

    B. ANSI

    C. IBM

    D. Cisco

13. ISL works over what types of network links?

    A. FDDI

    B. Fast Ethernet

    C. HDLC

    D. ATM

14. 802.10 theoretically allows for how many VLANs?

    A. 256

    B. 1024

    C. 32768

    D. Over 4,000,000,000

15. Each LEC is associated with how many VLANs?

    A. One

    B. Two

    C. Four

    D. Eight

16. How many LESs does Cisco support per VLAN in their implementation?

    A. One

    B. Two

    C. Three

    D. Four

17. Which LANE component handles broadcasts?

    A. LEC

    B. LES

    C. BUS

    D. LECS

18. How often does an LEC consult with the LECS?

    A. Once

    B. Each time a broadcast occurs

    C. Every 30 seconds

    D. Never

19. What is the VLAN number for the default TrCRF?

    A. 1
    B. 1003
    C. 1005
    D. 1023

20. What is one of the primary functions of the DRiP protocol?

    A. To provide SRB for Token Ring LANs
    B. LANE configuration
    C. To prevent duplicate TrCRFs
    D. Packet encapsulation

CISCO CERTIFIED NETWORK PROFESSIONAL

3

Placing Catalyst 5000 Series Switches in Your Network

Y ou have decided to implement a switched network for your office, campus, or corporation, using the Catalyst 5000 series switch. Now the fun begins! How do you equip and place the Catalyst 5000 series switch to take advantage of its benefits, while keeping everyone from the boardroom to the mailroom happy?

This chapter explores how to place the Catalyst 5000 series switch in your network to maximize the topology of the network while minimizing bottlenecks and congestion. This includes choosing the right chassis and module(s) to install, gathering the information needed to configure the switch once it is installed, and dealing with future expansion.

CERTIFICATION OBJECTIVE 3.01

Demand Nodes and Resource Nodes

When in the planning stages for deploying the Catalyst 5000 series switch, location of devices such as servers and workstations becomes important. Before the advent of the switched LAN environment, the Ethernet hub was used to connect workstations and servers to the LAN. As more devices were connected, the chances for congestion and collisions increased. This tended to make the media itself (10 Mbps Ethernet) an issue. While the media worked, response time began to suffer, due to the sheer numbers of workstations, servers, and other devices using LAN resources. Servers were placed in the data center, usually at the center of a star network topology that is at the center of the hub network.

Today's high-speed workstations demand more bandwidth to run multimedia applications and Internet applications such as browsers that use a wide range of helper applications. Trying to use today's workstations with yesterday's network topology, which utilized hubs mounted in the wiring closet, can result in a phone call from the user voicing his or her displeasure at the performance of the network.

The Catalyst 5000 series switch solves this problem by providing a wide range of modules that allow the switch to be integrated into just about any network topology. If you need 10 Mbps and 100 Mbps Ethernet, there are modules available to satisfy these needs. If your network is fiber based, the fiber module for Ethernet is just the ticket. Mounting a Catalyst 5000 series switch in the wiring closet to replace the hub will breathe new life into your network.

A demand node is a device that "demands" information from another device. In other words, a demand node sends out queries to determine the location of the information it needs, which will depend on the application. The most common form of demand node is an end-user workstation. An example of demand node operation would be a user at a workstation. The user needs to access a file located on a Windows NT server located on the local LAN. The user opens Network Neighborhood and selects the server, then locates the file and copies it to a local drive. The process of accessing the Windows NT server and copying the file is a demand node operation.

A resource node is a device where information that is being requested from a demand node is located. A resource node responds to queries received from the network. The most common resource nodes are file servers such as a Windows NT or Novell NetWare file server. Other examples would be print servers, mail servers, or a Cisco Router that is connected to an Internet Service Provider (ISP) for connectivity to the Internet.

In the past, LANs were implemented using hubs that grouped together demand and resource nodes in the same segment. The hub served as a quasi flow control device, limiting the amount of data the demand nodes were sending to the resource nodes. The limit was the bandwidth itself. Traffic became excessive, causing collisions and congestion. When the segment became congested due to nodes being added, new collision domains were created by adding new Ethernet segments. Demand nodes were placed on these segments, with a router or bridge connecting to the main segment. In some cases, the resource nodes were allocated a port off of the router or bridge, thus isolating the resource node on its own segment.

With the introduction of the LAN switch, the LAN administrator's life became much easier. Resource nodes can now be located on individual switch ports, and demand nodes located on other switch ports. The resource nodes no longer share bandwidth with the demand nodes. Demand nodes are now (depending on the number of users) allocated their own switch port or grouped together in small hub groups connected to a single switch port. However, the administrator still faces challenges.

Devices are now connected to a switch port with no flow control. Users complain that their applications are not responding as before. Complaints of poor response time pour into your voice mail and e-mail boxes. You break out the trusty LAN sniffer and after some evaluation and testing, you determine that the links to the resource nodes are congested. At this time, the links to the resource nodes are 10-Mbps Ethernet.

How do you, the administrator deal with this? After analyzing the current LAN topology, the number of users on the LAN, the information provided by the sniffer, and future expansion, you come up with a plan. You decide to speed up the links on the ports to which the resource nodes are connected. Conventional wisdom tells us that if the demand nodes are connected to 10-Mbps Ethernet ports, then the resource nodes, if possible, should be 10 times your current LAN bandwidth. This means the resource nodes will need to be connected to 100-Mbps switched Ethernet ports. This is where the Catalyst 5000 series switch comes into play.

When planning a switched LAN, in most cases, the demand and resource nodes will be located on different collision domains. This approach, sometimes called a tiered design, places the workstations in an "Access" tier, servers and other resource devices in a "Distribution" tier, and links to remote offices, or buildings within a campus on the "Core" tier. These tiers are normally separated by routers or switches.

Workstations would be connected to the access tier. The topology is usually 10 Mbps Ethernet or 16 Mbps Token Ring connecting to Catalyst 5000 series switches located in wiring closets across the campus or floor of an office building. On the network side of the switch, which connects to the distribution tier, connectivity can vary. 100 Mbps Ethernet is a common form of inter-switch connectivity. The introduction of Fast EtherChannel has made it a popular option for connectivity between switches. ATM is another option for connecting end users to the distribution tier with the advent of LANE (LAN Emulation) services over ATM.

The core tier serves as the backbone to the network, connecting both the access and distribution tiers to remote offices and/or other buildings on the campus or across a WAN. Connectivity options have recently been enhanced with the introduction of the Fast EtherChannel option on the Catalyst 5000 switch. Fast EtherChannel is a module that provides up to 400 Mbps (two-port configuration), 600 Mbps (three-port configuration) or 800 Mbps (four-port configuration) of full duplex Fast Ethernet bandwidth for switch trunks to handle today's high-performance networks.

Also available from Cisco is the Gigabit EtherChannel. Gigabit EtherChannel provides up to eight Gbps of bandwidth for switch trunks. This utilizes the Gigabit Ethernet module, providing nine ports of Gigabit Ethernet along with the Supervisor III module in the Catalyst 5000, 5009, and 550x chassis.

e x a m
ⓦ a t c h

Be aware of the differences between demand nodes and resource nodes. Demand nodes are basically workstations that are requesting (demanding) information from a resource. An example would be a workstation requesting a file from a file server. A resource node is a device that provides the information requested from a demand node. An example of a resource node is a file server or router.

CERTIFICATION OBJECTIVE 3.02

Local Resources and Remote Resources

When an Ethernet LAN is segmented, multiple collision domains are created. Within these segments, communication between demand and resource nodes occurs. This communication is called same-segment communication. Same-segment conversations between devices, along with inter-segment conversations between devices located on different collision domains create two resource types: local and remote.

Local Resources

A local resource is a resource node that is located on the same collision domain as the demand node. Collisions occur when more than one device on the segment transmits data at the same time. When an Ethernet LAN is broken into segments, capacity increases due to the separate conversation that is supported on each segment. In a switched environment, where the switch port is connected to only one device, local conversations are enabled for the node on the segment. When several devices are connected to a switch port (when the port is connected to a hub with several devices connected to the hub), local conversations are enabled for the nodes on that segment.

Collision domain capacity is measured by multiplying the speed of the medium by the number of local conversations that simultaneously occur. Since only one conversation can occur on any switch port, the capacity is equal to the port speed of the switch.

Remote Resources

A remote resource is a resource node that is not located on the same collision domain as the demand node. When dealing with remote resources, throughput becomes the factor that administrators deal with. Throughput is defined as a measurement of activity during a network conversation that is calculated in bits per second. Examples of remote resources would be servers, such as Novell NetWare or Windows NT, which are located on a different collision domain than the demand node.

To determine the throughput when dealing with remote resources, the number of simultaneous remote conversations is measured to determine the maximum number of conversations taking place at a given time that do not affect application performance.

exam
Ⓦatch

The difference between local resources and remote resources is the location of the resource with respect to the node that is demanding the information. A local resource is a device that is located on the same hub as the demand node. A remote resource is a device that is not located on the same hub as the demand node.

Bottlenecks and Buffer Overflows

Data that flows between demand nodes and resource nodes in a switched environment is analogous to water flowing through a funnel. If the amount of water that pours into the funnel is greater than the amount that is draining out, then water spills out over the top. Similarly, if the amount of data that is heading out of the pipe to the server is greater than the bandwidth, then data is lost. One workstation on a 10-Mbps Ethernet segment will not use all of the bandwidth available. But if many workstations are on a segment and are being used to access resource nodes, then the possibility for "spillage" increases. This is known as *buffer overflow* and there are several ways to deal with the problem.

In our water-through-the-funnel analogy, you could prevent spillage by increasing the size of the drain at the bottom of the funnel. On the other hand, if the drain is already at its maximum size, then you could decrease the amount of water flowing into the funnel.

In a switched environment, you can avoid buffer overflow by increasing the size of the pipe to the server. In the tiered network topology, the distribution tier is based on 100-Mbps Fast Ethernet connections. Today's high-performance servers are usually equipped with 100-Mbps network cards.

If the demand nodes are attached to 100-Mbps switch ports, then consider reducing these to 10-Mbps switch ports. Performance may actually increase as the amount of data flowing into the funnel is reduced to the point where the amount flowing in and out is equalized. An administrator could even group several nodes together with a hub, then let the nodes compete for and share the 10 Mbps on the switch port.

exam
watch

Bottlenecks and buffer overflow are the usual suspects when a problem occurs for which there is no obvious cause. To prevent problems, planning where to place the Catalyst 5000 switch is very important. Be able to identify the places in a network topology where bottlenecks are likely to occur. Understand how buffer overflow can affect network performance and how to make changes to correct this.

Congestion Management

Congestion management is a balancing act, keeping the resource nodes running as fast as possible and the demand nodes from killing the LAN. A switch offers little in the way of buffer tuning, other than the ability to adjust the buffer size, but the switch is usually not the problem when congestion occurs. More often than not, it is either the demand or resource node where the problems occur. If all the techniques we have discussed in the previous section to tune the network fail, buffering of data can be accomplished by forcing the demand nodes to traverse a router to reach the resources. The router will act as a buffering device, allowing data to flow in a more orderly manner to and from the resource and demand nodes.

There are general rules for configuring a switched network for demand and resource nodes. They are:

- Resource nodes are placed on dedicated switch ports

- Utilize 100-Mbps (Fast Ethernet) as much as possible for resource nodes

- If available, full duplex should be used as much as possible on the links to the resource nodes

- Resource nodes should be placed as close as possible to their demand nodes to prevent bottlenecks. If this is not possible, then make sure the number of switches between the demand and resource nodes are kept to a minimum. Consider VLANs as a way of keeping departments separated. Traffic that is within the VLAN will not be forwarded to other VLANs. Routers are used to carry traffic meant for both resource and demand nodes that are located outside the VLAN.

on the
!Job

When planning to convert a traditional hub-based LAN to a switched LAN, I find the concept of KISS applies. "Keep it simple, stupid" means keep the planning simple, but make the goal of a successful conversion achievable. For network designers and engineers who have not taken on the task of implementing a switched network, this may seem like an impossible task, but in reality, it is not. Depending on the number of users in the office, campus, or corporation, the designer will need to decide whether to provision each user a dedicated switch port on the Catalyst 5000 series switch. This is also a cost decision. The designer needs to determine the cost per port, depending on which model Catalyst switch is being used. To drive down the cost, the designer may choose to implement small hub groups, allowing several users to share a switch port. This minimizes the port costs and makes the investment in a switched network seem like a no-brainer. Traffic costs also come into play; the goals are to maximize the traffic per switch port and to minimize the possibility of congestion on the port.

Putting It All Together

So, based on the information presented to this point, how do you place Catalyst 5000 series switches into your network? The answer to this question is . . . it depends. Now this may seem like a vague answer, but there are as many different solutions as there are different networks. The following information should serve as a guideline in determining how to place the Catalyst 5000 series switch in your network to take advantage of the benefits it offers.

Number of Users

The number of users that are on the network dictates the number of collision domains needed. This can be broken down further to say how many users are "power" users, use bandwidth intensive applications, or have high-performance workstations, possibly with 100-Mbps Ethernet network cards. Along with this is the question of how many "regular" users there are; that is, which users are not using bandwidth-intensive applications or do not have 100-Mbps Ethernet network cards. Even the most powerful workstation equipped with a 100-Mbps Ethernet card can send no more than 8 Mbps of data at any one moment.

The advantage that the Catalyst 5000 series switch has in the area of planning is the fact that it is a "modular" chassis. You can add a module to a chassis to expand the number of switch ports available in a closet. If new users are added to a section of the office, just add another module to the chassis and assign the ports accordingly. Along with the modular chassis, the Catalyst 5000 series' support of VLANs allows administrators to add ports to a particular VLAN without having to move bodies around. Figure 3-1 shows a typical switched network using a tiered approach. Workstations attached to the access tier via 10 Mbps Ethernet, while a server and a Cisco 7000 router are connected to the distribution tier via 100 Mbps Fast Ethernet.

If the number of users does not justify the deployment of Catalyst 5000 series switches into each wiring closet, an alternative is to deploy a smaller switch chassis such as the Catalyst 1900, 2820, 2900, or 5002 series switches. In turn, these switches can connect to a central location or to a distribution tier Catalyst 5000, or 550*x* series switch. These switches have lower port density due to the smaller chassis, but still offer the same high-performance LAN connectivity as the Catalyst 5000 series switches.

If your company is located on a single floor of an office building with resource nodes in a single location or data center, it may be cost-effective to centrally locate a Catalyst 550*x* switch to handle the LAN connectivity needs. The features of the 1900, 2820, 2900, and 5002 switches are covered in other chapters in this guide.

Network topology

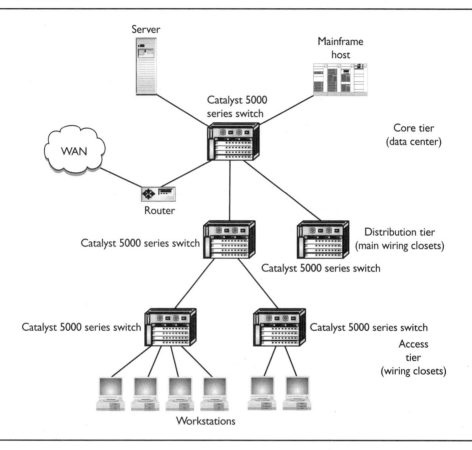

Size and Layout of the Office or Campus

The size and layout of the office or campus is also a consideration when it comes to placing the Catalyst 5000 series switch in your network. In a building with several floors, with several wiring closets per floor, one or possibly two switches are placed in the closets to provide the access tier. These switches would then be connected via trunk links directly to the data center. The number of switches placed in each closet would depend on the size of the office or floor, and the number of users on the floor.

The trunks connecting the closet switches to the distribution switch or the data center would be high-speed links such as Fast Ethernet, or, in the case of a campus, ATM or FDDI. In the cases of an established building where the cost would be prohibitive to run new wiring, you could employ two levels of closet switches. The first level would connect the users to the local wiring closet using the existing wiring. The second level would be a Catalyst 5000 switch in a central location on the floor. This switch would serve as the collection point for the closets on the floor, using 100-Mbps Ethernet to connect to the closets. This switch would then connect to the data center using FDDI or 100-Mbps Ethernet (or again, in the case of a campus setting, ATM). Figure 3-2 shows a three-switch network with FDDI interconnecting the switches.

Locating the server with respect to access by the users has become critical. The Catalyst 5000 series switch was designed with this consideration in mind. Connectivity to the data center has been covered. Now let us focus on placement of the servers.

In the past, servers were usually located in an office or lab on the floor of a building. Connectivity was usually to the same hub as the workstations. As applications became more bandwidth intensive, workstations became faster, the number of collisions increased, congestion occurred, and the users complained. Today, servers are grouped together in server farms, placed in the data center in racks, and treated in the manner that they should be: as sensitive devices that deserve respect. If the server crashes, everybody suffers.

Server farms are dedicated network segments reserved for servers only. Each server has a 100-Mbps switched Ethernet port dedicated for that server only. This design has worked, although it has been proven a poor design. Since the Catalyst 5000 series switch is modular, a Catalyst 5000 equipped with twelve-port Fast Ethernet modules is sufficient to provide dedicated port density for servers (each server resides on a dedicated switch port). If more capacity is needed, add another module. If redundancy is needed, then use two Catalyst 5000 switches with Fast Ethernet modules that connect to the servers (if they are equipped with two 100-Mbps Ethernet cards).

FIGURE 3-2   Server Location

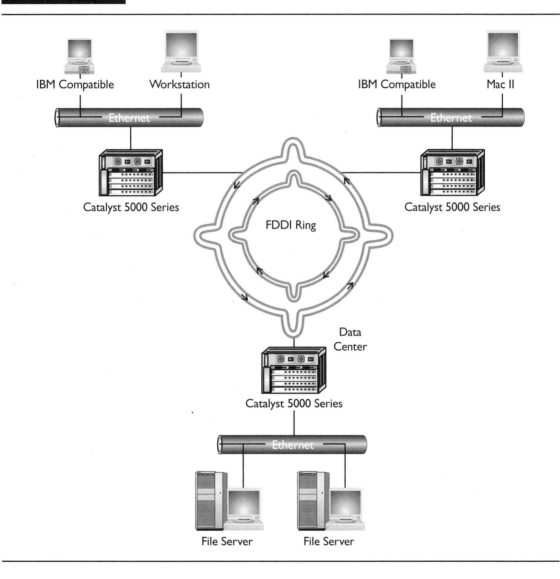

CERTIFICATION SUMMARY

We have learned in this chapter that today's high-performance workstations are running on yesterday's hub-based Ethernet networks. As companies grow and technology advances, the hub networks are showing their age. To bring the LAN into today's world, we speed up the network by introducing the Catalyst 5000 series LAN switch. The Catalyst allows the existing wiring to be used in a high-performance network that can handle today's high-performance devices. We introduced the concept of a node.

There are two types of nodes in a LAN, demand nodes and resource nodes. Demand nodes are devices that "demand" information or services from other devices. Resource nodes are devices that provide the information or service the demand node requests.

Demand and resource nodes can be further broken down into local and remote resources. Local resources are defined as resources that are located on the same hub or switch port as the demand nodes, while remote resources are located on a different physical hub.

We looked at the tiered approach to network topology. Demand nodes are located on the access tier; resource nodes such as file servers or routers are located on the distribution tier; and the links that connect buildings on the campus or remote offices to the home office comprise the core tier. We learned that the Catalyst now has the Fast EtherChannel and the Gigabit EtherChannel options for increasing the bandwidth on trunks between switches.

Bottlenecks and buffer overflow are analogous to water flowing through a pipe. Water (data) flows into the funnel (resource node). This needs to be maintained at a constant, smooth flow. If not, then spillage occurs.

We asked the question; With all of this information, how do we place the Catalyst 5000 series switch into a network? The answer is a combination of the number of users, office or campus layout, and location of the resource nodes. Port cost is also a consideration. The goal is to maximize the use of the resource at the lowest cost in terms of money. The Catalyst 5000 series switch provides the best answer to all of these issues.

✓ TWO-MINUTE DRILL

❑ When in the planning stages for deploying the Catalyst 5000 series switch, location of devices such as servers and workstations becomes important.

❑ The Catalyst 5000 series switch provides a wide range of modules that allow the switch to be integrated into just about any network topology.

❑ A demand node is a device that "demands" information from another.

❑ A resource node is a device where information that is being requested from a demand node is located.

❑ When planning a switched LAN, in most cases, the demand and resource nodes will be located on different collision domains.

❑ Be aware of the differences between demand nodes and resource nodes. Demand nodes are basically workstations that are requesting (demanding) information from a resource. An example would be a workstation requesting a file from a file server. A resource node is a device that provides the information requested from a demand node. An example of a resource node is a file server or router.

❑ Same-segment conversations between devices, along with inter-segment conversations between devices located on different collision domains create two resource types: local and remote.

❑ A local resource is a resource node that is located on the same collision domain as the demand node.

❑ A remote resource is a resource node that is not located on the same collision domain as the demand node.

❑ The difference between local resources and remote resources is the location of the resource with respect to the node that is demanding the information. A local resource is a device that is located on the same collision domain as the demand node. A remote resource is a device that is not located on the same collision domain as the demand node.

❏ If many workstations are on a segment and are being used to access resource nodes, then the possibility for "spillage" increases. This is known as *buffer overflow.*

❏ In a switched environment, you can avoid buffer overflow by increasing the size of the pipe to the server.

❏ Bottlenecks and buffer overflow are the usual suspects when a problem occurs for which there is no obvious cause. To prevent problems, planning where to place the Catalyst 5000 switch is very important. Be able to identify the places in a network topology where bottlenecks are likely to occur. Understand how buffer overflow can affect network performance and how to make changes to correct this.

❏ Congestion management is a balancing act, keeping the resource nodes running as fast as possible and the demand nodes from killing the LAN.

❏ The number of users that are on the network dictates the number of collision domains needed.

❏ The advantage that the Catalyst 5000 series switch has in the area of planning is the fact that it is a "modular" chassis.

❏ The size and layout of the office or campus is also a consideration when it comes to placing the Catalyst 5000 series switch in your network.

❏ Locating the server with respect to access by the users is critical.

❏ *Server farms* are dedicated network segments reserved for servers only.

SELF TEST

The following Self Test questions will help you measure your understanding of the material presented in this chapter. Read all the choices carefully, as there may be more than one correct answer. Choose all correct answers for each question.

1. What device was used to connect devices to an Ethernet LAN before the Catalyst switch?

   A. Router
   B. MAU
   C. Hub
   D. Bridge

2. What LAN topology consisted of workstations accessing centrally located servers?

   A. Token Ring
   B. Ladder
   C. FDDI
   D. Star

3. What type of device requests information or services?

   A. Demand node
   B. Resource node
   C. Server
   D. Router

4. What device in a traditional, hub-based Ethernet network effectively limits bandwidth usage?

   A. MAU
   B. NIC
   C. Hub
   D. Transceiver

5. A router is an example of what type of device?

   A. Demand node
   B. Local hub
   C. Resource node
   D. Resource hub

6. To what tier would workstations be connected?

   A. Core tier
   B. Access tier
   C. Distribution tier
   D. None of the above

7. At what speed would Fast EtherChannel operate if in full-duplex mode using four ports?

   A. 800 Mbps
   B. 400 Mbps
   C. 200 Mbps
   D. 100 Mbps

8. What is a local resource?

   A. A resource located on a remote collision domain

   B. A resource located on a resource network

   C. A resource located at a remote site

   D. A resource located on the same collision domain as the demand node

9. A server located on a branch office network is defined as a:

   A. Local resource

   B. Remote resource

   C. Local demand node

   D. Remote demand node

10. Which of the following is a rule for configuring a switched network?

    A. Locate the resource nodes as far as possible from the demand nodes

    B. Use 10 Mbps for the links to the resource nodes

    C. Resource nodes should be placed as close as possible to their demand nodes to prevent bottlenecks

    D. None of the above

   Questions 11–20 follow Smith and Co.'s design and implementation of a switched Ethernet network utilizing Catalyst 5000 series switches. The company's current network topology is a hub-based Ethernet network with servers located in the various departments in the office. The CEO has given you the task of implementing a switched Ethernet network to improve network performance and to plan for future expansion.

11. Users are complaining of poor response when accessing file and application servers located in different departments. Which of the following is the probable cause of this problem?

    A. Congestion due to poor network design

    B. A malfunctioning MAU

    C. Congestion caused by too many users on the segments

    D. None of the above

12. Which of the following would be a good solution to the problem in the preceding question?

    A. Add more servers

    B. Locate the servers on a dedicated segment

    C. Add more hubs

    D. More servers onto the user segments

13. Smith and Co. will be erecting a new building on the campus. Which of the following physical media would be the best for the inter-building link?

    A. Optical fiber

    B. Serial

    C. UTP

    D. Microwave

14. The company has purchased new file servers. Which of the following would provide the best network access to the servers?

    A. Connecting the servers to a Token Ring

    B. Locating the servers on the same segment as the workstations

    C. Installing a bridge between the servers and workstations

    D. Installing 100 Mbps Ethernet cards and a Fast Ethernet module in a Catalyst 5000 switch

15. At which tier would the company locate a Cisco router that has a link to the Internet?

    A. Access

    B. Core

    C. Distribution

    D. Network

16. Which of the following would allow for faster response time on the distribution tier?

    A. Enable full-duplex communication

    B. Enable routing

    C. Disable error checking

    D. Enable bridging

17. Which of the following would serve as a flow control method for the company workstations?

    A. Enable error checking

    B. Set up small hub groups connected to a switch port

    C. Enable full-duplex communication

    D. None of the above

18. The company has opened a branch office. Which of the following methods is the best method for network connectivity?

    A. X.25

    B. Leased line

    C. ATM

    D. None of the above

19. Users in several departments are spread out in the office. How can the administrator connect each user to the proper LAN segments?

    A. Create one large LAN

    B. Create workgroups

    C. Enable routing

    D. Create VLANs on the switched network

20. The network administrator is locating all of the file servers in the data center with a dedicated Catalyst 5000 switch. Which of the following is the best method for connecting the dedicated switch to the other switches in the network?

    A. 100-Mbps Fast Ethernet

    B. Fast EtherChannel

    C. FDDI

    D. None of the above

4

Catalyst 5000 Series Switch Architecture

CERTIFICATION OBJECTIVES

A number of years ago, Cisco entered into the LAN switching business with the purchase of a few switching companies, including Crescendo Communications Inc., Kalpana, Inc., and Grand Junction. Cisco has aggressively gained new technologies through acquisition for years, and has gotten very good at integrating new product lines into the Cisco family very quickly. The Catalyst family of switches is an example of Cisco acquiring a technology (in this case, from more than one company) and within a few months producing a new set of products with new features. Within just a couple of years, Cisco has gone from not really being in the LAN switching market to dominating it. It has been several years since networking professionals have thought of Cisco only as the WAN/routing company.

The history of the Catalyst products is probably less important than what Cisco has done with them and where they are headed. Still, it might be helpful to keep in mind how the products grew up as we examine some of the individual components and features. For the CLSC test, Cisco does require some amount of rote memorization, perhaps more so than in other tests.

The current test covers the 1900/2800, 3000, and 5000 families of switches. This chapter is about the 5000 series architecture. Unless specifically noted otherwise, "Catalyst 5000 family" refers to the 5000 and 5500 series.

There are lots of new acronyms with the Catalyst 5000 series. The exact set of questions on the test is selected randomly, but you can bet there will be lots of questions from this chapter. This chapter discusses each component and feature in detail, but remember to take special care to learn what each acronym means, and learn its basic function or concept.

The overview of the Catalyst architecture begins with a discussion of buffering and congestion control. Then the switching engine and network management components are handled separately.

CERTIFICATION OBJECTIVE 4.01

Buffering and Congestion Control

The Catalyst 5000 series switches offer tremendous measures to ensure that frames are efficiently buffered as they flow through the switch, and that congestion is avoided at all costs. The hardware orientation itself aids in the rapid frame processing. And each port has a processor and its own memory to hasten the frame flow. But as many can argue, the additional CPU horsepower and raw storage can sometimes do nothing to avoid the congestion problem that plagues many LAN switches.

Cisco allows each switched port to benefit from the use of full-duplex operations. This feature cannot be used in a half-duplex environment, but can greatly influence the flow of frames to important nodes in the network.

The Catalyst 5000 switches also allow for multiple port-level priority levels. Both the administrator and the switch itself can toggle between these priority levels to ensure that frames do not get lost or neglected in any of the buffers.

There are also many port speeds available for the Catalyst switches. Originally, the Catalyst 5000 switches had only 10-Mbps and 100-Mbps ports. They even offered the capability to sense automatically the appropriate speed to use relative to the maximum possible speed of the end station. Today, the Catalyst 5000 switch has Gigabit Ethernet ports available. Raw bandwidth, although not a formal means of congestion control, can be used to evacuate buffers faster than they can overflow.

Per-Port Buffers

Each switched port of a Catalyst 5000 switch has its own buffer pool. In fact, there are no shared buffers whatsoever in the Catalyst switch. This architectural enhancement has an immediate improvement on the overall flow of frames through the switch. The concept of a LAN switch is to move frames through the switch as fast as possible. Most vendors claim that wire-speed throughput is possible. However, the placement and use of the internal frame buffers in a LAN switch have a tremendous impact on the ability to switch packets at wire speed.

A typical LAN switch uses a shared pool of memory for all frames that travel through the switch. At first glance, this may seem efficient. If memory becomes a problem, then one can simply add memory to the switch. However, adding more memory to a switch may only correct a symptom, not the actual cause. What makes the switch appear as if it does not have enough memory?

Typically, if the buffers overflow, then there is a memory problem. However, one must differentiate between packets that sit in the buffer system for an extended period of time and those that need a buffer when none is available. A no-buffer situation is caused either by a severe shortage of memory, or the failure to process the frames in the switch efficiently. If additional memory in the switch does nothing to cure the lack of buffers, then the true problem is how well the switch processes frames.

The Catalyst 5000 series switch has 192KB of buffer for each switched port. These buffers are divided into two pools, one for incoming frames, and one for outgoing. Since it is virtually impossible to control the pace of frames that are about to go onto any medium (too many clients on an Ethernet or Token Ring), there is a greater amount of memory set aside for outbound frames. There is 24KB of memory for inbound frames, and 168KB for outbound.

The per-port buffers ensure that no frame is stuck in a shared buffer somewhere in the switch. Each port stores its own frames as they arrive, and before they are sent onto the appropriate medium. And, since a shared buffer pool is avoided, each frame only crosses the switch backplane once. A frame only needs to travel from the inbound buffer of the receiving port to the outbound buffer of the destination port. This process is detailed later in this chapter.

Full vs. Half Duplex

How quickly a network conversation can occur can certainly influence whether congestion will occur in the switch itself. Aside from the speed of the data, the capability to both talk and listen simultaneously can improve the throughput.

A network conversation is comparable to a conversation between two people. Normally, two people do not speak to each other at the same time. If they do, the words and thoughts get mixed up and confused. Most people cannot converse in such a manner. People are typically half-duplex machines—when one speaks, others listen. Then, the others take their turn expressing their opinions.

This compares to a network built with multiport repeaters. Of course, most network administrators and designers never implemented a multiport repeater by name, but many networks have been built with hubs for years. A hub yields a conversation similar to a classroom discussion. When one speaks, all others in that room hear the ideas. Whether this idea was meant for one other person in the room (such as a question directed to the teacher), or all those present (such as a question for the class), everyone present hears the idea.

Although each end station has its own port to the hub, each does not have its own private use of the bandwidth. All machines on the hub share the bandwidth. Thus, the hub is a single-bandwidth domain, also called a collision domain. When one machine speaks, all others hear it, whether they want to or need to. In Ethernet, if multiple machines speak simultaneously, a collision occurs. And in Token Ring, there are no collisions, but there can be a tremendous wait for the token to come around the ring, which is called latency.

A LAN switch offers the capability for each port to be its own collision domain. And if each end station has its own collision domain, then there are no other devices sharing the wire. From the perspective of the end station, the network world consists of itself and the switch. And since there are separate transmit and receive wires in a category 5 cable, it is possible for both the switch and the end station to talk and listen simultaneously.

Thus, as long as two devices are directly connected to one another, then a full-duplex conversation is possible. Most intelligent devices connected to a switch can benefit from this. An end station, a router, or another switch can use full-duplex operations. Since a hub blindly repeats each frame to every other attached device, it cannot participate in a full-duplex conversation.

The positive impact of a full-duplex port is the effective doubling of the available bandwidth. If the port speed is 10 Mbps, then it becomes 20 Mbps at full duplex. If the port runs at 100 Mbps, you end up with 200 Mbps. And, in reality, a 10-Mbps half-duplex port cannot realistically achieve 10 Mbps. The effects of collisions limit the effective throughput to 5–6 Mbps. This consequence is seen even in a physical point-to-point environment.

Priority Levels

The Catalyst switch allows the administrator to configure two different priority levels for inbound traffic. These levels are used to represent the importance of the information that arrives on each port. For example, packets that come from a server should have precedence over those that arrive from a simple workstation. Packets that arrive from other switches or routers may be more important than those from simple end stations.

It is important to remember that the priority levels that the administrator can control are for inbound frames only. Once a decision is made on where the frame is destined, that frame must wait until the congestion on the destination wire clears up (collisions or latency). That is why there is so much memory set aside for outbound frames.

The inbound buffers are quite limited (24KB). If there are hundreds of ports simultaneously receiving frames, and only one frame can cross the backplane at a time, then the inbound buffers on each port may get busy and get close to filling up. If there is no special priority scheme, then frames reach the backplane on a first-in, first-out (FIFO) basis. This scheme does not take into account the volume of packets coming from any one source or the importance that an administrator places on arriving frames.

The Catalyst 5000 switch is a store and forward switch only. This means that an arriving frame is received in its entirety, the checksum is verified, and then it is forwarded out of the switch. In fact, no decision on forwarding the frame is made until the entire frame is present in the port-level inbound buffer. There is no special treatment given to any frame as it arrives. One frame is not switched any faster than another. Some switches employ other methods such as cut-through or modified cut-through, but not the Catalyst 5000.

The speed of the Catalyst 5000 backplane always exceeds the port speed. The fastest current port is 1 Gbps, while the backplane runs at 1.2 Gbps. Thus, one port does not have any special backplane speeds, either. The various priority levels determine the quantity of frames that each port can send across the backplane; not how fast the frames are processed through the switch.

The administrator can define one of two priority levels for any switched port with the following command:

```
Cat> (enable) set port level ?
Usage: set port level <mod_num/port_num> <normal|high>
```

By default, each port of the Catalyst 5000 switch is at normal switching level. This means that frames from each port are equal in the mind of the switch. To make one or more ports appear more important, one can change the level to high.

High priority ports get serviced at a 5:1 ratio relative to the normal ports. This means that if any port is set to high, it gets five packets out for every one packet of the normal ports. If multiple ports are set to high, they each send out four packets, and then all ports—normal and high—send out one.

If the inbound buffer system of any port get close to capacity, the port goes into machine mode. During this time, this one port has 100 percent access to the main switching bus. No other port is allowed access to the bus until the machine port is no longer critical. If multiple ports simultaneously reach machine mode, then they share access to the bus while all other ports stand by. The administrator does not have access to this machine level. This is set by the Catalyst only.

Additional Bandwidth

A final method of congestion control is to get the frames out of the switch as fast as possible. One can argue that if the outbound interfaces are faster than normal, then there is less contention for the outbound port. Thus, the more bandwidth that is available, the less time a frame may spend in the outbound buffers.

Throwing bandwidth at a network problem is like tossing additional memory into a chassis to solve an apparent problem. Sometimes, the additional bandwidth does not help, and one may only be fighting a symptom, not the actual problem. However, the bandwidth solution in today's LANs is very viable. Unlike the WAN, where excessive bandwidth can be unrealistically expensive, LAN-based bandwidth is relatively cheap, if not free. Since most networks today consist of Category 5 cable, the ability to run Gigabit speeds is already in place. The simple purchase or lease of some new hardware is all it takes. And if the network is built on a fiber structure, then there is certainly no fear of Gigabit speeds. Granted, it was not until recently that the standard for Gigabit Ethernet included a copper medium, but the writing was on the wall long ago. After all, how could such a standard emerge and completely ignore the physical infrastructure of most networks in existence today?

Such tremendously high bandwidth options are typically seen between switches and routers. Most end stations cannot really benefit from the new, super-high-speed NIC cards. Although the card may be able to send frames that fast across the wire, the end station cannot generate frames fast enough to fill up the wire. This typically relates to processor and internal bus speeds of the end stations. True, there are some devices that can make exceptional use of such high bandwidth, but they do not represent the majority of installed client and server machines today.

Switching Components

The key to understanding the Catalyst 5000 architecture is not the features it has, but rather the components of the switch and how they interact. We have already discussed the features that these components enable. This section provides a deeper insight into the workings of the Catalyst 5000 family, and explains why some features work the way they do. This section contains many of the acronyms you were warned about at the beginning of the chapter.

This section starts at a high level, and drills down. The Catalyst 5000 switches contain several main pieces: The Network Management Processor (NMP), the switching bus, the management bus, the index bus, and in models in the 5500 family, the ATM switch fabric. Within these larger pieces, there are other components that are discussed in detail. These include the Encoded Address Recognition Logic (EARL), bus arbiter, Flash, DRAM, console port, and application-specific integrated circuits (ASICs).

It makes some sense to separate the 5000 models and 5500 models here, as there are a few significant differences.

Catalyst 5000

The Catalyst 5000 was the beginning of the Catalyst switch family. Each switched port in the chassis has its own 192KB frame buffer memory, and the administrator can configure priority levels to control access to the main switching bus. The switching bus is 48 bits wide, and runs at 25 MHz. If you multiply out 48 bits times 25 MHz, you'll come up with 1.2 Gbps.

Line cards connect to the backplane via a 192-pin connector that Cisco calls a *future bus* connector. The name implies a certain amount of "future proofing" as part of the design, and so far, Cisco seems to have done a good job of this. New supervisor and line cards work in the Catalyst 5000 chassis, and cards for the 5000 work in the newer 5500 chassis.

The 5000 supports dual power supplies. If both are installed, each runs at approximately 50 percent and they share the power requirements of the switch. Should one power supply fail, the remaining one immediately ramps up to 100 percent to serve the needs of the entire switch. The power supplies are modular, and can be changed individually by the administrator any time.

The Catalyst 5000 also has a little brother called the Catalyst 5002. Where the Catalyst 5000 has five slots, with one dedicated to the supervisor, the 5002 has only two slots, with the same supervisor requirement. The 5002 supports all of the line cards that the 5000 can. The 5002 also offers two power supplies, but they are imbedded in the chassis. They cannot be accessed by the administrator, and the entire chassis must be returned if one of the power supplies fails. Although the switch continues to operate with only a single power supply, there is no way to repair or replace the failed one.

The Catalyst 5000 supports the following types of line modules:

- Ethernet
- Fast Ethernet
- Gigabit Ethernet
- FDDI/CDDI
- Token Ring
- ATM LAN Emulation
- Route-Switch Module

The Catalyst 5000 switch has five slots, the first of which is reserved for the supervisor. Cisco originally had a maximum port density of 192 10BaseT ports. This was achieved by installing four 48-port line cards. Each port was not fully switched. They were, in Cisco's terminology, group-switched. This meant that a group of the ports was one collision domain. In this case, ports 1–12 were one collision domain, ports 13–24 were another, and so on. It's logically equivalent to a four-port card, each with a 12-port hub attached. This card has since been declared end-of-life, and Cisco now makes available a fully switched 48-port 10BaseT card. Other cards have been declared end-of-life as well, such as the Supervisor I.

Cisco offers wire-speed connections for all ports. Since the backplane runs at 1.2 Gbps, it is faster than any one port that the chassis supports. A frame arrives at its wire speed, gets transferred to the destination port faster than its arrival speed, and then exits the switch at the destination port speed.

Theoretically, one can swamp the backplane of the Catalyst 5000. If you had 12 100 Mbps ports, then you would have 1.2 Gbps of traffic. What happens when you add another card of 100 Mbps ports? The backplane capacity would be instantly exceeded, and packets would be dropped.

Realistically, the only time one can swamp a Catalyst (without filling it with Gigabit Ethernet ports) is with artificial traffic designed to do just that. This only happens during lab tests for switch throughput, and the Catalyst has always done well in those tests.

EARL

The Encoded Address Recognition Logic is responsible for Layer 2 address management within the switch. Recall that switches learn MAC addresses as they pass through the switch, and save them into memory to use in forwarding decisions. In the Catalyst 5000 switch, the EARL performs that function. It saves the VLAN number and port number along with the MAC address. The EARL also participates in the forwarding of frames, as we shall see shortly.

In reality, the inbound ports help EARL in its switching decision. Each port records the port number and VLAN, and adds a checksum to each frame as it arrives. This information is transferred across the bus to all ports and EARL, when granted permission by the arbiter. EARL reads this information and simply compares it to the forwarding table that it maintains.

EARL has a couple of logic "friends" that help in the decision process. The local target logic (LTL) helps EARL determine if the destination MAC address of the frame is present in the forwarding table. Then, the color blocking logic (CBL) ensures that that destination port is in the same VLAN as the source port. As is true with any switch, if EARL determines that there is no matching MAC address in the forwarding table, then the frame is flooded out every port in the same VLAN.

EARL also has some more recent revisions that increase its capabilities. EARL+ allows the use of the Token Ring card in the Catalyst 5000 switch. The normal EARL only understands Ethernet frames. And EARL2 allows Layer 3 routing table lookups if a NetFlow card is used. Both of these "new" EARLs are possible only on the Supervisor II and Supervisor III cards.

The EARL hardware is separate from the network management function, so it can operate independently if those components fail. There is actually a separate processor for all of the network management (SNMP) and remote management (RMON) functions. This processor could fail and the Catalyst switch could still move frames. Of course, you would lose your ability to remotely monitor the switch and gather statistics, but the users would never know the difference.

Bus Arbitration

As mentioned earlier, the Catalyst 5000 has a 1.2-Gbps, 48-bit switching bus. There is a second bus called the management bus. The management bus is used to communicate with cards in the switch for monitoring performance, controlling configuration, and updating software on each module. EARL also uses a third bus, called the index bus, as a private communications channel. As already mentioned, EARL makes the forwarding decision for every frame that passes through the switch. EARL communicates its decisions to each port individually across the index bus. In this manner, the frame flow across the switching bus is not interfered with.

On the supervisor card, in addition to the network management engine and EARL, there is a bus arbitration function, which controls which ports get access to the bus. When a port has a frame to transmit, it posts a request to the bus arbiter, and once that is accepted, it transmits the frame onto the bus. The arbiter is needed because only one frame can be on the bus at a time.

This is where the EARL enters back into the picture. When a frame is transmitted onto the bus, all ports receive and buffer it. The EARL is responsible for tracking which ports the frame actually needs to go to. If it is a single, known port, the EARL instructs that particular port, via the index bus, to transmit the frame, and tells all the other ports to discard their copy of the frame. If the destination of the frame is unknown, the EARL tells all ports in the same VLAN (except the one it came into originally) to transmit the frame. This accomplishes the flooding of frames for which the destination is unknown. The same process is used for broadcast and multicast frames.

This process of moving frames through the Catalyst switch is extremely efficient. Each frame crosses the backplane only once. EARL spends most of the time waiting for the frame to finish being transmitted. Consider a typical Ethernet frame. It has an eight-byte preamble, followed by the six-byte destination MAC address. The inbound port adds a four-byte VLAN identifier, and a four-byte source port tag to the beginning of each frame. Thus, EARL must read a total of 22 bytes of each frame before it can make a forwarding decision.

Since 48 bits, or six bytes, travel across the switching bus at a time, it takes four clock pulses for EARL to get the necessary forwarding information. After the decision is made, EARL must wait until that frame completes its transfer across the switching bus, and the next frame is granted permission to cross.

ASIC

With respect to the Catalyst 5000, Cisco makes reference to a port ASIC that is part of the architecture. The term ASIC (application-specific integrated circuit) is a general term for a class of custom-designed chips. Many hardware companies, not just Cisco, use ASICs. There are other components in the Catalyst 5000 that are implemented as ASICs as well (EARL, for example). However, for test purposes, the ASIC refers to the port-level chips that perform specific framing and checksum duties.

Each switched port on a line card in a Catalyst 5000 switch has its own ASIC. (On some cards, Cisco may implement multiple logical ASICs onto one physical chip.) This ASIC performs a number of functions. It contains the frame buffer, it buffers frames, it holds the MAC address for the port, and it handles negotiating control of the bus in order to place frames onto it.

Since the Catalyst 5000 is a store and forward switch, the ASIC performs the initial checksum of the frame as it arrives. The ASIC is responsible for adding the 12 additional bytes of information to the frame before it crosses the backplane. Of these 12 bytes, four are for the VLAN ID, four are for the port ID, and four are for a new checksum. Port-level ASICs remove these 12 bytes before the frame returns to any wire.

The ASIC chips are also responsible for creating any trunk frame formats. The Ethernet and Token Ring ports can use ISL trunks to communicate multiple VLANs out a single port. The port-level ASICs both create this format to be sent and interpret the trunk frame as it is received. Newer Ethernet ASICs can also perform the open standard 802.1Q trunking. On the FDDI card, the ASIC performs the 802.10 trunking.

It is important to note that not all Ethernet port-level ASICs can perform these trunking functions. Some are only capable of the memory management and internal format options. If ISL and/or 802.1Q trunking are necessary, verify that the card purchased is capable of that feature.

Frame Flow Through the Switch

Enough of the switch components have been covered to follow a frame through the switch. What follows is a "day in the life" of a frame as it travels through a Catalyst switch. Of course, in reality, it takes far less than a day for a frame to accomplish all this.

1. A frame is received on a port of the switch. The entire frame is received and stored in the buffer, as the Catalyst 5000 is a store and forward switch.

2. As the frame is stored, the port-level ASIC adds the internal encapsulation of VLAN ID, source port ID, and a new checksum. EARL uses the VLAN ID and the source port ID to make the final forwarding decision.

3. The ASIC sends a request to the local card arbiter, which sends a request to the main arbiter to transmit the frame onto the bus.

4. As the frame is transmitted across the bus, each ASIC begins to make a copy of the frame and store it in its buffer.

5. After four clock pulses, EARL has received all the information necessary to make a switching decision. EARL informs the ports which should keep and which should drop the now-arriving frame via the index bus. Those that are supposed to keep it continue receiving the frame. Those that should ignore the frame drop it from their buffers.

6. The frame continues to be copied across the switching bus until the checksum is transmitted and received by all ports directed by EARL.

7. The frame now sits in the destination ports' outbound buffers and waits for wire contention.

8. The switching bus is now ready to process another frame, and EARL tells the arbiter to get another one.

Catalyst 5500

Let's now turn to the architecture of the Catalyst 5500. The 5500 builds upon the features of the 5000, adding a number of new capabilities and increasing performance and expandability. Introduced along with the 5500 was a new supervisor card, the Supervisor II.

Rather than repeat the features that are the same as the 5000 (and much is the same) this section simply explores the differences.

5500 Slots

The first, obvious difference is the number of slots. The 5000 is a five-slot box, while the 5500 has 13 slots. Like the 5000, slot 1 is reserved for a supervisor card. Optionally in the 5500, slot 2 can be used for a supervisor card, too. If a redundant supervisor is not desired, slot 2 can be used for a regular line card. A single supervisor can run in slot 2, but slot 1 cannot be used for line cards. This might be done if eventually a redundant supervisor will be used, and you do not want the slot used up accidentally.

It is important to note that if dual supervisors are used, only one is actually active. The second one is there for backup purposes only. The second does maintain the same operating system and configuration file as the primary in case the primary does fail, but it does not aid in day-to-day

FROM THE CLASSROOM

Choking on Alphabet Soup

At this point in the class, most students are about ready to tattoo a few keyboard keys onto their foreheads. Regardless of how the information is presented, if one is not interested in hardware statistics and acronyms, they are difficult to retain. For those who struggle through the topic, a wealth of information is provided, which is quite helpful in gaining a better understanding of the Catalyst 5000 architecture, and just might help those interested in pursuing the CCNP certification.

What can really be gained from this discussion is the extreme optimization that Cisco has employed in the Catalyst 5000 series switches regarding packet flow. Great care has been taken to ensure that each frame only crosses the bus one time. Many switch vendors do not employ the port-level buffers, and opt instead for a shared buffer pool for all ports. This immediately means that each frame must cross the switching bus twice: once coming in and once going back out.

The Catalyst 5000 architecture also has a single decision-maker: EARL. This chip makes all switching decisions for all frames. Some switching vendors have port-level switching engines. These may or may not add to the overall switching speed. In the case of the Catalyst 5000, only one frame can cross the switching bus at a time. Thus, even if the individual ports had the intelligence to decide where the frame is destined, it could do nothing to get the frame there faster.

Having a single processor ensures that the same information is getting to each individual processor, or that each of the other processors is working correctly. One of the challenges of a multiprocessor environment is the synchronization of data and work. The Catalyst 5000 has absolutely no worries about these tasks.

The alphabet soup of all the chips and processors can quickly overwhelm students. Unfortunately, they are expected to know such details for the certification test. Both rote memorization and actual understanding are needed to reach the CCNP level. Relatively speaking, the hardware and architectural overview could have been much worse. Remember that Cisco decided to have only a single frame switching bus, and a single processor. The logic needed to replicate these functions would only have added to the acronym confusion.

—Neil Lovering, CCIE, CCSI

operations in any way. This is why the second processor is called the redundant processor.

Here are a few rules about 5500 slots:

- No more than 7 IOS-based modules (RSM and LANE) may be installed in a single 5500.

- Line cards can be places in slots 2–12. The only exception to this is if there is a supervisor present in slot 2.

- Slot 13 cannot be used for regular line cards (see the following section on ATM). If you are not using the ATM functionality of the 5500, then only 12 slots of the 5500 are usable.

The 5500 also has two smaller cousins. The 5505 is the exact same size as the 5000, and contains five slots. The 5505 benefits from the enhanced features of the 5500 (detailed in the coming sections). There is also a 5509, which is a nine-slot version of the 5500. Like the 5505, it has all the added benefits of the 5500. Neither the 5505 nor 5509 have the additional ATM backplane.

ATM

Another major new feature of the Catalyst 5500 is the addition of a separate ATM switch fabric backplane, running at 5 Gbps. To use this feature, an ATM Switch Processor (ASP) needs to be installed in slot 13. The ASP performs a function for the ATM backplane similar to what the supervisor does for the switching backplane. Slots 9–12 are dual purpose slots. They can contain either Catalyst 5000-style line cards, or they can contain ATM cards. The ATM cards are of the same type used in the LightStream 1010 product, and are compatible between the two. The slots 9–12 are logically equivalent to ATM slots 0–4 of the LightStream 1010, when used for ATM cards. The ASP even displays them as such. Figure 4-1 illustrates the layout of the Catalyst 5500.

Performance

On the 5500, the switching backplane throughput has been increased to 3.6 Gbps. This was accomplished by creating what Cisco calls a *three-bus*. This is simply the equivalent of three of the 1.2-Gbps buses previously described

FIGURE 4-1   Block layout of Catalyst 5500 (not to scale)

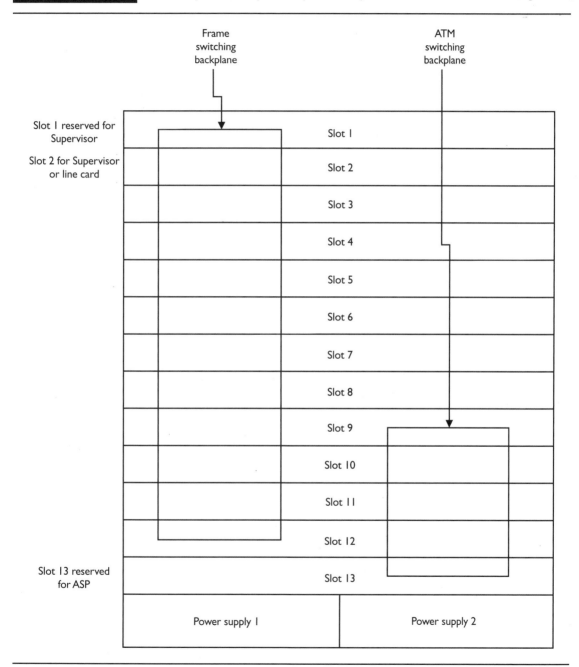

(index, switching, and management). This way, older cards that can only communicate over the one 1.2-Gbps bus can still function, cards that can use all three buses can take advantage of the extra speed, and all cards can work together. This is possible because Cisco left enough of the 192 pins available for future expansion. A Supervisor III is required, because the new bus arbiter has to manage the extra buses.

Supervisor II

The Supervisor II adds a few new features. First are a few new uplink options from the supervisor itself, mostly Fast Ethernet-over-fiber variants. The default amount of memory and flash has been increased to 20MB of RAM, and 8MB of flash. The other major feature is a space for the NetFlow Feature Card (NFFC).

The Supervisor II CPU is three times as fast as its predecessor, the Supervisor I. The Supervisor II is also the minimum type of supervisor required for the 5500 series of switches. Since it can be operated in a 5500, the Supervisor II supports redundancy. As noted earlier, this means that a second Supervisor II can be present and resume switch operations should the primary fail.

The Supervisor II also supports Fast EtherChannel. If both of the 100 Mbps links on the Supervisor module connect to the same destination Catalyst switch, they can appear as a single collision domain to EARL. This way, the Spanning Tree Protocol (STP) does not block traffic across one of the redundant links. Fast EtherChannel allows for dynamic load balancing of traffic in a switched environment.

Supervisor III

Currently, the Supervisor III is available, and all new Catalyst 5000s ship with it. The difference between the III and the II is much greater than the difference between the I and the II. First, the CPU used in the Supervisor III is ten times faster than the Supervisor I, since it uses a new type of CPU. Second, the Supervisor III is needed to support the three 1.2 Gbps switching buses on the 5500 chassis. The Supervisor III can operate in the 5000 chassis, but the three bus structures are not present.

Additionally, the Supervisor III changes a number of connectors and expansion options. They are not large architectural changes, but they make maintenance and management much easier. Among these changes:

- The flash has been changed from a SIMM that required the supervisor be removed to upgrade, to two cardbus (PCMCIA) slots on the front of the Supervisor, similar to the Flash on a 7500 family router RSP.

- The console port has been changed from a DB-25 port, wired DCE, to 2 RJ-45 serial ports (Console and AUX) wired DTE. The pinouts are the same as the 2500, 2600, and 3600 routers. This makes attaching a modem much easier, and may save you from having to carry around yet another type of serial cable.

- The uplink ports go up to gigabit speeds, and can be purchased in a modular style. The modular ports are called gigabit interface coupler (GBIC) ports, and they are front-loading, meaning the supervisor can stay in the chassis, while the GBICs are swapped. GBICs come in a variety of speeds and media, from 10 Mbps up to gigabit.

- If you decide to stay with the 100 Mbps ports, they are 10/100 Mbps autosensing ports. The previous Supervisor modules had 100 Mbps ports only.

- The Supervisor III now ships with the NFFC standard. It is no longer an option.

CERTIFICATION OBJECTIVE 4.03

Network Management Components

Now that the switching engine has been described in detail, the chapter will focus on the network management components.

The network management components are a key piece of the Catalyst 5000 architecture, though unlike some other switches, not every function is dependent on it. To some extent, the Catalyst 5000 switches can function even if these components become disabled, because the EARL will keep performing the learning and forwarding functions.

The network management function lives on the supervisor card. Even though the Catalyst can function somewhat without that function, other key components live on the supervisor cards, and the Catalyst cannot function at all without a supervisor card in one of the supervisor slots.

These management functions are part of the Network Management Processor. The NMP controls overall operation of the switch, and controls the network management as well as switching functions. All of the NMP components live on the supervisor.

What services does the NMP provide? As the name implies, it performs mostly management functions. These include things like switch bootup and initialization, configuration storage, configuration changes, line card recognition and initialization, SNMP communications, and the command line interface.

The Catalyst 5000 products have a separate, dedicated management bus on the backplane. The network management processor communicates with and manages the other cards in the chassis using this bus.

The two main remote management interfaces to the Catalyst 5000 are the command line interface and SNMP. They are complimentary and there is some overlap, but as will be explained shortly, both are required to manage a Catalyst switch fully. Some information is available via the command line but not SNMP, and vice-versa. The command line is better suited to manual configuration and maintenance, while SNMP is more useful for automated management software.

CERTIFICATION OBJECTIVE 4.04

Remote Access

The Catalyst 5000 has a number of features available for accessing it remotely. This includes not only the switch itself, but also the capability to collect information about stations attached to the switch.

Like a lot of network equipment, the Catalyst switches can pass traffic for a variety of protocols, but they themselves are designed to be managed via TCP/IP. The switch itself can be connected for management via Telnet, SNMP, direct console access, and dial-up console access via SLIP. For monitoring attached stations, the switch includes two features, remote monitoring (RMON) and Switched Port Analyzer (SPAN).

Each of these topics is covered briefly here from an architectural point of view. Information on how to use the remote management features can be found in Chapter 6, and more detailed information on the remote monitoring options can be found in Chapter 8.

Direct Console Access

If you ever have to set up a new Catalyst out of the box, you'll need to become familiar with the direct console access option. The reason is that none of the other access options can be used until at least some minimal setup has been done via the console port.

You use the console port by attaching a "dumb terminal" with the cables that Cisco provides with the equipment. You need not use an actual dumb terminal, since a PC of some sort will work fine if it has a serial port. For example, Windows includes either Terminal or HyperTerminal depending on the version of Windows. By default, the settings for the console port of the Catalyst are 9600 bps, no parity, eight data bits, and one stop bit. This is often abbreviated as 9600, N, 8, 1.

If everything is set up and connected properly, you should be able to attach your terminal or launch your terminal program, power on the switch, and watch the switch boot sequence. How to troubleshoot your serial connection is beyond the scope of this chapter, but naturally you should make sure you have a working console set up. Even if you normally manage your switches via another mechanism, you will someday need a console available in an emergency. You'll be really happy if you have a known working console set up before the emergency happens, so you're not scraping one together during the crisis.

on the
job

Where I work, we keep an actual dumb terminal on a shelf near all the routers and switches, a DEC VT420. I built a DB-25 adapter for it, which is used to connect to the larger routers and the Catalysts with Supervisor Is or IIs. I also built an adapter so that the equipment that uses RJ-45 connectors for console ports can be used as well.

DEC terminal equipment tends to use DEC proprietary connectors, called Modified Modular Jack (MMJ) connectors. These are very similar to RJ connectors, except the clip is offset to one side, so that to make an MMJ cable, you need an MMJ crimper, MMJ heads, and MMJ DB-25 adapters. I don't work in a DEC shop; I just happen to have a DEC terminal. On this terminal, I had an MMJ cable, which went to an MMJ-to-DB25 adapter.

One day, while I was moving the terminal connector between routers, the adapter came apart in my hand. I was a bit annoyed, but it was the end of the day and I wanted to get home. I left the adapter on top of a router, used a nearby PC to Telnet in and finish my work, and left. I assumed that I would just fix the terminal cable and adapter in the morning.

I was on call that week and was paged at 2:30 A.M. because a router was down. By 3:00, I was standing in front of a dead terminal, cursing myself. My console cables were missing from my laptop bag; someone had "borrowed" them. Since I had just about the only MMJ cable setup in the company, there were no ready-made cables that would work. So there I was at 3:00 in the morning, in the middle of an outage, half-asleep, building serial cables. I didn't have an MMJ crimper or any MMJ heads. It occurred to me that I could substitute a standard RJ-45 head and adapter if I just cut off one end of the cable. So I cut the head off, crimped on an RJ-45 head with the wires in the same position, and built an adapter to match the old MMJ adapter. Somehow, I managed to get it to work. This was fortunate, since the router that was down was involved in our Internet access, so I wouldn't have been able to get to CCO to get pinouts if I'd had to.

The moral of the story is to make sure you've got a good set of console cables, and a backup set for when you break them.

Dial-up console access is more or less the same as having a directly attached console terminal. The "less" part has to do with how you have to configure the modem. Modem setup on a Catalyst isn't quite as nice as it is on the routers.

A portion of the difficulty in setting up a modem is that the Supervisor II pinned out as data communications equipment (DCE) and not data terminal equipment (DTE). A modem, for example, is DCE, while a terminal is DTE. Normally, one connects DTE to DCE for dialup. This means that you would use a straight-through serial cable to connect your terminal (or PC) to a modem. In this case, you need to connect DCE to DCE. You need a special null-modem cable for this application. A regular null-modem cable will not work because Cisco did not reverse all of the pins, just some. If it is not built correctly, you could potentially damage the serial port. Cisco has "fixed" this on the Supervisor III, which is now DTE.

Telnet Access

Many network managers manage their Catalyst switches via Telnet. Since Telnet runs on top of IP, IP must be properly configured on the Catalyst before you can Telnet into the switch. See Chapter 6 for instructions on how to perform this configuration.

Once the IP configuration has been done, you can Telnet into the switch either by address or by name, if you have DNS set up. On either Windows or UNIX, from the command line the command is Telnet *hostname*, where *hostname* is either the name or address of the switch. It may look something like this:

```
>telnet cat
Cisco Systems Console
Enter password:
cat>
```

It does not echo, but a password was entered at the Enter password: prompt.

Up to eight people can Telnet to a switch at one time, and it is typically faster than connecting at the actual console. This is due to LAN speeds versus the limited console speed. Other than that, it is very similar to being connected via a terminal to the console port. The command line interface is the same.

There are a couple of things that can be done via the console port that cannot be done via Telnet. For example, the password recovery procedure must be done via the console, as the switch must be turned off and turned back on, which breaks Telnet connectivity. Recovery from a failed software upgrade must be done via the console. So again, make sure you have a console port set up that you can use when necessary.

SNMP

A full discussion of SNMP can take up an entire book, so this section takes a high-level view at SNMP itself, and discuss a few details in relation to Catalyst switches. SNMP also runs on top of IP, so IP must be configured for SNMP to work. In addition, SNMP uses its own set of passwords, called community strings, for access control. Information on configuring a switch to use SNMP can be found in Chapter 6. A full discussion of SNMP takes place in Chapter 8.

SNMP is very different from the type of interface you get when you Telnet to a switch or connect to the console. People use command line access, so commands and displays are formatted to make sense to a person typing and reading the screen. SNMP is used by automated systems. SNMP functions by sending small commands, or retrieving small bits of information. These commands and bits of information can be chained together to perform a more complex operation or view a trend. Often this is done over time, and the information is plotted as a graph.

SNMP activity, usually called SNMP "get" and SNMP "set," is almost always done by an application designed for this purpose. A prime example of such an application is CiscoWorks. CiscoWorks is capable of "discovering" your network (automatically building a logical map), plotting graphs of utilization per interface over time, tracking error conditions, and a wide variety of other things. Most of these functions are done via SNMP.

This brief discussion of SNMP is a bit abstract, but more concrete examples will be provided in Chapter 8. This section discusses the parts of SNMP that are specific to the Catalyst 5000 family.

Obviously, if pieces of information are to be exchanged, their format and the means to find them have to be specified somewhere. These specifications are called Management Information Bases (MIBs). An SNMP application and SNMP-manageable device will share a particular set of MIBs, so that the application knows what type of information it can retrieve from a network device.

In the case of the Catalyst 5000 family, this includes MIBs for Ethernet, FDDI, ATM, bridging, IP, RMON and others. This also includes some Cisco proprietary MIBs, such as those for VTP and CDP.

The proprietary MIBs are key to managing the extra features available in the Catalyst 5000 switches. The standards group (IETF) that produces MIB standards is a bit behind the industry in features. They have simple definitions for things like requesting bridge information, or a list of MAC addresses, but they have nothing regarding VLANs, VTP, CDP, or any of the other features that Cisco has added.

This is where Cisco's network management application (CiscoWorks) has an advantage over one that was not specifically designed for Cisco equipment. CiscoWorks includes excellent support for all of Cisco's features. If you already own a different network management application, you can download the Cisco MIBs from CCO.

SLIP

SLIP is how the world used to dial up to IP networks before PPP became popular. SLIP is the Serial Line Internet Protocol. PPP has effectively replaced it, because PPP is superior in just about every respect. For example, PPP can automatically assign IP address, subnet mask, default gateway, and DNS information to dialup clients. For SLIP, these must be configured manually. But SLIP is all that Cisco uses to dial up to Catalyst switches, so this section examines that protocol.

When you dial a Catalyst switch, you are connected to the console, and are able to issue console commands as if you were a dumb terminal. But what if you needed to connect to other things on your network, and that was your only dialup option? Cisco provides a way for you to be an IP node rather than a dumb terminal. That is where SLIP comes in. While dialed up to the console, you issue a command to tell the console to switch to SLIP mode. Then, you switch your computer from dumb terminal mode to SLIP mode as well. If all is configured properly, you should now have IP connectivity to the network that the switch is on.

Once you have a network connection, you can do a number of things, including running an SNMP application, Telneting to a number of switches, and performing uploads and downloads. Most of what you would need to do, even to other network devices, can be done while you are in dumb terminal mode. You can Telnet to other devices from the switch. Still, if you are stuck at some point, SLIP might make a useful "back door." You don't even have to set it up ahead of time, as long as the modem is already set up. You can do the entire SLIP configuration in console mode before you switch to SLIP. Be warned, though, that SLIP configuration on your client might be less than obvious if you are used to the relative ease of PPP. If you think you might need to use SLIP at some point, it would be worth your while to try it sometime before you really need it.

exam
ⓦatch

Useful or not, you'll need to know a few things about the SLIP capabilities of the Catalyst for the test. You'll need to know, for example, that the Catalyst supports SLIP, and not PPP.

RMON

Remote monitoring is a term used to describe a particular set of standardized statistics that can be gathered about a network connection. RMON information is not available directly from the command line, but much of the same information can be seen via SHOW PORT commands. RMON features are divided into groups. Each group will provide a certain set of features, and some of them are interrelated. The Catalyst 5000 family has four groups: statistics, history, alarm, and event. These four groups provide basic statistics and event reporting (for example, if utilization goes over a certain amount). Other RMON groups (which don't come built in) can provide for full frame capture. For frame capture, Cisco provides the SPAN feature.

The idea that Cisco wants you to understand about the RMON feature is that it's built in. RMON used to be implemented mostly as dedicated probes on shared-media networks. Cisco has taken some of the capabilities of dedicated RMON probes and built them into the port ASICs. RMON is built in, but Cisco sells a separate license for it. If you use the RMON feature, you are obligated to purchase the RMON agent license.

SPAN

The Switch Port Analyzer feature provides extra flexibility in network monitoring. Using it, you can attach a protocol analyzer (a Sniffer) to a port on the switch and monitor an exact copy of traffic from elsewhere in the same switch. You can monitor either a single port or an entire VLAN—provided the port you're attached to can handle the traffic load, of course. As we saw in our discussion of bus components, the architecture of the Catalyst 5000 switches makes it easy for Cisco to implement SPAN, and does not add a lot of overhead. This feature is a way to put back the network monitoring capability that existed on shared-media networks, which switches are often put in to replace. Switches don't pass all frames by default, so network monitoring "breaks" to some degree. The SPAN feature addresses that loss of capability.

Unfortunately, as nice as SPAN is, it could be slightly better. For example, it is only possible to monitor one VLAN at a time, unless you want to program manually a list of ports for the other VLANs that you are interested in. Also, you can only define one destination port, so it is only possible to use one protocol analyzer at a time.

Other Modules

There are a couple of other modules available now that are worth mentioning. These add functions on top of the core switching function of the Catalyst 5000.

RSM

Cisco sells a Route Switch Module for the Catalyst 5000 family, which adds a complete LAN routing function to the switch. This has two great advantages over traditional routers: speed and number of ports. Optionally, you can purchase a VIP2 card as a companion to the RSM, and add more router ports, including WAN interfaces. In some cases, you will still want a traditional router for WAN interfaces, if you cannot fit them all on the VIP2 card.

The RSM puts a full router on a Catalyst line card. Its management is independent of the Catalyst, meaning it has its own IP address, passwords, and Flash. You have to administer it as if it were a separate device. In terms of performance, the RSM is approximately equivalent to an RSP2.

QUESTIONS AND ANSWERS

What's the best way to achieve a high-availability LAN environment?	Take a good look at the 5500, with dual supervisors and dual power supplies. If you need to do better than that, and your budget allows for it, you can run dual 5500 chassis with cross-links.
I have a number of Catalyst 5000s. Can these be upgraded in some way?	The Supervisor II and Supervisor III let you take advantage of the NetFlow features, if the NFFC is installed. You can also install an RSM module. However, due to the 5000's limited backplane speed (compared to the 5500) and the limited number of slots, you might consider upgrading to a 5500.
What's the best way to set up a large LAN installation using Catalyst switches?	In terms of how to interconnect switches and routers, probably the best topology (budget allowing) is to have a master LAN router Catalyst with an RSM (or bigger model with equivalent feature built in), or even a pair. From those, connect all other Catalysts back to that central point.
What's the best way to monitor traffic passing through a Catalyst switch?	It depends on what type of monitoring equipment you have. Do you already own a Sniffer or RMON probe? If you have to purchase new monitoring gear, you might consider the NAM.
What am I going to be tested on?	Make certain you know the meaning of all the acronyms, and what each item does. For example, know what EARL stands for, and what the EARL does.

Connecting a traditional router to a switch must be done via one of the ports on the line cards of the switch. This limits you to the available bandwidth of that port. The RSM, however, connects to the backplane of the Catalyst at 400 Mbps (200 Mbps full duplex), which is higher than any 100 Mbps port on a Catalyst at present. On the RSM, the router interfaces are defined by the VLAN number, and are virtual interfaces.

This brings us to the number of interfaces available. The RSM can support all of the available VLAN numbers as interfaces, giving more than 1000 virtual router ports. This is possible with traditional routers that speak ISL as well, but with the extra bandwidth going to and from the RSM, the Catalyst with an RSM begins to be very attractive as a LAN router. The RSM reads the slightly modified Ethernet frames created by the port-level ASICs to determine the appropriate source VLAN for each frame. It then routes the packet based on the network layer information, and adjusts the VLAN tag before the frame is placed back on the backplane for EARL to switch.

NAM

As was hinted at earlier, the built-in RMON features of the Catalyst do not provide every monitoring feature that might be needed. There is always the SPAN port and a full protocol analyzer, but that may be overkill in some cases. These needs used to be filled by deploying RMON probes on shared-media networks. You can always use an RMON probe and the SPAN feature to get some of these effects back, but this leaves a couple of things to be desired. Cisco has a solution, called the Network Analysis Module (NAM).

The NAM is a card that goes into a line card slot in the Catalyst chassis. The NAM is, in fact, an RMON2 probe, but it has some Catalyst-specific features. Like the RSM, the NAM connects via the backplane, giving it greater bandwidth to the switch than if it had to connect via a port on the front. It also is able to decode ISL and 802.1Q trunked frames, giving it the capability to monitor traffic for several VLANs if a trunk port is what is being monitored.

CERTIFICATION SUMMARY

All switches must have a mechanism for dealing with congestion. Cisco's Catalyst 5000 family allows the administrator to configure full-duplex ports, to configure various priority levels on the ports, and to upgrade to higher bandwidth cards. Also, the per-port buffer system eases the memory squeeze felt by shared buffer systems.

The two main pieces of the Catalyst 5000 switches (from an architectural point of view) are the switching engines and the management components. The Catalyst 5000 architecture maintains separate processing and control hardware for each, so the Catalyst can still function partially under certain failure conditions. In addition, the Catalyst 5000 family allows for duplication of some hardware, such as the power supplies and supervisor cards.

The switching engines consist of the backplane, which is implemented as a 192-pin connector for each slot, called the future-bus connector. In the original Catalyst 5000 model, this bus is 48 bits wide and runs at 25 MHz, for a throughput of 1.2 Gbps. Starting with the 5500 model, the throughput was increased to 3.6 Gbps by "turning on" additional pins on the backplane. This provides for extra bandwidth and backward compatibility. In reality, the 5500 switches use three 1.2-Gbps buses.

In addition to the backplane, other key components of the switching engine are the EARL (responsible for MAC address management), the switch ASICs on each port (controls buffering of frames and placing them onto the backplane), and the bus arbiter (controls which devices have access to the bus at a given moment).

The 5500 introduced a separate ATM switch fabric, which supports ATM line cards independent of the frame-switching backplane. Use of this requires an ATM Switch Processor.

The Network Management Processor controls the monitoring and configuration functions of the Catalyst 5000. The NMP consists of a general-purpose CPU, RAM, Flash, software, and a console port. The software provides functions such as statistics collection, the command-line interface, and the SNMP interface.

The console port can be used to connect either a dumb terminal (or equivalent) or a modem. The modem can be used for dialup either in dumb terminal mode or in SLIP mode. SLIP mode provides for IP connectivity to the network the Catalyst is connected to. The console port must be used to configure a new Catalyst, or one that has had its configuration erased, before most of the other features can be used. Once it has been configured with an IP address and related information, it can be managed across an IP network.

Other features of the Catalyst architecture include a few built-in RMON groups (this function lives on the switch ASICs) and a SPAN feature, which allows the use of external packet analyzers or RMON probes. Switches in the Catalyst 5000 family can be made to be full LAN routers with the addition of a Route Switch Module.

✓ TWO-MINUTE DRILL

- ❑ The current CLSC test covers the 1900/2800, 3000, and 5000 families of switches.
- ❑ Remember to take special care to learn what each acronym means, and learn its basic function or concept.
- ❑ The Catalyst 5000 series switches offer tremendous measures to ensure that frames are efficiently buffered as they flow through the switch, and that congestion is avoided at all costs.
- ❑ The Catalyst 5000 switches also allow for multiple port-level priority levels.
- ❑ Each switched port of a Catalyst 5000 switch has its own buffer pool. In fact, there are no shared buffers whatsoever in the Catalyst switch.
- ❑ The per-port buffers ensure that no frame is stuck in a shared buffer somewhere in the switch.
- ❑ The hub is a single-bandwidth domain, also called a collision domain. When one machine speaks, all others hear it.

❑ In Ethernet, if multiple machines speak simultaneously, a collision occurs.

❑ In Token Ring, there are no collisions, but there can be a tremendous wait for the token to come around the ring, which is called latency.

❑ A LAN switch offers the capability for each port to be its own collision domain.

❑ The positive impact of a full-duplex port is the effective doubling of the available bandwidth.

❑ The Catalyst switch allows the administrator to configure two different priority levels for inbound traffic.

❑ The Catalyst 5000 switch is a store and forward switch only.

❑ The more bandwidth that is available, the less time a frame may spend in the outbound buffers.

❑ The Catalyst 5000 switches contain several main pieces: The Network Management Processor (NMP), the switching bus, the management bus, the index bus, and in models in the 5500 family, the ATM switch fabric.

❑ Within these larger pieces, there are other components: the Encoded Address Recognition Logic (EARL), bus arbiter, Flash, DRAM, console port, and application-specific integrated circuits (ASICs).

❑ The Catalyst 5000 supports the following types of line modules:

    ❑ Ethernet

    ❑ Fast Ethernet

    ❑ Gigabit Ethernet

    ❑ FDDI/CDDI

    ❑ Token Ring

    ❑ ATM LAN Emulation

    ❑ Route-Switch Module

❑ The 5500 builds upon the features of the 5000, adding a number of new capabilities and increasing performance and expandability. Introduced along with the 5500 was a new supervisor card, the Supervisor II.

❑ The network management function lives on the supervisor card.

❑ The Network Management Processor (NMP) controls overall operation of the switch, and controls the network management as well as switching functions.

❑ The Catalyst 5000 has a number of features available for accessing it remotely.

❑ If you ever have to set up a new Catalyst out of the box, you'll need to become familiar with the direct console access option.

❑ Many network managers manage their Catalyst switches via Telnet. Since Telnet runs on top of IP, IP must be properly configured on the Catalyst before you can Telnet into the switch.

❑ SNMP activity, usually called SNMP "get" and SNMP "set", is almost always done by an application designed for this purpose such as CiscoWorks.

❑ SLIP is all that Cisco uses to dial up to Catalyst switches.

❑ Remote monitoring (RMON) is a term used to describe a particular set of standardized statistics that can be gathered about a network connection.

❑ Cisco has taken some of the capabilities of dedicated RMON probes, and built them into the port ASICs.

❑ The Switch Port Analyzer (SPAN) feature provides extra flexibility in network monitoring.

❑ A couple of other modules worth mentioning that add functions on top of the core switching function of the Catalyst 5000 are:

    ❑ Route Switch Module (RSM)

    ❑ Network Analysis Module (NAM)

SELF TEST

The following Self Test questions will help you measure your understanding of the material presented in this chapter. Read all the choices carefully, as there may be more than one correct answer. Choose all correct answers for each question.

1. How much buffer space does each switched port have?

    A. 192KB

    B. 168KB

    C. 24KB

    D. There is only shared memory in the Catalyst 5000

2. Which devices can benefit from full duplex? (Choose all that apply.)

    A. Directly attached workstations

    B. Hub-attached workstations

    C. Other switches

    D. Servers

3. How many different user-defined priority levels are there in the Catalyst 5000?

    A. One

    B. Two

    C. Three

    D. Four

4. How does the Catalyst 5000 compare to the Catalyst 5002?

    A. The 5000 is smaller

    B. The 5002 is smaller

    C. The 5002 has only a single power supply

    D. The 5000 has fewer slots

5. In any Catalyst 5000 switch, which slot is always reserved for the supervisor?

    A. 2

    B. 4

    C. The bottom slot

    D. The top slot

6. Which chip is responsible for all switching decisions in the Catalyst 5000?

    A. LTL

    B. CBL

    C. EARL

    D. ASIC

7. What benefit does EARL+ offer?

    A. It is a newer, better EARL

    B. It allows for Gigabit Ethernet cards

    C. It allows for Token Ring cards

    D. It allows for ATM LANE cards

8. How many unique buses are there in the Catalyst 5000 switch?

    A. One

    B. Two

    C. Three

    D. Four

9. Which of the following functions is performed by the port-level ASICs?

   A. Initial frame checksum verification

   B. Final switching decision

   C. Frame translation

   D. Packet routing

10. What is the major enhancement to the Catalyst 5500 series of switches?

   A. Greater number of slots

   B. New, unique line cards

   C. Greater number of power supplies

   D. Enhanced backplane capacity

11. What does Fast EtherChannel do?

   A. It makes the Fast Ethernet pipes even faster

   B. It combines multiple Fast Ethernet links into a single collision domain for STP

   C. It turns regular Ethernet ports into Fast Ethernet ports

   D. It turns Fast Ethernet ports into Gigabit Ethernet ports

12. Which supervisor module supports the three 1.2 Gbps frame buses in the Catalyst 5500 series switches?

   A. Supervisor I

   B. Supervisor II

   C. Supervisor III

   D. All Supervisor modules support this feature

13. What are the default settings for the console port?

   A. 9600, N, 8, 1

   B. 9600, N, 8, 2

   C. 9600, N, 7, 1

   D. 9600, E, 8, 1

14. To which router can the RSM be compared?

   A. 2500

   B. 7200

   C. RSP-2

   D. RSP-4

15. How are the port-level buffers divided up?

   A. 50/50

   B. 24KB out, 168KB in

   C. Buffers are dynamically allocated

   D. 24KB in, 168KB out

16. Which switching mode does the Catalyst 5000 offer?

   A. Store and forward

   B. Cut-through

   C. Modified cut-through

   D. Cisco-proprietary Direct Destination Switching (DDS)

17. How do high-priority ports compare to normal ones?

   A. High ports operate faster

   B. Normal ports are randomly disabled to offer high ports greater access

   C. High ports have a 5:1 ratio of frames passed to the backplane

   D. Normal ports cannot operate in full-duplex mode

18. What does EARL do with a frame with an unknown destination MAC address?

    A. Drops it

    B. Forwards it to all ports within the same VLAN

    C. Forwards it to all ports regardless of VLAN

    D. Sends it only to the monitor port

19. What does the port-level ASIC add to each frame before it crosses the backplane?

    A. Nothing

    B. An additional checksum

    C. The VLAN tag

    D. The VLAN, source port, and checksum tags

5

Catalyst 5000 Series Switch Hardware

CERTIFICATION OBJECTIVES

E arlier chapters explained the Catalyst 5000 family switch architecture. This gave you the necessary input to proceed further in understanding switch hardware in detail. We will look into the individual switch components that make up the Catalyst 5000 switch.

We will examine the Catalyst 5000 family of switches in detail. This will include explanations regarding the Catalyst 5000, Catalyst 5002, Catalyst 5509, Catalyst 5505, and Catalyst 5500 switches. There is a table provided for quick reference about the features of these switches.

We will learn about the different modules that plug into the switch and provide detailed features for each. This includes a description of the supervisor engine module. There are different types of supervisor engine modules, and it is very important to understand the application of each. The front panel LED on the module provides functioning status of the switch. We will examine these LEDs in this chapter.

Catalyst switches have fault tolerance and redundancy built into them in order to limit network outages. The switch needs at least a supervisor engine module for its operation. This module provides all the switching and management functions within the box. If the supervisor module fails, the switch will not work.

In large campus networks, it may be necessary to have a backup supervisor engine module, should the primary module fail. This is called *redundant supervisor engine operation* and is implemented by using two Supervisor Engine type II (or above) modules. (This feature is only available on the Catalyst 5500, Catalyst 5505, and Catalyst 5509 switches.) Both of the supervisor engine modules must be plugged into the same Catalyst switch. One should be configured as the primary, and the other as the secondary module. When the primary fails, the second supervisor module will take over. We will look into the redundant operation of the modules later in this chapter.

Catalyst switches are all modular, which allows for many different types of network connections. We will introduce most of the modules used in a Catalyst switch, and examine the features of each one.

Catalyst 5000 Switch Hardware Description

Cisco Catalyst 5000 family switches are well suited for small to mid-range enterprise backbones. These switches provide high-density Ethernet, Fast Ethernet, and Gigabit Ethernet ports for high-end applications. First, let us introduce you to the physical description of the Catalyst 5000 family. Then we will provide detailed explanation of the specific modules in the switch.

The Catalyst 5000 switch gives switched connections to servers, workstations, and LAN segments using twisted-pair cables (STP or UTP) and fiber-optic cable. Since the switch has a backplane of 1.2 Gbps, it is capable of supporting Ethernet and Fast Ethernet connections to different backbone connections, including ATM, FDDI, and CDDI. Catalyst 5000 series switches support the following network types: Ethernet, Fast Ethernet, Gigabit Ethernet, ATM LANE, FDDI, CDDI, and Token Ring. Remember that these switches are modular—the modules used in the switch can be selected as per the requirement.

Cisco's Catalyst 5000 chassis are designed to meet networking requirements by supporting slots for the modules. This family of switches supports two, five, nine, and 13 slots, depending on the switch. The most advantageous feature with these chassis is that they all accommodate the same set of modules. These modules can be swapped between the chassis, allowing for interoperability and backup. The Catalyst 5500 switch has a special feature that makes it more suitable for high-end applications. We will look into the Catalyst 5500 in detail later.

Catalyst 5002 Switch

The Catalyst 5002 switching system (Figure 5-1) is a fully modular device supporting up to two modules, and is rack mountable in a standard 19-inch rack. This switch is similar to the five-slot Catalyst 5000 switch and uses the

FIGURE 5-1

Catalyst 5002 switch

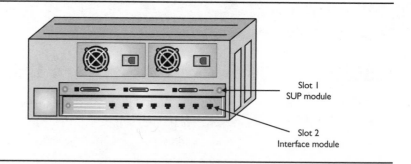

Slot 1
SUP module

Slot 2
Interface module

same hardware and software. The Catalyst 5002 switch is a compact chassis suitable for a wiring closet and small networks.

The Catalyst 5002 has a 1.2-Gbps, media-independent backplane, which supports Ethernet, Fast Ethernet, Token Ring, Fiber Distributed Data Interface (FDDI), and Asynchronous Transfer Mode (ATM).

Slot 1 is reserved for the supervisor engine module, which provides switching and network management functions. This module is necessary for all the Catalyst 5000 family switches because it is the main system processor. This module has a Layer 2 switching engine, and it also maintains and executes management functions that control the system. These modules store all interface configurations in nonvolatile memory.

Any of the Catalyst 5000 line cards can be used to plug into the second slot in the Catalyst 5002 switch. Most widely used modules to satisfy the current wiring-closet requirements used in slot 2 are high-density, switched Fast Ethernet, Ethernet, and group-switched Ethernet modules. We can implement Fast EtherChannel solutions for server connectivity applications.

The Catalyst 5002 provides smooth integration of the legacy LAN with the ATM networks by acting as ATM LAN Emulation (LANE) client and server. This is achieved by connecting the ATM LANE module in slot 2 and configuring the LANE software. Thus, the Catalyst 5002 functions as a compact, high-performance LANE client and server.

The Catalyst 5002 has two power supplies. A single supply is sufficient to support any configuration for reliable operation. The switch meets this requirement with a dual power supply, which will be functioning in load sharing and redundant mode. During normal operation, both power supplies share the load carried by the switch. If one of the power supplies fails, the other power supply takes over the load automatically and achieves redundant operation with zero down time.

Catalyst 5000 Switch

The Catalyst 5000 platform is a five-slot chassis, which goes into a standard 19-inch rack, as shown in Figure 5-2. This switch is able to support most data center applications.

The first slot is used for the supervisor engine module; slots 2–5 can be used for interface modules. The supervisor engine module is needed for the switching function. It also provides management functions for both local and remote management features. Additionally, this module has two uplink interfaces for connectivity to other network devices, including switches. We will see more detail about the supervisor engine module further on in this chapter.

The Catalyst 5000 has a switching backplane that supports up to 1.2 Gbps bandwidth. This switching fabric is independent of any medium

FIGURE 5-2

Catalyst 5000 switch

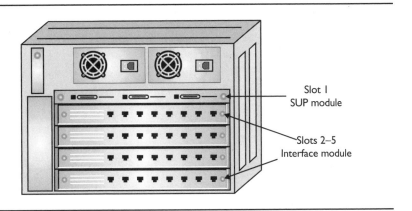

or module. The backplane provides a path for the interface modules and the supervisor engine modules to communicate with each other. The maximum speed at which this communication can take place is 1.2 Gbps.

The Fast Ethernet interfaces are used most of the time to provide interconnectivity among the switches. Gigabit Ethernet is now becoming a popular option, also. FDDI and ATM interfaces are also used for providing connectivity between switches and routers. If more bandwidth is required, then we have to implement Gigabit EtherChannel modules for interswitch connectivity. This gives up to 8 Gpbs full-duplex connectivity.

We can use either dual AC or DC power supplies for the switch. Power supply redundancy is achieved with two power supplies in the switch. If one of the power supply units fails, the other unit will automatically take over the functionality. During normal operation with both units working, each unit will provide half of the power to the switch. During redundant operation, the unit that takes over the functionality will provide full power to the switch.

Both power supplies are active all the time. When both are working, they mutually provide 50 percent of the power to the box. When one fails, the other automatically ramps up to a full 100 percent capacity.

Catalyst 5505 Switch

The Catalyst 5505 chassis (Figure 5-3) has five slots. This switch supports redundant supervisor engine operation, and is more suitable for high-end and critical applications.

As with the aforementioned switches, slot 1 is for the supervisor engine module, which provides switching, local and remote management, and dual uplink interfaces. Slot 2 can contain an additional supervisor engine in case the first module fails. This additional module provides redundancy for the supervisor engine module. This is a widely used feature implemented in mission-critical networks. Under redundancy operation, even if one of the supervisor engines fails, the other supervisor engine will take over without affecting the functionality of the network. If slot 2 is not used for a redundant supervisor engine module, then it is like the other remaining slots and can be used for an interface module.

FIGURE 5-3

Catalyst 5505 switch

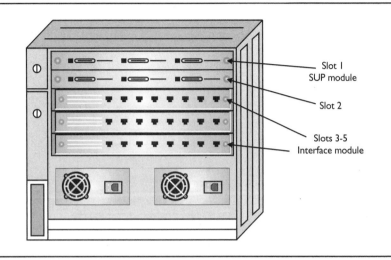

Slot 1
SUP module

Slot 2

Slots 3-5
Interface module

There is a difference between the backplane of the Catalyst 5505 switch and that of the Catalyst 5000. Catalyst 5505 has multiple 1.2-Gbps input, which can be used to obtain a 3.6-Gbps switching backplane. The standard switching modules will be utilizing the 1.2 Gbps for intermodule communication. The switching fabric supports Ethernet, Fast Ethernet, Gigabit Ethernet, FDDI/CDDI, ATM LAN Emulation, ATM DS3, Route Switch Module (RSM), and Versatile Interface processor (VIP2) modules. By having Supervisor Engine module III in slot 1, all three 1.2-Gbps backplanes can be activated to result in 3.6-Gbps support. Better utilization of the 3.6-Gbps backplane has been observed by combining the Gigabit modules.

Catalyst 5509 Switch

The Catalyst 5509 switch (Figure 5-4) is a high-end modular switch with a high-capacity backplane suitable for large enterprise networking. The switch has a nine-slot chassis, with slot 1 reserved for the supervisor engine module. The switch fits into a standard 19-inch rack. The unit can operate with only a single power supply. With an additional power supply, the switch provides power supply redundancy.

FIGURE 5-4

Catalyst 5509 switch

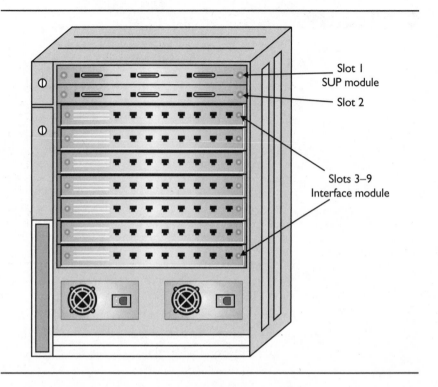

The switch supports Supervisor Engine II or III on slot 1 and slot 2. The switching engine redundancy is obtained with two Supervisor Engines II or III in slot 1 and slot 2. If the active supervisor engine in slot 1 has failed, the standby supervisor engine in slot 2 will take over the switching operation. If slot 2 does not have a supervisor engine, it will accommodate any other interface modules.

Slots 2–9 support standard switching modules. The switching backplane is similar to the Catalyst 5505 switch that supports 3.6-Gbps accessibility. The 3.6-Gbps, media-independent fabric supports Ethernet, Fast Ethernet, Gigabit Ethernet, FDDI/CDDI, ATM LANE, ATM dual PHY DS3, RSM, and RSM/VIP2 modules.

Catalyst 5500 Switch

Catalyst 5500 switch (Figure 5-5) is a high-end modular switch with a more capable backplane. This switch is more suitable for high-end and mission-critical applications. Let us examine the product features in detail.

The switch has a 13-slot chassis, with slot 1 reserved for Supervisor Engine II or III. The switch will operate only with Supervisor Engine II or III. Slot 2 can be used for a redundant Supervisor Engine module II (or III). If redundant operation is not required, slot 2 can be used for other interface modules.

FIGURE 5-5

Catalyst 5500 switch

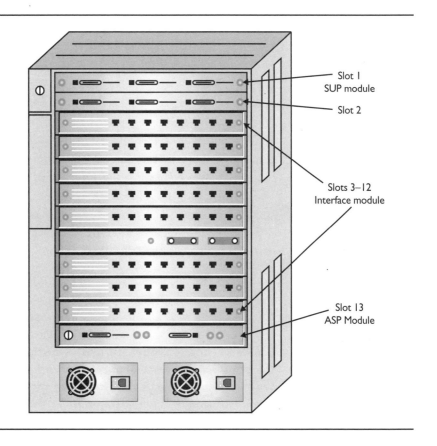

Slot 1
SUP module

Slot 2

Slots 3–12
Interface module

Slot 13
ASP Module

The switch accepts ATM modules in chassis slots 9–12. The ATM modules are the same as those from the LightStream 1010. Slot 13 is a dedicated slot, which accepts only the ATM Switch Processor (ASP) module. Catalyst 5500 is well suited for large, campuswide networks involving ATM technology. When the switch is used as an ATM backbone switch, then Catalyst 5500 with LightStream 1010 ASP module is required. This module will be plugged into slot 13. With this module, the switch can be connected to ATM Workgroup switches at various locations in the campus.

The switch backplane is similar to that of the Catalyst 5505 switch. This switch also has three 1.2-Gbps, media-independent switch fabrics and a 5-Gbps, cell-switch fabric. The backplane provides the connectivity among supervisor engines, interface modules and backbone modules. The 1.2-Gbps, media-independent fabric supports Ethernet, Fast Ethernet, Gigabit Ethernet, FDDI/CDDI, ATM LAN Emulation, and RSM modules. With the inclusion of the Supervisor Engine III, all the three 1.2-Gbps backplanes will be utilized. This results in a total bandwidth of 3.6 Gbps. The 5-Gbps, cell-based fabric supports an ATM Switch Processor (ASP) module and ATM Port Adapter Modules (PAMs). The communication between the ASP module and the other ATM modules in the switch takes place using the 5-Gbps, cell-switching backplane.

Table 5-1 summarizes features of all the Catalyst 5000 series switches. Use this table as a quick reference about the switches.

For more information about the Catalyst 5000 Series hardware description, refer to the following URL:

http://www.cisco.com/warp/public/729/c5000/literature.shtml

exam
Ⓦatch

Cisco's Catalyst 5000 series switches have been widely accepted by the information technology industry. Large enterprise networks have demanded cost-effective, stabilized intranets. You should be aware of the practical differences among the various models of Catalyst 5000 series switches. As a part of the certification process, or for network administration, it is essential to understand the design implications involved in these switches. The major differences among the models are the support for redundant supervisor engine operation and support for a large number of modules of different types. In the certification exam, you will be tested to select the best switch model for a particular networking requirement.

TABLE 5-1 Product Features of Catalyst 5000 Series Switches

Switch Model	Description	Features
Catalyst 5002	Two-slot switch	One Supervisor Engine (I, II, or III)
		One switching module (Ethernet, Fast Ethernet, Gigabit Ethernet, FDDI, CDDI, ATM LANE, and Token Ring)
		Supports one RSM module, but not the VIP2 module
		Redundant AC or DC power supplies are available
Catalyst 5000	Five-slot switch	One Supervisor Engine (I, II, or III)
		Up to four switching modules (Ethernet, Fast Ethernet, Gigabit Ethernet, FDDI, CDDI, ATM LANE, and Token Ring)
		Supports the RSM and VIP2 modules
		Redundant AC or DC power supplies are available
Catalyst 5505	Five-slot switch	One Supervisor Engine (II or III only)
		Up to four switching modules (Ethernet, Fast Ethernet, Gigabit Ethernet, FDDI, CDDI, ATM LANE, and Token Ring)
		Supports the RSM and VIP2 modules
		Redundant AC or DC power supplies are available
Catalyst 5509	Nine-slot switch	Supervisor Engines II or III only
		Supports a redundant supervisor engine for failover (must be identical models)
		Up to eight switching modules (Ethernet, Fast Ethernet, Gigabit Ethernet, FDDI, CDDI, ATM LANE, and Token Ring)
		Supports the RSM and VIP2 modules
		Redundant AC or DC power supplies are available

TABLE 5-1		Product Features of Catalyst 5000 Series Switches *(continued)*
Switch Model	**Description**	**Features**
Catalyst 5500	13-slot switch	Supervisor Engines II or III only
		Supports a redundant supervisor engine for failover (must be identical models)
		Up to eleven switching modules (Ethernet, Fast Ethernet, Gigabit Ethernet, FDDI, CDDI, ATM LANE, and Token Ring)
		Supports the RSM and VIP2 modules
		Redundant AC or DC power supplies are available
		Slot 13 is reserved for the optional Lightstream 1010 ATM Switch Processor (ASP)
		Slots 9-12 can host either 5000-series switching modules or 1010-series ATM modules

CERTIFICATION OBJECTIVE 5.02

Supervisor Engine Module

In this section, we will discuss the components of the supervisor engine module and examine in detail the redundancy operation of the supervisor engine.

The supervisor engine modules are classified into three types: Supervisor Engine I, Supervisor Engine II, and Supervisor Engine III. Catalyst 5002 supports Supervisor Engine I and II modules. The Catalyst 5000 switch supports all three supervisor engine modules. Catalyst 5509, Catalyst 5500, and Catalyst 5505 also support Supervisor Engines II and III.

The common features of Supervisor Engines I, II, and III are listed here for quick reference.

- Each module has a switching engine that is needed for providing a path for data transfer between the modules. This module controls the flow of traffic between the units.

- The module has two Fast Ethernet ports, which can also be used for load sharing. Supervisor Engine III supports a modular uplink port up to 1000 Mbps.

- The Fast Ethernet interfaces can be RJ-45, media-independent interface (MII) connectors, Fast Ethernet multimode fiber (MMF), or single-mode fiber (SMF) interfaces using SC connectors.

- The switch fabric interface is capable of over one million packets per second.

- The supervisor engine module can support 1024 VLANs.

- The hardware can hold up to 50,000 active MAC addresses. It can also hold information regarding the VLANs allocated dynamically among active ports.

- Supervisor Engines I and II have a 25-MHz Motorola MC68EC040 Network Management Processor (NMP). Supervisor Engine module III has a 150-MHz IDT R4700 Reduced Instruction Set Computing (RISC) processor.

- The module also provides management functions for monitoring the interfaces and unit status. This is essential in order to keep constant watch on the modules and the overall switching processes.

- Memory configuration varies depending on the Catalyst switch used. Dynamic random-access memory (DRAM) is used for the default system software. Flash memory is used for downloading the system software, and the configuration file is stored in the NVRAM. Supervisor III has 32MB DRAM, 4MB Flash, and 512KB NVRAM.

Supervisor Engine II has 16MB DRAM, 8MB Flash, and 256KB of NVRAM. Similarly, Supervisor Engine I has 20MB DRAM, 4MB Flash, and 256KB NVRAM.

Supervisor engine modules support *hot swapping*. The advantage with this feature is that the modules can be added or removed from the chassis without any interruption to the system power, without making any changes to the system software, and without bringing down any interfaces. It should be noted here that if there is only one supervisor engine module in the switch, you should not remove the module from the switch during normal operation. If the module is removed, the switch stops functioning. Similarly, if the active Supervisor is removed, the switch reboots to activate the standby Supervisor.

The supervisor engine module is capable of running diagnostic tests on the new modules when they are plugged into the chassis. It performs a series of tests on each of the new interfaces. If the tests are successful, the system will function normally. If there is a problem with the new module, the system will operate normally but leave any failing interfaces disabled. The supervisor engine module will automatically update the configuration file on the switch.

Each of the supervisor engine modules has erasable programmable read-only memory (EEPROM). This is used to store information regarding the modules plugged into the chassis. The information is the module serial number, part number, controller type, hardware version, and configuration information. The supervisor engine also stores more specific information about each of the modules. The EEPROM also stores an address allocator, which keeps a table of 1,024 MAC addresses used by the switch, with one address allocated per VLAN.

The Supervisor Engine II is almost the same as the Supervisor Engine I. The Supervisor Engine II comes with more features for redundancy of operation. A Catalyst 5500 switch with Supervisor Engine II supports redundancy operation if two Supervisor Engine II modules are used. If one of the modules fails, the other supervisor engine will take over the functionality.

Figure 5-6 gives a view of the front panel in a supervisor engine module. By observing the indication of each of the LEDs on the front panel, we can collect information on the supervisor engine, power supplies, and the fan assembly.

Table 5-2 details the information that can be determined based on the indication of each of the LEDs.

There is a Reset button in the front panel of the module. The Reset button is used to restart the switch. The console port is used for configuring the switch from the command-line interface. We can also monitor the network statistics, download the latest software to the switch, and configure SNMP agent parameters.

For more information on the supervisor engine modules, you can refer the following URL:

http://www.cisco.com/univercd/cc/td/doc/product/lan/cat5000/ cnfg_nts/supvr/4825_01.htm

The latest Supervisor Engine III is used widely in large enterprise backbone networks. Catalyst 5500 switches are mostly equipped with Supervisor Engine III.

The specific features of Supervisor Engine module III are:

- The three switching buses of 1.2 Gbps can run simultaneously and independent of each other. This will add to the total bandwidth of the backplane. In this type of configuration, the total throughput will be 3.6 Gbps, if traffic does not have to cross bus segments.

- The switching function is performed with a 150-MHz IDT R4700 RISC processor

- The module hardware is capable of supporting up to 4096 VLANs

---

FIGURE 5-6

Front panel details of Supervisor Engine II

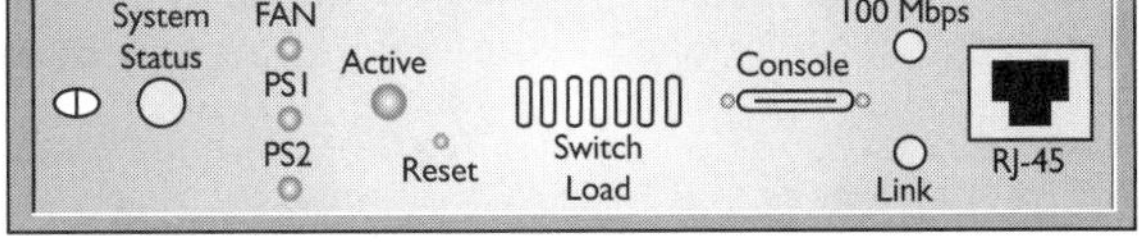

TABLE 5-2

Supervisor Engine II Front Panel LED Indications

LED	Indications
System Status	Green, if the self-test observes that all the components of the switch are performing normally
	Red, if the switch finds that unit is not functioning properly
	Red, when the switch is booting
	Red, if the module is disabled
	Orange, if the redundant power supply is installed but not turned on or receiving input
Fan	Green, when fan is operational
	Red, when fan is not operational
	Orange, if supervisor engine observes a malfunction in this module
PS1	Green, if the left power supply bay is operational
	Red, if the left bay is not operational, switched off, or not receiving any input power
	Off, if there is no power supply in the left bay
PS2	Green, if the power supply in the right bay is operational
	Red, if the power supply in the right bay is not operational
	Off, if the power supply in the right bay is not installed
Switch Load	Visual indication of the current traffic on the backplane
Active	Green, if the supervisor engine is operational and active
	Orange, if the module goes into standby mode
100 Mbps	Green, if the 100-Mbps uplink ports on the module are operating properly
Link	Green, if the link is operational
	Orange, if the software disables the link
	Orange flashing, if the link is bad and has been disabled due to a hardware failure
	Off, if no signal is detected

TABLE 5-3   Supervisor Engine for Catalyst 5000 Series Switches

Switch Model	Supervisor Engine I	Supervisor Engine II	Supervisor Engine III
Catalyst 5002	Yes	Yes	No
Catalyst 5000	Yes	Yes	Yes
Catalyst 5505	No	Yes	Yes
Catalyst 5509	No	Yes	Yes
Catalyst 5500	No	Yes	Yes

Table 5-3 shows which Catalyst 5000 series switch supports which particular type of supervisor engine module.

CERTIFICATION OBJECTIVE 5.03

Redundant Supervisor Engine Operation

We have examined supervisor engine modules in general. We also have introduced the hardware features of the module. The different types of modules were also discussed. Let us now examine the redundant supervisor engine operation.

Catalyst 5500, Catalyst 5509, and Catalyst 5505 switches support redundant supervisor engine operation. As discussed earlier, the supervisor engine is a must for the functionality of a switch. Without a backup supervisor engine, the switch performance is always in jeopardy. By installing a second supervisor engine along with the existing module, you provide a high-speed, fault-tolerant environment. Many environments require this type of redundant operation to support mission-critical applications. The second supervisor engine will take over automatically if the primary supervisor engine fails.

We have to note here that supervisor engine resilience is available on the Catalyst 5505, Catalyst 5509, and Catalyst 5500 switches with Supervisor Engine II and Supervisor Engine III only. It is important to note that only similar modules should be used in slots 1 and 2 of the switch for redundancy. That means if slot 1 is with Supervisor Engine II, then slot 2 should be with Supervisor Engine II only for redundant operation.

Supervisor Engines II and III are capable of performing redundancy operation because of the following specific features:

- Each module has separate hardware that supports switching and management functions.

- This hardware allows the main processor to forward packets across the bus even if the network management processor fails.

- There is sophisticated fault-detection logic that contacts the second Supervisor Engine II or III over a dedicated serial channel.

The actual redundancy operation of the module is as follows:

1. The supervisor engine module is installed in the first slot of the chassis. The second supervisor engine is installed in the second slot. Initially, the first supervisor engine becomes the active module and the second module goes into the standby mode.

2. Each supervisor engine stores the interface configuration and related functions of the switch in NVRAM configuration. The active supervisor engine first compares its NVRAM details with the standby supervisor engine. The active module sends information to the standby supervisor engine to update the NVRAM with what exists in the active module. If the active module finds that the software image on the standby module is different from the active module, then automatically the active module downloads its image to the standby supervisor engine module.

3. During the bootup sequence, both supervisor engines do the initial testing of the other modules. This test verifies the components of the modules. If the tests on both modules are successful, the modules communicate over the backplane. After these tests, the modules will be able to cooperate during switching-bus diagnostics.

Let's examine what happens if the active supervisor engine detects a problem. If the background diagnostics fail, then the active supervisor engine will automatically reset. When this happens, the standby module detects the reset operation and automatically takes over the active module operation. Now the active module will not do anything, but the standby module will take over and become the active module.

There is another special feature of this operation. When the standby module finds that the active supervisor engine is not functioning properly, it can force a reset. This results in the standby module becoming the active module. When the faulty module is replaced, it will become the standby module.

FROM THE CLASSROOM

A Point of Reference

In a classroom environment, nothing can drag down morale more quickly than spending huge quantities of time covering the speeds and feeds of various circuit boards and chip sets. A technical reference, white paper, documentation CD, or the Web itself are all great sources for such information. In the classroom, students want to tinker with the equipment, not be lectured about it.

A reference such as this book gives anyone instant access to small details that may otherwise be missed or forgotten in a classroom environment. Any valuable information source, whether it's a Cisco-certified instructor or a well-written

technical reference, lays out all the options possible to the prospective user. Since these options are more useful during the purchase or upgrade phases of running a network, hardcopy or softcopy information is best.

An instructor may point out a new feature or card, but nothing can beat the complete list. Once the card is obtained, the configuration chore begins. However, great care should be taken to select the proper card with the correct ports for the appropriate switch chassis up front. This chapter provides this form of necessary research as well as any classroom can, and at your own pace.

—Neil Lovering, CCIE, CCSI

When the new supervisor engine module is plugged in as replacement for the faulty module, the new module communicates with the active supervisor engine after performing initial, module-level diagnostics. Since the active module is switching traffic over the backplane, the new module does not perform switching-bus diagnostics; it goes into standby mode to avoid interrupting the current traffic flow. The active module will verify the software and configuration information of the new module and download related information, if needed.

You must install the redundant supervisor engine modules in the first two slots of the chassis. The supervisor engine modules are hot-swappable, and the system continues to operate with the same configuration after switching over to the redundant supervisor engine.

on the Job

One of our team got a pager message indicating that a switch was operating in redundant supervisor mode. This message came automatically from the management station, which was running SNMP-based CiscoView software configured to respond with a pager message whenever there was failover. We went to the site and found that the primary supervisor engine had failed. The front panel Status LED was lit in red and the standby supervisor module was active. We then pulled the faulty module out and plugged the new supervisor engine into slot I. The new module went into standby mode without disrupting the normal traffic. The overall process did not affect the normal operation.

CERTIFICATION OBJECTIVE 5.04

Ethernet and Fast Ethernet Switching

Catalyst switches support Ethernet and Fast Ethernet switching modules. In order to provide connectivity between the server and workstations or between server and hub directly, the Ethernet or Fast Ethernet switching module can be used. In a typical Ethernet network, ports on a hub are connected to a common backplane within the hub, and devices connected to the hub share the bandwidth. The overall network performance is always dependent on the way two stations communicate. If two stations continually use excessive bandwidth, the network performance for all other stations connected to the hub is degraded.

Catalyst series switches with Ethernet and Fast Ethernet switching modules will reduce the degradation problem. The switch treats each port as an individual segment. Now, when two stations on different ports need to communicate with each other, the Catalyst switch will switch the frames from one port to the other port at very high speed—usually at wire speed. The advantage here is that each connection gets the full 10/100 Mbps of bandwidth. The network performance will not be affected due to the sharing of bandwidth.

The switching of the frames is done at the Layer 2 level. The switch maintains an address table in hardware, called the MAC address table. This table has MAC addresses of the sending station associated with the port on which the frame was received. If a frame is received for a station that is not listed in the MAC address table, then the switch will flood the frame to all the ports except the port from which the packet was received. If the frame is received for a station on a different VLAN, the switch has to route the frame between the VLANs.

When the destination station replies, the switch will update the MAC address table. Then the switch will forward the next incoming frames to that single port without flooding to all the ports. The Catalyst series is capable of storing 16,000 address entries without having to flood any entries.

In a real-time networking environment, you will observe multiple switches interconnected. Each of the switches has its own MAC address table, which will be related to the workstations connected to its network. A switch is capable of supporting up to 50,000 MAC addresses, but in practice, a switch need not store so many MAC addresses to function.

Ethernet usually operates in half-duplex mode. This means stations can either receive or transmit at any time. Catalyst series switches provide the option of configuring each port on the switch for full-duplex communication. With full-duplex mode, stations can transmit and receive at the same time. The advantage here is that total bandwidth of the

Ethernet doubles from 10 Mbps to 20 Mbps for 10BaseT ports. The Fast Ethernet port will operate to provide bandwidth of 200 Mbps, with full-duplex communication.

The features of Ethernet and Fast Ethernet modules can be summarized as follows:

- Switch ports can be configured for half- or full-duplex operation

- The modules have hot-swappable capability

- With the Ethernet and Fast Ethernet modules in a switch, connectivity to an FDDI or ATM backbone is possible. The switch houses FDDI or ATM modules along with Ethernet or Fast Ethernet modules to achieve this.

- The modules have 192KB buffers on each interface to support bursty traffic

- The frame transfer is from one port to another port at wire speed

Ethernet Modules

Ethernet and Fast Ethernet modules can be classified into various categories. The Catalyst 5000 series supports the following Ethernet modules.

Group Switching Ethernet Module (WS-X5020)

This module provides 48 switched ports of 10BaseT. The medium supported is a standard 10BaseT Category 3 unshielded twisted-pair (UTP). There are four half-duplex Ethernet ports using RJ-21 telco connectors on the front panel. Each of these connectors provides 12 ports per connector. The numbering scheme on these connectors starts from the left. The first segment of telco connector ports is numbered 1–12; the second is numbered 13–24; the third is numbered 25–36; the last is numbered 37–48.

The module has LEDs on the front panel. This gives visual indication about the status of the module.

- The switch performs diagnostic tests on the unit. If the unit passes all the tests, the Status LED is green. If a test fails, the LED is red.

The LED will be orange during system boot, during self-test, or if the module is disabled.

■ The Link LED from ports 1–48 will be green when ports are working. It will flash orange if the port is bad due to hardware failure, or if the port is disabled by software. If the port could not detect any signal, the Link LED will be off.

Ethernet Switching Module (WS-X5010)

This module is similar to the group-switching module. The special feature observed in this module is that it supports full-duplex operation.

This module provides 24 switched 10-Mbps 10BaseT Cat 3 UTP ports. Each port is capable of operating in half- or full-duplex mode. The 24 ports are grouped into two telco RJ-21 connectors, with 12 ports per connector.

The LEDs on the front panel give the status information of the module.

Ethernet Switching Module (WS-X5013)

This module provides 24 switched, 10-Mbps 10BaseT Cat 3 UTP ports. The ports support full- or half-duplex Ethernet. The major difference here is that all the 24 ports are RJ-45 type connectors, and not RJ-21 type. The module also has Status and Link LEDs on the front panel. The functionality of these LEDs is the same as on the other modules.

Ethernet Switching Module (WS-X5012)

This module is similar to the WS-X5020 group-switching module. This also has 48 switched, 10-Mbps 10BaseT ports grouped into four RJ-21 telco connectors. The major difference here is that the individual ports are switched and support both half- and full-duplex operation. The group-switching module only supports half-duplex mode.

Ethernet Switching Module (WS-X5011)

This module provides 12 switched, 10-Mbps 10BaseFL ports with half- or full-duplex mode of operation. The ports support only multimode, fiber-optic cable. The connectors to be used are straight-type (ST), fiber-optic connectors. The module also has Status and Link LEDs on the front panel, giving visual indication of the module operation.

Fast Ethernet Modules

The Catalyst 5000 series of switches support the following Fast Ethernet modules.

10/100-Mbps Workgroup Fast Ethernet Switching Modules (WS-X5224)

The module provides 24 switched, 10/100-Mbps RJ-45 Fast Ethernet ports. Each of the ports can be a half-duplex or full-duplex mode. Cat 5 UTP cable is used for connecting the port to the devices. The port can be operating at 10 or 100 Mbps, depending upon the device with which it is interacting.

This module also has Status and Link LEDs on the front panel. The Link LEDs from ports 1–24 will be green when ports are working. An LED will be flashing orange if the port is bad due to hardware failure or if the port is disabled by software. If the port could not detect any signal, the Link LED will be off.

There is another LED, SP, to indicate the bandwith at which the port is operating. The SP LED will be green if the port is operating at 100 Mbps; the LED will be off when the port is at 10 Mbps.

10/100-Mbps Fast EtherChannel Switching Modules (WS-X5203, WS-X5225R)

These modules support Fast EtherChannel trunking, a feature that combines multiple ports so they appear as a single high-speed trunk port. This feature enables 200, 400, or 800 Mbps bandwidth between switches while avoiding problems with Spanning Tree loops. Combined with ISL or 802.1Q trunking, VLANs can span multiple switches using these high-speed links.

The WS-X5203 provides 12 UTP ports with RJ-45 connectors. The WS-X5225R provides 24 UTP ports with RJ-45 connectors. In addition to the normal Status and Link LEDs, these modules include an SP LED to indicate port speed. When operating at 100 Mbps the LED is green; at 10Mbps, the LED is not illuminated.

Group Switching Fast Ethernet Module (WS-X5223)

This module provides half-duplex Fast Ethernet ports: 24 shared, 100-Mbps (100BaseTX) ports in three groups of eight repeated ports each. There are 24 RJ-45 connectors on the front panel, with three groups of eight RJ-45 ports per segment. The numbering on the segments starts from the left. The first repeated segment of RJ-45 connector ports starting on the left is numbered 1–8; the second segment is numbered 9–16; the third segment is numbered 17–24.

The module has Status and Link LEDs on the front panel.

Fast Ethernet Switching Modules (WS-X5111 and WS-X5201)

These module types are similar. The major difference between the two is that the WS-X5201 module supports Fast EtherChannel operation, and the WS-X5111 does not. The number of ports in the modules remains the same. Each module provides connection to 12 switched, 100-Mbps (100BaseFX multimode, fiber-optic) devices. The port can be a full- or half-duplex mode. Each port is a Fast Ethernet port with SC fiber-optic connectors.

Fast Ethernet Switching Module Single-Mode/Multimode Fiber (WS-X5114)

This module is a combination of single-mode and multimode fiber connectors. The module provides 12 switched, 100-Mbps (100BaseFX), half- or full-duplex Fast Ethernet ports, using six single-mode and six multimode SC fiber-optic connectors.

10/100-Mbps Fast Ethernet Switching Module (WS-X5225R)

This module provides 24 switched, 10/100-Mbps (10/100BaseTX) ports with Cat 5 UTP support. The ports can be configured as full- or half-duplex Fast Ethernet ports using 24 RJ-45 connectors. Besides the Status and Link LEDs, there is an SP LED to indicate the bandwidth at which the port is operating. If the SP LED is off, the port is at 10 Mbps; if it is green, the port is at 100 Mbps.

For more information about the Ethernet modules, you can refer to the following URL:

http://www.cisco.com/univercd/cc/td/doc/product/lan/cat5000/
c5k3_1/mod_ig/04ether.htm#31407

Token Ring Modules

The following sections provide information regarding the Catalyst 5000 series switch with various, non-Ethernet technology modules. We will cover Token Ring, FDDI, CDDI, ATM LANE, and RSM.

Let us start with Token Ring switching modules in a Catalyst 5000 series switch. Large Token Ring networks have many smaller rings interconnected. The purpose of subdividing large rings into smaller ones and having fewer workstations on a single ring is to give each station more chances to transmit and receive information. The common method of interconnecting the rings is with a source-routing bridge. But introducing a bridge or router within a network will drastically affect the performance of the network. This will result in overloading of the backbone ring.

To avoid these problems, large Token Ring networks usually have a Token Ring switch as a local, collapsed backbone device. The inclusion of a Token Ring switch within the network will enhance performance by reducing the interstation latency.

Catalyst 5000 series switches support both 4-Mbps and 16-Mbps Token Ring networks.

Token Ring Module (WS-X5030)

The Token Ring Module provides up to 16 shielded RJ-45 connectors for Token Ring connections. These ports allow either full- or half-duplex operation with other switches, hubs, or end workstations.

The module has LEDs on the front panel providing visual information on the status of the module. There are Status (Module), Status (Port), and Activity (Port) LEDs.

The Status (Module) LED gives information regarding the initial diagnostic test on the module. Status (Port) LED gives indication of the port status of the module. Activity (Port) LED indicates whether there is some activity between the port and the end station connected to it.

The features of a Token Ring module used in a Catalyst 5000 series switch can be summarized as follows:

- The module gives up to 16 Token Ring ports. Each port is individually programmable and capable of running in 4-Mbps or 16-Mbps rates, full-or half-duplex.

- The module forwards frames between ports and modules

- Spanning-Tree Protocol is supported

- Up to 1024 VLANs per switch

- SNMP-based management with CiscoView graphical monitoring

Fiber Token Ring Module (WS-X5031)

This module has 16 Volition VF-45 socket connectors for Token Ring connections. The ports on the fiber Token Ring module support 16 multimode fixed-fiber connections via ST to Volition VF-45 or via SC to Volition VF-45 patch cords.

The INS LED indicates whether the particular port is inserted to the ring or not. If the INS LED is green, it means that port is inserted. The ACT LED indicates the port activity. For more information about the Token Ring modules, you can refer to the URL:

http://www.cisco.com/univercd/cc/td/doc/product/lan/cat5000/hardware/modules/08tknrng.htm

FDDI and CDDI Modules

We will now look into the FDDI and CDDI modules used in Catalyst 5000 series switches. FDDI is a LAN technology defined by the ANSI X3T9.5 group. This is a 100-Mbps, token-passing network. Fiber-optic cable is the medium used for achieving 100 Mbps bandwidth. FDDI can support transmission distances of up to two kilometers. FDDI provides high redundancy in the network because of its dual-ring architecture. FDDI technology is observed mostly in campus-area designs or large enterprise backbone networks.

Similarly, CDDI is the implementation of FDDI protocols over shielded twisted-pair and unshielded twisted-pair cabling. CDDI transmits data at 100 Mbps over relatively short distances (about 100 meters). CDDI also provides redundancy using dual-ring architecture.

The following sections describe the actual modules used in a Catalyst 5000 series switch.

CDDI Module (WS-X5103)

This module provides two 100-Mbps CDDI interfaces using two RJ-45 interfaces. The module provides a single-attachment station (SAS) or dual-attachment station (DAS) connection to two Category 5 UTP 100-Mbps CDDI interfaces using two RJ-45 connectors.

The LEDs on the CDDI module provide status information for the module and for the individual CDDI port connections. The Status LED will be green if the switch passes all diagnostic tests. The LED will be red if the module fails, and orange during boot sequence.

The Ring OP LED indicates whether the ring is operational. If the ring is operational, the LED is green. If the ring is not operational, the LED is off. If ports A and B of the CDDI/FDDI module are connected to the primary and secondary rings, the Thru LED is green; otherwise, it is off.

The Wrap A LED is green if port **B** is connected to the ring and port **A** is isolated. Similarly, the Wrap **B** LED is green if port **A** is connected to the ring and port **B** is isolated.

Port A LED and Port B LED provide status information on the individual ports. If Port A LED is green, it is connected to the ring. If Port A receives a signal but fails to connect, then the LED is orange. The LED is turned off if no receive signal is detected. Similarly, Port B LED will be green when it is connected to the ring. If port B receives a signal but fails to connect, or a dual-homing condition exists, the LED is orange. The LED is turned off if no receive signal is detected.

FDDI Module Multimode Fiber (WS-X5101)

This FDDI module provides an SAS or DAS connection to a FDDI ring via two media interface connector (MIC) fiber-optic ports. This version of the FDDI module supports multi-mode fiber (MMF). It has the same indicator LEDs as the CDDI module, plus a "Bypass" port and an "In" LED.

The Bypass port is a six-pin mini-DIN connector used to attach an external optical bypass switch. With a DAS-type connection, the optical bypass switch keeps the FDDI ring intact when the FDDI module is offline. This is an important option, since FDDI can only self-heal a single break in the ring.

When the FDDI module is online, the bypass switch passes traffic to the FDDI module and the "In" LED is lit. When the FDDI module is offline, the bypass switch re-routes the fiber connection around the FDDI module, "healing" this break in the FDDI ring.

FDDI Module Single-Mode Fiber (WS-X5104)

This module is similar to the FDDI Multimode Fiber module. It provides an SAS or DAS connection to the 100-Mbps FDDI backbone network using two single-mode, ST fiber-optic connectors (for an SAS); or four single-mode, ST fiber-optic connectors (for a DAS). This module also has a Bypass connector. When this switch is activated, the FDDI module SMF is inserted into the ring.

ATM LANE Modules

We will now look into ATM LANE switching modules used in Catalyst 5000 series switches. Catalyst 5000 series switches support ATM LANE switching modules using unshielded twisted-pair, single-mode fiber, multimode fiber, and coaxial cables.

ATM LANE technology is widely implemented in current enterprise-wide networks to support the integration of the legacy Ethernet networks into ATM networks. Catalyst 5000 series ATM switching modules support ATM connectivity by using LANE technology. LANE allows an ATM network to behave as a LAN backbone for Ethernet switches. The advantage is that it makes an ATM interface look like one or more Ethernet interfaces. It also allows upper-layer protocols that expect connectionless service to use connection-oriented ATM switches.

ATM LANE Module Features

ATM LANE modules allow end stations to communicate through a LAN-to-ATM switch with an ATM-attached device such as a file server, without requiring the traffic to pass through a more complex device such as a router. LANE requires a switch that supports User-Network Interface (UNI) 3.0 or 3.1 and point-to-multipoint signaling.

ATM LANE Single PHY Modules

There are three types of modules supported under this class of ATM LANE Single Physical-layer Interface (PHY) modules:

- **UTP (WS-X5153)** This module provides a direct connection between the 155-Mbps ATM network and the Catalyst 5000 series switch using one RJ-45 connector on Category 5 UTP cables. Using a straight Cat 5 UTP cable, one can connect an ATM network to the switch. The module supports LANE technology so that we can integrate an Ethernet network onto the same switch.

- **MMF (WS-X5155)** This module provides direct connections between the 155-Mbps ATM network and the Catalyst 5000 series switch, using one multimode, SC fiber-optic connector.

- **SMF (WS-X5154)** This module provides direct connections between the 155-Mbps ATM network and the Catalyst 5000 series switch, using one single-mode, SC fiber-optic connector.

The ATM LANE modules in this list have Status, TX, RX, and Link LEDs. The Status LED will be green if the switch passes all the diagnostic tests. If a test fails, the LED is red. During the initial boot sequence, or when the module is disabled, the LED is orange.

When the port is receiving cells from the connected station, the RX LED is green; otherwise it is off. The TX LED will be green whenever the port is transmitting a cell. The Link LED displays the link status of the ATM port.

If the link integrity is good, the LED is green; if a fault is discovered, then the LED blinks.

ATM LANE Dual PHY Modules

There are three types of modules supported under this class of ATM LANE Dual PHY module:

- **UTP (WS-X5156)** This module provides two direct connections between the ATM network and the switch, using two RJ-45 connectors. The module is capable of reassembling 256 packets simultaneously. It also supports up to 4096 virtual circuits and ATM adaptation layer (AAL) 5.

- **MMF (WS-X5158)** This module provides two direct connections between the ATM network and the switch, using two multimode, SC fiber-optic connectors. The module is capable of reassembling 256 packets simultaneously. It also supports up to 4096 virtual circuits and ATM AAL 5. The module supports ATM LANE 1.0, which includes LAN Emulation Client (LEC), LAN Emulation Server (LES), broadcast and unknown server (BUS), and LAN Emulation Configuration Server (LECS).

- **SMF (WS-X5157)** This module provides two direct connections between the ATM network and the switch, using two single-mode (SC) fiber-optic connectors. This module also supports ATM AAL 5 and ATM LANE 1.0.

The previously mentioned ATM LANE modules have Status, TX, RX, and Link LEDs. The Status LED will be green if the switch passes all the diagnostic tests. If a test fails, the LED is red. During the initial boot sequence, or when the module is disabled, the LED is orange.

When the port is receiving cells from the connected station, the RX LED is green; otherwise it is off. The TX LED will be green whenever the port is transmitting a cell. The Link LED displays the link status of the ATM port. If the link integrity is good, LED is green; if a fault is discovered, then the LED blinks.

If you would like to have some more information about these modules, you can refer to the URL:

http://www.cisco.com/univercd/cc/td/doc/product/lan/cat5000/hardware/modules/06atm.htm

RSM

In earlier sections of this chapter, we introduced you to modules supported by the Catalyst 5000 series switches. These modules integrated various technology networks. For example, ATM networks can be integrated with legacy Ethernet networks using ATM LANE modules in the switch. Let us now find out more about the latest module, Route Switch Module (RSM), supported by Catalyst series switches. In short, this module makes the switch behave like a router.

The Catalyst 5000 series RSM is an RSP2-based router module running Cisco IOS software, which connects directly into the Catalyst 5000 switch backplane. RSM will be like any other module in the switch with one MAC address. However, this MAC address (port) has some special features. It does not have any attributes, such as media type or speed, as other modules do. Within this port, RSM can route between VLANs. With optional Versatile Interface Processor 2 (VIP2), the RSM module behaves like a Cisco 7500 series router.

Catalyst 5000 series switches support the RSM and the RSM/VIP2. The following sections describe these modules.

Route Switch Module (WS-X5302)

This RSM module plugs directly into the Catalyst 5000 series switch backplane. The module runs Cisco IOS router software. With the software, the module is capable of providing multiprotocol routing for the Catalyst 5000 series Ethernet interfaces. For the switch, it sees RSM as another module, but the IOS within the module performs the routing functionality.

The front panel of the RSM module has PCMCIA slots, a Reset button, an AUX port, and a CON port. The IOS within the module is stored in

Flash memory. If necessary, the slots can be used to plug in PCMCIA Flash cards storing IOS images. The slots can be used to house PCMCIA cards acting as file servers with other routers, accessing them in the same manner as the remote clients.

The Reset button is used to make the RSM module go into ROM monitor mode. Under this mode, as observed in a typical router, diagnostic commands and recovery utilities can be executed. To reset, press the Reset button with a pointed device.

The AUX port on the front panel is used to connect to a modem for remote access to the RSM. The CON port allows connecting a terminal to the RSM for configuration and monitoring.

There are front panel LEDs on the module to provide visual indication of the module performance.

- The Status LED will be green if the switch passes the initial self-test and diagnostics. If not, the Status LED will be red.

- The CPU Halt LED is a very important LED on the RSM module. It gives the hardware status of the module. The LED is on during normal operation of the module. If the processor hardware fails, the LED goes off.

- The Enabled LED is on when the IOS is loaded and RSM is operational.

- PCMCIA Slot 0 and PCMCIA Slot 1 are on when the respective slot is used with Flash memory and RSM is using it.

- The TX and RX LEDs will be green only when the port is transmitting and receiving, respectively.

You can find more information at this URL:

http://www.cisco.com/univercd/cc/td/doc/product/lan/cat5000/cnfg_nts/rsm/4780vip2.htm

Route Switch Module/VIP2 Module

Adding another module can enhance the RSM features. This module is called the Versatile Interface Processor 2 module. The RSM without the

VIP2 will act as stand-alone inter-VLAN router. With the VIP2 module, we can have direct connections with external networks of different media types, with the same port adapters as used on Cisco 7500 series routers. This Catalyst VIP2 module supports any combination of port adapter-based network interface types. With a Catalyst VIP2 module, the RSM will occupy two consecutive slots in the chassis. The Catalyst VIP2 module requires that the RSM run Cisco IOS release 11.2(9) P or later.

QUESTIONS AND ANSWERS

Can I achieve redundant supervisor engine operation with Catalyst 5002?	No. You have to use Catalyst 5505, Catalyst 5509, or Catalyst 5500.
I need to swap a supervisor engine module from the switch, when the switch is online. Can I do it?	Yes. You can swap the supervisor engine module if it is in standby mode or not active. If it is the only module in the switch, then removing the module will halt the functioning of the switch.
When the standby supervisor engine module is swapped with a new supervisor engine module, do I need to restart the switch for the standby module to get the configuration information?	No. When the new supervisor engine module is connected, it automatically goes into standby mode. The active module will interact with the standby module and transfer the configuration file.
How do I know whether the supervisor engine module has failed?	There are two ways. The front panel Status LED gives information about the status of the module. The other method is to use the SNMP Management software, which collects the traps generated by the module and represents the data in a visual format.
Is it always necessary to have two supervisor engine modules in a switch?	The switch is capable of operating effectively with a single supervisor engine. But you have to make the decision based on the criticality of the network. If the network applications demand zero down time, then obviously you have to go in for a redundant supervisor engine configuration.
Which is better, Supervisor Engine II or Supervisor Engine III?	Both modules have their own specific features suitable for specific applications. If Supervisor Engine II is used, it will utilize the 1.2-Gbps backplane in the switch. If Supervisor Engine III is used, it will be capable of utilizing all three 1.2-Gbps backplanes in a Catalyst 5500 switch, enabling 3.6 Gbps operation.

The Catalyst VIP2 module uses a single motherboard with up to two port adapters. The Catalyst VIP2 port adapters provide WAN or LAN/WAN interface ports for the Catalyst 5000, Catalyst 5505, and Catalyst 5500 switches. You can remove the RSM/VIP2 module combination from the switch chassis while power is on and the system is operating. The Catalyst VIP2 CPU is a RISC, Mips 4700 processor, with an internal operating frequency of 100 MHz, and a 50-MHz system bus interface. The Catalyst VIP2 module has a 128KB NVRAM.

exam
ⓦatch

You have to understand the entire concept of routing within a switch. The RSM module is capable of doing this, but the most important application has to be the RSM with VIP2 module in it. On the exam, you will be tested about the RSM module types and their features. You have to know the LEDs on the front panel and their functions. You can use the CiscoView software to look into the status of the unit from a remote location. You have to be aware of the application of SNMP-based management in a real networking environment.

CERTIFICATION SUMMARY

You have been exposed to various Catalyst 5000 series switches in this chapter. The objectives of this chapter were to understand supervisor engine modules and redundancy supervisor operation, and to get an overview of modules supported by each switch.

The chapter provided the necessary information to meet the objectives. At the same time, for you to face the certification exam and to be an effective network engineer, practical exposure to the units discussed is essential. You should experiment in the labs with Catalyst 5000 series switches. This should include installation and configuration of the switches. For more information regarding the practical installation of the equipment, refer to the Installation and Configuration Manual supplied by Cisco along with the equipment. Another valuable reference is the Cisco Web site or the Cisco Documentation CD.

Cisco's Catalyst 5000 family offers a complete set of enterprise switching solutions spanning everything from the campus backbone to desktop. The chapter described the hardware and operation of the Catalyst 5000 series switches. The switches are capable of integrating frame and cell switching with full support for Cisco IOS-based routing, full support for Fast EtherChannel and ATM, and a migration to future Gigabit Ethernet. These switches are the most widely used for campus backbones, since they protect the future investment as the requirement in bandwidth grows.

For the switch to operate effectively, it needs the supervisor engine module. The switch cannot function without this module. The switch software and interface configuration are stored and maintained by the supervisor module. Each series switch supports different supervisor engine modules.

The supervisor engine module must be functioning all the time for the switch to keep working. If this module fails, the switch stops functioning. Catalyst 5500 and Catalyst 5505 switches provide redundant supervisor engine operation. Catalyst 5500 has a 13-slot chassis with support for 11 different switching modules. This switch is widely used for large-enterprise, mission-critical networks. Obviously, the failure of the entire network should not depend on a single supervisor engine module. These switches support Supervisor Engine II and III in slots 1 and 2. Two similar modules are plugged into the unit and configured for fail-over.

In any major enterprise backbone network, different networking needs arise. You might have observed situations in which it was necessary to integrate ATM networks with Ethernet, or to have FDDI/CDDI backbone connectivity or Token Ring network support. Catalyst 5000 series switches provide flexible architecture with high-end backplane. With support for Token Ring, ATM, CDDI/FDDI, Ethernet, and Fast Ethernet modules, the Catalyst 5000 switch will meet the current and future networking demands with less investment.

Route Switch Module (RSM) will make the switch behave like a typical Cisco 7500 series router. Catalyst 5000 series switches with RSM will provide full multiprotocol routing. You should be aware of the advantages of making the switch emulate a router.

To understand the subject thoroughly, and to equip yourself for the certification exam, we strongly recommend that you implement the concepts discussed in this chapter.

TWO-MINUTE DRILL

❑ Catalyst switches are all modular, which allows for many different types of network connections.

❑ Cisco Catalyst 5000 family switches are well suited for small to mid-range enterprise backbones.

❑ The Catalyst 5000 switch gives switched connections to servers, workstations, and LAN segments using twisted-pair cables (STP or UTP) and fiber-optic cable.

❑ Catalyst 5000 series switches support the following network types: Ethernet, Fast Ethernet, Gigabit Ethernet, ATM LANE, FDDI, CDDI, and Token Ring.

❑ The Catalyst 5002 switching system is a fully modular device supporting up to two modules, and is rack mountable in a standard 19-inch rack.

❑ The Catalyst 5000 platform is a five-slot chassis, which goes into a standard 19-inch rack. This switch is able to support most data center applications.

❑ The Catalyst 5505 chassis has five slots, supports redundant supervisor engine operation, and is more suitable for high-end and critical applications.

❑ The Catalyst 5509 switch is a high-end modular switch with a high-capacity backplane (9 slots) suitable for large enterprise networking.

❑ Catalyst 5500 switch is a high-end modular switch with a more capable backplane (13 slots). It is more suitable for high-end and mission-critical applications.

❑ You should be aware of the practical differences between the various models of Catalyst 5000 series switches. As a part of the certification process, or for the network administration, it is essential to understand the design implications involved in these switches. The major differences among the models are in the support for redundant supervisor engine operation and support for a large number of modules of different types. In the certification exam, you will be tested to select the best switch model for a particular networking requirement.

❑ The supervisor engine modules are classified into three types: Supervisor Engine I, Supervisor Engine II, and Supervisor Engine III.

❑ Supervisor engine modules support hot swapping.

❑ The supervisor engine module is capable of running diagnostic tests on the new modules when they are plugged into the chassis.

❑ Each of the supervisor engine modules has erasable programmable read-only memory (EEPROM).

❑ Catalyst 5500, Catalyst 5509, and Catalyst 5505 switches support redundant supervisor engine operation.

❑ Catalyst switches support Ethernet and Fast Ethernet switching modules.

❑ Catalyst series switches with Ethernet and Fast Ethernet switching modules will reduce degradation problems.

❑ Large Token Ring networks usually have a Token Ring switch as a local, collapsed backbone device. The inclusion of a Token Ring switch within the network will enhance performance by reducing the interstation latency.

❑ FDDI is a LAN technology defined by the ANSI X3T9.5 group. This is a 100-Mbps, token-passing network. Fiber-optic cable is the medium used for achieving 100 Mbps bandwidth.

❑ CDDI is the implementation of FDDI protocols over shielded twisted-pair and unshielded twisted-pair cabling. CDDI transmits data at 100 Mbps over relatively short distances (about 100 meters).

❑ Catalyst 5000 series switches support ATM LANE switching modules using unshielded twisted-pair, single-mode fiber, multimode fiber, and coaxial cables.

❑ ATM LANE technology is widely implemented in current enterprise-wide networks to support the integration of the legacy Ethernet networks into ATM networks.

❑ The Catalyst 5000 series RSM is an RSP2-based router module running Cisco IOS software, which connects directly into the Catalyst 5000 switch backplane.

❑ You have to understand the entire concept of routing within a switch. The RSM module is capable of doing this, but the most important application has to be the RSM with VIP2 module in it. On the exam, you will be tested about the RSM module types and their features. You have to know the LEDs on the front panel and their functions. We can use the CiscoView software to look into the status of the unit from a remote location. You have to be aware of the application of SNMP-based management in a real networking environment.

SELF TEST

The following Self Test questions will help you measure your understanding of the material presented in this chapter. Read all the choices carefully, as there may be more than one correct answer. Choose all correct answers for each question.

1. What is the major factor that decides the type of modular switch in the Catalyst 5000 series switches?

   A. Supervisor engine module
   B. Speed of the backplane
   C. Number of slots in the chassis
   D. Ethernet modules

2. The first slot in a Catalyst 5000 series switch should always be used for:

   A. Power supply module
   B. Route switch module
   C. Fast Ethernet module
   D. Supervisor engine module

3. What is the purpose of the switching fabric in the Catalyst 5000 series switch?

   A. To connect chassis together
   B. To provide connectivity between supervisor engine modules
   C. To provide connectivity between power supply and interface modules
   D. To supply power to the unit

4. Which of the Catalyst 5000 series switches support redundant supervisor engine operation?

   A. Catalyst 5000
   B. Catalyst 5505
   C. Catalyst 5500
   D. Catalyst 5002

5. Which type of Catalyst 5000 series switch supports Supervisor Engine II?

   A. Catalyst 5500
   B. Catalyst 5505
   C. Catalyst 5000
   D. All the above

6. Which are the specific features observed in a Catalyst 5500 switch with Supervisor Engine III?

   A. Supports supervisor engine redundancy
   B. Supports three switching buses with 3.6 Gbps bandwidth
   C. Has RISC processor at 150 MHz
   D. All the above

7. Which of the following features of Supervisor Engine II aids in redundancy operation?

   A. The module has hardware fault-detection logic built in
   B. The module has separate switching and management functions
   C. ASIC hardware forwards packets even if the processor fails
   D. All the above

8. Where do you have to install the two supervisor engines for redundant operation?

    A. Slot 13 in Catalyst 5500

    B. Slots 1 and 2

    C. Slot 4

    D. Slot 3

9. What is the advantage of full-duplex communication supported by Catalyst switching modules?

    A. Bandwidth will be doubled

    B. Data can be transmitted and received at the same time in both directions

    C. Data can be sent only in one direction

    D. None of the above

10. What would be the reason the Status LED on the Ethernet modules is lit red?

    A. Module is transmitting more data

    B. Module is not operating properly

    C. Switch is off

    D. None of the above

11. Which Ethernet module supports Fast EtherChannel operation?

    A. WS-X5213

    B. WS-X5012

    C. WS-X5013

    D. WS-X5010

12. Which Token Ring modules are supported by Catalyst 5000 series switches?

    A. WS-X5030

    B. WS-X5031

    C. WS-X5013

    D. All of the above

13. What is the maximum bandwidth FDDI technology supports?

    A. 10 Mbps

    B. 100 Mbps

    C. 200 Mbps

    D. All of the above

14. If the Bypass LED on an FDDI module is turned on, what can you infer?

    A. The module is working fine

    B. The module is in Thru mode

    C. Module is in diagnostic mode

    D. All of the above

15. Which media types do the ATM switching modules support?

    A. UTP

    B. Single-mode fiber (SMF)

    C. Multimode fiber (MMF)

    D. All of the above

16. The Catalyst 5000 series switch can act as a router with which module?

    A. FDDI module

    B. ATM module

    C. RSM module

    D. None of the above

17. What is the purpose of the PCMCIA slots in the front panel of the RSM module?

    A. To load the IOS

    B. To connect other I/O devices

    C. To plug in the Flash card

    D. All of the above

18. What is the use of the Reset button in the front panel of the RSM module?

    A. To make the RSM enter ROM monitor mode

    B. To boot the router module

    C. To reset the entire switch

    D. To reset the configuration of the unit

19. What happens if the power supply in a Catalyst 5002 switch fails during operation?

    A. The switch stops working

    B. The switch will work with backup power supply

    C. The switch still works without power supply

    D. None of the above

20. How can you make a switch connect directly to an external network with different media types, with the same port adapters as used on a Cisco 7500 series router?

    A. Use an RSM/VIP2 module

    B. Use FDDI with an RSM module

    C. Load new software to the switch

    D. All the above

CISCO CERTIFIED NETWORK PROFESSIONAL

6

Configuring the Catalyst 5000 Series Switches

CERTIFICATION OBJECTIVES

I f you have experience configuring other Cisco equipment, you will be amazed to learn that Cisco's Catalyst series switches actually do useful work right out of the box! Unlike the router products, which require significant manual configuration prior to forwarding data, the Catalyst switches get to work as soon as you plug in power and network connections. For instance, a "naked" Catalyst will carry traffic through any connected Ethernet or Token Ring interface. It auto-detects the speed of attached interfaces. It prevents broadcast storms by blocking ports involved in topology loops. Most important, the Catalyst switch, without any user configuration, will improve throughput in your network by providing media rate switching services to lots of users. I'm no longer surprised at the number of customer sites I visit where Catalysts are employed in exactly this fashion, essentially as fast-switching hubs.

These customers are perfectly happy with the operation of their Catalysts and the performance boost they experience in their networks. As a consultant, it's fun to point out some operating enhancements available through a few simple modifications to the default configuration. With the commands and examples detailed in this chapter, you will transform your Catalyst from a dusty piece of communications equipment relegated to your wiring closet, to an essential tool in preserving and monitoring your organization's networking capital.

In this chapter you will learn to navigate the Catalyst Network Management Processor (NMP) Image Command Line Interface. You will want to make special note of the commands to determine how your Catalyst is performing and whether it has detected correctable errors on your network. We will be interested in configuring services that make your Catalyst into a powerful network monitoring and maintenance tool. You will select from several methods how best to manage your Catalyst switch in a variety of situations. We will also consider the vitally important topic of backing up your configuration.

CERTIFICATION OBJECTIVE 6.01

SET, SHOW, and CLEAR Commands

Most of the commands that perform these functions fall into three broad families: the SET commands, the CLEAR commands, and the SHOW commands. SET and CLEAR commands generally modify the behavior of the Catalyst NMP image by changing its configuration. The SHOW commands, on the other hand, do not change the configuration of the switch. Rather, they provide a powerful tool kit for monitoring the operation of the Catalyst and all the networks attached to it.

We take some of these commands out for a spin in the sections that follow, but first we must consider details of how we talk to the Catalyst.

Accessing the Command Line Interface

The CLI is the most popular mechanism for configuring the Catalyst 5000 family of switches—primarily because it is free. You can access CLI through the EIA/TIA-232 Console port on the Catalyst Supervisor Module, through a Telnet virtual terminal session, or through a dial-up connection using the SLIP protocol. The latter two methods most commonly require configuration changes on the switch. Accordingly, you will need to make your first connection to the Catalyst using the console cable supplied by Cisco.

The Supervisor Module versions I and II use a 25-pin male connector for the console port, while the Supervisor III uses a RJ-45 female port. When connecting a PC to the Supervisor I and II, a "rolled" Cisco terminal cable is used. With a Supervisor III, a straight-through cable (for example, an Ethernet patch cable) is used. You will need a RJ-45 terminated cable with pin-out similar to a Category 5 straight-through unshielded twisted-pair (UTP) cable for connecting to the Supervisor III.

The default communications settings for the PC terminal emulation software or terminal connecting to the Supervisor console port are shown in Table 6-1. It is common practice to use no flow control when connecting to Cisco console ports. Under certain circumstances, it is possible to use hardware flow control, but most experienced professionals would suggest no flow control.

When you complete your connection to the Supervisor console port, press ENTER and you are prompted for a password. This is true even when no password has been previously configured. If this is the case, you will enter a null password by pressing the ENTER key on your PC or terminal. The CLI responds with the "User Mode" prompt:

```
Console>
```

TABLE 6-1	Terminal Communication Parameter	Default Setting
Default Console Port Communication Parameters	Speed	9600 bps
	Data Bits	8
	Parity	None
	Stop Bits	1
	Flow Control	None or Hardware

User mode permits us to issue a set of commands that help us monitor the Catalyst's operation without modifying it in any important way. A second mode of CLI operation gives us access to commands, including those that change the configuration. This is the privileged mode of CLI operation. It is commonly called the enable mode after the command syntax:

```
Console> enable
```

The CLI responds with another password prompt and the prompt changes to reflect the CLI mode. This is the purpose of having two modes of operation. Commands that might negatively affect the forwarding of traffic are protected by a second password. With this double password scheme, it is possible for less experienced personnel to monitor the status of a Catalyst without necessarily having the ability to modify its configuration. In the next section we configure the commands to set both the user and enable mode passwords. If you are used to Cisco router configuration, you may be surprised to learn that the Catalyst will prompt you for user and enable mode passwords even when none have been set. In this case, you would press the ENTER key to send a blank password.

The Configuration Process

As you learned earlier, the CLI commands SET and CLEAR change the behavior of the Catalyst software and thus the operation of the switch in your network. Most commands take effect immediately after you enter them. Some require that specific hardware be restarted before you see their results.

When you issue a command that changes the operation of the Catalyst NMP Image, that command is stored in nonvolatile RAM (NVRAM) storage on the Supervisor card. The configuration commands live in a data structure called the configuration file.

The NVRAM configuration file, often just called the config file, provides the set of instructions that the NMP image executes when the switch is reset or powered up. You can look at your Catalyst's configuration file now by issuing this command:

```
Console> (enable) show config
```

Your config file should look something like the following default configuration file. Unlike the Cisco router CLI you may be used to, the default configuration file shows the default value for all parameters.

```
begin
set password $1$FMFQ$HfZR5DUszVHIRhrz4h6V70
set enablepass $1$FMFQ$HfZR5DUszVHIRhrz4h6V70
set prompt Console>
set length 24 default
set logout 20
set banner motd ^C^C
!
set system baud  9600
set system modem disable
set system name
set system location
set system contact
!

#snmp
set snmp community read-only       public
set snmp community read-write      private
set snmp community read-write-all secret
set snmp rmon disable
set snmp trap disable module
set snmp trap disable chassis
set snmp trap disable bridge
set snmp trap disable repeater
set snmp trap disable vtp
set snmp trap disable auth
```

```
set snmp trap disable ippermit
set snmp trap disable vmps
!
#ip
set interface sc0 1 0.0.0.0 0.0.0.0 0.0.0.0

set interface sl0 0.0.0.0 0.0.0.0
set arp agingtime 1200
set ip redirect    enable
set ip unreachable    enable
set ip fragmentation enable
set ip alias default          0.0.0.0
!
#Command alias
!
#vmps
set vmps server retry 3
set vmps server reconfirminterval 60
set vmps tftpserver 0.0.0.0 vmps-config-database.1
set vmps state disable

!
#dns
set ip dns disable
!
#tacacs+
set tacacs attempts 3
set tacacs directedrequest disable
set tacacs timeout 5
set authentication login tacacs disable
set authentication login local enable
set authentication enable tacacs disable
set authentication enable local enable
!
#bridge
set bridge ipx snaptoether    8023raw
set bridge ipx 8022toether    8023
set bridge ipx 8023rawtofddi snap
!
#vtp
set vtp domain Cisco
set vtp mode client
set vtp pruneeligible 2-1000
clear vtp pruneeligible 1001-1005
!
```

```
#spantree
#uplinkfast groups
set spantree uplinkfast disable
#vlan 1
set spantree enable       1
set spantree fwddelay 15     1
set spantree hello     2       1
set spantree maxage    20      1
set spantree priority 32768 1
#vlan 1003
set spantree enable       1003
set spantree fwddelay 15     1003
set spantree hello     2       1003
set spantree maxage    20      1003
set spantree priority 32768 1003
set spantree portstate 1003 auto 0
set spantree portcost 1003 80
#vlan 1005
set spantree enable       1005
set spantree fwddelay 15     1005
set spantree hello     2       1005
set spantree maxage    20      1005
set spantree priority 32768 1005
set spantree multicast-address 1005 ieee
!
#cgmp
set cgmp disable
set cgmp leave disable
!
#syslog
set logging console enable
set logging server disable
set logging level cdp 2 default
set logging level cgmp 2 default
set logging level disl 5 default
set logging level dvlan 2 default
set logging level earl 2 default
set logging level fddi 2 default
set logging level ip 2 default
set logging level pruning 2 default
set logging level snmp 2 default
set logging level spantree 2 default
set logging level sys 5 default
set logging level tac 2 default
set logging level tcp 2 default
```

```
set logging level Telnet 2 default
set logging level tftp 2 default
set logging level vtp 2 default
set logging level vmps 2 default
set logging level kernel 2 default
set logging level filesys 2 default
set logging level drip 2 default
!
#ntp
set ntp broadcastclient disable
set ntp broadcastdelay 3000
set ntp client disable
clear timezone
set summertime disable
!
#permit list
set ip permit disable
!
#drip
set tokenring reduction enable
set tokenring distrib-crf disable
!
#module 1 : 2-port 100BaseTX Supervisor
set module name     1
set vlan 1     1/1-2
set port channel 1/1-2 off
set port channel 1/1-2 auto
set port enable     1/1-2
set port level      1/1-2  normal
set port duplex     1/1-2  half
set port trap       1/1-2  disable
set port name       1/1-2
set port security   1/1-2  disable
set port broadcast  1/1-2  100%
set port membership 1/1-2  static
set cdp enable     1/1-2
set cdp interval 1/1-2 60
set trunk 1/1   auto 1-1005
set trunk 1/2   auto 1-1005

set spantree portfast     1/1-2 disable
set spantree portcost     1/1-2 19
set spantree portpri      1/1-2 32
set spantree portvlanpri 1/1  0
```

```
set spantree portvlanpri 1/2  0
set spantree portvlancost 1/1  cost 18
set spantree portvlancost 1/2  cost 18
!
#module 2 : 24-port 10BaseT Ethernet
set module name     2
set module enable   2
set vlan 1     2/1-24
set port enable      2/1-24
set port level       2/1-24  normal
set port duplex      2/1-24  half
set port trap        2/1-24  disable
set port name        2/1-24
set port security    2/1-24  disable
set port broadcast   2/1-24  0
set port membership 2/1-24   static
set cdp enable     2/1-24
set cdp interval 2/1-24 60
set spantree portfast     2/1-24 disable
set spantree portcost     2/1-24 100
set spantree portpri      2/1-24 32
!
#module 3 empty

#module 4 : 2-port MM OC-3 Dual-Phy ATM
set module name     4
set port level       4/1  normal
set port name        4/1-2
set cdp enable     4/1


set spantree portcost     4/1 14
set spantree portpri      4/1 32
set spantree portvlanpri 4/1  0
set spantree portvlancost 4/1  cost 13

#module 5 empty
!
#switch port analyzer

!
#cam
set cam agingtime 1,1003,1005 300

end
```

Because configuration changes are automatically stored in NVRAM, we need not worry about the Cisco IOS router concept of running versus backup configuration files. On a Catalyst 5000, the running config file is always identical to the saved config file in normal operation. As you saw earlier, the SET and CLEAR commands change the behavior of the Catalyst software and thus the operation of the switch in your network. Most commands take effect immediately after you issue them. Some of them require that specific hardware be restarted before you see the result.

Take a look at the "#system" section of the default config file listing. This SET SYSTEM NAME line provides a name for your Catalyst when it communicates with other devices using the Simple Network Management Protocol (SNMP). We will have a great deal to say about the SNMP later in the chapter, but for now let's use this command to explore changing the Catalyst's configuration. To that end, enter this command on your Catalyst:

```
Console> (enable) set system name TEST
```

Now reissue the command to display the Catalyst's config file:

```
Console> (enable) show config
```

Do you see the result of your SET command? Figure 6-1 shows us the modified config file. Notice the change to the third line in the "#system" section. Now, when another SNMP speaking device on our network requests the name of our Catalyst, we will respond with the text string "TEST."

Suppose that you wish to move your Catalyst to another location in your network. It may be appropriate in this circumstance to eliminate all the configuration changes from the switch. Use this syntax to accomplish this task:

```
Console> (enable) clear config all
```

When the prompt returns, issue the SHOW CONFIG command again to display the config file. Examine Figure 6-2, the cleared config file, and you will notice that the system name has been set back to a null field. Note also, the More prompt at the bottom of the page. The "cleared" config file still contains several pages of commands. This is the default configuration. These commands make the Catalyst useful even before you manually change the configuration.

FIGURE 6-1

Configuration file SET
SYSTEM NAME command

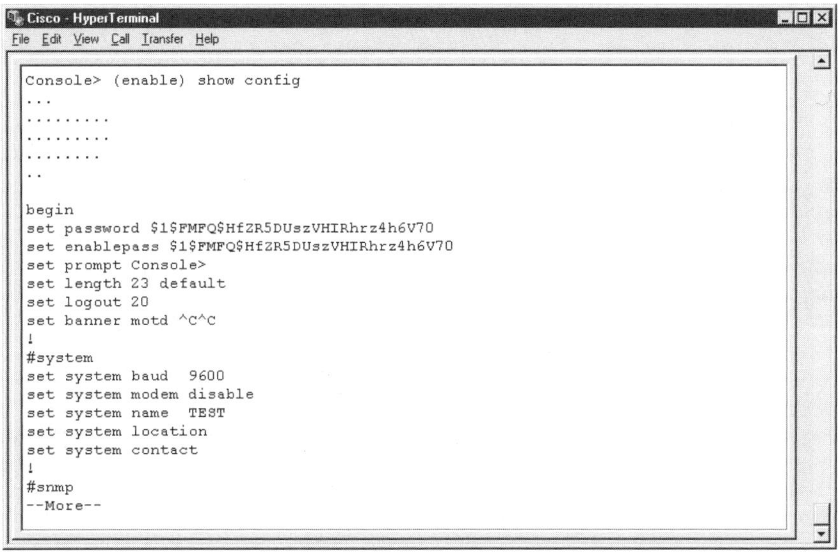

```
Cisco - HyperTerminal                                              _ □ ✕
File  Edit  View  Call  Transfer  Help

Console> (enable) show config
...
.........
.........
........
..

begin
set password $1$FMFQ$HfZR5DUszVHIRhrz4h6V70
set enablepass $1$FMFQ$HfZR5DUszVHIRhrz4h6V70
set prompt Console>
set length 23 default
set logout 20
set banner motd ^C^C
↓
#system
set system baud  9600
set system modem disable
set system name   TEST
set system location
set system contact
↓
#snmp
--More--
```

FIGURE 6-2

Configuration file cleared

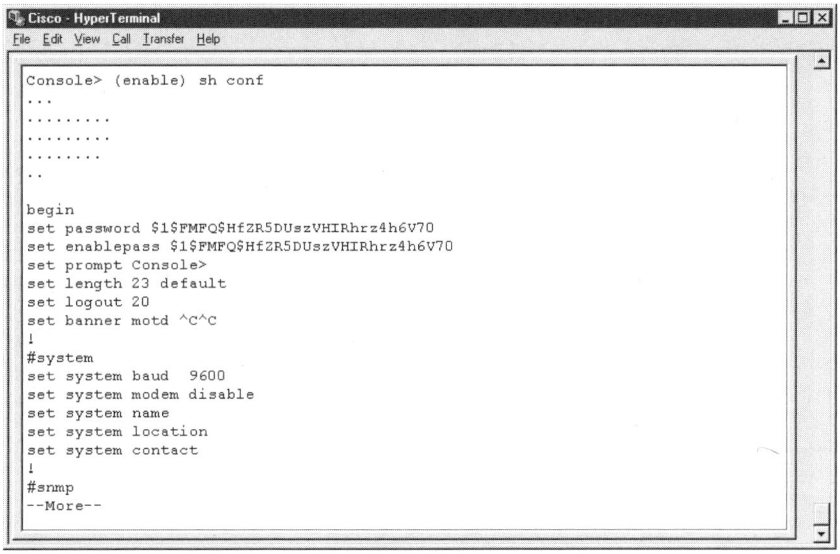

```
Cisco - HyperTerminal                                              _ □ ✕
File  Edit  View  Call  Transfer  Help

Console> (enable) sh conf
...
.........
.........
........
..

begin
set password $1$FMFQ$HfZR5DUszVHIRhrz4h6V70
set enablepass $1$FMFQ$HfZR5DUszVHIRhrz4h6V70
set prompt Console>
set length 23 default
set logout 20
set banner motd ^C^C
↓
#system
set system baud  9600
set system modem disable
set system name
set system location
set system contact
↓
#snmp
--More--
```

In a Catalyst 5000, the running config is always the same as the saved config file with the exception of commands that require hardware reset to become active. We will point out the commands that require hardware restart as we proceed through this chapter and the next.

exam
ⓦatch

Remember, in a Catalyst 5000, the running config is always the same as the saved config file with the exception of commands that require hardware reset to become active.

CLI Basics

With practice, you will master many of the commands illustrated in the default configuration file. Others you will use seldom, if at all. To assist you in remembering the meaning and use of its commands, the CLI provides a Help facility. While the intent of the Catalyst's Help facility is the same as that in Cisco's Router IOS, you will find that the implementation differs significantly.

In fact, the Catalyst Help facility bears more resemblance to UNIX command line Help. In general, you can expect the Catalyst CLI help to provide a terse usage message that identifies the parameters available with the command. As an example, let's take the SET command we used in the last section.

One way to invoke command line Help is to append a question mark after the command keyword. Let's try this:

```
Console>(enable) set ?
```

If you are familiar with the Cisco IOS-based routers, you may have been surprised to see that you have to press the ENTER key to see the Help message. Figure 6-3 shows the output from this command.

Some commands have multiple levels of help, while others provide only one message. Recall that we were curious about the command used to configure the SNMP system name. We need to examine the SYSTEM option of the SET command to learn more. Try this command syntax:

```
Console>(enable)set system ?
```

From Figure 6-4, you can guess that the usage message for setting the SNMP system name is available in the sixth line.

FIGURE 6-3

Catalyst CLI Help facility

```
Cisco - HyperTerminal                                                    _ □ ×
File  Edit  View  Call  Transfer  Help

Console> (enable) set ?
Set commands:
----------------------------------------------------------------------
set alias            Set alias for command
set arp              Set ARP table entry
set authentication   Set TACACS authentication
set banner           Set message of the day banner
set bridge           Set bridge, use 'set bridge help' for more info
set cam              Set CAM table entry
set cdp              Set cdp, use 'set cdp help' for more info
set cgmp             Set CGMP (enable/disable)
set enablepass       Set privilege mode password
set fddi             Set FDDI, use 'set fddi help' for more info
set help             Show this message
set interface        Set network interface configuration
set ip               Set IP, use 'set ip help' for more info
set length           Set number of lines in display (0 to disable 'more')
set logging          Set system logging configuration information
set logout           Set number of minutes before automatic logout
set module           Set module, use 'set module help' for more info
set multicast        Set multicast router port
set ntp              Set NTP, use 'set ntp help' for more info
set password         Set console password
--More--_
```

FIGURE 6-4

Second-level Help

```
Cisco - HyperTerminal                                                    _ □ ×
File  Edit  View  Call  Transfer  Help

Console> (enable) set system ?
Set system commands:
----------------------------------------------------------------------
set system baud          Set system console port baud rate
set system contact       Set system contact
set system help          Show this message
set system location      Set system location
set system modem         Set system modem control (enable/disable)
set system name          Set system name
Console> (enable)
```

Typing a ? on a blank command line results in a display of almost all the commands available to you. Some commands, however, do not show up in the Help display. These so-called "hidden commands" are often useful programs left over from the product development effort. Cisco does not officially support these commands, nor does it guarantee to include them in any future release of the software, but as long as they are available, they can make your life as a Catalyst administrator much easier. We will point out a number of the hidden commands in this chapter and the next.

One command that is listed in the Help facility is the HISTORY command. To see the Catalyst NMP Image History facility in action, enter the following:

```
Console>(enable) history
```

The output in Figure 6-5 is a buffer of commands recently entered at the command line.

FIGURE 6-5

Catalyst CLI History buffer

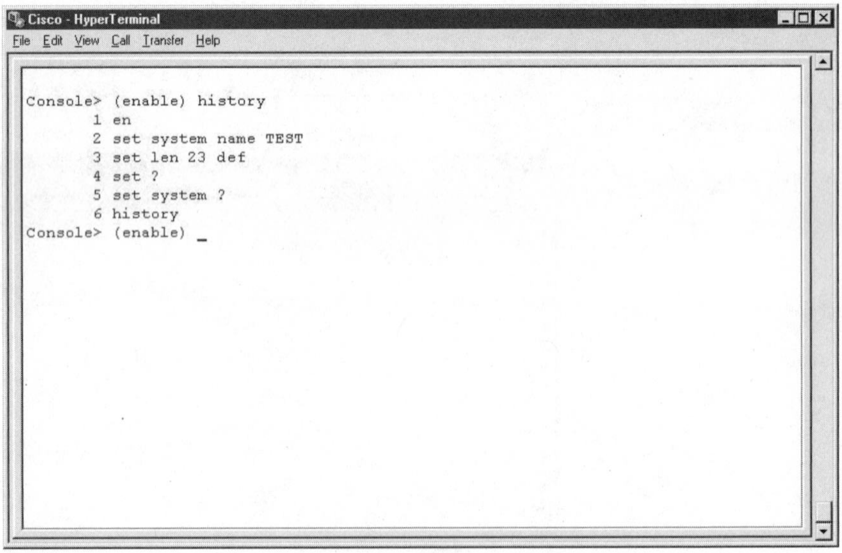

```
Cisco - HyperTerminal
File  Edit  View  Call  Transfer  Help

Console> (enable) history
        1 en
        2 set system name TEST
        3 set len 23 def
        4 set ?
        5 set system ?
        6 history
Console> (enable) _
```

This buffer will save you lots of time when configuring and troubleshooting your switch. For instance, you can recall the last command from the history buffer with this syntax:

```
Console>(enable) !!
```

(The !! is pronounced "double bang" by native UNIX speakers). Take a look at Figure 6-6 to see this syntax at work.

You can recall a command from the history buffer by referencing its line number or matching text from the command itself. You can even choose to edit a command from the buffer before it is executed. Experiment with the syntax from Table 6-2 to make the History facility come to life.

FIGURE 6-6

Command recall using the History buffer

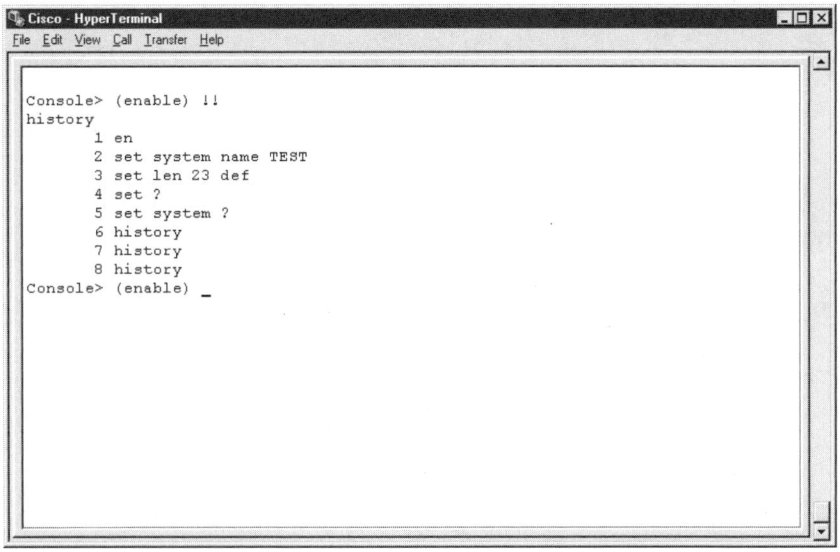

```
Cisco - HyperTerminal
File  Edit  View  Call  Transfer  Help

Console> (enable) !!
history
      1 en
      2 set system name TEST
      3 set len 23 def
      4 set ?
      5 set system ?
      6 history
      7 history
      8 history
Console> (enable) _
```

TABLE 6-2	History Facility Hidden Command	Result
The Catalyst NMP Image History Facility	!!	Issue the most recent command
	!5	Issue the command listed as 5 by the HISTORY command.
	!-5	Issue the command located fifth from the bottom of the HISTORY command buffer
	!SH	Issue the most recent command that starts with the letters SH
	?CONF	Issue the most recent command that includes the string CONF
	!! ENABLE	Issue the most recent command with the characters ENABLE appended
	^SHOW^SET	Issue the most recent command but change the first instance of the characters SHOW to the string SET
	!5 DISABLE	Issue the fifth most recent command but add the string DISABLE

CERTIFICATION OBJECTIVE 6.02

Administrative Commands

Now that the preliminary work of connecting to the Catalyst and exploring the CLI is complete, we are ready to begin configuring the Catalyst NMP Image to suit our needs. None of the commands in this section is required in order to cause data to move through our networks. These administrative configuration commands render the Catalyst itself secure and manageable in a network or internetwork. For this reason, no administrator of a production network should neglect them.

The Catalyst IP Stack

You may choose to configure your Catalyst in any combination of the following six ways:

- Access the CLI using EIA-232 on the console port
- Access the CLI using SLIP on the console port
- Use the Catalyst NMP Image TFTP client
- Use an SNMP Management Station
- Use the VTP protocol
- Access the CLI using EIA-232 on the Supervisor III Aux port

Three of these six methods require that you configure the TCP/IP protocol on the Catalyst NMP Image for proper operation.

The Catalyst NMP Image implements a simple IP stack to facilitate using these management tools. It should be noted that the Catalyst NMP Image does not route IP or any other traffic. The IP stack in question should be thought of as just another client on your network.

The Catalyst NMP Image IP stack requires a valid IP address and mask. The address you choose depends on the configuration of other devices in your network, but it must be unique within the set of devices that can reach your Catalyst. The IP address is used whenever the NMP image generates or receives traffic, including ICMP echo request and echo response packets (ping traffic).

We will demonstrate manually configuring an IP address for your IP stack when we look at the SET INTERFACE command later in this chapter. For now we consider two protocols that automatically configure an IP address: the BOOTP and RARP protocols.

When the Catalyst is first powered, it performs a series of self tests. Then the NMP Image is loaded and a file of configuration commands is read. If this file contains a SET INTERFACE command that sets the IP address to 0.0.0.0 with a mask of 0.0.0.0, it is interpreted as an instruction to obtain an address automatically. One of the methods the Catalyst uses is called

BOOTP. The NMP Image, acting as a BOOTP client, sends a BOOTP request using UDP port 68. If a previously configured BOOTP server hears the request, it will respond on port 67 with the IP address our Catalyst should use. The Catalyst NMP concurrently makes requests using the older Reverse ARP (RARP) process.

Both of these processes require an external server that is preconfigured with the Media Access Control (MAC) address of the Catalyst switch. In order to determine the MAC address of your switch, use this command:

```
Console>(enable) show module
```

exam
ⓦatch

To configure a BOOTP server, you use the first MAC address listed for the active Supervisor by the SHOW MODULE command. This MAC address will be assigned the IP address you configure in the BOOTP server.

You should note that the Catalyst does not implement the newer DHCP protocol for configuring IP. The console screen looks like Figure 6-7 while your Catalyst attempts to obtain an IP address.

FIGURE 6-7

Catalyst NMP BOOTP and
RARP request

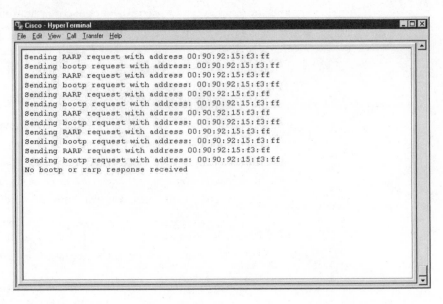

As you see, the process eventually times out and your Catalyst is left without an IP address. Many management functions, including the PING program, the TFTP client program, the Telnet client and server programs, and the SNMP process will not be available until you use the SET INTERFACE command to configure an address manually.

SNMP

Once an IP address is configured—through BOOTP, RARP, or the SET INTERFACE command—we can manage and monitor the Catalyst using the Simple Network Management Protocol. SNMP provides a mechanism whereby a Network Management Station like Cisco Works 2000 can gather certain information stored in the Catalyst. The information is kept in a data structure called a Management Information Base or MIB object. Among the information available in various MIB objects are counters that keep track of how many bytes of network traffic have transited our Catalyst, the number of errors and collisions experienced, and the state of all the ports on the Catalyst. Using SNMP, a device called a Network Management Station (NMS) can collect these counters and present them to us. The NMS can also configure MIB objects on a Catalyst. One of the objects included in the so-called Enterprise MIB allows the NMS to issue configuration commands on the Catalyst. In this fashion, we can manage our switches using SNMP.

This very powerful capability of SNMP can be thought of as a two-edged sword. Configuration and management of a Catalyst can be greatly facilitated by SNMP, but our system is also vulnerable to misconfiguration through malice or accident. SNMP v1 provides a password scheme in which each SNMP message carries a text string that can be used to authenticate the messages sent and received by the protocol. These passwords are called *community strings*. Unfortunately, in SNMP v1 the community strings are carried as plain rather than encrypted text in the SNMP messages. We will look in a moment at the commands that configure the community string passwords. First we need to look at several commands that start and customize the SNMP process within the Catalyst NMP Image.

The SNMP protocol specification makes mandatory a MIB object called the System MIB. It stores for us a name of our Catalyst on its network, a description of its physical location, and contact information for the administrator of the system. To configure the System MIB on your Catalyst, you might use these commands:

```
Console>(enable) set system name syngress
Console>(enable) set system contact Tony_Costa
Console>(enable) set system location Waltham_Mass
```

SNMP provides three levels of access to MIBs on the Catalyst. An NMS like Cisco Works 2000 can make read-only access to the Catalyst, read-write access, or read-write-all access. Read-only access allows the NMS to retrieve MIB objects from the Catalyst, including the one that represents the configuration file of commands currently active on the switch. Read-write access allows retrieval of MIB objects as well as placement of them on your Catalyst 5000. Read-write-all access is identical to read-write access except that it allows the NMS to learn and modify the SNMP community strings. The default settings for SNMP community strings are shown in Table 6-3.

Since any NMS can send configuration changes to your Catalyst, it makes a great deal of sense to protect your network by changing the default community strings to a value of your choice. Use these configuration statements to effect these changes:

```
Console>(enable) set snmp community read-only pass1
Console>(enable) set snmp community read-write pass2
Console>(enable) set snmp community read-write-all pass3
```

TABLE 6-3	Community	Community String
Default Settings for SNMP Community Strings	read-only	public
	read-write	private
	read-write-all	secret

SNMP can do more than just move MIB objects back and forth across your network! When the Catalyst detects an error condition, the SNMP software generates a message called a trap and sends it to the NMS. Configuring your Catalyst NMP Image to report traps is a two-step process. First you must identify the NMS that should receive the traps, and next you select the types of errors that SNMP should report. Use this syntax to accomplish these tasks:

```
Console>(enable) set snmp trap 10.2.3.100 read-only
Console>(enable) set snmp trap enable all
```

In these lines, 10.2.3.100 represents the IP address of the NMS, READ-ONLY represents the community to use when sending traps to this NMS, and ALL refers to the types of traps to send to this NMS. You may choose from the following traps in place of ALL:

- MODULE
- CHASSIS
- BRIDGE
- REPEATER
- AUTH
- VTP
- IPPE

RMON

The port ASICs SAINT, SAGE, and BODEGA are responsible for counting bytes of traffic received and forwarded through the port. You can view many of these counters using SHOW commands:

```
Console>(enable) show mac
Console>(enable) show port counters
```

```
Console>(enable) show counters
Console>(enable) show biga
Console>(enable) show spantree stat 1/1 1
```

As you can see from examining the output from the SHOW MAC command in Figure 6-8, many of the counters have cryptic names that make them less than useful for analyzing and troubleshooting in your network. A solution that makes these statistics easier to comprehend can be found in the remote monitoring (RMON) protocol.

RMON, described in RFC 1757, allows software on a management station such as Cisco's Switch Probe to gather these and many other statistics from the Catalyst switch and present them in a much more readable format. The port ASICs provide a hardware implementation of a mini RMON agent. The agent provides counters in four RMON groups: History, Stats, Alarms, and Events.

FIGURE 6-8

Catalyst CLI SHOW MAC command

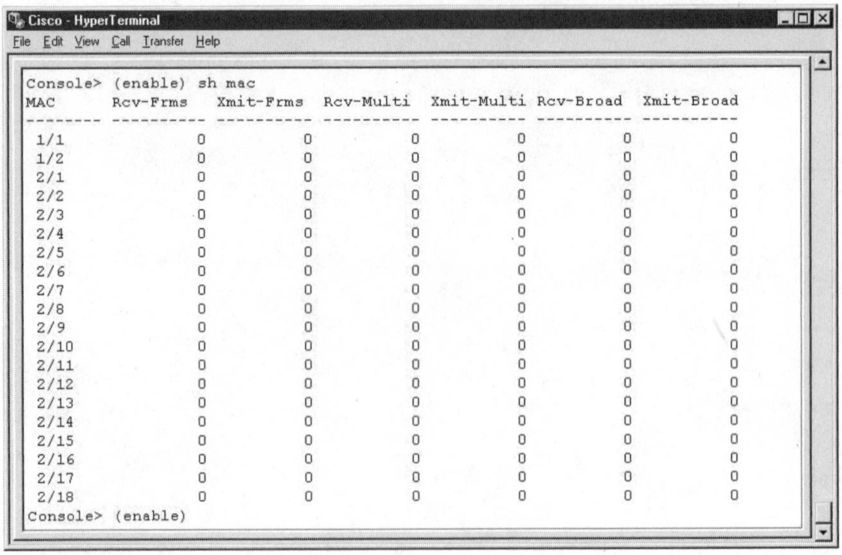

While the counters gather statistics from the port ASICs by default, you must configure the Catalyst NMP Image to report these statistics to a management station. Use this syntax:

```
Console>(enable) set snmp rmon enable
```

This command starts RMON processing on your Supervisor's CPU. RMON support is included in the NMP Image shipped with your Catalyst. Using it with the SET SNMP RMON ENABLE command requires that you pay an additional licensing fee.

To verify your SNMP and RMON configurations use this command at the CLI:

```
Console>(enable) show snmp
```

Your results should resemble Figure 6-9. Notice that this command presents the results not only of our RMON ENABLE command, but also the changes to the trap receiver address, the traps enabled, and the modifications of the community passwords. You can also use the SHOW CONFIG command to see the actual command lines that make the changes.

FIGURE 6-9

Catalyst CLI SHOW
SNMP command

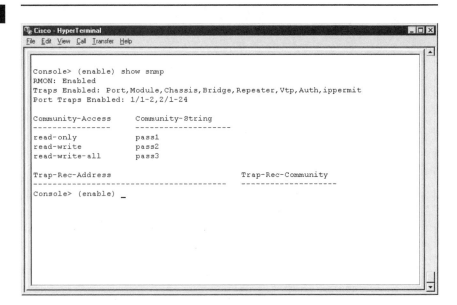

Password Configuration

The Catalyst CLI provides two levels of password protection. By default both passwords are blank. As you learned earlier in this chapter, one simply presses ENTER when prompted for a password. It should go without saying that using blank passwords in your network is not a good idea. To configure the user mode password that permits access to the SHOW commands, use this syntax:

```
Console>(enable) set password
```

Notice that I did not have you type in a new password as you would with Cisco's router IOS. Instead, this command starts a dialog with you that asks for the current password and only allows you to enter a new password if you correctly enter the old one. Figure 6-10 demonstrates using the dialog to set the new user-level password to TEST.

We use similar syntax to configure the privileged mode password. Since we enter privileged mode using the command ENABLE, we often call

---

FIGURE 6-10

Setting the user
mode password

```
Console> (enable) set password
Enter old password:
Enter new password:
Retype new password:
Password changed.
Console> (enable) _
```

privileged CLI mode the enable mode. When the CLI operates in enable mode, we have access to almost the entire command set of the Catalyst NMP Image, including the SET and CLEAR commands that we have described in this chapter. Using these commands, we configure the Catalyst switch for optimized Layer 2 data transport in our networks. In unskilled hands, the same SET and CLEAR commands could hamper or disable data forwarding in portions of a network far removed from this particular switch. This is the reason for having a separate password to grant access to the more dangerous commands. Use this syntax to start a dialog for configuring the enable mode password:

```
Console>(enable) set enablepass
```

Refer to Figure 6-11 for an example of the dialog in action.

Let's take a look now at how the Catalyst CLI stores passwords that you've entered through these dialogs. Do you remember the command to display the Catalyst configuration file? Try this:

```
Console>(enable) show config
```

FIGURE 6-11

Setting the enable
mode password

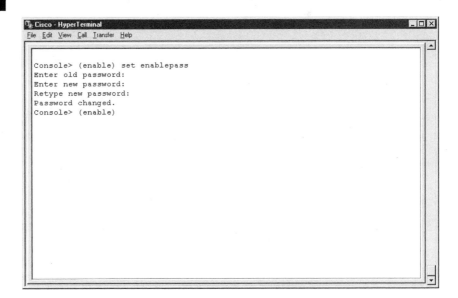

```
Cisco - HyperTerminal
File  Edit  View  Call  Transfer  Help

Console> (enable) set enablepass
Enter old password:
Enter new password:
Retype new password:
Password changed.
Console> (enable)
```

Take a look at the following output to see the changes in our modified configuration file so far (note that portions unchanged from the previous default configuration file have been deleted for clarity).

```
Console> (enable) show config
begin
set password $1$0o8Z$HGVG4gzWe4WUbLbPNZV0Q0
set enablepass $1$CBqb$w5k2PFuHNUsJfahpAKibh/
set prompt Console>
set length 0 default
set logout 20
set banner motd ^C^C
!
#system
set system baud  9600
set system modem disable
set system name
set system location
set system contact
!
#snmp
set snmp community read-only       pass1
set snmp community read-write      pass2
set snmp community read-write-all pass3
set snmp rmon enable
set snmp trap enable  module
set snmp trap enable  chassis
set snmp trap enable  bridge
set snmp trap enable  repeater
set snmp trap enable  vtp
set snmp trap enable  auth
set snmp trap enable  ippermit
set snmp trap disable vmps
(Text Deleted . . .)
```

Notice that the passwords you configured in the preceding steps do not show up in the SET PASSWORD and SET ENABLEPASS commands. Instead only an encrypted text string is displayed. This feature of the Catalyst NMP Image plugs a security hole associated with keeping documentation of your configuration files. You do not want to compromise the security of your network equipment by storing a hard copy of your Catalyst config files, as they might be accessed by unauthorized personnel. Yet a good disaster recovery plan would require that network managers maintain configuration documentation for all configurable devices. To solve this dilemma, the Catalyst NMP Image performs a one-way hash function whenever you type in a new user or enable mode password. The hash function, known as MD5, causes the passwords to be stored in encrypted text in the config file. Anyone attempting unauthorized access to your Catalyst must enter the passwords in clear text, rather than the encrypted string that they might read in your network documentation.

Password Recovery

Should you forget or lose your passwords, you will be unable to access the CLI to change them. To alleviate the obvious "Catch-22," the Catalyst provides several methods by which a lost password can be recovered or defeated. In this section we will examine one method specific to Catalysts with Supervisor I or Supervisor II, and a separate method for Supervisor III-equipped Catalysts.

Password recovery on the Supervisor I and II is relatively straightforward. You must be able to gain physical access to the Catalyst Chassis itself and configure an EIA-232 console session with the CLI. At this point we assume you do not have either user mode or privileged mode passwords for the Catalyst NMP Image. You need only power-cycle the switch to defeat the passwords. This is so because the NMP Image will accept both the configured passwords as well as the ENTER key for the first 30 seconds after it loads from Flash memory. If your Catalyst is equipped with dual power supplies, you must switch both of them off before attempting to "break in" to the Catalyst.

After restarting your Catalyst, the power-on self tests (POST) run and the NMP Image is loaded. It issues the user mode password prompt. You press ENTER now and the user mode prompt appears. You must act quickly to issue the ENABLE command, as you only have 30 seconds total to complete both tasks. When the enable mode password prompt appears, press ENTER again. Now the enable mode prompt displays and you have effectively defeated the configured passwords. Because the SET PASSWORD and SET ENABLEPASS dialogs require that you provide the old password before entering a new one, restoring passwords can be a bit tricky. The brute-force method is to save the entire config file to a notepad file on your terminal, then wipe the existing config with the CLEAR CONFIG ALL command. With the passwords cleared in this way, you can paste the config file from the notepad, less the SET PASSWORD and SET ENABLEPASS commands. Now when the dialog asks for the existing password, you would press the ENTER key.

Password recovery for the Supervisor III is significantly different because this hardware provides several components lacking on the Supervisor I and Supervisor II. We will examine three of these components, the ROM Monitor, the Virtual Config Register, and Configurable Flash RAM. The ROM Monitor is a small program that exists on Supervisor III independent of the Catalyst NMP Image that normally controls your switch. On Supervisor III, the ROM Monitor is responsible for loading the NMP Image and handing control of the NMP CPU to it. Certain behaviors of the NMP Image can be modified at load time while the ROM Monitor is in control. We will refer to a location in NVRAM that retains configuration settings for these behaviors as the *configuration register* or *confreg* for short. One of the behaviors that can be modified by a configuration register parameter is executing the NVRAM copy of the configuration file. This parameter, referred to as IGNORE-CONFIG will allow us to defeat password protection on a Catalyst with Supervisor III installed. The default setting for IGNORE-CONFIG is disabled. The double negative (disabling the IGNORE-CONFIG parameter) can be thought of as enabling the reading of config file information.

You can examine the state of your Supervisor III configuration register using this command:

```
Console>(enable) show boot
```

Figure 6-12 indicates that a hexadecimal value of 0x102 corresponds to disabling the IGNORE-CONFIG feature. That is, a Supervisor III with a configuration register setting of 0x102 will cause the config file to be read from NVRAM upon startup.

If our Supervisor III is configured as the one shown in Fig 6-12, it will read the configuration file in NVRAM, including the SET PASSWORD and SET ENABLEPASS commands. As was not the case with the Supervisor I and Supervisor II, these commands take effect immediately, so we can not defeat passwords through speedy typing. Instead we must interrupt the ROM Monitor's program before the Catalyst NMP Image is loaded, and modify the configuration register. Then when the NMP Image does load, it can be instructed to IGNORE-CONFIG and leave us with blank user and enable mode passwords.

The process that follows may seem a bit complicated, but that is actually a good thing. Breaking into a network device worth up to $100,000 should not be a process that any casual user can accomplish. You would like to know that only experienced personnel are gaining access to the most dangerous CLI commands through defeated passwords.

Just as with the Supervisor I and Supervisor II processes, you must have physical access to the Catalyst chassis to accomplish this procedure. First, power-cycle the Catalyst switch. Keep in mind that both power supplies must be turned off if your Catalyst employs dual power supplies. After the Cisco copyright notice appears on your console screen, you have 60 seconds during which you can interrupt the ROM Monitor. When this interval of time elapses, the ROM Monitor loads the Catalyst NMP Image.

FIGURE 6-12

Normal Supervisor III configuration register settings

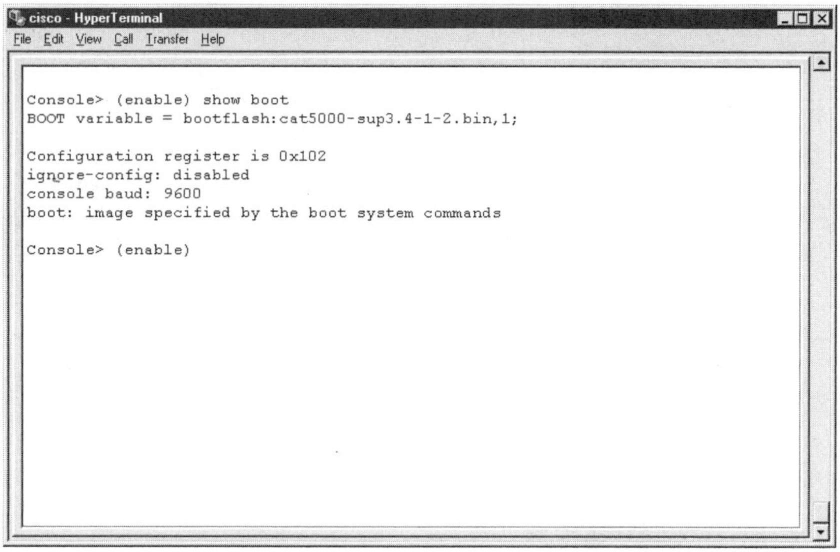

```
 cisco - HyperTerminal                                                    _ □ ×
File  Edit  View  Call  Transfer  Help

 Console> (enable) show boot
 BOOT variable = bootflash:cat5000-sup3.4-1-2.bin,1;

 Configuration register is 0x102
 ignore-config: disabled
 console baud: 9600
 boot: image specified by the boot system commands

 Console> (enable)
```

You will interrupt the ROM Monitor by sending a specific character to the Console port. The interrupt character can be generated on most terminal programs by holding the CTRL key while simultaneously pressing the BREAK key. The ROM Monitor program responds with its own command line:

```
ROMMON >
```

Many options for troubleshooting and diagnosing Catalyst problems exist in ROM Monitor mode. We will use the CONFREG command to alter the value of the configuration register. Our goal is to enable the IGNORE-CONFIG feature. We do this by changing the hexadecimal value of the configuration register from its default of 0x102 to 0x142. This value corresponds to turning on the seventh bit when counting from the right side of the Register. The seventh bit, which goes by the unlikely name of Bit 6, controls the IGNORE-CONFIG feature. Use this syntax at the ROM Monitor command line to enable IGNORE-CONFIG:

```
ROMMON > confreg 0x142
```

Your Catalyst ROM Monitor responds with a message suggesting you power-cycle the switch to make use of the new configuration register setting. The ROM Monitor command set includes an instruction to initialize the Catalyst. This software reboot will not cause your configuration register to be reset to the new CONFREG configured value. Only when power is removed and reapplied will the IGNORE-CONFIG feature be active. If your design requires that password recovery be available from off site, you may wish to investigate an external battery backup unit such as that manufactured by American Power Conversions, which allows to you turn off power to the outlet where your Catalyst is plugged in.

When you next cycle power by whatever means, the Catalyst NMP Image loads the default config file, which has blank passwords for user and enable mode. To complete the process, press ENTER in response to the user mode password prompt, then use the ENABLE command with a similar blank password to access the privileged CLI mode.

Now that we have defeated the passwords again, let's look at the state of the configuration register. Do you recall the command?

```
Console>(enable) show boot
```

In Figure 6-13, notice that the configuration register value is now 0x142 and the IGNORE-CONFIG feature is enabled. This is the result of our earlier ROM Monitor CONFREG command. In normal operation we would like to have the Catalyst NMP Image read and apply the configuration file from NVRAM. So we need to reset the configuration register back to its default state, 0x102. Use this syntax from the NMP Image privileged CLI mode:

```
Console>(enable) set boot config 0x102
```

Once the configuration register is set back to hexadecimal 0x102, the Catalyst NMP Image will read and apply commands (including passwords) in the NMRAM configuration file.

FIGURE 6-13

Password recovery
Supervisor III configuration
register setting

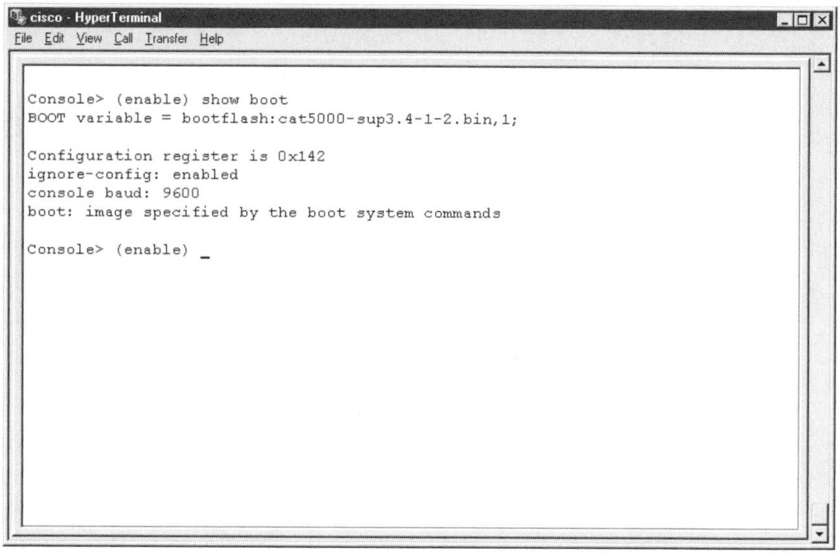

```
Console> (enable) show boot
BOOT variable = bootflash:cat5000-sup3.4-1-2.bin,1;

Configuration register is 0x142
ignore-config: enabled
console baud: 9600
boot: image specified by the boot system commands

Console> (enable) _
```

SET INTERFACE Command

While it may be convenient to use the BOOTP or RARP processes to assign an address for the Catalyst IP stack, you usually should configure an address manually and avoid the extra work of setting up and maintaining an external BOOTP or RARP server. When you manually configure the address you will supply a network or subnet mask and an optional broadcast address. The basic syntax to configure an IP address manually is as follows:

```
Console>(enable) set interface sc0 1 10.1.2.1 255.255.255.0 10.1.2.255
```

In this command, 10.1.2.1 is a valid IP address that we want the Catalyst stack to use; the subnet mask is 255.255.255.0; and we have indicated that we want the IP stack to use a directed broadcast address of 10.1.2.255 whenever it has broadcast traffic to send. Notice that two other parameters are included in the command. The term SC0 refers to one of two possible virtual interfaces for your Catalyst NMP Image IP stack and the numeral 1 refers to the VLAN your IP stack participates in. The sc0 virtual interface should not be confused with the physical console connection on the Supervisor module. We will see in later sections how to use the IP address associated with the sc0 virtual interface for in-band management and troubleshooting tasks.

The sc0 interface can be thought of as an abstraction of an Ethernet NIC used by the OSI model data-link control (DLC) functions in the Catalyst NMP image. IP usually expects to determine which of several possible interfaces should be used to transmit traffic based on a process called *comparison under mask*. Once the comparison determines which interface is best for transmitting a given datagram, that traffic is handed to DLC software, which prepares it for transmission and queues it in a physical buffer associated with an Ethernet NIC. Since the Catalyst has potentially many physical ports that may transmit a given frame of data, some modifications are required.

When the NMP Image IP stack creates traffic, it is actually placed on the Catalyst switching bus, where the EARL causes it to be transmitted out of each physical port that should carry it. The sc0 interface thus provides a software substitute for the single physical NIC interface that the DLC and upper-layer software in the Catalyst NMP Image IP stack expects.

A VLAN can be thought of as a logical broadcast domain. When the Catalyst NMP Image's IP stack participates in any given VLAN, it will only hear broadcasts that originate on other hosts in the same VLAN. For example, if we attach a station directly to our Catalyst and use static VLAN configuration to place that station in VLAN 2, but use the command just described to place the sc0 virtual interface in VLAN 1, the station will not be able to communicate with any of the software services available in the Catalyst NMP Image, because the sc0 interface will not hear ARP broadcasts from the station.

The second virtual interface that the Catalyst NMP Image makes available to us is called sl0. This interface is used when we wish to communicated with the Catalyst NMP Image services using a Serial Line IP (SLIP) connection on the Supervisor console port. This arrangement constitutes the "out-of-band" management capability for the Catalyst switch. By contrast, when we "Telnet" to the IP address configured on the Catalyst's sc0 virtual interface we are exercising its "in-band" management capability. This question often arises: if there are two interfaces with two different addresses, is it possible to route traffic from a SLIP network attached to the Catalyst console port to the Ethernet or other networks connected to the Catalyst line modules. The answer is no. It isn't possible as the Catalyst NMP Image lacks a routing process.

We will configure our Catalyst for out-of-band management in the next section. For now, let us examine more details of the in-band management capabilities. The sc0 virtual interface is enabled in the default configuration, even though it may not have a valid address assigned. If we wish to disable the interface, perhaps to prevent attacks from an entrusted network, we can do so with the following syntax:

```
Console>(enable) set interface sc0 disable
```

If you later wish to make use of the in-band management capabilities use this syntax to turn the interface up:

```
Console>(enable) set interface sc0 enable
```

We have mentioned several in-band management tools available in the Catalyst NMP Image, such as the SNMP agent and the mini-RMON agents. Two more tools bear discussion here, as they both depend on correct configuration of the sc0 interface address. The most important in-band management tool is the Telnet server. The Catalyst NMP Image will support up to eight concurrent Telnet sessions and can act either as a Telnet server receiving connections from workstation on your LAN, or as a client to start Telnet sessions with other networked devices. When a device establishes a Telnet session to the Catalyst NMP Image's IP address, the user mode password prompt is always presented. Once authenticated, the CLI is available to the so-called virtual terminal session.

In Chapter 7 we will examine methods for authenticating users who access the Catalyst through these virtual terminal sessions. For now it will suffice to point out that the Catalyst software gives us a command to filter on the source address of stations that wish to Telnet to our address. In the default state, any station can start a Telnet session with the Catalyst NMP Image Telnet server and access the CLI. Using the following command, we can cause the Catalyst to reject Telnet requests from nonconfigured addresses. Try this statement on your Catalyst:

```
Console>(enable) set ip permit 10.2.3.100
```

Using this statement, we have restricted the stations allowed to Telnet into our CLI to those that represent themselves at IP address 10.2.3.100. This is by no means perfect security—for instance, a host could easily pretend to be 10.2.3.100 in an attack called spoofing. Nevertheless, IP PERMIT will stop casual hackers gaining access to your Catalyst.

The Catalyst NMP Image also provides the network diagnostic used by more administrators than any other for detecting and troubleshooting connectivity problems: the venerable PING program. PING works by sending an Internet Control Message (ICMP) echo request packet through an IP network to a particular IP address. The IP stack that hears the echo request in most cases will send an ICMP echo-response back to the sending station. Use this syntax at the user or enable mode command prompt to send echo requests to 10.1.2.100:

```
Console>(enable) ping 10.1.2.100
```

You can also set up a continuous stream of PINGs using this command:

```
Console>(enable) ping -s 10.1.2.100
```

In Chapter 7, we will see that this syntax is particularly useful for measuring convergence time for the spanning-tree algorithm.

SLIP

SLIP is an OSI Layer 2 protocol that can provide dial-up access to IP networks. The Catalyst NMP Image implements SLIP as a mechanism for out-of-band access to the CLI. With SLIP, you can access the Catalyst CLI from a dial-up Telnet session through the Catalyst console port. When the port is configured for SLIP access, it is no longer available for EIA-232 terminal communication. The two management methods are mutually exclusive. You should, therefore, make an in-band Telnet connection to your Catalyst NMP Image CLI before you configure the console port for SLIP access.

If you issue the **SLIP attach** command to start SLIP processing, your Catalyst NMP Image expects only SLIP encoded data to arrive on the physical console port. Any traffic from your terminal emulation program, Hyperterm for example, will be interpreted as transmission errors by the SLIP configured console port. Since configuration changes like the **SLIP attach** command are automatically copied to the Catalyst's NVRAM config file, it is possible to render the supervisor inoperable with this command. The best way to avoid this situation is to first configure an in-band management capability. In other words, you want to configure the **sc0** interface with a valid IP address and mask so that you can Telnet to the Catalyst. When you are ready to configure and test your SLIP management capability, you should do so from a Telnet session. This way, if your SLIP configuration doesn't work, you can back it out from the Telnet CLI session.

Successful SLIP implementation requires that you provide specific physical connectivity as well as a workstation that also supports SLIP communication. Most UNIX implementations provide SLIP communication as a free option. The Microsoft Dial-Up Networking application sets up the newer Point-to-Point Protocol (PPP) by default, but you can select SLIP. The Catalyst NMP Image does not support PPP for out-of-band management. Your Catalyst console port and the SLIP workstation may be directly connected using a null modem serial cable or using a pair of modems. Keep in mind that the maximum data rate for the Supervisor I and Supervisor II console ports is 9600 bps.

Once you have established an in-band Telnet session with the Catalyst NMP Image and entered enable mode, use the following syntax to configure your sl0 virtual interface to provide an out-of-band connection:

```
Console>(enable) set interface sl0 enable
Console>(enable) set interface sl0 1 10.2.3.4 255.255.255.0 10.2.3.255
```

In these lines, 10.2.3.4 represents the sl0 interface's IP address; 10.2.3.255 is a default gateway on the network formed by the Catalyst sl0 and the workstation.

Use the following command to start SLIP processing on the Supervisor console port:

```
Console>(enable) slip attach
```

The principal benefit of SLIP is providing remote management capability when misconfiguration or network failures make the Catalyst NMP Image CLI unreachable through in-band means. Use caution when configuring this command from an EIA-232 terminal session. If you have not properly configured for in-band connectivity by setting a valid IP address on the sc0 interface and enabling it, you may render your Supervisor unusable. In the next section we will see that since the Supervisor image makes all configuration changes part of the configuration file in NVRAM, you may have no way to undo a SLIP ATTACH command unless you can make an in-band connection to the CLI.

QUESTIONS AND ANSWERS

I can't PING my Catalyst from a PC that is directly connected to it. What should I do?	Approach this problem from the point of view of the OSI layered model. PING is a program that tests connectivity at Layer 3 of the model. To troubleshoot Layer 3 problems, first make sure that the PC and the Catalyst have IP addresses in the same network number. Use the SET INTERFACE SC0 command on the Catalyst NMP Image CLI and the Network Neighborhood | Properties control panel on MS Windows PCs to set the IP address of both devices.

If this doesn't resolve the problem, examine Layer 2 of the model. At the data-link layer we are concerned with the VLAN configuration of the Catalyst. Use the SHOW PORT and SHOW INTERFACE commands to ensure that the port with which your PC connects and the sc0 interface both belong to the same VLAN. If they are configured in separate VLANs, the Catalyst IP stack can't hear your PC sending an ARP request. Use the SET INTERFACE SC0 command and the SET PORT commands to reconfigure VLANs.

If Layer 2 appears to be correctly configured, move on to Layer 1. In order to test connectivity at the physical layer, look at the SHOW PORT command again to see if the port state is Connected and that the port speed and duplex mode match the settings of your PCs NIC. Use the SET PORT commands to modify any of these settings on the Catalyst, but keep in mind that you may have to reset the port after reconfiguration with the SET PORT DISABLE and SET PORT ENABLE commands. |
| I'm worried about security for my Catalyst. What options do I have? | You have the ability to filter Telnet and SNMP access to the Catalyst NMP Image IP stack based on the source IP address. Recall the SET IP PERMIT LIST command. You can also prevent all access to your Catalyst IP stack by disabling the sc0 interface. Use the SET INTERFACE SC0 DISABLE command to prevent all IP access to the Catalyst NMP Image. |
| Help! I disregarded your advice about configuring the SLIP ATTACH command from a Telnet session. Now I can't communicate with the switch. Is there any hope of redemption for me? | If you have messed up Supervisor II or III and you have a Catalyst 5500, you are in luck. The dual-Supervisor feature of the Catalyst 5500 can be used as a recovery method by installing the misconfigured Supervisor as the backup Supervisor. This causes the good IOS and configuration to be copied onto it from the primary Supervisor, effectively recovering the situation. Lacking this recovery option, you may need to replace the bootflash SIMM. |

Saving Configuration Files to and from a TFTP Server

The configuration file stored in NVRAM is critically important to your Catalyst's normal functions. Network outages are almost certain if the config file is accidentally erased on a Catalyst in a production network. In the CLI enable mode, for instance, it is possible to wipe the configuration file with a single command:

```
Console>(enable) clear config all
```

To avoid serious disruption to your network's operation, Cisco provides several methods for backing up config files to other devices on your network. If you use an SNMP Network Management Station like Cisco Works 2000 or Cisco Resource Manager, you can conveniently copy the configuration files of all your Cisco Catalyst switches and IOS routers. Alternatively, you can also use the Trivial File Transfer Protocol (TFTP) to move configurations and other files from your Catalysts to a server in your network.

The TFTP employs an exchange of messages between a client device and a server device to copy files across an IP network or internetwork. The Catalyst NMP Image provides a TFTP client that will copy either configuration files, the NMP Image itself—or on a Supervisor III, any file that can reside in Flash RAM. There are at least two prerequisites for using TFTP to save your Catalyst's configuration file. Since a TFTP client uses IP to communicate with a server, the Catalyst NMP Image IP stack must be configured with a valid IP address. The address may be obtained through the BOOTP or RARP automatic configuration process or manually configured with the SET INTERFACE SC0 command. Also, you will need to have configured a device on your network as a TFTP server.

Providing a TFTP server is not difficult. Most variants of UNIX provide a TFTP daemon (tftpd) that will save files for you. There are numerous free and shareware TFTP servers as well available for 32-bit MS Windows platforms. Cisco customers can obtain a TFTP server through the Cisco Connection Online (CCO) at http://www.cisco.com.

Saving Configuration Files to the TFTP Server

Once the prerequisites have been met, issue this simple command to back up your config file to a TFTP server:

```
Console>(enable) write network
```

This command invokes the dialog shown in Figure 6-14. You may supply the address of the TFTP server or, if name resolution has been configured as shown in Chapter 7, you may supply a domain name for the server. When choosing the name of the configuration file when it is stored on the server, it is wise to choose something descriptive for the Catalyst in

FIGURE 6-14

The WRITE NETWORK dialog

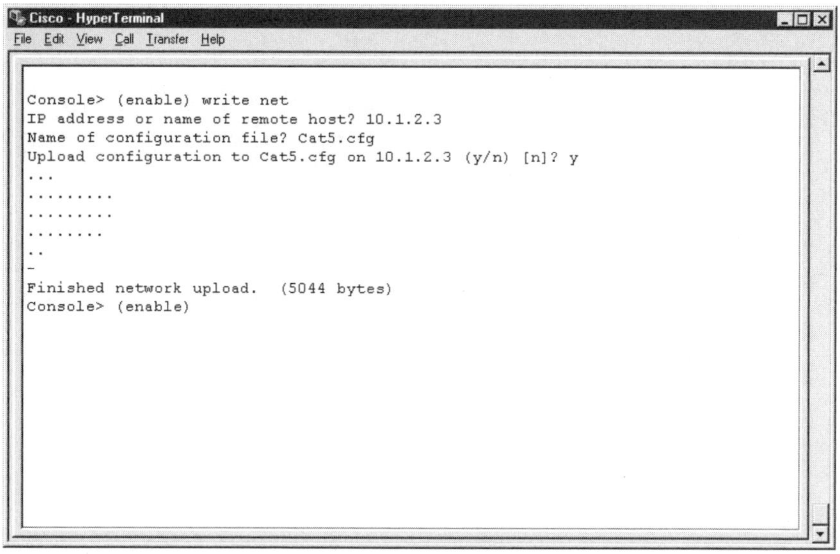

```
Console> (enable) write net
IP address or name of remote host? 10.1.2.3
Name of configuration file? Cat5.cfg
Upload configuration to Cat5.cfg on 10.1.2.3 (y/n) [n]? y
...
.........
.........
........
..
-
Finished network upload.  (5044 bytes)
Console> (enable)
```

question. This avoids a well-known weakness of TFTP: the server doesn't care that it is writing over a good file when you send it one with the same name. Most UNIX TFTP servers require that the file exist prior to its use to save your configuration file. If this is the case for your network, you can use the UNIX TOUCH or CAT commands to create the file first. Microsoft-based TFTP servers don't suffer this restriction.

You can use a syntactic shortcut if you wish. Instead of supplying the server address and file name in a dialog, you may choose to type them all on the same command line:

```
Console>(enable) write 10.1.2.3 Cat5.cfg
```

Figure 6-15 shows an example of the shortcut in action. As was true with the dialog version of the command, you may substitute a host name if name resolution has been configured.

FIGURE 6-15

The WRITE command shortcut

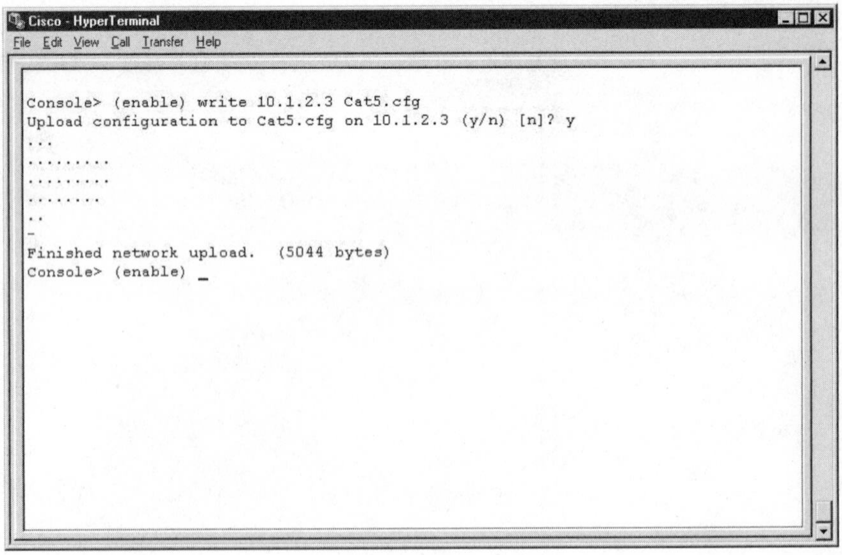

```
Cisco - HyperTerminal                                          _ □ X
File  Edit  View  Call  Transfer  Help

Console> (enable) write 10.1.2.3 Cat5.cfg
Upload configuration to Cat5.cfg on 10.1.2.3 (y/n) [n]? y
...
.........
.........
........
..
-
Finished network upload.  (5044 bytes)
Console> (enable) _
```

*Several Catalyst NMP Image commands like the WRITE NET and
WRITE commands are polymorphic. Cisco expects that you will be
able to recognize all the forms of a given command and select the
proper parameters for each when answering questions on the
certification exam.*

Retrieving a Config File from a TFTP Server

Now that your configuration file is safely deposited on your TFTP server,
you are ready for disaster. Suppose a fire destroys one of your organization's
wiring closets. Your task will be restoring network services as soon as
possible. When a new Catalyst 5000 arrives, you will be able to quickly
duplicate the operation of the original switch.

The new Catalyst will require an IP address, which may be configured
manually with the SET INTERFACE SC0 command or through the
BOOTP or RARP automatic configuration process. If your TFTP server is
not on the local subnet, you will also need to configure the default gateway
with the SET IP ROUTE command. Once these tasks are accomplished,
use the following syntax to retrieve a stored configuration file from the
TFTP server:

```
Console>(enable) config network
```

This command also invokes a dialog with the Catalyst NMP Image. At
the top of the listing that follows you can see the dialog. Below this you
notice that the Catalyst NMP Image applies each command as it arrives
through the TFTP client process. The Image provides a message after each
command to indicate success or failure. You will note several commands in
this file that were not successful. This is because the NMP Image does not
always overwrite a command in the current configuration when a similar
command arrives through TFTP.

```
Console> (enable) config network
IP address or name of remote host? 10.1.2.3
Name of configuration file? Cat5.cfg
Configure using Cat5.cfg from 10.1.2.3 (y/n) [n]? y
```

```
Finished network download.  (5044 bytes)
>> set password $1$0o8Z$HGVG4gzWe4WUbLbPNZV0Q0
Password changed.
>> set enablepass $1$CBqb$w5k2PFuHNUsJfahpAKibh/
Password changed.
>> set prompt Console>
>> set length 23 default
Screen length set to 23.
>> set logout 20
Sessions will be automatically logged out after 20 minutes of idle time.
>> set banner motd
MOTD banner cleared
>> set system baud  9600
System console port baud rate set to 9600.
>> set system modem disable
Modem control lines disabled on console port.
>> set system name
System name cleared.
>> set system location
System location cleared.
>> set system contact
System contact cleared.
>> set snmp community read-only        pass1
SNMP read-only community string set.
>> set snmp community read-write       pass2
SNMP read-write community string set.

>> set snmp community read-write-all pass3
SNMP read-write-all community string set.
>> set snmp rmon enable
SNMP RMON support enabled.
>> set snmp trap enable   module
SNMP module traps enabled.
>> set snmp trap enable   chassis
SNMP chassis alarm traps enabled.
>> set snmp trap enable   bridge
SNMP bridge traps enabled.
>> set snmp trap enable   repeater
SNMP repeater traps enabled.
>> set snmp trap enable   vtp
SNMP vtp traps enabled.
>> set snmp trap enable   auth
```

```
SNMP authentication traps enabled.
>> set snmp trap enable  ippermit
SNMP IP Permit traps enabled.
>> set snmp trap disable vmps
SNMP VMPS traps disabled.
>> set interface sc0 1 10.1.2.1 255.255.255.0 10.1.2.255
Interface sc0 vlan, IP address, netmask and broadcast address set.
>>
>> set interface sl0 0.0.0.0 0.0.0.0
Interface sl0 slip and destination address set.
>> set arp agingtime 1200
ARP aging time set to 1200 seconds.
>> set ip redirect    enable
ICMP redirect messages enabled
>> set ip unreachable    enable
ICMP Unreachable message enabled.

>> set ip fragmentation enable
Bridge IP fragmentation enabled.
>> set ip route 0.0.0.0        10.1.2.254       1
Route exists.
>> set ip alias default        0.0.0.0
IP alias updated.
>> set vmps server retry 3
Client retry count per VMPS set to 3
>> set vmps server reconfirminterval 60
Client to VMPS reconfirmation interval set to 60 min.
>> set vmps tftpserver 0.0.0.0 vmps-config-database.1
IP address of the TFTP server set to 0.0.0.0
VMPS configuration filename set to vmps-config-database.1
>> set vmps state disable
Vlan Membership Policy Server previously disabled.
>>
>> set ip dns disable
DNS is disabled
>> set tacacs attempts 3
Tacacs number of attempts set to 3.
>> set tacacs directedrequest disable
Tacacs direct request has been disabled.
>> set tacacs timeout 5
Tacacs timeout set to 5 seconds.
>> set authentication login tacacs disable
```

```
Tacacs Login authentication set to disable
>> set authentication login local enable
Local Login authentication set to enable.
>> set authentication enable tacacs disable
Tacacs Enable authentication set to disable.
>> set authentication enable local enable

Local Enable authentication set to enable.
>> set bridge ipx snaptoether    8023raw
Bridge snaptoether default IPX translation set.
>> set bridge ipx 8022toether    8023
8022 to ETHER translation set.
>> set bridge ipx 8023rawtofddi snap
8023RAW to FDDI translation set.
>> set vtp mode server
VTP domain  modified
>> set vtp v2 disable
This command will disable the version 2 function in the entire management domain.
Warning: trbrf & trcrf vlans will not work properly in this mode.
VTP domain  modified
>> set vtp pruning disable
This command will disable the pruning function in the entire management domain.
VTP domain  modified
>> set vtp pruneeligible 2-1000
Vlans 2-1000 eligible for pruning on this device.
VTP domain  modified.
>> clear vtp pruneeligible 1001-1005
Vlans 1,1001-1005 will not be pruned on this device.
VTP domain  modified.
>> set spantree uplinkfast disable
uplinkfast already disabled for bridge.
>> set spantree enable     1
Spantree 1 enabled.
>> set spantree fwddelay 15    1
Spantree 1 forward delay set to 15 seconds.
>> set spantree hello     2     1
Spantree 1 hello time set to 2 seconds.
>> set spantree maxage    20    1

Spantree 1 max aging time set to 20 seconds.
>> set spantree priority 32768 1
Spantree 1 bridge priority set to 32768.
>> set spantree enable     1003
Spantree 1003 enabled.
>> set spantree fwddelay 15    1003
```

```
Spantree 1003 forward delay set to 15 seconds.
>> set spantree hello     2     1003
Spantree 1003 hello time set to 2 seconds.
>> set spantree maxage    20    1003
Spantree 1003 max aging time set to 20 seconds.
>> set spantree priority 32768 1003
Spantree 1003 bridge priority set to 32768.
>> set spantree portstate 1003 auto 0
VLAN number must be in the range 1..1005.
>> set spantree portcost 1003 80
Token Ring CRF 1003 path cost set to 80.
>> set spantree enable     1005
Spantree 1005 enabled.
>> set spantree fwddelay 4     1005
Spantree 1005 forward delay set to 4 seconds.
>> set spantree hello     2     1005
Spantree 1005 hello time set to 2 seconds.
>> set spantree maxage    6     1005
Spantree 1005 max aging time set to 6 seconds.
>> set spantree priority 32768 1005
Spantree 1005 bridge priority set to 32768.
>> set spantree multicast-address 1005 ieee
Trbrf 1005 is not currently running ieee spanning tree
>> set cgmp disable
CGMP support for IP multicast disabled.

>> set cgmp leave disable
CGMP leave processing disabled.
>> set logging console enable
System logging messages will be sent to the console.
>> set logging server disable
System logging messages will not be sent to the configured syslog servers.
>> set logging level cdp 2 default
System logging facility <cdp> set to severity 2(critical)
>> set logging level cgmp 2 default
System logging facility <cgmp> set to severity 2(critical)
>> set logging level disl 5 default
System logging facility <disl> set to severity 5(notifications)
>> set logging level dvlan 2 default
System logging facility <dvlan> set to severity 2(critical)
>> set logging level earl 2 default
System logging facility <earl> set to severity 2(critical)
>> set logging level fddi 2 default
System logging facility <fddi> set to severity 2(critical)
```

```
>> set logging level ip 2 default
System logging facility <ip> set to severity 2(critical)
>> set logging level pruning 2 default
System logging facility <pruning> set to severity 2(critical)
>> set logging level snmp 2 default
System logging facility <snmp> set to severity 2(critical)
>> set logging level spantree 2 default
System logging facility <spantree> set to severity 2(critical)
>> set logging level sys 5 default
System logging facility <sys> set to severity 5(notifications)
>> set logging level tac 2 default
System logging facility <tac> set to severity 2(critical)
>> set logging level tcp 2 default

System logging facility <tcp> set to severity 2(critical)
>> set logging level Telnet 2 default
System logging facility <Telnet> set to severity 2(critical)
>> set logging level tftp 2 default
System logging facility <tftp> set to severity 2(critical)
>> set logging level vtp 2 default
System logging facility <vtp> set to severity 2(critical)
>> set logging level vmps 2 default
System logging facility <vmps> set to severity 2(critical)
>> set logging level kernel 2 default
System logging facility <kernel> set to severity 2(critical)
>> set logging level filesys 2 default
System logging facility <filesys> set to severity 2(critical)
>> set logging level drip 2 default
System logging facility <drip> set to severity 2(critical)
>> set ntp broadcastclient disable
NTP Broadcast Client mode disabled
>> set ntp broadcastdelay 3000
NTP Broadcast delay set to 3000 microseconds
>> set ntp client disable
NTP Client mode disabled
>> clear timezone
Timezone name and offset cleared
>> set summertime disable
Summertime is disabled and set to ''
>> set ip permit disable
IP permit list disabled.
>> set tokenring reduction enable
>> set tokenring distrib-crf disable
```

```
>> set module name    1
Module name cleared.

>> set vlan 1     1/1-2
VLAN  Mod/Ports
----  ---------------------
1     1/1-2
      2/1-24
      4/1-2
      >> set port channel 1/1-2 off
Port(s) 1/1-2 channel mode set to off.
>> set port channel 1/1-2 auto
Port(s) 1/1-2 channel mode set to auto.
>> set port enable    1/1-2
Ports 1/1-2 enabled.
>> set port level     1/1-2  normal
Ports 1/1-2 port level set to normal.
>> set port duplex    1/1-2  half
Ports 1/1-2 set to half-duplex.
>> set port trap      1/1-2  enable
Ports 1/1-2 up/down trap enabled.
>> set port name      1/1-2
Ports 1/1-2 name cleared.
>> set port security  1/1-2  disable
Ports 1/1-2 port security disabled
>> set port broadcast 1/1-2  100%
Port 1/1-2 broadcast traffic unlimited.
>> set port membership 1/1-2  static
Ports 1/1-2 vlan assignment set to static.
>> set cdp enable   1/1-2
CDP enabled on ports 1/1-2.
>> set cdp interval 1/1-2 60
CDP message interval set to 60 seconds for ports 1/1-2.
>> set trunk 1/1  auto 1-1005

Port(s) 1/1 allowed vlans modified to 1-1005.
Port(s) 1/1 trunk mode set to auto.
>> set trunk 1/2  auto 1-1005
Port(s) 1/2 allowed vlans modified to 1-1005.
Port(s) 1/2 trunk mode set to auto.
>> set spantree portfast     1/1-2 disable
Spantree ports 1/1-2 fast start disabled.
>> set spantree portcost     1/1-2 19
Spantree ports 1/1-2 path cost set to 19.
```

```
>> set spantree portpri    1/1-2 32
Bridge ports 1/1-2 port priority set to 32.
>> set spantree portvlanpri 1/1  0
Port 1/1 vlans 1-1005 using portpri 32.
>> set spantree portvlanpri 1/2  0
Port 1/2 vlans 1-1005 using portpri 32.
>> set spantree portvlancost 1/1  cost 18
Port 1/1 VLANs 1-1005 have path cost 19.
>> set spantree portvlancost 1/2  cost 18
Port 1/2 VLANs 1-1005 have path cost 19.
>> set module name    2
Module name cleared.
>> set module enable  2
Module 2 enabled.
>> set vlan 1    2/1-24
VLAN  Mod/Ports
---- ---------------------
1    1/1-2
     2/1-24
     4/1-2
     >> set port enable    2/1-24
Ports 2/1-24 enabled.

>> set port level      2/1-24  normal
Ports 2/1-24 port level set to normal.
>> set port duplex     2/1-24  half
Ports 2/1-24 set to half-duplex.
>> set port trap       2/1-24  enable
Ports 2/1-24 up/down trap enabled.
>> set port name       2/1-24
Ports 2/1-24 name cleared.
>> set port security   2/1-24  disable
Ports 2/1-24 port security disabled
>> set port broadcast  2/1-24  0
Ports 2/1-24 broadcast traffic unlimited.
>> set port membership 2/1-24  static
Ports 2/1-24 vlan assignment set to static.
>> set cdp enable    2/1-24
CDP enabled on ports 2/1-24.
>> set cdp interval 2/1-24 60
CDP message interval set to 60 seconds for ports 2/1-24.
>> set spantree portfast    2/1-24 disable
Spantree ports 2/1-24 fast start disabled.
```

```
>> set spantree portcost    2/1-24 100
Spantree ports 2/1-24 path cost set to 100.
>> set spantree portpri     2/1-24 32
Bridge ports 2/1-24 port priority set to 32.
>> set module name     4
Module name cleared.
>> set port level        4/1  normal
Port 4/1-2 level set to normal.
>> set port name         4/1-2
Ports 4/1-2 name cleared.
>> set cdp enable    4/1

CDP enabled on port 4/1-2.
>> set cdp interval 4/1 60
CDP message interval set to 60 seconds for port 4/1-2.
>> set trunk 4/1  on 1-1005
Port(s) 4/1-2 allowed vlans modified to 1-1005.
Port(s) 4/1-2 trunk mode set to on.
>> set spantree portcost    4/1 14
Spantree port 4/1-2 path cost set to 14.
>> set spantree portpri     4/1 32
Bridge port 4/1-2 port priority set to 32.
>> set spantree portvlanpri 4/1   0
Port 4/1 vlans 1-1005 using portpri 32.
>> set spantree portvlancost 4/1  cost 13
Port 4/1 VLANs 1-1005 have path cost 14.
>> set span disable
Disabled monitoring of VLAN 1 transmit/receive traffic by Port 1/1
>> set cam agingtime 1,1003,1005 300
Vlans 1,1003,1005 CAM aging time set to 300 seconds.
```

You can think of TFTP as a means of merging the current operating configuration with one stored on the TFTP server. For this reason, administrators commonly clear their Catalysts' config files (except the IP address!) prior to copying a backup config file from a TFTP server. To selectively clear the configuration from a particular module *n*, use the following command:

```
Console>(enable) clear config n
```

In this command, *n* refers to the slot where the module is installed. Figure 6-16 shows the results of this command.

FIGURE 6-16

Clearing configuration
on a module

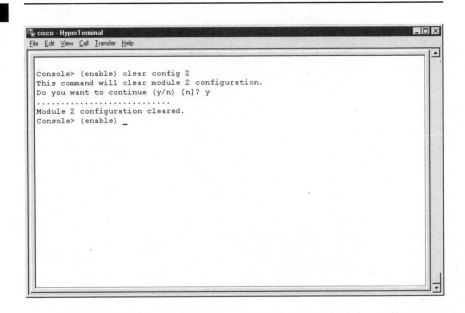

```
cisco - HyperTerminal

File  Edit  View  Call  Transfer  Help


Console> (enable) clear config 2
This command will clear module 2 configuration.
Do you want to continue (y/n) [n]? y
........................
Module 2 configuration cleared.
Console> (enable) _
```

CERTIFICATION OBJECTIVE 6.05

Downloading and Uploading Software Images

The Catalyst NMP Image resides in a Flash memory device on the
Supervisor Module. Supervisor I and Supervisor II Flash memory holds
only a single copy of the NMP Image. Supervisor III differs in that its Flash
is manageable and can hold multiple copies of the NMP Image as well as
a variety of other useful files. This capability is particularly useful when
upgrading to a new version of the NMP Image. With the manageable Flash
on the Supervisor III, you can retain a known good version of software
while testing a newer Image. If you encounter problems with your upgrade,
it is easy to restart the Catalyst with the older software.

You can look at the contents of your Catalyst's Flash memory using this command:

```
Console>(enable) show flash
```

Figure 6-17 displays typical output from this command.

You can get more information on the hardware and firmware components that cooperate with your NMP Image with this syntax:

```
Console>(enable) show version
```

See Figure 6-18 for an example of the SHOW VERSION command.

Just as we used TFTP to save and restore Catalyst configuration files, we can save and recall the Catalyst NMP Image itself. Software upload and download procedures differ depending on which Supervisor version and software version you are using in your Catalyst. Despite the differences in these details, using TFTP to move software requires that you properly configure the sc0 interface and IP address as well as provision a TFTP server.

FIGURE 6-17

Catalyst NMP Image
SHOW FLASH command

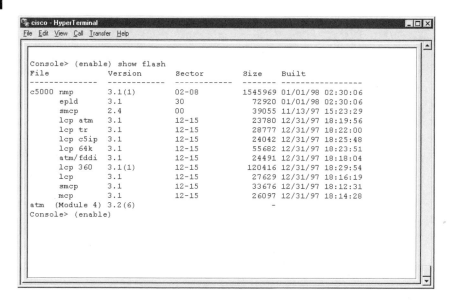

FIGURE 6-18

Catalyst NMP Image
SHOW VERSION
command

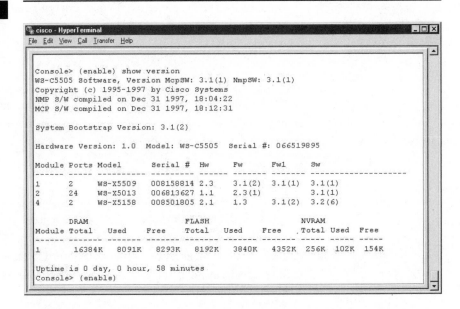

```
Console> (enable) show version
WS-C5505 Software, Version McpSW: 3.1(1) NmpSW: 3.1(1)
Copyright (c) 1995-1997 by Cisco Systems
NMP S/W compiled on Dec 31 1997, 18:04:22
MCP S/W compiled on Dec 31 1997, 18:12:31

System Bootstrap Version: 3.1(2)

Hardware Version: 1.0  Model: WS-C5505  Serial #: 066519895

Module Ports Model       Serial #    Hw     Fw      Fw1     Sw
------ ----- ----------  ----------  ------ ------- ------- --------------------
1      2     WS-X5509    008158814   2.3    3.1(2)  3.1(1)  3.1(1)
2      24    WS-X5013    006813627   1.1    2.3(1)          3.1(1)
4      2     WS-X5158    008501805   2.1    1.3    3.1(2)  3.2(6)

       DRAM                      FLASH                    NVRAM
Module Total   Used    Free     Total   Used    Free    Total Used  Free
------ ------- ------- -------   ------- ------- ------- ----- ----- -----
1      16384K  8091K   8293K     8192K   3840K   4352K   256K  102K  154K

Uptime is 0 day, 0 hour, 58 minutes
Console> (enable)
```

Copying NMP Images to Supervisor I or Supervisor II

If your Catalyst uses either Supervisor I or Supervisor II modules with
NMP Image 2.x or 3.x, use this command to copy a new image to your
Catalyst:

```
Console>(enable) download 10.2.3.4 C5000_312a.bin
```

Figure 6-19 illustrates the process. Note the message indicating that the
image is being stored in Flash memory. The Supervisor I and Supervisor II
modules lack a manageable Flash device. Therefore, only one copy of the
NMP Image can exist in Flash at a time. When we invoke the TFTP client to
copy software to the Catalyst with the DOWNLOAD command, the Image
is copied from the server, its checksum is verified, and then it replaces the
existing image in Flash memory on a sector-by-sector basis. The Supervisor I

FIGURE 6-19

Downloading software to
the Supervisor I or
Supervisor II

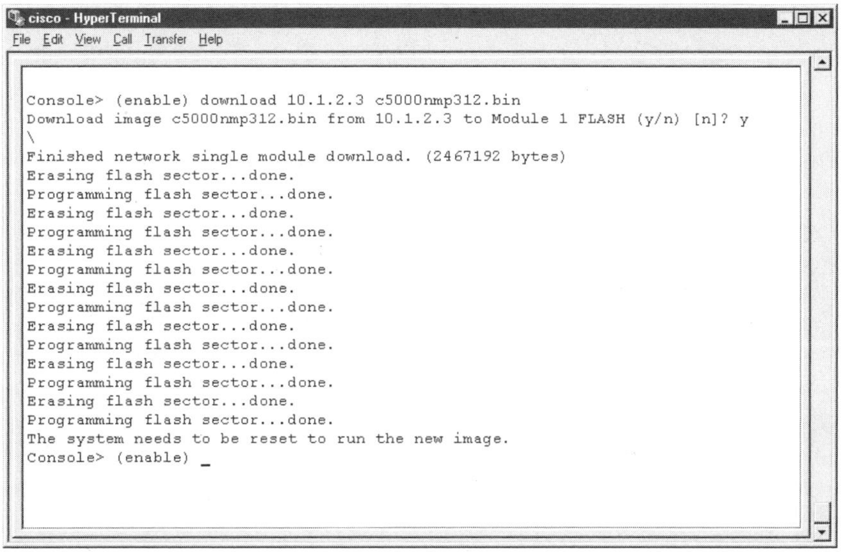

```
cisco - HyperTerminal                                                    _ □ X
File  Edit  View  Call  Transfer  Help

Console> (enable) download 10.1.2.3 c5000nmp312.bin
Download image c5000nmp312.bin from 10.1.2.3 to Module 1 FLASH (y/n) [n]? y
\
Finished network single module download. (2467192 bytes)
Erasing flash sector...done.
Programming flash sector...done.
Erasing flash sector...done.
Programming flash sector...done.
Erasing flash sector...done.
Programming flash sector...done.
Erasing flash sector...done.
Programming flash sector...done.
Erasing flash sector...done.
Programming flash sector...done.
Erasing flash sector...done.
Programming flash sector...done.
Erasing flash sector...done.
Programming flash sector...done.
The system needs to be reset to run the new image.
Console> (enable) _
```

or Supervisor II can be rendered inoperable if the sector copy process is
interrupted for any reason! Should this happen, either you or Cisco's
maintenance engineers will have to replace the Flash memory device. It is
also possible to debilitate the Supervisor I or Supervisor II engine during the
download process by moving to a newer image incorrectly. It is imperative
that you study the Catalyst NMP Image release notes for any new version you
wish to deploy. Some versions of software require that you downgrade to an
older version before upgrading to a newer one.

To copy your NMP Image from the Supervisor I or Supervisor II engine
to a TFTP server, use this syntax:

```
Console>(enable) upload 10.1.2.3 C5000_312a.bin
```

Recall from our discussion of the DOWNLOAD command that the
address may be replaced by a domain name in certain circumstances.

The 2.*x* and 3.*x* releases of the NMP Image software support an alias for the DOWNLOAD and UPLOAD commands that should seem familiar if you have experience using and configuring Cisco's IOS-based router products. The COPY command takes two command line parameters. The first is the source of an NMP Image; the second is the destination where the NMP Image should be copied. In the command:

```
Console>(enable) copy flash tftp
```

the source of a NMP Images is the Catalyst's Flash memory device. The destination for this command is a TFTP server. The COPY command starts a dialog with the NMP Software that has the same effect as the upload command. Take a look at Figure 6-20 for an example of the alternate syntax.

In the NMP version 4.*x* Image on any Supervisor model, the COPY command entirely replaces the UPLOAD and DOWNLOAD command structure.

FIGURE 6-20

The COPY command

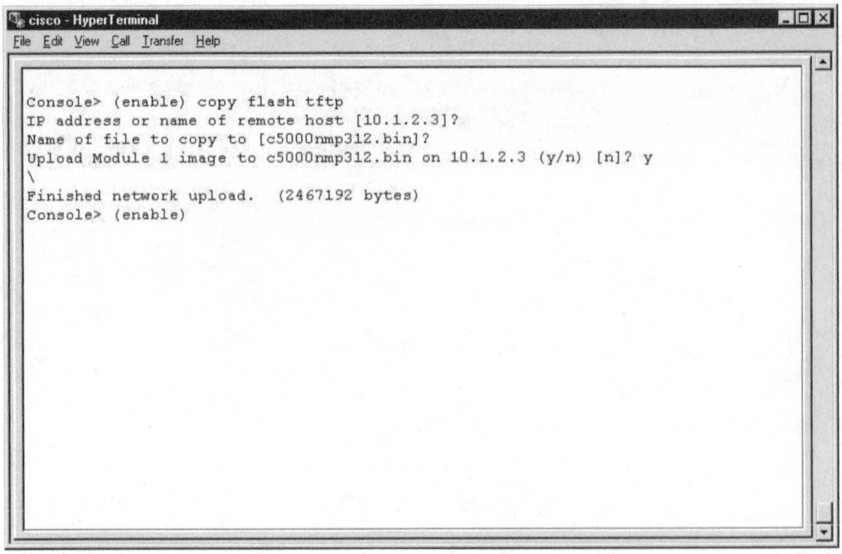

```
cisco - HyperTerminal                                          _ □ X
File  Edit  View  Call  Transfer  Help

Console> (enable) copy flash tftp
IP address or name of remote host [10.1.2.3]?
Name of file to copy to [c5000nmp312.bin]?
Upload Module 1 image to c5000nmp312.bin on 10.1.2.3 (y/n) [n]? y
\
Finished network upload.   (2467192 bytes)
Console> (enable)
```

Configuring Token Ring, Ethernet, and Fast Ethernet Modules

So far, we have configured administrative commands that help us prepare the Catalyst switch to work in our network. Now we turn our attention to configuration tasks that cause the switch to carry traffic and earn its keep. The commands introduced in the rest of this chapter configure the Catalyst to carry user traffic rapidly through your networks. That is, after all, the reason you purchased it in the first place.

Recall from Figure 6-1 that the Catalyst implements a default configuration file right out of the box. This default configuration enables all the Ethernet, Fast Ethernet, and Token Ring ports including the "uplink" ports on the Supervisor module. All of the ports are defined as Normal priority level for purposes of the Catalyst's bus arbitration process. On modules that support multiple port speeds such as the 24-Port 10/100 Ethernet Switching Module, the ports are set by default to auto-detect the speed and transmission mode of the attached stations. In contrast, on ports that are set to a fixed speed, the mode defaults to half-duplex transmission.

Port Configurations

Your network design determines which of these default settings need to be changed. One design issue of note is the location of the "resource" nodes in your networks. One characteristic of a resource node is that it offers a high-bandwidth traffic stream to the Catalyst switch. The port that receives this data is a good candidate for the High arbitration priority level. The command to change a port's arbitration level from the default of Normal to High state looks like this:

```
Console>(enable) set port level 1/1 high
```

1/1 represents the first port on the Supervisor module in slot 1.

Design issues also influence our decisions on the speed settings for many ports on the switch. When a host supports both 100 Mbps Fast Ethernet and 10 Mbps Ethernet, and is attached to the switch by a dedicated point-to-point link, it makes sense for that link to run at 100 Mbps. The Catalyst switch and most Fast Ethernet NICs implement auto-detection of link speed. Unfortunately, at least two significantly different mechanisms exist for link speed detection. It is not uncommon on links where both sides of the connection implement auto-detection for the speed setting to toggle from 10 Mbps to 100 Mbps and back to 10 Mpbs as the two NIC's fail to negotiate the speed correctly. Accordingly, it is often more reliable to have one end of the link specify a speed through manual configuration and allow the other side to auto-detect it. To avoid sub-optimal network performance it is often desirable to have the Catalyst set to the highest speed on multiple-speed ports rather than the default setting of auto-detect. Use this command to make it so:

```
Console>(enable) set port speed 1/2 100
```

1/2 denotes the second port on the Supervisor module in slot 1. If you wish to manually configure a port to run at 10 Mbps for the sake of an older NIC or a shared Ethernet configuration, use the following syntax:

```
Console>(enable) set port speed 3/1 10
```

3/1 represents the first port on the module in slot 3. If you would like the Catalyst to auto-detect link speed, use the key word AUTO, as in:

```
Console>(enable) set port speed 2/12 auto
```

If your design includes dedicated point-to-point links between the Catalyst and some host, you will experience a marked increase in throughput by disabling the Ethernet Media Access Control (MAC) algorithm. This procedure, which goes by the ungainly name of Carrier Sense Multiple Access with Collision Detection (CSMA/CD), requires that an Ethernet station listen to its Receive circuit for a period called the Guard Time prior to sending traffic. This reduces the likelihood that a station will interrupt the transmission of another station. If the channel is in use, the station with traffic ready to go is required to defer its transmission until a Guard Time worth of silence has been heard on the Receive circuit. This behavior unnecessarily eats a significant amount of bandwidth on a point-to-point link.

When we disable the CSMA/CD MAC algorithm, we enable full-duplex transmission. Two full-duplex connected stations (like the Catalyst Ethernet port and a directly connected PC) are allowed to send and receive at the same time. On a Fast Ethernet link operating in full-duplex transmission mode, we can see an aggregate data rate up to 200 Mbps. This is the sum of two 100 Mbps traffic streams crossing the channel at the same time.

To change your Catalyst's ports from the default half duplex to full-duplex operation, use this command:

```
Console>(enable) set port mode 4/1 full
```

If you would like the Catalyst to determine the transmission capabilities of its directly connected neighbor when the link is initialized, use this form:

```
Console>(enable) set port mode 4/1 auto
```

Since the change of duplex state to auto can only occur at link initialization time, this is one of the few commands that will not take effect until the port is reset. To accomplish a port reset, use these commands in sequence:

```
Console>(enable) set port disable 1/1
Console>(enable) set port enable 1/1
```

FROM THE CLASSROOM

Connecting to the Outside World

The SC0 interface of the Catalyst 5000 series switch provides the IP path to and from the outside world. Without an IP address on the SC0 interface, it is impossible to Telnet from the switch to any other IP destination. It is also impossible to ping or Telnet to the switch from some IP device in the network, or use any SNMP applications.

Many students think that since the IP address is applied to the SCO interface, then only the "console port" has this IP address, and that each port of the switch would need its own IP address to be unique. This is not the case. One cannot pretend that the switch acts like a router. The IP address of the SC0 interface represents the IP identity of the entire Catalyst switch. This IP address can be reached through any port *except* the console port. Remember that the console port is attached to an out-of-band device, which does not speak IP. When you enable or disable the SC0 interface, this simply enables or disables the IP stack of that interface. It does not affect the operation of the directly attached console device.

The VLAN assignment of the SC0 is another source of pain for the network administrator. Many times, students cannot determine why their Ethernet-attached PC cannot talk to their own switch. It gets worse when other devices clear across the network can reach the switch, and their PC still has no luck.

The VLAN is the answer here. A VLAN represents a broadcast domain. In router terms, the broadcast domain is an IP subnet. If the SC0 interface is in one broadcast domain, and the PC is in a separate one, then a router is needed to have connectivity. In other words, if device A is on subnet 1, and device B is on subnet 2, then without a router, there is no connectivity. VLANs offer impenetrable defenses, since each switch knows that it cannot send packets across VLAN boundaries. After all, that is what routers have done for many years. Why change now?

—Neil Lovering, CCIE, CCSI

CERTIFICATION SUMMARY

As is the case with each chapter of this guide, the author's purpose is to provide coverage of key concepts that will allow you quickly to become productive in a Cisco Catalyst network. The CCNP certification demonstrates this proficiency in a tangible way.

In this chapter you learned how to access the CLI through a serial EIA-232 connection to the Supervisor console port and through a SLIP-attached workstation. We accessed the privileged CLI mode using the ENABLE command and examined the three classes of commands used in this mode: SET commands, SHOW commands, and CLEAR commands. You prepared your Catalyst to participate in a SNMP environment by configuring the System MIB variables and enabling SNMP processing.

You recall that SNMP requires a correctly configured IP address for the sc0 virtual interface. We used the SET INTERFACE command to configure this address manually. Likewise, we discussed the conditions under which out-of-band management might prove useful. Following that discussion, you configured the sl0 virtual interface and started SLIP processing on the physical console port.

You next experimented with the Catalyst NMP Image's TFTP client and used it to copy configuration files and NMP Images around your network. Finally, we configured the Catalyst Ethernet, Fast Ethernet, and Token Ring ports to operate at various speeds, and in various transmission modes.

With these tools you will be well prepared for challenging implementations and troubleshooting scenarios in real Catalyst networks. Remembering these items during either the Foundation Routing and Switching (FRS) or Cisco LAN Switching Configuration (CLSC) exams will amply demonstrate your competence.

✓ TWO-MINUTE DRILL

❑ SET and CLEAR commands generally modify the behavior of the Catalyst NMP image by changing its configuration.

❑ The SHOW commands, on the other hand, do not change the configuration of the switch. They provide a powerful tool kit for monitoring the operation of the Catalyst and all the networks attached to it.

❑ You can access CLI through the EIA/TIA-232 Console port on the Catalyst Supervisor Module, through a Telnet virtual terminal session, or through a dial-up connection using the SLIP protocol.

❑ The configuration commands live in a data structure called the configuration file.

❑   The NVRAM configuration file, often just called the config file, provides the set of instructions that the NMP image executes when the switch is reset or powered up.

❑   Remember, in a Catalyst 5000, the running config is always the same as the saved config file with the exception of commands that require hardware reset to become active.

❑   To assist you in remembering the meaning and use of its commands, the CLI provides a Help facility.

❑   Typing a **?** on a blank command line results in a display of almost all the commands available to you.

❑   Administrative configuration commands render the Catalyst itself secure and manageable in a network or internetwork.

❑   The Catalyst NMP Image implements a simple IP stack to facilitate using the management tools.

❑   The Catalyst NMP Image IP stack requires a valid IP address and mask. To communicate outside its subnet, you must configure an IP route which identifies the default gateway.

❑   To configure a BOOTP server, you use the first MAC address listed for the active Supervisor by the SHOW MODULE command. This MAC address will be assigned the IP address you configure in the BOOTP server.

❑   While it may be convenient to use the BOOTP or RARP processes to assign an address for the Catalyst IP stack, you usually should configure an address manually and avoid the extra work of setting up and maintaining an external BOOTP or RARP server.

❑   SNMP provides a mechanism whereby a Network Management Station like Cisco Works 2000 can gather certain information stored in the Catalyst.

❑   The port ASICs SAINT, SAGE, and BODEGA are responsible for counting bytes of traffic received and forwarded through the port.

❑   RMON, described in RFC 1757, allows software on a management station such as Cisco's Switch Probe to gather these and many other statistics from the Catalyst switch and present them in a much more readable format.

❑   The Catalyst CLI provides two levels of password protection.

❑ To alleviate the obvious "Catch-22," the Catalyst provides several methods by which a lost password can be recovered or defeated.

❑ The Catalyst NMP Image also provides the network diagnostic used by more administrators than any other for detecting and troubleshooting connectivity problems: the venerable PING program.

❑ The Catalyst NMP Image implements SLIP as a mechanism for out-of-band access to the CLI.

❑ If you use an SNMP Network Management Station like Cisco Works 2000 or Cisco Resource Manager, you can conveniently copy the configuration files of all your Cisco Catalyst switches and IOS routers.

❑ You can also use the Trivial File Transfer Protocol (TFTP) to move configurations and other files from your Catalysts to a server in your network.

❑ Several Catalyst NMP Image commands like the WRITE NET and WRITE commands are polymorphic. Cisco expects that you will be able to recognize all the forms of a given command and select the proper parameters for each when answering questions on the certification exam.

❑ Supervisor I and Supervisor II Flash memory holds only a single copy of the NMP Image.

❑ Supervisor III differs in that its Flash memory is manageable and can hold multiple copies of the NMP Image as well as a variety of other useful files.

❑ On modules that support multiple port speeds such as the 24-Port 10/100 Ethernet Switching Module, the ports are set by default to auto-detect the speed used by stations on the attached network.

❑ One characteristic of a resource node is that it offers a high-bandwidth traffic stream to the Catalyst switch. The port that receives this data is a good candidate for the High arbitration priority level.

SELF TEST

The following Self Test questions will help you measure your understanding of the material presented in this chapter. Read all the choices carefully, as there may be more than one correct answer. Choose all correct answers for each question.

1. Which is not a way to obtain an address for the sc0 interface?

   A. BOOTP

   B. RARP

   C. DHCP

   D. SET INTERFACE command

2. How many IP addresses may be configured on the Catalyst Supervisor?

   A. One

   B. Two

   C. Three

   D. Four

3. Which best describes the purpose of CLI SET commands?

   A. Configures Ethernet port operations

   B. Configures Catalyst administrative parameters

   C. Displays Catalyst operational parameters

   D. Modifies Catalyst configuration parameters

4. Which best describes the purpose of CLI SHOW commands?

   A. Configures Ethernet port operations

   B. Configures Catalyst administrative parameters

   C. Displays Catalyst operational parameters

   D. Modifies Catalyst configuration parameters

5. Which is not a command used to configure the Catalyst for out-of-band management?

   A. SET INTERFACE SL0 ENABLE

   B. SET INTERFACE SL0 1 10.2.3.4 255.255.255.0 10.2.3.255

   C. SET SLIP ATTACH

   D. SLIP ATTACH

6. Which of the following is required for in-band management?

   A. SET INT SC0 UP

   B. SET INT SC0 ENABLE

   C. SET INT SL0 ENABLE

   D. SET INT SC0 1 10.2.3.4 255.255.255.0 10.2.3.255

7. Which command would be rejected by the Catalyst NMP Image version 4.*x*?

   A. SET INTERFACE SC0 1 192.168.10.10 255.255.255.0

   B. SET INTERFACE SL0 1 192.168.10.10 255.255.255.0

   C. SET INTERFACE SL0 1 191.168.10.10 255.255.0.0

   D. SET INT SC0 1 192.168.10.10 255.255.255.0

8. Which command would be rejected by the Catalyst NMP Image version 4.*x*?

   A. WRITE NETWORK

   B. CONFIG NETWORK

   C. COPY FLASH TFTP

   D. UPLOAD HOST

9. Which command would back up the Catalyst config file?

   A. WRITE CONFIG

   B. WRITE TERM

   C. CONFIG NET

   D. WRITE TFTP

10. Which command would be used to upgrade the Catalyst NMP Image?

   A. UPLOAD TFTP

   B. UPLOAD NET

   C. COPY TFTP FLASH

   D. COPY FLASH TFTP

11. What is the command to enter privileged CLI mode?

   A. PRIVILEGE

   B. LOGIN

   C. ENABLE

   D. LOGON

12. Which command forces a Catalyst Fast Ethernet port into full-duplex transmission mode?

   A. SET PORT DUPLEX 1/1 FULL

   B. SET PORT DUPLEX FULL 1/1

   C. SET PORT MODE 1/1 FULL

   D. SET PORT MODE FULL 1/1

13. What is the default transmission mode for a Catalyst 10/100 Ethernet port?

   A. 10 Mbps

   B. 100 Mbps

   C. Auto

   D. Half

14. What is the default transmission speed for a Catalyst Ethernet port that can be configured for either 10 Mbps or 100 Mbps operation?

   A. 10 Mbps

   B. 100 Mbps

   C. Auto

   D. Half

15. Which of the following acts as a password inside SNMP messages?

   A. Password string

   B. Community string

   C. Security ID

   D. Public key

16. Which of the following is the default community string for SNMP read-write-all mode?

   A. Password

   B. Secret

   C. Private

   D. Public

17. Which condition causes the NMP Image to issue BOOTP requests?

    A. SET BOOTP command

    B. CLEAR IP ADDRESS command

    C. Address of 0.0.0.0

    D. Mask of 255.255.255.255

18. What is the default value of the Supervisor III configuration register?

    A. IGNORE-CONFIG enabled

    B. Load NVRAM

    C. 0x102

    D. 0x142

19. Which of the following management tools does not depend on the IP stack?

    A. SLIP

    B. CLI

    C. TFTP

    D. SNMP

20. What value of the Supervisor III configuration register is useful for password recovery?

    A. IGNORE-CONFIG disabled

    B. Load NVRAM

    C. 0x102

    D. 0x142

CISCO CERTIFIED NETWORK PROFESSIONAL

7

Catalyst 5000 Series Switch Software

CERTIFICATION OBJECTIVES

The Catalyst NMP Image controls the operation of the Catalyst 5000 family of switches. The NMP Image also provides several ways to modify the operation of the switch through configuration changes. In Chapter 6, we used the command line interface (CLI) to prepare the Catalyst for operation in our networks. In this chapter, we will configure a set of Catalysts to implement a highly redundant network with multiple virtual LANs.

NMP Image Features

Your life as a CCNP will be calmer if you work with properly designed networks. A well-designed network, in this sense, is one that is reliable, scalable, and maintainable. When deploying Catalyst switches into such a network, care must be taken to ensure that the power and flexibility of the Catalyst NMP Image software does not detract from these characteristics.

The NMP Image has evolved rapidly to include an increasingly complex set of functions. Each major revision of the NMP Image provides extra features to use in your networks. One step in a structured design methodology is the selection of the appropriate set of features to be implemented in a given network. Not all features are warranted for every network. In certain network topologies, for instance, some services may cause an unacceptable increase in overhead traffic. In others, certain capabilities of the Catalyst NMP Image may cause instability or unacceptable recovery times when a link or piece of equipment fails. In order to build a reliable, scalable, maintainable network that provides the functionality you desire at a cost you can afford, it is essential that you understand the capabilities of various Catalyst NMP Image releases.

Features of Release 2.x

Release 2.1 of the Catalyst NMP Image marked the first release to support the Catalyst 5000 family of Ethernet switches from Cisco. The 5000 family owes much of its architectural heritage to the Catalyst 3000 series of switches, as you will see in the final chapters of this guide. The software for the Catalyst 5000 family, though, is radically different and provides significant additional functionality. Most significant was the CLI user interface. Other features of the Catalyst NMP Image release 2.*x* are described in this section.

TACACS+

Cisco has supported three different versions of Terminal Access Controller Access Control System (TACACS) security protocol on various products. One characteristic that is shared among all three flavors is the capability to authenticate command line access to communications equipment in a TCP/IP network. The Catalyst NMP Image is able to use the TACACS+ version of the protocol to authenticate your access to the NMP Image CLI.

Using TACACS+ requires that you configure a UNIX or MS Windows NT server to be a TACACS+ server. The server runs a process (CiscoAssure) that listens for network access server (NAS) messages from your Catalyst on TCP port 49. When the server receives a TCP connection from your Catalyst, it sends a username prompt that is displayed on your console terminal, Telnet, or SLIP session. When you respond, the username is returned to the TACACS+ server, which returns a password prompt to you. When you enter a password, TACACS+ responds with one of four messages to your Catalyst.

exam
ⓦatch

Since TACACS+ is carried in a TCP session, your Catalyst must have a valid IP address. You may manually configure an IP address using the CLI. You can automatically configure an address with a BOOTP or RARP server.

If the Catalyst NMP Image receives an *accept* message, you are authenticated and you will see the user mode prompt. If the TACACS+ server sends an error message, the Catalyst will attempt to authenticate you with the locally configured PASSWORD and ENABLEPASS. If the Catalyst NMP Image receives a reject message from the server, authentication has failed and you must reconnect to the CLI to try again.

You can use TACACS+ to authenticate both the user mode and the enable mode passwords. You may also choose to use encrypted NAS packets for the TACACS+ message exchange. To configure your Catalyst for TACACS+ authentication, choose from the following commands:

```
Console> (enable) set authentication login tacacs enable
Console> (enable) set authentication enable tacacs enable
Console> (enable) set tacacs server 10.1.2.50 primary
Console> (enable) set tacacs server 10.1.2.51
Console> (enable) set tacacs server 10.1.2.52
```

In this sequence of commands, you have enabled user mode TACACS authentication in the first line, and enable mode authentication in the second. The next three lines configure addresses for three TACACS+ servers. If TCP session setup to the primary server fails, the Catalyst NMP Image will attempt to contact the next two in sequence. If you neglect the PRIMARY keyword on one of the servers, your Catalyst attempts to set up sessions to the servers in the order that they appear in the config file.

NTP

When the NMP Image creates messages for logging purposes, it reports the time in Y2K-compliant fashion. You can set the clock used to timestamp these messages manually or you can specify that the Catalyst act as an Network Time Protocol (NTP) client. NTP provides a mechanism for automatic time synchronization between the Catalyst NMP Image and hosts called *time servers* on your network or on the Internet.

NTP uses UDP port 123 to send time synchronization messages across an IP network. Server mode NTP devices identify the trustworthiness of their time information. This degree of authority is called the *stratum* level of the time server. A stratum 1 device is directly connected to an Atomic Clock-based or radio-based time source. Other time servers use the stratum level to identify how far removed (by how many time sources) from a stratum 1 source they are. Thus, a time source that synchronizes itself to a stratum 1 time source would identify itself as stratum 2. The stratum levels allow an NTP client mode device to synchronize to the best time source, if multiple sources disagree on the correct time.

The Catalyst NTP client program can operate in two modes. As a broadcast client, NTP can update the local clock, based on NTP messages sent by any broadcast time server. Alternatively, when you use one or more specific time servers, your client can be restricted to receiving messages from a time server at that address. While the NMP Image does not function as an NTP time server, you can configure Cisco's router IOS to act as an NTP time server. In the NMP Image 2.*x* releases, the NTP program will only act as an NTP client. Later releases add the functionality of the NTP broadcast client configuration.

Figure 7-1 demonstrates the NTP commands and sets up NTP in client (rather than broadcast client) mode.

DNS

The NMP Image 2.2 release introduced a program that affords you the ability to use names for the catalysts and other hosts in your network rather than identifying them by their IP addresses. Your Catalyst can take advantage of the Domain Name System (DNS) to resolve host names into IP addresses for you.

FIGURE 7-1

Configuring the Catalyst NMP Image for NTP time synchronization

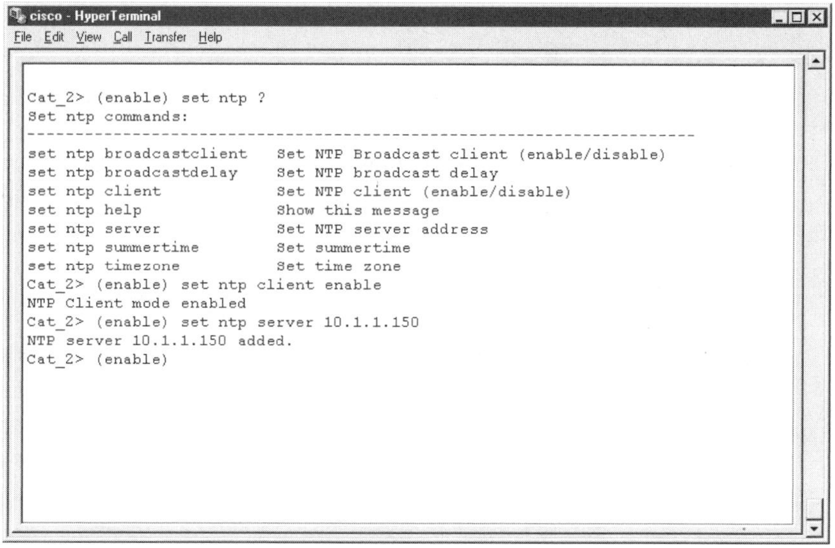

```
cisco - HyperTerminal
File  Edit  View  Call  Transfer  Help

Cat_2> (enable) set ntp ?
Set ntp commands:
-------------------------------------------------------------------
set ntp broadcastclient    Set NTP Broadcast client (enable/disable)
set ntp broadcastdelay     Set NTP broadcast delay
set ntp client             Set NTP client (enable/disable)
set ntp help               Show this message
set ntp server             Set NTP server address
set ntp summertime         Set summertime
set ntp timezone           Set time zone
Cat_2> (enable) set ntp client enable
NTP Client mode enabled
Cat_2> (enable) set ntp server 10.1.1.150
NTP server 10.1.1.150 added.
Cat_2> (enable)
```

DNS is implemented as a distributed database of hostname-to-IP address mappings. The database is stored on devices called name servers that exist throughout the Internet and very likely in your organization's networks as well. A DNS client program interprets your use of a host name such as www.syngress.com as a request for name resolution, and creates a name request. The request is sent to a name server. Generally, the location of your closest name server is either configured on your workstation or obtained through the process that allows you to access your organization's network.

A name server is usually configured with specific information for a certain domain or host names. In the preceding example, "syngress.com" is the domain. The "www" represents one host in the "syngress.com" domain. The name server locally configured with specific host names for a certain domain is called the *primary* name server for that domain. All primary name servers that supply DNS services in the Internet are registered with the InterNIC network information center, and their addresses are loaded into the so-called *root* name servers' databases.

If your local name server doesn't know the IP address for www.syngress.com, it sends a message to a root server requesting the address of the primary name server for the zone "syngress.com." Once your local name server has this information, the name request you originally created is forwarded to the primary server. When it responds with an address for the host www.syngress.com, the local name server caches the information and forwards it to your workstation.

The NMP Image can act as a DNS client. When you type a command at the CLI (the SET NTP SERVER command, for instance) and use a host name, the DNS client is invoked to resolve the name to an address.

Configuring your Catalyst NMP Image for DNS requires that you enable the DNS client and supply the address for a DNS server. You may optionally configure your DNS client with a default domain name. This optional step will relieve you from specifying the entire DNS name, called the *Fully Qualified Domain Name*, when you specify hosts in your own domain. Figure 7-2 illustrates the steps for setting up the DNS client on your Catalyst.

Configuring the Catalyst
NMP Image for DNS
name resolution

```
cisco - HyperTerminal                                          _ □ ×
File  Edit  View  Call  Transfer  Help

Cat_2> (enable) set ip dns ?
Set ip dns commands:
-------------------------------------------------------------
set ip dns enable        Set DNS enable/disable
set ip dns disable       Set DNS enable/disable
set ip dns domain        Set default DNS domain name
set ip dns help          Show this message
set ip dns server        Set DNS server address
Cat_2> (enable) set ip dns enable
DNS is enabled
Cat_2> (enable) set ip dns domain syngress.com
Default DNS domain name set to syngress.com
Cat_2> (enable) set ip dns server 10.1.1.100
10.1.1.100 added to DNS server table as primary server.
Cat_2> (enable) show ip dns
DNS is currently enabled.
The default DNS domain name is: syngress.com

DNS name server                          status
-------------------------------------    -------
10.1.1.100                               primary
Cat_2> (enable)
Cat_2> (enable) _
```

Port Security

The Catalyst NMP Image provides a number of mechanisms to increase the security of your switched internetwork. One such mechanism, provided by NMP Image release 2.2 and later, is called *Port Security*. Port Security allows you to ensure that unauthorized users of your network are not allowed access to it through your Catalysts.

To use Port Security, you create a list of MAC addresses that are allowed to participate in your network. The Catalyst NMP Image can learn the list of addresses by examining the CAM table, or you can configure the list manually. When your Catalyst NMP Image detects traffic generated on a host other than one in the allowed list, it disables the port that heard the offending traffic. You can optionally configure the NMP Image to also generate an SNMP trap to warn an NMS of the attempted attack.

Configuring the NMP Image for Port Security is simple. If you want to specify the actual MAC addresses that exist in your network, you enter them on the CLI. You may choose to allow the MAC addresses that your

Catalyst has registered in its CAM table when Port Security is enabled, but disallow any MAC address that is presented in the future. Use the syntax presented in Figure 7-3 to make it so.

In Figure 7-4 we test Port Security by sending ICMP traffic to the Catalyst from an unauthorized MAC address. Note that the "Shutdown" column in the SHOW PORT SECURITY output lists a state "yes" after the PING. This indicates that the port has been disabled because of the unauthorized traffic. The port LED on the Catalyst itself will illuminate orange in color and you will need to clear the condition manually with the SET PORT ENABLE command.

Dynamic VLAN Assignment

One reason often cited in justifying the cost of implementing a switched network solution for an organization is the savings to be had in administration of users' access to network resources. One costly component of managing users' access to the network is the adds, moves, and changes category.

FIGURE 7-3

Configuring Catalyst NMP Image Port Security

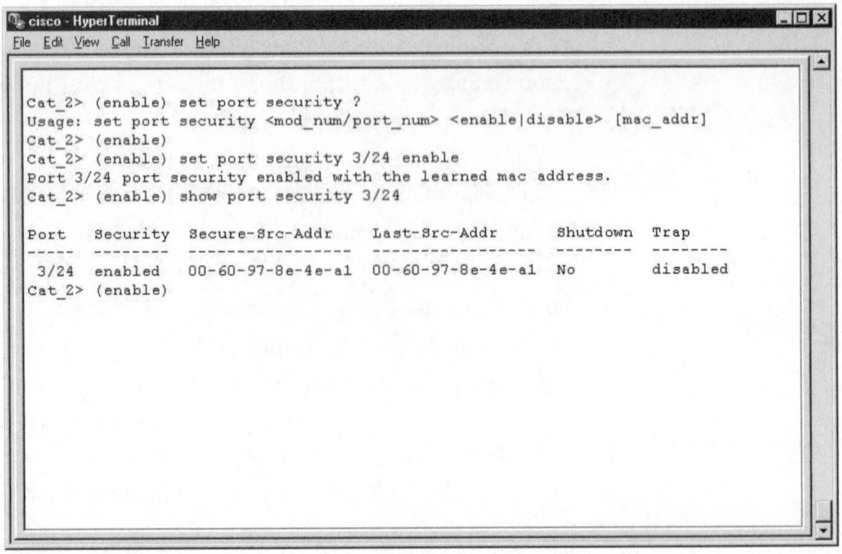

```
Cat_2> (enable) set port security ?
Usage: set port security <mod_num/port_num> <enable|disable> [mac_addr]
Cat_2> (enable)
Cat_2> (enable) set port security 3/24 enable
Port 3/24 port security enabled with the learned mac address.
Cat_2> (enable) show port security 3/24

Port   Security  Secure-Src-Addr    Last-Src-Addr       Shutdown  Trap
-----  --------  -----------------  -----------------   --------  --------
 3/24  enabled   00-60-97-8e-4e-a1  00-60-97-8e-4e-a1   No        disabled
Cat_2> (enable)
```

FIGURE 7-4

Testing Catalyst NMP
Image Port Security

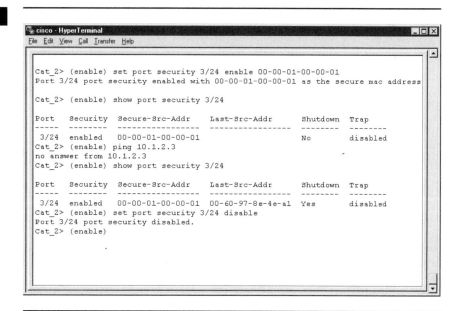

```
cisco - HyperTerminal
File  Edit  View  Call  Transfer  Help

Cat_2> (enable) set port security 3/24 enable 00-00-01-00-00-01
Port 3/24 port security enabled with 00-00-01-00-00-01 as the secure mac address

Cat_2> (enable) show port security 3/24

Port    Security   Secure-Src-Addr    Last-Src-Addr      Shutdown  Trap
-----   --------   ----------------   ----------------   --------  --------
 3/24   enabled    00-00-01-00-00-01                      No        disabled
Cat_2> (enable) ping 10.1.2.3
no answer from 10.1.2.3
Cat_2> (enable) show port security 3/24

Port    Security   Secure-Src-Addr    Last-Src-Addr      Shutdown  Trap
-----   --------   ----------------   ----------------   --------  --------
 3/24   enabled    00-00-01-00-00-01  00-60-97-8e-4e-a1  Yes       disabled
Cat_2> (enable) set port security 3/24 disable
Port 3/24 port security disabled.
Cat_2> (enable)
```

In a traditional routed network, when a user wishes to move his host to a different location, he is obliged to obtain a new address appropriate to the geographic location of his new office. Addressing workstations properly and ensuring that resources are available to a device with a new address are typically the province of highly paid network administrators. Thus there is a cost in terms of network administration time whenever a user changes offices.

Because of the flexibility introduced to traditional networks by VLAN configuration, it is no longer necessary to re-address workstations when they move from one Catalyst switch to another. Using dynamic VLAN assignment, we can configure the NMP Image to recognize the source address of frames of traffic, and to make a VLAN assignment for that frame on the fly. Now when you move a workstation from one location to another, the Catalyst that receives your traffic will examine the source MAC address to determine to which VLAN your traffic belongs.

To support dynamic VLAN assignment, you will need to build a database of the MAC addresses of devices in your network, and the VLAN to which each address belongs. The database can be a text file that you code manually on a TFTP server in your network, or you can make use of a Cisco management application called CiscoWorks 2000. CiscoWorks 2000 can discover the MAC addresses of all the devices connected to your switched internetwork and assist you in assigning them to VLANs.

When the database has been built, configuring the Catalyst to take advantage of dynamic VLAN assignments is simple. You first point the Catalyst at the server where CiscoWorks 2000 resides in the SET VMPS SERVER command, and then enable dynamic VLAN assignment on a particular port. We will examine the configuration in detail after explaining several key concepts in this section.

Other Features

Catalyst NMP Image releases in the 2.*x* series provide a number of other services that you will make use of in your own networks. For instance, you can configure your Catalyst to present security warnings to users who attempt to establish a Telnet VTY session with the device. The message is configured with the SET BANNER MOTD command. Another useful feature of the Catalyst NMP Image's Telnet client helps you copy new operating software to specific modules in your Catalyst, such as the LAN Emulation or Route Switch Module. The feature, called *multiple module download* or MMD, is useful when attempting to diagnose and solve operating software-related problems like recovering a lost password on the LAN Emulation module.

While the 2.x releases of the Catalyst NMP Image provided significant benefits in your network, they also have several serious shortcomings. If your Catalysts still use one of these software releases, you can make your network much more reliable and scalable by upgrading to current software.

Features of Release 3.x

NMP Image 3.*x* enhancements include software support for new hardware features of the Supervisor III module and enhancements to the standard IEEE Spanning-Tree Protocol. The 3.*x* release family also adds a new Layer 2 protocol for automatic configuration of Fast EtherChannel load sharing. We'll describe the latter feature first.

Port Aggregation Protocol

A port channel group is a collection of Fast Ethernet links that originate and terminate on the same Fast EtherChannel-capable or Gigabit EtherChannel-capable switch, router, or host. Using this group of links, you can configure high-speed paths useful for the aggregation of many users' conversations. These high-speed paths can provide from 200 Mbps to 8 Gbps of throughput in your networks.

Prior to the 3.x NMP Image releases, creation of port groups required manual configuration on both sides of the connection. The Port Aggregation Protocol (PAgP) provides you with the ability to configure your data center switch to detect a port channel-capable device like a Catalyst Fast EtherChannel module, and to create the channel automatically. We will use PAgP to establish Fast EtherChannel port groups in later sections of this chapter.

Uplink Fast

The spanning-tree algorithm provides a mechanism for configuring multiple redundant links in a bridged network without the risk of duplicating transmissions on the multiple redundant links. One weakness of the algorithm is that communication between end stations can be disrupted while the algorithm determines a loop-free topology. Cisco has provided several mechanisms that reduce or eliminate the loss of connectivity during these topology change events. One of these is the Uplink Fast feature.

Uplink Fast allows a wiring closet Catalyst to use an alternate path immediately in the event that communication to a data center Catalyst is lost over the preferred path. When such a failure is detected, the two remaining Catalysts exchange messages designed to allow the MAC database to be quickly rebuilt on the new switch.

Configurable Flash Memory Support

One hardware enhancement available on the Supervisor version III is configurable Flash memory. You may choose to use your Supervisor III Flash to hold multiple copies of the NMP Image, perhaps representing your operating copy and some new version of the Image for testing purposes. You can also place extra copies of the configuration file in Flash memory to archive prior known good configurations. The commands to manage flash memory on the Catalyst Supervisor version III are similar to the commands available in Cisco's router IOS.

Other Features

Starting with the 3.*x* releases, the spanning-tree algorithm does not treat each link in a Fast EtherChannel port group as a redundant path. You no longer need to disable spanning tree on devices where Fast EtherChannels will be configured.

Another new feature of the Spanning-Tree Protocol allows you to choose the forwarding versus blocking status of multiple ports manually, on a VLAN-by-VLAN basis. This capability leads to configuring multiple paths for load sharing without the intervention of a Layer 3 routing protocol. We will configure this feature later in this chapter.

SPAN

The Switched Port Analyzer (SPAN) function has also been enhanced in 3.*x* releases of the software. SPAN now permits mirroring of multiple source ports simultaneously, even when the ports reside on different modules in the Catalyst.

Features of Release 4.x

Release 4.*x* of the NMP Image is the first to offer support for the Supervisor III Net Flow Feature Card. In addition to new hardware, release 4.*x* offers several new features that enhance scalability and add Layer 3 switching features.

DTP

Dynamic Trunk Protocol (DTP) replaces the earlier Dynamic Inter-Switch Link protocol for configuring Trunk connections automatically for either the ISL or IEEE 802.1Q trunking protocols. We will examine the operation of DISL and DTP later in this chapter.

MLS

Starting with NMP Image 4.1, the Catalyst provides Multi-Layer Switching (MLS) services. MLS is a technology that allows Catalyst 5000 switches to act as Layer 3 devices. In order to implement MLS, your Catalyst must be equipped with a NetFlow Feature Card (NFFC) on a Supervisor III to act as the switching engine (MLS-SE). In addition, MLS requires a Cisco router with an MLS-capable IOS Image to act as the route processor (MLS-RP). You may use either a Cisco 7*xxx* series router or the Catalyst Route Switch Module (RSM) for your MLS-RP.

MLS services require that the MLS-SE and the MLS-RP exchange certain information using the Multi-Layer Switching Protocol (MLSP). MLSP exchanges allow the switch engine to recognize the MAC address or addresses used by the MLS-RP. When a host station sends traffic to an MLS-RP MAC address through the Catalyst Switch, the MLS-SE considers the packet as a candidate for Multi-Layer Switching. If the same packet reappears on the Catalyst after it has been routed by the MLS-RP, certain characteristics of the packet will be saved in a *flow record*. The flow record caches the routing decision and header information from the packet that transits the Catalyst after passing through the MLS-RP. Subsequent packets that belong to the same conversation are rewritten by the NFFC and retransmitted not to the MLS-RP but directly to the destination host as though they had passed through a router. In this way, MLS greatly increases throughput between two hosts by eliminating delay at the router.

Gigabit EtherChannel

The 4.2(1) NMP Image release provides support for Gigabit EtherChannel when used in Catalyst 550*x* models with Supervisor Engine III modules. In order to implement Gigabit EtherChannel with Supervisor I or Supervisor II modules, you should use the NMP Image 4.3(1) or later.

Like Fast EtherChannel, Gigabit EtherChannel creates port groups that provide a form of load sharing over multiple, parallel Gigabit Ethernet links.

CERTIFICATION OBJECTIVE 7.02

Multiple VLAN Configuration

To this point, our discussion of Catalyst NMP Image configuration has centered on providing services with a single VLAN. The default VLAN, which we call the *Management VLAN* or *VLAN 1*, is capable of carrying user traffic in your organization, but such a configuration is neither desirable nor recommended. When management traffic and user traffic compete for bandwidth and processor attention within a given Catalyst, it is possible for critical traffic such as spanning tree Bridge Protocol Data Units (BPDU) to be discarded. When this happens excessively, normal operation of the entire switched internetwork can be impaired. You can prevent situations like this in your infrastructure by segregating user traffic from management traffic in different VLANs. (On an ISL trunk, BPDUs only travel in VLAN 1.)

As we mentioned earlier, a VLAN can be thought of as a logical broadcast domain that extends over multiple Catalyst switches. Our goal in designing a switched network for TCP/IP is to create a separate VLAN for each IP subnet number. This is not the only way to design your switched network, but it is sensible since IP assumes that a single transmission to a directed broadcast address will reach all the members of a subnet.

Creating VLANs

Two tasks are required for creating a new VLAN. First, the Catalyst NMP Image must be configured to advertise the existence of the new VLAN before it is created. Even it you don't want your Catalysts to learn about new VLANs through advertisements, the NMP Image CLI parser will reject your attempt to create a new VLAN until you meet this prerequisite. We will use the SET VTP DOMAIN command to configure VLAN advertisement. Next, we will use the SET VLAN command to create the new VLAN. Before examining these commands in detail, we will review some background material with the goal of placing the command syntax in context.

VLAN Review

You will be happy to learn that the Catalyst NMP Image gives you the management VLAN for free. You must do a little work to create the second and subsequent VLANs to map to the IP subnets in your switched network design. Using the Catalyst NMP Image, it is possible to configure up to 1000 VLANs in your switched network infrastructure and it is possible to locally support ports on one Catalyst that represent up to 255 different VLANs.

When two Catalysts are directly connected to each other, we must provide a path for each VLAN to transit between the switches. Recall that the Catalyst port ASICs (SAINT, SAGE, or BODEGA) must classify received traffic into some VLAN before it can be switched across the Synergy bus. There are three methods the port ASICs can use to classify traffic: *static* configuration, *dynamic* configuration, or *VLAN tagging*. Of these three, we normally use either static configuration or VLAN tagging to classify traffic on a Catalyst-to-Catalyst link.

If we use static VLAN configuration, all traffic received on a Catalyst port will be classified into the VLAN configured on that port. In order to connect two Catalysts in this fashion, we would need one physical link for each VLAN in our switched network infrastructure. By implication, we would need one switch-to-switch link for each IP subnet we support. Provisioning links in this way has some advantages in terms of dedicating bandwidth to the traffic of a given VLAN, but it suffers from lack of scalability. For example, if you configure 200 VLANs, you would need to create 200 statically configured Catalyst-to-Catalyst links—one for each VLAN. That represents a lot of typing and a lot of switchports.

To solve this scalability problem, Cisco provides a variety of mechanisms whose goal is to allow the traffic from multiple VLANs to be multiplexed (travel together) over the same physical link. Connections of this sort are called *trunks*. The Catalyst implements a trunk by creating and placing a *frame tag* onto a LAN frame before it is transmitted by the outbound port ASIC. The tag contains an indication of the VLAN where the frame originated. When a Catalyst receives a frame on a port configured for trunking, it reads the frame tag to demultiplex the traffic and classifies the frame according to the indicated VLAN.

The Catalyst 5000 family does not implement frame filtering, an early mechanism for multiplexing the traffic of several VLANs over a single connection. In frame filtering, the MAC database of each switch is transmitted to the other switches on a periodic basis in much the same manner as a distance vector routing protocol periodically sending its routing table.

The format of the frame tag differs according to the trunking protocol we choose. Each protocol is specific to the physical network topology that carries it. For Ethernet trunking, we can choose either Cisco's Inter-Switch Link (ISL) trunking protocol or the IEEE standard 802.1Q frame-tagging protocol. On Token Ring connections between Catalysts, we can choose Token Ring ISL. On FDDI and certain wide-area network topologies, we may use Cisco's custom implementation of the IEEE 802.10 Secure Ethernet Protocol as a mechanism to tag frames. You can also think of ATM LAN emulation as a trunking protocol, where the VPI/VCI fields in each cell header imply a frame tag through operation of the common part convergence sublayer.

With these concepts in place, let us now return to our examination of the steps that will result in multiple VLANs in our switched infrastructure.

VTP

The NMP Image CLI parser requires us to configure the Catalyst to advertise the existence of new VLANs prior to their creation. The protocol that carries these advertisements goes by the unfortunate name of *VLAN Trunk Protocol* or *VTP*. It is a confusing name, as it implies that VTP might be necessary for configuring the ISL or IEEE 802.1Q trunk protocol. In point of fact, this is not the case. VTP might be better described as a VLAN information protocol, since its role is to inform one Catalyst about the VLANs configured elsewhere in the switched network. In only one of its many uses will we see VTP play a role in configuring the VLANs eligible to run on a trunk link.

VTP Modes

A program running on the Catalyst Supervisor module's CPU implements VTP. The VTP software sends and receives messages that advertise the existence, creation, and destruction of VLANs in a collection of Catalyst switches called a *management domain*. The VTP program, which is part of the NMP Image, operates in one of three modes: *server* mode, *client* mode, or *transparent* mode. In server mode, the VTP program is allowed to create a new VTP message containing information about VLANs created or destroyed in the management domain. In client mode, the VTP program will request and receive advertisements with information about these VLANs and update its local list of VLANs with this information. The client must retransmit VTP messages periodically but cannot create a new message. When a Catalyst running server mode VTP receives a VTP message with new VLAN information, it also updates its local VLAN table. The big difference between client and server mode operation is the ability to create new VTP messages. Since a client mode device can't originate a VTP message, you cannot create a new VLAN at the CLI of a VTP client mode Catalyst.

The VTP protocol specifies three different messages that VTP speaking devices can send each other: *VTP advert request*, *VTP summary advert*, and *VTP subset advert*. A VTP client mode device sends an advert request when it is initialized. A server mode or client mode device that hears the request will answer with an advert request followed by one or more subset requests. The purpose of this exchange is to allow the client mode Catalyst joining a switched network to learn about all the VLANs in the management domain. Client mode devices do not store a VLAN list in NVRAM when they are powered off or otherwise disconnected from the switched network.

Server mode devices, in contrast, do not send an advert request upon power-up. Instead, they read a VLAN list from their config file in NVRAM and send VTP advertisements to their directly connected neighbors, which recreate the VLAN list that was in place at the time the server mode device was powered off. One consequence of this behavior is that a server mode device that has been offline for some time may, in certain circumstances, disrupt an existing switched network when it is reattached.

Each of these three VTP messages is sent as a Layer 2 multicast over all trunk links to which the Catalyst is connected. The multicast address falls into the range of addresses that must be locally sunk according to the IEEE 802.1J specification. This ensures that a VTP message will never radiate more than one bridge or switch away from the originating Catalyst.

VTP implements a form of reliable delivery at Layer 2 of the protocol model. When a device sends an advert request, it includes the number of VLANs that will be advertised in subsequent subset request messages. If a receiver hears a summary advert that is not followed by the correct number of subset advert messages, it can use the advert request to initiate retransmission.

VTP requires that each server and client mode device periodically retransmit its most recent VTP information as summary and subset advert messages. If a device receives advertisements with information more recent than that held in its local VLAN table, it updates itself with the new information. In order to determine which information might be more recent, the VTP advertisements carry within themselves a *Configuration Revision* field. The configuration revision acts as a time stamp on VLAN information. When a device receives a message with a Configuration Revision field not heard before, it uses the advertised VLANs to update its internal list of VLANs. If a device hears an advertisement with a configuration revision that it has previously received, it discards the information. A particular VLAN may time out and be removed from the management domain if VTP advertisements of its existence are not received in this periodic fashion.

Each VTP advertisement also carries a field called the Management Domain Name. When a device sends a VTP advertisement (in the form of an advert request and multiple subset requests), it fills the Management Domain Name field with a text string. You will locally configure the management domain name with the SET VTP DOMAIN command that VTP uses to create this text field. When a device receives a VTP advertisement, it first checks the management domain name in the messages and compares it to the management domain name locally configured. If the names match, the VLAN information is evaluated and acted on. If the management domain names in the message and local configuration do not match, the VLAN information received in the message is discarded. Devices that send and look for messages with the same Management Domain Name field are said to belong to the same VTP management domain.

Both VTP server and client mode devices periodically retransmit the latest configuration revision that they have seen and installed. In this fashion, we gain a measure of security against accidental or intentional misconfiguration of our networks through VTP. We can also choose to send a password in our VTP messages. If the Catalyst NMP Image receives a VTP message with a password other than the one for which we have configured it, VTP will discard that message. We have additional flexibility to choose plain-text or MD5-encrypted passwords in our VTP messages.

VTP Management Domain

If your Catalyst has not been configured for VTP since the most recent use of CLEAR CONFIG ALL, it is possible for the NMP Image to learn and implement a management domain name by virtue of hearing VTP messages from existing server or client mode devices. While this is convenient when adding a new Catalyst to your network, it is considered good practice to configure the management domain name manually in order to reduce the possibility of VTP misconfiguration.

We will use the SET VTP command syntax to accomplish several tasks. We will configure a management domain name, specify the VTP mode of operation, and configure VTP password security—all in the same command. Figure 7-5 illustrates the process for starting VTP in server mode with the management domain name of "Syngress," and password security enabled.

FIGURE 7-5

VTP server mode configuration

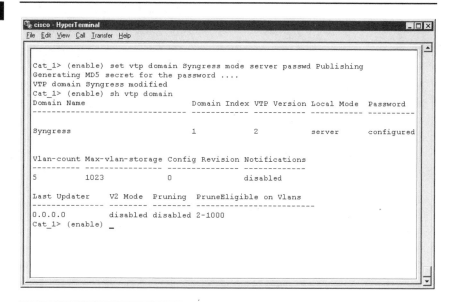

Contrast this with Figure 7-6, where we configure a directly connected Catalyst to participate as a VTP client mode device in the same management domain.

Examine the SHOW VTP DOMAIN commands that follow the SET VTP command in each example. Notice the "Local Mode" column that describes the operation of VTP on each Catalyst.

Create VLANs

Now that we have configured a device to advertise a new VLAN upon creation, we are ready to create VLANs. We will use the SET VLAN command in two forms when creating VLANs and assigning ports to them. The first form of the command that we will use has the effect of creating a VLAN without assigning any ports on the local Catalyst. Use this syntax to create VLAN 2 and name it "Sales_Dept":

```
Cat_1> (enable) set vlan 2 name Sales_Dept
```

FIGURE 7-6

VTP client mode configuration

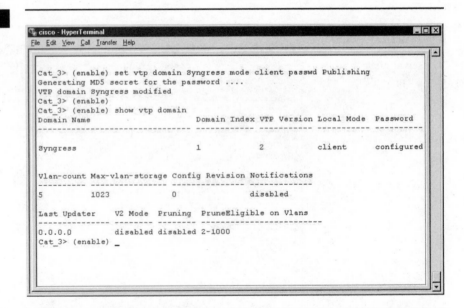

To see the local effect of this command on our Catalyst, use the SHOW VLAN command as shown in Figure 7-7.

Notice that the "Type" field reports that our new VLAN has taken on type "enet," which means an Ethernet-type VLAN. The other options are appropriate if we want the VLAN to include ports on a Token Ring switching module or on Cisco's FDDI switching module. You will also note that the default Max Transmission Unit (MTU) size for the VLAN defaults to the Ethernet interface MTU size.

Referring again to Figure 7-7, compare the list of ports in VLAN 1 with VLAN 2. Creating the VLAN in this instance did not cause assignment of ports into the new VLAN. To accomplish static port assignment, we will use a slightly different form of the SET VLAN command. Use the following syntax to configure Ethernet ports on Module 2 to participate in the newly created VLAN 2:

```
Cat_1> (enable) set vlan 2 1/1-2
```

FIGURE 7-7

Catalyst NMP Image
SHOW VLAN command

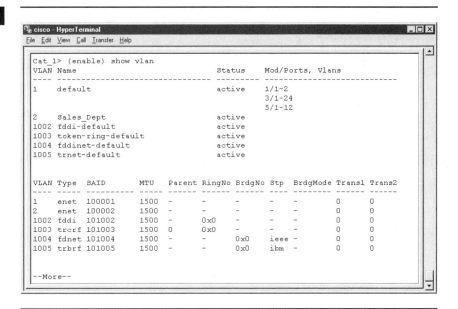

Before we leave the topic of VLAN configuration, let's look again at VTP operation. You recall that we can only create and advertise a new VLAN on a VTP server mode device. How does the NMP Image respond if we attempt to create a new VLAN on a client mode device? In a word, the command parser squawks at you! In the example shown in Figure 7-8, we enable VTP in client mode on our Cat_2 switch.

VLAN Routing

We now turn our attention to a most important topic, inter-VLAN communication. Cisco provides two methods for inter-VLAN communication: routing and Multi-Layer Switching (MLS). In this section we will examine routing with Cisco's RSM and external routers. Before launching into a discussion of the mechanics of the two technologies, it is a good idea to become comfortable with some of the terminology.

The simplest way to route traffic between two VLANs is to configure a device that is able to participate in both the source and destination VLAN. One such device is the Catalyst Route Switch Module (RSM). The Catalyst

---

FIGURE 7-8

VTP client mode operation

```
Cisco - HyperTerminal                                                    _ □ ×
File  Edit  View  Call  Transfer  Help

Cat_2> (enable) set vtp domain Syngress mode client passwd Publishing
Generating MD5 secret for the password ....
VTP domain Syngress modified
Cat_2> (enable) set vlan 2
Cannot add/modify VLANs on a VTP client.
Cat_2> (enable) _
```

RSM occupies a slot in the frame bus portion of the chassis. The RSM has two 100 Mbps full-duplex channels to the Synergy bus. The RSM is a modified version of Cisco's Route Switch Processor (RSP-2) used in the 7500 series routers.

When we configure the RSM to route traffic between VLANs, we will create a virtual interface in the RSM that will map to each of the VLANs configured in our management domain. We then configure an IP address on each VLAN's virtual interface that falls into the same subnet as is configured on the hosts connected to that VLAN. This address will be the default gateway used by other devices in the VLAN when they wish to transmit traffic to nonlocal destinations.

The syntax for configuring these tasks on the RSM is similar in many respects to the syntax that would be used on a discrete router. But first, to access the RSM through the console port, we will initiate a session to the slot where the RSM is installed:

```
Cat_1> (enable) session 6
Router>
```

Notice that the CLI prompt changes when we communicate with the RSM using the SESSION command. Since we are now configuring a router, we must move to privileged EXEC mode and global configuration mode before issuing configuration commands. The sequence will look like the following:

```
Router>enable
Router#configure terminal
Router(config)#
```

Figure 7-9 shows an example of this configuration for the RSM in Cat_1.

The next tasks, illustrated in Figure 7-10, involve creating a virtual interface and binding it to one of the VLANs. The term virtual interface may be unfamiliar to you if you have not explored the functions of Cisco's router IOS. On a Cisco router, each physical interface is represented to the IOS software by a data structure called the Interface Descriptor Block (IDB). When the communications circuitry in the physical interface receives a transmission from a network, say a 100 Mbps Fast Ethernet, the electronic signal is converted to bits and stored in buffer space allocated to the IDB.

FIGURE 7-9

Configuring the RSM

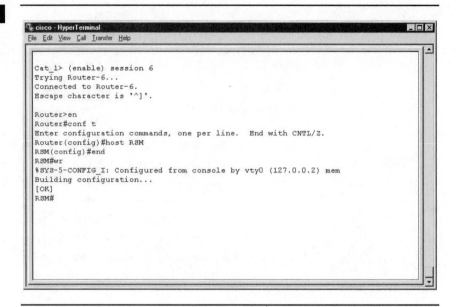

```
Cat_1> (enable) session 6
Trying Router-6...
Connected to Router-6.
Escape character is '^]'.

Router>en
Router#conf t
Enter configuration commands, one per line.  End with CNTL/Z.
Router(config)#host RSM
RSM(config)#end
RSM#wr
%SYS-5-CONFIG_I: Configured from console by vty0 (127.0.0.2) mem
Building configuration...
[OK]
RSM#
```

The routing software then decides where the packet should be sent next.
When IOS needs to transmit traffic, it selects the appropriate interface to
reach the destination address and hands the packet or datagram to the IDB
representing that interface. Once stored by the IDB, the bits making up the
packet are converted and transmitted as electronic signals.

Some technologies, RSM routing among them, employ a virtual interface.
This is an IDB associated not with a physical interface but with a parent
IDB. You can configure up to 255 virtual interfaces on a router (or RSM)
that uses IOS revision 11.2 or earlier. The 11.3 and later IOS images support
1000 virtual interfaces. A physical interface IDB is called the *parent interface*
to one or more virtual interfaces. Each parent may have many different
children interfaces or as few as one. We will create a separate virtual interface
for each VLAN configured on our Catalyst.

This simple picture of the relationship of virtual interfaces to a parent
physical interface is slightly more complicated when we consider the
RSM. On the RSM, the "physical interface" is in reality another software
abstraction. The actual connectivity between the Catalyst Synergy switching
bus and the IOS routing software consists of a pair of SAGE ASICs. Since
the SAGE can operate in full-duplex mode, the RSM can send a total of

Configuring the RSM for
VLAN 1 routing

```
cisco - HyperTerminal                                          _ □ ×
File  Edit  View  Call  Transfer  Help

RSM#conf t
Enter configuration commands, one per line.  End with CNTL/Z.
RSM(config)#int VLAN 1
RSM(config-if)#
%LINEPROTO-5-UPDOWN: Line protocol on Interface Vlan1, changed state to down
RSM(config-if)#ip address 10.1.1.254 255.255.0.0
RSM(config-if)#no shutdown
RSM(config-if)#
%LINEPROTO-5-UPDOWN: Line protocol on Interface Vlan1, changed state to up
RSM(config-if)#
%LINK-3-UPDOWN: Interface Vlan1, changed state to up
RSM(config-if)#end
%SYS-5-CONFIG_I: Configured from console by vty0 (127.0.0.2)
RSM#ping 10.1.1.1

Type escape sequence to abort.
Sending 5, 100-byte ICMP Echos to 10.1.1.1, timeout is 2 seconds:
.!!!!
Success rate is 80 percent (4/5), round-trip min/avg/max = 1/1/4 ms
RSM#
```

200 Mbps and concurrently receive 200 Mbps as well. Thus, the total
theoretical throughput may be as high as 200 Mbps full-duplex.

The SAGE ASICs represent separate channels (perversely referred to as
VLAN 0 and VLAN 1 in some of Cisco's documentation) from the Synergy
switching bus to the routing software. The challenge for Cisco's clever
software designers was to treat the two channels as a single physical interface.
The BIGA Ethernet interface is their answer. When we configure virtual
interfaces on the RSM, the BIGA interface is their parent. We will use one
virtual interface for each of the VLANs configured on our Catalyst switch.

Our first task in configuring a router for inter-VLAN routing is to create
a virtual interface. Next we must bind a particular VLAN to the new virtual
interface. Finally, we configure the virtual interface for all of the protocols
that it will service. The specific syntax for the RSM version of IOS differs in
one important respect from that on a discrete router like a Cisco 7206 or
Cisco 7513: Using an RSM, the first two steps are accomplished in the
same statement. The syntax is as follows:

```
RSM(config)#interface VLAN 1
RSM(config-if)#
```

In this example, the INTERFACE statement creates a new IDB with the BIGA Ethernet as its parent. The numeral 1 binds VLAN 1 from the Catalyst to this interface. In other words, whenever a broadcast frame is received on a VLAN 1 port in the Catalyst, a copy of it will be transferred across the Synergy bus to the RSM through one of the SAGE ASICs, which will place it in a buffer allocated to the interface VLAN 1 IDB.

The difference between this configuration for the RSM and the similar configuration for a discrete router is that creating the virtual interface and binding a VLAN to it are two separate steps. If our Catalyst switch were connected to a Cisco 7206 router with a Fast Ethernet Port Adapter Module (PAM), the command sequence to accomplish similar configuration of the router would look like this:

```
Router(config)#interface fastethernet 1/0
Router(config-if)#encapsulation isl
Router(config-if)#interface fastethernet 1/0.1
Router(config-subif)#isl encapsulation 1
Router(config-subif)#
```

We create the virtual interface with the third configuration statement in this example. We select the parent interface with the INTERFACE FASTETHERNET 1/0 portion of the statement and denote the virtual interface with the .1 notation. When we create the virtual interface with this syntax, EXEC changes to a new mode of operation called subinterface configuration mode. You will notice that the prompt changes to indicate that configuration commands entered in this mode will affect the operation of the newly created virtual interface. Thus, in the fourth statement, the numeral 1 binds VLAN 1 to the virtual interface. The second configuration statement provides a means for distinguishing the various VLANs' traffic from each other when it leaves the Catalyst and loses the VLAN ID header it carries inside the Catalyst. In the next section we will take up the topic of multiplexing traffic from multiple VLANs over the same physical connections. We call this function trunking, and the ISL referred to in the second statement of the preceding example is one trunking protocol.

To put this discussion in context, Figure 7-10 continues the configuration for inter-VLAN routing by creating a virtual interface for VLAN 1 on the RSM in Catalyst Cat_1. You will next want to configure the interface for IP by assigning an address to the interface. Most commonly, we will use a single subnet for all the hosts participating in a VLAN. In order for these hosts to communicate with stations outside their own subnet, you will need to configure them with a default gateway address that is the same as the address you configure on the RSM's VLAN interface. Of course, both the RSM's address and the hosts' addresses must belong to the same subnet in order to see successful routing!

Before the hosts can communicate with the RSM interface, we must ensure that the interface is enabled. Notice in Figure 7-10 that after we create the VLAN 1 interface, IOS reports the state of its line protocol as "Down." Enable the interface by issuing the NO SHUTDOWN command in interface configuration mode. The router responds by telling us that the VLAN 1 interface now has its line protocol "Up." This is the state you need in order to communicate to and through the router's interface. I always suggest that you verify proper configuration of the VLAN interface after enabling it by sending some PINGs to it. In Figure 7-10 we do so by exiting configuration mode and typing a PING command to the address applied to the VLAN 1 virtual interface. The exclamation marks represent receipt of an ICMP echo response for each ICMP echo packet sent. The first period is an ICMP echo that timed out before the ICMP echo response arrived. Why do you think one PING may have timed out while the remaining four succeeded?

exam
Watch

When one IP station wishes to send unicast traffic to another one on the same subnet, it must map the known destination IP address of the station to a possibly unknown MAC address. The mechanism for accomplishing this mapping when the media involved is one of the IEEE 802 LANs is an Address Resolution Protocol (ARP) request. The mapping learned through ARP is cached by most IP stacks for a period of typically five minutes to possibly several days. A small delay in communication may be noticed when sending IP traffic to a station whose MAC address is not cached in the local ARP table.

Now we are halfway to a complete routing configuration. Next we must create the configuration for VLAN 2. In Figure 7-11, we create another virtual interface, bind VLAN 2 to the interface, and configure the IP protocol by assigning an address. When we attempt to enable the interface, we encounter another "learning opportunity." (Some might call it a problem.)

FIGURE 7-11

Configuring the RSM for
VLAN 2 routing

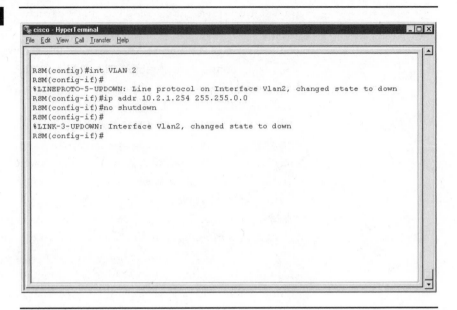

```
RSM(config)#int VLAN 2
RSM(config-if)#
%LINEPROTO-5-UPDOWN: Line protocol on Interface Vlan2, changed state to down
RSM(config-if)#ip addr 10.2.1.254 255.255.0.0
RSM(config-if)#no shutdown
RSM(config-if)#
%LINK-3-UPDOWN: Interface Vlan2, changed state to down
RSM(config-if)#
```

It turns out that the Catalyst RSM observes a tricky little rule regarding
enabling a VLAN virtual interface. By default, the interface cannot be enabled
for any VLAN that does not have at least one "connected" port on your
Catalyst. In other words, you can configure a virtual interface for VLAN 2
on the RSM, but until you create VLAN 2 using a command like

```
Cat_1>(enable)set vlan 2
```

on the Catalyst NMP CLI, the line protocol on the RSM will remain in the
"down" state and you will not be able to ping that interface's address. This
is the situation we are observing in Figure 7-11.

This feature will prevent unnecessary traffic in a VLAN when you have
multiple Catalyst switches equipped with RSMs. If, on the other hand, you
have several Catalysts in your environment but just one RSM, this feature
may seem like a serious limitation. You will need to waste several ports for
each VLAN in your environment in order to route traffic for the VLANs
your RSM-equipped Catalyst isn't directly connected to.

It is possible to modify this behavior using the RSM_AUTOSTATE variable. In Figure 7-12, we will have returned to the Catalyst NMP CLI (by exiting our session to the RSM). Using the SHOW VLAN 2 command, we see that VLAN 2 exists but that no ports have been connected to it. When we disable RSM_AUTOSTATE as shown in the figure, we are able to bring up the RSM virtual interface without a connected port.

You can verify this for yourself by following the steps shown in Figure 7-13. You will save yourself long hours of frustrating troubleshooting by keeping this RSM personality quirk in mind.

Now that we have a router interface configured for VLAN 2, it is possible for stations attached to it to communicate with stations attached to VLAN 1. You will follow a procedure similar to this one for each VLAN in your switched internetwork. We can demonstrate this by sending PING traffic from the SC0 IP stack on Cat_1 to the RSM VLAN 2 interface. If the ICMP echo packets originating in VLAN 1 are answered by ICMP echo reply packets from VLAN 2, we will conclude that our RSM configuration is correct.

FIGURE 7-12

RSM and the
AUTOSTATE variable

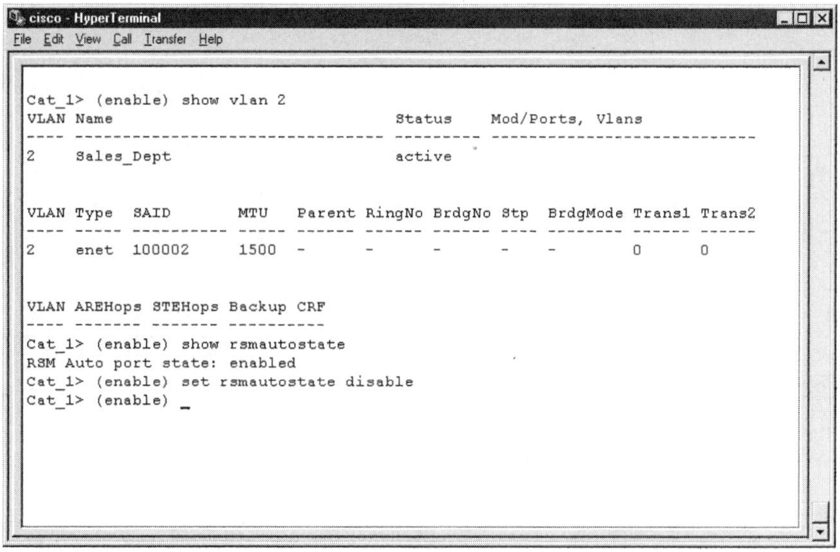

```
cisco - HyperTerminal
File  Edit  View  Call  Transfer  Help

Cat_1> (enable) show vlan 2
VLAN Name                             Status    Mod/Ports, Vlans
---- -------------------------------- --------- ---------------------------
2    Sales_Dept                       active


VLAN Type  SAID       MTU   Parent RingNo BrdgNo Stp  BrdgMode Trans1 Trans2
---- ----- ---------- ----- ------ ------ ------ ---- -------- ------ ------
2    enet  100002     1500  -      -      -      -    -        0      0


VLAN AREHops STEHops Backup CRF
---- ------- ------- ----------
Cat_1> (enable) show rsmautostate
RSM Auto port state: enabled
Cat_1> (enable) set rsmautostate disable
Cat_1> (enable) _
```

FIGURE 7-13

Virtual interface state with
RSM-AUTOSTATE disabled

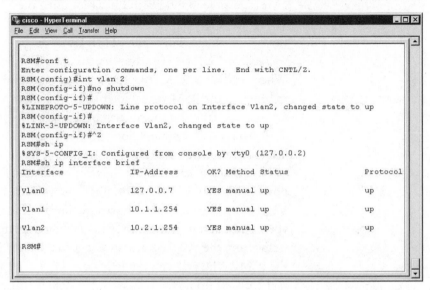

```
RSM#conf t
Enter configuration commands, one per line.  End with CNTL/Z.
RSM(config)#int vlan 2
RSM(config-if)#no shutdown
RSM(config-if)#
%LINEPROTO-5-UPDOWN: Line protocol on Interface Vlan2, changed state to up
RSM(config-if)#
%LINK-3-UPDOWN: Interface Vlan2, changed state to up
RSM(config-if)#^Z
RSM#sh ip
%SYS-5-CONFIG_I: Configured from console by vty0 (127.0.0.2)
RSM#sh ip interface brief
Interface           IP-Address      OK? Method Status            Protocol

Vlan0               127.0.0.7       YES manual up                up

Vlan1               10.1.1.254      YES manual up                up

Vlan2               10.2.1.254      YES manual up                up

RSM#
```

In Figure 7-14, we have to do a little more work on the Catalyst. The
SC0 IP stack must be informed that a default gateway now exists in VLAN
1. We use the SET IP ROUTE statement with a default route of 0.0.0.0
to configure the default gateway address 10.1.1.254. If you have already
installed a default route, you will need to delete it before following the
example in Figure 7-14. This is because the NMP CLI parser won't
overwrite an existing route. Use the command:

```
Cat_1> (enable) clear ip route all
```

to remove existing static routes before configuring a new default route.
You can verify proper configuration of your default gateway by entering
the command:

```
Cat_1> (enable) show ip route
```

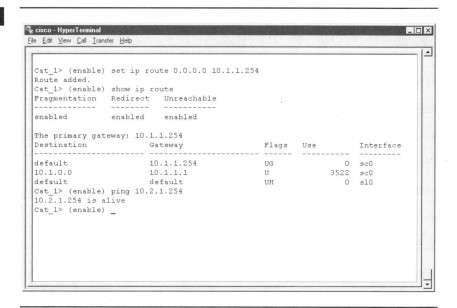

FIGURE 7-14

Configuring the default gateway on Cat_1

```
Cat_1> (enable) set ip route 0.0.0.0 10.1.1.254
Route added.
Cat_1> (enable) show ip route
Fragmentation    Redirect    Unreachable
-------------    --------    -----------
enabled          enabled     enabled

The primary gateway: 10.1.1.254
Destination              Gateway                Flags   Use          Interface
---------------------    ---------------------  ------  -----------  ---------
default                  10.1.1.254             UG               0   sc0
10.1.0.0                 10.1.1.1               U             3522   sc0
default                  default                UH               0   sl0
Cat_1> (enable) ping 10.2.1.254
10.2.1.254 is alive
Cat_1> (enable) _
```

on the
job

Most of the hosts on your network will require default gateway configuration just like the Catalyst IP client. In a network with a single router or RSM, all of your clients may lose connectivity if the router fails. The router in this design constitutes a single point of failure. Even when you install two or more routers, the hosts using each one as a default gateway will lose connectivity when that particular router fails. To combat this problem, Cisco offers a feature called Hot Standby Routing Protocol (HSRP) as part of the IOS. With HSRP, two or more routers can share a virtual IP address. If one of the routers fails, the remaining router will carry traffic for the virtual IP address. You configure your hosts to use this virtual address and they will not notice the failure of a router.

We are now ready to test inter-VLAN connectivity using PINGs from SC0. In Figure 7-14, we see the result of this configuration is successful communication between VLAN 1 and VLAN2.

FROM THE CLASSROOM

Routers and Switches: Not Mutually Exclusive

Every student that comes to a Catalyst 5000 class wants to know how to get the routers to work with the switches. And yet, there are people out there who say that routers are going away?

The important concept to remember when dealing with both switches and routers simultaneously is that each one speaks a different language. Switches understand VLANs; routers do not. Routers understand subnets and networks; switches have no clue. The common glue that brings these two devices together is the broadcast domain. It so happens that a broadcast domain equals both a VLAN and a subnet (convenient).

Now, the trick is to map the two different concepts of a broadcast domain together. The RSM makes life easy. The VLAN interface on the RSM must equal a VLAN number on the supervisor. Any client or server in that broadcast domain (VLAN) must share the IP subnet or IPX network number that you assign to this interface. If not, the client or server loses. (After all, the router is always correct, right?)

A key concept to remember is that every packet that travels to the RSM across the Catalyst backplane is an ISL frame. In other words, you are trunking to the RSM whether you want to or not (and you really want to). This trunking concept must also be stretched out to external routers if you want the switches and routers to interoperate.

Thus, the ISL frame that goes from a Catalyst switch to an external router is read by a Fast Ethernet interface configured for trunking. The ENCAPSULATION ISL <VLAN> command accomplishes this. The VLAN tag at the end specifies which VLAN is assigned to each logical subinterface that you have created. The subinterface number has nothing to do with the proper operation here, although it helps to keep them the same for sanity purposes.

The ENCAPSULATION statement is not needed on the RSM, since the VLAN interface *is* the ISL map. For both the RSM and external routers, you need to trunk the packets to the router, read the ISL header, and determine in which VLAN (IP subnet) the packet belongs.

—Neil Lovering, CCIE, CCSI

VLAN Trunking (ISL, 802.1Q, 802.10, and LANE)

In a large, switched internetwork, you may reasonably expect to configure tens of VLANs to support all of the subnets your customers use. If your design includes WAN switching (using ATM service, for instance) you may possibly configure hundreds of VLANs. In order to scale to this degree, a number of technologies will be required to reduce the amount of time spent in manual configuration and maintenance of your switched internetwork design.

Several such technologies allow you to provision a single physical path between two Catalyst switches, but carry the traffic from several different VLANs along the path. These technologies, referred to collectively as trunk protocols, allow you to minimize the physical configuration of switch-to-switch links in your network. When you add a new VLAN, a trunk protocol will allow traffic from that VLAN to transit between all the switches in your internetwork without the addition of new physical switch to switch links dedicated to the new VLAN.

The network shown in Figure 7-15 is a good example of a candidate for VLAN trunking. In this internetwork, two wiring closet switches are connected by trunk lines to a single data-center Catalyst switch.

If the User's computers are connected to ports that are statically configured in different VLANs, communication between them will require that traffic from all of these VLANs be capable of transiting the two switch-to-switch links.

Cisco's paradigm for carrying multiple VLANs over a single path requires that a VLAN tag be applied to the frames generated by the host computers when they transit between switches. The tag is used by the receiving Catalyst to determine the origin VLAN of the frame. Recall that the switch uses its CAM table to determine the port for forwarding a received frame. The EARL ASIC will only forward a frame to ports that belong to the same VLAN as the frame's origin. Thus it is critically important that any Catalyst in your internetwork determines the source VLAN of each frame of data it receives.

FIGURE 7-15   Multiple Catalysts in a switched internetwork

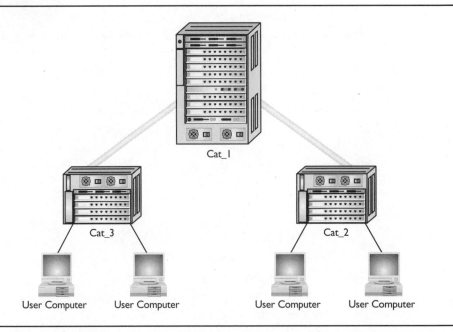

The format of the VLAN tag applied to any frame of data depends on the trunking protocol you choose for a given switch-to-switch link. Most network types have a single trunk protocol available. Ethernet, it turns out, has two trunk protocols available. Cisco's Inter-Switch Link (ISL) protocol and IEEE 802.1Q both permit you to configure multiple VLANs to run over a single port. On Token Ring ports you will use a slightly modified version of ISL to carry multiple VLANs on a single link. You can accomplish the same configuration on a FDDI ring using Cisco's implementation of the IEEE 802.10 protocol. This method of tagging frames also allows you to carry VLANs into your WAN if you choose Cisco's HDLC encapsulation.

The remaining trunking protocol, ATM LAN Emulation (LANE), breaks the frame tagging paradigm. Instead of reading an explicit VLAN number in the frame tag, the receiving Catalyst LANE switch infers the originating VLAN from the virtual circuit number that receives the cells comprising a frame. We will consider the configuration of ATM LANE in Chapter 11. The other trunking protocols are considered in the sections that follow.

Cisco ISL

Examining Figure 7-16, you can guess why we refer to the frame tagging methods as encapsulation methods. The Ethernet frames created by the user's computers are prepended with a 26-byte Header field, and followed by a new 32-bit CRC. Within the ISL header, a VLAN ID field uses 10 bits to number up to 1023 VLANs.

Four modes of operation describe Cisco's ISL. You assign a mode of operation to a port on the Catalyst in order to start using ISL on a switch-to-switch link. The default mode of operation for all Fast Ethernet ports on your Catalyst is auto. In this mode, your Catalyst listens for a request message from a neighboring switch and starts to send ISL encapsulated traffic in response. The request message is sent by a Catalyst whose Fast Ethernet port has been configured to ISL mode desirable. When two Catalysts are connected by ports that are both in the auto mode, no ISL encapsulated traffic will be sent. When either one of the switches is changed to desirable mode, ISL frame tagging will result.

The messages sent between auto and desirable mode ports are, strictly speaking, part of the Dynamic Trunk Protocol. You may choose to prevent an ISL trunk from forming by disabling DTP. Configure ISL trunk mode Off to accomplish this. In certain situations involving multiple trunk connections, you may wish to disable DTP while still allowing ISL. You would choose ISL mode On in this case.

The command to establish an ISL trunk through DTP looks like this:

```
Cat_1> (enable) set trunk 5/1 desirable isl
```

Here we list the Fast Ethernet port 5/1 that connects Cat_1 to Cat_2. It isn't necessary to create a matching configuration on Cat_2. Since its default ISL mode is auto, the Fast Ethernet port on Cat_2 will hear the DTP request from Cat_1 and start ISL encapsulation.

FIGURE 7-16

Cisco ISL frame format

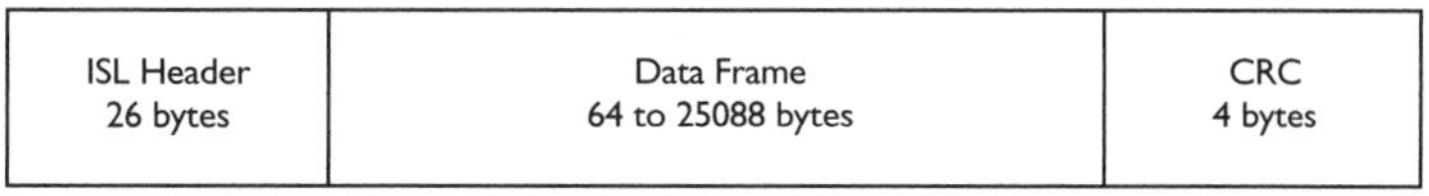

ISL Header 26 bytes	Data Frame 64 to 25088 bytes	CRC 4 bytes

We will examine this configuration again when we look at Fast EtherChannel technology. First, we will consider two other ways to support multiple VLANs on a single line that do not depend on frame tagging.

Frame Filtering

An early attempt to introduce VLANs into switched internetworks depended on sharing forwarding information between adjacent switches. This technique, known as *frame filtering* worked much like a routing protocol. The difference was that two switches would advertise the end stations they could reach, rather than advertising reachable network numbers, as a routing protocol might do.

Cisco switches, including the Catalyst 5000 family, do not implement frame filtering because it requires that reachable end-station MAC addresses be advertised periodically. In addition to the waste of bandwidth, the technique is prone to all the weaknesses of the distance vector routing protocols.

Dynamic VLANs

Even though Cisco shuns frame filtering, we do have a method for recognizing the VLAN of a particular frame of traffic without resorting to static configuration or VLAN trunking. We may choose to classify traffic dynamically into a VLAN by examining the source address of the station that sent the frame. When the Catalyst receives a frame on a port configured for dynamic VLAN assignment, it queries a VLAN Management Policy Server (VMPS) to determine the source address to VLAN mapping. When the VMPS responds to the query, the Catalyst can classify future traffic from the same source address without additional queries.

Using dynamic VLANs requires that you set up an external host with the source address-to-VLAN mappings. You can capture the MAC addresses of all your hosts and manually configure the VMPS with the VLAN number for each, or you can use Cisco Works 2000 to learn the addresses. Your Catalyst can support a maximum of 50 hosts per dynamic VLAN port.

CERTIFICATION OBJECTIVE 7.03

Fast EtherChannel

We have seen the role VLAN trunking plays in allowing us to implement larger, switched internetworks. As your networks grow, another limit to scalability will become apparent: the amount of switch-to-switch traffic will increase until a single 100 Mbps link will be saturated. You can alleviate this problem by configuring a Fast EtherChannel (FEC).

Cisco's FEC implementation on the Catalyst switch is a hardware-based service that multiplexes switch-to-switch traffic onto two, three, or four independent links as though they were the same physical path. A Fast EtherChannel forms when a Catalyst on each side of the link sends messages indicating that FEC is desired. The messages belong to the Port Aggregation Protocol (PAgP). Like DTP, PAgP allows FEC to operate in four different modes. By default, all the ports on an FEC-capable line card or supervisor module recognize PAgP auto mode. A port in PAgP auto mode will respond to PAgP requests but will not initiate them. When we wish to configure FEC using PAgP, we must set a port on one Catalyst to PAgP desirable mode. This initiates request messages and allows one of the Catalysts to reconfigure certain operating parameters of its neighbor. If you attempt configuration of multiple Fast EtherChannels on a single Catalyst, the automatic reconfiguration feature of PAgP will prove troublesome. We will consider these problems again after discussing the parameters that are subject to reconfiguration by PAgP, namely those of the Spanning-Tree Protocol.

How fast is a Fast EtherChannel? You can configure up to four Fast Ethernet links into an FEC channel. In a half-duplex arrangement, four links give us a total of 400 Mbps throughput. If you choose to configure the ports that make up the channel as full-duplex links, you get 400 Mbps in each direction, up to 800 Mbps. You should be aware that your mileage may vary. Let's see why.

FEC might be described as an "address" multiplexing scheme. When the EARL determines that a particular frame must be retransmitted through an FEC, it is the function of the Ethernet bundling controller to decide which link in the channel will transmit the frame. The decision criterion is a mathematical operation (Exclusive OR, in case you were interested) on the lower two bits of the source MAC address and destination MAC address in the frame. Because all the frames sent between two stations will always end up on the same link, it is not uncommon to see one link in an FEC bundle overutilized when compared to the rest.

Actually configuring Cisco's Fast EtherChannel takes a lot less time than describing it. The command syntax is as follows:

```
Cat_1> (enable) set port channel 5/1-2 on
```

In the example of Figure 7-17, we see the result for a two-port channel.

If you choose to create multiple channels on a single Catalyst, as in Figure 7-18, you may see your channels fail because of interaction between PAgP and the Spanning-Tree Protocol described in the following sections. In this situation, I've found the most stable configuration is to use the "on" mode for both channels, with manual configuration of spanning-tree link priorities and costs.

FIGURE 7-17

Configuring Fast
EtherChannel
without PAgP

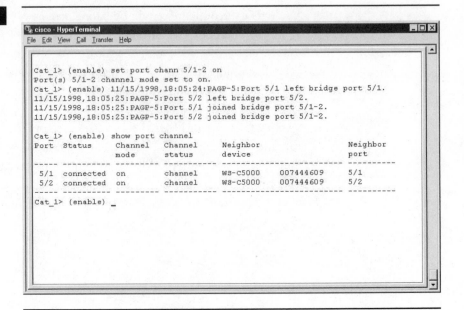

FIGURE 7-18

Problems with Multiple FEC and PAgP

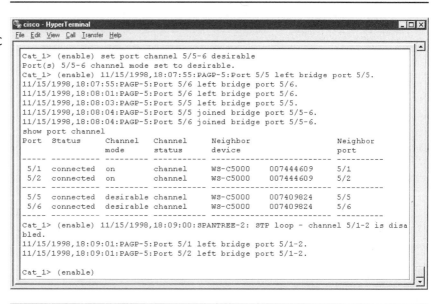

```
Cat_1> (enable) set port channel 5/5-6 desirable
Port(s) 5/5-6 channel mode set to desirable.
Cat_1> (enable) 11/15/1998,18:07:55:PAGP-5:Port 5/5 left bridge port 5/5.
11/15/1998,18:07:55:PAGP-5:Port 5/6 left bridge port 5/6.
11/15/1998,18:08:01:PAGP-5:Port 5/6 left bridge port 5/6.
11/15/1998,18:08:03:PAGP-5:Port 5/5 left bridge port 5/5.
11/15/1998,18:08:04:PAGP-5:Port 5/5 joined bridge port 5/5-6.
11/15/1998,18:08:04:PAGP-5:Port 5/6 joined bridge port 5/5-6.
show port channel
Port  Status      Channel    Channel     Neighbor                           Neighbor
                  mode       status      device                             port
----- ---------- --------- ----------- ------------------------   ---------- ----------
 5/1  connected   on         channel     WS-C5000      007444609    5/1
 5/2  connected   on         channel     WS-C5000      007444609    5/2
----- ---------- --------- ----------- ------------------------   ---------- ----------
 5/5  connected   desirable channel     WS-C5000      007409824    5/5
 5/6  connected   desirable channel     WS-C5000      007409824    5/6
----- ---------- --------- ----------- ------------------------   ---------- ----------
Cat_1> (enable) 11/15/1998,18:09:00:SPANTREE-2: STP loop - channel 5/1-2 is disa
bled.
11/15/1998,18:09:01:PAGP-5:Port 5/1 left bridge port 5/1-2.
11/15/1998,18:09:01:PAGP-5:Port 5/2 left bridge port 5/1-2.

Cat_1> (enable)
```

CERTIFICATION OBJECTIVE 7.04

Spanning-Tree Protocol and VLANs

When configuring VLANs in a switched internetwork, you will no doubt want to provide some redundancy in your links and networking equipment. In a traditional routed environment, redundancy comes from provisioning multiple paths to any given destination. We can add a redundant link to the example network of Figure 7-15 by connecting Cat_2 and Cat_3. This modified network is shown in Figure 7-19.

With this internetwork design, if the link between Cat_1 and Cat_2 fails, traffic will take the path from Cat_1 to Cat_3, then to Cat_2. We have enhanced reliability in our design. Sadly, we have also introduced a problem. You recall that the Catalyst switch will flood a broadcast packet to every port that belongs to the VLAN where the broadcast was generated. In Figure 7-20, let's imagine that the NMP Image on Cat_1 generates an ARP broadcast.

FIGURE 7-19 Redundant links in a switched internetwork

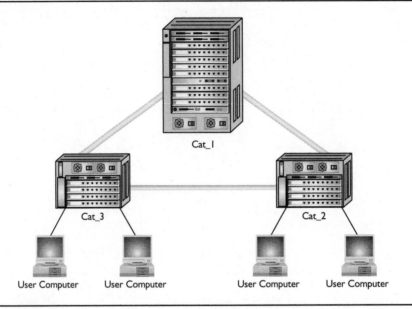

FIGURE 7-20 Broadcasts in a loop topology

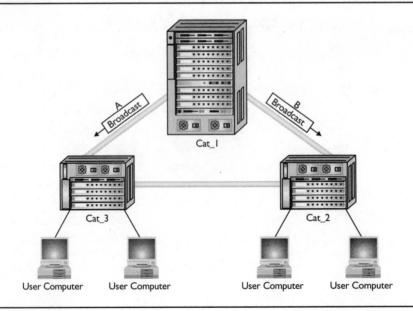

A copy of the broadcast frame is transmitted on both of the links from Cat_1. This is appropriate, since the broadcast is intended to find one of the PCs attached to Cat_2 or Cat_3. When the switches receive the frame, they forward a copy to each of the PCs; but in Figure 7-21, you notice that they also send copies of the frames onto the switch-to-switch link.

What do you imagine the Catalysts will do when these broadcasts arrive? In Figure 7-22, you see that they will forward them, just as you expected.

We refer to this behavior of topology loops as a broadcast storm. In Figure 7-23, the frames are retransmitted by Cat_1 again, and the storm continues. If we want to build redundancy into our switched internetworks, we must solve this problem.

The Spanning-Tree Protocol (STP) is the solution. STP operates by designating one device responsible for locating a topology loop and disabling one or more interfaces to eliminate continuous retransmissions. The device so designated is the "root" of the Spanning-Tree and is called the *root bridge*. The root bridge sends small frames of data called spanning-tree Bridge Protocol Data Units (BPDU) to adjacent devices to detect redundant paths.

FIGURE 7-21   Cat_2 and Cat_3 broadcast flooding

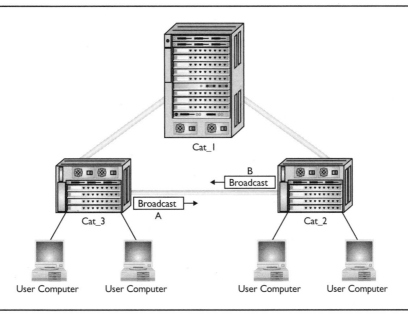

FIGURE 7-22   Start of a broadcast storm

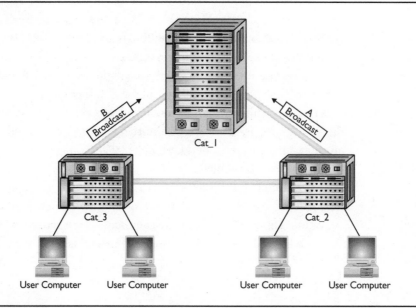

FIGURE 7-23   The broadcast storm never ends

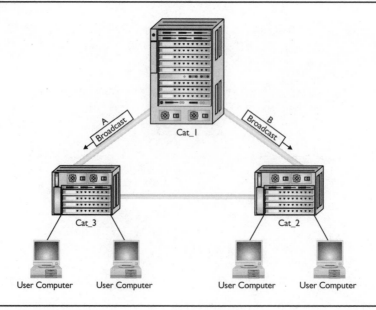

Devices adjacent to the root bridge incorporate certain information in the BPDU and send another BPDU to all of their neighbors. Devices involved in a topology loop will recognize an explorer that originated on the root bridge coming to them from more than one interface. When a topological loop is recognized, STP determines which interface provides the best path back to the root bridge. STP then blocks traffic entering or leaving on the less desirable path or paths. We think of STP as having blocked the less desirable interface while the best path is forwarding. Blocking the interface prevents one of the links involved in the loop from transmitting broadcast or unicast frames. The link thus blocked is likewise incapable of offering traffic to the Catalyst switch.

Redundancy arises when the root bridge periodically re-explores the network. If a link that had previously formed part of a topology loop disappears (perhaps someone unplugged a hub), STP will recognize the fact and unblock the remaining interface such that communication is reestablished. The root bridge sends BPDUs at two-second intervals by default.

Cisco's implementation of STP for the Catalyst family of switches provides a different spanning tree for each VLAN. Figure 7-24 illustrates several important operating parameters of the Spanning-Tree Protocol for VLAN 1.

A device will become the root bridge (called the Designated Root in Figure 7-24) if it has a lower priority than other devices in the internetwork. If two devices share the same priority (as is the case in this example), the device with the lower MAC address will become the root bridge. STP decides which of several paths should actually carry traffic to the root bridge by examining the total cost of the path. If two paths have the same cost to the root bridge, STP can use the interface priority to break the tie.

In Figure 7-25, we use the CLI help facility to examine the commands that adjust these parameters.

VLAN Load Sharing across Trunks

When we build a network with redundant links, it seems a shame that some of them should always sit unused in the blocking state. Since Cisco has provided us with a separate instance of STP for each VLAN, we can have one link in the topology loop carrying traffic for a given VLAN, but blocking traffic for other VLANs.

FIGURE 7-24

VLAN 1 spanning tree

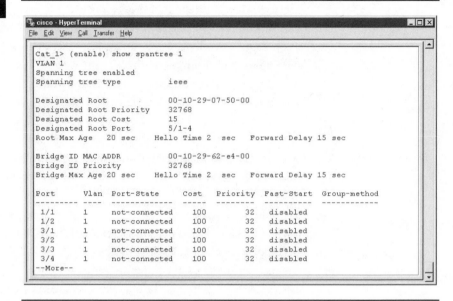

```
Cat_1> (enable) show spantree 1
VLAN 1
Spanning tree enabled
Spanning tree type        ieee

Designated Root            00-10-29-07-50-00
Designated Root Priority   32768
Designated Root Cost       15
Designated Root Port       5/1-4
Root Max Age  20 sec    Hello Time 2  sec   Forward Delay 15 sec

Bridge ID MAC ADDR         00-10-29-62-e4-00
Bridge ID Priority         32768
Bridge Max Age 20 sec    Hello Time 2  sec   Forward Delay 15 sec

Port    Vlan  Port-State     Cost   Priority  Fast-Start  Group-method
------- ----  -------------  -----  --------  ----------  ------------
 1/1     1    not-connected  100        32    disabled
 1/2     1    not-connected  100        32    disabled
 3/1     1    not-connected  100        32    disabled
 3/2     1    not-connected  100        32    disabled
 3/3     1    not-connected  100        32    disabled
 3/4     1    not-connected  100        32    disabled
--More--
```

FIGURE 7-25

Tuning STP parameters

```
Cat_1> (enable) set spantree ?
Set spantree commands:
-------------------------------------------------------------------------
set spantree disable         Disable spanning tree
set spantree enable          Enable spanning tree
set spantree fwddelay        Set spantree forward delay
set spantree hello           Set spantree hello interval
set spantree help            Show this message
set spantree maxage          Set spantree max aging time
set spantree portcost        Set spantree port cost
set spantree portfast        Set spantree port fast start
set spantree portpri         Set spantree port priority
set spantree portstate       Set spantree logical port state
set spantree portvlancost    Set spantree port cost per vlan
set spantree portvlanpri     Set spantree port vlan priority
set spantree priority        Set spantree priority
set spantree root            Set switch as primary or secondary root
set spantree uplinkfast      Enable or disable uplinkfast groups
set spantree multicast-address  Set multicast address type for trbrf's
set spantree backbonefast    Enable or disable fast convergence
Cat_1> (enable) _
```

We can use either the port cost or port priority to configure the asymmetry in blocking vs. forwarding states for a given VLAN. If we use cost, the modification to the path made on one Catalyst will influence decisions made by other Catalysts. If, on the other hand, we choose to modify the priority, the change remains local to one Catalyst. We use the command:

```
Cat_1> (enable) set spantree portvlanpri
```

to cause one of a set of equal-cost links to have a better priority than the others. If links have different costs, use the command:

```
Cat_1> (enable) set spantree portvlancost
```

to determine which link will forward traffic. Referring to the network diagram of Figure 7-19, we use the PORTVLANPRI form of the command in Figure 7-26 to cause VLAN 1 traffic to forward the link to the left of Cat_1; VLAN 2 traffic chooses the link to the right.

FIGURE 7-26

VLAN load balancing with PORTVLANPRI

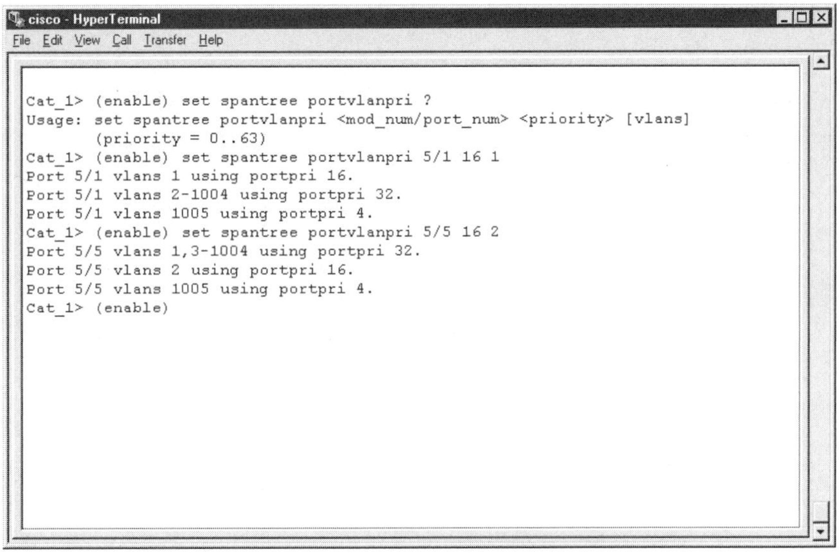

```
cisco - HyperTerminal                                                    _ □ ×
File  Edit  View  Call  Transfer  Help

Cat_1> (enable) set spantree portvlanpri ?
Usage: set spantree portvlanpri <mod_num/port_num> <priority> [vlans]
       (priority = 0..63)
Cat_1> (enable) set spantree portvlanpri 5/1 16 1
Port 5/1 vlans 1 using portpri 16.
Port 5/1 vlans 2-1004 using portpri 32.
Port 5/1 vlans 1005 using portpri 4.
Cat_1> (enable) set spantree portvlanpri 5/5 16 2
Port 5/5 vlans 1,3-1004 using portpri 32.
Port 5/5 vlans 2 using portpri 16.
Port 5/5 vlans 1005 using portpri 4.
Cat_1> (enable)
```

VTP Pruning

When distributing VLANs onto multiple parallel paths using PORTVLANPRI or PORTVLANCOST, we should take care to prevent the broadcast traffic of one VLAN from radiating to parts of the switched internetwork, where no stations are configured to receive it. When a VLAN is created, it is added to all trunk connections in the switched internetwork through VTP. If a particular trunk connection leads to a Catalyst where we have no ports statically configured for a given VLAN, we can implement VTP pruning to remove that VLAN automatically from the list of those that carry traffic on the trunk. This action prevents broadcast traffic from the "pruned" VLAN from wasting bandwidth on trunk links. If a client of the missing VLAN is added later, VTP will advertise the new configuration, and broadcast traffic will again transit the trunk.

Pruning VLANs is a two-step process. First, you must configure VTP to permit pruning. Next you will select the VLANs that can be pruned. Use the following commands to accomplish the configuration:

```
Cat_1> (enable) set vtp domain Training pruning enable
Cat_1> (enable) set pruneeligible 1-1000
```

If you have already configured trunks before configuring VTP pruning, you will have to clear and restart the trunking protocol on the links in your internetwork.

CERTIFICATION OBJECTIVE 7.05

Multicast Services

The learning bridge functions performed by a Catalyst present a problem when our network traffic includes IP multicasts. In general, we can't represent a multicast destination address in the Catalyst CAM table. This is so because the CAM represents a one-to-one relationship between a MAC address and a port. The consequence is that multicast traffic is flooded to all ports in the VLAN that receives a multicast. This behavior has the potential for wasting a huge amount of bandwidth on links where no multicast clients reside.

To cope with this problem, Cisco provides two ways to keep track of which links have multicast clients, and to forward multicast traffic only to them. The first technique, called Cisco Group Management Protocol (CGMP), can be configured on any Catalyst 5000 model. The second service, Internet Group Management Protocol (IGMP) snooping, can only be configured on Catalyst 5000 models equipped with the Supervisor III module and a NetFlow Feature Card.

CGMP uses an IGMP-capable Cisco router to keep track of the physical MAC addresses of stations that have joined various multicast sessions. The IGMP router informs the CGMP software running on the Catalyst NMP of these MAC addresses. When traffic addressed to a multicast MAC address arrives on the switch, the NMP Image forwards it to just those ports where the corresponding physical MAC addresses identified by the IGMP router live. To configure the Catalyst NMP Image to support CGMP, you must enable the service to identify the port where the IGMP-capable router communicates with the switch. The commands are as follows:

```
Cat_1> (enable) set cgmp enable
Cat_1> (enable) set multicast router 1/1
```

1/1 represents the port that connects to a Cisco router.

IGMP Snooping

IGMP snooping uses the traffic inspection capability of the NFFC to interpret the join and leave messages sent by IGMP multicast client stations. With this information, the NFFC builds its own table of physical MAC-to-multicast address mappings. Many administrators prefer IGMP snooping over CGMP, as it requires no extra overhead on the link between the Catalyst and router. To configure IGMP snooping on a properly configured Catalyst switch you need only turn it on with this command:

```
Cat_1> (enable) set igmp snoop enable
```

SPAN

Before we end our discussion of configuring the Catalyst NMP Image, we should look for a moment at the challenges of maintaining a switched internetwork. When we design such a network, we would like to see a result that is robust and very reliable. Most administrators of routed networks would readily admit that a traffic analyzer is indispensable in locating network problems and diagnosing their cause.

In traditional shared-media network environments, capturing traffic for analysis is as easy as plugging your analyzer into an available port on the appropriate hub. If we have configured point-to-point Ethernet links for full-duplex operation, the situation in our switched network is drastically altered. As you know, a Catalyst switch does not forward all Ethernet frames out of its ports. Instead, the EARL consults the CAM table to determine a single port from which a frame can be retransmitted to reach the intended destination address. Now, instead of using a traffic analyzer to obtain a copy of every frame that appears on a particular Ethernet segment, we must find a logical means to copy such frames to the Catalyst port where the analyzer is attached.

Early Ethernet switch manufacturers accommodated the requirement by equipping their products with a special Ethernet port that could mirror all the frames actually sent or received on a normal switch port. This capability allowed the network administrator to monitor the traffic on a port that might be experiencing a problem.

The Catalyst 5000 NMP Image generalizes this capability by allowing us to make any port into such a monitoring port. The service is called

Switched Port Analyzer (SPAN). Using the Catalyst SPAN port, you can monitor traffic offered to a port in the inbound direction, sent from a port in the outbound direction—or both simultaneously. You can even monitor more than one port at a time. Keep in mind, though, that frames are copied to the SPAN port over the Catalyst Synergy bus. This means that you will only monitor valid Ethernet frames using the SPAN capabilities. If, for example, your problem is caused by a workstation with a failing NIC, which sends frames with an incorrect or missing FCS, SPAN will not be able to help you.

You configure SPAN service for mirroring traffic from port 1/1 to an analyzer connected to port 5/1 on the Catalyst 5000 with the following syntax:

```
Cat_1> (enable) set span 1/1 5/1 both
Cat_1> (enable) set span enable
```

QUESTIONS AND ANSWERS

When I configure my RSM with a new subinterface, I often find that I can't ping it right away. The #SHOW INTERFACE display says that it is up and up. What's up?	You are experiencing an interaction between the Catalyst CAM table learning function and the RSM software. The fastest way to clear this condition is to ping the Catalyst SC0 IP client address from the RSM. This forces the RSM's MAC address into the CAM table, resolving the problem.
I think a PC with a jabbering NIC is attached to my switch. When I configure SPAN on the suspect port, I don't see any bad frames. What's going on?	Since the Catalyst uses store and forward switching, only frames that pass the FCS test are carried to the Synergy switching bus. In order to diagnose this problem with your Catalyst, you will need the Catalyst Management module, which implements a switch probe on the blade.

CERTIFICATION SUMMARY

This chapter presented essential information for configuring the services provided by the Catalyst NMP Image. You should recall the details of VTP operation, ISL trunking, and FEC for your certification. Likewise, understanding Cisco's STP per VLAN to configure load balancing over parallel links will prove invaluable. Scalability features provided by the NMP Image reduce your administrative burden when implementing and maintaining a switched internetwork. You should be comfortable with the operation and configuration of features like VTP pruning for certification.

 # TWO-MINUTE DRILL

- ❑ The Catalyst NMP Image controls the operation of the Catalyst 5000 family of switches.

- ❑ A well-designed network is one that is reliable, scalable, and maintainable. When deploying Catalyst switches into such a network, care must be taken to ensure that the power and flexibility of the Catalyst NMP Image software does not detract from these characteristics.

- ❑ Release 2.1 of the Catalyst NMP Image marked the first release to support the Catalyst 5000 family of Ethernet switches from Cisco.

- ❑ Cisco has supported three different versions of Terminal Access Controller Access Control System (TACACS) security protocol on various products.

- ❑ Since TACACS+ is carried in a TCP session, your Catalyst must have a valid IP address. You may manually configure an IP address using the CLI or an NMS. You can automatically configure an address with a BOOTP or RARP server.

- ❑ Your Catalyst can take advantage of the Domain Name System (DNS) to resolve host names into IP addresses for you.

- ❑ Port Security allows you to ensure that unauthorized users of your network are not allowed access to it through your Catalysts.

- ❑ Using dynamic VLAN assignment, we can configure the NMP Image to recognize the source address of frames of traffic, and to make a VLAN assignment for that frame on the fly.

❑ NMP Image 3.*x* enhancements include software support for new hardware features of the Supervisor III module and enhancements to the standard IEEE Spanning-Tree Protocol.

❑ Release 4.*x* of the NMP Image is the first to offer support for the Supervisor III module. Release 4.*x* also offers several new features that enhance scalability and add Layer 3 switching features.

❑ A VLAN can be thought of as a logical broadcast domain that extends over multiple Catalyst switches. In designing a switched network for TCP/IP you can create a separate VLAN for each IP subnet number.

❑ The Catalyst NMP Image must be configured to advertise the existence of the new VLAN before it is created.

❑ The Catalyst 5000 family does not implement *frame filtering*, an early mechanism for multiplexing the traffic of several VLANs over a single connection. In frame filtering, the MAC database of each switch is transmitted to the other switches on a periodic basis in much the same manner as a distance vector routing protocol periodically sending its routing table.

❑ Cisco provides two methods for inter-VLAN communication: routing and Multi-Layer Switching (MLS).

❑ When one IP station wishes to send unicast traffic to another one on the same subnet, it must map the known destination IP address of the station to a possibly unknown MAC address. The mechanism for accomplishing this mapping when the media involved is one of the IEEE 802 LANs is an Address Resolution Protocol (ARP) request. The mapping learned through ARP is cached by most IP stacks for a period of from one minute to possibly several days. A small delay in communication may be noticed when sending IP traffic to a station whose MAC address is not cached in the local ARP table.

❑ Several technologies allow you to provision a single physical path between two Catalyst switches, but carry the traffic from several different VLANs along the path. These technologies, referred to collectively as trunk protocols.

❏ Cisco's FEC implementation on the Catalyst switch is a hardware-based service that multiplexes switch-to-switch traffic onto two, three, or four independent links as though they were the same physical path.

❏ When configuring VLANs in a switched internetwork, you will no doubt want to provide some redundancy in your links and networking equipment.

❏ The Spanning-Tree Protocol (STP) operates by designating one device responsible for locating a topology loop and disabling one or more interfaces to eliminate continuous retransmissions.

❏ Cisco has provided us with a separate instance of STP for each VLAN, we can have one link in the topology loop carrying traffic for a given VLAN, but blocking traffic for other VLANs.

❏ When distributing VLANs onto multiple parallel paths using PORTVLANPRI or PORTVLANCOST, we should take care to prevent the broadcast traffic of one VLAN from radiating to parts of the switched internetwork, where no stations are configured to receive it.

❏ Pruning VLANs is a two-step process. First, you must configure VTP to permit pruning. Next you will select the VLANs that can be pruned.

❏ Cisco provides two ways to keep track of which links have multicast clients, and to forward multicast traffic only to them.

 ❏ Cisco Group Management Protocol (CGMP), can be configured on any Catalyst 5000 model.

 ❏ Internet Group Management Protocol (IGMP) snooping, can only be configured on Catalyst 5000 models equipped with the Supervisor III module and a NetFlow Feature Card.

 ❏ Using the Catalyst Switched Port Analyzer (SPAN) port, you can monitor traffic offered to a port in the inbound direction, sent from a port in the outbound direction—or both simultaneously. You can even monitor more than one port at a time.

SELF TEST

The following Self Test questions will help you measure your understanding of the material presented in this chapter. Read all the choices carefully, as there may be more than one correct answer. Choose all correct answers for each question.

1. Which well known TCP port does Cisco's TACACS+ use?

   A. 53

   B. 69

   C. 130

   D. 49

2. Which well known UDP port does Cisco's implementation of NTP use?

   A. 53

   B. 69

   C. 123

   D. 49

3. What action does the NMP Image take when unauthorized traffic appears on a port where Port Security is configured?

   A. The amber Port Warning LED is illuminated

   B. The port is disabled

   C. The NMP Image reboots

   D. None of the above

4. Which protocol does DTP replace in NMP Image 4.*x*?

   A. VTP

   B. DHCP

   C. DISL

   D. DISP

5. Which protocol is not a mechanism for classifying traffic by VLAN?

   A. Immediate configuration

   B. Dynamic configuration

   C. Static configuration

   D. VLAN tagging

6. Which is a VTP operating mode?

   A. Client

   B. Server

   C. Transparent

   D. All of the above

7. Which of the following are VTP messages?

   A. VTP summary advert

   B. VTP advert response

   C. VTP advert request

   D. VTP subset advert

8. What is the default MTU for a FDDI VLAN on a Catalyst switch?

   A. 1500 bytes

   B. 1518 bytes

   C. 4480 bytes

   D. 16384 bytes

9. Which Catalyst NMP Image CLI command allows you to access the RSM EXEC interface?

   A. Console> (enable) SESSION

   B. Console> (enable) RSM

   C. Console> (enable) SET RSM-AUTOSTATE

   D. Console> (enable) ROUTER

10. If your RSM is running IOS version 11.2(7)P, what is the largest number of virtual interfaces can you create?

    A. 100

    B. 255

    C. 512

    D. 1000

11. Where would you look for VLAN 0 on your Catalyst?

    A. NMP

    B. EARL

    C. RSM

    D. EIEIO

12. Which configuration command binds a VLAN to a virtual interface?

    A. Console> (enable) SET VLAN

    B. Router(config)# INTERFACE VLAN

    C. ATM(config)# BIND VLAN

13. Which command removes a default gateway configured on the Catalyst NMP?

    A. CLEAR IP ROUTE *

    B. CLEAR IP ROUTE ALL

    C. CLEAR DEFAULT-NETWORK

    D. CLEAR DEFAULT-GATEWAY

14. Which technology is not a frame tagging method?

    A. ISL

    B. IEEE 802.1Q

    C. IEEE 802.10

    D. LANE

15. What is the range of VLAN numbers allowed by the ISL protocol?

    A. 0–1000

    B. 0–1023

    C. 1–255

    D. 1–1023

16. Which of the following is a DTP mode for ISL?

    A. Auto

    B. Server

    C. Translucent

    D. Client

17. Which Catalyst model implements frame filtering?

    A. Catalyst 5002

    B. Catalyst 1912

    C. Catalyst 5505

    D. None of the above

18. Which device has a special role in STP?

    A. Master switch

    B. Designated bridge

    C. Root bridge

    D. Root switch

19. If the bridge priorities of two switches are the same, how is the root bridge determined?

    A. Bridge cost
    B. MAC address
    C. Bridge priority
    D. None of the above

20. What hardware is required for IGMP snooping?

    A. Ethernet Switch module
    B. NetFlow Feature Card
    C. Inline rewrite module
    D. None of the above

CISCO CERTIFIED NETWORK PROFESSIONAL

8

Managing the Catalyst 5000 Series Switches

Once your switch is up and running, you will need to manage it. Your management needs may range from occasional checking and changes, to constant monitoring of traffic levels, and monitoring traffic for security reasons. The Cisco Catalyst 5000 switches provide for the whole spectrum of needs.

We'll take a look at each of the ways to manage the switch, and then focus on those that are emphasized on the exam.

CERTIFICATION OBJECTIVE 8.01

Management Options

Cisco provides a variety of ways to manage their switches. They can be managed via the command line interface, via SNMP, or with external monitoring devices. The first section of this chapter deals with command line methods, and the second deals with SNMP and related features, and external devices.

Command Line Interface

When a Catalyst 5000 switch is first unpacked, or after the configuration file has been erased, it must be programmed via the console port using the command line interface. Well, that's not strictly true, since all ports are members of VLAN 1 by default, and right out of the box the Catalyst can be used as a single broadcast domain switch. In that mode, however, hardly any of the features are used. You may want to program your switch so that it is fully manageable across a network.

There are several different ways to get to the command line of a Catalyst 5000 switch:

- Direct console access
- Dial-up access
- Telnet

Direct Console Access

In order to configure a Catalyst 5000 that currently does not have a configuration file, you must use the console port. The console port is EIA/TIA-232 (previously called RS-232). On the Supervisor I and II, the connector is DB-25; on the Supervisor III, it is an RJ-45. The Supervisor III has a console port and aux port, which match the 2500, 2600, and 3600 routers. In either case, the Catalyst comes with a console cable kit appropriate to the Supervisor ordered. The cable kit can be used to hook up an actual dumb terminal, or for connection to the serial port of a PC. If the cables are lost, additional cable kits can be ordered from Cisco, or they can be built using pinout information found on Cisco's Web site. If you use a Mac or some other device with a serial connector besides DB-25 or DB-9, you'll have to buy or make a special cable.

Here is a quick review of the configuration steps you may want to perform, once the connection is made:

- Configure line and enable passwords
- Configure IP address, subnet mask, default gateway, and DNS server(s)
- Configure SNMP community names
- Configure VLANs and VTP
- Configure trunk links, if there is another switch

This is just a small list of possible configuration steps—the ones most relevant to remote management of the switch. Full details for performing each of these steps can be found in Chapters 6 and 7 of this book.

Modem Console Access

Most of the same capabilities of direct console access also apply to modem console access. Modem console access is really just a dumb terminal across a modem, instead of a serial cable. There are some special considerations for hooking a modem up to a Supervisor I or II. (See Chapter 4 of this book for more information.) It's a bit easier on a Supervisor III, and the modem would connect to the aux port instead of the console port.

Don't forget your security considerations when hooking up a modem. Be absolutely certain to apply passwords to the switch, and be careful to log out before hanging up a modem, or else the next caller may find himself already logged in with enable privileges, without having to supply a password.

SLIP

There is an additional feature available for dial-up modem access, and that's SLIP. SLIP is the Serial Line Internet Protocol, a precursor to PPP for IP modem access. There are a few things you can do via SLIP that you can't do when acting as a dumb terminal, most notably SNMP. SNMP is covered in detail later in this chapter. When you use SLIP, you're connected to the switch via TCP/IP rather than as a dumb terminal. The reason that SLIP is required to use SNMP is that SNMP access is not available via the command line, only via TCP/IP. So, in order to use SNMP across a modem, you must be acting as a network client, and not as a terminal.

For information on how to configure SLIP, see Chapter 6 of this book.

Telnet

Telnet access gives you a virtual console port on the Catalyst. More than one person at a time can Telnet to a Catalyst, while the console or a modem is limited to one person at a time. (Or someone on the console port and another on the aux port, in the case of the Supervisor III.) The IP information on the switch must be correctly configured for Telnet access to function. Telnet gives access to the same set of command line options as the console, with at least one exception: Password recovery or a bad image upload may require physical console access.

Many Catalyst administrators, after the initial configuration, use Telnet exclusively to make configuration changes to their switches. Don't forget to have a console setup of some sort for troubleshooting, though.

Command Line Management Commands

Now that you know how to get command line access to the Catalyst, what can you do with it? One of the obvious uses is making configuration changes. However, configuration commands are covered in detail elsewhere in this book, so we won't repeat those. We'll concern ourselves primarily with statistical information.

FROM THE CLASSROOM

Management Tools

Many students come to class and never really think about how they are going to manage the Catalyst switches back in their shops. SNMP is the assumed method, but the potential security holes are never outlined to most students as they are in this chapter. Some prefer the Telnet option to the direct console, so they do not have to leave their comfortable office for the cold computer room. Others turn to SLIP for the remote site manned by non-network-literate personnel. Modem access certainly beats a long car ride or frequent airline flights.

When using Telnet as a remote management tool, a few items should be considered. When you establish a virtual terminal session to the switch, you reach the IP address and VLAN of the SC0 interface. From a security perspective, all the switches in the network should be in a separate VLAN from the users. This prevents direct access to the network devices from any user or server. In order to reach the switches, traffic would normally flow through a router, where security can be enforced with access lists.

By having the SC0 interface in a unique VLAN, the SNMP traffic also flows through the network without being monitored by others in user-based VLANs. The network management stations should reside in the same VLAN as the switches to provide this additional layer of safety.

Administrators sometimes forget to allow the management VLAN access to the switch. If the SC0 interface is in VLAN 1 (the recommended management VLAN), then you need either a port configured in VLAN 1 or a trunk into the switch. VLAN 1 is always configured across a trunk and cannot be disabled—another great reason to use VLAN 1 for management. At remote sites, sometimes only a single VLAN is needed, and thus a trunk is not configured to that site. In that case, management of the switch (Telnet or SNMP) is lost.

Don't forget about the dynamics of VLAN management when it comes to physical management of the Catalyst switches.

—Neil Lovering, CCIE, CCSI

The majority of the information we'll be looking at is the output of SHOW commands. Let's examine some of the most interesting ones. Some of the commands we're about to look at may only be available in the newer software versions. It will be noted if that is the case. Cisco is continually adding features to their switches, so if you have a newer software version, additional information may be shown.

SHOW PORT

Here's the output of a SHOW PORT command for a particular port:

```
Cat> (enable) show port 6/29
Port  Name               Status     Vlan       Level  Duplex Speed Type
----- ------------------ ---------- ---------- ------ ------ ----- ------------
 6/29                    connected  91         normal half      10 10BaseT

Port  Security Secure-Src-Addr   Last-Src-Addr     Shutdown Trap     IfIndex
----- -------- ----------------- ----------------- -------- -------- -------
 6/29 disabled                                     No       disabled 83

Port      Broadcast-Limit Broadcast-Drop
-------- --------------- --------------
 6/29                  -              0

Port  Align-Err  FCS-Err    Xmit-Err   Rcv-Err    UnderSize
----- ---------- ---------- ---------- ---------- ---------
 6/29        259          0          0          0         0

Port  Single-Col Multi-Coll Late-Coll  Excess-Col Carri-Sen Runts     Giants
----- ---------- ---------- ---------- ---------- --------- --------- ---------
 6/29      10844       3691          0          0         0       259         0

Last-Time-Cleared
-------------------------
Sat Jun 5 1999, 14:07:45
```

In the SHOW PORT command, a particular port was specified, so only output for that port is shown. Here we see some basic information about the port: the number, the name (if given one; this one was not), whether it has connected, which VLAN it belongs to, and which duplex and speed it is running at.

Next is some information pertaining to port security. In this example, security is disabled, so most of the fields are not filled in. Finally, we have a number of fields that count collisions and errors. As seen later in this chapter, some of these fields are tracked by the RMON logic in the port ASIC.

SHOW MAC

What you may have noticed missing from the output of the SHOW PORT command is the amount of traffic successfully transferred. That's available with the SHOW MAC command.

```
cat> (enable) show mac 6/29
Port      Rcv-Unicast             Rcv-Multicast           Rcv-Broadcast
--------  --------------------    --------------------    --------------------
 6/29                 520334                        0                        1

Port      Xmit-Unicast            Xmit-Multicast          Xmit-Broadcast
--------  --------------------    --------------------    --------------------
 6/29                 298292                    32587                    60891

Port      Rcv-Octet               Xmit-Octet
--------  --------------------    --------------------
 6/29              681752728                 32206879

MAC       Dely-Exced MTU-Exced  In-Discard Lrn-Discrd In-Lost    Out-Lost
--------  ---------- ---------- ---------- ---------- ---------- ----------
 6/29              0          0          0          0          0          0

Last-Time-Cleared
--------------------------
Sat Jun 5 1999, 14:07:45
```

We can see the switch keeps separate counts for both transmitted and received frames, and displays whether they were unicast, multicast, or broadcast. We can also see some additional error statistics.

SHOW TOP

In many cases, you do not know which specific ports you are interested in, and you might like an overall picture of what is going on in your switch. The SHOW TOP command is particularly useful for that purpose. The SHOW TOP command will give the top N ports for a particular category. This command was added in version 4.1 of the software.

Let's look at what the SHOW TOP command can display.

```
Cat> (enable) show top ?
Usage: show top [N] [metric] [interval <interval>] [port_type] [background]
       show top report [report_number]
       (N = 1..maximum number of physical ports. Default is 20.
        metric = util, bytes, pkts, bcst, mcst, errors, overflow.
                Default is util.
        interval = 0, 10..999 seconds. Default is 30 seconds.
        port_type = all, tr, fddi, eth, fe, ge. Default is all.)
```

The on-line help is a bit terse. Here is an explanation of the available options

- ■ **[N]** The number of ports you want to display. If you want the top 10, then N would be 10.

- ■ **[metric]** The counter by which you want to sort. Available metrics are: utilization, number of bytes, number of packets, number of broadcast packets, number of multicast packets, number of errors, and number of overflows.

- ■ **Interval** Number of seconds you want to measure. Your switch will take this many seconds to process your report. If you specify 60 seconds, you'll wait a full minute to get your report.

- ■ **[port_type]** You can limit what types of ports you look at. Available types are Token Ring, FDDI, Ethernet, Fast Ethernet and Gigabit Ethernet. Other options may be introduced in later software versions, if Cisco introduces new network types.

In the following example, we ask for the top 10 ports that pass the most bytes (by default, in 30 seconds):

```
Cat> (enable) show top 10 bytes
Start Time:     06/06/1999,00:46:44
End Time:       06/06/1999,00:47:16
PortType:       all
Metric:ytes (Tx + Rx)
Port  Band-  Uti Bytes              Pkts        Bcst        Mcst        Error Over
      width  %   (Tx + Rx)          (Tx + Rx)   (Tx + Rx)   (Tx + Rx)   (Rx)  flow
----- -----  --- ----------------   ----------  ----------  ----------  ----- ----
 5/6   100    0           3988633        17267          20          53      0    0
11/1   100    0           3684979        13533           1          30      0    0
 9/9   100    0           1187169         1878          12          36      0    0
 9/7   100    0           1020647         3578           5          39      0    0
 9/5   100    0            989390         6144          16          33      0    0
 9/4   100    0            979226         2965          24          47      0    0
 3/3   100    0            901913         3435          13          32      0    0
 7/22 a-100   0            877069         4677          20          50      0    0
 4/9  a-100   0            874865         5848           1          31      0    0
 4/6   100    0            802370         1722           1          30      0    0
```

As you can see, we can also ask for errors, multicasts, broadcasts, and frames. These can be used to help isolate errors, sources of high bandwidth utilization, and broadcast storms.

Additional commands, specifically for troubleshooting, will be presented in Chapter 9.

Embedded RMON

Stop to consider which devices might be collecting the statistics we've seen so far. The Catalyst 5000 switches are store and forward switches, meaning that they must receive an entire frame intact, and verify the checksum, before they forward the frame along. Malformed frames are discarded. Where are the frames discarded? And—more relevant to this discussion—which component counts them? The port ASIC is the device that checks the frames as they arrive and keeps statistics about them.

The set of standards that determines what kinds of statistics the switch tracks is the RMON standard. RMON stands for "remote monitor." It is a standard designed to allow information to be collected about network links. RMON is an Internet Engineering Task Force (IETF) standard, which means it is documented in Request For Comment (RFC) format. RMON is documented in RFC 1757, which can be found at:

http://www.ietf.org/rfc/rfc1757.txt

RMON statistics are organized into groups. An RMON group is simply several items of related information. The Catalyst 5000 switches support four RMON groups without the addition of a dedicated RMON probe. The RMON standard defines 10 groups of RMON. Some of these groups allow for full packet capture. The four groups that Cisco supports are statistics, history, alarm, and event. Cisco supports the embedded RMON feature on its Catalyst Ethernet ports. Cisco supports these four groups because that's what they designed into their Ethernet ASICs. Cisco at one point had to make a trade-off decision about which RMON features were cost-effective to include. Full packet capture on every port might have been nice, but it would likely have been cost prohibitive. Let's take a look at what the four supported groups cover.

Statistics Group

These are the counters kept under the statistics group:

- **Drops**   Number of frames dropped
- **Octets**   Number of octets (bytes) passed
- **Packets**   Number of packets (frames) passed
- **Broadcast Packets**   Number of broadcast packets (frames) passed
- **Multicast Packets**   Number of multicast packets (frames) passed
- **CRC Align Errors**   Number of frames that had CRC alignment errors
- **Undersize Packets**   Number of undersized frames (runts)
- **Oversize Packets**   Number of oversize frames (giants)
- **Fragments**   Number of frame fragments
- **Jabbers**   Number of jabber errors
- **Collisions**   Number of collisions
- **64 Octets**   Number of frames that are 64 bytes
- **65 to 127 Octets**   Number of frames between 65 and 127 bytes
- **128 to 255 Octets**   Number of frames between 128 and 255 bytes
- **256 to 511 Octets**   Number of frames between 256 and 511 bytes
- **512 to 1023 Octets**   Number of frames between 512 and 1023 bytes
- **1024 to 1518 Octets**   Number of frames between 1024 and 1518 bytes

The statistics group is also called the Ethernet Statistics Group.

History Group

The history group tracks the following items per each time interval set:

- Drops
- Octets
- Packets
- Broadcast Packets
- Multicast Packets
- CRC Align Errors

- Undersize Packets
- Oversize Packets
- Fragments
- Jabbers
- Collisions
- Utilization

Note that utilization is the only counter that did not appear in the statistics group.

Each of these counters is stored into a *bucket* for the time period specified. For example, the switch can be programmed to sample these statistics every minute, and it will take a count of how many of each of these items occurred in that minute, and store them separately. The utilization is a mean average of the utilization over that period (octets divided by time).

Using the history mechanism, a network manager can plot what the network looks like over time.

Alarm Group

The alarm group does not keep its own set of statistics. Instead, it watches other statistics to see if they cross a particular threshold in a given time interval. If that mark (set by the network manager) is crossed, an alarm is generated, and further action can be taken.

For example, the network manager may want to set an alarm for a particular number of bytes in a given amount of time. This means that he wants an alarm generated if the utilization is higher than a particular amount. Another example might be that the network manager wants to know if N number of errors occur in a particular time period.

An alarm is generated when the monitored item goes above the threshold. To avoid constantly generating alarms while the item is above the threshold, no further alarms are generated until that item first goes back below the threshold.

When an alarm occurs, an event is generated. Please see the event group in the next section.

Event Group

The event group is similar to, and related to, the alarm group. It does not track specific statistics, but rather reacts to events occurring on the switch. The switch can be set to perform a specific action when a specific event occurs. Our example from the alarm group is the threshold event. When this occurs, an SNMP trap (SNMP is discussed in the next section) is generated and sent.

Another example of an event action might be to shut off a port in response to some error.

exam
Watch

Try to memorize what types of statistics are tracked in the statistics group. Also be sure to memorize the names and functions of the four embedded RMON groups that are supported on the Catalyst 5000 Ethernet ports. Cisco tests you on which ones are supported, and what they do. For example, you may be asked to identify which group tracks statistics over time (the history group.)
A typical application of the RMON feature is utilization graphing. It's often very useful to see what a network looks like over time. A common use is to graph what a particular network port (which may be a single machine, a whole subnet, or a trunk link) looks like over a day, a week, a month, or a special time period such as year-end closing. Using such a graph, a network manager can look for peaks or low spots, which may help decide what times network backups should run, for example.

SNMP

So far, we've talked about what RMON can do without discussing how a network manager communicates with a switch to collect RMON information. We saw in the discussion of the command line interface that some of the information is available via SHOW commands. This is fine for a person who is checking something manually, but is poorly suited to automatic polling and collection of information by a software application.

The answer to these issues is the Simple Network Management Protocol (SNMP). SNMP runs on top of the IP, and uses the UDP transport protocol. For this reason, configuring an IP address for the switch is essential if you wish to use SNMP and services like RMON that depend on it.

Another item that is essential to configure for the use of SNMP is community names. A community name is a short string that is sent by SNMP management software to identify itself, so the switch knows what kind of operations it's permitted to do. It is, in essence, a password. The basic SNMP operations are read and write. On the switch, you can configure three levels of SNMP access: read-only, read-write, and read-write-all.

- **Read-only** Grants read-only access to all information on the switch except the community strings

- **Read-write** Grants read-write access to all information on the switch except the community strings

- **Read-write-all** Grants read-write access to all information on the switch, including the community strings

There are default community strings for the Catalyst. Before you configure an IP address on the Catalyst, you should change or remove them. This is very important for security reasons, as these community strings are widely known, and people with SNMP write access to your switch can change any portion of the configuration they want. Via SNMP (if the community strings are known), an attacker can change VLAN assignments, shut off ports, control SPAN, shut down the switch, or upload and download entire configurations. The default community strings are:

- **Read-only** Public
- **Read-write** Private
- **Read-write-all** Secret

These represent a significant security risk if they aren't changed. On the plus side, they do give you an initial set of community names to use in order to change the community names via SNMP.

MIB

We've mentioned an SNMP management application a couple of times now, so let's define what that is. A SNMP management application is a piece of software that knows how to communicate with a networking device via the SNMP protocol. Basic SNMP applications can get and set pieces of information on network devices via command line tools. The command line in this instance is the command line of a workstation or server operating system, such as UNIX or Windows.

Some of the more full-featured (usually commercial) SNMP management applications perform functions such as building a visual map of the network, keeping a database of IP address and community strings for devices to be managed, and network auto-discovery (automatic building of logical network topology).

We'll take a closer look at one such SNMP management application, CiscoWorks for Switched Internetworks (CWSI), later in the chapter. In the meantime, let's consider the question of how SNMP software knows what pieces of information it can get and set for a particular network device.

The SNMP standards (which are documented in IETF RFCs, like RMON) specify a Management Information Base (MIB), which documents the types of information available on various pieces of network equipment. Clearly, not all network equipment performs all network functions (for example, there's little point in asking an Ethernet switch for FDDI statistics), so not all portions of a MIB will apply to all devices.

In fact, this problem is handled through modularization. This means that there are many MIBs, all covering different aspects of networking. This still leaves a small challenge for the SNMP management application: Which MIBs does a given piece of networking equipment support? There are a couple of ways SNMP managers handle this. One is simply trial and error. One can try to access a particular piece of information from a MIB and see if it fails. The second is for the SNMP manager to have a database of which equipment supports which MIBs.

The information that all network equipment supports (if it supports SNMP at all) is the manufacturer, model, and software version. Those three pieces of information are enough for an SNMP manager to look up which

MIBs that device is supposed to support. Again, some trial and error may be required, as some of those features can be turned on and off individually.

To get an idea of the variety of MIBs available, and to see that MIB support does change with the software version, look for a list of MIBs supported on the Catalyst 5000, by software version, at the following address:

http://www.cisco.com/public/mibs/supportlists/wsc5000/supportlist.html

Next to each MIB is the RFC that documents that MIB, if you're interested.

The items in a MIB are referenced via MIB variables. A MIB variable consists of a string of numbers separated by periods. It may also have a name associated with it. MIB variables may be readable, writeable, or both.

Cisco has created some proprietary (though published) MIBs to support some of their proprietary features. For example, Cisco has MIBs to access CDP information, VTP information, and VLAN information. In the case of the VLAN MIB, Cisco has released a proprietary MIB as an interim solution for managing VLANs in a Catalyst, since the IETF has not yet released a standard VLAN MIB, and probably won't for a couple of years. If history is any indicator, when the standard MIB is finally released, Cisco will support it in addition to their proprietary MIBs. Proprietary MIBs are explicitly allowed in the MIB standards for these exact reasons.

For ease of use, CiscoWorks supports all of the MIBs Cisco's equipment supports out of the box. The proprietary MIBs can be obtained from Cisco and used with third-party network management software.

SNMP Operations

SNMP works via the operations get, get next, and set. UDP is connectionless, and SNMP specifies a maximum packet size, so information requests that return a large amount of data must be done in pieces.

- **Get** Retrieves a single piece of information, or starts a list of information
- **Get next** Retrieves the next piece of information in a list by referencing the previous piece
- **Set** Sets the value of a variable on a network device

These operations are small and simple, but when put together in an intelligent way, some very powerful network management applications can be created.

SNMP Traps

SNMP traps were mentioned briefly in the section on RMON, as part of the event group. There is one real problem with the model of get, get next, and set mentioned in the preceding section, and that is that all the work is done by the SNMP manager. In that model, the network device sits passively, waiting for the SNMP manager to tell it what to do. The problem with that model is that if the SNMP manager is waiting for a particular event to happen, it has to check (poll) frequently to see if it has occurred. If many events are being watched for, polling must happen frequently for a number of MIB variables. All of this polling adds up to a significant amount of traffic. This could have a very detrimental impact on the network if the polling is being done across a small WAN link.

The solution to this problem is SNMP traps. An SNMP management application can set a trap on a network device. A trap is simply a threshold or event that the device waits for. In our RMON examples, we mentioned utilization going over a particular amount as one example, and N number of errors in a given time period as another.

SNMP traps place some of the work back on the network device, to cut down on the amount of polling required. When an SNMP trap occurs, the network device initiates an SNMP trap connection back to the SNMP manager. The SNMP manager waits for traps, and then responds appropriately, possibly sending an SNMP set to change something, or possibly paging a human to take action.

CDP

It was mentioned that some SNMP management applications include the capability to auto-discover a network. What does that mean, and how does it work? We'll see a better example in the next section on CWSI, but for now a brief description will suffice. Most commercial network management packages include the capability to build a visual representation of a network, perhaps superimposed on a map of the world, with links between network devices. The purpose of such a network map is to get a quick visual of the health of the network, with problem areas usually shown in a different color.

How is such a layout built? If you want to show where in the world devices are, you'll probably have to do that manually, but many network management applications can automatically figure out the *logical* layout of your network. They can't tell you where a device is, but they can show you how it's connected.

How do they determine this? One way is brute force: send SNMP queries to every IP address in a given range. With luck, all the devices you're interested in will answer to the community string you're using for queries. This works for the most part, but is wasteful, time-consuming, and inaccurate. It can also create security issues, since it sends the community string to every IP device on your network. If you use such a discovery method, use a read-only community string, or one that you intend to change immediately afterwards.

What other discovery options are there? Cisco has added to its equipment a proprietary protocol called the Cisco Discovery Protocol (CDP). CDP is a Layer 2 protocol that broadcasts information about that device, using a destination address of 01-00-0C-CC-CC-CC. This information includes model, software version, Layer 3 addresses, name, and capabilities. Here's an example from a Catalyst switch:

```
Cat1> show cdp neighbor detail
Device-ID: 069014313(Cat2)
Device Addresses:
  IP Address: 10.1.50.116
Holdtime: 165 sec
Capabilities: TRANSPARENT_BRIDGE SR_BRIDGE SWITCH
Version:
  WS-C5500 Software, Version McpSW: 3.2(3) NmpSW: 3.2(3)
  Copyright (c) 1995-1998 by Cisco Systems
Platform: WS-C5500
Port-ID (Port on Device): 11/5
Port (Our Port): 3/1
```

Here we see that the first Catalyst has another Catalyst for a "neighbor." It even shows which ports on both ends the connection is on. In our example, we can see:

- The IP address

- Holdtime (how long the CDP information should be considered valid)

- What capabilities the device has (in this case transparent bridging, source-route bridging, and switching)

- The software type (WS-C5500, or a Catalyst 5500)

- The software versions (switching and NMP software, which for all Catalysts so far match)

- The copyright notice

- The platform (hardware)

- Which port the other device is connected by

- Which port the other device is connected to on the local switch

The connected port implies that it only works for directly connected devices, which is true. CDP can only detect an immediate Layer 2 neighbor. If two devices do not share a Layer 2 broadcast domain, the frames will not make it though.

What does this have to do with auto-discovery? You start with one Cisco device on your network, and ask it (via SNMP) for its list (we're only showing one neighbor in the example above) of neighbors. Then, you contact each neighbor, ask it for its list of neighbors, and so on. If all goes well, soon you'll have a logical map of your network.

In practice, most networks will include some non-Cisco devices, or SNMP passwords will be different, or a device will be unreachable. So some manual work, or brute-force discovery, probably still will be necessary.

CWSI

OK, so we've discussed conceptual network management software quite a bit. Let's take a look at an actual package. Cisco sells an application to manage their equipment, called CiscoWorks for Switched Internetworks (CWSI). Cisco recently realigned the product line, and the overall family is called CiscoWorks 2000 (CW2000). Individual components include CWSI Campus, Resource Manager, and the Y2K Compliance Assessment Tool. Our particular interest is in a few particular parts of these applications, as that's what's tested. Figure 8-1 shows the CWSI main view.

This is the logical view of an auto-discovered network. Notice the boxes that are Xed-out. Those are devices that CWSI knows are there because of the CDP list on another device, but it cannot contact them for some reason.

FIGURE 8-1   CWSI main view

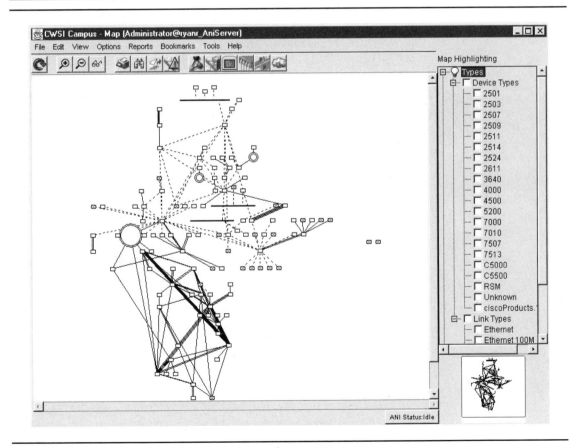

Here are some of the components of CWSI:

- **TrafficDirector**   Used for statistics gathering via SNMP and RMON

- **ATMDirector**   Used for various ATM switch management and discovery functions

- **VLANDirector**   GUI for managing VLANs on Catalyst switches

- **UserTracker**   Displays end station information retrieved from switches and routers, including the capability to track down a MAC address of a particular station

- **Resource Manager**   Used for managing configuration and inventory information

- **CiscoView**   Used to display and manage individual devices

- **Resource Manager Essentials**   Used for keeping inventory, updating software versions, and managing syslog information

exam
ⓦatch   *For the CLSC test, Cisco doesn't expect you to know a great deal of detail about CWSI, but they do expect you to know the names of each of the individual applications in the packages, and their major functions. Do your best to memorize the list.*

If you're interested in doing further reading about CW2000, Cisco makes the documentation available at the following address:

http://www.cisco.com/univercd/cc/td/doc/product/rtrmgmt/cw2000/index.htm

If you're interested in learning more about SNMP and network management tools, including some free, open-source tools, read Chapter 8 in *CCNP Cisco Internetwork Troubleshooting 4.0 Study Guide* (Osborne/McGraw-Hill, 1999).

SPAN

If all of the network management options we've gone over so far aren't enough, there is one final option, the Switch Port Analyzer (SPAN). Put simply, SPAN can be used to take a copy of the network traffic for any ports or single VLAN on a switch. This is a very useful tool for protocol analysis and troubleshooting.

A typical use for the SPAN feature is to attach a protocol analyzer to the switch to monitor traffic going to and from a station or set of stations. Protocol analyzers of this sort are often called *sniffers* generically, although Sniffer is actually the name of a product from Network Associates. Another possible use for the SPAN port is as a network-based intrusion detection system (IDS).

The reason this feature exists is that, when you go from a shared-media network to a switched network, you lose the ability to monitor traffic as conveniently. On shared-media networks, all stations get copies of all traffic; they just drop it if it isn't for them. Switches do not do this. Many protocol analyzers and dedicated RMON probes took advantage of this for troubleshooting and statistics purposes. To make up for this, Cisco added a mechanism to the switch to allow for this type of monitoring.

Let's take a look at the command for using SPAN:

```
Cat> (enable) set span ?
Usage: set span enable
       set span disable
       set span <src_mod/src_ports...> <dest_mod/dest_port>
              [rx|tx|both] [inpkts <enable|disable>]
       set span <src_vlan> <dest_mod/dest_port>
              [rx|tx|both] [inpkts <enable|disable>]
```

Basically, your options are to select the ports (or VLAN) to be monitored, decide where to send the traffic, and then enable it. Your two choices for the source (what to be monitored) are either a VLAN number or a list of ports. The destination module and port are the same in both cases, and that's the port you want the traffic sent to. Note that this will turn off trunking on the selected destination port, so take care which port you choose. The [RX|TX|BOTH] option controls which direction(s) of traffic you will monitor. You can monitor traffic to that port(s) (RX), traffic from the port(s) (TX), or both. Starting in version 4.2, the INPKTS option was added, which allows the switch to accept packets as it normally would into the port, if it weren't being used as a SPAN destination. Previously, the port wasn't usable for normal network activity while being used as a SPAN destination.

on the job

It is very important to be absolutely certain that you select what it is you want to monitor before you set SPAN ENABLE. I found this out the hard way. If you don't specify what source and destination ports you wish to use, and go ahead and do the SET SPAN ENABLE command, the switch will take all traffic running through the box, and send it out port 1/1. Many switch administrators use port 1/1 for a trunk link. This will have the effect of killing your box, requiring a reboot. When I first discovered this feature, I managed to shut down three live production switches before I figured it out.

You will of course need to attach your monitoring device to whichever port you are sending traffic to. You will probably want to make sure your destination port is as fast or faster than the port you are monitoring.

Here's an example of turning SPAN on:

```
Barefoot> (enable) set span 5/1 5/48 both
Enabled monitoring of Port 5/1 transmit/receive traffic
by Port 5/48
Barefoot> (enable) set span enable
Enabled monitoring of Port 5/1 transmit/receive traffic
by Port 5/48
```

The resulting message is a little misleading, since in the first command we're just setting which ports to use, and we haven't actually enabled SPAN yet. In the second case, we've turned SPAN on, and the resulting message is exactly the same.

Here's how to turn SPAN off:

```
Barefoot> (enable) set span disable
Disabled monitoring of Port 5/1 transmit/receive traffic
by Port 5/48
```

QUESTIONS AND ANSWERS

How do I use RMON to track network traffic?	You'll need a network management application to take advantage of RMON information. You can use a commercial application like CiscoWorks, or find a free package like the Multi Router Traffic Grapher (MRTG). Do a Web search to track down MRTG. In general, CiscoWorks will have better support of Cisco devices than other packages. MRTG requires much more manual setup.
What's the easiest way to spot-check network health?	If you have only a few switches, it's probably easier to use Telnet and do a few SHOW commands to determine how things are going. If you have a large network, or you need to keep any kinds of trends or history, you'll probably have to take a look at an SNMP package for automatic monitoring.
Commercial SNMP packages are expensive. Is there anything cheaper?	You can get free SNMP packages, such as the CMU SNMP applications. The problem is, they tend to have fewer features than the commercial packages. They also require a minimum of programming experience, and a lot more manual work to get going. Still, you can't beat the price. Even if you have a commercial package, the free packages may be useful for special applications, Web page building, or something similar.
How can I manage my switches securely?	Unfortunately, almost all of the mechanisms for managing Catalyst switches have some security issues. SNMP and Telnet both send passwords as clear text, meaning that if anyone is able to monitor your management traffic, they can see your passwords. With a modem, you have to be concerned about who might dial up. If you're truly paranoid, you can always keep your Catalysts locked in the wiring closets and manage them via the console port only. For console and Telnet access, a TACACS+ server can be added to your network to support centralized user-specific IDs and password control.

CERTIFICATION SUMMARY

Cisco allows you to manage your switch via a command line interface, or with SNMP. You can also use an external monitoring device via the SPAN feature. When you first unpack a Catalyst 5000 switch, it must be configured before you can use Telnet or SNMP to manage it. Typical configuration steps include applying passwords, configuring IP address information, and setting SNMP community strings. This initial configuration must be done using the console port and a dumb terminal, or a PC emulating a dumb terminal. A modem can also be connected to the console port to provide either remote command line access or SLIP access.

There are a number of SHOW commands that can be used at the command line to collect statistical information about the switch. SHOW PORT gives information about the configuration of that port, as well as error counters. SHOW MAC displays information about how many good frames have passed through that port, broken down by unicast, multicast, and broadcast, for both sent and received. SHOW TOP displays the top *N* ports in a requested category.

To aid in network management, Cisco has included four embedded RMON groups in their Ethernet ports. These four groups are statistics, history, alarm, and event. RMON is an IETF standard for statistics collecting and reporting for network traffic. Many of the counters that RMON tracks are also available via the SHOW PORT and SHOW MAC commands. RMON information is retrieved from the switch via a SNMP management application.

SNMP is another IETF standard, used to communicate with network devices for management purposes. On the Catalyst 5000 family, Cisco divides the SNMP access into read-only, read-write, and read-write-all. The level of access granted to SNMP applications is determined by the SNMP community string (password) being used. SNMP works by sending get and set requests to network devices to retrieve and send pieces of information. Network devices can also support SNMP traps, which allow the network device to do a limited amount of self-monitoring, and report back to the management station when some event occurs. The bits of information are called MIB variables, and are defined in MIBs. Cisco equipment supports many MIBs, providing a variety of management features.

Cisco has created a proprietary protocol called CDP, which is used for locating neighboring pieces of Cisco network equipment. This is particularly useful for network management applications that wish to build a logical map of the network.

Cisco produces an application called CWSI, which can be used to manage a network. CWSI takes advantage of the CDP information on Cisco equipment to build a map of the network automatically. CWSI consists of several components, used for various network management tasks.

Cisco provides a feature called SPAN on its switches, which can be used to monitor arbitrary traffic passing through its switches. This feature exists to make up for the loss of ability to monitor the network that existed on shared-media networks. Protocol analyzers or dedicated RMON probes can be attached to a SPAN port to monitor traffic passing thorough the switch.

✓ TWO-MINUTE DRILL

- ❑ Cisco provides a variety of ways to manage their switches. They can be managed via the command line interface, via SNMP, or with external monitoring devices.

- ❑ There are several different ways to get to the command line of a Catalyst 5000 switch:
  - ❑ Direct console access
  - ❑ Dial-up access
  - ❑ Telnet

- ❑ Once you know how to get command line access to the Catalyst, you can use the SHOW commands, such as the following to obtain statistical information:
  - ❑ SHOW PORT
  - ❑ SHOW MAC
  - ❑ SHOW TOP

- ❑ The Catalyst 5000 switches are store and forward switches, meaning that they must receive an entire frame intact, and verify the checksum, before they forward the frame along.

❑ The set of standards that determines what kinds of statistics the switch tracks is the RMON standard.

❑ Try to memorize what types of statistics are tracked in the statistics group. Also be sure to memorize the names and functions of the four embedded RMON groups that are supported on the Catalyst 5000 Ethernet ports. Cisco tests you on which ones are supported, and what they do. For example, you may be asked to identify which group tracks statistics over time (the history group.)
A typical application of the RMON feature is utilization graphing. It's often very useful to see what a network looks like over time. A common use is to graph what a particular network port (which may be a single machine, a whole subnet, or a trunk link) looks like over a day, a week, a month, or a special time period such as year-end closing. Using such a graph, a network manager can look for peaks or low spots, which may help decide what times network backups should run, for example.

❑ SNMP runs on top of IP, and uses the UDP transport. For this reason, configuring an IP address for the switch is essential if you wish to use SNMP and services like RMON that depend on it.

❑ Cisco has added to its equipment a proprietary protocol called the Cisco Discovery Protocol (CDP).

❑ CDP is a Layer 2 protocol that broadcasts information about that device, using a destination address of 01-00-0C-CC-CC-CC. This information includes model, software version, Layer 3 addresses, name, and capabilities.

❑ Cisco sells an application to manage their equipment, called CiscoWorks for Switched Internetworks (CWSI).

❑ For the CLSC test, Cisco doesn't expect you to know a great deal of detail about CWSI, but they do expect you to know the names of each of the individual applications in the packages, and their major functions. Do your best to memorize the list.

❑ The Switch Port Analyzer (SPAN) can be used to take a copy of the network traffic for any ports or single VLAN on a switch. This is a very useful tool for protocol analysis and troubleshooting.

❑ It is very important to be absolutely certain that you select what it is you want to monitor before you set SPAN ENABLE.

SELF TEST

The following Self Test questions will help you measure your understanding of the material presented in this chapter. Read all the choices carefully, as there may be more than one correct answer. Choose all correct answers for each question.

1. In order to first configure a Catalyst, you must use:

    A. The console port

    B. Telnet

    C. SNMP

    D. CDP

2. What can be done via SLIP that can't be done in dial-up terminal mode?

    A. SET commands

    B. Rebooting the switch

    C. Password changes

    D. SNMP

3. What must be configured to be able to Telnet to a Catalyst?

    A. RMON

    B. SNMP

    C. IP

    D. SLIP

4. Which of the following cannot be done via Telnet?

    A. Password recovery

    B. Password changes

    C. SET commands

    D. Rebooting

5. Which SHOW command will give you error statistics for a particular port?

    A. SHOW MAC

    B. SHOW PORT

    C. SHOW TOP

    D. SHOW CDP NEIGHBOR DETAIL

6. Which SHOW command will give you the number of bytes successfully transferred?

    A. SHOW MAC

    B. SHOW PORT

    C. SHOW TOP

    D. SHOW CDP NEIGHBOR DETAIL

7. Which show command will give the top talkers?

    A. SHOW MAC

    B. SHOW PORT

    C. SHOW TOP

    D. SHOW CDP NEIGHBOR DETAIL

8. RMON statistics are organized into:

    A. Buckets

    B. Ports

    C. Packets

    D. Groups

9. Which of the following are the correct four embedded RMON groups on the Catalyst 5000?

   A. Statistics, history, event, alarm

   B. Statistics, history, event, errors

   C. Statistics, topN, event, alarm

   D. Statistics, history, filter, alarm

10. An RMON alarm generates:

    A. An SNMP trap

    B. An event

    C. Port shutdown

    D. A log entry

11. An RMON event usually generates:

    A. An SNMP trap

    B. An event

    C. Port shutdown

    D. A log entry

12. Utilization is tracked in which RMON group?

    A. Statistics

    B. History

    C. Alarm

    D. Event

13. SNMP runs over:

    A. TCP/IP

    B. UDP/IP

    C. RMON

    D. SLIP

14. Which SNMP access type allows viewing of the community strings?

    A. Read-only

    B. Read-write

    C. Read-write-all

    D. Write-only

15. The SNMP standard was created by which standards group?

    A. Cisco

    B. EIA/TIA

    C. IETF

    D. RFC

16. Which SNMP command is used to retrieve additional items in a list?

    A. Get

    B. Get next

    C. Set

    D. List

17. What happens when an SNMP trap occurs?

    A. A log entry is created

    B. A port is shut down

    C. An RMON event is triggered

    D. An SNMP trap message is sent to the management station

18. What is the Layer 2 protocol used to find neighboring switches?

    A. SNMP

    B. CDP

    C. RMON

    D. SPAN

19. Which CWSI application can be used to find which switch a MAC address is on?

    A. TrafficDirector

    B. VLANDirector

    C. UserTracker

    D. CiscoView

20. To use a protocol analyzer with your switch, which feature do you turn on?

    A. RMON

    B. SNMP

    C. SPAN

    D. CDP

9

Troubleshooting the Catalyst 5000

I n previous chapters, you learned about the hardware and software parts of the Catalyst switch and configuring the VLANs. The main objective of this chapter is to troubleshoot the Catalyst switch-based network. Although troubleshooting is a vast subject with immense possibilities, this chapter concentrates on problems related to the Catalyst 5000 series switch. This chapter introduces the bootup sequence and messages, interpretation of these messages, built-in basic diagnostic tools available with the switch, and other switch commands from the command line interface (CLI) used to view and diagnose problems in the switch-based network.

Some of the basic diagnostic commands available on Cisco Catalyst 5000 switch are described. In most cases, these are general-purpose tools. Even though some of these commands have been presented in previous chapters, this chapter examines those commands from a different perspective—to help keep the network up and running. Later in this chapter, troubleshooting at the physical, data link, and network layers is explored.

The general steps involved in troubleshooting are:

1. Define the problem

2. Collect the symptoms or necessary data

3. Track down the problem and isolate the fault

4. Resolve the problem and document for future reference

CERTIFICATION OBJECTIVE 9.01

Catalyst 5000 Power-Up Sequence

Like most networking equipment, Catalyst switches have the power-on self test (POST) sequence. Understanding the behavior of the switch during the normal operation helps in troubleshooting the switch in the event of failure. Since the switch has operating system software, it performs all the diagnostic tests and enables the different modules for connectivity. The various LEDs on the switch modules indicate that the power-on sequence as well as the bootup messages can be seen on the terminal connected to the console port of the switch.

When the Catalyst 5000 series LAN switch is powered on, the normal operation sequence is as follows:

1. All LEDs start red.

2. During the boot process, the Status LED will turn orange, indicating that it is in the boot process.

3. The PS1 and PS2 LEDs on the supervisor engine module faceplate turn green, indicating that both the power supply modules are functional (assuming that you have two power supplies). If a power supply is not operational, the LED will be red.

4. The fan LED on the supervisor engine module should come on, indicating normal operation of the cooling fan. In normal operations, the fan LED will be green. If the fan is not operational, the LED will turn red.

5. The Status LED on the supervisor engine module remains orange until the switch bootup is complete. At this point, all LEDs on the module are green.

6. During initialization, the Status LED on the supervisor module turns from red to orange and finally to green when all the software is loaded into memory.

7. After the self test, the active ports on the supervisor module turn green, while the LEDs on other modules remain orange.

8. After completing self tests of the other modules, the Status LEDs on each module turn green if they pass; the active ports on the modules turn green as well. The exceptions to this are the ATM and FDDI modules. These modules have a separate operating system and perform internal boot processes that are not part of the supervisor module.

If a terminal is connected to the console port, it displays bootup messages similar to the following. The console generates different messages at different times of the boot-up process. The LED state changes described in the preceding list are in synchronization with the system's bootup messages displayed on the terminal screen.

```
ATE0
ATS0=1
ROM Power Up Diagnostics of Feb 19 1998   --> LED's are RED at this point
```

LEDs turn ORANGE for this portion of the boot process:

```
Init NVRAM Log
LED Test  ................. done
ROM Checksum  .............. passed
Dual Port RAM r/w Test  ..... passed
ID PROM  .................. passed
System DRAM Size(mb)  ....... 16
DRAM Data Bus Test  ........ passed
DRAM Address Test  ......... passed
DRAM Byte/Word Access Test .. passed
EARL Test  ................ passed
BOOTROM Version 3.1(2), Dated Feb 19 1998 11:05:50
BOOT date: 03/21/99 BOOT time: 13:23:42
Uncompressing NMP image. This will take a minute...
Downloading epld sram device please wait ...
Programming successful for Altera 10K10 SRAM EPLD
Running System Diagnostics from this Supervisor (Module 1)
This may take up to 2 minutes....please wait
Cisco Systems Console
3/21/1999,13:24:25:SYS-5:Module 1 is online
3/21/1999,13:24:48:SYS-5:Module 2 is online
3/21/1999,13:24:54:SYS-5:Module 3 is online
3/21/1999,13:24:57:SYS-5:Module 4 is online
3/21/1999,13:25:00:SYS-5:Module 5 is online
```

At this point, if all tests are successful, all LEDs will be green.

```
Enter password:
```

Depending on the number of the modules present, the module online messages is displayed, indicating that all modules have passed systems diagnostics and are ready for operation. It should be noted that it is normal for the modules to come online at different times, meaning the modules will not always come online in order. Any abnormal behavior in the bootup sequence can indicate faults in various switch subsystems and require troubleshooting. If a module LED starts flashing orange, this indicates the link is bad and has been disabled.

Before understanding how to isolate problems to different subsystems, let's first learn about the different subsystems available in Catalyst 5000 series LAN switches:

- **Power subsystem**   Consisting of the power supplies and power supply fans
- **Cooling subsystem**   Consisting of the chassis fan assembly
- **Processor and interface subsystem**   Consisting of the supervisor engine module (which contains the system operating software), the network interfaces, and all associated cabling

Troubleshooting the Power Subsystem

The following list indicates the steps to be taken if any of the components of the power subsystem fails during the boot process. Again, check the LEDs on the supervisor module for symptoms of the problem.

1. Check to see if the PS1 LED is on. If it is not, ensure that the power supply is connected properly and that it is flush with the back of the chassis. Make sure that captive installation screws are tight.

2. Verify the AC source and the power cable. Connect the power cord to another power source if one is available, and turn the power back on. If the LED fails to go on after you connect the power supply to a new power source, replace the power cord. In the case of DC power, verify that the DC power source is active and providing power, and check the terminal block on the back of the chassis to ensure that the screws on the terminal block are tight and making contact with the wires.

3. If the LED fails to go on when the switch is connected to a different power source with a new power cord, the power supply is probably faulty. If a second power supply is available, install it in the second power supply bay.

4. If the power cord and power source are good, but the power supply still does not work, then it is possible the power supply is bad. You would then need to contact Cisco to report the bad power supply and arrange to have a replacement shipped and the bad unit sent back for repair.

5. Repeat these steps for the second power supply, if present.

Note: When working with power supplies and associated power cords, care should always be taken to prevent an electric shock.

Troubleshooting the Cooling Subsystem

The following steps should be taken if the cooling subsystem for the Catalyst 5000 series switch fails during the boot process.

1. Check to see if the Fan LED on the supervisor engine module is green. If it is not, check the power subsystem to see if it is operational. If the power subsystem is not operating, follow the steps explained in the section Troubleshooting the Power Subsystem.

2. If the Fan LED is red, the fan assembly might not be seated properly in the chassis. To ensure that the fan assembly is seated properly, turn off the power supply(s), loosen the captive installation screws, remove the fan assembly, and reseat it. Tighten all captive installation screws and restart the power supply(s). The fan assembly is designed to be hot swappable, but if at all possible, the power should be turned off while removing and installing the fan assembly. The exception to this is the Catalyst 5002 switch, where the cooling subsystem is not a field replaceable unit (FRU).

3. If the Fan LED is still red, the system has probably detected a fan assembly failure. Normal operating temperatures for the Catalyst 5000 series switch are 32–104°F (0–40° C). The system should not be operated without the fan assembly. Immediately shut the system down, as severe damage can occur to the Catalyst switch if it is operated without the fan assembly.

If the switch hardware is faulty, contact your customer support representative for further assistance.

Troubleshooting the Processor and Interface Subsystem

The following steps cover the troubleshooting process for the processor and interface subsystem.

1. Check the supervisor engine module Status LED. This should be green if all diagnostic and self tests were successful and ports are operational. If the Status LED is red, this indicates that a portion of the boot self or diagnostic tests has failed. If the Status LED remains orange after the boot process, this indicates the module is disabled. Refer to the section Catalyst 5000 Power-up Sequence for more information.

2. Check the LEDs on individual interface modules. The LED will be green (or should flicker green in the case of transmit and receive LEDs) if the interface is functioning correctly.

3. Check all cabling and connections. Replace any faulty cabling. This is described in detail in the next section.

Performing a SHOW VERSION command would give you more information on the hardware and software details of the switch.

```
Cat5000 (enable) sh version
WS-C5000 Software, Version McpSW: 3.1(1) NmpSW: 3.1(1)
Copyright (c) 1995-1997 by Cisco Systems
NMP S/W compiled on Dec 31 1997, 18:04:22
MCP S/W compiled on Dec 31 1997, 18:12:31
```

```
System Bootstrap Version: 3.1(2)
 Hardware Version: 1.3  Model: WS-C5000  Serial #: 059041051

Module Ports Model         Serial #  Hw    Fw      Fw1     Sw
------ ----- ----------    --------- ----- ------- ------- -----------
1      2     WS-X5509      008782829 2.3   3.1(2)  3.1(1)  3.1(1)
2      24    WS-X5013      006733762 1.1   2.3(1)          3.1(1)
3      12    WS-X5213A     006826557 2.1   3.1(1)          3.1(1)
4      24    WS-X5224      002413608 1.3   3.1(1)          3.1(1)
5      1     WS-X5302      005709377 6.0   20.7    3.1(1)  11.2(12a.P1)P1

        DRAM                        FLASH                   NVRAM
Module Total   Used    Free    Total   Used    Free    Total Used  Free
------ ------- ------- ------- ------- ------- ------- ----- ----- -----
1      16384K  8136K   8248K   8192K   3840K   4352K   256K  100K  156K

Uptime is 0 day, 0 hour, 25 minutes
```

The output of this command displays the software set used on different modules, memory availability and usage, and the system uptime. This output can be used to verify the software and hardware versions. The output can also be used to find any incompatibility issues with the switch. The primary software for the Catalyst is the NMP (Network Management Processor) image. The other software image is the MCP (Master Communication Processor), which is shown separately in the preceding listing. The ATM and FDDI modules also contain operating system software that runs separately from the switch operating system software.

The output from the SHOW VERSION command is broken down into the following information:

- **McpSw**   Software version for the Master Communication Processor
- **NmpSw**   Software version for the Network Management Processor
- **NMP S/W version compiled**   The date the NMP software was compiled
- **MCP S/W version compiled**   The date the MCP software was compiled
- **System Bootstrap version**   Bootstrap software
- **Hardware version**   Hardware version number

- **Serial number**   Chassis serial number

- **Module**   The module number. Corresponds to the slot number in which the module is installed.

- **Ports**   The number of ports on the module

- **Model**   The module's model number

- **Serial #**   Module serial number

- **HW**   The module's hardware version

- **SW**   The module's software version number

- **FW**   The module's firmware version number

- **FW1**   The module's second firmware version number (if equipped)

- **DRAM**   The total dynamic RAM installed

- **FLASH**   The total amount of Flash memory installed

- **NVRAM**   The total amount of nonvolatile RAM installed

- **Used**   The amount of memory used

- **Free**   The amount of free memory

CERTIFICATION OBJECTIVE 9.02

Physical and Data Link Layers

In this section, we troubleshoot the switched network at the physical (cabling) and data link layers. In the next section, we will review troubleshooting at the network layer. Although the LAN switch is a data link layer device, troubleshooting at the network layer is required if the switch is hosting the Route Switch Module (RSM).

The physical layer is the most basic level at which to start the network troubleshooting process. Though physical layer connectivity is quite apparent, most of the time problems at this layer go unnoticed due to negligence or overconfidence.

As we learned from earlier chapters, the switch provides connectivity for workstations, servers, and other devices in a switched LAN. Most cabling used in today's data-communication networks consist of twisted-pair and fiber-optic cables. Within the structured cabling environment, the physical star topology commonly used helps to isolate problems within a segment of cable to a particular network or node.

Troubleshooting at the Cabling Level

The basic diagnostic tool that is available to troubleshoot cable-level problems is the LED indications on the switch modules. Besides the Status LED, which indicates the general health of the entire module, every port on the switch module has a Link LED, indicating various states of the physical connectivity between the switch and the device connected to that port. The state of the Link LED can help you narrow down the problem. Table 9-1 indicates the different states of the Link LEDs and their meaning.

From these basic physical inspections of the module ports, the fault can be isolated to a specific area or component in the physical layer of the network. Once it is concluded that the problem is with a cable, third-party tools are available to test it. They can perform tests from the basic continuity test to more complex tests like locating the exact position of the fault within the cable. These tools are cable scanners or time domain reflectometers (TDR).

TABLE 9-1		
	Link LED Indicator	**Status of the Link**
Link LED Indications	Solid green	Normal link signal on the port
	Solid orange	Port is disabled by software, a bad port, or an incorrect VLAN configuration
	Flashing orange	Bad link or port hardware failure
	Off	No link signal, because remote node is not powered on, the cable is cut, there is improper cabling, or there is a problem with the remote node/device NIC

The simplest and least expensive cable testers are called *continuity testers*, which simply verify the connectivity of wires. The better ones test pairs individually to make sure that some of the wires have not been crossed with another pair. Most of these testers operate as a pair of devices, one at each end of a wire, with LEDs on them. Some of the testers use combinations of LED colors to indicate proper operation, while some may display a graph of the pin-to-pin connectivity for the entire cable (twisted-pair cables). Continuity testers are available in wiring stores and communications catalogs.

The more expensive wire testers are capable of performing a TDR test. Basically, a TDR test is used to measure the length of a cable, or the distance to a break. This is accomplished by sending a signal down a wire and measuring how long it takes for an echo of the signal to bounce back. This type of test was slightly more useful when coax cable was more popular, but TDRs can still be handy when cable runs are behind walls or under floors. They're also very useful for certifying your cable plant. Part of certifying your cable plant involves making sure that none of your cable runs exceed the maximum allowed distance for the media. In the case of fiber-optic cables, optical time domain reflectometers (OTDR) are used to troubleshoot and to verify the quality of the cabling. These tools would also indicate a loss of signal strength within the cables or at the connectors, which play important role in FO cabling.

For example, for 10BaseT or 100BaseT wiring, the maximum allowed length (according to the spec) is 100 meters, or about 328 feet. With a TDR-capable tester, you can pick a few cable runs that you think are farthest from your wiring closet, and test for length. If you're under the limit, you're probably okay. But if you're beyond it, you know to keep an eye out for trouble. 10BaseT is a lot more forgiving than 100BaseT. Don't forget to consider the length of the patch cables at both ends.

Other testers are capable of performing *signal-quality testing*. You may have heard the terms *NEXT* and *attenuation* in relation to network cabling. NEXT stands for near-end cross talk. This refers to the tendency for signals to "jump" pairs near the ends of wires, where the pairs have been separated and untwisted. Attenuation is the tendency for signals to get weaker over distance. The physics behind the phenomenon isn't all that important; what matters is whether your wire is "in spec" or "out of spec." Most of the high-end testers are fairly easy to use. They usually require a calibration for your cable type; after that you usually just have to press a single button. They perform continuity, length, NEXT, and attenuation tests (and possibly others) and report pass or fail. When the cable fails, the tester usually displays what failed.

Replacing the cable—whether a patch cord replacement or running new cable from the patch panel to the destination—can rectify most of the networking problems related to cabling. But a problem at the logical level or at higher-layer levels needs more research and time. Troubleshooting the problems at the data link layer involves console login or Telneting to the Catalyst switch.

Once you connect the terminal via the console port or by Telnet, press ENTER until you see the switch console prompt. Once you establish proper connection with the switch console port, what you see is called the command line interface, which would be as follows:

```
Cisco Systems Console
Enter password:
Console>
Console> enable                 .....to enter the privileged mode
Enter Password:
Console> (enable)               .....privileged mode prompt
```

If you have not configured for password, just press ENTER when asked to enter a password.

As has been discussed in earlier chapters, the CLI is the basic interface for the Catalyst switch configuration and maintenance. From the CLI, different SHOW commands can be issued to check the status of various subsystems, modules, and ports. These are the primary tools in troubleshooting the switch connectivity after the basic cable tests. We will look at the important SHOW commands from the basic troubleshooting point of view.

- SHOW MODULE
- SHOW PORT
- SHOW MAC
- SHOW CAM

SHOW MODULE

This command displays a summary of all the modules present in the Catalyst switch and their status. The "OK" in the last column shows their normal behavior. Any other status such as "fail" or "disable" indicates the cause of the problem, which can be rectified by action such as enabling the module or replacing the faulty module.

```
cat5000 (enable) sh module
Mod Module-Name    Ports Module-Type          Model      Serial-Num Status
--- ------------- ----- -------------------- --------- --------- -------
1                  2     100BaseTX Supervisor WS-X5509   008789029 ok
2                 24     10/100BaseTX Ethernet WS-X5224  007235608 ok
3                 12     10/100BaseTX Ethernet WS-X5213A 007389057 ok
4                 24     10BaseT Ethernet     WS-X5013   006737662 ok
5                  1     Route Switch         WS-X5302   005407377 ok

Mod MAC-Address(es)                           Hw     Fw      Sw
--- ------------------------------------ ------ ------- ----------------
1   00-90-92-d8-c0-00 thru 00-90-92-d8-c3-ff  2.3    3.1(2)  3.1(1)
2   00-10-7b-f2-b3-d8 thru 00-10-7b-f2-b3-ef  1.3    3.1(1)  3.1(1)
3   00-10-7b-d9-5e-f8 thru 00-10-7b-d9-5f-03  2.1    3.1(1)  3.1(1)
4   00-e0-ee-47-5b-40 thru 00-e0-ee-47-5b-57  1.1    2.3(1)  3.1(1)
5   00-e0-1e-f1-fa-68 thru 00-e0-1e-f1-fa-69  6.0    20.7    11.2(12a.P1)P1
```

The output that is displayed by the SHOW MODULE command is as follows:

- **Mod** The module number as installed in the switch

- **Module Name** The name of the module. This is an optional setting that is set in the configuration of the module.

- **Ports** The number of ports on the module

- **Module-Type** The type of module installed (Ethernet, Route Switch)

- **Model** Model number of the module

- **Serial-Num** Serial number for the module

- **Status** Current status of the module

- **MAC Address(es)** MAC or MAC address range for the module (if used)

- **Hw** Hardware version of the module

- ■ **Fw**   Module firmware number
- ■ **Sw**   Module software version

All Catalyst 5000 series switches support hot swapping, which lets you install, remove, replace, and rearrange switching modules without turning off the system power. When the system detects that a switching module has been installed or removed, it runs a diagnostic and discovery routine automatically, acknowledges the presence or absence of the module, and resumes system operation with no operator intervention. Care should be taken while replacing any faulty module, since the components are ESD sensitive.

SHOW PORT

The SHOW PORT command can be used as the next step in troubleshooting a problem at the port level, once it is concluded that the cable and module are functioning properly. This command shows detailed status of the port in question. It shows the port speed, half or full duplex, VLAN membership, and collisions or errors. From this output, inference can be drawn as to where the problem lies.

```
cat5000 (enable) sh port 1/1
Port  Name              Status      Vlan      Level   Duplex Speed Type
----- ---------------   ---------   -------   ------  ------ ----- -----------
 1/1                    connect     1         normal  half    100  100BaseTX

Port  Security  Secure-Src-Addr   Last-Src-Addr       Shutdown  Trap
----- --------  ----------------  ----------------    --------  --------
 1/1  disabled                                        No        disabled

Port     Broadcast-Limit Broadcast-Drop
-------- --------------- --------------
 1/1            -              -
Port  Align-Err  FCS-Err    Xmit-Err   Rcv-Err    UnderSize
----- ---------- ---------- ---------- ---------- ---------
 1/1       0          0          0          0          0
Port  Single-Col Multi-Coll Late-Coll  Excess-Col Carri-Sen Runts   Giants
----- ---------- ---------- ---------- ---------- --------- ------- -------
 1/1       0          0          0          0          0         0       0

Last-Time-Cleared
--------------------------
Sun Mar 21 1999, 13:24:01
```

The output from the SHOW PORT command is as follows:

- **Port**   Port number that has been queried
- **Name**   Name of the port (Optional)
- **Status**   Port status
- **VLAN**   The VLAN to which the port belongs
- **Level**   Setting for the level of the port (Choices are low or high)
- **Duplex**   Whether the port is in full-duplex or half-duplex mode
- **Speed**   Port speed (10, 100, auto)
- **Type**   The type of port (10BaseT, 100BaseT)
- **Security**   Whether port security is enabled
- **Secure-Src-Addr**   Displays the MAC address of the security-enabled port
- **Last-Src-Addr**   Displays the MAC address of the last packet received by the port
- **Shutdown**   Indicates whether the port was shut down due to a security violation
- **Trap**   Indicates if port trap has been enabled
- **Broadcast-Limit**   Displays the port broadcast limit setting
- **Broadcast-Drop**   Displays the number of packets dropped that exceed the limit
- **Align-Err**   Number of frames received with alignment errors (packets with an uneven number of octets, and CRC errors)
- **FCS-Err**   Number of frame check sequence errors
- **Xmit-Err**   Number of transmit errors. This is an indication of a full transmit buffer.
- **Rcv-Err**   Number of receive errors. This indicates a full receive buffer.
- **UnderSize**   Number of frames that were less than 64 octets
- **Single-Col**   The number of single collisions that occurred before the frame was transmitted successfully

- **Multi-Coll**   The number of multiple collisions that occurred before the frame was successfully transmitted

- **Excess-Col**   The number of excessive collisions that occurred. This indicates that the frame encountered 16 collisions and was discarded.

- **Carri-Sen**   The number of times the port has detected a carrier

- **Runts**   The number of runt frames (frames smaller than the IEEE 802.3 specification)

- **Last-Time-Cleared**   The last time the counters were cleared for the port

SHOW PORT SECURITY

One more command of interest would be SHOW PORT SECURITY, which displays the security assigned to the port in question. This command is used to determine whether the port needs to be disabled due to eavesdropping. If any other node with a different MAC address were attached to this port, the port would not forward that traffic.

```
Cat5000 (enable) show port security
 Port    Security  Secure-Src-Addr    Last-Src-Addr      Shutdown  Trap
 -----   --------  ----------------   ----------------   --------  --------
 1/1     disabled                                        No        disabled
 1/2     disabled                                        No        disabled
 2/1     enabled   00-80-5e-20-d2-10  00-80-5e-20-d2-10  No        disabled
 2/2     disabled                                        No        disabled
 2/3     disabled                                        No        disabled
 2/4     disabled                                        No        disabled
```

If an SNMP management application such as CiscoWorks were monitoring the switch, then eavesdropping would generate trap messages for the SNMP console.

SHOW MAC

The SHOW MAC command displays the total number of frames transmitted and received by the individual ports, along with the types of frames, such as broadcast or multicasts.

```
Cat5000 (enable) sh mac 1/1
MAC       Rcv-Frms   Xmit-Frms  Rcv-Multi  Xmit-Multi Rcv-Broad· Xmit-Broad
--------  ---------- ---------- ---------- ---------- ---------- ----------
  1/1           67         89          7         56         34          4
MAC       Dely-Exced MTU-Exced  In-Discard Lrn-Discrd In-Lost    Out-Lost
--------  ---------- ---------- ---------- ---------- ---------- ----------
  1/1            0          0          0          0          0          0
Port      Rcv-Unicast        Rcv-Multicast       Rcv-Broadcast
--------  ------------------- ------------------- -------------------
  1/1                     5                   7                  34
Port      Xmit-Unicast       Xmit-Multicast      Xmit-Broadcast
--------  ------------------- ------------------- -------------------
  1/1                    23                  67                   0
Port      Rcv-Octet          Xmit-Octet
--------  ------------------- -------------------
  1/1                   748                1256
Last-Time-Cleared
-------------------------
Sun Mar 21 1999, 13:24:01
```

The information that is displayed by the SHOW MAC command is as follows:

- **MAC**   The module and port number in question
- **Rcv-Frms**   The number of frames received
- **Xmit-Frms**   The number of frames transmitted
- **Rcv-Multi**   The number of multicast frames received
- **Xmit-Multi**   The number of multicast frames transmitted
- **Rcv-Broad**   The number of broadcast frames received
- **Xmit-Broad**   The number of broadcast frames transmitted
- **Dely-Exced**   The number of aborted frames due to exceeded deferral
- **MTU-Exced**   The number of frames that exceeded the MTU size
- **In-Discard**   The number of discarded frames because there was no need to forward
- **Lrn-Discard**   The number of content-addressable memory (CAM) entries that have been discarded due to EARL page being full

- **In-Lost** The number of incoming frames lost due to insufficient buffer space

- **Out-Lost** The number of outgoing frames lost due to insufficient buffer space

- **Rcv-Unicast** The number of unicast frames received

- **Rcv-Multicast** The number of multicast frames received

- **Rcv-Broadcast** The number of broadcast frames received

- **Xmit-Unicast** The number of unicast frames sent out

- **Xmit-Multicast** The number of multicast frames sent out

- **Xmit-Broadcast** The number of broadcast frames sent out

- **Rcv-Octet** Total number of octets received

- **Xmit-Octet** Total number of octets transmitted

- **Last-Time-Cleared** The last time the counters were cleared

To troubleshoot, you can send traffic such as a PING from a node connected to a port on the switch. After you verify reception of the PING on the switch, you can use the *show mac* command to verify packet receive and transmit by noting the counters.

SHOW CAM

The SHOW CAM command displays the bridging table in the switch. This table lists all the MAC addresses the switch has learned and their respective ports. The switch forwards frames to ports based upon the CAM table entries. If a destination MAC address for a frame is not found, it is sent to all ports that are in the same VLAN. The switch creates CAM entries dynamically. The administrator can also create CAM statically. The aging time for dynamic entries is 300 seconds by default.

```
Cat5000 (enable) sh cam dynamic
VLAN  Dest MAC/Route Des  Destination Ports or VCs
----  ------------------  ----------------------------------------
5     00-10-e3-20-2d-10   4/1
10    00-80-ff-23-ed-5f   4/2
Total Matching CAM Entries Displayed = 2
```

The information displayed using the SHOW CAM DYNAMIC command is as follows:

- **VLAN**   The VLAN to which the device belongs
- **Dest MAC/Route Des**   The MAC address of the device found
- **Destination Ports or VCs**   The port or virtual circuit to which the device is connected

The SHOW CAM command used in conjunction with a MAC address will display the same information for the device specified by the device's MAC address.

```
Cat5000 (enable) sh cam 00-10-e3-20-2d-10
* = Static Entry. + = Permanent Entry. # = System Entry.
VLAN  Dest MAC/Route Des  Destination Ports or VCs
----  ------------------  ----------------------------------------------
5     00-10-e3-20-2d-10   4/1
Total Matching CAM Entries Displayed = 1
```

The following SHOW commands are also helpful with troubleshooting at the data link layer.

- SHOW VLAN
- SHOW TRUNK
- SHOW VTP DOMAIN
- SHOW SPANTREE

SHOW VLAN

The SHOW VLAN command displays the list of VLANs present on the switch and the switch ports assigned to them. VLANs are identified by assigned numbers 1–1024. While the numbers 1 and 1001–1024 are reserved, 1002–1005 are default VLANs defined for any Token Ring or FDDI modules installed in the switch. VLAN 1 is defined as the management VLAN and is already configured in the switch by default. VLANs 1–1000 can be assigned to the various ports available on the switch, depending on the modules installed in the chassis. Membership of the port to specific VLANs indicates whether the node attached to that port could communicate with other ports. If you are troubleshooting for connectivity issues, this command should be helpful in finding the VLAN membership and thus isolating any issues with VLAN configuration in the switch.

```
Cat5000 (enable) sh vlan
VLAN Name                             Status    Mod/Ports, Vlans
---- -------------------------------- --------- ---------------------------
1    default                          active    1/1-2
                                                2/1-12
                                                3/1-12

1002 fddi-default                     active
1003 token-ring-default               active
1004 fddinet-default                  active
1005 trnet-default                    active


 VLAN Type  SAID     MTU    Parent RingNo BrdgNo Stp  BrdgMode Trans1 Trans2
 ---- ----- -------- -----  ------ ------ ------ ---- -------- ------ ------
 1    enet  100001   1500   -      -      -      -    -        0      0
 1002 fddi  101002   1500   -      0x0    -      -    -        0      0
 1003 trcrf 101003   1500   0      0x0    -      -    -        0      0
 1004 fdnet 101004   1500   -      -      0x0    ieee -        0      0
 1005 trbrf 101005   1500   -      -      0x0    ieee -        0      0


VLAN   AREHops STEHops Backup CRF
----   ------- ------- ----------
1003    7       7       off
```

The information displayed with the SHOW VLAN command is as follows:

- ■ **VLAN**   VLAN number
- ■ **Name**   The name of the VLAN, if this option has been configured
- ■ **Status**   The current state of the VLAN (active or suspend)

- **Mod/Ports, VLANs** The ports assigned to the VLAN

- **Type** The media used for the VLAN

- **SAID** The Security Association ID for the VLAN

- **MTU** The maximum transmission unit size for the VLAN

- **Parent** The parent VLAN, if this has been configured

- **RingNo** Ring number for the VLAN, if ring media is used

- **BrdgNo** Bridge number for the VLAN, if used

- **Stp** Defines which Spanning-Tree Protocol is in use for the VLAN

- **BrdgMode** The bridging mode being used. The choices are SRB and SRT. Default setting is SRB.

- **Trans1** The translation VLAN used to translate FDDI or Token Ring frames to Ethernet

- **Trans2** The second translation VLAN used to translate FDDI or Token Ring frames to Ethernet

- **AREHops** The number of hops for all-routes explorer frames. The default setting is seven. The range of values that can be used is 1–13.

- **STEHops** The number of hops for spanning-tree explorer frames. The default setting is seven. The range of values that can be used is 1–13.

- **Backup TrCRF** Indicates whether the TrCRF is to be used as a backup path for switch traffic

You can use the SHOW VLAN command to view a specific VLAN, as in the following example:

```
Cat5000 (enable) show vlan 12
```

SHOW TRUNK

The output of the SHOW TRUNK command lists the ports that are in trunk mode and are used for inter-switch, high-speed links. It also displays the VLANs that are allowed to pass through these trunks. This command can be helpful in troubleshooting connectivity issues between switches. Of course, there are other factors to consider while troubleshooting inter-switch connections.

```
Cat5000 (enable) sh trunk
Port      Mode          Status
--------  -----------   ------------
 5/1      on            trunking


Port      Vlans allowed on trunk
--------  --------------------------------------------------------
 5/1      1-1005


Port      Vlans allowed and active in management domain
--------  -------------------------------------------------------
 5/1
 Port      Vlans in spanning tree forwarding state and not pruned
--------  -------------------------------------------------------
 5/1
```

The information displayed by the SHOW TRUNK command is as follows:

- **Port**   The port being used for a VLAN trunk
- **Mode**   The current state of the port. The choices are on, off, auto, and desirable
- **Status**   Indicates whether the port is or is not trunking
- **Vlans allowed on trunk**   Indicates which VLANs are able to use the trunk
- **Vlans allowed and active in management domain**   The range of active VLANs in the allowed range
- **Vlans in spanning-tree forwarding state and not pruned**   The VLANs that are on trunk with the spanning-tree forwarding state.

By default the Catalyst switch assigns trunk ports to the RSM and ATM LANE modules, if present in the switch.

SHOW VTP DOMAIN

The SHOW VTP DOMAIN command lists the VTP domain in which the switch resides. By default the Catalyst switch does not reside in any domain. A switch can reside in one and only one VTP domain. The display of the SHOW VTP DOMAIN command shows the VTP domain mode for the switch. This command can be used to troubleshoot the LAN switch environment with the VLANs being spanned across the switches. The most important information in this command is the mode of the switch. The modes for which the switch can be configured are:

- **Client**   The switch will get its VTP information from another switch in the domain
- **Server**   The switch will be the storage device for VTP information for all devices in the domain
- **Transparent**   The administrator will configure VTP information manually on all of the switches in the domain

```
Cat5000 (enable) sh vtp domain
Domain Name                   Domain Index VTP Version Local Mode  Password
----------------------------- ------------ ----------- ----------- ----------
disable                            1            2          server      -

Vlan-count Max-vlan-storage Config Revision Notifications
---------- ---------------- --------------- -------------
6          1023             2               disabled

Last Updater    V2 Mode  Pruning  PruneEligible on Vlans
--------------- -------- -------- ------------------------
192.168.75.1    disabled disabled 2-1000
```

The information that is displayed with the SHOW VTP DOMAIN command is as follows:

- **Domain Name**   Name of the domain (if configured)
- **Domain Index**   The index number for the domain
- **VTP Version**   The version of VTP the switch is running

- **Local Mode**   The VTP mode the switch is running

- **Vlan-count**   The number of VLANs in the domain

- **Max-vlan-storage**   The maximum number of VLANs that can be supported on the switch

- **Config Revision**   The revision number of VTP. This is used to exchange VLAN information between the switches in the domain.

- **Notifications**   Indicates whether SNMP information will be forwarded to SNMP workstations

- **Last Updater**   The IP address of the device that made the last VTP configuration changes

- **V2 Mode**   Indicates if VTP V2 mode is enabled or disabled

- **Pruning**   Indicates whether VTP pruning is enabled

- **PruneEligible on Vlans**   Indicates if VTP pruning is allowed on the domain

SHOW SPANTREE

The SHOW SPANTREE command comes in handy when the switches are interconnected by multiple links and there are possible loops. The spanning-tree algorithm (STA) per VLAN is enabled in Catalyst by default. So whenever the switch encounters a loop, it puts one of the ports in blocked mode to create a loop-free network. By default, the SHOW SPANTREE command displays information from VLAN 1. To display information for other configured VLANs on the switch, the VLAN number must be specified.

```
Cat5000 (enable) sh spantree
VLAN 1
Spanning tree enabled
Spanning tree type          ieee

Designated Root             00-10-42-4e-c0-00
Designated Root Priority    32768
Designated Root Cost        0
Designated Root Port        1/0
Root Max Age    20 sec    Hello Time 2  sec    Forward Delay 15 sec
```

```
Bridge ID MAC ADDR          00-10-42-4e-c0-00
Bridge ID Priority          32768
Bridge Max Age 20 sec     Hello Time 2  sec    Forward Delay 15 sec

Port      Vlan  Port-State      Cost   Priority  Fast-Start  Group-method
--------- ----  -------------   -----  --------  ----------  ------------
  1/1     1     connected         19        32   disabled
  1/2     1     connected         19        32   disabled
  2/1     1     connected         19        32   disabled
  2/2     1     not-connected    100        32   disabled
```

The information displayed by the SHOW SPANTREE command is as follows:

- **VLAN**   Indicates which VLAN's information is being displayed

- **Spanning tree**   Indicates the current status of Spanning Tree

- **Designated Root**   Displays the MAC address of the designated root bridge

- **Designated Root Priority**   The designated root bridge priority

- **Designated Root Cost**   The total path cost to the root bridge

- **Designated Root Port**   The port in which the designated root bridge can be reached

- **Root Max Age**   The length of time a BPDU packet is considered valid

- **Hello Time**   The number of times a root bridge sends out a BPDU

- **Forward Delay**   The length of time the port remains in listening or learning mode

- **Bridge ID MAC ADDR**   The MAC address of the bridge

- **Bridge ID Priority**   The priority of the bridge

- **Bridge Max Age**   The maximum age of the bridge

- **Hello Time**   Indicates how often the bridge sends out BPDU's

- **Forward Delay**   The length of time the bridge remains in listening or learning mode

- **Port**   The port number for ports in the VLAN

- **Vlan** The VLAN to which the port belongs

- **Port-State** The port state of Spanning Tree. Options are disabled, inactive, not connected, blocking, listening, learning, forwarding, and bridging.

- **Cost** Port cost

- **Priority** Port priority

- **Fast-Start** Indicates whether the port is configured to use FastStart

FROM THE CLASSROOM

The Importance of SHOW Commands

When it comes to troubleshooting any switched-based network, many parallels can be drawn to the generic router-based networks. At the physical layer, are the cables properly working and pinned out? Do the various components show Link lights? Are there any activity lights that seem to show packets flying out a particular port? All of these pointers are important to a Networking 101 course. They are common in any network, with any protocol.

However, when you add LAN switches to your network, some of these rules tend to bend a bit. In the old days, if you had physical connectivity, you pretty much had a guarantee that the packets would travel the wires. The friendly green Link light helped to verify basic cable integrity. But that is no longer enough with the advent and implementation of VLANs in the networks.

Since each VLAN is an independent broadcast domain, traffic is logically blocked between different VLANs by the switches. It takes some routing function to connect VLANs together and allow packets to flow between them. For quite some time, routers have been seen as the evil, slow, tough-to-configure boxes in the network. If not properly configured, you get no traffic flow. Switches and bridges forward traffic by default. Thus, folks get comfortable thinking that once you attach to a switch, the packets will get to the destination. VLANs are the unexpected speed bump.

There are a few key commands within the Catalyst 5000 switch line that help a network administrator determine the scope of the applied VLANs within a switched network. The SHOW VLAN command lists all VLANs that any switch is aware of, and then shows the ports that each VLAN is associated with (or not). It is important to note that just because a switch has knowledge of a VLAN does not mean that the VLAN must be used on some port in that switch.

FROM THE CLASSROOM

Disaster has struck many switched networks when remote administrators removed VLANs that they felt did not belong in their switches. The VLAN Trunk Protocol (VTP) ensures that if a VLAN is added or removed from one switch, the behavior is echoed across all switches. In other words, if somebody removes a VLAN that he is not using, but you are, you lose that VLAN. The severe downside of this is that any ports you have that reside in that ex-VLAN are instantly disabled (orange lights).

The SHOW PORT command shows similar information to SHOW VLAN. This time, the ports are listed first, and eventually the VLAN association is shown. If you are not local to the switch to verify port light colors, this command helps to determine the status of any port in the Catalyst switch. This can also help you determine that a port that was once operational is now dead due to the loss of a VLAN.

Ideally, once a network is physically wired, not too many wiring changes occur. If it can be assured that such changes are a thing of the past, yet problems continue to plague a switch-based network, then the VLAN status is probably the root of the problems. The SHOW TRUNK command helps one to see that multiple VLANs are properly crossing the trunk interface. Of course, if a VLAN has been removed, then it would be absent from the trunk.

A final useful command is SHOW CAM DYNAMIC. This lists all known MAC addresses associated with each port of the switch. The tough part about using this particular command is that the administrator must be well versed in all the MAC addresses used throughout the network. Since most administrators do not track this information, it is difficult to verify if a particular user is properly connected. However, this command is very powerful since any MAC address is tracked in every switch that it travels through. The administrator can execute this command on various switches to verify frame flow across an STP-defined path through the network.

STP itself introduces interesting situations. Adding or removing a network device from a switch makes STP determine whether there is a loop there or not. This process can take 30–60 seconds in average-sized networks. Thus, the friendly green Link light means nothing until Spanning Tree releases the port and allows frames to be forwarded. The SHOW SPANTREE <*VLAN*> command allows the administrator to examine the status of STP on each port in the switch per VLAN. Remember that you must add the appropriate VLAN to this command to see ports that are configured in a particular VLAN.

—Neil Lovering, CCIE, CCSI

Network Layer

It should be understood that the switch creates multiple collision domains but uses a single broadcast domain, unless VLANs are configured to create separate broadcast domains. For all inter-VLAN communication, a Layer 3 routing process is required, which the Route Switch Module or an external router can provide.

To troubleshoot the network layer, first Telnet to the switch to get to the CLI. The switch should be assigned an IP address on its sc0 interface. This can be done with the following command from the console connection.

```
Console>(enable) set interface sc0 192.168.1.1 255.255.255.0
```

Once the IP is assigned, you can Telnet to the switch from any IP host that can reach the switch management in-band interface IP address.

```
Router# telnet 192.168.1.1
Trying 192.168.1.1...
Connected to Catalyst.
Escape character is '^]'.

Cisco Systems Console
Enter password:
Catalyst>
```

If you are connecting through a router, check the default gateway setting and subnet mask on both the IP host and Catalyst switch. The default gateway in the switch is used to route the traffic meant for the sc0 interface. SNMP response packets (to communicate with the management station) also use the default gateway. Up to three default gateways can be defined in the switch. The priority can be set with the keyword **primary** as the suffix. Refer to the following example.

```
cat5000 (enable) sh interface
sl0: flags=51<UP,POINTOPOINT,RUNNING>
        slip 0.0.0.0 dest 0.0.0.0
sc0: flags=63<UP,BROADCAST,RUNNING>
    vlan 1 inet 192.168.1.1 netmask 255.255.255.0 broadcast 192.168.1.255
Cat5000 (enable) sh ip route
Fragmentation   Redirect   Unreachable
-------------   --------   -----------
enabled         enabled    enabled

Destination          Gateway                  Flags  Use         Interface
-----------------    ----------------------   ------ ----------   ---------
192.168.1.0          192.168.1.254            U           0       sc0
default              default                  UH          0       sl0
```

The SHOW INTERFACE command will display information for the SLIP and in-band Ethernet interface that are used for LAN and remote access to the switch. This information includes the following:

- **sl0**   The interface name. In this case, the interface is the SLIP interface.

- **flags**   Describes the current state of the interface; with the decoded information also displayed

- **slip**   Shows the IP address of the SLIP interface

- **dest**   Shows the destination IP address of the interface

- **sc0**   The interface name. This section is for the in-band Ethernet interface.

- **vlan**   The VLAN number of which the interface is part. VLAN 1 is the management VLAN.

- **inet**   The IP address of the interface

- **netmask**   The subnet mask for the interface

- **broadcast**   The broadcast address for the interface

The SHOW IP ROUTE command displays information that is contained in the switch's routing table.

- **Fragmentation**   Indicates whether IP fragmentation is enabled
- **Redirect**   Indicates whether ICMP redirect is enabled
- **Unreachable**   Indicates whether ICMP unreachable messages are enabled
- **Destination**   Displays the destination IP addresses currently in the table
- **Gateway**   Displays the next-hop address used to reach the destination
- **Flags**   The flags associated with the entry. Possible flags are:
  U = Up
  G = Gateway
  H = Host
- **Use**   The number of times the route was used to reach the destination
- **Interface**   The interface used to reach the destination

exam
ⓦatch

The sl0 interface is used for the SLIP interface to log in remotely via modem through the console port. The sc0 and sl0 cannot be in the same subnet. If you configure both interfaces in the same subnet, the switch will shutdown one of the interfaces. By default, both the interfaces are assigned the 0.0.0.0 IP address.

As seen in earlier chapters, there are different ways for interconnecting the VLANs. If you are using the RSM module for inter-VLAN communication, then you may need to log into the module to verify the configuration. This can be done from the switch CLI mode itself. The SESSION command connects to the RSM, which in the following example is in the fourth slot of the chassis:

```
Console> (enable) session 4
Trying Router-4...
Connected to Router-4
Enter Password:
Router>
```

The RSM CLI interface is the same IOS that is used on Cisco routers. Once you get into the RSM, the configuration can be checked by SHOW RUNNING-CONFIG or SHOW STARTUP-CONFIG commands. In these situations, the logical VLAN interfaces are created and assigned an IP address from the subnet of the VLAN. Also, you may want to see the routing protocol used if the switch or RSM is connected to any other external router. Make sure that the routing table has entries for all the networks that you want to reach or a default route entry.

Two examples of these commands would be the SHOW IP ROUTE and SHOW IP INTERFACE commands. The SHOW IP ROUTE command displays all of the routes that are contained in the RSM's routing table, and the origin of the routes—whether they are static routes or learned from an IP routing protocol such as RIP or OSPF. The SHOW IP INTERFACE command displays which interfaces are routing IP traffic, and other information such as whether any access lists are active on the interface.

If the inter-VLAN communication is not functional, you may want to verify the configuration of the RSM to see that the VLANs specified have the correct IP address from the VLAN's IP subnet.

Besides these SHOW commands, there are two other important utilities available in the switch that can be used to check the connectivity, especially for IP protocols. These are PING and TRACEROUTE.

PING

This command is a basic tool for troubleshooting connectivity in multiprotocol networks. Unlike Cisco routers, where the PING utility can be used for protocols like IPX and AppleTalk, in the Catalyst switch it is available only for the IP protocol. This command sends the ICMP echo request to the remote host and waits for the echo reply.

```
Cat5000 (enable) ping -s 10.16.1.1 1000 -4
PING 10.16.1.3: 1000 data bytes
1008 bytes from 10.16.1.1: icmp_seq=0. time=6 ms
1008 bytes from 10.16.1.1: icmp_seq=1. time=5 ms
1008 bytes from 10.16.1.1: icmp_seq=2. time=6 ms
1008 bytes from 10.16.1.1: icmp_seq=3. time=6 ms
----10.16.1.1 PING Statistics----
4 packets transmitted, 4 packets received, 0% packet loss
round-trip (ms) min/avg/max = 5/5/6
Console> (enable)
```

If you were pinging to a host on a different subnet, then you would need to define the default gateway or enter a static IP route in the switch. The -s option in the preceding example specifies that response time and success rate information is displayed. The -4 option specifies that four PING packets should be sent to the remote host. If you don't specify any parameters to the PING command except the remote host IP address, it will just state whether the host is reachable or not. It will not provide the PING statistics.

TRACEROUTE

This is a tool used in conjunction with the PING mainly to troubleshoot in an IP routing environment. This tool displays the route taken by the IP packet to reach to the destination, by displaying Layer 3 devices such as routers. TRACEROUTE is used to find the routing point in the network where a problem could occur.

```
Cat5000 (enable) traceroute 192.168.2.100
traceroute to 192.168.2.100 (192.168.2.100), 30 hops max, 40 byte packets
1 10.16.1.1 (10.16.1.1) 1 ms 2 ms 1 ms
2 10.16.1.33 (10.16.1.100) 2 ms 2 ms 2 ms
3 192.168.1.1 (198.168.1.100) 3 ms 4 ms 3 ms
4 192.168.2.100 (10.16.1.100) 4 ms 4 ms 3 ms
```

The information that is displayed with the TRACEROUTE command is as follows:

- **1**   This is the first hop in the path to the destination. Each hop in the path to the destination will have a number from 1 to the destination. When a TRACEROUTE is executed, the default maximum hop number is 30.

- **10.16.1.1**   This is the IP address of the next-hop device

- **(10.16.1.1)**   This is the device name or ID of the device

- **1 ms**   This number (in milliseconds) represents the average length of time the packet took to reach this point in the path

- **2 ms**   This number (in milliseconds) represents the longest length of time the packet took to reach this point in the path

- **1 ms**   This number (in milliseconds) represents the shortest length of time the packet took to reach this point in the path

TRACEROUTE generates UDP packets with the destination IP address, but with TTL starting at 1. Any router that receives the packet decrements the TTL; when it sees that the TTL is 0, it discards the packet generating the ICMP TTL-exceeded message back to originating station. Thus the originating station (the switch, in this case) would come to know about the next hop in the direction of the destination. When the switch again sends a packet with TTL=2, the second-hop router on the path towards the destination will discard it. When there is no response from certain hops, we can infer that the problem lies at that point in the internetwork. No response shows that the router at that location either does not have a route to reach the destination network, or the host is not alive.

CERTIFICATION SUMMARY

This chapter took you through the necessary steps in troubleshooting the Catalyst LAN-based switched network. The main issues covered were the connectivity problems and addressing these issues at the physical and logical level of the network. In addition to the switch-based commands presented in this chapter, there are a number of other tools and techniques that can be used to manage your entire network. Most of the troubleshooting can be done at the switch level using the built-in tools or commands. These are again limited to the physical, data link, and to some extent the network layer. Any troubleshooting at higher levels needs clear understanding of protocols and their handshake sequence, and may require the assistance of sophisticated tools such as protocol analyzers.

The Catalyst switch CLI can be used as a basic diagnostic tool in network troubleshooting. The obvious advantage of using network equipment for troubleshooting (rather than special devices or software) is that the network equipment is already installed at the location where the problem is occurring. The types of troubleshooting that can be done with a LAN switched environment would be at the physical level. (For example: cabling connectivity, verification of the port status, VLAN configurations and port membership, and inter-VLAN communication via router process.)

For the CSLC exam, it is important to understand the various commands and their usage in troubleshooting the network in case of failure. The examples offered in this chapter give you the troubleshooting steps. It is always recommended to have practical experience in real-life situations. A major benefit is to have documentation of the problems for future reference.

At the end of the chapter, we introduced important utilities to verify connectivity in the internetwork. These tools come in handy to troubleshoot at the network layer.

TWO-MINUTE DRILL

❑ The general steps involved in troubleshooting are:
  ❑ Define the problem.
  ❑ Collect the symptoms or necessary data.
  ❑ Track down the problem and isolate the fault.
  ❑ Resolve the problem and document for future reference.

❑ Understanding the behavior of the switch during the normal operation helps in troubleshooting the switch in the event of failure.

❑ Any abnormal behavior in the bootup sequence can indicate faults in various switch subsystems and require troubleshooting.

❑ When troubleshooting the Power Subsystem:
  ❑ Check the LEDs on the supervisor module for symptoms of the problem.
  ❑ Check to see if the PS1 LED is on.
  ❑ Verify the AC source and the power cable.

❑ When troubleshooting the Cooling Subsystem:
  ❑ Check to see if the Fan LED on the supervisor engine module is green.
  ❑ If the Fan LED is red, the fan assembly might not be seated properly in the chassis.
  ❑ If the Fan LED is still red, the system has probably detected a fan assembly failure.

- ❏ When troubleshooting the Processor and Interface Subsystem:
    - ❏ Check the supervisor engine module Status LED.
    - ❏ Check the LEDs on individual interface modules.
    - ❏ Check all cabling and connections.
- ❏ Performing a SHOW VERSION command would give you more information on the hardware and software details of the switch.
- ❏ Although the LAN switch is a data link layer device, troubleshooting at the network layer is required if the switch is hosting the Route Switch Module (RSM).
- ❏ The physical layer is the most basic level at which to start the network troubleshooting process.
- ❏ The basic diagnostic tool that is available to troubleshoot cable-level problems is the LED indications on the switch modules.
- ❏ The SHOW MODULE command displays a summary of all the modules present in the Catalyst switch and their status.
- ❏ The SHOW PORT command shows detailed status of the port in question. It shows the port speed, half or full duplex, VLAN membership, and collisions or errors.
- ❏ SHOW PORT SECURITY displays the security assigned to the port in question. This command is used to determine whether the port needs to be disabled due to eavesdropping.
- ❏ The SHOW MAC command displays the total number of frames transmitted and received by the individual ports, along with the types of frames, such as broadcast or multicasts.
- ❏ The SHOW CAM command displays the bridging table in the switch. This table lists all the MAC addresses the switch has learned and their respective ports.
- ❏ The SHOW VLAN command displays the list of VLANs present on the switch and the switch ports assigned to them.
- ❏ The output of the SHOW TRUNK command lists the ports that are in trunk mode and are used for inter-switch, high-speed links.
- ❏ The SHOW VTP DOMAIN command lists the VTP domain in which the switch resides.

❑ The SHOW SPANTREE command comes in handy when the switches are interconnected by multiple links and there are possible loops.

❑ It should be understood that the switch creates multiple collision domains but uses a single broadcast domain, unless VLANs are configured to create separate broadcast domains.

❑ The SHOW INTERFACE command will display information for the SLIP and in-band Ethernet interface that are used for LAN and remote access to the switch.

❑ The SHOW IP ROUTE command displays information that is contained in the switch's routing table.

❑ The sl0 interface is used for the SLIP interface to log in remotely via modem through the console port. The sc0 and sl0 cannot be in the same subnet. If you configure both interfaces in the same subnet, the switch will shutdown one of the interfaces. By default, both the interfaces are assigned the 0.0.0.0 IP address.

❑ The PING command is a basic tool for troubleshooting connectivity in multiprotocol networks.

❑ TRACEROUTE is used to find the routing point in the network where a problem could occur.

SELF TEST

The following Self Test questions will help you measure your understanding of the material presented in this chapter. Read all the choices carefully, as there may be more than one correct answer. Choose all correct answers for each question.

1. How can different VLANs be interconnected?

   A. Using RSM

   B. Using an external router

   C. Using Supervisor III module with NetFlow cards

   D. All of the above

2. What command displays information on the SLIP and in-band Ethernet ports for the Catalyst 5000 series switch?

   A. SHOW HARDWARE

   B. SHOW MODULE

   C. SHOW INTERFACE

   D. None of the above

3. What command is used to display routing information?

   A. DISPLAY ROUTES

   B. SHOW IP ROUTE

   C. SHOW ROUTE TABLE

   D. DISPLAY IP ROUTE

4. How is the Route Switch Module accessed?

   A. From the console port

   B. From the Catalyst port

   C. Telnet from the Catalyst

   D. From the Catalyst CLI

5. What needs to be checked when a power supply LED is not lit when it is powered on?

   A. Check the supervisor module to verify that it is plugged in

   B. Verify that the power cord is plugged in to a power source

   C. Verify that the chassis is grounded

   D. Verify that the power supply is seated into the chassis

6. With respect to wiring, what does NEXT means?

   A. The next patch panel

   B. The next bridge hop

   C. The next router hop

   D. Near-end crosstalk

7. The cooling fan LED is red. Which of the following is the correct step for checking the fan assembly?

   A. Verify that the assembly is seated into the chassis

   B. Turn the cooling fans on

   C. Plug in the power cord for the assembly

   D. None of the above

8. What command is used to verify that there are no hardware incompatibilities?

   A. SHOW SWITCH

   B. DISPLAY SWITCH HARDWARE

   C. SHOW VERSION

   D. DISPLAY VERSION

9. What command will display the status of a particular module installed in the chassis?

   A. SHOW TEST

   B. DISPLAY TEST

   C. SHOW MODULE

   D. SHOW ALL MODULES

10. What type of test is used to determine cable length or the distance to cable breaks?

    A. PING

    B. TDR

    C. NEXT

    D. Attenuation

11. Which command will give detailed information on the ports for an installed module?

    A. SHOW PORT

    B. SHOW PORT MODULE

    C. SHOW PORT STATUS

    D. SHOW STATUS PORT

12. What information does the SHOW VLAN command display?

    A. VLAN routing information

    B. Ports set to No Negotiate

    C. VLAN MAC information

    D. VLAN information

13. Which command can be used to see what VLANs are passed across the trunk port?

    A. SHOW VLAN

    B. SHOW PORT TRUNK

    C. SHOW TRUNK

    D. SHOW PORT *trunking-port*

14. You are not able to Telnet to the switch from your workstation even if the link is good and both IP hosts are in the same subnet. What could be the reason?

    A. Your port and the sc0 port could be in different, nonconnected VLANs

    B. The switch may be configured to filter traffic on the TCP port number

    C. Your machine may be listed in the IP filter list

    D. You may not have defined the default gateway for the switch

15. Which tool built into the switch will you use to check the connectivity at IP protocol level?

    A. SHOW PORT

    B. PING

    C. TRACE

    D. SHOW VLAN

16. What command is useful in determining if there are loops in a switched network?

    A. SHOW LOOPS

    B. SHOW SWITCH

    C. SHOW TREE

    D. SHOW SPANTREE

17. The port link Status LED is orange. What does that indicate?

    A. Port disabled

    B. Port blocked by STP

    C. Port in trunk mode

    D. Port shutdown by security violation

18. What type of trunking encapsulation is allowed on the Fast Ethernet and Gigabit Ethernet ports?

    A. ISL

    B. 802.3

    C. 802.10

    D. 802.1q

19. How can you see the MAC address learned by the ports in the switch?

    A. SHOW MODULE

    B. SHOW BRIDGE TABLE

    C. SHOW CAM

    D. SHOW MAC

20. With what software does the RSM operate?

    A. CLI

    B. DOS

    C. IOS

    D. None of the above

21. What will the switch do with the frame destined for MAC addresses not available in the bridging table?

    A. The frame is discarded

    B. The frame is forwarded on all ports

    C. The frame is forwarded on all ports within the same VLAN

    D. None of the above

10

Catalyst 5000 Series Switch FDDI Module

Typical Catalyst switched environments use Ethernet, Fast Ethernet, and now Gigabit Ethernet. Some environments also deploy ATM with LAN Emulation to achieve greater distances in their campus environment.

But what if we have to integrate our Catalyst equipment with an existing building or campus backbone—one that has been in place for several years? Chances are that backbone is a Fiber Distributed Data Interface (FDDI) ring. The Catalyst 5000 FDDI card provides connectivity to that FDDI backbone for clients on other networks attached to the switch.

The Catalyst equipment can also take advantage of the existing FDDI infrastructure as a trunking medium. Cisco uses a frame format compatible with the IEEE 802.10 Secure FDDI Frame format to provide a frame tagging mechanism. Since it is a shared-media environment, many switches can participate in the same trunk link. Cisco routers with FDDI interfaces can route between VLANs for the switches.

This chapter describes and explores the uses of the Catalyst FDDI card. You will be able to implement and troubleshoot the FDDI card in both trunked and nontrunked environments.

CERTIFICATION OBJECTIVE 10.01

FDDI/CDDI Review

The ANSI X3T9.5 committee created the FDDI standard in the mid-1980s to address high-speed, longer distance networking needs. FDDI is a 100-Mbps shared-media networking standard, using a token passing scheme over fiber-optic cable. Using fiber optics allows for much greater distance with immunity from interference problems associated with copper cables. The fiber-optic cabling comes in two varieties, single-mode and multimode. Single-mode fiber uses a single strand of 8–10 micron glass. Multimode fiber uses a much thicker diameter strand of glass (50–150 microns), and is sometimes even made using plastic instead of glass. Plastic multimode fiber is the cheapest to install and use, but it has distance limitations of less than two kilometers without repeaters.

FDDI equipment is linked together in a physical ring topology. Data is transferred from upstream neighbor to downstream neighbor, with stations releasing data onto the ring when they can claim the token. FDDI operates much like Token Ring, with key differences being speed (100 Mbps vs. 16 or 4 Mbps) and physical ring topology (FDDI) instead of logical ring topology (Token Ring).

Since this networking standard potentially involves miles of cabling, replacement of cut or damaged cabling or equipment can be a time-consuming event. To ensure that the ring is still operational even if there is a physical failure, FDDI actually uses a dual ring structure. During normal operation, data is sent on the primary ring only. If there is a failure, the FDDI adapters beacon, signaling a ring problem. The beaconing process helps find the operational FDDI devices at each end of the problem. Those devices will be responsible for *wrapping* data onto the secondary ring to bypass the problem. This beaconing and wrapping phase is fast enough for most end stations not to notice a loss of connectivity.

FDDI adapters with connections to both the primary and secondary rings are called Class A stations. A more popular term for this is a dual attachment station (DAS). If you look at an FDDI adapter and it has cabling attached to both the A port and the B port, then the adapter is a DAS. Adapters that do not need to participate in the redundancy, just to send and receive data, are attached to the primary ring only. They are called Class B stations. The more popular term for this is single attachment station (SAS). You can tell a SAS because it only has a connector plugged into the A port or the B port, but not both.

With its high speed and high availability, FDDI became a popular LAN technology in places with high bandwidth demands for their workstations. The problem was that FDDI adapters were very expensive, as was laying fiber-optic cable to each desktop. This put FDDI technology out of the reach of most people. To lower the cost per workstation, a variation on the FDDI standard emerged that used Category 5 copper twisted-pair cabling instead of fiber optics. This standard is called Copper Distributed Data Interface (CDDI). Less expensive desktop adapters could be purchased and cabled with less expensive copper cabling. The functionality of CDDI is identical to FDDI—still 100 Mbps, token-passing, shared-media technology. The sacrifice is distance. The copper cabling severely limits the width of the CDDI ring. An additional sacrifice is that interference is more prevalent.

Typical environments had CDDI Class B adapters attached to a concentrator. The concentrator was attached to an FDDI ring with a Class A adapter. This way, the bulk of the stations could get 100 Mbps throughput without having to have multiple copper drops or fiber drops. The concentrators are basically FDDI-to-CDDI hubs. Since they are few in number, it is okay to dual-attach them with fiber.

CERTIFICATION OBJECTIVE 10.02

Catalyst 5000 FDDI/CDDI Features

The Catalyst 5000 FDDI card is a high-speed translating bridge. Frames seen on the FDDI interface are translated into Ethernet and forwarded onto the switching bus. The biggest difference in the cards is the connector type. The FDDI card comes in single-mode and multimode fiber versions. There is also a Category 5 twisted-pair card, the CDDI model. Since the CDDI card is identical to the FDDI card except for the kind of cabling used, the rest of the chapter will refer to the Catalyst 5000 card as the FDDI card. Each of the cards has two ports, an A port and a B port. If the card is participating fully in the FDDI ring as a DAS, the A port connects the card to the upstream neighbor and the B port connects the card to the downstream neighbor. If the card is being used as a SAS, either the A port or the B port can be used to attach the card to an FDDI (or CDDI) concentrator.

APaRT Overview

To translate FDDI frames to the proper Ethernet frame type, the card possesses its own MAC address table and keeps track of frame formatting parameters for each host it has seen. This process is done with logic called

Automated Packet Recognition/Translation (APaRT). This logic is described in more detail in a later section of this chapter.

IP Features

If the frames being translated contain IP messages, the card can perform extra functions to ensure delivery of traffic. If the FDDI server sends frames larger than 1500 bytes to an Ethernet host, the FDDI card fragments the packet. MTU discovery is also used to find the largest packet size available for FDDI and Ethernet sides of the bridge.

Spanning Tree Support

The FDDI card supports 802.1d Spanning Tree, allowing you to use a FDDI ring as a redundant backbone for your core switches. Since the card can function as a trunking interface, it also supports the VLAN Trunking Protocol (VTP). If trunking is enabled on the FDDI card, each VLAN uses a separate copy of Spanning Tree.

Trunking Support Overview

If the FDDI card is trunking, the frames leaving the FDDI interface are tagged with VLAN information. This process is very similar to the process used by Ethernet ports that are trunking. Remember from previous chapters that tagged frames are not translated. They are merely wrapped in a header and shipped to other Catalyst switches. In the Ethernet environment, it does not matter that the frames are illegal, as long as both ends of the full-duplex link understand what is happening.

However, since FDDI is a shared environment, you cannot create radically different (or illegal) frames on the FDDI ring without causing problems for the legacy devices. Cisco handles this by using the IEEE 802.10 frame type to carry tagged frames. Traditional FDDI interfaces using the ANSI frame format see these frames as valid frames for some other device and pass them along. Catalyst switches on the FDDI ring see these frames for what they contain, tagged Ethernet frames. A more detailed discussion is presented later in this chapter.

exam
ⓦatch

IEEE 802.10 was originally created to provide a method of securing FDDI data in a metropolitan-area network environment. The IEEE frame format is compatible with ANSI FDDI devices; it just contains a secured data carrier that they can not decode. Cisco uses the capabilities of the IEEE 802.10 frame to provide trunking service and make it transparent to ANSI FDDI devices.

CERTIFICATION OBJECTIVE 10.03

APaRT

Novell devices communicating through Ethernet media use one of four possible frame types in their transmission. These types are Ethernet version 2, IEEE 802.3 with IEEE 802.2 Logical Link Control, IEEE 802.3/802.2 with SNAP header extensions, and Novell's interpretation of IEEE 802.3. The Novell client software configuration determines the frame type to use. Other link layer transmission media do not exhibit the diversity of Ethernet. FDDI, our media of concern, only has two possible frame types available for data transmission. These types are ANSI X3T9.5 and ANSI X3T9.5 with IEEE SNAP header extensions. The Novell client software still picks one of the two frame types to use. As long as all the clients on the FDDI ring agree on which frame type to use per network layer stack, everyone can communicate with each other.

Our problem occurs when you try to send a data stream from a Novell device on an Ethernet segment to a Novell device on a FDDI segment, and vice versa. How do you make sure that the FDDI frames get converted into the expected Ethernet frame type? How do we make sure that the Ethernet data gets converted into the expected FDDI frame type?

What if you just watch all of the frames on the FDDI segment and the frames on the Ethernet segment, writing down what frame type(s) each device is using? The Catalyst FDDI card keeps track of all this information in a cache on the card itself. Whenever data must be translated from Ethernet to FDDI or vice versa, the cache information can be used to make sure that the proper frame type is used.

APaRT, Automated Packet Recognition and Translation, performs just that function. This logic updates information in the content-addressable memory (CAM) on the FDDI card and handles making sure the proper frame type is picked during translation. If your network is completely TCP/IP-based, APaRT is not really necessary, since TCP/IP chooses one particular frame type on Ethernet segments and one particular frame type on FDDI segments. In a Novell network, however, the frame type is user-selectable in both Ethernet and FDDI environments. In this environment, without APaRT you must make sure all Ethernet-based Novell clients are using the same frame type. The same applies to the FDDI segment. With APaRT, this is not necessary; APaRT will keep track of which client is doing what.

on the job

Several years ago, I had a LAN support assignment that involved moving from a hub-based environment to a switched Ethernet environment. Several hundred workstations needed access to their local Novell servers and two campus-wide servers. The original idea was that the workstations would be on switched Ethernet ports along with their workgroup servers. This was before the days of VLANs, so the workgroup servers were on the same switch as the workstations, just using multiple Ethernet adapters to get extra bandwidth. The Enterprise servers were going to be placed on a FDDI ring, to get the 100 Mbps bandwidth they needed. However, the switches only supported one Ethernet and one FDDI frame format for their translation technology. This would mean that several hundred workstations in a half dozen buildings would need to be changed. We ended up using router technology instead for the servers, just because changing things was not feasible with our short timeframe. If we had APaRT then, the routers (and the FDDI interface for them) would not have been necessary to accomplish our goal.

FDDICHECK

Think about the following scenario: an Ethernet PC needs to talk to a file server on the FDDI segment. The PC sends out an Ethernet frame addressed to the fileserver's MAC address, starting the conversation. The Catalyst FDDI card translates the frame into an ANSI FDDI frame and forwards it onto the ring the next time it has the token. When the frame has traveled around the ring and comes back to the Catalyst, the FDDI card strips off the finished frame and awaits the next time it receives the token. Sounds just like Token Ring? It's very similar to the operation of Token Ring. There is one difference, though. In FDDI, the sender puts a special frame on the ring immediately following the data frame. This is called a *void* frame. Once the Catalyst has sent the frame and the void, it strips incoming data off the ring until it sees the void frame. At that point, the source adapter knows that it is finished stripping data and can start listening again for data from other adapters.

As long as all the adapters follow FDDI specifications, this works great. Token, then data, then void. You can send data when you have the token. If you have the token and have sent data, you remove your data from the ring and let the next adapter in line use the ring.

Suppose we have an adapter that is not compliant with the FDDI specifications. Suppose the adapter releases void frames onto the ring when it does not have the token? If we had a ring composed of just FDDI devices, it would not be a big deal. Once the device sees that the current data on the ring is from its own source address, it can try to restart everything and clean up. But in this case, it is more complicated. The original source of the message was an Ethernet PC. The catalyst is just translating and forwarding a message from that Ethernet device. The Catalyst will not realize that the Ethernet source is data that it generated on behalf of the PC. By default, it will assume that the data was generated by some FDDI device and keep propagating it. Since nobody on the ring has that source MAC address, nobody cleans up the ring.

Cisco has a feature that allows the FDDI card to keep track of which frames it has forwarded from Ethernet sources. In that case, when it sees that bad frame, the card realizes that it is the source and cleans up the ring properly. This feature is called FDDICHECK. However, it is rarely needed, since almost all adapters are FDDI specifications-compliant, so the feature is turned off by default. Turn it on only if you need it. If you decide to turn on FDDICHECK, make sure that APaRT is enabled.

FDDI VLANs and 802.10

The hardest part about working with the FDDI card is understanding when the card uses ANSI frames and when the card uses IEEE frames. In a trunked environment, it will use both. So we need to spend a little time talking about the differences in the frames and when they are used in order to configure and troubleshoot the card.

Here is a mind blower: the FDDI card belongs to an Ethernet VLAN, not an FDDI VLAN. Huh? Take a look at a Catalyst fresh out of the carton: the FDDI module belongs to VLAN 1—the default VLAN—an Ethernet VLAN. What this actually means is that the FDDI card treats the FDDI ring as part of one of the Ethernet VLANs. It translates Ethernet frames from that VLAN into ANSI FDDI frames. When FDDI frames need to be forwarded to Ethernet (broadcasts, for instance) they are forwarded as part of whichever Ethernet VLAN the FDDI card belongs to. If you want a group of Ethernet PCs in VLAN 342 to talk with their server on the FDDI ring, for instance, you make the FDDI ports part of VLAN 342. The bigger implication here is that servers and other devices on the FDDI ring have to belong to the same IP subnet or IPX network as one of the groups of Ethernet PCs.

What if we do not have any servers on the FDDI ring and we just want to use it as a carrier medium for trunking purposes? In that case, we need to tell the Catalyst to create IEEE 802.10 frames for the data, not ANSI frames. When the Catalyst uses 802.10 frames, it does not translate the Ethernet data. Instead, it wraps the entire Ethernet frame with an IEEE 802.10 header and trailer, inserts VLAN information into the frame in the field normally used for encryption type data, then ships the data across the ring.

Other Catalysts that are also trunking see the 802.10 frame, realize that this is trunked data, and unwrap the Ethernet frame for shipment across the switching bus, looking at the VLAN information tagged in the frame to pick the proper Ethernet VLAN of the frame. You should realize from previous chapters that this sounds like the operation of ISL. It is the same procedure, but it is on a different medium, so you need a different frame format.

Look at the IEEE 802.10 frame as employed by the Catalyst switch, shown in Figure 10-1. The destination MAC address is a multicast address recognized by other trunking Catalyst switches. The source MAC address is the address of the source FDDI card. Then, in the Clear Header part, the magic happens. The 802.10 LSAP field is used to say, "This is a Cisco Tagged Frame." The next field, the Security Association Identifier (SAID) identifies to which VLAN the wrapped frame belongs. The Catalyst receiving this tagged frame can look up the SAID value in the VLAN list (each VLAN created has a SAID value associated with it) and pass the frame along properly.

Luckily, you do not really have to worry about SAID values or how to implement them to make all this work. Whenever you create a VLAN, a default SAID value is automatically assigned to the VLAN. This value is given in a formula: SAID=100,000+VLAN index number. If you create VLAN 10, for instance, the SAID value assigned to that VLAN is 100010.

When you create VLANs, you have the option to implement your own SAID values if you do not want to use Cisco's defaults. However, usually there is no reason to stray from the default values unless you happen to have true IEEE 802.10-compliant FDDI devices on your FDDI ring. If you did have real 802.10 devices on the ring, you may need to change SAID values to prevent conflicts with those devices. Since there are very few devices that actually implement IEEE 802.10, that is normally not a problem. If you do decide to change SAID values when creating VLANs, just remember that you must have a unique SAID value assigned to each VLAN you create.

Cisco interpretation of the IEEE 802.10 frame format

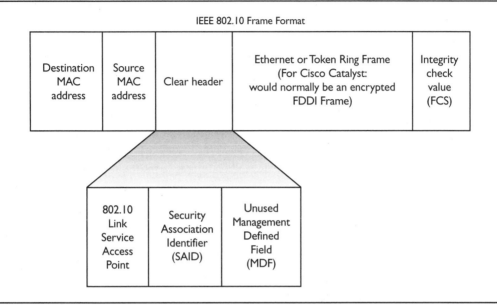

IEEE 802.10 Frame Format

| Destination MAC address | Source MAC address | Clear header | Ethernet or Token Ring Frame (For Cisco Catalyst: would normally be an encrypted FDDI Frame) | Integrity check value (FCS) |

| 802.10 Link Service Access Point | Security Association Identifier (SAID) | Unused Management Defined Field (MDF) |

Given all this, you might be thinking: OK, if trunking is on, the source Catalyst takes the Ethernet data, looks up the SAID of that Ethernet VLAN, builds the 802.10 frame, and ships it on the ring. Then the destination Catalyst grabs the 802.10 frame, looks up the SAID to figure out which Ethernet VLAN it belongs to, and then ships the Ethernet frame across the backplane. Indeed, that is almost the full procedure. To make things a little more interesting, the Catalysts do not use the SAID value of the Ethernet VLAN. For each of the VLANs trunked across the FDDI ring, you create a VLAN of type FDDI to act as a carrier. It is the SAID of this FDDI VLAN that is used in the 802.10 frame as the data crosses the ring. On each switch, you build a mapping of which FDDI VLAN goes with which Ethernet VLAN.

When you create VLANs of type FDDI, you are creating IEEE 802.10 carriers. These carriers are mapped on a one-to-one basis with whichever source VLANs should be in the payload section of the frame. Any Ethernet or Token Ring VLAN that has a corresponding FDDI VLAN mapped to it is trunked across the ring. Any other Ethernet or Token Ring VLAN is not trunked across the ring. As with most rules, there is one exception.

Remember that the FDDI card actually belongs to an Ethernet VLAN. As long as all Catalysts on the FDDI ring have their FDDI ports belonging to the same VLAN (and they should), that VLAN does not really have to be trunked. The Catalyst FDDI cards will translate Ethernet to ANSI FDDI for that particular VLAN. When the other Catalysts see the ANSI FDDI frames, they will translate them back to Ethernet and pass them to the switching bus. Thus, as stated at the beginning of this section, the FDDI card actually uses both ANSI FDDI frames and 802.10 frames. It uses ANSI for one VLAN and 802.10 for every other VLAN that is mapped into a FDDI VLAN.

CERTIFICATION OBJECTIVE 10.06

Mapping Ethernet and FDDI VLANs Together

If you want to do trunking in the FDDI environment, you must create a FDDI VLAN for each Ethernet or Token Ring VLAN to be carried. The SET VLAN command is used to create these FDDI VLANs. Suppose, for instance, that a campus contained VLANs 50–55 (50, 51, 52, 53, 54, 55). You might want to trunk those six VLANs across the FDDI ring. The first thing you would have to do is create IEEE 802.10 carriers for each of the Ethernet VLANs, so you would use the following commands from privileged mode on the switch:

```
set vlan 650 name FDDI_FOR_50 type fddi
set vlan 651 name FDDI_FOR_51 type fddi
set vlan 652 name FDDI_FOR_52 type fddi
set vlan 653 name FDDI_FOR_53 type fddi
set vlan 654 name FDDI_FOR_54 type fddi
set vlan 655 name FDDI_FOR_55 type fddi
```

This is the same SET VLAN command that has been previously used to create Ethernet VLANs. The only difference is that you add the TYPE

FDDI parameter at that end. The Catalyst creates the default SAID value for each of these VLANs, using the formula mentioned earlier.

Now that the FDDI VLANs are created, you have to tell the Catalyst which Ethernet VLAN maps to which FDDI VLAN. In the creation commands, you happened to pick a numbering scheme and naming convention that would make it easy for you to figure out what is going on. The Catalyst cannot make assumptions about what you have done and must be explicitly told, so you should use the following commands to tell the Catalyst what is going on:

```
set vlan 50 translation 650
set vlan 51 translation 651
set vlan 52 translation 652
set vlan 53 translation 653
set vlan 54 translation 654
set vlan 55 translation 655
```

The TRANSLATION version of the SET VLAN command creates a mapping from the Ethernet VLAN (the first number in each command) to the FDDI VLAN (the second number in each command). You could have just as easily used these commands:

```
set vlan 650 translation 50
set vlan 651 translation 51
set vlan 652 translation 52
set vlan 653 translation 53
set vlan 654 translation 54
set vlan 655 translation 55
```

The idea is that it does not matter whether you specify Ethernet or FDDI numbers first, as long as you do one of these commands for each mapping you want to create. Now when you turn on trunking with the SET TRUNK command, the FDDI card uses IEEE 802.10 frames for VLANs 50–55.

exam
⊕atch

Remember that the TRANSLATION command must go from either Ethernet or Token Ring frame types to FDDI, and vice versa. Be on the lookout for questions that try to translate Ethernet VLANs to Ethernet VLANs or Token Ring to Token Ring. There should be a FDDI VLAN on one side of the TRANSLATION parameter and either a Token Ring or Ethernet VLAN on the other.

FROM THE CLASSROOM

Old Meets New

Although FDDI may not be the backbone or server farm of choice today, there are countless networks that have huge FDDI installations. "If it's not broke, don't fix it" comes into play here. Why replace FDDI with some newer technology if the existing technology works fine?

Since FDDI will probably stick around for a while, and switches have arrived with force over the last few years, the two will meet in a dark wiring closet somewhere. To make this meeting a friendly one, Cisco has developed a trunking mechanism for the Catalyst switches to move as many Ethernet VLANs as necessary across the FDDI backbone. This backbone may be within a building or across an entire campus.

The FDDI module in the Catalyst 5000 can translate Ethernet frames to FDDI frames to access the FDDI network. However, if the packets only need to get across the FDDI ring to get to another Ethernet, why bother translating the packet twice (once from Ethernet into FDDI, and a second time to get it back into Ethernet)? To save CPU cycles and increase overall throughput, FDDI trunking simply wraps the Ethernet frame into a unique FDDI frame to travel across the FDDI backbone.

There is one catch, however. You can only map one Ethernet VLAN to a FDDI network (to the FDDI port). If there are multiple Ethernet VLANs that need to traverse the FDDI, they are not allowed to leap onto the FDDI ring as Ethernet VLANs. Only FDDI VLANs can cross FDDI networks, which makes sense. But an Ethernet VLAN and an FDDI VLAN cannot share the same VLAN number. Thus, the broadcast domain that is represented by that VLAN is not extended across the FDDI.

The solution is mapping the Ethernet VLANs into FDDI VLANs. There is a one-to-one ratio here. If you had 10 Ethernet VLANs, you would need 10 FDDI VLANs to trunk all across the FDDI backbone. The SET VLAN ... TRANSLATION ... command accomplishes this. Just realize that this command does not translate anything; it wraps one VLAN type into another.

The FDDI card translates Ethernet to FDDI by default. The TRANSLATION command carries the Ethernet packets across inside an FDDI frame. With this understanding, FDDI trunks become simple.

—*Neil Lovering, CCIE, CCSI*

Configuring the FDDI/CDDI Module

In the default configuration, the FDDI card is configured with the port in VLAN default (VLAN 1), no names associated with the A and B ports (A=port 1 and B=port 2), APaRT enabled, and FDDICHECK disabled. IP fragmentation and MTU discovery support are also enabled by default. Trunking is off for the card and the ports are half duplex, normal priority.

Naming FDDI Ports

Probably the first things you want to set up are names for the ports. Usually, you might give the A port a name that will help you identify who the upstream neighbor is, and the B port a name that identifies the downstream neighbor. This way, if there is a problem and the card goes into a wrap state, you know where to look for cable or adapter problems. To set the name for you FDDI ports:

```
set port name 3/1  LINK_FROM_5thFloor_Closet
set port name 3/2 LINK_TO_Resource_Building
```

As you can see, the SET PORT NAME command is used to create descriptions for each port. This example assumes the FDDI card is in slot 3 of the switch. Port 1 is the A port and Port 2 is the B port.

Turning Off APaRT

There are not many other configuration options that need to be set in a normal environment, except for creating a trunking environment or changing the VLAN that is translated. If you want to get a little more horsepower out of the translations, and you have an all-IP environment (no IPX), you can turn off the APaRT feature. This enables the FDDI card to translate frames a little bit faster. If you have IPX, don't disable APaRT!

Should you decide to live dangerously and turn it off, use the following command:

```
set bridge apart disable
```

Turning On FDDICHECK

Should you decide that FDDICHECK is valuable to you, you can enable it with the following command:

```
set bridge fddicheck enable
```

You probably won't ever have to do this, but if you detect problems with the same frame from an Ethernet source continuously on the ring (using a sniffer, perhaps), you can turn on FDDICHECK to clean them up.

CERTIFICATION OBJECTIVE 10.08

Multiswitch VLAN without Trunking

Once the FDDI card is physically connected and running, you have to decide to which Ethernet VLAN should it belong? If there are no FDDI servers or workstations involved, just Catalyst switches, then you are trying to use the FDDI ring as a trunk medium. If that is the case, then simply leave the FDDI card as part of VLAN 1.

If there are FDDI servers and workstations on the ring, but your Ethernet hosts do not need to access them, you still do not need to worry. Just treat the FDDI ring as if those hosts do not exist. In this case, too, you leave the FDDI card as part of VLAN 1. Keep in mind that those FDDI hosts are isolated from the rest of your campus if the Catalysts are the only path on and off the ring.

If you need Ethernet-to-FDDI connectivity, you have to plan a little bit more. You need to make sure that the FDDI card can translate Ethernet to FDDI for you. This means you need to figure out which Ethernet hosts need to talk to the FDDI servers. If those hosts are spread out among several Ethernet VLANs, we need to figure out which VLAN needs those hosts the most—or which one has the most Ethernet PCs involved. The other VLANs are going to have to route to this Ethernet VLAN first and then get translated onto the FDDI ring. Once you figure out which Ethernet VLAN should be used, then you use the SET VLAN command to make the FDDI card part of that Ethernet VLAN. For instance, if the FDDI card in slot 3 of your switch needs to be part of Ethernet VLAN 342, use the command SET VLAN 342 3/1.

There is one other thing to consider when doing this. Remember that now the FDDI ring is going to be an extension of one of the Ethernet VLANs (342 in the our example). So that means, from an IP perspective, that the FDDI ring should be part of the same subnet as the Ethernet VLAN. In this example, all of the FDDI servers should be a part of whatever subnet VLAN 342 represents. When implementing this, think about which is easier: changing those FDDI server addresses (few in number but have been around for a long time) or changing the workstation addresses (not implemented yet, if you are lucky). There has to be a match.

What if the FDDI ring represents a totally different subnet and you cannot change the IP addressing information on servers or workstations? Then create a new Ethernet VLAN that is used to represent the FDDI ring. Make sure that the FDDI ports are part of that new VLAN and a router port is also part of that VLAN. Yes, it means that we route from the PCs to those servers on the FDDI ring.

CERTIFICATION OBJECTIVE 10.09

Configuring FDDI VLANs

This section concentrates on the steps necessary to get IEEE 802.10 configured and working. Most of the necessary information has already been presented, but this section will break the process out step by step.

1. Turn on trunking.

2. Create FDDI VLANs.

3. Map Ethernet VLANs to FDDI VLANs.

Turning On Trunking

Turn on trunking on the FDDI ports on all of the Catalysts attached to the
FDDI ring. This ensures that VTP information can flow from Catalyst to
Catalyst. If you turn on trunking first, then as you do the next steps on one
switch, the information will propagate across the ring to all the other
switches. Assuming the FDDI card is in slot 3, use the following command
to turn on trunking:

```
set trunk 3/1 on
```

Remember to repeat this on all the Catalysts on the FDDI ring. In using
the trunking command on an FDDI port, you will notice one major
difference from the Ethernet ports used in previous chapters. That is that
trunking in a FDDI environment is either on or off. With Ethernet trunking,
there are four possible states for trunking status: on, off, auto, and desirable.
This means that trunking is not negotiated in a FDDI environment; you
must turn it on physically on every switch that participates. That's why you
have to remember to repeat the trunking command on all Catalysts on the
FDDI ring.

Creating FDDI VLANs

On one of the Catalysts, create an FDDI VLAN for each Ethernet and
Token Ring VLAN you wish to trunk. If you have 50 Ethernet VLANs
and you want to trunk them all across the FDDI ring, you need to create
50 FDDI VLANs as part of this step. Aren't you glad that you turned on
trunking in the preceding step, so you do not have to do this on all 30
switches attached to the ring? The one exception to this step is VLAN 1
(default). There is already a FDDI VLAN (VLAN 1001) created for VLAN 1,
so you do not have to create one.

As we did earlier in the chapter, let's say we have six Ethernet VLANs
(50–55) to trunk. We use the following commands:

```
set vlan 650 name FDDI_FOR_50 type fddi
set vlan 651 name FDDI_FOR_51 type fddi
set vlan 652 name FDDI_FOR_52 type fddi
set vlan 653 name FDDI_FOR_53 type fddi
set vlan 654 name FDDI_FOR_54 type fddi
set vlan 655 name FDDI_FOR_55 type fddi
```

As you create each of these VLANs, VTP propagates the information to the other switches on the ring.

Mapping Ethernet VLANs to FDDI VLANs

On one of the Catalysts—let's say the one from which you just created the FDDI VLANs—do the Ethernet-to-FDDI mapping statements. This lets the Catalysts know which IEEE 802.10 carriers go with which Ethernet VLAN. Using the same example as in the preceding step:

```
set vlan 50 translation 650
set vlan 51 translation 651
set vlan 52 translation 652
set vlan 53 translation 653
set vlan 54 translation 654
set vlan 55 translation 655
```

As you perform each of these set VLAN commands, VTP propagates the information to the other switches, just as it propagated the FDDI VLAN information. At this point, you may want to check the VLAN list on other switches attached to the FDDI ring and make sure the new VLANs appear.

QUESTIONS AND ANSWERS

When should I use the FDDI/CDDI Card?	Whenever campus connectivity to (through) a legacy FDDI ring is required.
To which VLAN should the FDDI card belong if it is being used for trunking only?	Leave the FDDI card as part of VLAN 1 unless there are devices on the FDDI ring that need connectivity to Ethernet PCs.
Do I have to trunk all of my VLANs, or can I trunk only a subset?	You will trunk any VLANs for which you have created FDDI mappings. If you wish to only trunk a subset (corporate-wide VLANs) of your campus, then only create FDDI VLANs for the subset and use the TRANSLATION command for only that subset.
Is the FDDI card hot swappable?	The FDDI card supports online insertion and removal like all Catalyst line cards.
Can I use the FDDI card to do full-duplex FDDI switching?	No, the Catalyst FDDI card is half duplex only.

Also, try to send some information from a PC in VLAN 50 on one of the switches to another device in VLAN 50 on another switch.

Trunking has four states in Ethernet: on, off, auto, and desirable. The FDDI card does not support the auto or desirable states. Trunking must be turned on manually when it is required. Watch out for questions trying to make the FDDI card support the auto or desirable states.

CERTIFICATION SUMMARY

The Cisco Catalyst 5000 switches support your existing legacy FDDI infrastructure. The FDDI or CDDI modules allow Ethernet-based workstations to communicate with servers and hosts attached directly to the FDDI ring. This is supported with translational bridging. The existing FDDI medium can be reused as a longer-distance trunking backbone by enabling IEEE 802.10 frames on the Catalyst 5000 card.

When translating frames, the card will use the ANSI X3T9.5 standard MAC frame on the FDDI ring. These frames will be generated for whichever Ethernet VLAN the FDDI card belongs. You can set which VLAN is translated by using the SET VLAN command to change the FDDI ports to some Ethernet VLAN other than the default VLAN (1).

To aid in translation of Ethernet and FDDI frame formats, the FDDI card uses the APaRT feature. This feature allows the FDDI card to discover and record the frame format of all devices being translated. This feature is enabled by default and should only be turned off in pure IP environments.

The FDDICHECK feature allows the FDDI card to integrate with some nonstandard FDDI adapters. This feature forces the FDDI card to pay more attention to the source of each frame on the ring, making sure that any frame it sources from Ethernet devices does not circle the ring endlessly. Basically, it becomes a ring monitor for all of its translated frames. Since this feature is not needed if all stations are FDDI standards-compliant, it is disabled by default.

To enable IEEE 802.10 frames for trunking purposes, you must create an FDDI VLAN for each Ethernet VLAN you wish to trunk. When you create a VLAN of type FDDI, you tell the switch to create an FDDI carrier VLAN with a particular SAID value. The SAID value is in effect the VLAN tagging number used to let other switches know which IEEE 802.10 carrier is coming across the ring. Don't worry about SAID values; just realize that they are by default 100,000+VLAN number.

Once the IEEE 802.10 carriers are created, you must tell the Catalyst which Ethernet VLAN translates to which carrier. You use a special form of the SET VLAN command to do this: SET VLAN (*Ethernet#*) TRANSLATION (*FDDI#*) or SET VLAN (*FDDI#*) TRANSLATION (*Ethernet#*).

Trunking has two states for FDDI cards, on and off. If you have trunking on, the Catalyst will use IEEE 802.10 frames for any translations that exist. For Ethernet VLANs that do not have translations to FDDI VLANs, their traffic will not be trunked. Whichever Ethernet VLAN the port belongs to will not be trunked; it will be translated instead.

✓ TWO-MINUTE DRILL

- ❑ FDDI is a 100-Mbps shared-media networking standard, using a token passing scheme over fiber-optic cable.

- ❑ Copper Distributed Data Interface (CDDI) allows for less expensive desktop adapters to be purchased and cabled with less expensive copper cabling. The functionality of CDDI is identical to FDDI—still 100 Mbps, token-passing , shared-media technology.

- ❑ The Catalyst 5000 FDDI card is a high-speed translating bridge. The FDDI card comes in single-mode and multimode fiber versions.

- ❑ There is also a Category 5 twisted-pair card, the CDDI model.

- ❑ To translate FDDI frames to the proper Ethernet frame type, the card possesses its own MAC address table and keeps track of frame formatting parameters for each host it has seen.

❑ If the frames being translated contain IP messages, the card can perform extra functions to ensure delivery of traffic.

❑ The FDDI card supports 802.1d Spanning Tree, allowing you to use a FDDI ring as a redundant backbone for your core switches.

❑ If the FDDI card is trunking, the frames leaving the FDDI interface are tagged with VLAN information.

❑ IEEE 802.10 was originally created to provide a method of securing FDDI data in a metropolitan-area network environment. The IEEE frame format is compatible with ANSI FDDI devices; it just contains a secured data carrier that they can not decode. Cisco uses the capabilities of the IEEE 802.10 frame to provide trunking service and make it transparent to ANSI FDDI devices.

❑ Novell devices communicating through Ethernet media use one of four possible frame types in their transmission.

❑ APaRT (Automated Packet Recognition and Translation) logic updates information in the content-addressable memory (CAM) on the FDDI card and handles making sure the proper frame type is picked during translation.

❑ Cisco has a feature that allows the FDDI card to keep track of which frames it has forwarded from Ethernet sources. This is called FDDICHECK

❑ One difficulty when working with the FDDI card is understanding when the card uses ANSI frames and when the card uses IEEE frames.

❑ When the Catalyst uses 802.10 frames, it does not translate the Ethernet data. Instead, it wraps the entire Ethernet frame with an IEEE 802.10 header and trailer, inserts VLAN information into the frame in the field normally used for encryption type data, then ships the data across the ring.

❑ When you create VLANs, you have the option to implement your own SAID values if you do not want to use Cisco's defaults.

❑ Remember that the FDDI card actually belongs to an Ethernet VLAN. As long as all Catalysts on the FDDI ring have their FDDI ports belonging to the same VLAN (and they should), that VLAN does not really have to be trunked.

❑ If you want to do trunking in the FDDI environment, you must create a FDDI VLAN for each Ethernet or Token Ring VLAN to be carried.

❑ Remember that the TRANSLATION command must go from either Ethernet or Token Ring frame types to FDDI, and vice versa. Be on the lookout for questions that try to translate Ethernet VLANs to Ethernet VLANs or Token Ring to Token Ring. There should be a FDDI VLAN on one side of the TRANSLATION parameter and either a Token Ring or Ethernet VLAN on the other.

❑ In the default configuration, the FDDI card is configured with the port in VLAN default (VLAN 1), no names associated with the A and B ports (A=port 1 and B=port 2), APaRT enabled, and FDDICHECK disabled.

❑ Probably the first things you want to set up are names for the ports.

❑ If you want to get a little more horsepower out of the translations, and you have an all-IP environment (no IPX), you can turn off the APaRT feature.

❑ Trunking has four states in Ethernet: on, off, auto, and desirable. The FDDI card does not support the auto or desirable states. Trunking must be turned on manually when it is required. Watch out for questions trying to make the FDDI card support the auto or desirable states.

SELF TEST

The following Self Test questions will help you measure your understanding of the material presented in this chapter. Read all the choices carefully, as there may be more than one correct answer. Choose all correct answers for each question.

1. What does the acronym APaRT stand for?

   A. Advanced Packet Recognition Technology

   B. Automated Packet Recognition and Translation

   C. Automated Packet Recognition Technology

   D. A Packet is Recognized and Translated

2. Which of the following is true about FDDICHECK?

   A. It ensures that FDDI cabling is correct

   B. It is enabled by default

   C. It ensures that frames translated from Ethernet are removed by the FDDI card

   D. It performs FDDI compliance testing on neighboring adapters

3. Which of the following features of the FDDI card is not true?

   A. The card is available in single-mode fiber and multimode fiber versions

   B. The card performs IP fragmentation and MTU discovery

   C. The card can be used as a single DAS connection or two SAS connections

   D. The card supports IEEE 802.1d Spanning Tree

4. If you create Ethernet VLAN 321, what is the default SAID value associated with this VLAN?

   A. 100321

   B. 1321

   C. 321

   D. SAID values are only created for FDDI VLANs

5. What does the following command do?

   SET VLAN 34 TRANSLATION 43

   A. Creates a translation between Ethernet VLAN 34 and FDDI VLAN 43

   B. Creates a new FDDI VLAN 34

   C. Creates a new Ethernet VLAN 43

   D. Does nothing; it is invalid

6. Assuming VLAN 34 is an Ethernet VLAN, and an FDDI card is in slot 4 of a catalyst switch, what does the following command do?

   SET VLAN 34 4/1

   A. Makes the FDDI card part of Ethernet VLAN 34

   B. Enables Ethernet-to-ANSI FDDI translation for VLAN 34

   C. Both A and B

   D. Neither A or B

7. Which of the following statements is true of the command SET VLAN 34 TYPE FDDI?

   A. It will create a VLAN for trunking for Ethernet VLAN 34

   B. It will create an FDDI VLAN with SAID 100034

   C. It will return an error

   D. It will create a VLAN for trunking Token Ring number 34

8. How is turning off APaRT accomplished?

   A. SET FDDI APART DISABLE

   B. SET 3/1 APART DISABLE

   C. SET BRIDGE APART DISABLE

   D. APaRT can't be turned off

9. Which of the following is true about the FDDI/CDDI card?

   A. If you put two FDDI cards in a Catalyst, you get true FDDI switching between them

   B. The FDDI card is a high-speed translational bridge

   C. The CDDI version of the card offers the longest cabling distance

   D. The FDDI card does not allow half-duplex operation

10. In setting up IEEE 802.10 trunking, which of the following statements is correct?

   A. If you use the SET TRUNK command before creating the FDDI VLANS and translations, you will have to recreate the commands on every switch

   B. If you use the SET TRUNK command before creating the FDDI VLANS and translations, VTP will propagate the VLAN information for you

   C. Using the SET TRUNK command first has no effect

   D. The SET TRUNK command is only used for ISL trunking

11. CDDI stands for:

   A. Copper Data to Data Interface

   B. Copper Data Distributed Interface

   C. FDDI over Copper

   D. Copper Distributed Data Interface

12. FDDI is specified by which ANSI specification?

   A. ANSI 802.11

   B. ANSI X833

   C. ANSI X3T9.5

   D. None of the above

13. Dual attachment stations are also known as:

   A. Class A stations

   B. Class B stations

   C. CDDI stations

   D. FDDI stations

14. A Class B station would have which connector in use?

   A. The A port connector

   B. The B port connector

   C. Both, for redundancy

   D. A port or B port, but not both

15. Void frames have what purpose in FDDI?

    A. They signal the beginning of a data frame

    B. They signal the end of a data frame

    C. They are used to purge the ring if there are problems

    D. They have no purpose

16. Which of the following is not a valid Ethernet frame type?

    A. IEEE 802.3

    B. Ethernet Version 2

    C. AppleTalk IEEE 802.3

    D. IEEE 802.3/802.2/SNAP

17. Which of the following is true about the IEEE 802.10 frame?

    A. It is used by the Catalyst to perform trunking

    B. Ethernet frames are translated into IEEE 802.10 before leaving the catalyst

    C. The ICV is the void frame released after the data

    D. None of the above

18. Which of the following commands will name the A port of the FDDI card in slot 3 to upstream?

    A. SET FDDI 3/1 NAME UPSTREAM

    B. SET PORT NAME 3/1 UPSTREAM

    C. SET PORT 3/1 NAME UPSTREAM

    D. SET PORT NAME UPSTREAM 3/1

19. Which of the following is not true about turning off APaRT?

    A. Turning it off will speed up translations

    B. Turning it off in an all-IP environment is usually safe

    C. Turning it off in an all-IPX environment is usually safe

    D. Turning it off in an IPX environment means setting encapsulation types on servers and clients

20. Which of the following best describes how SAID values are used with trunking?

    A. The SAID value of the Ethernet VLAN is included in the 802.10 frames

    B. The SAID value of the FDDI VLAN is included in the 802.10 frames

    C. A random SAID value is used, since it is not used by the Catalysts

    D. A formula adding the Ethernet SAID and FDDI SAID is included in the 802.10 frames

21. If there are hosts on the FDDI ring that need access to Ethernet PCs, we enable translation by:

    A. Putting the FDDI card in the Ethernet VLAN of the PCs

    B. Putting the FDDI card into a FDDI VLAN and using a TRANSLATION command to turn on translation

    C. Adding a TRANSLATION command to the switch

    D. The catalyst card is a trunking device only

11

ATM LANE

L ocal-area network emulation (LANE) is a technology gaining popularity for providing Asynchronous Transfer Mode (ATM) service without the expense of deploying ATM to every desktop. With LANE, PCs can benefit from the extra bandwidth that ATM provides without replacing their Ethernet or Token Ring Network Interface Cards (NICs) or modifying the ODI or NDIS drivers currently installed.

LANE accomplishes this by allowing the point-to-point topology of an ATM network to emulate a point-to-multipoint LAN. Why would you want to emulate LAN topologies? Many of the protocols used in LANs were developed to run over broadcast-capable physical media like Ethernet or Token Ring. The NetBEUI protocol, for instance, uses a name query broadcast to map a device's name to an Ethernet or Token Ring network address. In Figure 11-1, the NetBEUI protocol assumes that the name server C will hear the name query broadcast from station A, because all stations on the local network are obligated to copy the broadcast from the wire and process it.

ATM, in contrast, is a point-to-point network without a native capability to broadcast to all stations. In the ATM network shown in Figure 11-2, Workstation A has multiple logical connections with the other stations, called virtual circuits. When the NetBEUI protocol on Workstation A generates a name query broadcast, it must be converted into ATM cells and transmitted over the ATM physical connection. Since ATM is a connection-oriented protocol, the ATM device must somehow create one copy of the cells to send over the Virtual Circuit 1 and another copy to send over Virtual Circuit 2. The processing and bandwidth overhead required by LANE to provide this sort of broadcast emulation and other related services makes it ill suited to many PC and workstation platforms.

In this chapter, an ATM configuration that solves this problem is considered. By utilizing fast hardware on a Catalyst LANE module, the Catalyst is configured to proxy ATM duties for a collection of host stations. The LANE networks might use ATM connections between Catalyst switches with Fast Ethernet or Token Ring connections to workstations, as shown in Figure 11-3. The Catalyst switch proxy device, acting as a LANE Client (LEC), carries broadcasts between Ethernet-connected or Token Ring-connected hosts using the ATM network as the bridge path.

FIGURE 11-1   A connectionless, broadcast-capable topology

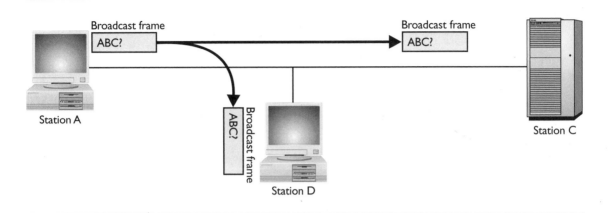

FIGURE 11-2   A connection-oriented ATM network

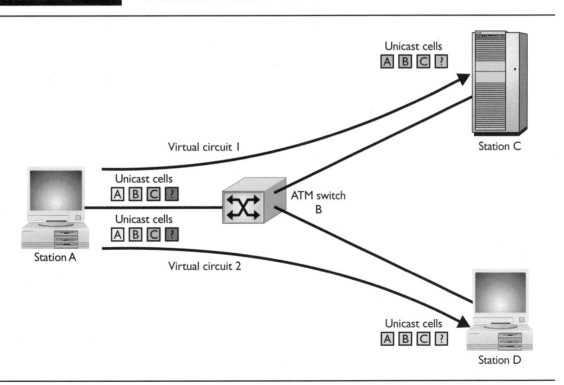

In the illustration, Ethernet and Token Ring switches with ATM LANE connections provide the proxy service. The Catalyst switch receives the name query on one of its Ethernet ports, converts it to cells for the ATM network, and forwards one copy of the cells to the directly connected ATM switch. The ATM network then replicates the cells to Station C and Station D. The steps involved in accomplishing this nontrivial configuration are examined in the sections that follow. First, though, a few words of ATM background.

FIGURE 11-3   An ATM network emulating a broadcast-capable network with LANE

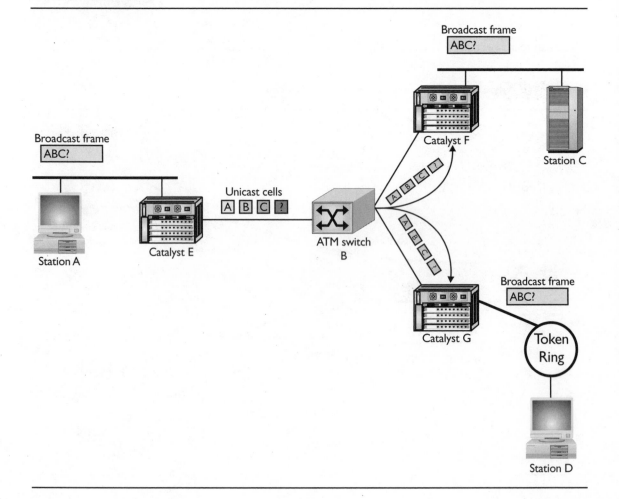

ATM Boot Camp

ATM communication provides a protocol model for very high-bandwidth networking. The high bandwidth is achieved by simplifying many aspects of the forwarding process. For instance, ATM networks send and receive small, fixed-size data units called cells. The fixed size permits lower latency in the forwarding process, as the receiving device need not scan the incoming data for a bit pattern representing the end of the cell. Its beginning implies the end of each cell. Zen networking!

SAR

A high-bandwidth network is of little value unless interesting data goes into and out of it reliably. Several standards exist to provide client station access to the ATM infrastructure. LANE is the newest of these. One advantage that LANE sports is preservation of existing upper-layer software on the ATM-connected station. LANE functions begin when an OSI Layer 2 process like IEEE 802.3 on a host hands a frame of data to the LANE ATM Adaptation Layer. The Layer 2 frame must pass through several transformations before it is ready to be presented to the ATM network as 53-byte cells.

Examining the protocol stack in Figure 11-4, you see that ATM receives data from an OSI data link layer process in order to deliver it to a cooperating process on the receiving station.

Once the Layer 2 frame is presented to ATM, and specifically to the ATM adaptation layer (AAL) (see Figure 11-5), the common part convergence sublayer (CPCS) adds trailer information so that the resulting CPCS-PDU is exactly 48 octets in length.

Next, the CPCS-PDU is chopped up by the segmentation and reassembly (SAR) process. SAR on the sending side takes 48-octet chunks and hands them off to the ATM layer with an indication as to which of these SAR-PDUs is the last fragment of the CPCS-PDU. The speed of the SAR process determines in large part how well any given vendor's ATM equipment performs. Cisco's Catalyst LANE products use fast, hardware-based SAR to operate at full "wire" speed.

FIGURE 11-4   ATM Protocol Stack

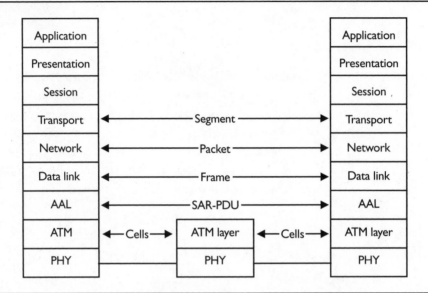

Having received a SAR-PDU, the sending ATM layer creates a five-octet cell header like the one shown in Figure 11-6 for the ATM User-Network Interface. The header contains two distinct addressing fields, the virtual path ID and the virtual channel ID, which permit a receiving ATM switch to forward a newly received cell to the next destination on the virtual circuit. In this regard, cell addressing in ATM is similar to addressing with DLCI numbers in a Frame Relay network. That is, each cell carries in its header a virtual path ID and a virtual channel ID. The combination VPI/VCI is locally significant to two directly connected devices, just as the DLCI number is locally significant between a Frame Relay DTE device and its directly connected Frame Relay switch.

Creation of an ATM permanent virtual circuit (PVC) or switched virtual circuit (SVC) requires establishing a series of point-to-point VPI/VCI links between a series of systems from one ATM end system (ES) to another, through one or more ATM switches. In ATM LANE, this chapter considers the use of point-to-point bidirectional virtual circuits and point-to-multipoint unidirectional virtual circuits. We refer to them collectively as virtual channel connections (VCC).

FIGURE 11-5   Encapsulation in ATM

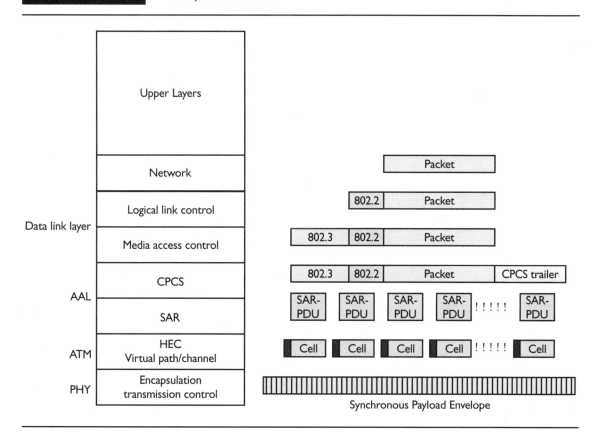

FIGURE 11-6   UNI 3.1 cell header

Field name	GFC	VPI	VCI	PT	C L P	HEC	Payload ! ! !
Field length (in bits)	4	8	16	3	1	8	384

The ATM layer has the job of addressing the SAR-PDU in preparation for transmission. The ATM layer infers which VPI/VCI to prefix onto a given cell from the SAR service access point that provided the SAR-PDU. The VPI/VCI numbers are either locally configured or learned by the ATM device through an SVC signaling and call setup process. With the address and other header information created and applied to the cell, the ATM layer hands the nearly completed cell to the physical layer through the PHY service access point.

The first PHY sublayer, the transmission control sublayer, has the job of creating an error detection code in order to recognize a bit error occurring in transmission of the cell header. The header error control (HEC) field does not detect errors in the 48-octet data field. Rather it allows the receiving station to correct or discard a cell if an error might have changed the VPI/VCI numbers or other header information. The HEC can also be used in place of a synchronized clocking transmission facility between sender and receiver. In other words, the receiver can determine the start of a cell by looking for HEC fields in the received bit stream.

The complete cell is now encapsulated by the physical medium dependant sublayer and queued for transmission. If the receiving station is an ATM switch, the VPI and/or VCI fields of the cell header are examined and compared with entries in a switching table to determine where the cell payload should be sent next. Table 11-1 shows a sample switching table for the ATM switch shown in Figure 11-7.

TABLE 11-1	Inbound			Outbound		
Example ATM Switching Table	Port	VPI	VCI	Port	VPI	VCI
	1	10	20	2	30	40
	2	30	40	1	10	20

FIGURE 11-7   Example ATM switching table network

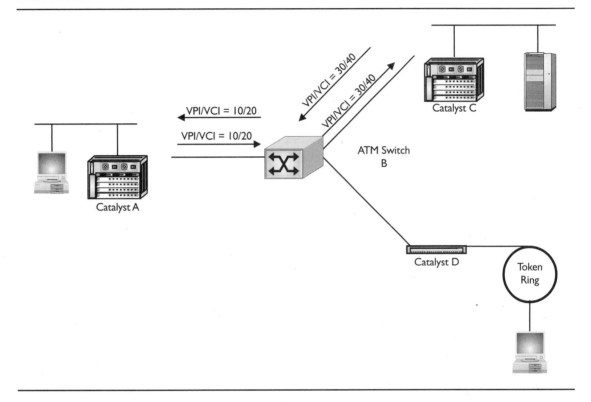

When the LANE module in Catalyst A sends a cell with VPI/VCI fields set to 10/20, the ATM switch receives it on Port 1. The switch examines the table and determines that cells received inbound on Port 1 with VPI/VCI of 10/20 should be forwarded outbound from Port 2 with VPI/VCI set to 30/40. The ATM switch creates a new cell header as shown in Table 11-1, with the VPI/VCI set to 30/40. The switch then transmits the cell outbound from Port 2.

The path between Catalyst A and the ATM switch represented by the VPI/VCI combination 10/20 can be considered a one-way, or unidirectional, virtual link between the two ATM-connected devices. The combination of the 10/20 virtual link from A to the switch and the 30/40 virtual link from the switch to the LANE module in Catalyst C constitute a complete virtual circuit between A and C. The virtual circuit represented by this switching table is a unidirectional point-to-point virtual circuit, allowing A to send cells to C only.

A separate virtual circuit is needed if C wishes to send cells to A. In Figure 11-7, this virtual circuit is formed from the 30/40 virtual link between C and the switch and the 10/20 virtual link between the switch and A. In general, the virtual links used to communicate between an end station and its directly connected intermediate station need not have the same VPI/VCI in both directions. This pair of unidirectional virtual circuits allows two-way, or bidirectional, communication between End Systems A and C. We will call a pair of virtual circuits that allow bidirectional communication between two ATM devices a point-to-point VCC.

ATM LAN emulation makes extensive use of point-to-point VCCs as well as point-to-multipoint VCCs. The point-to-multipoint VCC is a collection of virtual circuits that allows one ATM-connected device (either ES or IS) to communicate with more than one ATM-connected device. If you recall that one reason for implementing LANE in your network is to allow ATM-connected devices to emulate the broadcast capability of Ethernet-connected devices, you can see the importance of the point-to-multipoint VCC. The point-to-multipoint VCC will be the vehicle for carrying broadcast traffic to all the members of an emulated LAN.

ATM Addressing

At this point, you have spent some time learning ATM terminology and concepts. While none of these concepts is particularly difficult, you will no doubt agree that there is a lot to grasp. You will be pleased that there is a payoff for all the hard work of understanding these concepts. With LANE, you can create a large number of VCCs with just a few configuration statements on each Catalyst switch.

An ATM signaling protocol called System Services Connection-Oriented Protocol (SSCOP) facilitates a call setup process that LANE uses to create VCCs between ATM end systems like your Catalyst. SSCOP requires that the end systems be identified by an address. Just as the public telephone network requires a unique address for each local loop (the phone number), ATM devices must have unique addresses identifying each station in call requests. The addresses we use in ATM networks are called network service access point (NSAP) addresses.

ATM Address Formats

You may choose from several formats for NSAP addresses in your ATM network. If your network will connect to a public ATM network, you will likely use a format called E.164. You can easily tell if your provider is using E.164 addresses by looking at the leading byte in the address. If the hexadecimal value of the first byte is 0x45, you are using an E.164 address. The addressing scheme used by default on Cisco ATM devices is called International Code Designator (ICD). It is distinguished by having the hexadecimal number 0x47 as its high-order byte. The third popular address format, the Data Country Code (DCC) format, uses addresses that start with 0x39. This is the address format specified in the BellCore recommendations.

ATM NSAP addresses must be globally unique in order for different organizations' ATM networks to interoperate. There are three different popular formats because three international standards bodies take responsibility for maintaining uniqueness in the address spaces they manage. The British National Standards Institute is responsible for assigning unique address ranges for Data Country Code format address space. In the United States, the Commerce Department of the federal government assigns ICD addresses. Uniqueness is guaranteed in E.164 addresses by embedding an international dial-plan telephone number in the address. The ITU-T is responsible for assignment of E.164-formatted addresses. The three formats for addresses are shown in Figure 11-8.

Each of the formats shares some fields. For instance, the Authority and Format Indicator (AFI) is the first byte in each of the address formats. A field that differs depending on the format follows the AFI. It is either called the Data Country Code (DCC) or the International Code Designator (ICD). The combination of the AFI and DCC or ICD is called the Initial Domain Indicator (IDI) field. The next field is the Domain Specific Part (DSP) of the address. The DSP can be divided into a Higher-Order DSP, the End System ID (ESI) field, and a final field called the Selector byte. These last two fields, the 48-bit ESI and the eight-bit Selector, will prove most important to us in configuring LANE. A sample ICD address is shown in Figure 11-9.

FIGURE 11-8 ATM NSAP address formats

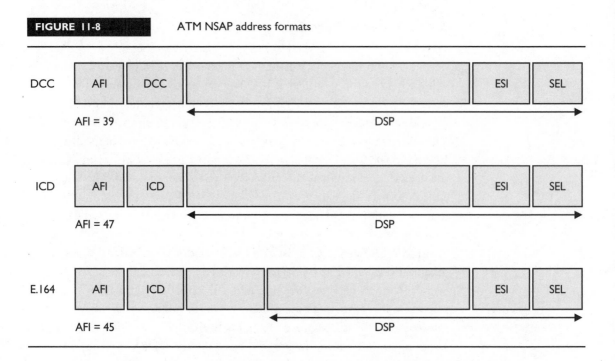

The entire NSAP address is twenty bytes, or 160 bits, in length. ATM routing protocols allow you to allocate addresses in hierarchical fashion to reduce the number of ATM addresses stored in each ATM device. Cisco implements the hierarchical addressing concept in its address auto-configuration service. When you choose to auto-configure addresses for your Cisco ATM equipment, IOS will supply the ESI and Selector portions of your ATM addresses. The rest of the address, the IDI and HO-DSP, are learned through a remarkable protocol called the Integrated Link Management Interface (ILMI). Some Cisco documentation still refers

FIGURE 11-9 A sample ICD address

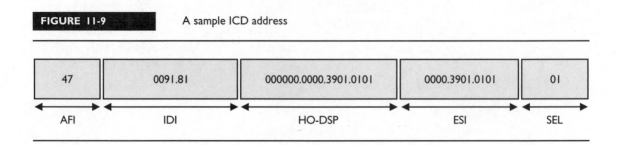

to ILMI as "Interim Link Management Interface," the term used before completion of the ATM Forum LANE specification.

ILMI

The ILMI is defined in specifications produced by the ATM Forum. ILMI is similar in concept to the IP Simple Network Management Protocol (SNMP) or the OSI Common Management Interface Protocol (CMIP) in that it allows ATM-connected devices to "get" and "put" information between each other. Among the ATM operating parameters that ILMI can transfer are the IDI and HO-DSP portions of an ATM switch's addresses. When an ATM end system incorporates these fields into its ATM NSAP addresses, the ATM switch can represent all of its connected end systems with a single advertisement.

The ATM end system uses well-known PVCs to query its directly connected ATM switch. The ILMI PVC is identified by the VPI/VCI combination 0/16. Some Cisco ATM equipment requires that you manually configure this PVC to support ILMI. The Catalyst LANE module, which we examine later in this chapter, includes the ILMI well known PVC in its default configuration. This feature greatly eases the burden of configuring ATM addressing for use with LANE.

ATM Signaling

ATM NSAP addresses enable a key ATM technology used by LANE. They permit one device to dynamically establish a VCC to another device. The process, ATM signaling, requires that an ATM end system with data to transmit make a request to its directly connected ATM switch for an SVC to a destination ATM end system. The request is carried to the ATM switch over a specific ATM virtual circuit. Like ILMI, the Signaling ATM adaptation layer (QSAAL) used by LANE requires a specific virtual circuit for its operation. The default VPI/VCI for QSAAL is 0/5.

The destination of the signaling request is represented by its unique NSAP address. As long as the switch has resources to spare for the new connection, it consults its route table and determines which switch or end system provides a path to the destination address. Once the determination is made, the ATM switch forwards the request to the next hop, where the process repeats. When the call request is received by the destination end system, it returns a call accepted message to complete creation of the SVC. In order to best utilize resources in the ATM network, end stations may tear down their SVCs when they are no longer needed.

The ATM building blocks used by LANE have now been examined. In the next section, we look at when and how these components are used to make the point-to-point, connection-oriented ATM network emulate a broadcast-capable LAN.

CERTIFICATION OBJECTIVE 11.02

LANE Components

LANE enjoys a reputation as an "expert friendly" protocol—that is, a difficult service to configure and maintain. One reason for this bad publicity is the number and complexity of the services that comprise a LANE internetwork. In this section, the components of LAN emulation are explored. We define an emulated LAN and examine how one is created when the LANE Client, the LANE Server, the broadcast and unknown server (BUS), and the LAN Emulation Configuration Server work together.

ELAN

The purpose of LANE is to allow hosts (as shown in Figure 11-10) to communicate as though they belonged to the same broadcast domain. Stations that can hear each other's broadcasts over a LANE infrastructure are said to belong to the same Emulated LAN (ELAN). You may be able to recognize in this definition a parallel to the IP subnet. IP assumes that all stations that are hosts on the same subnet number are able to communicate with each other using link-layer broadcasts. This is the foundation of the Address Resolution Protocol (ARP). In fact, the similarity is so strong that you should usually design your LANE solutions such that an IP subnet corresponds to a single ELAN.

FIGURE 11-10   Sample LANE topology

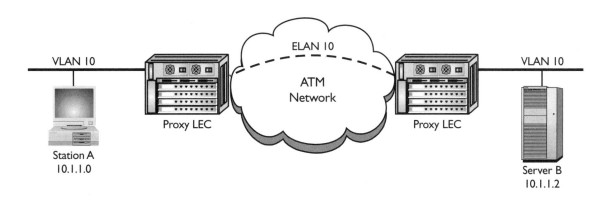

The goal of LANE is to allow PCs and other hosts to communicate over an ATM infrastructure, while avoiding the costs of deploying ATM technology to each desktop. In Figure 11-10, the PCs belong to a single Ethernet broadcast domain, even though they are attached to different Catalyst switches. It should be easy to see that an Ethernet VLAN is similar to the ATM ELAN in this regard. Again, this feature is utilized in LANE designs by mapping each ATM ELAN to a single IP subnet number and, in turn, to a single Ethernet VLAN, where that subnet number is implemented.

LAN Emulation Client

LANE functions are implemented by software that must run on any ATM device that participates as a client to an ELAN. Once the software has registered an ATM device in a particular ELAN, the device is called a LANE Client or LEC. If the LEC is a switch or router, the software will provide transport service to Ethernet-connected or Token Ring-connected hosts. LEC software operating on an ATM-connected host station allows connection to an ATM LANE network without the need to replace the OSI Layer 2 software drivers (ODI or NDIS drivers) used on the host.

LEC software tasks can be divided into control functions and data-forwarding functions. The LEC first performs its control functions when it joins an ELAN. Joining an ELAN requires that the LEC locate other services in the ELAN and set up various VCCs to them. Later, the LEC software performs call setup functions when it wishes to send data to or through another LEC in the ELAN. This call setup process creates bidirectional, point-to-point virtual channel connections between the LECs in an ELAN. These VCCs are used to transmit traffic from LAN-connected hosts across the ATM network.

The LEC software is also responsible for forwarding data to and from the ATM network. The data may originate in LAN-connected devices, and transit through an ELAN to other LAN-connected devices, as shown in Figure 11-11. Alternatively, it may be sourced by, or destined for, an ATM-connected host. Regardless of whether a LEC provides transit service or not, it must map the OSI Layer 2 MAC address specified in the upper-layer frame to an ATM address that represents a destination LEC.

FIGURE 11-11   LEC topology

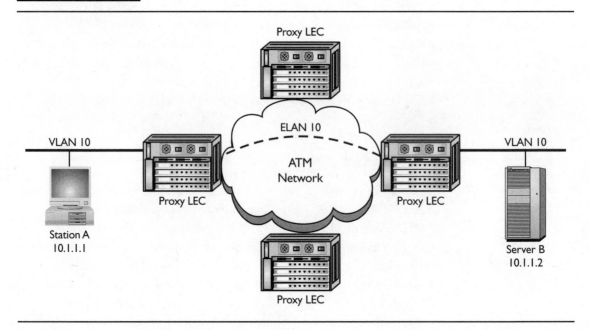

In some cases, a LEC acts like a traditional learning bridge. In order for a LEC to forward traffic to a MAC-addressed host station, it must consult a database that associates a destination MAC address with a VCC that can reach it. If a database record does not exist for a particular MAC address, the LEC must initiate a LANE ARP (LE-ARP) to determine which ATM address can reach the destination MAC. The LES answers the LE-ARP request if it has cached the MAC address in question. LES functions, including the LE-ARP process, are examined in the next section.

LAN Emulation Server

Each LEC must register itself to become a member of an emulated LAN. The LES handles the registration process. The LEC first sets up a bidirectional virtual circuit to the LES for the ELAN it wishes to join. Using the virtual circuit, the LEC must register its ATM addresses, and may optionally register the IEEE MAC addresses it can reach as well. The registered addresses are later used by the LES to resolve LAN-connected MAC addresses to the ATM NSAP-addressed LECs that can forward traffic to them. This address resolution is referred to as the LAN Emulation Address Resolution Protocol (LE-ARP). ATM addresses learned through LE-ARP are used to set up the point-to-point VCCs that LECs use to transmit to each other.

During the registration process, the LES may optionally authenticate an LEC's request to join an ELAN. A LANE service called the LAN Emulation Configuration Server (LECS) provides authentication and other services that we will examine shortly. Once the LES accepts a new LEC into its ELAN, it also registers the new member LEC with a LANE service called the broadcast and unknown server (BUS). As its name implies, the BUS has the job during data forwarding of creating and sending cells to each member LEC so that LAN-originated broadcast frames arrive at all stations in the ELAN. The BUS has other control and data forwarding functions that we will examine next.

Broadcast and Unknown Server

When registering itself in an ELAN, a LEC is added to a point-to-multipoint VCC called the *multicast forward* VCC. The BUS uses this VCC to copy cells to each member of an ELAN. Using the point-to-multipoint VCC, the BUS lets the ELAN mimic the broadcast capability of Ethernet or Token Ring LANs.

As noted earlier, in some cases a LEC acts like a traditional learning bridge. In order for a LEC to forward traffic to a MAC-addressed host station, it must consult a database that associates a destination MAC address with a VCC that can reach it. If a database record doesn't exist for a particular MAC address, the LEC must initiate a LE-ARP to determine which ATM address can reach the destination MAC.

LAN Emulation Configuration Server

Thus far the LANE discussion has focused on operation of a single ELAN. In fact, your LANE implementation will very likely include several ELANs. For instance, in a switched IP network, a subnet is usually mapped to a single virtual LAN (VLAN). Since a subnet is also a broadcast domain, separate ELANs provide an effective means to transport traffic for many IP networks over the same ATM backbone.

In order to participate in an ELAN, an LEC must first locate the LES for the ELAN and register themselves. To locate a LES for any ELAN, a LEC initiates a point-to-point VCC with a LANE service called the LAN Emulation Configuration Server (LECS). The LECS (not to be confused with multiple LECs, the LANE Clients) answers the question, "Where is the LES for my ELAN?" With the ATM address supplied by the LECS, a LEC can initiate a point-to-point VCC to the LES and join the ELAN.

You must manually configure LES NSAP addresses on the LECS. Since LANE uses 20-byte addresses, this configuration step is subject to error. It is easy to mistype one of the 40 hex digits that represent the 20-byte address. Figure 11-12 shows our LANE network with ATM addresses applied to the LECs.

As already noted, the LECS can answer a second question. Optionally, it may provide authentication services for an emulated LAN. When the LEC requests participation in an ELAN, the LES can query the LECS and ask whether a particular LEC ATM address is authorized in the ELAN. If the LECS has not been preconfigured to recognize the ATM address of the requesting LEC, the LES must refuse to register the LEC. This capability is essential if LANE is to be provided over public ATM networks.

FIGURE 11-12   Cisco NSAP address configuration

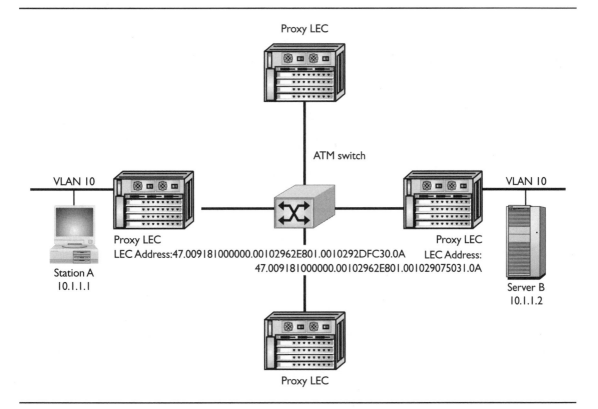

Proxy LEC

ATM switch

VLAN 10

Proxy LEC
LEC Address:47.009181000000.00102962E801.0010292DFC30.0A

VLAN 10

Proxy LEC
LEC Address:
47.009181000000.00102962E801.001029075031.0A

Station A
10.1.1.1

Server B
10.1.1.2

Proxy LEC

LANE Internetworking

An ATM device can participate in many ELANs. A device would use a separate instance of the LEC software to join each ELAN. The same device may also provide one or more of the other LANE services. That is, one device may be a LEC in several ELANs, while at the same time providing LES service to one or more of the ELANs, and acting as the LECS as well. Since each of these roles is provided through software, CPU utilization can be a concern when configuring multiple LANE roles for an ATM device.

An ELAN represents a broadcast domain. It is common to configure one ELAN to bridge traffic within a single IP subnetwork or IPX network number. In a switched environment, one ELAN is configured to transport traffic through the ATM network for a single VLAN. Like VLANs traffic between ELANs must be forwarded by a router. You can review the details of configuring a router in a switched network in Chapter 7.

ATM Switch

The LES address is found in the LECS, but how does the LEC find the LECS address? There are several ways to answer that tongue-twisting riddle. Using Cisco equipment, the simplest way for a LEC to learn the NSAP address of the LECS is to configure the ATM switch to provide the answer. In Figure 11-12, the ATM switch would point each LEC to the Cisco Catalyst 5000 labeled B when they request an LECS address. The mechanism used to request and learn the LECS address is our old friend, ILMI.

LEC, LES, BUS, and LECS Addresses

Each of the LANE software components—the LEC, LES, BUS, and LECS—are identified in the ATM network by their NSAP address. Even if several components operate on the same Catalyst switch, they must all have different ATM NSAP addresses. If you choose to do so, you can make up any unique NSAP address you wish for each component. If your design permits, you will usually find it much simpler to use Cisco's automatic address configuration service.

Cisco makes use of two fields in the ATM NSAP address format to create unique addresses: the End System ID (ESI) field and the NSAP

Selector field. Cisco Catalyst LANE modules create a template of NSAP addresses where each possible component (LEC, LES, BUS, and LECS) has a different ESI. The ESI for the template comes from MAC addresses burned into the LANE module. Each MAC address is inserted into the ESI field to give a different NSAP for each type of service.

If a LEC is configured on a Catalyst LANE module, its ESI will be the first NSAP address from the pool supplied by the LANE module. If multiple LECs are configured on the LANE module, each one shares the same ESI. Each LEC also shares the higher-order portion of the address that is learned from the directly connected ATM switch through ILMI. You may at this point question how we arrive at a unique address for each LEC on this Catalyst. The remaining field in the ATM NSAP address format, the NSAP Selector, is different for each LEC on our Catalyst. This ensures that we maintain unique addresses for each component.

The LANE module provides an IOS command line interface (CLI) exactly like that found on most of Cisco's router products. When LANE services are configured on the module, you create subinterfaces whose parent interface is interface atm 0, and start the LANE component software on the new subinterface. Cisco takes the value for the NSAP selector byte from the number of the ATM subinterface where we configure the component. For instance, if you choose to create a LEC service on subinterface 1, the NSAP selector byte for that LEC's address is 1. You must create a different subinterface for each LEC you configure on your Catalyst. In our configuration section, you will see the potential for confusion when using decimal numbers for subinterfaces and hexadecimal numbers for the NSAP selector byte.

CERTIFICATION OBJECTIVE 11.03

LANE Operation

Thinking of LANE operation proceeding in two phases can help to clarify details. First, a LEC registers itself in an ELAN during a setup phase. Then information moves between LANE clients during the data transfer phase. During the setup phase, several VCCs are created between the LEC and other LANE services. During data transfer phase, LECs create point-to-point VCCs to each other, and use them to carry ELAN traffic between the clients.

Prior to the setup phase, the LANE services must be configured and started. The LECS must have the addresses of LESs for each ELAN. The LES and BUS need the name of the ELAN that they serve. Once the services are configured and started, a LEC may begin its setup operations by joining an ELAN.

Setup Phase

Setup phase begins when a LEC is initialized. The LEC first determines the address of a LECS. As noted above, the simplest way to find the LECS address is to query the directly attached ATM switch using ILMI. Alternatively, the LEC can be locally configured with the LECS ATM address, or the LEC can attempt to find the LECS at a well-known address.

Using the LECS's ATM address, the LEC initiates a call to the LECS that results in a bidirectional point-to-point VCC called the *configuration direct* VCC, as shown in Figure 11-13. Over the configuration direct VCC, the LEC asks for the ATM addresses of the LES. In Cisco's LAN emulation, the LES and BUS are implemented in the same software module, so we often refer to the combined LES/BUS functions.

FIGURE 11-13   Configuration direct VCC

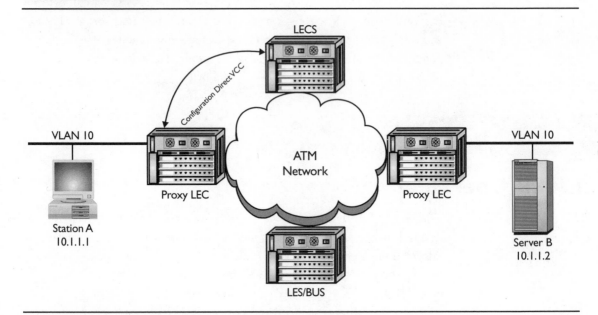

The next step the LEC takes in the setup phase is joining the ELAN. First the LEC initiates a call to the LES, which results in another point-to-point VCC called the control direct VCC. Over the control direct VCC, the LEC passes its NSAP ATM address and optionally may pass a list of MAC addresses that can be reached through it. The LES also sets up a virtual circuit to the LEC called the *control distribute* VCC. Both the control direct and control distribute VCCs are used during the data forwarding phase by the LE-ARP process. LES virtual circuit setup results are shown in Figure 11-14.

Next, the LEC uses the LE-ARP process to locate the NSAP address of the BUS component of the ELAN. The LEC sends a request for the NSAP corresponding to the broadcast MAC address. This is the address of the BUS software that will carry broadcasts during the data-forwarding phase.

FIGURE 11-14   Control direct and control distribute VCCs

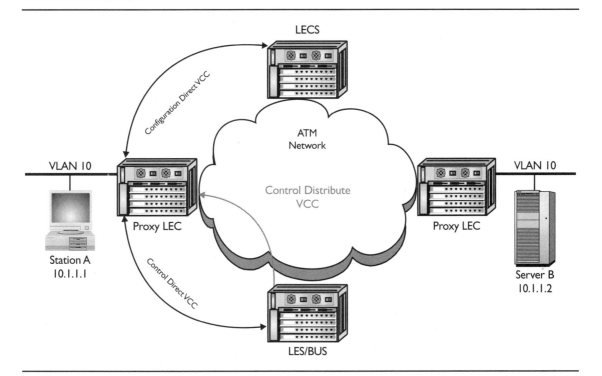

Once the BUS address is retrieved, the LEC initiates a bidirectional point-to-point and a unidirectional multipoint virtual circuit to the BUS. Both the point-to-point *data direct* VCC and the point-to-multipoint *data distribute* VCC are used to emulate a broadcast network during data forwarding. Establishment of this collection of virtual channel connections completes the setup phase for an individual LEC. The LANE network now resembles the one shown in Figure 11-15.

Each LEC performs similar setup functions to join an ELAN. Since many ELANs may exist in a LANE network, practical limits on the number of supported virtual circuits determine the maximum number of LECs that can be configured. For this and several other reasons that we shall consider shortly, LANE does not scale well to very large networks.

| FIGURE 11-15 | Multicast send VCC and multicast forward VCC |

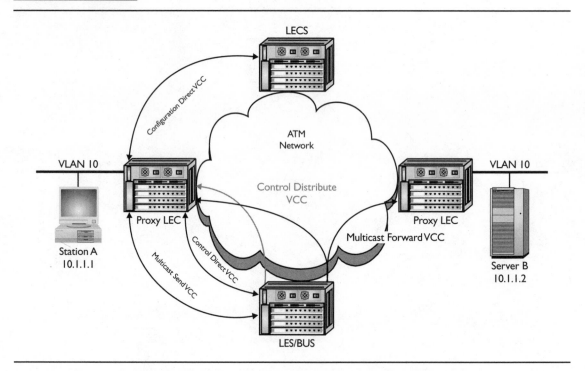

Data Forwarding Phase

This phase begins when OSI Layer 2 software on the LEC determines that it wishes to send data across the LANE network. This may occur when an ATM-connected host computer wishes to transmit to another device, or when a switch or router configured to use LANE receives traffic from a host on one of its Ethernet or Token Ring interfaces. In either case, the LEC software checks the OSI Layer 2 destination address in the frame and consults a local database of destination MAC addresses to determine if a virtual circuit has been mapped to that destination address. If no match for the destination MAC address exists, the LEC software creates an LE-ARP request and forwards it to the LES over the control direct VCC, as shown in Figure 11-16. The LE-ARP requests an NSAP address through which the destination MAC address may be reached.

FIGURE 11-16　　　　LE-ARP process

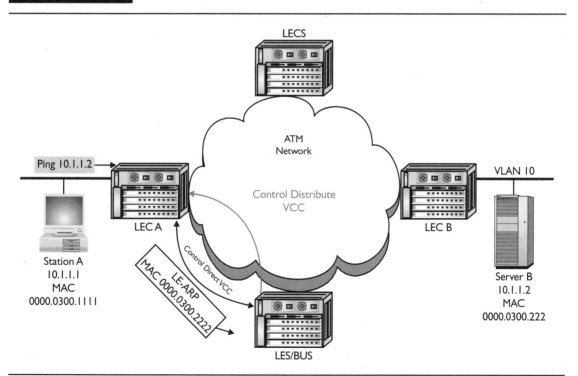

At the same time, the LEC begins chopping the OSI Layer 2 frame into cells and forwarding them to the BUS over the data direct VCC. The BUS then floods these cells to all LECs configured in the ELAN. This flood ensures that the initial frames will reach the destination MAC address without waiting for LE-ARP to complete.

When the LES software receives the LE-ARP, a local LE-ARP table is checked for the destination MAC address. If the address has been cached, the LES responds to the LE-ARP with the desired NSAP address. Otherwise, the LES forwards the LE-ARP to all LECs in the ELAN using the control distribute VCC. When a LEC receives an LE-ARP from the LES, it will consult its local MAC address database and respond if it has an entry for the destination MAC address. The response, which contains the NSAP address of the LEC with the destination MAC, goes to the LES, which notes the destination MAC-to-NSAP mapping in its LE-ARP table for future reference. The LES then forwards the LE-ARP response to the requesting LEC.

In Figure 11-17, the LEC labeled A has received data that should be sent to MAC address 0000.0300.2222. Concurrent with sending an LE-ARP to the LES/BUS, LEC A also begins sending cells to the broadcast and unknown server using the same physical ATM connection but a different VCC. These cells are duplicated by the BUS function and sent to all the LECs in the ELAN, including LEC B.

Meanwhile, in Figure 11-18, the LES software has determined that it does not know which LEC can reach the destination MAC 0000.0300.2222. The LES software therefore duplicates cells of the LE-ARP and sends them to all the LECs in the ELAN. Since the host PC with the destination MAC is attached to the LEC labeled B, only this device will respond to the LE-ARP by sending its ATM NSAP address back to LEC A via the LES.

FIGURE 11-17 Sending "unknown" cells to the BUS

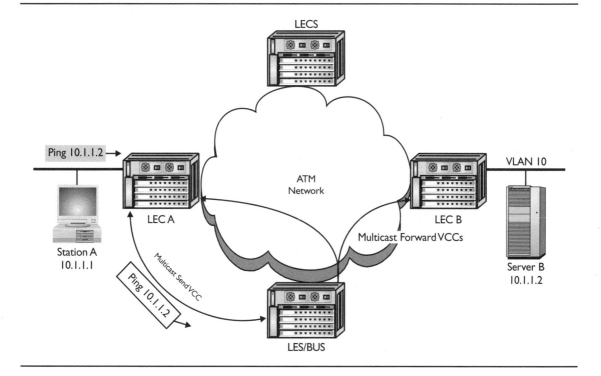

With the NSAP address of the destination now in its possession, the LEC checks to see if a point-to-point bidirectional VCC already exists to carry the data to the destination. If so, the LEC updates its local MAC database to indicate that the destination MAC is available through a specific VPI/VCI. Otherwise, the LEC must initiate call setup to create a data direct VCC to the destination NSAP address, also shown in Figure 11-18.

FIGURE 11-18 Forwarding LE-ARP to all LANE Clients

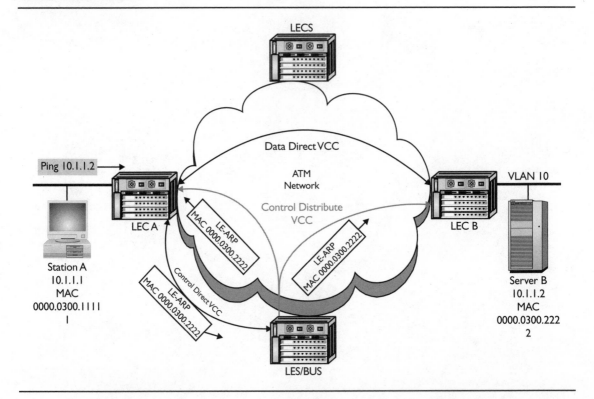

Once call setup is complete, the LEC must ensure that all cells that were sent to the BUS software have been delivered. The receiving LEC lacks the ability to recognize cells arriving out of order. If the sending LEC uses two different paths for cells at the same time—one starting with the *multicast send* VCC to the BUS and the other starting with the data direct VCC to the receiving LEC—the possibility for cells to arrive out of order exists. Cisco's solution to the problem is a flush message to the BUS software. When the flush message arrives at the BUS, it is retransmitted through the multicast distribute VCC to all LECs in the ELAN. When the originating LEC hears its own flush message returned, it concludes that the destination LEC has likewise received all cells that were first sent through the BUS. At this point, the LEC may begin sending the remaining cells from the original Layer 2 frame, using the more efficient data direct VCC.

All of the pieces of LANE are now in place to allow data forwarding between the two Ethernet-connected hosts stations using the ATM network as a bridge path. Theory is a fine thing, but nothing cements the concept like a hands-on example. In the next section, the configuration steps required to implement the simple LANE network with two ELANs are detailed.

CERTIFICATION OBJECTIVE 11.04

Configuring **LAN Emulation**

In the Cisco Catalyst-based LANE network shown in Figure 11-19, ATM LANE is configured with one ELAN called Management. Next, a second ELAN called Sales is configured to illustrate the concepts of multiple LECs running on the same Catalyst LANE module. In order to understand the necessary configuration steps, the capabilities of the Catalyst LANE module are examined first.

FIGURE 11-19   LANE configuration example network

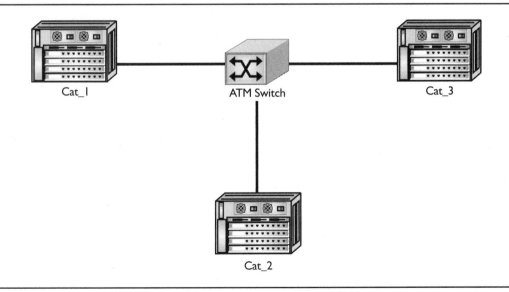

Cat_1   ATM Switch   Cat_3

Cat_2

ATM LANE Module

Cisco's LAN emulation module for the Catalyst 5000 series switches supports up to 255 LAN Emulation Clients concurrently. With the maximum memory installed, it can terminate up to 4,096 ATM virtual circuits. The module performs its SAR functions with two ASICs that each can segment and reassemble 512 frames concurrently.

Cisco's LANE modules come with two PHY (physial interface) ports, of which only one can be active at any time. The backup PHY may be connected to an ATM switch and used to fail-over the connection should the primary link fail. Both PHY ports are represented in the CLI as "interface atm 0." Should the link to the preferred ATM switch fail, the entire ATM 0 configuration will be applied to the backup PHY acting as interface ATM 0.

The LANE module processes its operating software with an IDT RISC CPU. This feature allows the LANE module to be configured independent of the Catalyst 5000. Use the SESSION command in the Catalyst CLI to communicate with the LANE module CLI.

Configuring the Catalyst 5000 Series ATM LANE Modules

The process for configuring the LANE module has, in essence, four steps:

1. Configure the LECS and populate its database with the ATM NSAP addresses of the LESs.

2. Configure the ATM switch with the address of the LECS. This permits ILMI responses to LECs when they make requests for the LECS NSAP address.

3. Start the LES software for the Management and Sales ELANs.

4. Start an instance of the LEC for both ELANs on each server. When the LEC is initialized, it kicks off the registration process. Once the LEC has successfully joined the ELAN, it is ready for data forwarding. You can observe data forwarding by sending PING packets across the ATM network from one Catalyst switch to the other.

Configuring the LECS

In Figure 11-19, Cat_2 has been chosen to configure the LECS software. This choice was arbitrary, as it could just as well have been configured on any of the Catalysts, or on the ATM switch for that matter. First, access the LANE module using the NMP image command SESSION. You can review the details of the SESSION command in Chapter 7.

```
Cat_2> enable
Password:
Cat_2 (enable)> session 4
ATM_Cat_2> enable
Password:
ATM_Cat_2#
```

Now you must gather information for the LECS database. The address templates on Cat_2 and Cat_3 are examined. These devices act as the LESs for the network. In order to populate the LECS database with the NSAP address of each LES, you must use the SHOW LANE DEFAULT command. Figure 11-20 shows the results of this command on Cat_2.

FIGURE 11-20   Results of SHOW LANE DEFAULT on Cat_2

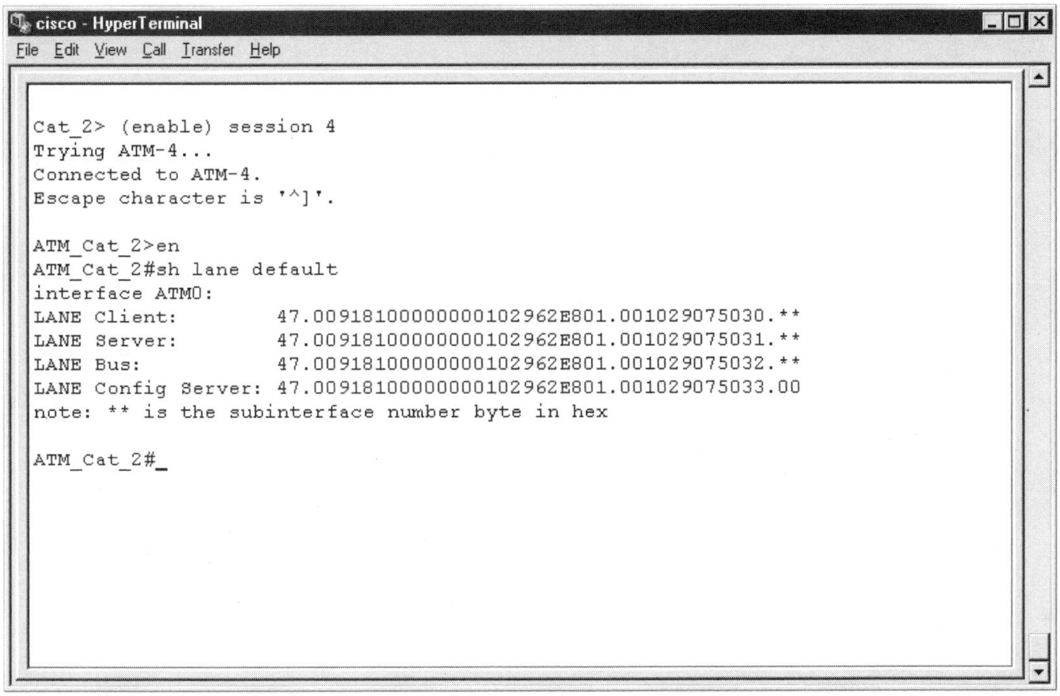

```
cisco - HyperTerminal
File  Edit  View  Call  Transfer  Help

Cat_2> (enable) session 4
Trying ATM-4...
Connected to ATM-4.
Escape character is '^]'.

ATM_Cat_2>en
ATM_Cat_2#sh lane default
interface ATM0:
LANE Client:          47.00918100000000102962E801.001029075030.**
LANE Server:          47.00918100000000102962E801.001029075031.**
LANE Bus:             47.00918100000000102962E801.001029075032.**
LANE Config Server:   47.00918100000000102962E801.001029075033.00
note: ** is the subinterface number byte in hex

ATM_Cat_2#_
```

Examining Figure 11-20, you notice in the LANE address displayed that the last two hexadecimal digits for the LEC, LES, and BUS are shown as **. This indicates to us that the addresses shown are just a template that may be used if you choose to implement any of the services on your LANE module. When a LEC or LES is started on the LANE module, use a subinterface under ATM 0. The ** is replaced with the subinterface number in the real address. If you choose to start a LES on Cat_2, subinterface 1, it will have the hexadecimal address 47.00918100000000102962E801.001029075031.**01**

The address of a LES on Cat_3 will be different. Using the SHOW LANE DEFAULT command on Cat_3's LANE module yields Figure 11-21. Since the second ELAN is configured on Cat_3, the LES for it is created on subinterface 2. The benefit of this self-documentation in the configuration will be seen shortly. Having made this choice, the address for the LES on Cat_3 will be 47.00918100000000102962E801.0010292DFC31.**02**, where we have substituted 02 for the ** shown in the template.

FIGURE 11-21   Results of SHOW LANE DEFAULT on Cat_3

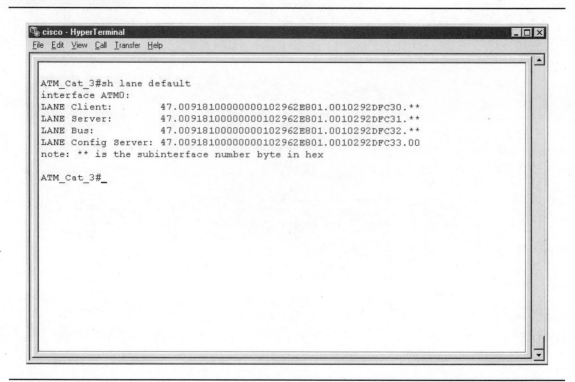

```
ATM_Cat_3#sh lane default
interface ATM0:
LANE Client:        47.00918100000000102962E801.0010292DFC30.**
LANE Server:        47.00918100000000102962E801.0010292DFC31.**
LANE Bus:           47.00918100000000102962E801.0010292DFC32.**
LANE Config Server: 47.00918100000000102962E801.0010292DFC33.00
note: ** is the subinterface number byte in hex

ATM_Cat_3#_
```

Armed with the addresses where the two LES instances run when configured, you can now create the LECS database. Use the global configuration command LANE DATABASE to create the LECS database. We cannot fit the entire command string on screen at one time. The IOS EXEC editor must scroll our text to the left or right to accommodate a command this long. Instead examine the following commands. The complete commands to create two database entries on Cat_3 look like this:

```
ATM_Cat_3(config)#lane database Cat_2_LECS_db
ATM_Cat_3(lane-config-database)#name Management server
47.00918100000000102962E801.001029075031.01
ATM_Cat_3(lane-config-database)#name Sales server
47.00918100000000102962E801.0010292DFC31.02
```

Now that the database is configured, you need to enter two more commands to activate the LECS. First, tell the LANE software to use the auto-configured addressing provided by ILMI to configure its NSAP address. The command looks like this:

```
ATM_Cat_3(config)#interface atm0
ATM_Cat_3(config-if)#lane config auto-config-atm-address
```

Configuring the LECS to answer requests using the LECS database we just created is the final step. Use this syntax while still in interface configuration mode:

```
ATM_Cat_3(config-if)#lane config database Cat_2_LECS_db
```

This command is described as binding the LECS database to the ATM 0 interface. Once the database is bound, the LECS is ready to serve the NSAP addresses of LESs to requesting clients. You want to insure the LECS is working properly. Use the SHOW LANE CONFIG command to see details of the LECS operation. In Figure 11-22, examine the "Admin State" line. Note that the LECS is up and operating. The next line provides information about an optional LANE service called the Simple Server Redundancy Protocol (SSRP), which will be discussed shortly. Also, note the NSAP address that the LANE server is using. The LECS is now ready to service requests, but you must first configure our ATM switch to provide the LECS NSAP address when a LEC requests it.

FIGURE 11-22   Results of SHOW LANE CONFIG on Cat_2

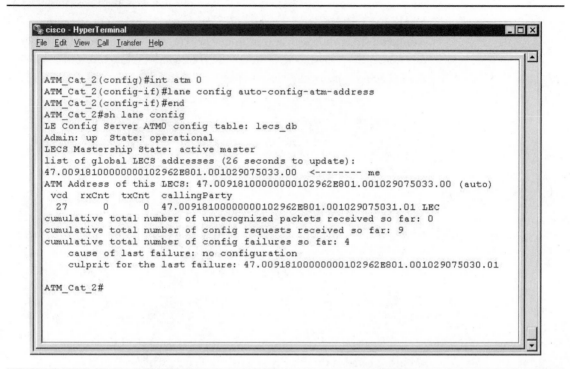

```
cisco - HyperTerminal                                          _ □ ✕
File  Edit  View  Call  Transfer  Help

ATM_Cat_2(config)#int atm 0
ATM_Cat_2(config-if)#lane config auto-config-atm-address
ATM_Cat_2(config-if)#end
ATM_Cat_2#sh lane config
LE Config Server ATM0 config table: lecs_db
Admin: up   State: operational
LECS Mastership State: active master
list of global LECS addresses (26 seconds to update):
47.00918100000000102962E801.001029075033.00  <-------- me
ATM Address of this LECS: 47.00918100000000102962E801.001029075033.00 (auto)
 vcd  rxCnt  txCnt  callingParty
  27     0      0   47.00918100000000102962E801.001029075031.01 LEC
cumulative total number of unrecognized packets received so far: 0
cumulative total number of config requests received so far: 9
cumulative total number of config failures so far: 4
    cause of last failure: no configuration
    culprit for the last failure: 47.00918100000000102962E801.001029075030.01

ATM_Cat_2#
```

ATM Switch ILMI Configuration

Recall that the LEC needs to find the LECS during the LANE setup phase.
The LEC can use any one of three methods to find the LECS.

- You can simply type the LECS address into the LEC configuration

- You can instruct the LECS to advertise at the well-known ATM NSAP address

- You can configure ILMI on your ATM switch to provide the LECS address

In this example, we will use the ILMI method. ILMI uses ATM VCI/VPI 0/16 by default for communication between the ATM switch and a directly connected LEC. Cisco's LANE module and the LS-1010 ATM switch both configure this virtual circuit by default. You need only provide the LECS address to configure ILMI. This address is placed on the ATM switch in either global or interface configuration mode. Use the configuration mode command ATM LECS-ADDRESS. Figure 11-23 shows us an example of this configuration step.

FIGURE 11-23 Configuring the ATM switch for ILMI

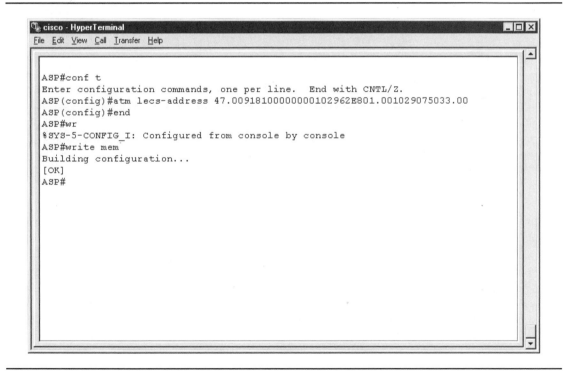

```
ASP#conf t
Enter configuration commands, one per line.  End with CNTL/Z.
ASP(config)#atm lecs-address 47.00918100000000102962E801.001029075033.00
ASP(config)#end
ASP#wr
%SYS-5-CONFIG_I: Configured from console by console
ASP#write mem
Building configuration...
[OK]
ASP#
```

Configuring the LES/BUS

The next step in configuring the LANE internetwork is starting the LES instances. You should keep in mind that we have already configured addresses for the LES instances when the LECS database was configured. The selector byte portion of the address is determined by the subinterface number used when configuring the LES. Since a selector byte of 0x01 was used when the NAME command was configured for ELAN Management, you must use subinterface 1 to start the LES for ELAN Management. Figure 11-24 illustrates the LANE SERVER-BUS command on the ATM LANE module installed in Cat_2. This command starts an instance of the LAN Emulation Server/broadcast and unknown server software on ATM subinterface 1 for the emulated LAN named Management.

FIGURE 11-24   Configuring and verifying the LES/BUS on Cat_2

```
cisco - HyperTerminal                                                    _ □ ×
File  Edit  View  Call  Transfer  Help


ATM_Cat_2#conf t
Enter configuration commands, one per line.   End with CNTL/Z.
ATM_Cat_2(config)#int atm 0.1 multipoint
ATM_Cat_2(config-subif)#lane server-bus ?
  ethernet   Emulate Ethernet

ATM_Cat_2(config-subif)#lane server-bus ethernet ?
  WORD   Name of the emulated LAN

ATM_Cat_2(config-subif)#lane server-bus ethernet Management
ATM_Cat_2(config-subif)#end
ATM_Cat_2#
ATM_Cat_2#
ATM_Cat_2#sh lane server
LE Server ATM0.1   ELAN name: Management  Admin: up   State: operational
type: ethernet          Max Frame Size: 1516
ATM address: 47.00918100000000102962E801.001029075031.01
LECS used: 47.00918100000000102962E801.001029075033.00 connected, vcd 40


ATM_Cat_2#_
```

Likewise in Figure 11-25, an instance of the LES/BUS for ELAN
Sales on subinterface 2 on Cat_3 is started. In both figures, notice that
the MULTIPOINT parameter is added to the LANE SERVER-BUS
command. This is necessary for all LANE subinterfaces, because each
will be the source or destination of more than one virtual circuit.
It is important at this point, to make sure that there are no errors in the
configuration. There are several diagnostic tools available. After the software is
started, use the SHOW LANE SERVER command. As you see in Figure 11-24
and Figure 11-25, the LES software has found the LECS at the indicated
address and set up a VCC to it. In both figures the VCC is referred to using
an index number called the virtual channel descriptor (VCD). Each VCC is
represented by its VCD. You can examine the VCD table using the enable
mode command SHOW ATM VC on each of your ATM devices.

FIGURE 11-25   Configuring and verifying the LES/BUS on Cat_3

```
cisco - HyperTerminal                                                    _ □ ×
File  Edit  View  Call  Transfer  Help

ATM_Cat_3#conf t
Enter configuration commands, one per line.  End with CNTL/Z.
ATM_Cat_3(config)#int atm 0.2 multipoint
ATM_Cat_3(config-subif)#lane server-bus ethernet Sales
ATM_Cat_3(config-subif)#end
ATM_Cat_3#
ATM_Cat_3#
ATM_Cat_3#
ATM_Cat_3#show lane server
LE Server ATM0.2  ELAN name: Sales  Admin: up  State: operational
type: ethernet       Max Frame Size: 1516
ATM address: 47.00918100000000102962E801.0010292DFC31.02
LECS used: 47.00918100000000102962E801.001029075033.00 connected, vcd 4

ATM_Cat_3#
```

Compare VCD 40 in Figure 11-24 with the same VCD in Figure 11-26. Now you can see the VPI/VCI combination 0/149 assigned to the VCC by the ATM signaling process and that the VCC is a LANE-LES type VCC. Notice that the interface originating the VCD is ATM 0.1, while the interface for two LECS VCCs is ATM0.

In Figure 11-27, you see only the ILMI and signaling VCCs on interface ATM 0 and the LANE-LES VCC on ATM 0.2, because there is no LECS running on the LANE module in Cat_3. Since you see the VCCs that we expected running on the correct subinterfaces, we conclude that the configuration is working up to this point. The final task is configuring LECs to join both of the ELANs.

FIGURE 11-26   Results of SHOW ATM VC on Cat_2

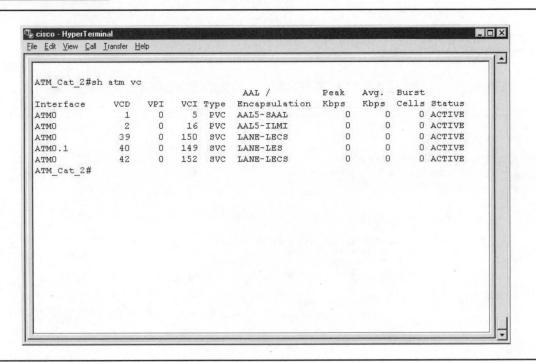

```
ATM_Cat_2#sh atm vc
                                    AAL /          Peak   Avg.   Burst
Interface     VCD   VPI   VCI Type  Encapsulation  Kbps   Kbps   Cells Status
ATM0          1     0     5   PVC   AAL5-SAAL      0      0      0 ACTIVE
ATM0          2     0     16  PVC   AAL5-ILMI      0      0      0 ACTIVE
ATM0          39    0     150 SVC   LANE-LECS      0      0      0 ACTIVE
ATM0.1        40    0     149 SVC   LANE-LES       0      0      0 ACTIVE
ATM0          42    0     152 SVC   LANE-LECS      0      0      0 ACTIVE
ATM_Cat_2#
```

FIGURE 11-27 Results of SHOW ATM VC on Cat_3

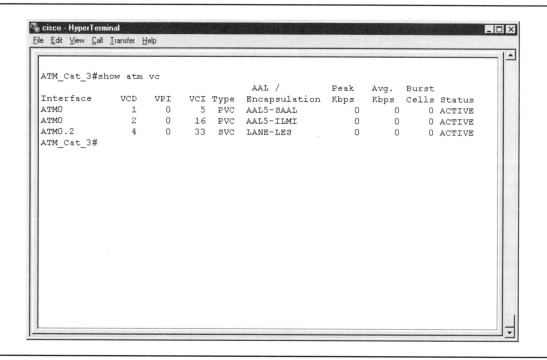

```
ATM_Cat_3#show atm vc
                                    AAL /          Peak   Avg.   Burst
Interface    VCD   VPI   VCI  Type  Encapsulation  Kbps   Kbps   Cells Status
ATM0          1     0     5   PVC   AAL5-SAAL         0      0       0 ACTIVE
ATM0          2     0    16   PVC   AAL5-ILMI         0      0       0 ACTIVE
ATM0.2        4     0    33   SVC   LANE-LES          0      0       0 ACTIVE
ATM_Cat_3#
```

LEC Configuration

Now configure two LECs. Recall that each instance of the LEC software must operate at a different ATM NSAP address. Also, each copy of the LEC software takes the same ESI from the pool of addresses available to auto-configuration. In order to maintain unique addressing, therefore, you must ensure that each instance of LEC software receives a different Selector field. Using different subinterfaces accomplishes this goal.

In Figure 11-28, the LANE CLIENT command is used to start the LEC for the Management ELAN and bind it to VLAN Ethernet 1 on the existing ATM 0.1 subinterface. A new subinterface, ATM 0.2, is created, and a LEC is configured to carry traffic between the Sales ELAN and VLAN Ethernet 2.

Similarly, in Figure 11-29, instances of both LECs on Cat_3 are configured. As soon as you configure a LEC instance, it starts the signaling process of the LANE setup phase. The results are seen with the SHOW ATM VC command again.

FIGURE 11-28   Configuring the LEC on Cat_2

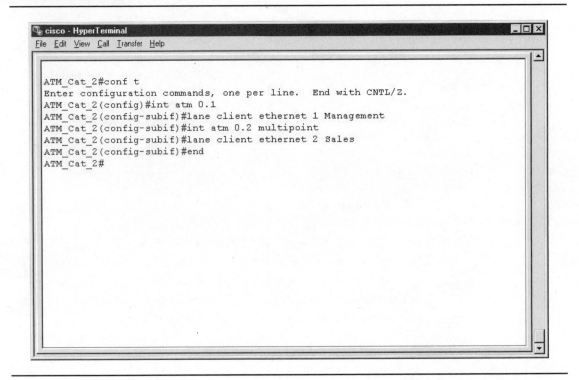

```
ATM_Cat_2#conf t
Enter configuration commands, one per line.  End with CNTL/Z.
ATM_Cat_2(config)#int atm 0.1
ATM_Cat_2(config-subif)#lane client ethernet 1 Management
ATM_Cat_2(config-subif)#int atm 0.2 multipoint
ATM_Cat_2(config-subif)#lane client ethernet 2 Sales
ATM_Cat_2(config-subif)#end
ATM_Cat_2#
```

FIGURE 11-29   Configuring the LEC on Cat_3

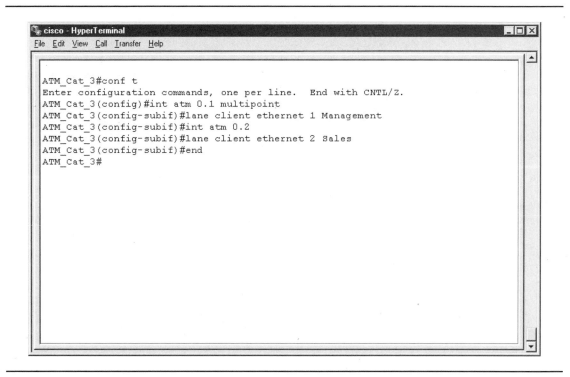

```
ATM_Cat_3#conf t
Enter configuration commands, one per line.  End with CNTL/Z.
ATM_Cat_3(config)#int atm 0.1 multipoint
ATM_Cat_3(config-subif)#lane client ethernet 1 Management
ATM_Cat_3(config-subif)#int atm 0.2
ATM_Cat_3(config-subif)#lane client ethernet 2 Sales
ATM_Cat_3(config-subif)#end
ATM_Cat_3#
```

Figure 11-30 and Figure 11-31 show the VCCs between each LEC and the LES and BUS for its ELAN. Notice that each of the new VCCs is associated with an ATM subinterface.

FIGURE 11-30   Results of SHOW ATM VC on Cat_2

```
ATM_Cat_2#sh atm vc
                                 AAL /          Peak  Avg.  Burst
Interface    VCD  VPI   VCI Type Encapsulation  Kbps  Kbps  Cells Status
ATM0           1    0     5 PVC  AAL5-SAAL         0     0      0 ACTIVE
ATM0           2    0    16 PVC  AAL5-ILMI         0     0      0 ACTIVE
ATM0          39    0   150 SVC  LANE-LECS         0     0      0 ACTIVE
ATM0.1        40    0   149 SVC  LANE-LES          0     0      0 ACTIVE
ATM0          42    0   152 SVC  LANE-LECS         0     0      0 ACTIVE
ATM0.1        55    0   166 SVC  LANE-LES          0     0      0 ACTIVE
ATM0.1        56    0   165 SVC  LANE-LEC          0     0      0 ACTIVE
ATM0.1        57    0   168 MSVC LANE-LEC          0     0      0 ACTIVE
ATM0.1        58    0   167 MSVC LANE-LES          0     0      0 ACTIVE
ATM0.1        59    0   170 SVC  LANE-BUS          0     0      0 ACTIVE
ATM0.1        60    0   169 SVC  LANE-LEC          0     0      0 ACTIVE
ATM0.1        61    0   172 MSVC LANE-LEC          0     0      0 ACTIVE
ATM0.1        62    0   171 MSVC LANE-BUS          0     0      0 ACTIVE
ATM0.2        65    0   175 SVC  LANE-LEC          0     0      0 ACTIVE
ATM0.2        66    0   176 MSVC LANE-LEC          0     0      0 ACTIVE
ATM0.2        67    0   177 SVC  LANE-LEC          0     0      0 ACTIVE
ATM0.2        68    0   178 MSVC LANE-LEC          0     0      0 ACTIVE
ATM_Cat_2#_
```

You can verify your configuration of LECs using the VCC table as well as the results of the SHOW LANE CLIENT command. Here is a sample:

```
ATM_Cat_2#show lane client
LE Client ATM0.1  ELAN name: Management  Admin: up  State: operational
Client ID: 1                  LEC up for 1 minute 23 seconds
Join Attempt: 1
HW Address: 0010.2907.5030   Type: ethernetMax Frame Size: 1516
VLANID: 1
ATM Address: 47.009181000000000102962E801.001029075030.01

VCD   rxFrames  txFrames  Type       ATM Address
  0          0         0  configure  47.009181000000000102962E801.001029075033.00
 56          1        44  direct     47.009181000000000102962E801.001029075031.01
 57         43         0  distribute 47.009181000000000102962E801.001029075031.01
```

```
60          0          44   send      47.009181000000000102962E801.001029075032.01
61          0           0   forward   47.009181000000000102962E801.001029075032.01

LE Client ATM0.2  ELAN name: Sales  Admin: up   State: operational
Client ID: 1                        LEC up for 1 minute 0 second
Join Attempt: 1
HW Address: 0010.2907.5030   Type: ethernetMax Frame Size: 1516
VLANID: 2
ATM Address: 47.009181000000000102962E801.001029075030.02

VCD  rxFrames  txFrames  Type       ATM Address
  0         0         0  configure  47.009181000000000102962E801.001029075033.00
 65         1         2  direct     47.009181000000000102962E801.0010292DFC31.02
 66         1         0  distribute 47.009181000000000102962E801.0010292DFC31.02
 67         0         0  send       47.009181000000000102962E801.0010292DFC32.02
 68         0         0  forward    47.009181000000000102962E801.0010292DFC32.02
ATM_Cat_2#
```

FIGURE 11-31   Results of SHOW ATM VC on Cat_3

```
cisco - HyperTerminal                                              _ □ ✕
File  Edit  View  Call  Transfer  Help

ATM_Cat_3#sh atm vc
                                 AAL /         Peak  Avg.  Burst
Interface    VCD  VPI  VCI Type  Encapsulation Kbps  Kbps  Cells Status
ATM0          1    0    5  PVC   AAL5-SAAL       0     0     0   ACTIVE
ATM0          2    0   16  PVC   AAL5-ILMI       0     0     0   ACTIVE
ATM0.2        4    0   33  SVC   LANE-LES        0     0     0   ACTIVE
ATM0.2        5    0   34  SVC   LANE-LES        0     0     0   ACTIVE
ATM0.2        6    0   35  MSVC  LANE-LES        0     0     0   ACTIVE
ATM0.2        7    0   36  SVC   LANE-BUS        0     0     0   ACTIVE
ATM0.2        8    0   37  MSVC  LANE-BUS        0     0     0   ACTIVE
ATM0.1       10    0   39  SVC   LANE-LEC        0     0     0   ACTIVE
ATM0.1       11    0   40  MSVC  LANE-LEC        0     0     0   ACTIVE
ATM0.1       12    0   41  SVC   LANE-LEC        0     0     0   ACTIVE
ATM0.1       13    0   42  MSVC  LANE-LEC        0     0     0   ACTIVE
ATM0.2       15    0   45  SVC   LANE-LES        0     0     0   ACTIVE
ATM0.2       16    0   44  SVC   LANE-LEC        0     0     0   ACTIVE
ATM0.2       17    0   46  MSVC  LANE-LEC        0     0     0   ACTIVE
ATM0.2       18    0   48  SVC   LANE-BUS        0     0     0   ACTIVE
ATM0.2       19    0   47  SVC   LANE-LEC        0     0     0   ACTIVE
ATM0.2       20    0   49  MSVC  LANE-LEC        0     0     0   ACTIVE
ATM_Cat_3#_
```

This display is helpful in troubleshooting, as it identifies the ATM NSAP address at the other end of each VCC. The SHOW LANE CLIENT display on Cat_3 looks like this:

```
ATM_Cat_3#show lane client
LE Client ATM0.1  ELAN name: Management  Admin: up  State: operational
Client ID: 2                 LEC up for 1 minute 12 seconds
Join Attempt: 1
HW Address: 0010.292d.fc30  Type: ethernet  Max Frame Size: 1516  VLANID: 1
ATM Address: 47.00918100000000102962E801.0010292DFC30.01

  VCD  rxFrames  txFrames  Type        ATM Address
   0         0         0  configure  47.00918100000000102962E801.001029075033.00
  10         1         2  direct     47.00918100000000102962E801.001029075031.01
  11        38         0  distribute 47.00918100000000102962E801.001029075031.01
  12         0         2  send       47.00918100000000102962E801.001029075032.01
  13        38         0  forward    47.00918100000000102962E801.001029075032.01

LE Client ATM0.2  ELAN name: Sales  Admin: up  State: operational
Client ID: 2                 LEC up for 1 minute 0 second
Join Attempt: 1
HW Address: 0010.292d.fc30  Type: ethernet  Max Frame Size: 1516 VLANID: 2
ATM Address: 47.00918100000000102962E801.0010292DFC30.02

  VCD  rxFrames  txFrames  Type        ATM Address
   0         0         0  configure  47.00918100000000102962E801.001029075033.00
  16         1         2  direct     47.00918100000000102962E801.0010292DFC31.02
  17         1         0  distribute 47.00918100000000102962E801.0010292DFC31.02
  19         0         0  send       47.00918100000000102962E801.0010292DFC32.02
  20         0         0  forward    47.00918100000000102962E801.0010292DFC32.02

ATM_Cat_3#
```

The Type field displayed by SHOW LANE CLIENT displays the VCC names described in the section on the LANE setup phase. The "configure" type VCD is the configuration direct VCC. You recall this is the VCC set up by the LEC to the LECS for the purpose of finding an address for the LES. Next you see that the LEC has a "direct" type VCD that corresponds to the control direct VCC initiated by the LEC to the LES. When the LEC sends a join request along this VCC, the LES responds by adding the new LEC to the control distribute VCC. You see the resulting VCD as the type "distribute" VCD in the output.

Continuing through the setup process, the LEC next requests the address of the BUS and then sets up the multicast send VCC, which we see identified as the "send" VCD. The BUS then adds the new LEC to the multicast forward VCC, which maps to the type "forward" VCD in the SHOW LANE CLIENT display. In troubleshooting the LEC configuration, we look for an Address field of all zeros to identify a VCC that failed to initialize. Most commonly, addressing of the LECS or of the LES in the LECS database is the root of LEC setup problems. Look for missing VCDs in your configuration for clues to where your configuration might be missing.

If we suspect a problem with a LEC finding the LES, you can examine the SHOW LANE SERVER command. In Figure 11-32, we see that the LES for ELAN Sales running on Cat_3 now recognizes a VCD to both the LEC configured on Cat_3 and the one on Cat_2. In the Figure 11-32, the LANE ARP table with the command SHOW LANE LE-ARP is also examined. Since no data has yet been sent across the LANE network, the LE-ARP table should be empty, as the display shows.

| FIGURE 11-32 | Results of SHOW LANE SERVER on Cat_3 |

```
cisco - HyperTerminal                                                    _ □ ×
File  Edit  View  Call  Transfer  Help

ATM_Cat_3#sh lane server
LE Server ATM0.2   ELAN name: Sales  Admin: up   State: operational
type: ethernet           Max Frame Size: 1516
ATM address: 47.00918100000000102962E801.0010292DFC31.02
LECS used: 47.00918100000000102962E801.001029075033.00 connected, vcd 4
control distribute: vcd 6, 2 members, 2 packets

proxy/ (ST: Init, Conn, Waiting, Adding, Joined, Operational, Reject, Term)
lecid ST vcd    pkts Hardware Addr  ATM Address
   1P O    5      2 0010.2907.5030 47.00918100000000102962E801.001029075030.02
   2P O   15      2 0010.292d.fc30 47.00918100000000102962E801.0010292DFC30.02

ATM_Cat_3#
ATM_Cat_3#show lane le-arp
Hardware Addr   ATM Address                              VCD   Interface
ATM_Cat_3#
```

Sending Data Over LANE

In the LANE CLIENT command described in the last section, a particular ELAN was mapped to a specific VLAN on the Catalyst 5000. Whenever a broadcast frame floods throughout such a VLAN, copies of the broadcast frame will be delivered by the LEC to all other LECs that have joined the ELAN. We can test this capability by sending a PING across the LANE network from one Catalyst to the other. Before sending the ICMP echo request, the IP client, sc0, on our Catalyst will send an ARP request as an Ethernet broadcast. In Figure 11-33, we use the PING command to cause ARP broadcasts and ICMP echo and echo-reply traffic to cross the ATM network.

Successfully pinging across the LANE network is the best indication that your configuration is sound. After the ARP broadcast transits the LANE

FIGURE 11-33   Sending data over LANE

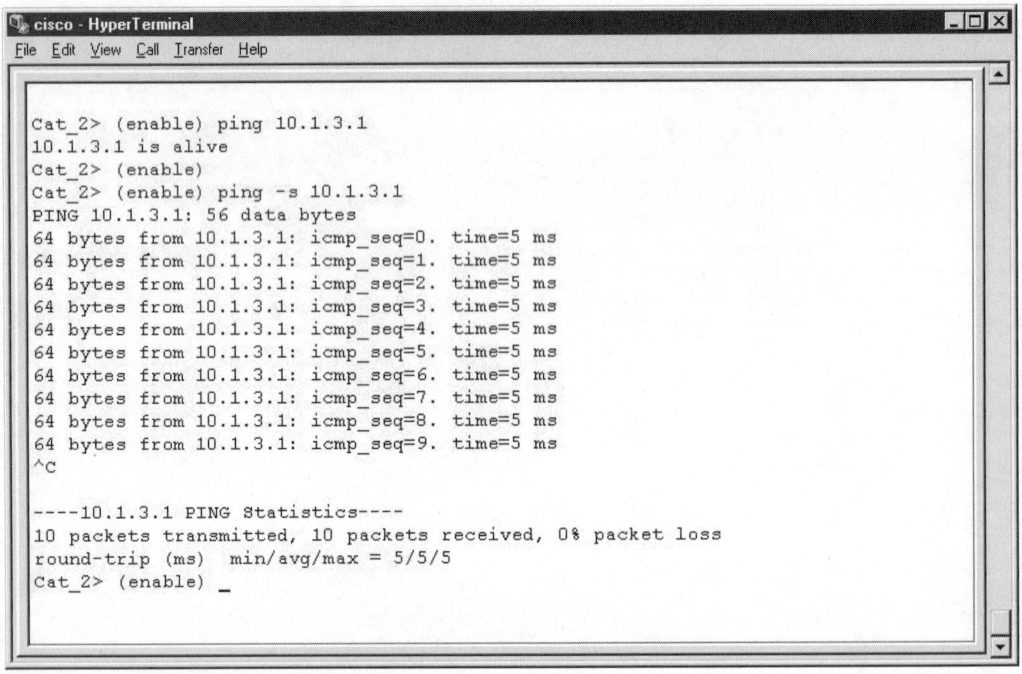

```
cisco - HyperTerminal
File  Edit  View  Call  Transfer  Help

Cat_2> (enable) ping 10.1.3.1
10.1.3.1 is alive
Cat_2> (enable)
Cat_2> (enable) ping -s 10.1.3.1
PING 10.1.3.1: 56 data bytes
64 bytes from 10.1.3.1: icmp_seq=0. time=5 ms
64 bytes from 10.1.3.1: icmp_seq=1. time=5 ms
64 bytes from 10.1.3.1: icmp_seq=2. time=5 ms
64 bytes from 10.1.3.1: icmp_seq=3. time=5 ms
64 bytes from 10.1.3.1: icmp_seq=4. time=5 ms
64 bytes from 10.1.3.1: icmp_seq=5. time=5 ms
64 bytes from 10.1.3.1: icmp_seq=6. time=5 ms
64 bytes from 10.1.3.1: icmp_seq=7. time=5 ms
64 bytes from 10.1.3.1: icmp_seq=8. time=5 ms
64 bytes from 10.1.3.1: icmp_seq=9. time=5 ms
^C

----10.1.3.1 PING Statistics----
10 packets transmitted, 10 packets received, 0% packet loss
round-trip (ms)  min/avg/max = 5/5/5
Cat_2> (enable) _
```

network through the BUS, the destination device (in this case, the sc0 interface on Cat-3) replies with a unicast frame of data directed to Cat_2's Ethernet MAC address. The unicast frame is divided into cells that are forwarded to the BUS. At the same time, the LEC on Cat_3 sends an LE-ARP request to the LES for ELAN Management. The LEC is looking for an NSAP address to send the remaining cells in the ARP reply. Since the LES has not yet cached this NSAP-to-MAC mapping, the request is forwarded to all LEC instances that belong to the Management ELAN. When the LEC on Cat_2 receives the LE-ARP, it will reply with its own NSAP address.

Now the LES for ELAN Management has sufficient information to cache a response and send it on to the LEC on Cat_3. You can see the cached response at the LES using the SHOW LANE LE-ARP command on Cat_2. In Figure 11-34, you see the MAC-to-NSAP mapping.

FIGURE 11-34   Examining the LE-ARP cache on Cat_3

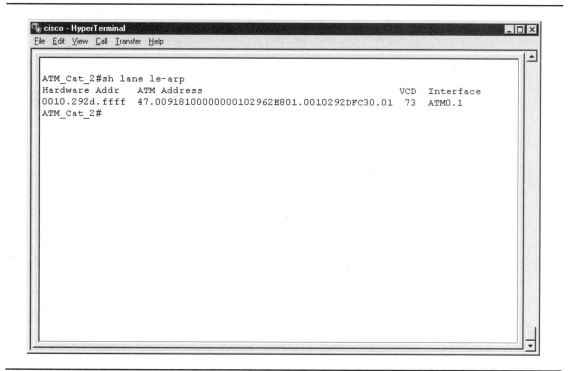

Compare this with the results of the SHOW MODULE command on Cat_3 in Figure 11-35. You notice that the MAC address cached by the LES matches the sc0 address from the pool provided by Cat_3's supervisor module.

As a final step in the process, the LEC on Cat_3 uses the NSAP address provided by the LE-ARP to create a VCC directly to the LEC on Cat_2. This is the data direct VCC that provides an efficient path from LEC to LEC in an ATM LANE network. You observe the data direct VCC using the SHOW ATM VC command. In Figure 11-36, we notice the new VCD number 73. The type associated with VCD 73 is LANE-DATA, indicating the data direct VCC. Congratulations on your first working LANE configuration!

FIGURE 11-35   Verifying Ethernet MAC addresses on Cat_2

```
Cisco - HyperTerminal
File  Edit  View  Call  Transfer  Help

Cat_3> (enable) show module
Mod Module-Name          Ports Module-Type            Model     Serial-Num Status
--- -------------------- ----- ---------------------- --------- ---------- -------
1                        2     100BaseTX Supervisor   WS-X5509  007409824  ok
2                        12    10/100BaseTX Ethernet  WS-X5203  007414720  ok
3                        1     Route Switch           WS-X5302  006806423  ok
4                        2     MM OC-3 Dual-Phy ATM   WS-X5158  008444034  ok
5                        24    10BaseT Ethernet       WS-X5013  006813503  ok

Mod MAC-Address(es)                        Hw     Fw      Sw
--- -------------------------------------- ------ ------- ------------------
1   00-10-29-2d-fc-00 to 00-10-29-2d-ff-ff 2.1    2.4(1)  4.2(2)
2   00-e0-1e-e8-86-7c to 00-e0-1e-e8-86-87 1.1    3.1(1)  4.2(2)
3   00-e0-1e-91-cd-c8 to 00-e0-1e-91-cd-c9 4.5    20.1    11.2(7)P, SHAR
4   00-10-7b-42-ab-56                       2.1    1.3     3.2(4)
5   00-e0-1e-90-34-48 to 00-e0-1e-90-34-5f 1.1    2.3(1)  4.2(2)

Mod Sub-Type Sub-Model Sub-Serial Sub-Hw
--- -------- --------- ---------- ------
1   EARL 1+  WS-F5511  0007461350 1.0
Cat_3> (enable) _
```

FIGURE 11-36 Verifying the data direct VCC

```
cisco - HyperTerminal                                                      _ □ ×
File  Edit  View  Call  Transfer  Help

ATM_Cat_2#sh atm vc
                                   AAL /        Peak   Avg.   Burst
Interface    VCD   VPI   VCI  Type Encapsulation Kbps  Kbps   Cells  Status
ATM0          1     0     5   PVC  AAL5-SAAL       0     0      0  ACTIVE
ATM0          2     0    16   PVC  AAL5-ILMI       0     0      0  ACTIVE
ATM0         39     0   150   SVC  LANE-LECS       0     0      0  ACTIVE
ATM0.1       40     0   149   SVC  LANE-LES        0     0      0  ACTIVE
ATM0         42     0   152   SVC  LANE-LECS       0     0      0  ACTIVE
ATM0.1       55     0   166   SVC  LANE-LES        0     0      0  ACTIVE
ATM0.1       56     0   165   SVC  LANE-LEC        0     0      0  ACTIVE
ATM0.1       57     0   168  MSVC  LANE-LEC        0     0      0  ACTIVE
ATM0.1       58     0   167  MSVC  LANE-LES        0     0      0  ACTIVE
ATM0.1       59     0   170   SVC  LANE-BUS        0     0      0  ACTIVE
ATM0.1       60     0   169   SVC  LANE-LEC        0     0      0  ACTIVE
ATM0.1       61     0   172  MSVC  LANE-LEC        0     0      0  ACTIVE
ATM0.1       62     0   171  MSVC  LANE-BUS        0     0      0  ACTIVE
ATM0.2       65     0   175   SVC  LANE-LEC        0     0      0  ACTIVE
ATM0.2       66     0   176  MSVC  LANE-LEC        0     0      0  ACTIVE
ATM0.2       67     0   177   SVC  LANE-LEC        0     0      0  ACTIVE
ATM0.2       68     0   178  MSVC  LANE-LEC        0     0      0  ACTIVE
ATM0.1       70     0   180   SVC  LANE-LES        0     0      0  ACTIVE
ATM0.1       71     0   181   SVC  LANE-BUS        0     0      0  ACTIVE
ATM0.1       73     0   183   SVC  LANE-DATA       0     0      0  ACTIVE
ATM_Cat_2#_
```

Optional LANE Configuration Steps

The simple LANE configuration that has been detailed so far provides excellent service for a lab environment or technology demonstration, but would not be suitable for a production network. The design suffers from several points of failure. For instance, if Cat 2 fails and the LECS is lost, the LES prevents communication over the ATM network. The LANE specification does not provide for duplicate services in a LANE network. Cisco adds the capability to create backup instances of the LES, BUS, and LECS services in your LANE network. Cisco calls the LANE extensions the Simple Server Redundancy Protocol (SSRP).

FROM THE CLASSROOM

ELANs and VLANs

So where are the trunk commands? We've spent the entire book talking about trunking multiple VLANs between switches. The SET TRUNK command has been used for Ethernet, Token Ring, and FDDI to activate the multi-VLAN ports. So why has that not been mentioned for LANE?

LANE itself, from a Catalyst switch, is only used to trunk multiple broadcast domains across the ATM network. LANE helps match the noisy, connectionless LAN protocols across the controlled, connection-oriented ATM world. In the LAN world, broadcasts are used to announce to, or request from, all machines.

ATM does not agree with this approach. To the ATM cloud, there is no all-stations packet (or cell). ATM only sends cells to predefined destinations. If the destination is not already known, then cells cannot go there. This is almost logical until you apply LAN protocols to the equation. LAN protocols basically say, "I have no idea of where I should go, so I'll go everywhere." This is an instant problem.

LANE solves this issue with the LANE devices covered in this chapter. The BUS is really the device that allows broadcast and unknown packets to travel the ATM cloud. Now, the cells are not allowed to wander the ATM network without an escort. The BUS replicates the cells that wish to visit everyone on all the appropriate virtual circuits.

Of course, "everyone" is defined as the LECs that have registered with the appropriate LES for the ELAN (broadcast domain). There truly is no way to speak to every device attached to the ATM cloud, unless all the devices are registered parts of the same ELAN. Since there are probably multiple ELANs out there, there is no one-cell-hits-all shot. Thus, the ELAN is the same broadcast domain as the VLAN.

Thus, to properly trunk across a LANE cloud, your Catalyst switch is configured as a client in each of the ELANs (VLANs) needed to get across the cloud. If all VLANs need to be in the trunk, then a client is needed in each ELAN. The simple presence of the configuration commands creates a LANE trunk.

—Neil Lovering, CCIE, CCSI

SSRP

SSRP adds a communication protocol between multiple LECS instances and all the LEC and LES/BUS instances that rely on them for configuration information. Using Cisco's SSRP, only one instance of each service is active at a given moment. Other instances act in a backup capacity until signaled by the current master LECS. To configure one or more backup LECS, you need only create the software instance on another Catalyst LANE module and configure ILMI on the ATM switch with additional ATM LECS-ADDRESS commands. The order of the commands is significant. The order of LECS addresses in the ATM switch determines the order in which they are used, should the first one fail.

You can also configure multiple copies of the LES and BUS service for each ELAN in the LANE network. Use the process we have described to create the services on multiple Catalyst LANE modules and add a NAME command to the LECS database for each one. The order of the commands in the LECS database determines which instance of LES and BUS is used first for a given ELAN.

Restricted and Unrestricted Membership ELANs

In the future, service providers may offer LANE service through public networks. If so, security of your LANE infrastructure may become an issue. To address such concerns, Cisco provides the capability to authenticate the identity of devices that attempt to join your ELANs. In the configuration described so far in this chapter, you have created unrestricted membership ELANs. If you wish to do so, you can configure the LECS to permit only specific LEC instances to join an ELAN, using the optional RESTRICTED parameter at the end of the NAME command in the LECS database. You then identify each LEC permitted to join the restricted ELAN, using the CLIENT-ATM-ADDRESS command. For example,

```
ATM_Cat_2(config)#client-atm-address
47.00918100000000102962E801.00102
9075030.01 name Management
```

After this command is issued, only this client is allowed to join the Management ELAN. You must specifically configure the address of each LEC that is used in a restricted membership ELAN.

CERTIFICATION SUMMARY

We have covered a significant amount of new ground in this chapter. For your Certification exam, you should make particular note of the way Cisco ATM NSAP address configuration creates unique addresses using four different ESI fields and the Selector field. You will also want to review the names of the various VCCs that are created during the setup phase and the one created during the operational phase.

ILMI provides a mechanism for LECs to find the LECS when they attempt to join an ELAN. You will want to review the process as well as the VPI/VCI 0/16 virtual circuit used by ILMI.

TWO-MINUTE DRILL

❑ Local-area network emulation (LANE) is a technology gaining popularity for providing Asynchronous Transfer Mode (ATM) service without the expense of deploying ATM to every desktop.

❑ ATM is a point-to-point network without a native capability to broadcast to all stations.

❑ ATM LAN emulation makes extensive use of point-to-point VCCs as well as point-to-multipoint VCCs.

❑ An ATM signaling protocol called System Services Connection-Oriented Protocol (SSCOP) facilitates a call setup process that LANE uses to create VCCs between ATM end systems like your Catalyst.

❑ ILMI is similar in concept to the IP Simple Network Management Protocol (SNMP) or the OSI Common Management Interface Protocol (CMIP) in that it allows ATM-connected devices to "get" and "put" information between each other.

❏ Certain LANE functions are implemented by software that must run on any ATM device that participates as a client to an ELAN. Once the software has registered an ATM device in a particular ELAN, the device is called a LANE Client or LEC.

❏ LEC software tasks can be divided into control functions and data-forwarding functions.

❏ Each LEC must register itself to become a member of an emulated LAN. The LES handles the registration process.

❏ When registering itself in an ELAN, a LEC is added to a point-to-multipoint VCC called the *multicast forward* VCC.

❏ Using Cisco equipment, the simplest way for a LEC to learn the NSAP address of the LECS is to configure an ATM switch to provide the answer.

❏ Each of the LANE software components—the LEC, LES, BUS, and LECS—are identified in the ATM network by their NSAP address.

❏ Cisco makes use of two fields in the ATM NSAP address format to create unique addresses: the End System ID (ESI) field and the NSAP Selector field.

❏ Cisco's LAN emulation module for the Catalyst 5000 series switches supports up to 255 LAN Emulation Clients concurrently.

❏ The LEC can use any one of three methods to find the LECS: you can simply type the LECS address into the LEC configuration; you can instruct the LECS to respond at the well-known ATM NSAP address; or you can configure ILMI on your ATM switch to provide the LECS address.

❏ You can verify your configuration of LECs using the VCC table as well as the results of the SHOW LANE CLIENT command.

❏ SSRP adds a communication protocol between multiple LECS instances and all the LEC and LES/BUS instances that rely on them for configuration information.

SELF TEST

The following Self Test questions will help you measure your understanding of the material presented in this chapter. Read all the choices carefully, as there may be more than one correct answer. Choose all correct answers for each question.

1. Which layer of the ATM protocol model performs the SAR function?

   A. AAL

   B. ATM

   C. PHY

   D. CPCS

2. Which of the following is a function of CPCS?

   A. Creating header error control code

   B. Segmenting cells

   C. Reassembling cells

   D. Padding frames

3. How many bits make up the VCI field in the ATM cell header?

   A. 12

   B. 16

   C. 24

   D. Depends on the UNI

4. The HEC can correct how many bit errors in a cell's Data field?

   A. Zero

   B. One

   C. Two

   D. Three

5. What does the acronym VCC stand for?

   A. Virtual circuit connection

   B. Virtual circuit connectionless

   C. Virtual channel circuit

   D. Virtual channel connection

6. Which is a protocol used by LANE to create a VCC?

   A. SS7

   B. SSCOP

   C. SSCP

   D. SSN

7. Which of the following is not an ATM address format?

   A. DCD

   B. DCC

   C. E.164

   D. ICD

8. Which of the following is the AFI field for an ICD ATM address?

   A. 0x41

   B. 0x39

   C. 0x47

   D. 0x45

9. The last field in an NSAP address is called?

   A. Selector

   B. HO-DSP

   C. End System ID

   D. AFI

10. What is the length of an ATM NSAP address?

    A. 25 octets

    B. 45 hex digits

    C. 160 bits

    D. Variable

11. What does the acronym ILMI stand for?

    A. Interim Link Management Integrated

    B. Integrated Link Management Interface

    C. Internal Line Management Interface

    D. Inverted Link Markup Interval

12. Which VPI/VCI does ILMI use?

    A. 0/16

    B. 0/17

    C. 0/2

    D. 0/5

13. Which VPI/VCI does QSAAL make use of?

    A. 0/16

    B. 0/17

    C. 0/2

    D. 0/5

14. Which of the following is not a component of LANE?

    A. BUCS

    B. LECS

    C. LES

    D. LEC

15. Which is a function of the LEC?

    A. Joining an ELAN

    B. Authenticating clients

    C. LE-ARP responses

    D. Replicating cells

16. Which is a function of the LECS?

    A. Joining an ELAN

    B. Authenticating clients

    C. LE-ARP responses

    D. Replicating cells

17. Which is a function of the BUS?

    A. Joining an ELAN

    B. Authenticating clients

    C. LE-ARP requests

    D. Replicating cells

18. Which is a function of the LES?

    A. Joining an ELAN

    B. Authenticating clients

    C. LE-ARP responses

    D. Replicating cells

19. Which VCC is set up between two LANE Clients when unicast data is sent?

    A. Control distribute VCC

    B. Configuration direct VCC

    C. Multicast forward VCC

    D. Data direct VCC

20. Which best describes Simple Server Redundancy Protocol?

    A. It is an ATM Forum standard for multiple LECS

    B. It allows multiple LANE Clients for each ELAN

    C. It is a more efficient LANE Client implementation

    D. It is Cisco's extension to ATM Forum LANE specification

CISCO CERTIFIED NETWORK PROFESSIONAL

12

Catalyst 1900 Series and Catalyst 2820 Switches

CERTIFICATION OBJECTIVES

The Cisco 1900 series and 2820 Catalyst switches are designed to provide low-cost, high-performance networking capabilities to today's high-performance Ethernet networks. The Catalyst 1900 series provides dedicated 10-Mbps Ethernet ports right to the desktop, along with 100-Mbps connectivity between workgroups. The Catalyst 2820 provides the same dedicated 10-Mbps Ethernet ports to the desktop, but also provides expansion slots for two plug-in modules that support 100BaseTX, 100BaseFX, ATM LANE, and FDDI connectivity for increased workgroup and/or WAN performance. The 1900 and 2820 Catalyst switches can also provide 100-Mbps connectivity to the desktop, but since the maximum number of 100-Mbps ports available on the 1900 and 2820 series is two, it is suggested that these ports be used for uplinks to the data center or the backbone.

In this chapter, we will discuss the concept of ClearChannel architecture, and how Cisco implements ClearChannel architecture in the 1900 series and 2820 Catalyst switches. We will also discuss the various features of both switches, configuration information for Ethernet, VLAN, SNMP, and ATM LANE. We will also cover the Standard and Enterprise editions of the Catalyst operating software—how they apply to the needs of the users, and the needs of those who maintain and monitor the network.

CERTIFICATION OBJECTIVE 12.01

ClearChannel Architecture

The ClearChannel architecture is implemented by Cisco to address the needs of high-performance networks in the area of bandwidth allocation. High-performance networks need a switch architecture that can handle the load that workgroups place upon the switch.

The ClearChannel architecture in use on the 1900 series and 2820 Catalyst switches has been developed as third-generation LAN switches. The following sections will provide a description of how ClearChannel architecture works, and how it has been incorporated into the 1900/2820 Catalyst switches.

There are four areas that Catalyst switches have been designed to address:

- Network management
- Bus architecture
- Packet forwarding
- Filtering and buffering of packets

Catalyst 1900 and 2820 support SNMP and RMON for advanced network management. They provide for loop-free network topology through the support of the Spanning-Tree Protocol, which identifies redundant links and backbone connections. These assist the network administrator by providing ease of use when installing and managing multiple switches in complex LAN environments.

The 1900/2820 Catalyst contains a one-gigabyte backplane bus. This bus provides access for the ports in an orderly fashion, to prevent problems caused by bandwidth delays. This allows the Catalyst to maintain the speed necessary for high-speed LAN access and usage. The 1900/2820 Catalyst also employs application-specific integrated circuit (ASIC) technology. Each ASIC contains eight 10BaseT ports, along with two port controllers and four Ethernet controllers. This allows for up to 24 10BaseT ports for the 2820 Catalyst.

The 1900/2820 Catalyst offers three different methods for frame forwarding. The first two are cut-through. They are FastForward and FragmentFree. A cut-through switch is defined as a switch that will begin forwarding a frame when it has received enough of the frame to determine the destination MAC address. The choice of cut-through method depends on your network. If your network has low latency along with a low collision rate, then FastForward is the best method. If your network has high latency and high collision rates, then FragmentFree is the answer. FragmentFree provides better error checking than FastForward, with no additional latency.

The other method of frame forwarding is store and forward. *Store and forward* is defined as a frame-forwarding method that stores the frame until all of the data is received, then forwards the frame to the appropriate exit port.

The methods of frame forwarding available on the 1900/2820 Catalyst give network administrators the advantage of being able to position switches and use a method to maximize network efficiency.

The 1900/2820 Catalyst switch has incorporated a packet-filtering and buffering scheme that allows the switch to maximize the memory available on the switch. This scheme allows for the dynamic allocation of buffer space to the ports as it is needed. Memory usage is also reduced by not allowing duplicate packets to be created during both broadcast and multicast packet transmission. This concept of shared memory is what allows the 1900/2820 Catalyst to handle more bursty traffic, while eliminating latency in today's high-speed LANs.

Overview of Architecture

The 1900/2820 Catalyst switches have been developed by Cisco as third generation, using ClearChannel architecture. The components that comprise ClearChannel architecture are the embedded control unit (ECU), forwarding engine, packet exchange bus (Xbus), and the shared memory buffer.

Embedded Control Unit

The ECU was developed to handle tasks that would normally take valuable hardware resources. These tasks include network management, configuration, and software images. There are three subsystems that make up the ECU. They are the embedded CPU, DRAM for the CPU (512KB), and 1MB of Flash memory for configuration files, statistical information, and for operating system software. The Flash memory is divided into three areas: a partition for the switch software image, a partition for switch configuration data, and a partition allocated for the boot sector.

The embedded control unit handles tasks that include the configuration of the switch, control of diagnostics and error reporting, the front panel display, Spanning-Tree Protocol, and inband/out-of-band management.

An example of in-band management would be control of the switch through an SNMP-based management such as CiscoWorks. Out-of-band management would be defined as access through the console port or serial link (remote access).

Forwarding Engine

The forwarding engine controls the central function of the switch. Tasks include examining packets arriving at the ports, checking the destination address, and then sending the packet to the appropriate exit port (packet processing). The forwarding engine also handles the collection and maintenance of statistical information. This is accomplished by monitoring the packet exchange bus. The forwarding engine counts packet length, errors, throughput, and exceptions, and makes this data available for collection by network management applications to provide accurate information that is used for network design or traffic pattern development.

Packet Exchange Bus (Xbus)

The packet exchange bus runs at 20 MHz and is 53 bits wide. The bandwidth allows data to be transferred on the Xbus at wire speed on all ports at the same time. The total bandwidth that is available on the Xbus is one Gbps.

Access to the Xbus is prioritized, with different functions having different priority depending on the nature of the data being placed on the bus. An example of bus priority would be buffer space requested for a packet yet to be placed on the bus getting a higher priority than a packet that is reaching the end of a transmission onto the bus. The Xbus is also used by the components of the switch itself for communications between the components. A master scheduler is used to control access to the Xbus.

Shared Buffer Memory

The 1900/2820 Catalyst uses 3MB of dynamic RAM for the shared buffer memory as a large packet buffer. This allows for a dynamic allocation of buffer memory to the individual ports. Through the use of a memory allocation mechanism, incoming packets are placed into buffers that are part of a pool that is available for use by all ports on the switch. Pointers are then linked to the correct queues for transport to the destination port when ready. Each port has a number of queues associated with it. Packets remain in the same location in memory until they are forwarded to the destination port(s). Buffers are dynamically allocated to ports as needed. Multicast and broadcast packets are not duplicated, thereby saving buffer space.

The forwarding engine retains a map of ports to which packet buffers need to be transmitted and keeps the memory allocated until the port has been transmitted to all destination ports.

The shared memory concept used on the 1900/2820 Catalyst switches is more efficient than port-based buffering. Head-of-line blocking, which is a common problem with port-based buffering, is eliminated, which can result in the switch becoming under-utilized. No single port can use more than 1.5MB of memory at any single time, leaving at least half of the memory available for other ports at any one moment.

exam
ⓦatch

Be familiar with the components that comprise the ClearChannel architecture. Be able to describe the different components and the tasks that each component performs. Also, know how the components communicate with each other to provide wire-speed switching capability.

CERTIFICATION OBJECTIVE 12.02

Catalyst 1900 and Catalyst 2820 Features

The 1900/2820 series of Catalyst switches have many features, which make them unique in the LAN switching industry. This section will examine each of the features and how these features make the Catalyst switches unique.

Cisco Group Management Protocol

The popularity of audio and video applications and playback, live financial information, and other new technologies has increased the demand for multicast-capable LAN switching technology. This technology uses a single source-to-multiple destination concept. Information originates from a single source (such as a workstation or server) and is sent to all workstations participating in the event. The problem that results is that switches will forward these packets (multicast packets) to all ports configured in the VLAN. This can cause bandwidth to be used unnecessarily. Cisco's answer to this problem is Cisco Group Management Protocol (CGMP).

CGMP was developed to prevent flooding of multicast packets to all ports in a VLAN. The 1900/2820 uses CGMP to communicate with Cisco routers to identify clients that are receiving multicast packets. The routers gather this Layer 3 information via the Internet Group Management Protocol (IGMP) from other routers in the network. With this information, the switch uses the forwarding engine to send these multicast packets only to the ports to which the destination clients are connected. CGMP allows for close communication between Catalysts and Cisco routers to handle the needs of Layer 3 and multicast information. This is a feature not found on other vendors' routers and switches.

Broadcast Storm Prevention

Broadcast storms occur when the amount of broadcast traffic gets to the point where application data is unable to use the available bandwidth. The source of a broadcast storm is usually a workstation on the LAN that has become faulty and starts to generate high amounts of broadcast packets.

To prevent broadcast storms, Cisco incorporated broadcast storm control within the IOS for the 1900/2820 series of Ethernet switches. This feature allows the port that is sending broadcast packets above the set threshold to be disabled from sending broadcast packets. Other packet types (unicast and multicast) are not affected by this; they will continue to be forwarded as usual. Once the amount of broadcast packets has fallen below the threshold, the switch will resume forwarding broadcast packets from the affected port. The administrator enables this feature, as it is disabled by default.

Multicast Packet Filtering

Packet filtering (specifically multicast traffic) is an important feature of the 1900/2820 Catalyst Ethernet switches. The Catalyst can filter multicast packets based on the multicast group number. The Catalyst keeps an up-to-date table of multicast groups and the ports the packets are being forwarded to. This multicast group/port number mapping eliminates the need for the switch to keep track of client MAC addresses. When the switch receives a multicast packet and the multicast group number is not listed in this table, the packet is flooded to all ports. The multicast group/port number matching is not automatic. The switch administrator must manually configure this information.

When combined with source port filtering, packet filtering has the ability to load-balance traffic across multiple ports. A good example would be two servers on the same VLAN (Servers A and B) that are also in the same multicast group. If the VLAN has multiple ports on the switch, the administrator can configure the switch to use certain ports for Server A and certain ports for Server B. This type of load balancing would be unnoticed by users, since the load balancing would be to the servers only.

Packet filtering gives administrators the advantage of being able to control multicast packet traffic in the absence of CGMP and routers that are running IGMP, at the expense of having to manually configure this information into the switch.

Support for Full-Duplex Ethernet

With the advent of unshielded twisted-pair (UTP) cabling for Ethernet networks, the 1900/2820 series of Catalyst switches can support full-duplex communication on the 100MB Fast Ethernet ports. This gives connections between devices such as routers with 100 Mbps Ethernet ports a full 200 Mbps of bandwidth (100 Mbps each for transmit and receive) for communication. Both devices must be configured for full-duplex operation to be able to take advantage of this capability.

This capability can be used for switch-to-switch, router-to-switch, or server-to-switch communication, where maximum speed is needed for optimum performance. When using a fiber connection between switches, full-duplex Ethernet can be extended to a maximum of 2.2km between the switches, routers, or servers. This is a feature that is not supported by older technology such as a repeater, which was used to extend Ethernet segments between buildings.

Spanning-Tree Protocol

Today's switched LANs often provide multiple paths from source to destination hosts. As a result, because switched LANs are switched, not routed, loops can occur if there is no control over multiple paths. To correct this problem, Cisco 1900/2820 employs the Spanning-Tree Protocol.

Spanning-Tree will detect and remove redundant links from the switched network topology. All switches in the network will use Spanning-Tree to create a loop-free path to all other switches in the network, using one switch as the "root switch" and then creating the loop-free path. Another feature of Spanning-Tree is that when a link or switch fails, the redundant links are used to re-create the topology around the failed switch or link.

In a VLAN configuration, the Catalyst originally supported up to four spanning trees, one for each supported VLAN. With the latest version of the Catalyst 1900 Enterprise switch, through the use of Inter-Switch Link (ISL) protocol, this number increases to 1000. Catalysts also support FastStart, which allows the switch's ports to activate and start participating in the spanning tree faster. This eliminates the situation in which devices attached to the switch experience delay in initial startup.

Switching Modes

The 1900/2820 series of Catalyst switches support three modes of switching. They are cut-through, modified cut-through, and store and forward. Each type has advantages and disadvantages when it comes to latency. Depending on the mode, the trade-off for faster latency is less error-checking capability. Changing switch modes is performed through the configuration menu. All modes allow for throughput at wire speed.

Store and Forward

A store and forward switch receives the entire packet (store) before sending the packet to the destination port (forward). The packet is checked for errors before it is forwarded. Packet latency depends on the size of the packet. Latency is measured from the moment the first bit is received until the first bit is forwarded. Normal latency for a Catalyst switch running in store and forward mode is about seven microseconds, not including the length of the packet.

Ports that are running different speeds use store and forward switching as opposed to cut-through. An example would be switching between a 10-Mbps and 100-Mbps Ethernet port. Because the Fast Ethernet is running at much higher speed, packet errors would occur, because the 100-Mbps port would run out of data before the 10-Mbps port has finished sending the packet.

The 100-Mbps port will store the packet and forward it when it has received the complete packet.

Cut-Through

In cut-through, or FastForward switching, the forwarding process is started once the port has received the first six bytes of the packet. This provides for very low latency, as the port has barely received the packet when it begins to forward.

The disadvantage to this mode is that there is very little error checking. Since the port begins forwarding once the first six bytes are received, there is no time taken for proper error checking. This mode is used mainly for LANs or VLANs that do not experience a lot of errors or collisions.

Modified Cut-Through

Modified cut-through, or FragmentFree switching, "stores" the first 64 bytes, then forwards the packet to the destination port. Ethernet collisions cause runt frames (frames that are less than 64 bytes in length) to exist on the wire. If the arriving frame is at least 64 bytes, then it cannot be a runt. Although a proper error check cannot be performed until the FCS arrives with the end of the frame, the frame is forwarded with very little additional latency.

FragmentFree provides the advantages of FastForward with low latency, and the advantage of the runt-free capabilities. Latency is about 70 microseconds when the switch is in FragmentFree mode.

exam
ⓦatch

Be able to describe the different switching options available on the 1900/2820 series of Catalyst switches. Know the benefits that each mode provides and how each is tailored to take advantage of different network topologies. Be able to identify which mode is used, based on network use.

Modules Supported

The hardware modules available on the 1900/2820 Catalyst switches use ASIC technology to provide wire-speed, low-latency operation. The use of ASICs combines components like Ethernet controllers, schedulers, forwarding engine, and Ethernet transceivers. Other tasks such as initialization, configuration, front panel display, and error diagnostics are handled by the CPU subsystem.

Quad Ethernet Controller ASIC

The Quad Ethernet Controller ASIC (QEC) contains four 10BaseT Ethernet controllers. The QEC handles the CSMA/CD aspect of the Ethernet protocol. Incoming packets are received by the QEC and placed onto the Xbus after they are arranged in 48-bit words. The QEC communicates with the master scheduler to ensure proper data communication with the Xbus. Outgoing packets are accepted by the QEC from the Xbus and arranged into the proper frame size for transmission out of the port.

The QEC also handles retransmissions. When the QEC detects a collision, it informs the forwarding engine that a collision has occurred and a new packet is needed. It will then receive the replacement data and handle it as it would any other packet.

There are six QEC ASICs on a board. This provides a total of 24 Ethernet ports per switch.

10BaseT Transceiver ASIC

The 10BaseT Transceiver ASIC handles Layer 1 tasks such as encoding and decoding of data as it is received from the LAN, signaling, and line-state monitoring.

Each ASIC handles eight 10BaseT transceivers, plus one additional 10BaseT or AUI-configurable connector for a drop cable configuration. Incoming data is received from the wire and passed to the correct QEC. Outgoing data is received from the QEC and sent out onto the LAN. Three ASICs handle 24 ports plus the extra AUI or 10BaseT port, and communicate with the six QEC ASICs.

High-Speed Ethernet Controller ASIC (Master Scheduler)

The Master Scheduler ASIC contains one 10BaseT Ethernet controller plus two 100-Mbps Fast Ethernet controllers. This ASIC also performs the same tasks as a QEC; it controls the movement of data across the Xbus.

The master scheduler (MS) generates Xbus cycles at set times to allow for the transfer of data to and from the Xbus.

Forwarding Engine ASIC

The heart of the 1900/2820 Catalyst switch is the Forwarding Engine ASIC. As stated earlier, the forwarding engine is the heart of the switch. The Forwarding Engine ASIC handles all decisions when it comes to forwarding packets. The FE ASIC also handles the collection and maintenance of switch statistics.

The master scheduler announces to the FE ASIC that a packet has been received. The FE will then transfer the packet to the buffer that the FE has made available for the packet. Once in buffers, the source and destination MAC addresses are noted. The addresses are compared to what is in the switch's content-addressable memory (CAM) table.

The FE then initiates a transmit process for the packet. With information from the CAM table, it identifies to which port(s) to send the packet. The packet is kept in the buffer until the QEC sends a message back indicating the packet was successfully transmitted. If an error occurs, the packet is then prepared for transmission again. Once a success message is sent from the QEC, the buffer is made available for use.

CPU

The CPU is an embedded processor in the 1900/2820 Catalyst. Network management for the switch is handled by the CPU. The CPU is responsible for in-band and out-of-band access to the switch. User commands such as configuration changes, statistics display, and other management tasks are performed by the CPU.

The CPU views two types of packets, broadcast and in-band management, when they are destined for the individual switch rather than the network. The CPU handles inter-switch communication sent with broadcast packets. An example of this is Cisco Discovery Protocol (CDP) used by the switches to gain information on neighboring switches. Other in-band communication would be Telnet and SNMP information, as these would be sent and responded to by the CPU.

The CPU processes packets identified by the forwarding engine that require CPU intervention. The FE flags the packet in buffer for the CPU to read. When the CPU needs to respond to these packets, it requests a buffer from the FE and places the packet in the buffer for the FE to forward to the appropriate destination port.

Cisco Discovery Protocol (CDP)

CDP was developed by Cisco as a tool for all Cisco products (routers and switches) to communicate with each other to gain detailed network topology information. Switches that are running CDP communicate with each other to learn and understand the network topology. CDP is built into the IOS software and is available on 1900/2820 Catalyst switches, even though the 1900/2820 switches do not run IOS. CDP is available on the Catalyst 1900/2820 series switches starting with software release version 5.

Network management programs such as VLANDirector use CDP information to build a low-level network graphical topology map.

Management Support

Full support for network management via SNMP is included in the 1900/2820 Catalyst switches. The SNMP MIB contains all of the information needed to configure and monitor the switch using SNMP management applications such as CiscoWorks and CiscoWorks for Switched Internetworks (CWSI).

RMON support for remote monitoring and statistics collection is supported via the RMON MIB. Using an RMON application, the switch queries for statistics, history, alarm, and event information that is stored in the switch's RMON MIB.

CERTIFICATION OBJECTIVE 12.03

Configuring Catalyst 1900 and Catalyst 2820 for VLANs, SNMP, and ATM LANE

The 1900/2820 Catalyst switches offer three methods for setup and configuration of the switch. The first is a Web-based graphical user interface

(GUI) that employs embedded HTML files located on Flash memory. The second is a menu-based interface, which is accessed either via the console port or Telnet access. The last method is via an SNMP-based network management application such as CiscoWorks.

on the **job**

When implementing the 1900/2820 series of Catalyst switches in your network, determining how the switch is to be utilized becomes important. In a corporate environment, the 1900/2820 is used to provide desktop connectivity to the corporate network by providing either 10-Mbps, or in some cases 100-Mbps Ethernet to the desktop. Determining which type of port to provide to the desktop user depends on the users themselves. For most users, 10 Mbps is sufficient even for the most powerful of desktop PCs. Today's servers, on the other hand, require 100 Mbps to be able to provide the performance the users require.

In a switched LAN environment, the most common topology is the tiered approach. The tiers are identified as the access tier, where the users are located, the distribution tier, where devices such as servers and routers would be located, and the core or backbone tier, which has the inter-office or inter-building links. The 1900/2820 Catalyst series switches are best used as the point of access for users in the three-tier network topology. With 10 Mbps to the desktops and 100-Mbps connectivity to the distribution tier for access to the servers and routers, the 1900/2820 is the ideal choice for today's switched network environments.

Web-Based Configuration

The Web console is an embedded HTML Web site that is contained in Flash memory. To be able to take advantage of the Web console, the switch must be configured with an IP address via the console port prior to accessing a Web browser. To access the Web console, you must have either Netscape Communicator 4.*xx* or Microsoft Internet Explorer 4.*xx* with JavaScript enabled.

The home page for the switch is the Basic Configuration page. This page will present the administrator with options for each port. The administrator can click a port and be presented with that port's settings and statistics.

At the top of the screen is a menu bar for navigating to the various pages corresponding to the different options available on the switch. The pages available are:

- **Home**   The basic configuration page. Used for changing passwords, switch image, and basic switch information.

- **Port**   Displays and defines port configuration

- **Address**   Displays and defines address information and port security information

- **SNMP**   Displays and defines SNMP community and SNMP trap information

- **STP**   Spanning-Tree Protocol information and configuration

- **CDP**   Displays and defines CDP information

- **SPAN**   Port monitoring parameters and configuration

- **Console**   Console port configuration, firmware upgrades

- **Statistics**   Statistical information

- **System**   System configuration

- **CGMP**   Multicast and CGMP configuration

Configuration Changes

Changing the configuration via the Web console is similar to selecting and providing information on an Internet Web page. Changes are made by entering information, checking boxes, and adding or removing components. Certain rules apply to certain types of changes. Some changes are immediate. An example of an immediate change would be a change to a console password. Changes made by clicking boxes or entering information in a field require the administrator to click the Apply button to make the change.

Changes made via the Web console or from the console port require about 30 seconds to be written to NVRAM (similar to copying the running configuration to startup configuration on a Cisco router). The administrator should wait before powering the switch off to ensure that the changes have been written.

FROM THE CLASSROOM

Configuration of the Future

The 1900 series and 2820 series of Catalyst switches represent a more cost-efficient solution to provide individual switched performance to each workstation. Due to the popularity of the Catalyst 5000 switches, network administrators are often confused with the menu-based operating system of the 1900/2820 series.

However, these switches offer one of the more powerful HTML-based interfaces. Once an IP address is assigned to the switch, the Web interface becomes active. Through any Java-enabled Web browser, virtually any parameter can be configured in the switches. The ability to point and click through the configuration options seems to run circles around the command line interface (CLI) of the 5000 series switches.

No longer are extensive labs needed in order to learn the various configuration details. The ability to browse through the configurations simplifies the learning process. The Web interface allows students and administrators alike to discover new commands and easily configure the switch. These switches are strategically placed at the end of the course. This way, students are not spoiled by the Web interface and then forced to endure the CLI for the remainder of the week.

Supposedly, this form of HTML interface is the future of configuration options. Once students discover this feature, the CLI pales in comparison. However, it may be quite some time before HTML and the Catalyst 5000s are joined together.

—Neil Lovering, CCIE, CCSI

The 1900/2820 Catalyst switch has been designed to operate in most network topologies with little or no configuration. Once the switch has been powered on, and compatible devices are connected to the switch, it begins forwarding frames.

Menu-Based Configuration

The Menu console is a menu-based interface for configuration and statistics display. Access to the Menu console is via either the console port or Telnet access. (Telnet access requires the switch to be configured with an IP address first).

When the administrator accesses the switch, it presents a login screen that gives the administrator the option to access the Menu console or the IP Configuration console. When the Menu option is selected, the switch displays the Menu console options. The options available are:

- **Console Settings**   Used to configure the console port
- **System**   System and broadcast storm configuration
- **Network Management**   SNMP, IP, Spanning-Tree, CDP, CGMP, and HTTP configuration
- **Port Configuration**   Port configuration and information
- **Port Addressing**   Unicast and multicast packet configuration
- **Port Statistics**   Port statistic and usage information
- **Monitoring Configuration**   System and port monitoring
- **Bridge Group Configuration**   Assign switch ports to bridge groups
- **Multicast Registration**   Define multicast groups and ports
- **Firmware Configuration**   Firmware upgrades
- **RS-232 Port Configuration**   Configure the Console port for connecting a terminal
- **Usage Summaries**   Usage and statistics (system)
- **Help**   Access to help
- **Exit**   Logout

Configuration Changes

When making changes to the switch configuration via the Menu console, changes take effect immediately, unlike the Web console, where some types of changes require the administrator to apply the changes. The administrator can restrict access to both the Web and Menu consoles by setting a password to access either console.

The information keyed in via the Menu console is not case-sensitive, with the exception of information that is used for descriptions. Each menu selection has an associated letter that is used to select that menu item. When a selection has been made, the switch displays the current configuration for that selection (with the exception of group parameters).

As with the Web console, the 1900/2820 Catalyst has been designed to operate with very little configuration. The default settings work with most networks.

SNMP-Based Configuration

The 1900/2820 Catalyst switches can also be configured from an SNMP management station. The switch is shipped with a diskette that contains the necessary MIB files to configure the switch from an SNMP management station.

Configuration of the switch is performed through GET-REQUEST, GET-NEXT-REQUEST, and SET-REQUEST commands. These commands assist the administrator with configuration settings and polling the switch to gain information on the performance of the switch. Applications such as CiscoWorks use the information provided by the administrator and, using these commands, access the MIB on the switch to enter the configuration or monitoring information.

To use an SNMP management station to configure a switch, the switch first must be configured with an IP address so the SNMP management station can access the switch across the Ethernet LAN.

exam
ⓦatch

Note which types of changes take effect immediately or are deferred. Menu console changes and some Web console changes take effect right away. Be aware there are some changes made via the Web console that need to be "applied" before the change takes effect.

Default Configuration

Out of the box, the 1900/2820 Catalyst has been designed to work with most networks with little or no configuration changes. Table 12-1 displays the default settings of the switch as soon as it is powered on.

TABLE 12-1	
Default Switch Configuration	

Setting	Default Configuration
IP address, subnet mask, and default gateway	0.0.0.0
CDP (Cisco Discovery Protocol)	Enabled
Switching mode	FragmentFree
ECC (Enhanced Congestion Control) for 10BaseT ports	Disabled
ECC for 100BaseT ports	Disabled
Duplex mode (10BaseT ports)	Half
Back pressure for half duplex	Disabled
Duplex mode (100BaseFX port)	Half
Duplex mode (100BaseTX port)	Automatic Negotiation
Broadcast Storm control	Disabled
Network port	None
CGMP	Enabled
Overlapping bridge groups	Disabled
Multicast store and forward	Disabled
Unicast packet Flooding	Enabled
Multicast packet Flooding	Enabled
Spanning-Tree	Enabled
Spanning-Tree PortFast (10BaseT ports)	Enabled
Spanning-Tree PortFast (100BaseT ports)	Disabled
Port monitoring	Disabled
Console password	None
Address violation	Suspend
Address security	Disabled
Trap Manager definition	None
Community Strings	Public/Private

CERTIFICATION SUMMARY

The Catalyst 1900/2820 series of switches take advantage of the ClearChannel architecture to provide wire-speed packet forwarding. The 1900/2820 is designed to bring low-cost, high-performance connectivity to the desktop. This is achieved through dedicated 10-Mbps and 100-Mbps Ethernet ports that can be configured based on your needs.

The ClearChannel architecture incorporates four components: the embedded control unit, the forwarding engine, the Xbus, and the shared memory buffer. Through the use of ClearChannel architecture and ASIC technology, the Catalyst 1900/2820 series switch provide a one-Gbps backplane bus for switching processes. Expansion modules available for the 1900/2820 include 100BaseTX and 100BaseFX, ATM LANE, and FDDI, to provide increased desktop or WAN connectivity.

Configuration options include a Web-based console that utilizes a Web browser to make configuration simple. A console port-based menu system is also available—just connect a terminal to the console port to gain access to the menu system. Full support for SNMP-based monitoring applications such as CiscoWorks and CiscoWorks for Switched Internetworks is included.

In most cases, the 1900/2820 is ready to start switching right out of the box. Add a few commands to provide access for the administrator, and a network management application, and the Catalyst 1900/2820 series of switches is ready to begin work providing high-speed, low-cost LAN switching to your network.

TWO-MINUTE DRILL

❑ The Cisco 1900 series and 2820 Catalyst switches are designed to provide low-cost, high-performance networking capabilities to today's high-performance Ethernet networks.

❑ The ClearChannel architecture is implemented by Cisco to address the needs of high-performance networks in the area of bandwidth allocation.

❑ There are four areas that Catalyst switches have been designed to address:

   ❑ Network management

   ❑ Bus architecture

   ❑ Packet forwarding

   ❑ Filtering and buffering of packets

❑ The components that comprise ClearChannel architecture are the embedded control unit (ECU), forwarding engine, packet exchange bus (Xbus), and the shared memory buffer.

❑ The 1900/2820 series of Catalyst switches have many features, which make them unique in the LAN switching industry.

❑ Cisco Group Management Protocol (CGMP) was developed to prevent flooding of multicast packets to all ports in a VLAN.

❑ To prevent broadcast storms, Cisco incorporated broadcast storm control within the IOS for the 1900/2820 series of Ethernet switches. This feature allows the port that is sending broadcast packets above the set threshold to be disabled from sending broadcast packets.

❑ The Catalyst can filter multicast packets based on the multicast group number. The Catalyst keeps an up-to-date table of multicast groups and the ports the packets are being forwarded to.

❑ With the advent of unshielded twisted-pair (UTP) cabling for Ethernet networks, the 1900/2820 series of Catalyst switches can support full-duplex communication on the 100MB Fast Ethernet ports.

❑ Spanning-Tree will detect and remove redundant links from the switched network topology.

❑ The 1900/2820 series of Catalyst switches support three modes of switching: cut-through, modified cut-through, and store and forward.

❑ Be able to describe the different switching options available on he 1900/2820 series of Catalyst switches. Know the benefits that each mode provides and how each is tailored to take advantage of different network topologies. Be able to identify which mode is used, based on network use.

❑ The hardware modules available on the 1900/2820 Catalyst switches use ASIC technology to provide wire-speed, low-latency operation.

❑ Full support for network management via SNMP is included in the 1900/2820 Catalyst switches.

❑ The 1900/2820 Catalyst switches offer three methods for setup and configuration of the switch:

  ❑ A Web-based graphical user interface

  ❑ A menu-based interface

  ❑ Via an SNMP-based network management application such as CiscoWorks

❑ To be able to take advantage of the Web console, the switch must be configured with an IP address via the console port prior to accessing a Web browser.

❑ The Menu console is a menu-based interface for configuration and statistics display. Access to the Menu console is via either the console port or Telnet access.

❑ The 1900/2820 Catalyst switches can also be configured from an SNMP management station.

❑ Note which types of changes take effect immediately or are deferred. Menu console changes and some Web console changes take effect right away. Be aware there are some changes made via the Web console that need to be "applied" before the change takes effect.

❑ Out of the box, the 1900/2820 Catalyst has been designed to work with most networks with little or no configuration changes.

SELF TEST

The following Self Test questions will help you measure your understanding of the material presented in this chapter. Read all the choices carefully, as there may be more than one correct answer. Choose all correct answers for each question.

1. Which of the following requirements do the 1900/2820 Catalyst switches fulfill?

   A. Network management

   B. Loop-free routing

   C. Packet forwarding

   D. Access list management

2. What is the backplane bus speed of the 1900/2820 Catalyst switch (per second)?

   A. One megabyte

   B. 256 gigabytes

   C. 400 MHz

   D. One gigabyte

3. What does ASIC stand for?

   A. Application-speed internal circuit

   B. Application-specific integrated chip

   C. Application-specific integrated circuit

   D. Application-speed internal chip

4. Which of the following switching modes are supported by the 1900/2820 Catalyst switch?

   A. Cut and forward

   B. Store and forward

   C. Modified store and forward

   D. Forward through

5. Which of the following is a component that comprises the ClearChannel architecture?

   A. Embedded Xbus

   B. Forwarding unit

   C. Forwarding engine

   D. Xbus engine

6. Which of the following controls access to the switch via the console port?

   A. Forwarding engine

   B. Shared memory buffer

   C. Xbus

   D. Embedded control unit

7. How does the forwarding engine collect statistical information?

   A. Querying the ECU

   B. Monitoring the Xbus

   C. SNMP requests

   D. None of the above

8. How much memory does the shared memory buffer use for packet forwarding?

   A. 3MB

   B. 1MB

   C. 6MB

   D. 1.5MB

9. What is the maximum amount of memory the shared memory buffer can allocate to a port?

   A. 3MB

   B. 1MB

C. 2MB

D. 1.5MB

10. What protocol is used by the 1900/2820 Catalyst switch to prevent multicast packets from being flooded to all ports?

   A. IGMP

   B. IGRP

   C. CGMP

   D. CMGP

11. What is the cause of a broadcast storm?

   A. A switch sending multiple broadcast packets

   B. A faulty device attached to a switch that sends multiple broadcast packets

   C. A faulty switch

   D. None of the above

12. How does the Catalyst prevent broadcast storms?

   A. By preventing broadcast packets

   B. By forwarding broadcast packets back to the source

   C. By deleting broadcast packets

   D. By identifying the source port and blocking broadcast packets

13. Which type of Ethernet can support full-duplex communication?

   A. 100 Mbps

   B. 10 Mbps

   C. 16 Mbps

   D. 4 Mbps

14. What protocol is used to prevent loops from occurring in a Catalyst switch network?

   A. Loop-Prevent Protocol

   B. Spanning-Tree Protocol

   C. Spanning-Trunk Protocol

   D. None of the above

15. How many Ethernet controllers are contained on the QEC ASIC?

   A. Six

   B. Ten

   C. Eight

   D. Four

16. What does the master scheduler notify when a packet has been received?

   A. The QEC ASIC

   B. The Forwarding Engine ASIC

   C. The CPU

   D. The destination port

17. Which component handles the operation of Cisco Discovery Protocol (CDP)?

   A. The forwarding engine

   B. Shared buffer memory

   C. CPU

   D. ASIC

18. Which of the following are methods for configuring the 1900/2820 Catalyst switch?

   A. ASCII

   B. SNMP

   C. Console port

   D. Ethernet

19. Which switching mode is the default mode at switch startup?

    A. Store and forward

    B. FragmentFree

    C. FastForward

20. What setting must be configured on the Catalyst switch to permit SNMP-based management and configuration?

    A. Routing must be configured

    B. Bridging must be configured

    C. The IP address must be configured

    D. None of the above

Scenerio for Questions 21–27: These questions cover Smith and Co.'s purchase and installation of a Catalyst 1900/2820 series switch. Smith and Co. currently has an Ethernet LAN installed, but due to expansion has decided to install several switches to upgrade the LAN and prepare for the expansion and allow for future network changes.

21. To allow other buildings to connect to Smith and Co.'s network via the campus FDDI network, which module is needed for the 1900/2820 switch?

    A. ATM module

    B. FDDI module

    C. 100Mbps module

    D. X.25 module

22. How does the administrator connect Smith and Co.'s Cisco router to the switch to allow users access to the company's Internet link?

    A. Via the console port

    B. Via the router module

    C. Via an Ethernet port

    D. None of the above

23. The company's file server has a 100-Mbps NIC installed that is capable of full-duplex communication. What needs to be configured on the Catalyst to support this?

    A. Enabling full duplex on the 100-Mbps port

    B. Enabling full duplex on the 10-Mbps ports

    C. Enabling half duplex on the 10-Mbps ports

    D. Enabling routing on the 100-Mbps port

    E. None of the above

24. Because of the number of users, Smith and Co.'s current network suffers from high latency and collision rates. Which switching method would best serve the company's needs?

    A. Routing

    B. Cut-through

    C. FastForward

    D. FragmentFree

25. The administrator has connected the Cisco router to the switch's Ethernet port. What protocol allows the switch and router to identify each other?

    A. ADP

    B. ATM

    C. CDP

    D. CTM

26. What is required for Smith and Co. to configure the switch from an SNMP management workstation?

    A. The SNMP module

    B. The SNMP MIB for the switch

    C. The routing module

    D. None of the above

27. Smith and Co. has decided to implement a tiered network topology. For which tier is the Catalyst 1900/2820 series switch best suited?

    A. Access tier

    B. Distribution tier

    C. Dial-up tier

    D. Core tier

13

Catalyst 3000 Series Switches

T his chapter will explore the Catalyst 3000 series of stackable LAN switches. The Catalyst 3000 series has been designed to work in a variety of LAN environments. Plug-in modules and the capacity to stack several switches together create a system providing both Layer 2 and Layer 3 switching that will support a variety of network connectivity options. The Catalyst 3000 series of switches come in three different versions.

The Catalyst 3000 features 16 10BaseT Ethernet ports, one AUI port, and expansion ports that allow two other modules to be added. To provide for the capability to stack switches, this model features an I/O port that is used to "daisy-chain" switches together. The Catalyst 3000 is known as a switch-stackable LAN switch, because it can stack several 3000 switches together. Used in conjunction with the Stack Port module, three to eight switches can be connected in a switch-stack environment.

The Catalyst 3100 has 24 10BaseT Ethernet ports, with one FlexSlot for use with either a 3000 expansion module, or a 3011 WAN access module. The Catalyst 3100 is known as a switch-flexible model, because it can provide an additional LAN module or the WAN access module, to provide WAN connectivity to branch offices.

The Catalyst 3200 is a modular chassis with seven expansion slots, one of which is a FlexSlot. The Catalyst 3200 is stackable with other 3200, 3100, or 3000 Catalyst switches with different expansion modules. The Catalyst 3200 also has a FlexSlot for use with the WAN access module.

CERTIFICATION OBJECTIVE 13.01

Catalyst 3000 System Architecture

The Catalyst 3000 series features a bus architecture that is known as the AXIS bus. The AXIS bus is a 480 Mbps switching bus, which all ports on the switch use to communicate. The 3000 series uses application-specific integrated circuit (ASIC) technology built into specific modules, such as the ATM or Fast Ethernet modules. Each port on the switch is a specific module. Modules are simple to install; just power down the switch, install the module, and restart the switch.

The following sections will describe the different ASIC modules for the Catalyst 3000 series of LAN switches.

Arbiter ASIC

The arbiter ASIC handles access to the switching bus. Working in conjunction with the CPU ASIC, the arbiter provides for orderly access to the switching bus by each of the individual LAN modules. This orderly access allows for wire-speed access to the bus with low latency.

CPU ASIC

The CPU ASIC contains the Intel i960 processor, which handles switch operations and also contains the IOS code used by the switch. The CPU ASIC also contains the console port interface for access to the switch for initial configuration and setup. The CPU operates at 16.25 MHz, not very fast when compared to today's 400 MHz PCs. But with the Catalyst 3000 series switch, this provides all the power needed to achieve wire-speed packet forwarding.

The master address table is on the CPU ASIC. This table contains the MAC addresses of devices on the LAN, which the switch uses to forward packets to the appropriate destination port.

exam
ⓦatch

You should be familiar with the Catalyst 3000 series AXIS bus architecture and how the modules use the bus to communicate with each other. Know the different components of the bus and how they function.

10 Mbps Ethernet Module

There are two versions of the Ethernet module for the Catalyst 3000 series of LAN switches. The most common is the four-port 10BaseT module. This module is ideal for connecting hubs for shared connectivity, or for connecting servers directly to the module for dedicated port access.

The other version of the Ethernet module is the three-port 10BaseFL module. This module is used for fiber-based LAN environments.

Both versions feature low latency (40 microseconds) and high throughput. This is achieved via the ASIC technology that all Catalyst 3000 modules share. The Ethernet module provides for full-duplex communications. Full-duplex communication gives the module a total of 20 Mbps of bandwidth (10 Mbps transmit and 10 Mbps receive) for today's high-speed server applications. Full- or half-duplex communication can be selected by the user or administrator through the use of DIP switches found on the back of the switch.

The 10 Mbps Ethernet module features 192KB of memory used to store, filter, and forward packets. The LAN module ASIC provides access to the AXIS bus and also determines how packets are buffered and sent either to the AXIS bus or to the 10BaseT or 10BaseFL ports.

Other features of the 10 Mbps Ethernet module include support for Switched Port Analyzer (SPAN). SPAN is used to connect a network analyzer or sniffer to the switch to collect statistics from the switch ports. The module is fully IEEE 802.3 compliant, meaning it supports all of the standards for 802.3 Ethernet.

As with other modules, the 10 Mbps Ethernet module is simple to install in the chassis with no special configuration changes required.

Fast Ethernet Module

The Fast Ethernet module comes in both single-port and dual-port configurations. As with the 10 Mbps Ethernet module, the Fast Ethernet is available in 100BaseT and 100BaseFX ports.

Both versions of the Fast Ethernet module use the high-speed port (HSP) ASIC to communicate with the AXIS bus and the CPU ASIC. A specific ASIC is used to communicate with the arbiter ASIC for access to the AXIS bus. Both versions contain 512KB of buffer (256 for inbound and 256 for outbound) to handle processing and forwarding of packets. Low latency with 512KB of buffer area provides for wire-speed switching.

The Fast Ethernet module supports the Ethernet MIB for the collection of port statistics by SNMP management packages such as CiscoWorks.

IEEE 802.1d spanning tree is also supported to prevent network loop conditions and to provide redundant link support.

The single-port module provides for both half- and full-duplex communication, with a total of 200 Mbps of available bandwidth when used in full-duplex mode. The port table can handle up to 1700 addresses, with the capability to purge older addresses based on user-configurable parameters.

The dual-port module will support the Inter-Link Switching (ISL) protocol to allow the switch to communicate with Cisco routers and other switches to create trunks and campus or wide-area VLANs. ISL also allows for redundant links between switches and/or routers. Load-sharing capabilities are also a benefit when multiple links are used.

Both modules can be installed in the chassis with ease. Just power down the switch, install the module, and power on the switch. Startup diagnostics provide information that assists administrators with troubleshooting.

ATM LANE Module

For campus and wide-area connectivity to ATM backbones, the ATM LAN emulation (LANE) module is used with the Catalyst 3000 series of switches. The ATM module has an OC3c optical interface operating at 155 Mbps. The ATM module supports both ATM UNI 3.0 and 3.1 specifications.

Version 2.1 of the ATM module software now supports the following services: LANE Server (LES), LANE Configuration Server (LECS), Broadcast and Unknown Server (BUS), and LANE Client (LEC). These services provide all of the necessary components to connect legacy LANs to today's ATM backbone and ATM campus networks.

Through the use of the Virtual LAN Trunking Protocol (VTP), multiple switches in an ATM campus or wide-area network can share VLAN or Emulated LAN (ELAN) information. This information allows the switches to map VLANs based on Fast Ethernet topology to ELANs that are ATM based. This will occur automatically through VTP.

The ATM module uses the high-speed port (HSP) ASIC to communicate with the AXIS bus and the arbiter ASIC. 1MB of inbound and 512KB of outbound buffer provide high-speed packet processing and forwarding.

In a stackable-switched environment, the Catalyst 3000 series of switches can support up to 16 ATM modules, with each module able to support 1912 Tx and 1912 Rx virtual channel circuits (VCCs). The memory on the ATM module can support up to 472 concurrent reassemblies at any one time.

The ATM module will inter-operate with third-party vendors' ATM switches that comply with the ATM Forum standards UNI 3.0 and 3.1, Q.2931 signaling protocols, Interim Local Management Interface (ILMI), and LANE 1.0.

100VG AnyLan Module

For corporate LANs that require high-speed access but cannot bear the cost of investing in wiring an existing building for fiber, the 100VG AnyLan module provides 100 Mbps connectivity using existing UTP facilities to connect 100VG devices to a switched network. There are two 100VG AnyLan modules available: one that has two 10BaseT ports for existing UTP topology, and a two-port fiber module with ST interfaces for existing fiber networks.

Both versions contain 512KB of buffer (256 for inbound and 256 for outbound) to handle processing and forwarding of packets. Low latency with 512KB of buffer area provides for wire-speed switching.

The 100VG AnyLan module supports the Ethernet MIB for the collection of port statistics by SNMP management packages such as CiscoWorks. IEEE 802.1d spanning tree is also supported to prevent network loop conditions and to provide redundant link support.

Each port can buffer up to 1700 addresses in its address table with a configurable demand-aging process to keep the address table current by purging old addresses. As with the other 3000 series modules, the 100VG AnyLan module is easily installed, with power-on diagnostics that aids troubleshooting.

3011 WAN Access Module

The 3011 WAN access module provides a fully functional Cisco 2503 router that plugs into the Catalyst 3000 series FlexSlot. The 3011 WAN access module is equipped with two serial ports, one ISDN BRI port, and aux port. The same IOS software images are available for the 2500 series router (IOS Release 11.1(6) and higher). All of the advantages of the 2500 series router with IOS are also included with the 3011.

The two serial ports provide both DCE and DTE connectivity—up to 2 Mbps in both synchronous and asynchronous mode. The serial ports support point-to-point, X.25, and Frame Relay connectivity. The ISDN BRI interface does not require an external terminal adapter and provides two 64-Kbps B channels for data and one 16-Kbps D channel for signaling.

As with the 2503 router, the 3011 WAN access module is equipped with 4MB of Flash memory and 2MB of RAM, which can be upgraded to 8MB and 16MB, respectively. This allows the 3011 to meet future needs for WAN connectivity.

Access to the 3011 is provided via the console port of the switch. The administrator selects the WAN interface via a menu system. Commands are issued via a submenu system.

The 3011 WAN access module provides all of the WAN connectivity needed for an entire stack of Catalyst 3000 series switches.

Catalyst Matrix

The Catalyst Matrix is a specialized module that allows up to eight Catalyst 3000 series switches to be connected to create a stack, which expands the number of ports that are available. Of course, this depends on how the various Catalyst 3000 series switches are configured. For example, the use of the Catalyst Matrix with eight Catalyst 3100 switches will provide 192 10BaseT Ethernet ports for connecting various Ethernet devices to the stack.

The Catalyst Matrix is an eight-port crosspoint matrix switch that allows from three to eight Catalyst 3000 series switches to connect to create a single stack switch. The Catalyst Matrix provides for 3.84 Gbps of switch-to-switch backbone. A fully redundant module, which includes both logic and power, is an option. This provides fully fault-tolerant switching.

The switches are connected to the Catalyst Matrix with a SCSI-2 connector that is installed on the I/O stack port on the rear panel of the Catalyst 3000 series switch.

Once the switches complete the power-on diagnostics, they will perform a stack discovery process that allows the switches to combine to create the stack. Switches can be connected or disconnected from the Matrix while it is powered on.

Once the stack discovery process is complete, each switch will be assigned a box number that identifies it to the other switches, and the switches will then combine their configurations to ensure that they share the same inter-box configuration. One switch will be chosen to be the location for this configuration information.

For more information on the Catalyst Matrix, you can access Cisco Connection Online at http://www.cisco.com/univercd/cc/td/doc/product/lan/cat3ks/c3ksug/cat3ks03.htm.

exam
ⓦatch

You should be familiar with the various Catalyst 3000 series modules and how they communicate on the AXIS bus. Be prepared to describe each of the modules, with emphasis on the Ethernet, FDDI, and ATM modules. Be aware of how the 3011 WAN access module is installed in the chassis (using the FlexSlot) and how to communicate via the Configuration menu. The Catalyst Matrix is a specialized module that allows multiple Catalyst 3000 switches to join together to form a stack.

Filtering Capabilities

The Catalyst 3000 series of switches offer three types of filtering. Administrators can:

- Set filters based on MAC address
- Set static entries to forward packets to certain ports or even multiple ports
- Use port security to allow or deny users connected to a port access to the network

The Catalyst 3000 series can support up to 100 filter entries per switch. In a stacked environment, 800 filters are supported. Each filter, whether a destination, source, or both, counts as one entry. So a MAC address that has both destination and source filters counts as two entries.

When used together, these three types of filters provide administrators the power to set both filters and security for a switched network. This section will examine each of the filters.

Port Security

Port security is as basic as shutting a port down to both the network and the devices that are connected to the port. This is achieved by disabling address learning, which prevents the switch from learning about new devices connected to the particular port, and by flushing the address table of addresses associated with the port. When this occurs, subsequent traffic coming from, and destined for the port is dropped.

There are two types of port security. They are source-secure and destination-secure modes. They are exactly as what their names imply. Source-secure mode will drop any packet that originates from the source port, while destination-secure mode will drop any packet with the port as the destination.

Port security, when used without address filters and static entries, gives little value to administrators. However, when it is used with address filters and static entries, it can provide a useful tool for network management by directing traffic to maximize the current network topology.

Static Entries

Static entries allow an administrator to direct packet traffic to and from certain ports. Similar to static routes, which route traffic based on IP addresses used on Cisco routers, static entries forward traffic based on the MAC (hardware) address of a device. As with port security, there are two types of static entries.

Source (or "allow-to") static entries permit packets originating from a particular MAC address to access some or all ports within a switched network. Ports that are not defined in the static entry are not accessible to the defined device.

Destination (or "force-to") static entries are just the opposite. Ports defined in a destination entry "force" packets with the defined MAC address to use a certain port or a group of ports. If this sounds familiar, it is. This type of entry works on the same concept as multicast addressing, where packets destined for a certain address are forced to use a set path (either a port or group of ports) to the destination.

Address Filters

Address filters do exactly that: deny access to either a source or destination MAC address. A source address filter is set on the source port. Packets originating from a source MAC address that has a filter entry are dropped at the port the source device is connected to.

A destination address filter is set on the source port of the destination MAC address. Packets destined for the device defined by the filter are allowed to transit the switch, but are dropped at the source port of the destination device.

VLANs and VTP

The Enhanced Catalyst 3000 series switch can support multiple VLANs as a stand-alone unit. Multiple VLANs can be configured, with each VLAN using a set number of ports. Packets are forwarded only to ports that are defined as members of the individual VLAN. Packets are not forwarded between VLANs.

VLAN Trunk Protocol (VTP) is used to configure and manage each VLAN defined in the switch. VTP will process and distribute information to all trunks defined for each VLAN. VTP is transmitted to all trunks, including Inter-Switch Link (ISL) trunks and ATM LANE trunks.

The information that is sent by VTP includes the management domain name, revision number, and any VLAN information learned by VTP. Other switches in the domain use this information to build a database of the network topology. This allows the configuration of a VLAN to be done on one switch, and allows VTP to broadcast this information to all switches in the domain.

We will explore the configuration of VLANs and VTP later in this chapter.

CERTIFICATION OBJECTIVE 13.02

Configuring the Catalyst 3000 Series Switches

Configuration of the Catalyst 3000 series of switches is performed via a menu-driven application that is accessed via a terminal or PC attached to the console port. Figure 13-1 shows the main configuration menu from a 3000 Catalyst.

Each menu selection provides further selections that change information for that component of the switch.

FIGURE 13-1

Main configuration screen

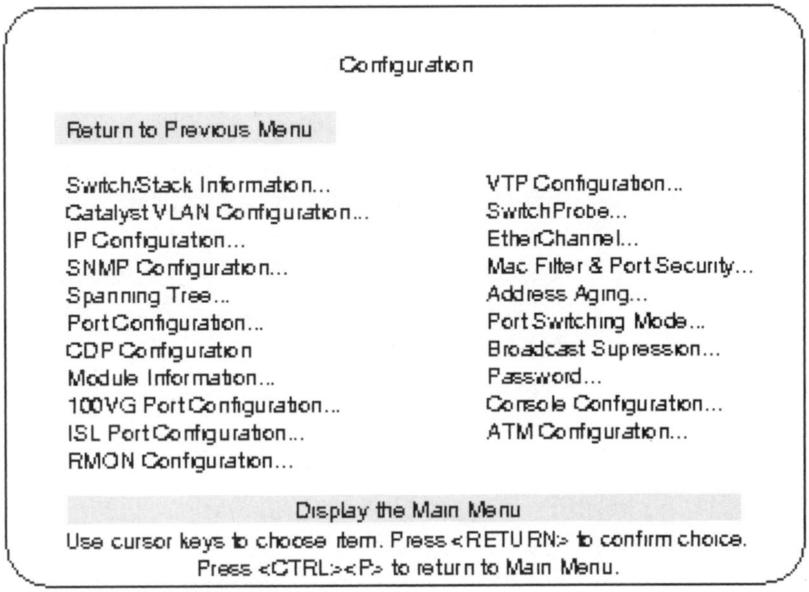
Configuration
Return to Previous Menu
Switch/Stack Information...
Catalyst VLAN Configuration...
IP Configuration...
SNMP Configuration...
Spanning Tree...
Port Configuration...
CDP Configuration
Module Information...
100VG Port Configuration...
ISL Port Configuration...
RMON Configuration...
VTP Configuration...
SwitchProbe...
EtherChannel...
Mac Filter & Port Security...
Address Aging...
Port Switching Mode...
Broadcast Supression...
Password...
Console Configuration...
ATM Configuration...
Display the Main Menu
Use cursor keys to choose item. Press <RETURN> to confirm choice.
Press <CTRL><P> to return to Main Menu.

For example, the Switch/Stack Information menu choice provides information on the switch and system information. The administrator can change information such as the system name, time/date, and location. The up and down arrow keys are used to navigate between the selections on each screen. CTRL-P is used to return to the Main Menu screen.

Basic Configuration

Unlike other members of the Catalyst family of LAN switches, such as the 1900/2820 series, the Catalyst 3000 series switch must be configured to establish port connectivity, Telnet, and SNMP access. This is usually performed from a terminal or PC attached to the console port of the switch. From the Main Menu, the administrator can choose from the following configuration types:

IP Configuration

To set the IP configuration, select IP Configuration from the Main Menu. The IP Configuration screen allows the administrator to set the IP address of the switch, the subnet mask, and default gateway. The menu also provides selections for using BOOTP. This allows the switch to access a BOOTP server to receive IP address information when the switch is booted.

The IP Configuration menu also has a PING facility that allows the administrator to verify that the switch is communicating with other devices on the LAN.

Port Configuration

From the Main Menu, select Port Configuration to configure the particular module's ports that are installed. Depending on the type(s) of modules installed, different options are available for configuring the individual ports:

- Speed of the port
- Switching mode
- Duplex setting (For Ethernet modules, this is not available via the Port Configuration menu; DIP switches located on the back panel are set and the menu display reflects those changes.)

■ Whether the port is enabled/disabled

Designing and installing today's switched LANs is not much different than designing and installing yesterday's non-switched LANs. Location of file and print servers is important. Today's high-performance file servers and workstations now are equipped with 100 Mbps Fast Ethernet NICs. Determining where to locate these devices is made simpler with the Catalyst 3000 series of switch. The 100 Mbps Fast Ethernet module enables network designers to connect servers directly to the switch, to avoid using Ethernet hubs. This eliminates the possibility of congestion and collision problems that can affect network performance. With the ability to connect servers directly to the switch, the network administrator's job is made easier by ensuring congestion-free and collision-free connectivity to the server.

Spanning Tree Configuration

Since the Catalyst 3000 series switch works on the same concept as bridges, Spanning Tree is used to manage all of the links in a switched network. If there were no management of the links, then loops would occur, which would render the network useless.

From the Main Menu, select the Spanning Tree Configuration menu.

VLANs and ISL Trunks

To be able to take advantage of the Catalyst 3000 series' capability to implement VLANs, you must have the enhanced version of the switch. With the VLAN feature, a switch can be configured for multiple VLANs, with specific ports assigned to individual VLANs.

From the Main Menu, select the VLAN configuration menu; then select the enhanced Catalyst 3000 series. To create a VLAN within a management domain on a Catalyst 3000 series switch, the administrator will need the following information.

■ VLAN number(s)

■ VLAN name(s)

■ Type of media (Ethernet, Token Ring)

- MTU (Maximum Transmission Unit) size, depending on media
- Security Association Identifier (SAID)
- Ring number (for Token Ring and FDDI LANs)
- Bridge ID
- Parent VLAN
- Type of Spanning Tree used

Note: When translating between media types, the switch requires a VLAN number to handle the translation (when using both Ethernet and Token Ring networks). This information is entered from the VLAN VTP Configuration menu. The administrator then can activate the VLAN.

Local VLAN Configuration

The Local VLAN configuration screen allows the administrator to assign ports to individual VLANs. Ports that will be assigned to trunks to other switches are also defined from this menu.

VTP Configuration

VTP configuration is also performed from the VLAN and VTP Configuration menu. Select VTP Administrative Configuration to define the domain that the switch is participating in, the mode in which the switch is running VTP, and other information that VTP needs to operate.

The modes that VTP can run in are Server, Client, or Transparent. Each mode provides the switch with different methods of VTP operation.

- **Server**   Server mode allows configuration changes to be made on the local switch. The switch must be able to store VLAN configuration for the domain. The maximum number of VLANs the switch can participate in is 68. The switch will enter Client mode if the number of VLANs exceeds 68.

- **Client**   If the switch is in Client mode, the switch will accept configuration changes only from other switches in the network. The switch will automatically enter Client mode when the number of VLANs configured is more than 68.

■ **Transparent** When in Transparent mode, the switch will pass VTP packets. The switch will also receive and store changes to the local VLAN configuration, but will not send the changes to other switches in the network.

ISL Trunks

A specialized module is needed to configure ISL trunks on the Catalyst 3000 series of switches. Access the Module Information menu from the Main Menu and verify that either the WS-X3009 or the WS-X3010 module is installed. The module must be active to be able to configure ISL trunks.

The ISL Port Configuration menu, which is accessed from the Main Menu, provides information to view and change the ISL port configuration settings. The port can be set for two modes, ISL and Non-ISL.

ISL mode will define the port as an ISL trunk port. Non-ISL mode defines the port as a 100 Mbps port that will not be operating as an ISL trunk port.

It must be noted that Enhanced mode must be turned on to allow ISL trunks to be configured. To turn on Enhanced mode, access the Switch/Stack submenu from the Main Menu screen.

Configuring ATM and LANE

The Catalyst 3000 series of switches support ATM LAN emulation. Using the ATM module, the 3000 series allows connectivity for LAN Emulation Clients (LECs) in an ATM network. The switch works along with Cisco 7500 and 4500 series routers connected to a LightStream ATM switch. Devices on the LAN will treat the Catalyst 3000 switch with the ATM interface running LANE as a single Ethernet port or several Ethernet ports.

Cisco's LANE product joins together LAN devices (such as devices on an Ethernet network) and ATM-attached devices. This connectivity also includes devices located at different physical locations that use an ATM network for remote or branch-office access. Cisco follows the ATM Forum ATM_FORUM 94-0035 specification for LAN emulation over ATM. The following services are defined within the specification:

■ LAN MAC driver services

- Connectionless services
- Multicast services

Existing LANs can take advantage of LANE services with no costly changes to update the physical wiring. LANE services exist at the MAC layer, so upper-layer services remain unchanged.

To configure a Catalyst 3000 series switch for ATM and LANE connectivity, the switch must have the WS-X3006A module installed and running to support ATM and LANE. Access the Module Information screen from the Main Menu to verify that the module is running and the mode is set to LANE. Then access the Port Configuration menu and verify that the port that contains the ATM module has the following settings:

- Port type is set to ATM155AF
- The link is up (The port has established communication with the ATM switch)
- Speed is set to 155 Mbps
- LANE is the current mode
- The port is enabled

Once this information has been verified, the administrator can check the Statistics menu for information such as whether master address table entries are being built and whether all of the 10BaseT or 100BaseT ports are up and forwarding packets.

LANE Configuration

Once ATM connectivity and LANE have been enabled, the following components are needed to configure LANE networking:

- Router interface and LANE configuration
- Location of LANE BUS server
- Location of the Catalyst 3000 series ATM module(s) and VLANs
- Name of the unrestricted emulated LAN

■ Name of the restricted emulated LAN

■ Name of the default emulated LAN (optional)

This information will be entered into the Catalyst 3000 series switch from the LANE Client Configuration submenu that is accessed via the ATM Configuration menu.

exam
⊕atch

ATM and LANE are fast becoming the choice for campus and LAN connectivity between remote offices. Catalyst switches can be configured for ATM and LANE connectivity with little difficulty. Be prepared to use your knowledge of configuring and monitoring the Catalyst 3000 series in an ATM/LANE environment.

CERTIFICATION SUMMARY

The Catalyst 3000 series switches are stackable, module-based LAN switches that provide connectivity for high-speed, switched networks. With a 480 Mbps AXIS bus and ASIC technology, the Catalyst 3000 allows for wire-speed switching with low latency.

The architecture that makes up the Catalyst 3000 switch includes the arbiter ASIC (which manages access to the AXIS bus by all of the various modules), the CPU ASIC (which controls switch operation and stores the IOS software for the switch), and the various physical media ASIC modules that provide the interface to the LAN media or ATM network.

Configuration and management of the Catalyst 3000 series switches are accomplished via a menu system accessed from a terminal connected to the console port, or via Telnet access from a terminal on the LAN, or through the use of a Network Management application such as CiscoWorks. The menu system provides various selections for setting up the switch (depending on the modules installed) for VLAN operation, ATM network connectivity, packet filtering, and access to the physical media.

Cisco announced the End Of Sales (EoS) for the Catalyst 3000 series of Ethernet stackable workgroup switches and line cards effective June 25, 1999. It also announced a trade-in promotion for up to $3000 for a Catalyst 3000 switch towards new 10/100/1000 Ethernet Catalyst solutions.

Catalyst 3016B, 3100B, and 3200B orders will be received only through June 25, 1999. Cisco Systems Customer Service must receive orders no later than June 25, 1999. These products will continue to be supported according to the standard Cisco EoS support policy.

For more information on this EoS notice, consult the following Web page: http://www.cisco.com/warp/customer/729/c3000/883_pp.htm

TWO-MINUTE DRILL

❑ The Catalyst 3000 series has been designed to work in a variety of LAN environments.

❑ The Catalyst 3000 features 16 10BaseT Ethernet ports, one AUI port, and expansion ports that allow two other modules to be added.

❑ The Catalyst 3000 series features a bus architecture that is known as the AXIS bus.

❑ The 3000 series uses application-specific integrated circuit (ASIC) technology built into specific modules, such as the ATM or Fast Ethernet modules.

❑ The arbiter ASIC handles access to the switching bus.

❑ The CPU ASIC contains the Intel i960 processor, which handles switch operations and also contains the IOS code used by the switch.

❑ You should be familiar with the Catalyst 3000 series AXIS bus architecture and how the modules use the bus to communicate with each other. Know the different components that comprise the bus and how they function.

❑ The four-port 10BaseT module (of the Ethernet module) is ideal for connecting hubs for shared connectivity, or for connecting servers directly to the module for dedicated port access.

❑ The three-port 10BaseFL module is used for fiber-based LAN environments.

❑ The Fast Ethernet module comes in both single-port and dual-port configurations. The Fast Ethernet is available in 100BaseT and 100BaseFX ports.

❏ For campus and wide-area connectivity to ATM backbones, the ATM LAN emulation (LANE) module is used with the Catalyst 3000 series of switches.

❏ For corporate LANs that require high-speed access but cannot bear the cost of investing in wiring an existing building for fiber, the 100VG AnyLan module provides 100MB connectivity using existing UTP facilities to connect 100VG devices to a switched network.

❏ The 3011 WAN access module provides a fully functional Cisco 2503 router that plugs into the Catalyst 3000 series FlexSlot.

❏ The Catalyst Matrix is a specialized module that allows up to eight Catalyst 3000 series switches to be connected to create a stack, which expands the number of ports that are available.

❏ You should be familiar with the various Catalyst 3000 series modules and how they communicate on the AXIS bus. Be prepared to describe each of the modules, with emphasis on the Ethernet, FDDI, and ATM modules. Be aware of how the 3011 WAN access module is installed in the chassis (using the FlexSlot) and how to communicate via the Configuration menu. The Catalyst Matrix is a specialized module that allows multiple Catalyst 3000 switches to join together to form a stack.

❏ The Catalyst 3000 series of switches offer three types of filtering.

❏ The Enhanced Catalyst 3000 series switch can support multiple VLANs as a stand-alone unit.

❏ VLAN Trunk Protocol (VTP) is used to configure and manage each VLAN defined in the switch.

❏ Configuration of the Catalyst 3000 series of switches is performed via a menu-driven application that is accessed via a terminal or PC attached to the console port.

❏ The Catalyst 3000 series switch must be configured to establish port connectivity, Telnet, and SNMP access.

❏ To be able to take advantage of the Catalyst 3000 series' capability to implement VLANs, you must have the enhanced version of the switch.

❏ A specialized module is needed to configure ISL trunks on the Catalyst 3000 series of switches.

- ❑ The Catalyst 3000 series of switches support ATM LAN emulation.
- ❑ Cisco's LANE product joins together LAN devices (such as devices on an Ethernet network) and ATM-attached devices.
- ❑ ATM and LANE are fast becoming the choice for campus and LAN connectivity between remote offices. Catalyst switches can be configured for ATM and LANE connectivity with little difficulty. Be prepared to use your knowledge of configuring and monitoring the Catalyst 3000 series in an ATM/LANE environment.

SELF TEST

The following Self Test questions will help you measure your understanding of the material presented in this chapter. Read all the choices carefully, as there may be more than one correct answer. Choose all correct answers for each question.

1. The AXIS bus operates at what speed on the Catalyst 3000 series switch?

   A. 10 Mbps

   B. 480 Kbps

   C. 10 Kbps

   D. 480 Mbps

2. Which of the following technologies is used by the Catalyst 3000 series switch?

   A. AISC technology

   B. ASIC technology

   C. IACS technology

   D. SACI technology

3. What is the task of the arbiter?

   A. Handles access and communication to the AXIS bus

   B. Handles communication to the ATM module

   C. Handles console access to the switch

   D. None of the above

4. Which ASIC contains the master address table?

   A. Arbiter ASIC

   B. IOS ASIC

   C. CPU ASIC

   D. Console ASIC

5. The 10BaseT module features high throughput at what latency speed?

   A. 10 Mbps

   B. 100 microseconds

   C. 10 milliseconds

   D. 40 microseconds

6. The 100BaseT and 100BaseFX modules use which type of ASIC?

   A. HSP ASIC

   B. LSP ASIC

   C. CPU ASIC

   D. HPS ASIC

7. Which version of the 100Base Ethernet modules features support for ISL?

   A. The single-port 100BaseT and 100BaseFX modules

   B. The dual-port 100BaseT and 100BaseFX modules

   C. The quad-port 100BaseT and 100BaseFX modules

   D. None of the above

8. The ATM module supports which of the following? (Choose all that apply.)

   A. The ATM Forum's UNI 3.0 specification

   B. The Frame Relay Forum's 1.0 specification

C. The ATM Forum's UNI 3.1 specification

D. The ATM Forum's UNI 4.6 specification.

9. Which release of the Catalyst 3000 operating system supports ATM LANE 1.0 services?

A. Version 1.0

B. Version 1.5

C. Version 2.1

D. Version 2.0

10. How much buffer memory is contained on the ATM module?

A. 155 Mbps

B. 1512MB

C. 1MB

D. 192KB

11. What is the total number of ATM modules supported by the Catalyst 3000 series of switches, when used in a stacked configuration?

A. 20

B. 10

C. 12

D. 16

12. Which of the following is an advantage of the 100VG AnyLan module?

A. Port density over 10BaseT hubs

B. The ability to use existing wiring for 100-Mbps LAN access

C. Connectivity to X.25 networks

D. None of the above

13. Where does the 3011 WAN access module connect to the Catalyst 3000 series chassis?

A. FlexSlot

B. Ethernet port slot

C. Expansion slot

D. Console port

14. How many filter entries will the Catalyst 3000 switch support?

A. 50

B. 25

C. 1000

D. 100

15. Where are packets dropped when a destination filter is in place?

A. The port from which the packet originated

B. The packet is not dropped

C. The port to which the destination device is connected

D. None of the above

16. What protocol is used to manage VLANs on the Catalyst 3000 series switch?

A. RIP

B. ISL

C. VTP

D. CDP

17. What version of the Catalyst 3000 series supports VLANs?

A. The Enhanced Catalyst 3000

B. The Advanced Catalyst 3000

C. The Super Catalyst 3000

D. None of the above

18. Which mode of VLAN allows for local configuration of the VLAN domain?

A. Client

B. Transparent

C. Server

D. Router

19. Which module is needed to support ISL trunks?

A. WS-2000

B. WS-X3009

C. WS-7500

D. XS-W3010

20. Which specification for LANE services over ATM does the Catalyst 3000 series switch support?

A. ATM Forum ATM_FORUM 94-0003

B. ATM Forum UNI 3.0

C. ATM Forum UNI 94-0035

D. ATM Forum ATM_FORUM 94-0035

Scenario for questions 21–30: ABC, Inc. has just purchased a Catalyst 3000 switch. The remaining questions concern the installation and configuration of ABC, Inc.'s Catalyst switch and its connection to their LAN. The questions and answers provide a scenario from initial installation to configuring the various ports and modules.

21. ABC, Inc.'s file server is able to transmit full duplex on its 100 Mbps Ethernet interface. How does the administrator configure full-duplex communication on the Catalyst Ethernet port?

A. From the Duplex Mode Configuration screen

B. From the Port Configuration screen

C. From the Module Configuration screen

D. None of the above

22. What menu does the administrator use to set the IP address of the switch?

A. The Main Menu screen

B. The IP Address menu screen

C. The IP Configuration menu screen

D. The Ethernet Module menu screen

23. ABC, Inc. has recently added a link to the Internet, via an Internet Service Provider, through the addition of the 3011 WAN access module. How does the administrator configure the module when installed?

A. Via the module's console port

B. From the Main Menu selection

C. Via Telnet access to the module

D. None of the above

24. ABC, Inc. is considering creating a VLAN for the corporate LAN. Which Ethernet module supports ISL trunking for VLAN environments?

A. The dual-port 100BaseT module

B. The four-port 10BaseT module

C. The single-port 10BaseT module

D. The ATM module

25. The company is planning the expansion of the corporate LAN. Additional switches are to be purchased to expand port capacity. What module is needed to create a Catalyst stack?

A. The ATM module

B. The Catalyst Stack module

C. The Catalyst Expansion module

D. The Catalyst Matrix

26. What is the total number of ports that are available when eight Catalyst 3100 switches are combined into a stack configuration?

A. 256

B. 192

C. 224

D. 300

27. What port on the Catalyst 3000 series switch is used to connect the switch to the Catalyst Matrix?

A. The I/O expansion port

B. The console port

C. The I/O stack port

D. None of the above

28. The administrator is connecting the Catalyst switches to the Catalyst Matrix. What type of cable is used for the connection?

A. V.35 DTE

B. 50-pin SCSI-2

C. RJ-45 Cat5

D. RS-232C

29. Which of the following is used to identify the various switches that are part of the stack?

A. Box number

B. IP address

C. Switch ID

D. VLAN number

30. ABC, Inc. has purchased new switches and a Catalyst Matrix to expand the network. What will occur when the switches are connected to the Matrix?

A. The switches will be configured by the Matrix

B. The VLAN will be created automatically

C. The switches will use stack discovery to gain switch and configuration information

D. Routing will be configured

CISCO CERTIFIED NETWORK PROFESSIONAL

A

Self Test
Answers

Chapter 1 Self Test

1. Which bridging method checks for the RIF and discards the frame if it is not present?

   A. Source-route bridging

   B. Source-route transparent bridging

   C. Source-route switching

   D. Source-route transparent switching
   A. Source-route bridging. This method does not check for MAC addresses, so if the RIF is not present, then the frame is discarded. Source-route transparent bridging and source-route switching do not work this way. Source-route transparent switching does not exist.

2. What is a benefit of using a router to segment networks?

   A. It reduces the number of routes on the network

   B. It increases the number of replications on the network

   C. It increases the number of protocols on the network

   D. It reduces the number of broadcasts on the network
   D. It reduces the number of broadcasts on the network. Routers do not pass broadcast traffic (unless configured to pass DHCP broadcasts), so they are very effective in reducing the size of broadcast domains. Routes are not reduced on the network, nor does the amount of replications and protocols increase just because a router is added.

3. Which forwarding method has a low latency rate?

   A. Store and forward

   B. Cut-and-store

   C. Cut-through

   D. Store-and-cut
   C. Cut-through. This method has low latency, especially when compared to store and forward. Cut-and-store as well as store-and-cut do not exist.

4. What port(s) on a Cisco Catalyst 3900 switch are used to connect to the ring in/ring out ports of a media access unit?

   A. 1

   B. 2

   C. 19

   D. 20
   C, D. Ports 19 and 20. These two ports are used to add the Catalyst 3900 switch to an existing Token Ring network. Ports 1 and 2 are used to add devices to the switch.

5. What type of network uses carrier sense multiple access with collision detection?

   A. Ethernet

   B. T1

   C. Token Ring

   D. OC-3
   A. Ethernet. Carrier sense multiple access with collision detection (CSMA/CD) is defined by IEEE in the 802.3 standard. Token Ring does not use CSMA/CD. T1 and OC-3 are point-to-point transmission links normally used on wide-area networks.

6. What type(s) of hardware can be utilized to segment local-area networks?

   A. Routers

   B. Switches

   C. Media altering unit

   D. Bridges

   A, B, D. Routers, switches, and bridges. These three devices can be used to segment local-area networks. Each device serves a specific purpose, so you need to select the correct device to suit your needs. Media altering unit does not exist.

7. What type of forwarding does the Catalyst 5500 use?

   A. Cut-through

   B. Store and forward

   C. FragmentFree

   D. FastForward

   B. Store and forward. The Cisco Catalyst 5500 uses this method of forwarding frames. The 5500 does not support cut-through, FragmentFree, or FastForward. FragmentFree and FastForward are Cisco variants of cut-through forwarding.

8. What happens to a Token Ring network if the cable connecting the switch to a port on the multistation access unit breaks?

   A. The network no longer functions

   B. The network continues to function, but the swtich or MSAU cannot communicate

   C. The network continues to function at a lower speed

   D. The network continues to function except for nodes on the switch

   D. The network continues to function except for nodes on the switch. Since the switch is plugged into the media access unit, it is seen as a device. The MAU excludes the port the switch is plugged into when it detects that the port is not acting properly. All other nodes on the MAU continue to function properly on the network. The only nodes that cease functioning are those located on the switch.

9. Which item(s) can negatively affect the performance on your network?

   A. FDDI

   B. Collisions

   C. ATM

   D. Broadcast domains

   B, D. Collisions and broadcast domains. Both of these items can negatively affect the performance on your network. FDDI and ATM are network technologies normally used for network backbones.

10. Which forwarding method performs a cyclic redundancy check on each frame?

   A. Store-and-cut

   B. Cut-through

   C. Store and forward

   D. Cut-and-forward

   C. Store and forward. This forwarding method performs a cyclic redundancy check on each frame that passes through it. The purpose of the CRC is to ensure that the data in the frame is not corrupt. Cut-through forwarding does not utilize CRCs. Cut-and-store as well as store-and-cut do not exist.

11. Why did vendors decide to invent the switch?

    A. As a replacement for repeaters

    B. As a replacement for ASIC

    C. As a replacement for SNA

    D. As a replacement for routers
       D. As a replacement for routers. In the early 1990s, the vendors wanted to develop an alternative to routers, which they considered to be too expensive to build and very difficult to configure correctly. Switches were not developed as a replacement for repeaters. SNA is a set of network protocols. ASIC is an acronym for application-specific integrated circuit.

12. Which of the following is another term for a switch?

    A. A multiport repeater

    B. A multiport bridge

    C. A multiport router

    D. A multiport segmentor
       B. A multiport bridge. Switches are nothing more than multiport bridges. They use the destination MAC address, just as bridges do, to forward frames to the correct port. Switches cannot be compared to multiport repeaters and multiport routers.

There is no such thing as a multiport segmentor.

13. What is the purpose of microsegmentation?

    A. It provides a decrease in available bandwidth to the end users

    B. It provides an increase in available ports to the end users

    C. It provides an increase in available bandwidth to the end users

    D. It provides a decrease in available ports to the end users
       C. It provides an increase in available bandwidth to the end users. Microsegmentation breaks the local-area network into smaller segments so that the bandwidth available to the end users is increased. It does not decrease the bandwidth, nor does it increase or decrease the ports that are available to the end users.

14. How does a switch know which port to forward a frame to?

    A. It reads the source MAC address

    B. It uses a MAC address table

    C. It reads the source ARP address

    D. It uses an ARP address table
       B. It uses a MAC address table. The switch monitors all network traffic and builds a table of MAC addresses. It uses this table to forward frames to the correct port. Switches do not use the source MAC address to forward frames. There is no such thing as the source ARP address, and switches do not have an ARP address table.

15. How can a switch transfer an Ethernet frame to an FDDI backbone?

    A. Translational switching

    B. Transmedial switching

    C. Transferral switching

    D. Transcrossial switching

       A. Translational switching. This method of switching allows dissimilar networks to communicate. The frame is translated into the format of the destination network at the switch. There is no such thing as transmedial, transferral, and transcrossial switching.

16. Which bridging method uses the IEEE Spanning-Tree Protocol?

    A. Source-route bridging

    B. Source-route transferral bridging

    C. Source-route switching

    D. Source-route transparent bridging

       D. Source-route transparent bridging. This bridging method uses the IEEE Spanning-Tree Protocol. It forwards frames based upon RIF. If the frame does not have RIF, then it forwards the frame based upon the MAC address. Source-route bridging and source-route switching do not work this way. Source-route transferral bridging does not exist.

17. Which forwarding method uses the most memory during normal operation?

    A. Cut-through

    B. FragmentFree

    C. FastForward

    D. Store and Forward

       D. Store and Forward. Store and Forward buffers the entire frame before forwarding. The other methods begin forwarding after only a few bytes have been received. However, all methods behave like Store and Forward when the destination port is busy or is operating at a different speed than the source port.

18. What item(s) does translational switching have to account for in networks?

    A. Differences in frame sizes

    B. Differences in redundancy

    C. Differences in the BRI rate

    D. Differences in MAC headers

       A, D. Differences in frame sizes and differences in MAC headers. Translational switching must take into consideration that frame sizes are different between different protocols, so it must make the necessary conversions when transferring between these protocols. Translational switching must also consider the differences in MAC headers, since different protocols send the address differently. Some protocols send the least significant bit first, whereas other protocols send the most significant bit first. Differences in redundancy and differences in BRI rate are irrelevant to translational switching.

19. What function makes switches superior to standard hubs?

    A. Increased driver availability

    B. Increased security

    C. Increased port availability

    D. Increased prioritization
       B. Increased security. Switches provide enhanced security to a network because no one can simply plug into an empty port and monitor the entire network segment, which can be done with a standard hub. Increased driver availability and increased port availability are not relevant to this question. Increased prioritization is an added feature of some switches, but is not present in switching technology in general.

20. What is the maximum frame size for FDDI?

    A. 1526 bytes

    B. 5400 bytes

    C. 2615 bytes

    D. 4500 bytes
       D. 4500 bytes. The maximum frame size for FDDI is 4500 bytes. Switches must take this into consideration when translating frames from another LAN specification such as Ethernet. 1526 bytes is the maximum frame size of Ethernet frames.

Chapter 2 Self Test

1. A VLAN is roughly equivalent to:

    A. A collision domain

    B. A broadcast domain

    C. A VTP domain

    D. A DNS domain
       B. A broadcast domain. Out of the choices given, a broadcast domain is most correct. This is less correct with Token Ring, but it's still the best answer in the group for that, too. A collision domain is a group of machines that can have collisions with each other on an Ethernet. It's common for switched-to-the-desktop Ethernet networks to have a collision domain of just the desktop station and the switch port it's plugged into, but the VLAN consists of many more stations than that. A VTP domain is used to propagate information about VLANs. DNS is used to map names to IP addresses.

2. What is the difference between a regular switch and a VLAN switch?

    A. VLAN switches can do SNMP

    B. VLAN switches have RMON

    C. VLAN switches can do multiple Layer 3 protocols

    D. VLAN switches can maintain separate broadcast domains
       D. VLAN switches can maintain separate broadcast domains. The main new feature of VLAN switches is that they can have separate broadcast domains in the same chassis. Most regular switches can do all the features mentioned in the other answers.

3. Static VLAN assignment is usually based on:

    A. Port

    B. MAC address

C. IP address

D. VLAN ID
    A. Port. Most static VLANs are port-assigned. Answers B and C are dynamic VLAN assignment criteria. VLAN ID exists after assignment has already taken place.

4. Which of the following are potential dynamic VLAN criteria? (Select two.)

    A. MAC address

    B. Slot number

    C. Port number

    D. IP address
        A, D. MAC address and IP address. Dynamic VLANs are usually based on some characteristic present in each frame. Slot number and port number don't usually change the frame in any way, unless and until it needs to be trunked.

5. Cisco supports which type of VLANs in their switches?

    A. Static

    B. Dynamic

    C. Both static and dynamic

    D. Neither static nor dynamic
        C. Both static and dynamic. Catalyst switches operate in static assignment mode, with the exception of LANE. It's possible with LANE essentially to have the station assigned to a VLAN based on MAC address.

6. VLANs can help with which of the following?

    A. Decreased cost

    B. Reducing latency

    C. Increased flexibility

    D. Consolidate WAN links
        A, C. Decreased cost and increased flexibility. Two characteristics specifically mentioned in this chapter were decreased cost (over an equivalent number of traditional switches to do the same number of LANs) and increased flexibility. VLANs don't improve latency any over regular switches or repeated networks. WAN links are still primarily the domain of routers, not switches.

7. How do VLANs increase security?

    A. By bridging between segments

    B. By providing RMON capabilities

    C. By isolating traffic to specific broadcast domains

    D. By providing a firewall feature
        C. By isolating traffic to specific broadcast domains. On the exam, look for terms like *isolate* and *segment* on VLAN security questions. Answer A provides no extra security. Answer B can work against security in the wrong hands. Answer D doesn't apply. VLAN switches don't have a proper firewall feature; that's usually implemented with a separate device.

8. Frame tagging is also known as: (Select two.)

A. Frame filtering

B. Trunking

C. Explicit tagging

D. Coloring
   C, D. Explicit tagging and coloring. Answer A is the other type of VLAN assignment (dynamic). It's theoretically possible to trunk without tagging frames, so answer B isn't the best answer.

9. What is a trunk?

   A. A VLAN tagging mechanism

   B. A way of passing more than one VLAN over a link

   C. An SRB to link TrCRFs

   D. A way to bridge between VLANs
      B. A way of passing more than one VLAN over a link. A trunk is a link designed to carry traffic for multiple VLANs. Trunks often use tagged frames as part of a trunk, but that's not what it actually is, so answer A isn't correct. As for answer D, to bridge between VLANs, a bridge group has to be defined somewhere (typically either in the switch or a router), but this bridge group is not a trunk.

10. Cisco switches support which kinds of trunk setup? (Select two.)

    A. Static

    B. Advertisement

    C. Auto-negotiation

    D. ISL
       A, C. Cisco supports static trunk setup, as well as auto-negotiation. Cisco doesn't really support trunking

based strictly on advertised capabilities, though VTP does part of that function. ISL is a trunk protocol, not a way to establish a trunk.

11. Which trunking protocols does Cisco support? (Choose all that apply.)

    A. ISL

    B. LANE

    C. 802.10

    D. STP
       A, B, C. ISL, LANE, and 802.10. These are all trunking protocols supported by Cisco. STP is not a trunking protocol.

12. Who created ISL?

    A. IEEE

    B. ANSI

    C. IBM

    D. Cisco
       D. Cisco created ISL independently, so it's considered a proprietary protocol, even if it becomes a de facto standard. The IEEE and ANSI are standards bodies, and IBM is another private company.

13. ISL works over what types of network links?

    A. FDDI

    B. Fast Ethernet

    C. HDLC

    D. ATM
       B. Fast Ethernet. So far, ISL only works over Fast Ethernet. 802.10 work over FDDI and HDLC links. If your backbone is ATM, you would use LANE.

14. 802.10 theoretically allows for how many VLANs?

    A. 256

    B. 1024

    C. 32,768

    D. Over 4,000,000
       D. Over 4,000,000. By using 32 bits, there are over four million possible VLAN IDs using 802.10. 256 is the number of VLANs the Catalyst originally supported; 1024 is the number they support now. 32,768 is how many VLANs can theoretically be supported with ISL, as it uses a 15-bit field for the VLAN ID.

15. Each LEC is associated with how many VLANs?

    A. One

    B. Two

    C. Four

    D. Eight
       A. One. Each LEC is associated with only one VLAN. If another VLAN is defined in an ATM switch, a new LEC is created to go with it.

16. How many LESs does Cisco support per VLAN in their implementation?

    A. One

    B. Two

    C. Three

    D. Four
       A. One. Cisco only supports one active LES per VLAN (although up to four LESs may be configured for redundancy).

17. Which LANE component handles broadcasts?

    A. LEC

    B. LES

    C. BUS

    D. LECS
       C. BUS. The broadcast and unknown server handles broadcasts in LANE.

18. How often does an LEC consult with the LECS?

    A. Once

    B. Each time a broadcast occurs

    C. Every 30 seconds

    D. Never
       A. Once. A LEC consults with the LECS once at startup to obtain configuration information.

19. What is the VLAN number for the default TrCRF?

    A. 1

    B. 1003

    C. 1005

    D. 1023
       B. 1003 is the VLAN number for the default TrCRF.

20. What is one of the primary functions of the DRiP protocol?

    A. To provide SRB for Token Ring LANs

    B. LANE configuration

    C. To prevent duplicate TrCRFs

    D. Packet encapsulation
       C. To prevent duplicate TrCRFs. Of

the choices given, answer C is the best answer. DRiP is the Duplicate Ring Information Protocol, and it's used with Token Ring networks. Token Ring stations and bridges handle the SRB function themselves. DRiP is not used with LANE. As for answer D, in the context of this chapter, packet encapsulation is trunking.

Chapter 3 Self Test

1. What device was used to connect devices to an Ethernet LAN before the Catalyst switch?

    A. Router
    B. MAU
    C. Hub
    D. Bridge
    C. Hub. The Ethernet hub connected devices to a LAN or Ethernet segment before the development of the Ethernet switch.

2. What LAN topology consisted of workstations accessing centrally located servers?

    A. Token Ring
    B. Ladder
    C. FDDI
    D. Star
    D. Star. The star LAN topology consisted of workstations connecting to centrally located servers. This type of topology is the most common topology in use.

3. What type of device requests information or services?

    A. Demand node
    B. Resource node
    C. Server
    D. Router
    A. Demand node. A demand node requests information or services from another device.

4. What device in a traditional, hub-based Ethernet network effectively limits bandwidth usage?

    A. MAU
    B. NIC
    C. Hub
    D. Transceiver
    C. Hub. Hubs effectively limit the amount of data that demand nodes can send to resource nodes because they must compete for access to the shared media.

5. A router is an example of what type of device?

    A. Demand node
    B. Local hub
    C. Resource node
    D. Resource hub
    C. Resource node. A resource node is a device that is the location of the information being requested from a demand node. It responds to queries received from the network.

6. To what tier would workstations be connected?

   A. Core tier

   B. Access tier

   C. Distribution tier

   D. None of the above
      B. Access tier. Workstations would be connected to the access tier. The topology is usually 10 Mbps Ethernet or 16 Mbps Token Ring connecting to Catalyst 5000 series switches located in wiring closets across the campus or floor of an office building.

7. At what speed would Fast EtherChannel operate if in full-duplex mode using four ports?

   A. 800 Mbps

   B. 400 Mbps

   C. 200 Mbps

   D. 100 Mbps
      A. 800 Mbps. Fast EtherChannel is a module that provides up to 400 Mbps (two-port configuration) or 800 Mbps (four-port configuration) of full-duplex Fast Ethernet bandwidth for switch trunks to handle today's high-performance networks.

8. What is a local resource?

   A. A resource located on a remote collision domain

   B. A resource located on a resource network

   C. A resource located at a remote site

   D. A resource located on the same collision domain as the demand node
      D. A resource located on the same collision domain as the demand node. A collision domain is defined as an Ethernet segment containing both demand and resource nodes.

9. A server located on a branch office network is defined as a:

   A. Local resource

   B. Remote resource

   C. Local demand node

   D. Remote demand node
      B. Remote resource. A remote resource is a resource node that is not located on the same collision domain as the demand node.

10. Which of the following is a rule for configuring a switched network?

    A. Locate the resource nodes as far as possible from the demand nodes

    B. Use 10 Mbps for the links to the resource nodes

    C. Resource nodes should be placed as close as possible to their demand nodes to prevent bottlenecks

    D. None of the above
       C. Resource nodes should be placed as close as possible to their demand nodes to prevent bottlenecks.

Questions 11–20 follow Smith and Co.'s design and implementation of a switched Ethernet network utilizing Catalyst 5000 series switches. The company's current network topology is a hub-based Ethernet network with servers located in the various departments in the office. The CEO has given you the task of implementing a switched Ethernet network to improve network performance and to plan for future expansion.

11. Users are complaining of poor response when accessing file and application servers located in different departments. Which of the following is the probable cause of this problem?

   A. Congestion due to poor network design

   B. A malfunctioning MAU

   C. Congestion caused by too many users on the segments

   D. None of the above
   A, C. Congestion due to poor network design and congestion caused by too many users on the segments. As applications became more bandwidth intensive, workstations became faster, the number of collisions increased, congestion occurred, and users complained of poor performance. Proper design prevents this.

12. Which of the following would be a good solution to the problem in the preceding question?

   A. Add more servers

   B. Locate the servers on a dedicated segment

   C. Add more hubs

   D. Move servers onto the user segments
   B. Locate the servers on a dedicated segment. To minimize congestion on an Ethernet network, servers should be located on a dedicated segment. This will eliminate much of the traffic on the segments where the workstations are located. To assist with flow control, a router could separate the segment from the workstation segments.

13. Smith and Co. will be erecting a new building on the campus. Which of the following physical media would be the best for the inter-building link?

   A. Optical Fiber

   B. Serial

   C. UTP

   D. Microwave
   A. Optical Fiber. For inter-building links in a campus environment, optical fiber offers a cost-effective solution for high-speed LAN traffic. Many modules for the Catalyst 5000 series switches are available in fiber-optic versions, allowing them to provide trunk connections over longer distances than with copper cabling.

14. The company has purchased new file servers. Which of the following would provide the best network access to the servers?

   A. Connecting the servers to a Token Ring

   B. Locating the servers on the same segment as the workstations

C. Installing a bridge between the servers and workstations

D. Installing 100 Mbps Ethernet cards and a Fast Ethernet module in a Catalyst 5000 switch

D. Installing 100 Mbps Ethernet cards and a Fast Ethernet module in a Catalyst 5000 switch. Today's high-performance servers can be equipped with 100 Mbps Ethernet NICs. To maximize their capabilities, a Catalyst 5000 series switch with the Fast Ethernet module will provide maximum network performance.

15. At which tier would the company locate a Cisco router that has a link to the Internet?

A. Access

B. Core

C. Distribution

D. Network

C. Distribution. In a tiered network topology, the distribution tier would contain the resource nodes such as routers and servers. These devices would be connected to the switch using 100-Mbps Ethernet.

16. Which of the following would allow for faster response time on the distribution tier?

A. Enable full-duplex communication

B. Enable routing

C. Disable error checking

D. Enable bridging

A. Enable full-duplex communication. The Catalyst 5000 series switch has full duplex communication capabilities. If the devices connected to the distribution tier (routers, servers) have full-duplex capability, this allows the Fast Ethernet to communicate at 200 Mbps.

17. Which of the following would serve as a flow control method for the company workstations?

A. Enable error checking

B. Set up small hub groups connected to a switch port

C. Enable full-duplex communication

D. None of the above

B. Set up small hub groups connected to a switch port. To control data flow from the access tier, the network designer can use an Ethernet hub with several workstations connected to it, and connect this hub to a switch port. This will allow the workstations to share and compete for bandwidth on the hub, effectively controlling data flow onto the switch.

18. The company has opened a branch office. Which of the following methods is the best method for network connectivity?

A. X.25

B. Leased line

C. ATM

D. None of the above

B. Leased line. Of these options, leased line is the best option. X.25 is rarely used today, and ATM is not widely available.

19. Users in several departments are spread out in the office. How can the administrator connect each user to the proper LAN segments?

    A. Create one large LAN

    B. Create workgroups

    C. Enable routing

    D. Create VLANs on the switched network
    D. Create VLANs on the switched network. The Catalyst 5000 switch's support of VLANs allows administrators to add ports to a particular VLAN without having to move bodies around.

20. The network administrator is locating all of the file servers in the data center with a dedicated Catalyst 5000 switch. Which of the following is the best method for connecting the dedicated switch to the other switches in the network?

    A. 100-Mbps Fast Ethernet

    B. Fast EtherChannel

    C. FDDI

    D. None of the above
    B. Fast EtherChannel. Fast EtherChannel is a module that provides up to 400 Mbps (two-port configuration) or 800 Mbps (four-port configuration) of full-duplex Fast Ethernet bandwidth for switch trunks to handle today's high-performance networks.

Chapter 4 Self Test

1. How much buffer space does each switched port have?

    A. 192KB

    B. 168KB

    C. 24KB

    D. There is only shared memory in the Catalyst 5000
    A. Each switched port has 192KB of buffer space.

2. Which devices can benefit from full duplex? (Choose all that apply.)

    A. Directly attached workstations

    B. Hub-attached workstations

    C. Other switches

    D. Servers
    A, C, D. Directly attached workstations, other switches, and servers. Anything directly attached to a switched port can benefit from FD operation.

3. How many different user-defined priority levels are there in the Catalyst 5000?

    A. One

    B. Two

    C. Three

    D. Four
    B. Two. The Catalyst 5000 allows the user to set normal or high priority levels on each switched port.

4. How does the Catalyst 5000 compare to the Catalyst 5002?

   A. The 5000 is smaller

   B. The 5002 is smaller

   C. The 5002 has only a single power supply

   D. The 5000 has fewer slots
      B. The Catalyst 5002 is smaller than the Catalyst 5000.

5. In any Catalyst 5000 switch, which slot is always reserved for the supervisor?

   A. 2

   B. 4

   C. The bottom slot

   D. The top slot
      D. The top slot, slot 1, is always reserved for the supervisor engine.

6. Which chip is responsible for all switching decisions in the Catalyst 5000?

   A. LTL

   B. CBL

   C. EARL

   D. ASIC
      C. EARL is in charge of all switching decisions. EARL is an ASIC that uses LTL and CBL to make the final decision.

7. What benefit does EARL+ offer?

   A. It is a newer, better EARL

   B. It allows for Gigabit Ethernet cards

   C. It allows for Token Ring cards

   D. It allows for ATM LANE cards
      C. It allows for Token Ring cards. EARL+ is required to understand Token Ring packets that the Token Ring cards send across the backplane.

8. How many unique buses are there in the Catalyst 5000 switch?

   A. One

   B. Two

   C. Three

   D. Four
      C. Three. The Catalyst 5000 series switch offers three different buses. The switching bus handles all frames; the management bus handles all inter-card communication; and the index bus handles communication between EARL and the switched ports.

9. Which of the following functions is performed by the port-level ASICs?

   A. Initial frame checksum verification

   B. Final switching decision

   C. Frame translation

   D. Packet routing
      A. Initial frame checksum verification. Of the features listed, the port-level ASICs only perform the initial frame checksum verification.

10. What is the major enhancement to the Catalyst 5500 series of switches?

    A. Greater number of slots

    B. New, unique line cards

    C. Greater number of power supplies

D. Enhanced backplane capacity
   D. Enhanced backplane capacity. All of the 5500 series switches benefit from a combined 3.6 Gbps backplane for frame-switching operations.

11. What does Fast EtherChannel do?

   A. It makes the Fast Ethernet pipes even faster

   B. It combines multiple Fast Ethernet links into a single collision domain for STP

   C. It turns regular Ethernet ports into Fast Ethernet ports

   D. It turns Fast Ethernet ports into Gigabit Ethernet ports
      B. It combines multiple Fast Ethernet links into a single collision domain for STP. FEC combines multiple FE ports into a single collision domain, thus making them appear as if within a single STP domain.

12. Which supervisor module supports the three 1.2 Gbps frame buses in the Catalyst 5500 series switches?

   A. Supervisor I

   B. Supervisor II

   C. Supervisor III

   D. All Supervisor modules support this feature
      C. The Supervisor III is required to support all three 1.2 Gbps frame buses in the Catalyst 5500 series chassis.

13. What are the default settings for the console port?

   A. 9600, N, 8, 1

   B. 9600, N, 8, 2

   C. 9600, N, 7, 1

   D. 9600, E, 8, 1
      A. 9600, N, 8, 1. The default settings for the console port are 9600 baud, no parity, eight data bits and one stop bit. Each of these parameters can be modified.

14. To which router can the RSM be compared?

   A. 2500

   B. 7200

   C. RSP-2

   D. RSP-4
      C. RSP-2. The RSM is an RSP-2 modified to operate in the Catalyst 5000.

15. How are the port-level buffers divided up?

   A. 50/50

   B. 24KB out, 168KB in

   C. Buffers are dynamically allocated

   D. 24KB in, 168KB out
      D. 24KB in, 168KB out. The 192KB port buffer is statically divided into 24KB for inbound traffic and 168KB for outbound.

16. Which switching mode does the Catalyst 5000 offer?

    A. Store and forward

    B. Cut-through

    C. Modified cut-through

    D. Cisco-proprietary Direct Destination Switching (DDS)
       A. Store and forward. The Catalyst 5000 is only a store and forward switch. Each frame is received in its entirety at the inbound port before it crosses the backplane.

17. How do high-priority ports compare to normal ones?

    A. High ports operate faster

    B. Normal ports are randomly disabled to offer high ports greater access

    C. High ports have a 5:1 ratio of frames passed to the backplane

    D. Normal ports cannot operate in full-duplex mode
       C. High ports have a 5:1 ratio of frames passed to the backplane compared to normal ones.

18. What does EARL do with a frame with an unknown destination MAC address?

    A. Drops it

    B. Forwards it to all ports within the same VLAN

    C. Forwards it to all ports regardless of VLAN

    D. Sends it only to the monitor port
       B. Unknown frames are flooded out all ports in the same VLAN.

19. What does the port-level ASIC add to each frame before it crosses the backplane?

    A. Nothing

    B. An additional checksum

    C. The VLAN tag

    D. The VLAN, source port, and checksum tags
       D. The VLAN, source port, and checksum tags. Inbound frames are adjusted to include the VLAN and source port, and to carry an additional checksum before crossing the main switching bus.

Chapter 5 Self Test

1. What is the major factor that decides the type of modular switch in the Catalyst 5000 series switches?

    A. Supervisor engine module

    B. Speed of the backplane

    C. Number of slots in the chassis

    D. Ethernet modules
       C. Number of slots in the chassis. All Catalyst 5000 series switches are modular types. Each of the chassis has a different number of slots. Catalyst 5000 series switches are classified based on the number of slots.

2. The first slot in a Catalyst 5000 series switch should always be used for :

   A. Power supply module

   B. Route switch module

   C. Fast Ethernet module

   D. Supervisor engine module
   D. Supervisor engine module. The slot 1 in any Catalyst 5000 series switch should be used as a supervisor engine module. This module decides the functionality of the switch. Other modules listed can be plugged in at any other slot.

3. What is the purpose of the switching fabric in the Catalyst 5000 series switch?

   A. To connect chassis together

   B. To provide connectivity between supervisor engine modules

   C. To provide connectivity between power supply and interface modules

   D. To supply power to the unit
   B, C. The switching fabric provides connectivity between the supervisor engine modules, and between the power supply and interface modules.

4. Which of the Catalyst 5000 series switches support redundant supervisor engine operation?

   A. Catalyst 5000

   B. Catalyst 5505

   C. Catalyst 5500

   D. Catalyst 5002
   B, C. Catalyst 5505 and Catalyst 5500 support Supervisor Engine II or

III in slot 1 and slot 2 of the chassis. These switches are capable of functioning even when the primary supervisor engine module fails.

5. Which type of Catalyst 5000 series switch supports Supervisor Engine II or III?

   A. Catalyst 5500

   B. Catalyst 5505

   C. Catalyst 5000

   D. All the above
   D. The Catalyst 5000 series switches all provide support to Supervisor Engine II. But not all the chassis support redundancy operation.

6. Which are the specific features observed in a Catalyst 5500 switch with Supervisor Engine III?

   A. Supports supervisor engine redundancy

   B. Supports three switching buses with 3.6 Gbps bandwidth

   C. Has RISC processor at 150 MHz

   D. All the above
   D. The Supervisor Engine III in a Catalyst 5500 switch is capable providing redundancy operations with three switching buses totaling 3.6 Gbps bandwidth support. The module has a RISC processor to take care of these functions.

7. Which of the following features of Supervisor Engine II aids in redundancy operation?

   A. The module has hardware fault-detection logic built in

B. The module has separate switching and management functions

C. ASIC hardware forwards packets even if the management processor fails

D. All the above
   D. Supervisor Engine II has separate ASIC hardware to support redundancy operation, with fault-detection logic for switch over from primary to standby module.

8. Where do you have to install the two supervisor engines for redundant operation?

   A. Slot 13 in Catalyst 5500

   B. Slots 1 and 2

   C. Slot 4

   D. Slot 3
   B. Slots 1 and 2 should be used for supervisor engine redundant operation.

9. What is the advantage of full-duplex communication supported by Catalyst switching modules?

   A. Bandwidth will be doubled

   B. Data can be transmitted and received at the same time in both directions

   C. Data can be sent only in one direction

   D. None of the above
   A, B. The Catalyst 5000 series Ethernet and Fast Ethernet modules support full duplex. Data can be sent or received simultaneously on the same pipe.

10. What would be the reason the Status LED on the Ethernet modules is lit red?

    A. Module is transmitting more data

    B. Module is not operating properly

    C. Switch is off

    D. None of the above
    B. Module is not operating properly. If the module is not operational, the Status LED goes red. During the diagnostic self-tests, if the module passes the test, the LED is green.

11. Which Ethernet module supports Fast EtherChannel operation?

    A. WS-X5213

    B. WS-X5012

    C. WS-X5013

    D. WS-X5010
    A. WS-X5213. This Ethernet module will use both the ports combined to achieve double the bandwidth.

12. Which Token Ring modules are supported by Catalyst 5000 series switches?

    A. WS-X5030

    B. WS-X5031

    C. WS-X5013

    D. All of the above
    A, B. WS-X5030 and WS-X5031. The Token Ring module with RJ-45 interface and the Token Ring module with fiber interface are supported by Catalyst 5000 series switches.

13. What is the maximum bandwidth FDDI technology supports?

    A. 10 Mbps

    B. 100 Mbps

    C. 200 Mbps

    D. All the above
       B. 100 Mbps. The FDDI module in a Catalyst 5000 series switch will support 100 Mbps as the maximum bandwidth with fiber-optic cabling.

14. If the Bypass LED on an FDDI module is turned on, what can you infer?

    A. The module is working fine

    B. The module is in Thru mode

    C. Module is in diagnostic mode

    D. All of the above
       B. The module is in Thru mode. In this mode, the module is operating in dual ring mode.

15. Which media types do the ATM switching modules support?

    A. UTP

    B. Single-mode fiber (SMF)

    C. Multimode fiber (MMF)

    D. All of the above
       D. The ATM switching module supports UTP, SMF, and MMF media types, depending upon the type of the module used.

16. The Catalyst 5000 series switch can act as a router with which module?

    A. FDDI module

    B. ATM module

    C. RSM module

    D. None of the above
       C. RSM module. With an RSM module in the switch, the unit will behave as a router. The module has to be configured appropriately for this function.

17. What is the purpose of the PCMCIA slots in the front panel of the RSM module?

    A. To load the IOS

    B. To connect other I/O devices

    C. To plug in the Flash card

    D. All of the above
       D. PCMCIA slots can be used for updating the IOS, plugging in additional Flashcards, or acting as clients for other units.

18. What is the use of the Reset button in the front panel of the RSM module?

    A. To make the RSM enter ROM monitor mode

    B. To boot the router module

    C. To reset the entire switch

    D. To reset the configuration of the unit
       B. The reset button causes the RSM to reboot, similar to the Reload command. During the boot cycle, a break can be issued at the console to enter the ROM monitor mode.

19. What happens if the power supply in a Catalyst 5002 switch fails during operation?

    A. The switch stops working

    B. The switch will work with backup power supply

    C. The switch still works without power supply

    D. None of the above
    B. The switch will work with backup power supply. The Catalyst 5002 will support dual power supplies. If one power supply fails, the other power supply automatically takes over.

20. How can you make a switch connect directly to an external network with different media types, with the same port adapters as used on a Cisco 7500 series router?

    A. Use an RSM/VIP2 module

    B. Use FDDI with an RSM module

    C. Load new software to the switch

    D. All the above
    A. Use an RSM/VIP2 module. By using RSM with VIP2, you can have direct connection with an external network using different media types, with the same port adapters used on a Cisco 7500 series router.

Chapter 6 Self Test

1. Which is not a way to obtain an address for the sc0 interface?

    A. BOOTP

    B. RARP

    C. DHCP

    D. SET INTERFACE command
    C. DHCP. The Catalyst NMP Image doesn't support DHCP. You may manually configure an IP address with the SET INTERFACE command, or the NMP Image will attempt to obtain one using RARP and BOOTP if the IP address is set to 0.0.0.0. This is the case in the Catalyst's default configuration file.

2. How many IP addresses may be configured on the Catalyst Supervisor?

    A. One

    B. Two

    C. Three

    D. Four
    B. Two. One for the sc0 interface and one for the sl0 interface. You should keep in mind, though, that the Catalyst NMP Image lacks the capability to forward traffic from the subnet configured on the sc0 interface to the sl0 interface. This is the function of a router.

3. Which best describes the purpose of CLI SET commands?

   A. Configures Ethernet port operations

   B. Configures Catalyst administrative parameters

   C. Displays Catalyst operational parameters

   D. Modifies Catalyst configuration parameters
   D. Modifies Catalyst configuration parameters. SET commands change the configuration. CLEAR commands also change configuration parameters.

4. Which best describes the purpose of CLI SHOW commands?

   A. Configures Ethernet port operations

   B. Configures Catalyst administrative parameters

   C. Displays Catalyst operational parameters

   D. Modifies Catalyst configuration parameters
   C. Displays Catalyst operational parameters. SHOW commands display the current configuration. For instance, use the SHOW PORT command to determine the connection status of a particular port on your Catalyst.

5. Which is not a command used to configure the Catalyst for out-of-band management?

   A. SET INTERFACE SL0 ENABLE

   B. SET INTERFACE SL0 1 10.2.3.4 255.255.255.0 10.2.3.255

   C. SET SLIP ATTACH

   D. SLIP ATTACH
   C. SET SLIP ATTACH. This is not a valid command. The SLIP ATTACH command starts SLIP processing on the physical console port.

6. Which of the following is required for in-band management?

   A. SET INT SC0 UP

   B. SET INT SC0 ENABLE

   C. SET INT SL0 ENABLE

   D. SET INT SC0 1 10.2.3.4 255.255.255.0 10.2.3.255
   D. SET INT SC0 1 10.2.3.4 255.255.255.0 10.2.3.255. Answer B is the default configuration. You need only issue this command if you have previously disabled the sc0 interface. Answer A is not a valid command. Answer C configures out-of-band management.

7. Which command would be rejected by the Catalyst NMP Image version 4.*x*?

   A. SET INTERFACE SC0 1 192.168.10.10 255.255.255.0

   B. SET INTERFACE SL0 1 192.168.10.10 255.255.255.0

   C. SET INTERFACE SL0 1 191.168.10.10 255.255.0.0

   D. SET INT SC0 1 192.168.10.10 255.255.255.0
   C. SET INTERFACE SL0 1 191.168.10.10 255.255.0.0. Recall that the SET INTERFACE command requires a valid IP address and mask configuration. Answer C uses a Class C address with a mask shorter than the Class A 24 bits.

8. Which command would be rejected by the Catalyst NMP Image version 4.*x*?

    A. WRITE NETWORK

    B. CONFIG NETWORK

    C. COPY FLASH TFTP

    D. UPLOAD HOST
    D. UPLOAD HOST. UPLOAD and DOWNLOAD commands are replaced by COPY commands in version 4.*x*.

9. Which command would back up the Catalyst config file?

    A. WRITE CONFIG

    B. WRITE TERM

    C. CONFIG NET

    D. WRITE TFTP
    A. WRITE CONFIG. This command copies the config file to a TFTP server. Answer B, the WRITE TERM command, displays the configuration file on the console. Answer C, the CONFIG NET command, will copy a configuration file from a TFTP server to your Catalyst.

10. Which command would be used to upgrade the Catalyst NMP Image?

    A. UPLOAD TFTP

    B. UPLOAD NET

    C. COPY TFTP FLASH

    D. COPY FLASH TFTP
    C. COPY TFTP FLASH. Recall that in the COPY commands, the first parameter is the source and the second parameter is the destination of the NMP Image file.

11. What is the command to enter privileged CLI mode?

    A. PRIVILEGE

    B. LOGIN

    C. ENABLE

    D. LOGON
    C. ENABLE. Privileged CLI mode is often called enable mode because of the syntax.

12. Which command forces a Catalyst Fast Ethernet port into full-duplex transmission mode?

    A. SET PORT DUPLEX 1/1 FULL

    B. SET PORT DUPLEX FULL 1/1

    C. SET PORT MODE 1/1 FULL

    D. SET PORT MODE FULL 1/1
    C. SET PORT MODE 1/1 FULL. This is the correct syntax described in the chapter. The duplex state of an Ethernet link is sometimes referred to as the transmission mode. Thus the syntax of the command.

13. What is the default transmission mode for a Catalyst 10/100 Ethernet port?

    A. 10 Mbps

    B. 100 Mbps

    C. Auto

    D. Half
    C. Auto. On 10/100 Ethernet ports, the default transmission mode is Auto when the port speed is also set to Auto. If the port speed is changed to 10 or 100 Mbps, the transmission mode changes to a default of half-duplex.

14. What is the default transmission speed for a Catalyst Ethernet port that can be configured for either 10 Mbps or 100 Mbps operation?

    A. 10 Mbps

    B. 100 Mbps

    C. Auto

    D. Half

    C. Auto. Multispeed-capable ports will attempt to auto-detect the link speed. Once auto-detection has selected a speed, you must reset the port to change its speed.

15. Which of the following acts as a password inside SNMP messages?

    A. Password string

    B. Community string

    C. Security ID

    D. Public key

    B. Community string. SNMP community strings act as a security mechanism within messages. In SNMP v1 the community string is sent in plain text. You should consider the security provided by community strings relatively weak.

16. Which of the following is the default community string for SNMP read-write-all mode?

    A. Password

    B. Secret

    C. Private

    D. Public

    B. Secret. It is important to modify this well-known default setting. The community string "public" is the default string for read-only mode. The string "private" is the default for read-write mode, and "secret" is the default string for read-write-all mode.

17. Which condition causes the NMP Image to issue BOOTP requests?

    A. SET BOOTP command

    B. CLEAR IP ADDRESS command

    C. Address of 0.0.0.0

    D. Mask of 255.255.255.255

    C. Address of 0.0.0.0. Answers A and B are invalid commands. Answer D would not cause a BOOTP request.

18. What is the default value of the Supervisor III configuration register?

    A. IGNORE-CONFIG enabled

    B. Load NVRAM

    C. 0x102

    D. 0x142

    C. The hexadecimal value 0x102 indicates IGNORE-CONFIG is disabled. Use this value in normal operation to ensure that the configuration file will be read from NVRAM on the next power cycle or restart.

19. Which of the following management tools does not depend on the IP stack?

    A. SLIP

    B. CLI

C. TFTP

D. SNMP

B. The CLI may be accessed from the console port when no IP address is configured. Use of SLIP, TFTP, and SNMP require that an IP address be correctly configured.

20. What value of the Supervisor III configuration register is useful for password recovery?

A. IGNORE-CONFIG disabled

B. Load NVRAM

C. 0x102

D. 0x142

D. 0x142. This value means IGNORE-CONFIG enabled. When the Catalyst is restarted with this value in the configuration register, the NMP Image will not load the config file from NVRAM. Instead, the Catalyst will restart with a default configuration. The default configuration will allow you to use the ENTER key for both the user mode and enable mode password prompts.

Chapter 7 Self Test

1. Which well known TCP port does Cisco's TACACS+ use?

A. 53

B. 69

C. 130

D. 49

D. 49. TACACS+ creates a TCP session between the Catalyst NMP Image and a TACACS+ server on Port 49.

2. Which well-known UDP port does Cisco's implementation of NTP use?

A. 53

B. 69

C. 123

D. 49

D. 123. Cisco's implementation of NTP uses the well-known port 123.

3. What action does the NMP Image take when unauthorized traffic appears on a port where Port Security is configured?

A. The amber Port Warning LED is illuminated

B. The port is disabled

C. The NMP Image reboots

D. None of the above

B. The port is disabled. When the NMP Image disables the port, an administrator must manually enable the port. The Port Disabled LED is also illuminated.

4. Which protocol does DTP replace in NMP Image 4.*x*?

A. VTP

B. DHCP

C. DISL

D. DISP

C. DISL. The Dynamic Trunk Protocol (DTP) replaces the older Dynamic InterSwitch Link (DISL) protocol for use in creating trunk connections. DTP is enhanced to allow creation of both ISL and IEEE 802.1d trunk connections.

5. Which protocol is not a mechanism for classifying traffic by VLAN?

    A. Immediate configuration

    B. Dynamic configuration

    C. Static configuration

    D. VLAN tagging
    A. Immediate configuration. Dynamic configuration uses the source MAC address in a frame to determine to which VLAN the frame belongs. Static configuration applies the same single-VLAN ID to every frame received on a port. When a link is configured as a trunk connection, the port ASIC reads a VLAN tag in the received frame to determine which VLAN sent the frame.

6. Which is a VTP operating mode?

    A. Client

    B. Server

    C. Transparent

    D. All of the above
    D. All of these are VTP operating modes. You configure a given Catalyst to participate in a VLAN management domain, and select an operating mode with the SET VTP DOMAIN command.

7. Which of the following are VTP messages?

    A. VTP summary advert

    B. VTP advert response

    C. VTP advert request

    D. VTP subset advert
    A, C, D. All of these are VTP messages. The VTP advert request is sent by client mode devices to learn the current VLAN configuration in the management domain. The VTP subset request and VTP advert request messages are used by both client mode and server mode devices to publish the latest VLAN configuration.

8. What is the default MTU for a FDDI VLAN on a Catalyst switch?

    A. 1500 bytes

    B. 1518 bytes

    C. 4480 bytes

    D. 16384 bytes
    A. 1500 bytes. All VLANs on a Catalyst switch share the 1500-byte MTU of Ethernet unless you select otherwise when creating them.

9. Which Catalyst NMP Image CLI command allows you to access the RSM EXEC interface?

    A. Console> (enable) SESSION

    B. Console> (enable) RSM

    C. Console> (enable) SET RSM-AUTOSTATE

    D. Console> (enable) ROUTER
    A. SESSION. The SESSION command initiates a Telnet session internal to the Catalyst, which allows you to configure the RSM.

10. If your RSM is running IOS version 11.2(7)P, what is the largest number of virtual interfaces can you create?

    A. 100

    B. 255

    C. 512

    D. 1000
       B. 255. IOS 11.2 in general allows only 255 virtual interfaces. If you upgrade to IOS 11.3, you can configure up to 1000 virtual interfaces.

11. Where would you look for VLAN 0 on your Catalyst?

    A. NMP

    B. EARL

    C. RSM

    D. EIEIO
       C. RSM. The RSM represents one of the SAGE ASIC channels to the Synergy bus as VLAN 0.

12. Which configuration command binds a VLAN to a virtual interface?

    A. Console> (enable) SET VLAN

    B. Router(config)# INTERFACE VLAN

    C. ATM(config)# BIND VLAN
       B. INTERFACE VLAN. When using the RSM to route traffic between VLANs, each VLAN is bound to a virtual interface using the INTERFACE VLAN command.

13. Which command removes a default gateway configured on the Catalyst NMP?

    A. CLEAR IP ROUTE *

    B. CLEAR IP ROUTE ALL

    C. CLEAR DEFAULT-NETWORK

    D. CLEAR DEFAULT-GATEWAY
       B. CLEAR IP ROUTE ALL. The Catalyst NMP Image represents a default gateway with a route to network 0.0.0.0. To add a new default network, you must remove the existing one.

14. Which technology is not a frame tagging method?

    A. ISL

    B. IEEE 802.1Q

    C. IEEE 802.10

    D. LANE
       D. LANE. LAN Emulation is a trunking method, but it doesn't use a VLAN tag to multiplex and demultiplex multiple VLANs onto the same link. Instead, LANE uses multiple virtual circuits to accomplish the same service.

15. What is the range of VLAN numbers allowed by the ISL protocol?

    A. 0–1000

    B. 0–1023

    C. 1–255

    D. 1–1023
       D. 1–1023. ISL uses a 10-bit field to number VLANs. While you can represent the numbers from 0 to 1023 with a 10-bit number, ISL does not permit a VLAN number of zero.

16. Which of the following is a DTP mode for ISL?

    A. Auto

    B. Server

    C. Translucent

    D. Client
    A. Auto. The default state of all ports on a Catalyst switch for Dynamic Trunk Protocol is auto. Answers B and D are modes of VTP operation.

17. Which Catalyst model implements frame filtering?

    A. Catalyst 5002

    B. Catalyst 1912

    C. Catalyst 5505

    D. None of the above
    D. None of the above. Cisco implements frame tagging rather than frame filtering to support multiple VLANs on the same link.

18. Which device has a special role in STP?

    A. Master switch

    B. Designated bridge

    C. Root bridge

    D. Root switch
    C. Root bridge. The root bridge is responsible for exploring the spanning tree. The other three devices don't really exist.

19. If the bridge priorities of two switches are the same, how is the root bridge determined?

    A. Bridge cost

    B. MAC address

    C. Bridge priority

    D. None of the above
    B. MAC address. STP chooses the lowest advertised MAC-addressed bridge as the root bridge.

20. What hardware is required for IGMP snooping?

    A. Ethernet Switch module

    B. NetFlow Feature Card

    C. Inline rewrite module

    D. None of the above
    B. NetFlow Feature Card. The NFFC is capable of recognizing the protocol of IGMP join and leave messages.

Chapter 8 Self Test

1. In order to first configure a Catalyst, you must use:

    A. The console port

    B. Telnet

    C. SNMP

    D. CDP
    A. The console port must be used to configure a new Catalyst. Telnet and SNMP won't work until an IP address has been configured on the box (via the console port) and CDP is not used for configuration.

2. What can be done via SLIP that can't be done in dial-up terminal mode?

A. SET commands

B. Rebooting the switch

C. Password changes

D. SNMP

    D. SNMP. There is no way to issue SNMP requests from the command line. All the other answers mentioned work just fine from the command line, dialed up. Since SNMP requires IP access to the switch, you must switch from being a dumb terminal to being a full network station.

3. What must be configured to be able to Telnet to a Catalyst?

A. RMON

B. SNMP

C. IP

D. SLIP

    C. IP. In order to Telnet to a Catalyst, it has to have a proper IP address configuration. The other answer choices also require IP, but Telnet does not require them. SNMP and RMON are alternative interfaces to the switch, as opposed to Telnet, which gives you command-line access. SLIP will also enable the use of Telnet while dialed up, but it's not required if you Telnet to the switch via a LAN.

4. Which of the following cannot be done via Telnet?

A. Password recovery

B. Password changes

C. SET commands

D. Rebooting

    A. Password recovery. In order to perform the password recovery procedure, you must be connected via the console port. The procedure requires reboot of the switch, and Telnet doesn't work while the switch is rebooting. All the other commands can be performed via Telnet.

5. Which SHOW command will give you error statistics for a particular port?

A. SHOW MAC

B. SHOW PORT

C. SHOW TOP

D. SHOW CDP NEIGHBOR DETAIL

    B. SHOW PORT. SHOW MAC doesn't give error counts. SHOW TOP only shows error counts for a particular port if it happens to be one of the top *N*. SHOW CDP doesn't have anything to do with port statistics.

6. Which SHOW command will give you the number of bytes successfully transferred?

A. SHOW MAC

B. SHOW PORT

C. SHOW TOP

D. SHOW CDP NEIGHBOR DETAIL

    A. SHOW MAC displays how many octets (bytes) were transferred. SHOW PORT gives errors, not good traffic counts. SHOW TOP would only work if the port desired were in the top *N*. SHOW CDP doesn't have anything to do with port statistics.

7. Which show command will give the top talkers?

   A. SHOW MAC

   B. SHOW PORT

   C. SHOW TOP

   D. SHOW CDP NEIGHBOR DETAIL
   C. SHOW TOP is used to show the top N ports for a particular category, one of which can be top talkers. SHOW PORT and SHOW MAC give statistics for fixed port ranges. The idea behind SHOW TOP is to have the switch do the work for you. SHOW PORT and SHOW MAC can show stats for groups of ports, but they are sorted by the slot/port number, not by the statistic.

8. RMON statistics are organized into:

   A. Buckets

   B. Ports

   C. Packets

   D. Groups
   D. Groups. RMON statistics are organized into named groups. Don't forget to learn the names of the four embedded groups (statistics, history, event and alarm). The key word in the question is "organized," which should give you a hint that groups are what are desired. History information is kept in buckets, but RMON isn't organized into buckets.

9. Which of the following are the correct four embedded RMON groups on the Catalyst 5000?

   A. Statistics, history, event, alarm

   B. Statistics, history, event, errors

   C. Statistics, topN, event, alarm

   D. Statistics, history, filter, alarm
   A. Statistics, history, event, alarm is the correct list of groups. You'll just have to memorize this list, unfortunately.

10. An RMON alarm generates:

    A. An SNMP trap

    B. An event

    C. Port shutdown

    D. A log entry
    B. An event. An RMON alarm generates an RMON event. RMON events are used inside the switch to indicate that a particular condition has occurred. This usually, but not always, generates a trap. You'll need to know that the alarm doesn't go straight to a trap. This can be a useful abstraction, and allows for other things besides traps to occur.

11. An RMON event usually generates:

    A. An SNMP trap

    B. An event

    C. Port shutdown

    D. A log entry
    A. An SNMP trap. An RMON event usually generates an SNMP trap. This is not always the case. In some cases, a

trap isn't generated at all. Someday Cisco may allow for events to perform some action locally in the switch without involving an SNMP management station at all.

12. Utilization is tracked in which RMON group?

    A. Statistics

    B. History

    C. Alarm

    D. Event

    B. History. Utilization is tracked under the history group. It's possible to derive it from information in the statistics group, but it isn't tracked there directly. The utilization information that can be derived from the statistics group isn't usually as detailed as what can be tracked in the history group. For example, if you know that the statistics group counters were zeroed an hour ago, you can only derive a utilization average over the whole hour. With the history group, you can have an average for the time period you tracked, say 10 seconds. With the 10-second tracking, spikes in traffic are much, much more apparent.

13. SNMP runs over:

    A. TCP/IP

    B. UDP/IP

    C. RMON

    D. SLIP

    B. UDP/IP. SNMP runs over UDP on top of IP. It doesn't run on top of

TCP, and RMON isn't a transport. It can run on top of SLIP, but answer B is a better answer, because it's more specific. Think back to the OSI layer model.

14. Which SNMP access type allows viewing of the community strings?

    A. Read-only

    B. Read-write

    C. Read-write-all

    D. Write-only

    C. Read-write-all. The difference between read-write and read-write-all is that read-write-all allows viewing of the community strings. There is no write-only. The significance of the viewing of the community strings is that those are essentially your passwords. If a read-only string could read the other strings, obtaining read-write access would be trivial.

15. The SNMP standard was created by which standards group?

    A. Cisco

    B. EIA/TIA

    C. IETF

    D. RFC

    C. IETF. SNMP was created by the IETF. The EIA/TIA is a different group. SNMP is documented in RFCs, but RFCs aren't a group. Cisco isn't a standards group.

16. Which SNMP command is used to retrieve additional items in a list?

A. Get

B. Get next

C. Set

D. List

   B. Get next. To retrieve a list, get next is used repeatedly. SNMP works by using a large number of small operations to form a more complex function.

17. What happens when an SNMP trap occurs?

   A. A log entry is created

   B. A port is shut down

   C. An RMON event is triggered

   D. An SNMP trap message is sent to the management station

   D. An SNMP trap is a message that is sent back to the management station. What the station does with the information is up to the management software. Any of the other items may be performed as a result of the trap, but that's up to the software on the management station.

18. What is the Layer 2 protocol used to find neighboring switches?

   A. SNMP

   B. CDP

   C. RMON

   D. SPAN

   B. CDP is the protocol that sends information to neighboring switches. SNMP and RMON are higher-layer protocols. SPAN isn't even a protocol. "Neighboring" means a direct, Layer 2 connection.

19. Which CWSI application can be used to find which switch a MAC address is on?

   A. TrafficDirector

   B. VLANDirector

   C. UserTracker

   D. CiscoView

   C. UserTracker can search the switches for a particular MAC address. This can be useful for tracking down a machine with a duplicate Layer 3 address. Don't forget to memorize the functions of each CWSI application.

20. To use a protocol analyzer with your switch, which feature do you turn on?

   A. RMON

   B. SNMP

   C. SPAN

   D. CDP

   C. SPAN is the feature that allows full use of a protocol analyzer with the Catalyst switch. SPAN lets you take a copy of the frames destined for a group of ports, and send copies to a SPAN destination port. This is exactly what a protocol analyzer needs to do its job.

Chapter 9 Self Test

1. How can different VLANs be interconnected?

   A. Using RSM

   B. Using an external router

   C. Using a Supervisor III module with NetFlow cards

D. All of the above
D. All of the above. RSM, and external router, and a Supervisor III module with NetFlow cards can all be used to interconnect different VLANs. A Layer 3 device is needed to handle the routing between the different VLANs.

2. What command displays information on the SLIP and in-band Ethernet ports for the Catalyst 5000 series switch?

    A. SHOW HARDWARE

    B. SHOW MODULE

    C. SHOW INTERFACE

    D. None of the above
    C. SHOW INTERFACE. The SHOW INTERFACE command will display information on the SLIP and the in-band Ethernet ports. This information includes the IP address, subnet mask, current state of the interface, and other VLAN information for the interfaces.

3. What command is used to display routing information?

    A. DISPLAY ROUTES

    B. SHOW IP ROUTE

    C. SHOW ROUTE TABLE

    D. DISPLAY IP ROUTE
    B. SHOW IP ROUTE. The SHOW IP ROUTE command will display information on routes that are in the switch's routing table. This information includes fragmentation information, destination and gateways available, and ICMP redirects.

4. How is the Route Switch Module accessed?

    A. From the console port

    B. From the Catalyst port

    C. Telnet from the Catalyst

    D. From the Catalyst CLI
    A, B, C, D. The RSM can be accessed via any of these methods.

5. What needs to be checked when a power supply LED is not lit when it is powered on?

    A. Check the supervisor module to verify that it is plugged in

    B. Verify that the power cord is plugged in to a power source

    C. Verify that the chassis is grounded

    D. Verify that the power supply is seated into the chassis
    B, D. Verify that the power cord is plugged into a power source and that the power supply is seated into the chassis. The power supply must be seated into the chassis and the power cord plugged into a power source. If the power supply does not power on, then check to ensure that the power cord is not defective. This is accomplished by using a different power source, or using the suspect power cord in a working power supply (if redundant power supplies are being used).

6. With respect to wiring, what does NEXT means?

    A. The next patch panel

    B. The next bridge hop

C.   The next router hop

D.   Near-end crosstalk
D. NEXT is the term used for near-end crosstalk, the tendency for signals to jump pairs at the ends of cables.

7.   The cooling fan LED is red. Which of the following is the correct step for checking the fan assembly?

A.   Verify that the assembly is seated into the chassis

B.   Turn the cooling fans on

C.   Plug in the power cord for the assembly

D.   None of the above
A. Verify that the assembly is seated into the chassis. If the assembly is seated correctly and still does not activate when the switch is powered on, then the fan assembly needs to be replaced.

8.   What command is used to verify that there are no hardware incompatibilities?

A.   SHOW SWITCH

B.   DISPLAY SWITCH HARDWARE

C.   SHOW VERSION

D.   DISPLAY VERSION
C. SHOW VERSION. The SHOW VERSION command displays information on the NMP and MCP software versions, the different modules installed in the chassis, and the software versions for each module.

9.   What command will display the status of a particular module installed in the chassis?

A.   SHOW TEST

B.   DISPLAY TEST

C.   SHOW MODULE

D.   SHOW ALL MODULES
C. SHOW MODULE. The SHOW MODULE command will display information on the installed modules. This includes the status of the module. If the module status is "OK", then the module is operating normally.

10.   What type of test is used to determine cable length or the distance to cable breaks?

A.   PING

B.   TDR

C.   NEXT

D.   Attenuation
B. TDR. Time Domain Reflectometry is the test related to cable length.

11.   Which command will give detailed information on the ports for an installed module?

A.   SHOW PORT

B.   SHOW PORT MODULE

C.   SHOW PORT STATUS

D.   SHOW STATUS PORT
A. SHOW PORT. The SHOW PORT command provides detailed information for ports on an installed module. This information includes the port speed, port status, the VLAN number to which the port belongs, as well as other information.

12. What information does the SHOW VLAN command display?

    A. VLAN routing information

    B. Ports set to No Negotiate

    C. VLAN MAC information

    D. VLAN information
        D. VLAN information. The SHOW VLAN command will display information on the VLANs configured in the switch and the ports that have been assigned to them.

13. Which command can be used to see what VLANs are passed across the trunk port?

    A. SHOW VLAN

    B. SHOW PORT TRUNK

    C. SHOW TRUNK

    D. SHOW PORT *trunking-port*
        C. SHOW TRUNK can show the VLANs that are passing across the trunk ports. The other commands listed do not give the desired output.

14. You are not able to Telnet to the switch from your workstation even if the link is good and both IP hosts are in the same subnet. What could be the reason?

    A. Your port and the sc0 port could be in different, nonconnected VLANs

    B. The switch may be configured to filter traffic on the TCP port number

    C. Your machine may be listed in the IP filter list

    D. You may not have defined the default gateway for the switch

A. Your port and the sc0 port could be in different, nonconnected VLANs. If this is the case, then a Layer 3 device (a router) needs to be installed to route between the nonconnected VLANs.

15. Which tool built into the switch will you use to check the connectivity at IP protocol level?

    A. SHOW PORT

    B. PING

    C. TRACE

    D. SHOW VLAN
        B, C. PING and TRACE. The tools available in the switch to check connectivity at the IP layer are PING and TRACE. The other commands listed can only show the port status and VLANs defined.

16. What command is useful in determining if there are loops in a switched network?

    A. SHOW LOOPS

    B. SHOW SWITCH

    C. SHOW TREE

    D. SHOW SPANTREE
        D. SHOW SPANTREE. The SHOW SPANTREE command displays useful information when a switched network has multiple links. By default the command displays information for VLAN 1.

17. The port link Status LED is orange. What does that indicate?

A. Port disabled

B. Port blocked by STP

C. Port in trunk mode

D. Port shutdown by security violation
   A, D. Port disabled or port shutdown by security violation. Both of these symptoms would cause the port Status LED to turn orange.

18. What type of trunking encapsulation is allowed on the Fast Ethernet and Gigabit Ethernet ports?

A. ISL

B. 802.3

C. 802.10

D. 802.1Q
   A, D. ISL and 802.1Q. The Ethernet trunk port can use one of these two encapsulations. ISL is Cisco proprietary, whereas the 802.1Q is standard across multiple vendors' switches.

19. How can you see the MAC address learned by the ports in the switch?

A. SHOW MODULE

B. SHOW BRIDGE TABLE

C. SHOW CAM

D. SHOW MAC
   C. SHOW CAM. The SHOW CAM command shows the active bridge forwarding table list. SHOW MAC displays the summary of traffic for all ports.

20. With what software does the RSM operate?

A. CLI

B. DOS

C. IOS

D. None of the above
   C. IOS. Since the Route Switch Module is a fully functional Cisco router, it will use the same IOS as a conventional Cisco router. The same troubleshooting commands used for routing and VLAN problems are available on the RSM.

21. What will the switch do with the frame destined for MAC addresses not available in the bridging table?

A. The frame is discarded

B. The frame is forwarded on all ports

C. The frame is forwarded on all ports within the same VLAN

D. None of the above
   C. Unlike a router, the switch will forward all the frames meant for unknown destinations to all ports within the same VLAN.

Chapter 10 Self Test

1. What does the acronym APaRT stand for?

A. Advanced Packet Recognition Technology

B. Automated Packet Recognition and Translation

C. Automated Packet Recognition Technology

D. A Packet is Recognized and Translated
   B. APaRT stands for Automated
   Packet Recognition and Translation.

2. Which of the following is true about
   FDDICHECK?

   A. It ensures that FDDI cabling is correct

   B. It is enabled by default

   C. It ensures that frames translated
   from Ethernet are removed by the
   FDDI card

   D. It performs FDDI compliance testing
   on neighboring adapters
   C. It ensures that frames translated
   from Ethernet are removed by the
   FDDI card. FDDICHECK keeps
   track of Ethernet sources that it has
   translated and ensures that the traffic
   from those Ethernet sources does
   not continuously circle the ring.
   Answer B is incorrect; FDDICHECK
   is disabled by default. Answers A and
   D are not possible.

3. Which of the following features of the
   FDDI card is not true?

   A. The card is available in single-mode
   fiber and multimode fiber versions

   B. The card performs IP fragmentation
   and MTU discovery

   C. The card can be used as a single DAS
   connection or two SAS connections

   D. The card supports IEEE 802.1d
   Spanning Tree
   C. The card cannot be used as two
   SAS connections. It is either a DAS or

a SAS connection. The other choices
are true statements about the
FDDI/CDDI card.

4. If you create Ethernet VLAN 321, what is
   the default SAID value associated with
   this VLAN?

   A. 100321

   B. 1321

   C. 321

   D. SAID values are only created for
   FDDI VLANs
   A. 100321. The formula
   100000+VLAN # is used to create
   SAID 100321 for this VLAN.
   Answers B and C don't use the
   formula. Answer D is wrong because
   SAID values are created for any
   VLAN you create; they are only
   necessary in FDDI and IEEE 802.10.

5. What does the following command do?
   SET VLAN 34 TRANSLATION 43

   A. Creates a translation between Ethernet
   VLAN 34 and FDDI VLAN 43

   B. Creates a new FDDI VLAN 34

   C. Creates a new Ethernet VLAN 43

   D. Does nothing; it is invalid
   A. Creates a translation between
   Ethernet VLAN 34 and FDDI VLAN
   43. This command maps VLAN 34 to
   VLAN 43. Technically, 34 could be
   the FDDI VLAN and 43 could be the
   Ethernet VLAN, since that
   information was not provided.

6. Assuming VLAN 34 is an Ethernet VLAN, and an FDDI card is in slot 4 of a catalyst switch, what does the following command do?
   SET VLAN 34 4/1

   A. Makes the FDDI card part of Ethernet VLAN 34

   B. Enables Ethernet-to-ANSI FDDI translation for VLAN 34

   C. Both A and B

   D. Neither A or B
   C. Both A and B. Makes the FDDI card part of Ethernet VLAN 34 and enables Ethernet-to-ANSI FDDI translation for VLAN 34. The command puts the FDDI module in VLAN 34, which enables translation of Ethernet frames into ANSI FDDI frames for that particular VLAN.

7. Which of the following statements is true of the command SET VLAN 34 TYPE FDDI?

   A. It will create a VLAN for trunking for Ethernet VLAN 34

   B. It will create an FDDI VLAN with SAID 100034

   C. It will return an error

   D. It will create a VLAN for trunking Token Ring number 34
   B. The command will create a FDDI VLAN with default SAID 100034. Answers A is incorrect, because the FDDI VLAN will be numbered 34, not the Ethernet VLAN to be trunked. You need a

   TRANSLATION command as well to trunk. Answer C is incorrect, as this command will work. Answer D is incorrect for the same reason as A.

8. How is turning off APaRT accomplished?

   A. SET FDDI APART DISABLE

   B. SET 3/1 APART DISABLE

   C. SET BRIDGE APART DISABLE

   D. APaRT can't be turned off
   C. SET BRIDGE APART DISABLE is the command that turns off APaRT.

9. Which of the following is true about the FDDI/CDDI card?

   A. If you put two FDDI cards in a Catalyst, you get true FDDI switching between them

   B. The FDDI card is a high-speed translational bridge

   C. The CDDI version of the card offers the longest cabling distance

   D. The FDDI card does not allow half-duplex operation
   B. The FDDI card is a high-speed, Ethernet-to-FDDI translating bridge. Answer A is incorrect, since the card always translates incoming FDDI frames into Ethernet frames. Answer C is incorrect; the single-mode fiber version of the card offers the longest distance. CDDI offers the shortest distance. Answer D is incorrect, since FDDI is always half duplex. The card cannot do full duplex.

10. In setting up IEEE 802.10 trunking, which of the following statements is correct?

    A. If you use the SET TRUNK command before creating the FDDI VLANS and translations, you will have to recreate the commands on every switch

    B. If you use the SET TRUNK command before creating the FDDI VLANS and translations, VTP will propagate the VLAN information for you

    C. Using the SET TRUNK command first has no effect

    D. The SET TRUNK command is only used for ISL trunking
       B. If you use the SET TRUNK command before creating the FDDI VLANS and translations, VTP will propagate the VLAN information for you. VTP will propagate VLAN and translation information for you if you turn on trunking first. Answer A is typically what happens if you turn on trunking last. Answers C and D are not valid comments.

11. CDDI stands for:

    A. Copper Data to Data Interface

    B. Copper Data Distributed Interface

    C. FDDI over Copper

    D. Copper Distributed Data Interface
       D. CDDI stands for Copper Distributed Data Interface.

12. FDDI is specified by which ANSI specification?

    A. ANSI 802.11

    B. ANSI X833

    C. ANSI X3T9.5

    D. None of the above
       C. The ANSI X3T9.5 committee specified the standards for FDDI.

13. Dual attachment stations are also known as:

    A. Class A stations

    B. Class B stations

    C. CDDI stations

    D. FDDI stations
       A. Dual attachment stations are called Class A stations.

14. A Class B station would have which connector in use?

    A. The A port connector

    B. The B port connector

    C. Both, for redundancy

    D. A port or B port, but not both
       D. A single attachment station can be connected with either the A or B port, but not both can be active.

15. Void frames have what purpose in FDDI?

    A. They signal the beginning of a data frame

    B. They signal the end of a data frame

    C. They are used to purge the ring if there are problems

    D. They have no purpose
       B. They signal the end of a data frame. Void frames are released after

the data so that the source adapter knows when to stop stripping data. Answer A is incorrect; if void frames were at the beginning, the source adapter would not know where to stop stripping data. Answer C is incorrect. The cleanup frame is a beacon or ring purge message.

16. Which of the following is not a valid Ethernet frame type?

   A. IEEE 802.3

   B. Ethernet Version 2

   C. AppleTalk IEEE 802.3

   D. IEEE 802.3/802.2/SNAP
      C. AppleTalk IEEE 802.3 is not a valid Ethernet frame type. Answers A, B, and D are all valid frame types.

17. Which of the following is true about the IEEE 802.10 frame?

   A. It is used by the Catalyst to perform trunking

   B. Ethernet frames are translated into IEEE 802.10 before leaving the catalyst

   C. The ICV is the void frame released after the data

   D. None of the above
      A. The IEEE 802.10 frame is used to carry trunked data from one catalyst to another over FDDI. Answer B is incorrect; the Ethernet frames are not translated, they are encapsulated by

the 802.10 header. Answer C is incorrect; the ICV is the checksum on the 802.10 frame.

18. Which of the following commands will name the A port of the FDDI card in slot 3 to upstream?

   A. SET FDDI 3/1 NAME UPSTREAM

   B. SET PORT NAME 3/1 UPSTREAM

   C. SET PORT 3/1 NAME UPSTREAM

   D. SET PORT NAME UPSTREAM 3/1
      B. SET PORT NAME 3/1 UPSTREAM will name the A port to upstream.

19. Which of the following is not true about turning off APaRT?

   A. Turning it off will speed up translations

   B. Turning it off in an all-IP environment is usually safe

   C. Turning it off in an all-IPX environment is usually safe

   D. Turning it off in an IPX environment means setting encapsulation types on servers and clients
      C. It is not true that turning APaRT off in an all-IPX environment is usually safe. In an IPX environment, APaRT should not be disabled, because you will have to ensure that all Ethernet hosts use the same encapsulation type and that all FDDI hosts use the same encapsulation type.

20. Which of the following best describes how SAID values are used with trunking?

    A. The SAID value of the Ethernet VLAN is included in the 802.10 frames

    B. The SAID value of the FDDI VLAN is included in the 802.10 frames

    C. A random SAID value is used, since it is not used by the Catalysts

    D. A formula adding the Ethernet SAID and FDDI SAID is included in the 802.10 frames
    B. The SAID of the FDDI VLAN is used in 802.10 frames on the FDDI ring. The Catalyst knows which Ethernet VLAN this corresponds to with the translation that has been set up.

21. If there are hosts on the FDDI ring that need access to Ethernet PCs, we enable translation by:

    A. Putting the FDDI card in the Ethernet VLAN of the PCs

    B. Putting the FDDI card into a FDDI VLAN and using a TRANSLATION command to turn on translation

    C. Adding a TRANSLATION command to the switch

    D. The catalyst card is a trunking device only
    A. Putting the FDDI card in the Ethernet VLAN of the PCs. Putting the FDDI card in the same Ethernet VLAN as the PCs will enable translation between the Ethernet PCs

and the FDDI servers. Answer B is incorrect, since the FDDI card cannot belong to an FDDI VLAN. It must belong to an Ethernet VLAN.

Chapter 11 Self Test

1. Which layer of the ATM protocol model performs the SAR function?

    A. AAL

    B. ATM

    C. PHY

    D. CPCS
    A. AAL. The segmentation and reassembly (SAR) process chops the CPCS-PDU into 48-octet SAR-PDUs before handing them to the ATM layer, where they become cells.

2. Which of the following is a function of CPCS?

    A. Creating header error control code

    B. Segmenting cells

    C. Reassembling cells

    D. Padding frames
    D. Padding frames. The common part convergence sublayer receives frames from OSI Layer 2 software and adds a trailer to it. One purpose of the trailer is to create a PDU that is evenly divisible by 48, in preparation for the SAR fuction.

3. How many bits make up the VCI field in the ATM cell header?

A. 12

B. 16

C. 24

D. Depends on the UNI
   B. 16. The Virtual Channel ID (VCI) field always uses 16 bits.

4. The HEC can correct how many bit errors in a cell's Data field?

A. Zero

B. One

C. Two

D. Three
   A. Zero. The Header Error Control (HEC) field checks for bit errors in the five-byte cell header only.

5. What does the acronym VCC stand for?

A. Virtual circuit connection

B. Virtual circuit connectionless

C. Virtual channel circuit

D. Virtual channel connection
   D. Virtual channel connection. A VCC can be regarded as a set of ATM virtual circuits.

6. Which is a protocol used by LANE to create a VCC?

A. SS7

B. SSCOP

C. SSCP

D. SSN
   B. SSCOP. The System Services Connection Oriented Protocol (SSCOP) is used by LANE for call

setup purposes. Signaling System 7 (SS7) performs similar functions in the Public Switched Telephone Network. System Services Control Point (SSCP) is an IBM Systems Network Architecture (SNA) communications function.

7. Which of the following is not an ATM address format?

A. DCD

B. DCC

C. E.164

D. ICD
   A. DCD. The three ATM addressing formats are International Code Designator (ICD), Data Country Code (DCC), and ITU-T E.164.

8. Which of the following is the AFI field for an ICD ATM address?

A. 0x41

B. 0x39

C. 0x47

D. 0x45
   A. 0x47. The ICD addresses, administered in this country by the U.S. Department of Commerce, use an Authority and Format Indicator byte of 0x47. E.164 addresses use 0x45; DCC addresses use an address 0x39.

9. The last field in an NSAP address is called?

A. Selector

B. HO-DSP

C. End System ID

D. AFI

A. Selector. The Higher-Order Domain Specific Part (HO-DSP) field precedes the End System ID (ESI) field. The AFI is the first field in the ATM address format. The Selector byte is the final field and is used by Cisco to distinguish between multiple copies of a LANE service running on the same LANE module.

10. What is the length of an ATM NSAP address?

A. 25 octets

B. 45 hex digits

C. 160 bits

D. Variable

C. 160 bits. An NSAP address is 20 bytes or octets in length. It can be written as 40 hex digits or 160 bits.

11. What does the acronym ILMI stand for?

A. Interim Link Management Integrated

B. Integrated Link Management Interface

C. Internal Line Management Interface

D. Inverted Link Markup Interval

B. Integrated Link Management Interface. The ILMI provides a communications protocol between an ATM end system and its directly connected ATM switch.

12. Which VPI/VCI does ILMI use?

A. 0/16

B. 0/17

C. 0/2

D. 0/5

A. 0/16. VPI/VCI combinations in the range 0/1 through 0/31 have been reserved by the ATM Forum for a variety of network management functions. The combination 0/16 is reserved for ILMI.

13. Which VPI/VCI does QSAAL make use of?

A. 0/16

B. 0/17

C. 0/2

D. 0/5

D. 0/5. VPI/VCI combinations in the range 0/1 through 0/31 have been reserved by the ATM Forum for a variety of network management functions. The combination 0/5 is reserved for QSAAL.

14. Which of the following is not a component of LANE?

A. BUCS

B. LECS

C. LES

D. LEC

A. BUCS. The LAN Emulation Configuration Server (LECS), the LAN Emulation Server (LES), the LAN Emulation Client (LEC), and the broadcast and unknown server (BUS) are all components of LANE. BUCS is not a component of LANE.

15. Which is a function of the LEC?

A. Joining an ELAN

B. Authenticating clients

C. LE-ARP responses

D. Replicating cells
   A. Joining an ELAN. The LAN Emulation Client is software that allows an ATM end system to participate in an ELAN. The LEC sends a join message to the LES for an ELAN as part of the setup phase.

16. Which is a function of the LECS?

   A. Joining an ELAN

   B. Authenticating clients

   C. LE-ARP responses

   D. Replicating cells
      B. Authenticating clients. The LAN Emulation Configuration Server (LECS) may be configured with a database of LEC addresses that are permitted access to the other services in an emulated LAN.

17. Which is a function of the BUS?

   A. Joining an ELAN

   B. Authenticating clients

   C. LE-ARP requests

   D. Replicating cells
      D. Replicating cells. The broadcast and unknown server is software that emulates a link-layer broadcast by causing cells to be replicated to all clients of an emulated LAN.

18. Which is a function of the LES?

   A. Joining an ELAN

   B. Authenticating clients

C. LE-ARP responses

D. Replicating cells
   C. LE-ARP responses. The LAN Emulation Server is software that maintains a cache of address mappings of Ethernet or Token Ring hosts and the ATM NSAP of the LEC that can reach them.

19. Which VCC is set up between two LANE Clients when unicast data is sent?

   A. Control distribute VCC

   B. Configuration direct VCC

   C. Multicast forward VCC

   D. Data direct VCC
      D. Data direct VCC. The LES uses the control distribute VCC to send LE-ARP messages to the LANE Clients. The LECS uses the configuration direct VCC to communicate with a LEC. The BUS uses the multicast forward VCC to replicate cells to all LANE Clients in an ELAN. The data direct VCC is created when a LEC has one or more unicast frames to send to another LEC.

20. Which best describes Simple Server Redundancy Protocol?

   A. It is an ATM Forum standard for multiple LECS

   B. It allows multiple LANE Clients for each ELAN

   C. It is a more efficient LANE Client implementation

   D. It is Cisco's extension to ATM Forum LANE specification

D. It is Cisco's extension to the ATM Forum LANE specification. SSRP permits multiple instances of the LECS service for backup purposes. The extensions also permit multiple instances of the LES and BUS for any ELAN, to avoid a single point of failure.

Chapter 12 Self Test

1. Which of the following requirements do the 1900/2820 Catalyst switches fulfill?

   A. Network management

   B. Loop-free routing

   C. Packet forwarding

   D. Access list management
   A, C. Network management and packet forwarding. These are two of the four areas that the Catalysts have been designed to address. The ClearChannel architecture uses network management, packet forwarding, bus architecture, and the buffering and filtering of packets as the bases for the Catalyst switch.

2. What is the backplane bus speed of the 1900/2820 Catalyst switch (per second)?

   A. One megabyte

   B. 256 gigabytes

   C. 400 MHz

   D. 1 Gbps
   D. 1 Gbps. The backplane bus of the 1900/2820 Catalyst has been

developed to provide orderly access to the backplane for all ports. This orderly access to the bus provides the speed needed to achieve wire-speed access for all ports to the backplane.

3. What does ASIC stand for?

   A. Application-speed internal circuit

   B. Application-specific integrated chip

   C. Application-specific integrated circuit

   D. Application-speed internal chip
   C. Application-specific integrated circuit. These specialized boards have been developed to integrate several components of the 1900/2820 Catalyst switch onto a single board. On the Catalyst 2820, a single ASIC can support 24 10BaseT Ethernet ports.

4. Which of the following switching modes are supported by the 1900/2820 Catalyst switch?

   A. Cut and forward

   B. Store and forward

   C. Modified store and forward

   D. Forward through
   B. Store and forward. Store and forward switching is defined as a switch receiving the entire packet into buffer space (store) and, once the entire packet has been received, forwarding to the appropriate destination ports (forward).

5. Which of the following is a component that comprises the ClearChannel architecture?

   A. Embedded Xbus
   B. Forwarding unit
   C. Forwarding engine
   D. Xbus engine
      C. Forwarding engine. The forwarding engine is considered the heart of the Catalyst switch. The forwarding engine, working along with the embedded control unit, the Xbus, and the shared memory buffer, comprise the ClearChannel architecture.

6. Which of the following controls access to the switch via the console port?

   A. Forwarding engine
   B. Shared memory buffer
   C. Xbus
   D. Embedded control unit
      D. Embedded control unit. The ECU controls the management of the console port. Allowing the ECU to handle tasks such as the console port, configuration changes, and in-band and out-of-band access frees up valuable hardware resources that would otherwise be used for these functions.

7. How does the forwarding engine collect statistical information?

   A. Querying the ECU
   B. Monitoring the Xbus

   C. SNMP requests
   D. None of the above
      B. Monitoring the Xbus. The forwarding engine monitors the Xbus for errors, collisions, packet length, and throughput. It collects this information, which can be display via monitoring commands and an SNMP network management workstation that is running an application such as CiscoWorks.

8. How much memory does the shared memory buffer use for packet forwarding?

   A. 3MB
   B. 1MB
   C. 6MB
   D. 1.5MB
      A. 3MB. The 1900/2820 Catalyst switch uses 3MB of dynamic RAM as the buffer for receiving and forwarding packets from the ports.

9. What is the maximum amount of memory the shared memory buffer can allocate to a port?

   A. 3MB
   B. 1MB
   C. 2MB
   D. 1.5MB
      D. 1.5MB. The maximum amount of memory that can be allocated to a single port is 1.5MB. This allows at least half of the shared memory buffer to be available to all ports at any given moment.

10. What protocol is used by the 1900/2820 Catalyst switch to prevent multicast packets from being flooded to all ports?

    A. IGMP

    B. IGRP

    C. CGMP

    D. CMGP

    C. CGMP. Cisco Group Management Protocol was developed to prevent flooding of multicast packets to ports that do not have multicast clients attached. By communicating with Cisco routers running IGMP, the Catalyst identifies which ports have multicast clients attached.

11. What is the cause of a broadcast storm?

    A. A switch sending multiple broadcast packets

    B. A faulty device attached to a switch that sends multiple broadcast packets

    C. A faulty switch

    D. None of the above

    B. A faulty device attached to a switch that sends multiple broadcast packets. A broadcast storm occurs when the amount of broadcast packets increases to the point where the bandwidth becomes unusable for regular network traffic.

12. How does the Catalyst prevent broadcast storms?

    A. By preventing broadcast packets

    B. By forwarding broadcast packets back to the source

    C. By deleting broadcast packets

    D. By identifying the source port and blocking broadcast packets

    D. By identifying the source port and blocking broadcast packets. The Catalyst will block the originating port when the amount of broadcast packets exceeds a set threshold. Other packet traffic is not affected and will be forwarded as usual. Once the amount of broadcast packets falls below the threshold, it will then begin to forward the packets as usual.

13. Which type of Ethernet can support full-duplex communication?

    A. 100 Mbps

    B. 10 Mbps

    C. 16 Mbps

    D. 4 Mbps

    A. 100 Mbps. 100-Mbps "Fast" Ethernet ports can support full-duplex communication. This provides 100 Mbps for transmit and 100 Mbps for receive, for a total combined bandwidth of 200 Mbps for communication on Fast Ethernet LANs.

14. What protocol is used to prevent loops from occurring in a Catalyst switch network?

    A. Loop-Prevent Protocol

    B. Spanning-Tree Protocol

    C. Spanning-Trunk Protocol

    D. None of the above

    B. Spanning-Tree Protocol. To identify redundant links in a network topology, the switch uses Spanning-Tree Protocol. When the redundant links are identified, the switch disables the link, but keeps the link available for use in case of a link or switch failure.

15. How many Ethernet controllers are contained on the QEC ASIC?

   A. Six

   B. Ten

   C. Eight

   D. Four
   D. Four. The QEC ASIC contains four 10BaseT Ethernet controllers.

16. What does the master scheduler notify when a packet has been recevied?

   A. The QEC ASIC

   B. The Forwarding Engine ASIC

   C. The CPU

   D. The destination port
   B. The Forwarding Engine ASIC. When a packet is received, the master scheduler informs the FE ASIC. The FE will allocate buffer space for the packet and place the packet in the buffer.

17. Which component handles the operation of Cisco Discovery Protocol (CDP)?

   A. The forwarding engine

   B. Shared buffer memory

   C. CPU

   D. ASIC
   C. The CPU handles the operation of CDP. The CPU reviews two types of

packets, broadcast and in-band management. A broadcast packet that contains inter-switch communication is an example of a packet that the CPU would handle.

18. Which of the following are methods for configuring the 1900/2820 Catalyst switch?

   A. ASCII

   B. SNMP

   C. Console port

   D. Ethernet
   B, C. SNMP or console port. There are three methods for configuring the 1900/2820 Catalyst switch. They are the Web console, Menu console, and SNMP. The Web console is accessed using a Web browser such as Netscape Communicator or Internet Explorer. The Menu console is accessed via the console port or Telnet, and via an SNMP management workstation.

19. Which switching mode is the default mode at switch startup?

   A. Store and forward

   B. FragmentFree

   C. FastForward
   B. FragmentFree. When in FragmentFree mode, the switch will receive the first 64 bytes of the packet, examine it for errors, then begin to forward the packet to the destination port.

20. What setting must be configured on the Catalyst switch to permit SNMP-based management and configuration?

A. Routing must be configured

B. Bridging must be configured

C. The IP address must be configured

D. None of the above
   C. The IP address must be configured.
   Before access to the switch can be accomplished for any of the configuration modes (except from the Menu console), the switch must be configured with an IP address.

Scenario for questions 21–27: These questions cover Smith and Co.'s purchase and installation of a Catalyst 1900/2820 series switch. Smith and Co. currently has a Ethernet LAN installed, but due to expansion has decided to install several switches to upgrade the LAN and prepare for the expansion and allow for future network changes.

21. To allow other buildings to connect to Smith and Co.'s network via the campus FDDI network, which module is needed for the 1900/2820 switch?

A. ATM module

B. FDDI module

C. 100Mbps module

D. X.25 module
   B. FDDI module. The Catalyst 1900/2820 series of switches offer two expansion slots for adding modules such as the FDDI module to provide connectivity to campus FDDI rings. Other modules available are the ATM module, and the 100BaseTX and 100BaseFX modules.

22. How does the administrator connect Smith and Co.'s Cisco router to the switch to allow users access to the company's Internet link?

A. Via the console port

B. Via the router module

C. Via an Ethernet port

D. None of the above
   C. Via an Ethernet port. Devices such as routers can connect right to a 10BaseT port on the Catalyst 1900/2820 series switch.

23. The company's file server has a 100-Mbps NIC installed that is capable of full-duplex communication. What needs to be configured on the Catalyst to support this?

A. Enabling full duplex on the 100-Mbps port

B. Enabling full duplex on the 10-Mbps ports

C. Enabling half duplex on the 10-Mbps ports

D. Enabling routing on the 100-Mbps port

E. None of the above
   A. Enabling full duplex on the 100-Mbps port. The 100-Mpbs and 10-Mbps ports on the Catalyst 1900/2820 series switch support full-duplex communication.

24. Because of the number of users, Smith and Co.'s current network suffers from high latency and collision rates. Which switching method would best serve the company's needs?

A. Routing

B. Cut-through

C. FastForward

D. FragmentFree

> **D. FragmentFree.** FragmentFree switching is used for networks that suffer from high latency and high collision rates. FragmentFree provides additional error-checking capability while providing the same latency as FastForward switching.

25. The administrator has connected the Cisco router to the switch's Ethernet port. What protocol allows the switch and router to identify each other?

A. ADP

B. ATM

C. CDP

D. CTM

> **C. CDP.** Cisco Discovery Protocol was developed by Cisco to allow devices to exchange information to form a topological map of the network. This allows network management applications to display the network topology with accurate information. CDP is enabled on the Ethernet ports via menu selections.

26. What is required for Smith and Co. to configure the switch from an SNMP management workstation?

A. The SNMP module

B. The SNMP MIB for the switch

C. The routing module

D. None of the above

> **B. The SNMP MIB for the switch.** Included with each Catalyst 1900/2820 switch is a diskette that contains the SNMP MIBS for the switch. This data enables an SNMP management workstation to access the switch. Once connectivity is established, the administrator can then configure the switch from the management workstation without the need to connect directly to the console port of the switch.

27. Smith and Co. has decided to implement a tiered network topology. For which tier is the Catalyst 1900/2820 series switch best suited?

A. Access tier

B. Distribution tier

C. Dial-up tier

D. Core tier

> **A. Access tier.** The Catalyst 1900/2820 series switch would replace Smith and Co.'s existing Ethernet hubs by providing switched connectivity right to the desktop. The switch would then use the 100-Mbps Fast Ethernet, FDDI, or ATM expansion modules to connect the switch to the distribution tier for access to application or file servers.

Chapter 13 Self Test

1. The AXIS bus operates at what speed on the Catalyst 3000 series switch?

   A. 10 Mbps

   B. 480 Kbps

   C. 10 Kbps

   D. 480 Mbps

   D. 480 Mbps. The AXIS switching bus is used by the various modules to communicate with each other and with both the master address table and arbiter, to provide wire-speed switching across all modules and ports.

2. Which of the following technologies is used by the Catalyst 3000 series switch?

   A. AISC technology

   B. ASIC technology

   C. IACS technology

   D. SACI technology

   B. ASIC technology. Application-specific integrated circuit technology is used by the Catalyst 3000 series to incorporate tasks onto a single module that is easily installed in the chassis. The ATM module contains all of the hardware needed to provide connectivity to an ATM network cloud.

3. What is the task of the arbiter?

   A. Handles access and communication to the AXIS bus

   B. Handles communication to the ATM module

   C. Handles console access to the switch

   D. None of the above

   A. The arbiter handles access and communication to the AXIS bus. All component modules use the arbiter for orderly and efficient communication with the AXIS bus. This allows for wire-speed communication for all modules on the switch.

4. Which ASIC contains the master address table?

   A. Arbiter ASIC

   B. IOS ASIC

   C. CPU ASIC

   D. Console ASIC

   C. CPU ASIC. The master address table, which contains all of the MAC addresses and the destination port of every device connected to the LAN, can contain up to 10,000 addresses. An on-demand aging process keeps the master address table current. The aging process is adjustable to clean the table either by time interval or by capacity.

5. The 10BaseT module features high throughput at what latency speed?

   A. 10 Mbps

   B. 100 microseconds

   C. 10 milliseconds

   D. 40 microseconds

   D. 40 microseconds. Through the use of ASIC technology, the 10BaseT and 10BaseFL Ethernet modules operate with 40 microseconds of latency. This is achieved through the use of cut-through switching.

Once the first six bytes are received from a port, the switch reads the destination MAC address and immediately starts forwarding the frame to the destination port.

6. The 100BaseT and 100BaseFX modules use which type of ASIC?

A. HSP ASIC

B. LSP ASIC

C. CPU ASIC

D. HPS ASIC

A. HSP ASIC. The high-speed port (HSP) ASIC is used by the high-speed modules, such as the 100BaseT and 100BaseFX modules, to communicate with the CPU and the AXIS bus. A separate, specific ASIC is used to communicate with the arbiter ASIC for access to the AXIS bus.

7. Which version of the 100Base Ethernet modules features support for ISL?

A. The single-port 100BaseT and 100BaseFX modules

B. The dual-port 100BaseT and 100BaseFX modules

C. The quad-port 100BaseT and 100BaseFX modules

D. None of the above

B. The dual-port 100BaseT and 100BaseFX modules. Both modules feature Inter-Switch Link Protocol, which supports VLAN trunking between the Catalyst 3000 switch and other switches or routers using ISL.

8. The ATM module supports which of the following? (Choose all that apply.)

A. The ATM Forum's UNI 3.0 specification

B. The Frame Relay Forum's 1.0 specification

C. The ATM Forum's UNI 3.1 specification

D. The ATM Forum's UNI 4.6 specification.

A, C. The ATM Forum's UNI 3.0 specification and the ATM Forum's UNI 3.1 specification. Both specifications cover the OC-3c multimode optical interface.

9. Which release of the Catalyst 3000 operating system supports ATM LANE 1.0 services?

A. Version 1.0

B. Version 1.5

C. Version 2.1

D. Version 2.0

C. Version 2.1. Version 2.1 supports the full range of ATM LANE services. These services include LANE Client (LEC), LANE Server (LES), LANE Configuration Server (LECS), and Broadcast and Unknown Server (BUS).

Earlier versions of the IOS for the Catalyst 3000 series switch only support LEC.

10. How much buffer memory is contained on the ATM module?

    A. 155 Mbps

    B. 1512MB

    C. 1MB

    D. 192KB

    B. 1512MB. The buffer memory on the ATM module is divided into 1MB of receive buffer and 512KB of transmit buffer. This memory division allows for wire-speed ATM cell switching with the ATM module.

11. What is the total number of ATM modules supported by the Catalyst 3000 series of switches, when used in a stacked configuration?

    A. 20

    B. 10

    C. 12

    D. 16

    D. 16. When used in a stacked configuration, three to eight Catalyst switches can be stacked to support up to 16 ATM modules, depending on the model used.

12. Which of the following is an advantage of the 100VG AnyLan module?

    A. Port density over 10BaseT hubs

    B. The ability to use existing wiring for 100-Mbps LAN access

    C. Connectivity to X.25 networks

    D. None of the above

    B. The ability to use existing wiring

for 100-Mbps LAN access. For older buildings with existing facilities, the 100VG AnyLan module provides high-speed LAN access without the cost of updating the existing wiring.

13. Where does the 3011 WAN access module connect to the Catalyst 3000 series chassis?

    A. FlexSlot

    B. Ethernet port slot

    C. Expansion slot

    D. Console port

    A. FlexSlot. The FlexSlot is available on the Catalyst 3100 and 3200 switches. This slot allows for the addition of the 3011 WAN access module to provide routing capabilities or Internet access for a switched network.

14. How many filter entries will the Catalyst 3000 switch support?

    A. 50

    B. 25

    C. 1000

    D. 100

    D. 100. The Catalyst 3000 supports 100 filter entries. In a stacked environment, the Catalyst 3000 series can support up to 800 filter entries. A filter entry consists of either a source or destination MAC address that causes the switch to drop the packet. A filter can be configured as a source or destination filter.

15. Where are packets dropped when a destination filter is in place?

    A. The port from which the packet originated

    B. The packet is not dropped

    C. The port to which the destination device is connected

    D. None of the above
       C. The port to which the destination device is connected. Address filters allow the packet to enter the switch, then will drop the packet at the port of the destination device. This allows the packet to be forwarded to other devices accepting packets from the source.

16. What protocol is used to manage VLANs on the Catalyst 3000 series switch?

    A. RIP

    B. ISL

    C. VTP

    D. CDP
       C. VTP. VLAN Trunk Protocol is used to distribute VLAN information to all ISL and ATM LANE trunks that are configured on the Catalyst 3000 switch. When a switch is booted, it will request VTP information from other switches in the network, in the form of VTP requests that are sent to all VLAN trunks. When a reply is received, the switch compares this with information already stored in memory. If no changes are noted, then the switch uses the information in memory. If new information is received, the switch then requests VTP information from the neighbor.

17. What version of the Catalyst 3000 series supports VLANs?

    A. The Enhanced Catalyst 3000

    B. The Advanced Catalyst 3000

    C. The Super Catalyst 3000

    D. None of the above
       A. The Enhanced Catalyst 3000. The Enhanced version of the Catalyst 3000 series switch is needed to support VLAN topologies. The Enhanced Catalyst 3000 can support multiple VLANs, and forwards packets only to the ports that are configured as a VLAN segments. ISL Protocol is used to transmit the VLAN information across VLAN trunks.

18. Which mode of VLAN allows for local configuration of the VLAN domain?

    A. Client

    B. Transparent

    C. Server

    D. Router
       C. Server. Server mode allows for local configuration of the VLAN domain. The other modes are Client and Transparent.
       In Client mode, the switch will only use changes to its VLAN configuration from other devices.
       In Transparent mode, the switch passes VTP information to other devices. VLAN configuration changes are saved to memory, but are not propagated to other devices.

19. Which module is needed to support ISL trunks?

    A. WS-2000

    B. WS-X3009

    C. WS-7500

    D. XS-W3010

       B. WS-X3009. This module (or the WS-X3010) allows the Catalyst 3000 to support VLAN trunks using ISL as the trunking protocol. The WS-X3009 is the product number for the 100BaseFX Fast Ethernet module. WS-X3010 is the product number for the 100BaseTX Fast Ethernet module.

20. Which specification for LANE services over ATM does the Catalyst 3000 series switch support?

    A. ATM Forum ATM_FORUM 94-0003

    B. ATM Forum UNI 3.0

    C. ATM Forum UNI 94-0035

    D. ATM Forum ATM_FORUM 94-0035

       D. ATM Forum ATM_FORUM 94-0035. This specification covers connectivity for LAN emulation services over an ATM network. These services include provisions for connectivity between ATM and LAN-attached devices, and for remote LAN devices using an ATM network for end-to-end connectivity.

Scenario for questions 21–30: ABC, Inc. has just purchased a Catalyst 3000 switch. The remaining questions concern the installation and configuration of ABC, Inc.'s Catalyst switch and its connection to their LAN. The questions and answers provide a scenario from initial installation to configuring the various ports and modules.

21. ABC, Inc.'s file server is able to transmit full duplex on its 10 Mbps Ethernet interface. How does the administrator configure full-duplex communication on the Catalyst Ethernet port?

    A. From the Duplex Mode Configuration screen

    B. From the Port Configuration screen

    C. From the Module Configuration screen

    D. None of the above

       D. None of the above. To set the Ethernet port to operate in full-duplex mode, you must set the dipswitch found on the back panel of the switch to set the port to operate in full-duplex mode. The change will take effect when the switch has been changed.

22. What menu does the administrator use to set the IP address of the switch?

    A. The Main Menu screen

    B. The IP Address menu screen

    C. The IP Configuration menu screen

    D. The Ethernet Module menu screen

       C. The IP address is set from the IP Configuration menu screen. The IP Configuration screen provides the selections to set the IP address, the subnet mask, the default gateway, and the IP state the switch will use at boot.

23. ABC, Inc. has recently added a link to the Internet, via an Internet Service Provider, through the addition of the 3011 WAN access module. How does the administrator configure the module when installed?

   A. Via the module's console port
   B. From the Main Menu selection
   C. Via Telnet access to the module
   D. None of the above
   B. From the Main Menu selection. When the module is installed in the Catalyst 3000 series chassis, access to the module is via the WAN Access menu. Selections for configuring the module are displayed from the WAN Access menu.

24. ABC, Inc. is considering creating a VLAN for the corporate LAN. Which Ethernet module supports ISL trunking for VLAN environments?

   A. The dual-port 100BaseT module
   B. The four-port 10BaseT module
   C. The single-port 10BaseT module
   D. The ATM module
   A. The dual-port 100BaseT module. This module supports ISL for setting up VLANs across multiple ports. This allows the Catalyst switch to communicate with other switches in a network to pass VLAN information between multiple switches. Along with

ISL, the Catalyst uses the Spanning Tree Protocol to identify redundant links.

25. The company is planning the expansion of the corporate LAN. Additional switches are to be purchased to expand port capacity. What module is needed to create a Catalyst stack?

   A. The ATM module
   B. The Catalyst Stack module
   C. The Catalyst Expansion module
   D. The Catalyst Matrix
   D. The Catalyst Matrix. This module enables up to eight Catalyst 3000 series switches to be connected to create switch stack. This allows expansion of the corporate LAN to be as simple as adding a switch to the stack.

26. What is the total number of ports that are available when eight Catalyst 3100 switches are combined into a stack configuration?

   A. 256
   B. 192
   C. 224
   D. 300
   B. 192. The Catalyst 3000 switch comes with 24 10BaseT Ethernet ports, so combining eight Catalyst 3100 switches in a stack configuration provides 192 10BaseT Ethernet ports.

27. What port on the Catalyst 3000 series switch is used to connect the switch to the Catalyst Matrix?

A. The I/O expansion port

B. The console port

C. The I/O stack port

D. None of the above
   C. The I/O stack port. The I/O stack port is used to connect the Catalyst 3000 switch to the Catalyst Matrix to create a switch stack. The port is located on the back panel of the switch.

28. The administrator is connecting the Catalyst switches to the Catalyst Matrix. What type of cable is used for the connection?

   A. V.35 DTE

   B. 50-pin SCSI-2

   C. RJ-45 Cat5

   D. RS-232C
      B. 50-pin SCSI-2 cable. This cable is used to connect the Catalyst 3000 switch to the Catalyst Matrix.

29. Which of the following is used to identify the various switches that are part of the stack?

   A. Box number

   B. IP address

   C. Switch ID

   D. VLAN number

A. **Box number.** When a switch is added to the Catalyst Matrix, a box number is assigned to the switch. This number is based on the port number on the Matrix to which the switch is connected.

30. ABC, Inc. has purchased new switches and a Catalyst Matrix to expand the network. What will occur when the switches are connected to the Matrix?

   A. The switches will be configured by the Matrix

   B. The VLAN will be created automatically

   C. The switches will use stack discovery to gain switch and configuration information

   D. Routing will be configured
      C. The switches will use stack discovery to gain switch and configuration information. Once this information is discovered, the switches will combine to create the stack. One switch will be chosen to be the central location of the combined stack configuration and the inter-box configuration.

B

About the CD

Installing the Personal Testing Center

This CD-ROM contains a browser-based testing product, the Personal Testing Center. The Personal Testing Center is easy to install on any Windows 95/98/NT computer.

Double clicking on the Setup.html file on the CD will cycle you through an introductory page on the *Test Yourself* software. On the second page, you will have to read and accept the license agreement. Once you have read the agreement, click on the Agree icon and you will be taken to the Personal Testing Center's main page.

On the main page, you will find links to the Personal Testing Center, to the electronic version of the book, and to other resources you may find helpful. Click on the first link to the Personal Testing Center and you will be taken to the Quick Start page. Here you can choose to run the Personal Testing Center from the CD or install it to your hard drive.

Installing the Personal Testing Center to your hard drive is an easy process. Click on the Install to Hard Drive icon and the procedure will start. An instructional box will appear, and walk you through the remainder of the installation. If installed to the hard drive, the "Personal Testing Center" program group will be created in the Start Programs folder.

Should you wish to run the software from the CD-ROM, the steps are the same as above until you reach the point where you would select the Install to Hard Drive icon. Here, select the Run from CD icon and the exam will automatically begin.

To uninstall the program from your hard disk, use the add/remove programs feature in your Windows Control Panel. InstallShield will run uninstall.

Test Type Choices

With the Personal Testing Center, you have three options in which to run the program: Live, Practice, and Review. Each test type will draw from a pool of over 300 potential questions. Your choice of test type will depend on whether you would like to simulate an actual Network+ exam, receive instant feedback on your answer choices, or review concepts using the testing simulator. Note that selecting the Full Screen icon on Internet Explorer's standard toolbar gives you the best display of the Personal Testing Center.

Live

The Live timed test type is meant to reflect the actual exam as closely as possible. You will have 90 minutes in which to complete the exam. You will have the option to skip questions and return to them later, move to the previous question, or end the exam. Once the timer has expired, you will automatically go to the scoring page to review your test results.

Managing Windows

The testing application runs inside an Internet Explorer 4.0 or 5.0 browser window. We recommend that you use the full-screen view to minimize the amount of text scrolling you need to do. However, the application will initiate a second iteration of the browser when you link to an Answer in Depth or a Review Graphic. If you are running in full-screen view, the second iteration of the browser will be covered by the first. You can toggle between the two windows with ALT-TAB, you can click your task bar to maximize the second window, or you can get out of full-screen mode and arrange the two windows so they are both visible on the screen at the same time. The application will not initiate more than two browser windows, so you aren't left with hundreds of open windows for each Answer in Depth or Review Graphic that you view.

Saving Scores as Cookies

Your exam score is stored as a browser cookie. If you've configured your browser to accept cookies, your score will be stored in a cookie named History. If you don't accept cookies, you cannot permanently save your scores. If you delete the History cookie, the scores will be deleted permanently.

Using the Browser Buttons

The test application runs inside the Internet Explorer 4.0 browser. You should navigate from screen to screen by using the application's buttons, not the browser's buttons.

JavaScript Errors

If you encounter a JavaScript error, you should be able to proceed within the application. If you cannot, shut down your Internet Explorer 4.0 browser session and relaunch the testing application.

Practice

When choosing the Practice exam type, you have the option of receiving instant feedback as to whether your selected answer is correct. The questions will be presented to you in numerical order, and you will see every question in the available question pool for each section you chose to be tested on.

As with the Live exam type, you have the option of continuing through the entire exam without seeing the correct answer for each question. The number of questions you answered correctly, along with the percentage of correct answers, will be displayed during the post-exam summary report. Once you have answered a question, click the Answer icon to display the correct answer.

You have the option of ending the Practice exam at any time, but your post-exam summary screen may reflect an incorrect percentage based on the number of questions you failed to answer. Questions that are skipped are counted as incorrect answers on the post-exam summary screen.

Review

During the Review exam type, you will be presented with questions similar to both the Live and Practice exam types. However, the Answer icon is not present, as every question will have the correct answer posted near the bottom of the screen. You have the option of answering the question without looking at the correct answer. In the Review exam type, you can also return to previous questions and skip to the next question, as well as end the exam by clicking the Stop icon.

The Review exam type is recommended when you have already completed the Live exam type once or twice, and would now like to determine which questions you answered correctly.

Questions with Answers

For the Practice and Review exam types, you will have the option of clicking a hyperlink titled Answers in Depth, which will present relevant study material aimed at exposing the logic behind the answer in a separate browser window. By having two browser windows open (one for the test engine and one for the review information), you can quickly alternate between the two windows while keeping your place in the exam. You will find that additional windows are not generated as you follow hyperlinks throughout the test engine.

Scoring

The Personal Testing Center post-exam summary screen, called Benchmark Yourself, displays the results for each section you chose to be tested on, including a bar graph similar to the real exam, which displays the percentage of correct answers. You can compare your percentage to the actual passing percentage for each section. The percentage displayed on the post-exam summary screen is not the actual percentage required to pass the exam. You'll see the number of questions you answered correctly compared to the total number of questions you were tested on. If you choose to skip a question, it will be marked as incorrect. Ending the exam by clicking the End button with questions still unanswered lowers your percentage, as these questions will be marked as incorrect.

Clicking the End button and then the Home button allows you to choose another exam type, or test yourself on another section.

CCNP
CISCO CERTIFIED NETWORK PROFESSIONAL

C

About the
Web Site

As you know by now, Global Knowledge is the largest independent IT training company in the world. Just by purchasing this book, you have also secured a free subscription to the Global Knowledge Web site and its many resources. You can find it at: http://access.globalknowledge.com

You can log on directly at the Global Knowledge site, and you will be e-mailed a new, secure password immediately upon registering.

What You'll Find There . . .

The wealth of useful information at the Global Knowledge site falls into three categories:

Skills Gap Analysis

Global Knowledge offers several ways for you to analyze your networking skills and discover where they may be lacking. Using Global Knowledge's trademarked Competence Key Tool, you can do a skills gap analysis and get recommendations for where you may need to do some more studying. (Sorry, it just might not end with this book!)

Networking

You'll also gain valuable access to another asset: people. At the Access Global site, you'll find threaded discussions, as well as live discussions. Talk to other certification candidates, get advice from folks who have already taken the exams, and get access to instructors.

Product Offerings

Of course, Global Knowledge also offers its products here, and you may find some valuable items for purchase—CBTs, books, or courses. Browse freely and see if there's something that could help you take that next step in career enhancement.

Glossary

10Base2   Ethernet specification using 50-ohm thin coaxial cable and a signaling rate of 10-Mbps baseband.

10Base5   Ethernet specification using standard (thick) 50-ohm baseband coaxial cable and a signaling rate of 10-Mbps baseband.

10BaseFL   Ethernet specification using fiber-optic cabling and a signaling rate of 10-Mbps baseband, and FOIRL.

10BaseT   Ethernet specification using two pairs of twisted-pair cabling (Category 3, 4, or 5): one pair for transmitting data and the other for receiving data, and a signaling rate of 10-Mbps baseband.

10Broad36   Ethernet specification using broadband coaxial cable and a signaling rate of 10 Mbps.

100BaseFX   Fast Ethernet specification using two strands of multimode fiber-optic cable per link and a signaling rate of 100-Mbps baseband. A 100BaseFX link cannot exceed 400 meters in length.

100BaseT   Fast Ethernet specification using UTP wiring and a signaling rate of 100-Mbps baseband. 100BaseT sends link pulses out on the wire when there is no data traffic present.

100BaseT4   Fast Ethernet specification using four pairs of Category 3, 4, or 5 UTP wiring and a signaling rate of 100-Mbps baseband. The maximum length of a 100BaseT4 segment is 100 meters.

100BaseTX   Fast Ethernet specification using two pairs of UTP or STP wiring and 100-Mbps baseband signaling. One pair of wires is used to receive data; the other is used to transmit. A 100BaseTX segment cannot exceed 100 meters in length.

100BaseX   100-Mbps baseband Fast Ethernet specification based on the IEEE 802.3 standard. 100BaseX refers to the whole 100Base family of standards for Fast Ethernet.

80/20 rule   General network standard that 80 percent of traffic on a given network is local (destined for targets in the same workgroup); and not more than 20 percent of traffic requires internetworking.

AAL (ATM adaptation layer)   Service-dependent sublayer of the Data Link layer. The function of the AAL is to accept data from different applications and present it to the ATM layer in 48-byte ATM segments.

AARP (AppleTalk Address Resolution Protocol)   The protocol that maps a data-link address to an AppleTalk network address.

ABR (area border router)   Router located on the border of an OSPF area, which connects that area to the backbone network. An ABR would be a member of both the OSPF backbone and the attached area. It maintains routing tables describing both the backbone topology and the topology of the other area.

access list   A sequential list of statements in a router configuration that identify network traffic for various purposes, including traffic and route filtering.

accounting   Cisco command option that, when applied to an interface, makes the router keep track of the number of bytes and packets sent between each pair of network addresses.

acknowledgment   Notification sent from one network device to another to acknowledge that a message or group of messages has been received. Sometimes abbreviated ACK. Opposite of **NACK**.

active hub   A multiport device that repeats and amplifies LAN signals at the Physical layer.

active monitor   A network device on a Token Ring that is responsible for managing ring operations. The active monitor ensures that tokens are not lost and that frames do not circulate indefinitely on the ring.

address   A numbering convention used to identify a unique entity or location on a network.

address mapping   Technique that allows different protocols to operate together by associating addresses from one format with those of another.

address mask   A string of bits, which, when combined with an address, describes which portion of an address refers to the network or subnet and which part refers to the host. *See also* **subnet mask**.

address resolution   A technique for resolving differences between computer addressing schemes. Address resolution most often specifies a method for mapping network layer addresses to Data Link layer addresses. *See also* **address mapping**.

Address Resolution Protocol   *See* ARP.

administrative distance   A rating of the preferability of a routing information source. Administrative distance is expressed as a value between 0 and 255. The higher the value, the lower the preference.

advertising   A process in which a router sends routing or service updates at frequent intervals so that other routers on the network can maintain lists of usable routes or services.

algorithm   A specific process for arriving at a solution to a problem.

AMI (alternate mark inversion)   The line-code type that is used on T1 and E1 circuits. In this code, zeros are represented by 01 during each bit cell, and ones are represented by 11 or 00, alternately, during each bit cell.

ANSI (American National Standards Institute)   An organization of representatives of corporate, government, and other entities that coordinates standards-related activities, approves U.S. national standards, and develops positions for the United States in international standards organizations.

APaRT (automated packet recognition/translation)
Technology that enables a server to be attached to CDDI or FDDI without necessitating the reconfiguration of applications or network protocols. APaRT recognizes specific data link layer encapsulation packet types; when these packet types are transferred to another medium, they are translated into the native format of the destination device.

AppleTalk   A suite of communications protocols developed by Apple Computer for allowing communication among their devices over a network.

Application layer   Layer 7 of the OSI reference model. This layer provides services to end-user application processes such as electronic mail, file transfer, and terminal emulation.

ARP (Address Resolution Protocol)   Internet protocol used to map an IP address to a MAC address.

ASBR (autonomous system bounder router)   An ASBR is an ABR connecting an OSPF autonomous system to a non-OSPF network. ASBRs run two protocols: OSPF and another routing protocol. ASBRs must be located in a non-stub OSPF area.

asynchronous transmission   Describes digital signals that are transmitted without precise clocking or synchronization.

ATM (Asynchronous Transfer Mode)   An international standard for cell relay suitable for carrying multiple service types (such as voice, video, or data) in fixed-length (53-byte) cells. Fixed-length cells allow cell processing to occur in hardware, thereby reducing latency.

ATM adaptation layer   *See* AAL.

ATM Forum   International organization founded in 1991 by Cisco Systems, NET/ADAPTIVE, Northern Telecom, and Sprint to develop and promote standards-based implementation agreements for ATM technology.

AUI (attachment unit interface)   An interface between an MAU and a NIC (network interface card) described in the IEEE 802.3 specification. AUI often refers to the physical port to which an AUI cable attaches.

auto-discovery   A mechanism used by many network management products, including CiscoWorks, to build a map of a network.

autonomous system   A group of networks under a common administration that share in a common routing strategy. Sometimes abbreviated AS.

B channel (Bearer channel)   An ISDN term meaning a full-duplex, 64-Kbps channel used to send user data.

B8ZS (binary 8-zero substitution)   The line-code type that is used on T1 and E1 circuits. With B8ZS, a special code is substituted whenever eight consecutive zeros are sent over the link. This code is then interpreted at the remote end of the connection.

backoff   The retransmission delay used by contention-based MAC protocols such as Ethernet, after a network node determines that the physical medium is already in use.

bandwidth   The difference between the highest and lowest frequencies available for network signals. The term may also describe the throughput capacity of a network link or segment.

baseband A network technology in which a single carrier frequency is used. Ethernet is a common example of a baseband network technology.

baud Unit of signaling speed equal to the number of separate signal elements transmitted in one second. Baud is synonymous with bits per second (bps), as long as each signal element represents exactly one bit.

Bearer channel *See* B channel.

BECN (backward explicit congestion notification) A Frame Relay network facility that allows switches in the network to advise DTE devices of congestion. The BECN bit is set in frames traveling in the opposite direction of frames encountering a congested path.

best-effort delivery Describes a network system that does not use a system of acknowledgment to guarantee reliable delivery of information.

BGP (Border Gateway Protocol) An interdomain path-vector routing protocol. BGP exchanges reachability information with other BGP systems. It is defined by RFC 1163.

binary A numbering system in which there are only two digits, ones and zeros.

bit stuffing A 0 insertion and deletion process defined by HDLC. This technique ensures that actual data never appears as flag characters.

BNC connector Standard connector used to connect coaxial cable to an MAU or line card.

BootP (Bootstrap Protocol) Part of the TCP/IP suite of protocols, used by a network node to determine the IP address of its network interfaces, in order to boot from a network server.

BPDU (Bridge Protocol Data Unit)   A Layer 2 protocol used for communication among bridges.

bps   Bits per second.

BRI (Basic Rate Interface)   ISDN interface consisting of two B channels and one D channel for circuit-switched communication. ISDN BRI can carry voice, video, and data.

bridge   Device that connects and forwards packets between two network segments that use the same data-link communications protocol. Bridges operate at the Data Link layer of the OSI reference model. A bridge will filter, forward, or flood an incoming frame based on the MAC address of the frame.

broadband   A data transmission system that multiplexes multiple independent signals onto one cable. Also, in telecommunications, any channel with a bandwidth greater than 4 KHz. In LAN terminology, a coaxial cable using analog signaling.

broadcast   Data packet addressed to all nodes on a network. Broadcasts are identified by a broadcast address that matches all addresses on the network.

broadcast address   Special address reserved for sending a message to all stations. At the Data Link layer, a broadcast address is a MAC destination address of all 1s.

broadcast domain   The group of all devices that will receive the same broadcast frame originating from any device within the group. Because routers do not forward broadcast frames, broadcast domains are typically bounded by routers.

buffer   A memory storage area used for handling data in transit. Buffers are used in internetworking to compensate for differences in processing speed between network devices or signaling rates of segments. Bursts of packets can be stored in buffers until they can be handled by slower devices.

bus   Common physical path composed of wires or other media, across which signals are sent from one part of a computer to another.

bus topology   A topology used in LANs. Transmissions from network stations propagate the length of the medium and are then received by all other stations.

byte   A series of consecutive binary digits that are operated upon as a unit, usually eight bits.

cable   Transmission medium of copper wire or optical fiber wrapped in a protective cover.

cable range   A range of network numbers on an extended AppleTalk network. The cable range value can be a single network number or a contiguous sequence of several network numbers. Nodes assign addresses within the cable range values provided.

CAM   Content-addressable memory.

carrier   Electromagnetic wave or alternating current of a single frequency, suitable for modulation by another, data-bearing signal.

Carrier Detect   *See* CD.

carrier sense multiple access with collision detection   *See* CSMA/CD.

Category 5 cabling   One of five grades of UTP cabling described in the EIA/TIA-586 standard. Category 5 cabling can transmit data at speeds up to 100 Mbps or higher.

CCITT (Consultative Committee for International Telegraphy and Telephony)   International organization responsible for the development of communications standards. Now called the ITU-T. *See also* ITU-T.

CCO (Cisco Connection Online)   Self-help resource for Cisco customers. Available 24 hours a day, seven days a week at http://www.cisco.com. The CCO family includes CCO Documentation, CCO Open Forum, CCO CD-ROM, and the TAC (Technical Assistance Center).

CD (Carrier Detect)   Signal that indicates whether a connection is established.

CDDI (Copper Distributed Data Interface)   The implementation of FDDI protocols over STP and UTP cabling. CDDI transmits over distances of approximately 100 meters, providing data rates of 100 Mbps. CDDI uses a dual-ring architecture to provide redundancy.

CDP (Cisco Discovery Protocol)   Used to discover neighboring Cisco devices, and used by network management software. The CiscoWorks network management software takes advantage of CDP.

cell   The basic data unit for ATM switching and multiplexing. A cell consists of a five-byte header and 48 bytes of payload. Cells contain fields in their headers that identify the data stream to which they belong.

CHAP (Challenge Handshake Authentication Protocol) Security feature used with PPP encapsulation, which prevents unauthorized access by identifying the remote end. The router or access server determines whether that user is allowed access.

checksum   Method for checking the integrity of transmitted data. A checksum is an integer value computed from a sequence of octets taken through a series of arithmetic operations. The value is recomputed at the receiving end and compared for verification.

CIDR (classless interdomain routing)   Technique supported by BGP4 and based on route aggregation. CIDR allows routers to group routes together in order to cut down on the quantity of routing information carried by the core routers. With CIDR, several IP networks appear to networks outside the group as a single, larger entity. With CIDR, IP addresses and their subnet masks are written as four octets, separated by periods, followed by a forward slash and a two-digit number that represents the subnet mask.

CIR (committed information rate)   The rate at which a Frame Relay network agrees to transfer information under normal conditions, averaged over a minimum increment of time. CIR, measured in bits per second, is one of the key negotiated tariff metrics.

circuit switching   A system in which a dedicated physical path must exist between sender and receiver for the entire duration of a call. Used heavily in telephone networks.

CiscoWorks   Network management package that provides a graphical view of a network, collects statistical information about a network, and offers various network management components.

client   Node or software program, or front-end device, that requests services from a server.

CLNS (Connectionless Network Service)   An OSI network layer service, for which no circuit need be established before data can be transmitted. Routing of messages to their destinations is independent of other messages.

CMU SNMP   A free command-line SNMP management package that comes in source code form. Originally developed at the Carnegie Mellon University, and available at http://www.net.cmu.edu/projects/snmp/.

collision   In Ethernet, the result of two nodes transmitting simultaneously. The frames from each device cause an increase in voltage when they meet on the physical media, and are damaged.

collision domain   A group of nodes connected such that any two or more of the nodes transmitting simultaneously will result in a collision.

congestion   Traffic in excess of link capacity.

connectionless   Term used to describe data transfer without the prior existence of a circuit.

console   A DTE device, usually consisting of a keyboard and display unit, through which users interact with a host.

contention   Access method in which network devices compete for permission to access the physical medium. Compare with **circuit switching** and **token passing**.

cost   A value, typically based on media bandwidth or other measures, that is assigned by a network administrator and used by routing protocols to compare various paths through an internetwork environment. Cost values are used to determine the most favorable path to a particular destination—the lower the cost, the better the path.

count to infinity   A condition in which routers continuously increment the hop count to particular networks. Often occurs in routing algorithms that are slow to converge. Usually, some arbitrary hop count ceiling is imposed to limit the extent of this problem.

CPE (customer premises equipment)   Terminating equipment, such as terminals, telephones, and modems, installed at customer sites and connected to the telephone company network.

CRC (cyclic redundancy check)   An error-checking technique in which the receiving device performs a calculation on the frame contents and compares the calculated number to a value stored in the frame by the sending node.

CSMA/CD (carrier-sense multiple-access/collision-detect)
Media-access mechanism used by Ethernet and IEEE 802.3. Devices use CSMA/CD to check the channel for a carrier before transmitting data. If no carrier is sensed, the device transmits. If two devices transmit at the same time, the collision is detected by all colliding devices. Collisions delay retransmissions from those devices for a randomly chosen length of time.

CSU (channel service unit)   Digital interface device that connects end-user equipment to the local digital telephone loop. Often referred to together with DSU, as CSU/DSU.

D channel   Data channel. Full-duplex, 16-Kbps (BRI) or 64-Kbps (PRI) ISDN channel.

DAS (dual attachment station)   Device that is attached to both the primary and the secondary FDDI rings. Provides redundancy for the FDDI ring. Also called a *Class A station. See also* **SAS**.

datagram   Logical unit of information sent as a network layer unit over a transmission medium without prior establishment of a circuit.

Data Link layer   Layer 2 of the OSI reference model. This layer provides reliable transit of data across a physical link. The Data Link layer is concerned with physical addressing, network topology, access to the network medium, error detection, sequential delivery of frames, and flow control. The Data Link layer is divided into two sublayers: the MAC sublayer and the LLC sublayer.

DCE (data circuit-terminating equipment)   The devices and connections of a communications network that represent the network end of the user-to-network interface. The DCE provides a physical connection to the network and provides a clocking signal used to synchronize transmission between DCE and DTE devices. Modems and interface cards are examples of DCE devices.

DDR (dial-on-demand routing)   Technique whereby a router can automatically initiate and close a circuit-switched session as transmitting stations demand. The router spoofs keepalives so that end-stations treat the session as active. DDR permits routing over ISDN or telephone lines using an external ISDN terminal adapter or modem.

de facto standard   A standard that exists because of its widespread use.

de jure standard   Standard that exists because of its development or approval by an official standards body.

DECNet   Group of communications products (including a protocol suite) developed and supported by Digital Equipment Corporation. DECNet/OSI (also called DECNet Phase V) is the most recent iteration and supports both OSI protocols and proprietary Digital protocols. Phase IV Prime supports inherent MAC addresses that allow DECNet nodes to coexist with systems running other protocols that have MAC address restrictions. *See also* **DNA**.

dedicated line   Communications line that is indefinitely reserved for transmissions, rather than switched as transmission is required. *See also* **leased line**.

default gateway   Another term for default router. The router that an IP host will use to reach another network when it has no specific information about how to reach that network.

default route   A routing table entry that is used to direct packets when there is no explicit route present in the routing table.

delay   The time between the initiation of a transaction by a sender and the first response received by the sender. Also, the time required to move a packet from source to destination over a network path.

demarc   The demarcation point between telephone carrier equipment and CPE.

demultiplexing   The separating of multiple streams of data that have been multiplexed into a common physical signal for transmission, back into multiple output streams. Opposite of **multiplexing**.

destination address   Address of a network device to receive data.

DHCP (Dynamic Host Configuration Protocol)   Provides a mechanism for allocating IP addresses dynamically so that addresses can be reassigned instead of belonging to only one host.

Dijkstra algorithm   Dijkstra's algorithm is a graph algorithm used to find the shortest path from one node on a graph to all others. Used in networking to determine the shortest path between routers.

discovery mode   Method by which an AppleTalk router acquires information about an attached network from an operational router and then uses this information to configure its own addressing information.

distance vector routing algorithm   Class of routing algorithms that use the number of hops in a route to find a shortest path to a destination network. Distance vector routing algorithms call for each router to send its entire routing table in each update to each of its neighbors. Also called Bellman-Ford routing algorithm.

DLCI (data-link connection identifier)   A value that specifies a virtual circuit in a Frame Relay network.

DNA (Digital Network Architecture)   Network architecture that was developed by Digital Equipment Corporation. DECNet is the collective term for the products that comprise DNA (including communications protocols).

DNIC (Data Network Identification Code)   Part of an X.121 address. DNICs are divided into two parts: the first specifying the country in which the addressed PSN is located and the second specifying the PSN itself. *See also* X.121.

DNS (Domain Name System)   System used in the Internet for translating names of network nodes into addresses.

DSP (domain specific part)   Part of an ATM address. A DSP is comprised of an area identifier, a station identifier, and a selector byte.

DTE (data terminal equipment)   Device at the user end of a user-network interface that serves as a data source, destination, or both. DTE connects to a data network through a DCE device (for example, a modem) and typically uses clocking signals generated by the DCE. DTE includes such devices as computers, routers and multiplexers.

DUAL (Diffusing Update Algorithm)   Convergence algorithm used in EIGRP. DUAL provides constant loop-free operation throughout a route computation by allowing routers involved in a topology change to synchronize at the same time, without involving routers that are unaffected by the change.

DVMRP (Distance Vector Multicast Routing Protocol)
DVMRP is an internetwork gateway protocol that implements a typical dense mode IP multicast scheme. Using IGMP, DVMRP exchanges routing datagrams with its neighbors.

dynamic routing   Routing that adjusts automatically to changes in network topology or traffic patterns.

E1   Wide-area digital transmission scheme used in Europe that carries data at a rate of 2.048 Mbps.

EIA/TIA-232   Common Physical layer interface standard, developed by EIA and TIA, that supports unbalanced circuits at signal speeds of up to 64 Kbps. Formerly known as RS-232.

EIGRP (Enhanced IGRP)   A multiservice routing protocol supporting IPX, AppleTalk, and IP. BGP is used for interconnecting networks and defining strict routing policies.

encapsulation   The process of attaching a particular protocol header to a unit of data prior to transmission on the network. For example, a frame of Ethernet data is given a specific Ethernet header before network transit.

endpoint   Device at which a virtual circuit or virtual path begins or ends.

enterprise network   A privately maintained network connecting most major points in a company or other organization. Usually spans a large geographic area and supports multiple protocols and services.

entity   Generally, an individual, manageable network device. Sometimes called an alias.

error control   Technique for detecting and correcting errors in data transmissions.

Ethernet   Baseband LAN specification invented by Xerox Corporation and developed jointly by Xerox, Intel, and Digital Equipment Corporation. Ethernet networks use the CSMA/CD method of media access control and run over a variety of cable types at 10 Mbps. Ethernet is similar to the IEEE 802.3 series of standards.

EtherTalk Apple Computer's data-link product that allows an AppleTalk network to be connected by Ethernet cable.

EtherWave A product from Netopia (formerly Farallon) used to connect AppleTalk devices with LocalTalk connectors to Ethernet networks. They are an alternative to LocalTalk-to-EtherTalk routers.

explorer packet Generated by an end-station trying to find its way through an SRB network. Gathers a hop-by-hop description of a path through the network by being marked (updated) by each bridge that it traverses, thereby creating a complete topological path.

Fast Ethernet Any of a number of 100-Mbps Ethernet specifications. Fast Ethernet offers a speed increase ten times that of the 10BaseT Ethernet specification, while preserving such qualities as frame format, MAC mechanisms, and MTU. Such similarities allow the use of existing 10BaseT applications and network management tools on Fast Ethernet networks. Based on an extension to the IEEE 802.3 specification. Compare with **Ethernet**. *See also* **100BaseFX; 100BaseT; 100BaseT4; 100BaseTX; 100BaseX; IEEE 802.3.**

FDDI (Fiber Distributed Data Interface) LAN standard, defined by ANSI X3T9.5, specifying a 100-Mbps token-passing network using fiber-optic cable, with transmission distances of up to 2 kilometers. FDDI uses a dual-ring architecture to provide redundancy. Compare with **CDDI.**

FECN (forward explicit congestion notification) A facility in a Frame Relay network to inform DTE receiving the frame that congestion was experienced in the path from source to destination. DTE receiving frames with the FECN bit set can request that higher-level protocols take flow-control action as appropriate.

file transfer Category of popular network applications that features movement of files from one network device to another.

filter   Generally, a process or device that screens network traffic for certain characteristics, such as source address, destination address, or protocol, and determines whether to forward or discard that traffic or routes based on the established criteria.

FIORL (fiber-optic interrepeater link)   Fiber-optic signaling methodology that is based on the IEEE 802.3 fiber-optic specfication. *See also* **10BaseFL**.

firewall   Router or other computer designated as a buffer between public networks and a private network. A firewall router uses access lists and other methods to ensure the security of the private network.

Flash memory   Nonvolatile storage that can be electrically erased and reprogrammed as necessary.

flash update   Routing update sent asynchronously when a change in the network topology occurs.

flat addressing   A system of addressing that does not incorporate a hierarchy to determine location.

flooding   Traffic-passing technique used by switches and bridges in which traffic received on an interface is sent out all of the interfaces of that device except the interface on which the information was originally received.

flow control   Technique for ensuring that a transmitting device, such as a modem, does not overwhelm a receiving device with data. When the buffers on the receiving device are full, a message is sent to the sending device to suspend transmission until it has processed the data in the buffers.

forwarding   The process of sending a frame or packet toward its destination.

fragment　Piece of a larger packet that has been broken down to smaller units.

fragmentation　Process of breaking a packet into smaller units when transmitting over a network medium that is unable to support a transmission unit the original size of the packet.

frame　Logical grouping of information sent as a Data Link layer unit over a transmission medium. Sometimes refers to the header and trailer, used for synchronization and error control, which surround the user data contained in the unit. The terms cell, datagram, message, packet, and segment are also used to describe logical information groupings at various layers of the OSI reference model and in various technology circles.

Frame Relay　Industry-standard, switched Data Link layer protocol that handles multiple virtual circuits over a single physical interface. Frame Relay is more efficient than X.25, for which it is generally considered a replacement.

Frame Relay Cloud　A generic term used to refer to a collective Frame Relay network. For Frame Relay carrier customers, it generally refers to the carrier's entire Frame Relay network. It's referred to as a "cloud" because the network layout is not visible to the customer.

frequency　Number of cycles, measured in hertz, of an alternating current signal per unit of time.

FTP (File Transfer Protocol)　An application protocol, part of the TCP/IP protocol stack, used for transferring files between hosts on a network.

full duplex　Capability for simultaneous data transmission and receipt of data between two devices.

full mesh A network topology in which each network node has either a physical circuit or a virtual circuit connecting it to every other network node.

gateway In the IP community, an older term referring to a routing device. Today, the term router is used to describe devices that perform this function, and gateway refers to a special-purpose device that performs an Application layer conversion of information from one protocol stack to another.

GB Gigabyte. Approximately 1,000,000,000 bytes.

Gb Gigabit. Approximately 1,000,000,000 bits.

GBps Gigabytes per second.

Gbps Gigabits per second.

giants Ethernet frames exceeding the maximum frame size.

GNS (Get Nearest Server) Request packet sent by a client on an IPX network to locate the nearest active server of a particular type. An IPX network client issues a GNS request to solicit either a direct response from a connected server or a response from a router that tells it where on the internetwork the service can be located. GNS is part of the IPX SAP.

half-duplex Capability for data transmission in only one direction at a time between a sending station and a receiving station.

handshake Sequence of messages exchanged between two or more network devices to ensure transmission synchronization.

hardware address *See* MAC address.

HDLC (High-level Data Link Control) Bit-oriented synchronous Data Link layer protocol developed by ISO and derived from SDLC. HDLC specifies a data encapsulation method for synchronous serial links and includes frame characters and checksums in its headers.

header Control information placed before data when encapsulating that data for network transmission.

Hello packet Multicast packet that is used by routers for neighbor discovery and recovery. Hello packets also indicate that a client is still operating on the network.

Hello protocol Protocol used by OSPF and other routing protocols for establishing and maintaining neighbor relationships.

hierarchical addressing A scheme of addressing that uses a logical hierarchy to determine location. For example, IP addresses consist of network numbers, subnet numbers, and host numbers, which IP routing algorithms use to route the packet to the appropriate location.

holddown State of a routing table entry in which routers will neither advertise the route nor accept advertisements about the route for a specific length of time (known as the holddown period).

hop Term describing the passage of a data packet between two network nodes (for example, between two routers). *See also* **hop count**.

hop count Routing metric used to measure the distance between a source and a destination. RIP uses hop count as its metric.

host A computer system on a network. Similar to the term *node* except that host usually implies a computer system, whereas node can refer to any networked system, including routers.

host number   Part of an IP address that designates which node is being addressed. Also called a host address.

hub   A term used to describe a device that serves as the center of a star topology network; or, an Ethernet multiport repeater, sometimes referred to as a concentrator.

ICMP (Internet Control Message Protocol)   A network layer Internet protocol that provides reports of errors and other information about IP packet processing. ICMP is documented in RFC 792.

IEEE (Institute of Electrical and Electronics Engineers)   A professional organization among whose activities are the development of communications and networking standards. IEEE LAN standards are the most common LAN standards today.

IEEE 802.3   IEEE LAN protocol for the implementation of the Physical layer and the MAC sublayer of the Data Link layer. IEEE 802.3 uses CSMA/CD access at various speeds over various physical media.

IEEE 802.5   IEEE LAN protocol for the implementation of the Physical layer and MAC sublayer of the Data Link layer. Similar to Token Ring, IEEE 802.5 uses token-passing access over STP and UTP cabling.

IGP (Interior Gateway Protocol)   A generic term for an Internet routing protocol used to exchange routing information within an autonomous system. Examples of common Internet IGPs include IGRP, OSPF, and RIP.

InARP (Inverse Address Resolution Protocol)   *See* Inverse ARP.

interface   A connection between two systems or devices; or in routing terminology, a network connection.

Internet   Term used to refer to the global internetwork that evolved from the ARPANET, that now connects tens of thousands of networks worldwide.

Internet protocol   *See* IP.

internetwork   Collection of networks interconnected by routers and other devices that functions (generally) as a single network.

internetworking   General term used to refer to the industry that has arisen around the problem of connecting networks together. The term may be used to refer to products, procedures, and technologies.

Inverse ARP (Inverse Address Resolution Protocol)   Method of building dynamic address mappings in a Frame Relay network. Allows a device to discover the network address of a device associated with a virtual circuit.

IP (Internet Protocol)   Network layer protocol in the TCP/IP stack offering a connectionless datagram service. IP provides features for addressing, type-of-service specification, fragmentation and reassembly, and security. Documented in RFC 791.

IP address   A 32-bit address assigned to hosts using the TCP/IP suite of protocols. An IP address is written as four octets separated by dots (dotted decimal format). Each address consists of a network number, an optional subnetwork number, and a host number. The network and subnetwork numbers together are used for routing, while the host number is used to address an individual host within the network or subnetwork. A subnet mask is often used with the address to extract network and subnetwork information from the IP address.

IPX (Internetwork Packet Exchange)   NetWare network layer (Layer 3) protocol used for transferring data from servers to workstations. IPX is similar to IP in that it is a connectionless datagram service.

IPXCP (IPX Control Protocol)   The protocol that establishes and configures IPX over PPP.

IPXWAN   A protocol that negotiates end-to-end options for new links on startup. When a link comes up, the first IPX packets sent across are IPXWAN packets negotiating the options for the link. When the IPXWAN options have been successfully determined, normal IPX transmission begins, and no more IPXWAN packets are sent. Defined by RFC 1362.

ISDN (Integrated Services Digital Network)   Communication protocol, offered by telephone companies, that permits telephone networks to carry data, voice, and other source traffic.

ISL (Inter-Switch Link)   Cisco's protocol for trunking VLANs over Fast Ethernet.

ITU-T (International Telecommunication Union Telecommunication Standardization Sector)   International body dedicated to the development of worldwide standards for telecommunications technologies. ITU-T is the successor to CCITT.

jabbers   Long, continuous frames exceeding 1518 bytes that prevent all stations on the Ethernet network from transmitting data. Jabbering violates CSMA/CD implementation by prohibiting stations from transmitting data.

jam pattern   Initiated by Ethernet transmitting station when a collision is detected during transmission.

KB   Kilobyte. Approximately 1,000 bytes.

Kb   Kilobit. Approximately 1,000 bits.

KBps   Kilobytes per second.

Kbps   Kilobits per second.

keepalive interval   Period of time between keepalive messages sent by a network device.

keepalive message   Message sent by one network device to inform another network device that it is still active.

LAN (local area network)   High-speed, low-error data network covering a relatively small geographic area. LANs connect workstations, peripherals, terminals, and other devices in a single building or other geographically limited area. LAN standards specify cabling and signaling at the physical and Data Link layers of the OSI model. Ethernet, FDDI, and Token Ring are the most widely used LAN technologies.

LANE (LAN Emulation)   Technology that allows an ATM network to function as a LAN backbone. In this situation LANE provides multicast and broadcast support, address mapping (MAC-to-ATM), and virtual circuit management.

LAPB (Link Access Procedure, Balanced)   The Data Link layer protocol in the X.25 protocol stack. LAPB is a bit-oriented protocol derived from HDLC.

LAPD (Link Access Procedure on the D channel)   ISDN Data Link layer protocol for the D channel. LAPD was derived from the LAPB protocol and is designed to satisfy the signaling requirements of ISDN basic access. Defined by ITU-T Recommendations Q.920 and Q.921.

LAPF   Data link standard for Frame Relay.

late collision   Collision that is detected only after a station places a complete frame of the network.

latency   The amount of time elapsed between the time a device requests access to a network and the time it is allowed to transmit; or, amount of time between the point at which a device receives a frame and the time that frame is forwarded out the destination port.

LCP (Link Control Protocol)   A protocol used with PPP, which establishes, configures, and tests data-link connections.

leased line   Transmission line reserved by a communications carrier for the private use of a customer. A leased line is a type of dedicated line.

LEC (LAN Emulation Client)   Performs data forwarding, address resolution, and other control functions for a single end system within a single ELAN. Each LEC has a unique ATM address, and is associated with one or more MAC addresses reachable through that ATM address.

LECS (LAN Emulation Configuration Server)   Assigns LANE clients to ELANs by directing them to the LES that corresponds to the ELAN. There can be logically one LECS per administrative domain, which serves all ELANs within that domain.

LES (LAN Emulation Server)   Implements the subscription function for an ELAN. There can be only one logical LES per ELAN. It has a unique ATM address.

link   Network communications channel consisting of a circuit or transmission path and all related equipment between a sender and a receiver. Most often used to refer to a WAN connection. Sometimes called a line or a transmission link.

link-state routing algorithm   Routing algorithm in which each router broadcasts or multicasts information regarding the cost of reaching each of its neighbors to all nodes in the internetwork. Link state algorithms require that routers maintain a consistent view of the network and are therefore not prone to routing loops.

LLC (Logical Link Control)   Higher of two Data Link layer sublayers defined by the IEEE. The LLC sublayer handles error control, flow control, framing, and MAC-sublayer addressing. The most common LLC protocol is IEEE 802.2, which includes both connectionless and connection-oriented types.

LMI (Local Management Interface)   A set of enhancements to the basic Frame Relay specification. LMI includes support for keepalives, a multicast mechanism; global addressing, and a status mechanism.

load balancing   In routing, the ability of a router to distribute traffic over all its network ports that are the same distance from the destination address. Load balancing increases the utilization of network segments, thus increasing total effective network bandwidth.

local loop   A line from the premises of a telephone subscriber to the telephone company central office.

LocalTalk   Apple Computer's proprietary baseband protocol that operates at the Data Link and Physical layers of the OSI reference model. LocalTalk uses CSMA/CA and supports transmissions at speeds of 230.4 Kbps.

loop   A situation in which packets never reach their destination, but are forwarded in a cycle repeatedly through a group of network nodes.

MAC (Media Access Control)   Lower of the two sublayers of the Data Link layer defined by the IEEE. The MAC sublayer handles access to shared media.

MAC address   Standardized Data Link layer address that is required for every port or device that connects to a LAN. Other devices in the network use these addresses to locate specific devices in the network and to create and update routing tables and data structures. MAC addresses are 48 bits long and are controlled by the IEEE. Also known as a hardware address, a MAC-layer address, or a physical address.

MAN (metropolitan-area network)   A network that spans a metropolitan area. Generally, a MAN spans a larger geographic area than a LAN, but a smaller geographic area than a WAN.

MAU   *See* MSAU.

MB   Megabyte. Approximately 1,000,000 bits.

Mbps   Megabits per second.

media   The various physical environments through which transmission signals pass. Common network media include cable (twisted-pair, coaxial, and fiber optic) and the atmosphere (through which microwave, laser, and infrared transmission occurs). Sometimes referred to as physical media.

Media Access Control   *See* MAC.

mesh   Network topology in which devices are organized in a segmented manner with redundant interconnections strategically placed between network nodes.

message   Application layer logical grouping of information, often composed of a number of lower-layer logical groupings such as packets.

MIB (Management Information Base)   Database for network management information; it is used and maintained by a network management protocol such as SNMP.

MSAU (multistation access unit)   A wiring concentrator to which all end stations in a Token Ring network connect. Sometimes abbreviated MAU.

multiaccess network   A network that allows multiple devices to connect and communicate by sharing the same medium, such as a LAN.

multicast   A single packet copied by the network and sent to a specific subset of network addresses. These addresses are specified in the Destination Address field.

multicast address   A single address that refers to multiple network devices. Sometimes called a group address.

multiplexing   A technique that allows multiple logical signals to be transmitted simultaneously across a single physical channel.

mux   A multiplexer device. A mux combines multiple input signals for transmission over a single line. The signals are demultiplexed, or separated, before they are used at the receiving end.

NACK (negative acknowledgment)   A response sent from a receiving device to a sending device indicating that the information received contained errors.

name resolution   The process of associating a symbolic name with a network location or address.

NAT (Network Address Translation)   A technique for reducing the need for globally unique IP addresses. NAT allows an organization with addresses that may conflict with others in the IP address space to connect to the Internet by translating those addresses into unique ones within the globally routable address space.

NBMA (nonbroadcast multiaccess)   Term describing a multiaccess network that either does not support broadcasting (such as X.25 and Frame Relay) or in which broadcasting is not feasible.

NBP (Name Binding Protocol)   AppleTalk transport level protocol that translates a character string name into the DDP address of the corresponding socket client.

NCP (Network Control Protocol)   Protocols that establish and configure various network layer protocols. Used for AppleTalk over PPP.

NDS (NetWare Directory Services)   A feature added in NetWare 4.0 as a replacement for individual bindaries. NDS allows NetWare and related resources to be grouped in a tree hierarchy to better provide central administration.

NetBIOS (Network Basic Input/Output System)   An application programming interface used by applications on an IBM LAN to request services from lower-level network processes such as session establishment and termination, and information transfer.

netmask   A number, usually used as a bit-mask, to separate an address into its network portion and host portion.

NetWare   A network operating system developed by Novell, Inc. Provides remote file access, print services, and numerous other distributed network services.

network   Collection of computers, printers, routers, switches, and other devices that are able to communicate with each other over some transmission medium.

network interface   Border between a carrier network and a privately owned installation.

Network layer   Layer 3 of the OSI reference model. This layer provides connectivity and path selection between two end systems. The Network layer is the layer at which routing takes place.

NIC (Network Interface Card)   An expansion card used to connect a computer to a local area network. Also known as a network adapter.

NLSP (NetWare Link Services Protocol)   Link-state routing protocol for IPX based on IS-IS.

node   Endpoint of a network connection or a junction common to two or more lines in a network. Nodes can be processors, controllers, or workstations. Nodes, which vary in their functional capabilities, can be interconnected by links, and serve as control points in the network.

NVRAM (nonvolatile RAM)   RAM that retains its contents when a device is powered off.

ODI   Novell's Open Data-link Interface. A specification for developing modular hardware drives and protocol stacks.

OSI reference model (Open System Interconnect reference model)   A network architectural framework developed by ISO and ITU-T. The model describes seven layers, each of which specifies a particular network. The lowest layer, called the Physical layer, is closest to the media technology. The highest layer, the Application layer, is closest to the user. The OSI reference model is widely used as a way of describing network functionality.

OSPF (Open Shortest Path First)   A link-state, hierarchical IGP routing algorithm, which includes features such as least-cost routing, multipath routing, and load balancing. OSPF was based on an early version of the IS-IS protocol.

out-of-band signaling   Transmission using frequencies, channels, or media other than those used for transfer of normal data. Out-of-band signaling is often used for error reporting when normal channels are unusable for communicating with network devices.

packet   Logical grouping of information that includes a header containing control information and (usually) user data. Packets are most often used to refer to network layer units of data. The terms datagram, frame, message, and segment are also used to describe logical information groupings at various layers of the OSI reference model, and in various technology circles. *See also* PDU.

packet analyzer   A software package (also sometimes including specialized hardware) used to monitor network traffic. Most packet analyzer packages will also do packet decoding, making the packets easier for humans to read.

packet burst   Allows multiple packets to be transmitted between Novell clients and servers in response to a single read or write request. It also allows file transfer to greatly improve throughput by reducing the number of acknowledgments.

packet starvation effect   On Ethernet, when packets experience latencies up to 100 times the average, or completely "starve out" due to 16 collisions. Occurs as a result of the CSMA/CD implementation.

PAP (Password Authentication Protocol)   Authentication protocol that allows PPP peers to authenticate one another. The remote router attempting to connect to the local router is required to send an authentication request. Unlike CHAP, PAP passes the password and host name or username in the clear (unencrypted). PAP does not itself prevent unauthorized access, but merely identifies the remote end. The router or access server then determines if that user is allowed access. PAP is supported only on PPP lines.

partial mesh   Term describing a network in which devices are organized in a mesh topology, with some network nodes organized in a full mesh, but with others that are only connected to one or two other nodes in the network. A partial mesh does not provide the level of redundancy of a full mesh topology, but is less expensive to implement. Partial mesh topologies are generally used in the peripheral networks that connect to a fully meshed backbone. *See also* **full mesh**; **mesh**.

PDU (protocol data unit)   The OSI term for a packet of data.

Physical layer   Layer 1 of the OSI reference model; it corresponds with the Physical control layer in the SNA model. The Physical layer defines the specifications for activating, maintaining, and deactivating the physical link between end systems.

ping (packet internet groper)   ICMP echo message and its reply. Often used in IP networks to test the reachability of a network device.

poison reverse updates   Routing updates that explicitly indicate that a network or subnet is unreachable, rather than implying that a network is unreachable by omitting it from updates. Poison reverse updates are sent to defeat large routing loops.

port   1. Physical interface on an internetworking device (such as a router). 2. In IP terminology, an upper-layer process that receives information from lower layers. Ports are numbered, and each numbered port is associated with a specific process. For example, SMTP is associated with port 25. Standardized port numbers are also called "well-known" ports. 3. To rewrite software or microcode so that it will run on a different hardware platform or in a different software environment than that for which it was originally designed.

PPP (Point-to-Point Protocol)   A successor to SLIP that provides router-to-router and host-to-network connections over synchronous and asynchronous circuits. Whereas SLIP was only designed to work with IP, PPP was designed to work with several network layer protocols, such as IP, IPX, and AppleTalk. PPP also has built-in security mechanisms, such as CHAP and PAP. PPP relies on two protocols: LCP and NCP. *See also* **CHAP; LCP; NCP; PAP; SLIP.**

Presentation layer   Layer 6 of the OSI reference model. This layer ensures that information sent by the Application layer of one system will be readable by the Application layer of another. The Presentation layer is also concerned with the data structures used by programs and therefore negotiates data transfer syntax for the Application layer.

PRI (Primary Rate Interface)   ISDN interface to primary rate access. Primary rate access consists of a single 64-Kbps D channel plus 23 (T1) or 30 (E1) B channels for voice or data. Compare to **BRI.**

protocol   Formal description of a set of rules and conventions that govern how devices on a network exchange information.

protocol stack   Set of related communications protocols that operate together and, as a group, address communication at some or all of the seven layers of the OSI reference model. Not every protocol stack covers each layer of the model, and often a single protocol in the stack will address a number of layers at once. TCP/IP is a typical protocol stack.

proxy ARP (proxy Address Resolution Protocol)   Variation of the ARP protocol in which an intermediate device (for example, a router) sends an ARP response on behalf of an end node to the requesting host. Enables very simple devices to communicate without knowing about the default gateway. *See also* **ARP.**

PVC (permanent virtual circuit)   PVCs avoid the delay, bandwith, and CPU load associated with dynamically creating SVCs. PVCs are suited to applications where a virtual circuit will be used regularly.

Q.921   ITU (International Telecommunication Union) standard document for ISDN Layer 2 (Data Link layer).

Q.931   ITU (International Telecommunication Union) standard document for ISDN Layer 3.

query   Message used to inquire about the value of some variable or set of variables. *See* SNMP.

queue   A backlog of packets stored in buffers and waiting to be forwarded over an interface.

RAM (random-access memory)   Volatile memory that can be read and written by a computer.

reassembly   The putting back together of an IP datagram at the destination after it has been fragmented either at the source or at an intermediate node. *See also* **fragmentation**.

reload   The event of a Cisco router or switch rebooting, or the command that causes the router to reboot.

reverse path forwarding   If a packet server receives a packet through different interfaces from the same source, the server drops all packets after the first.

reverse Telnet   Using a router to connect to a serial device, frequently a modem, in order to connect out. For example, telnetting to a special port on an access router in order to access a modem to dial out. Called "reverse" because it's the opposite of the router's usual function, to accept calls into the modem.

RFC (Request For Comments)   Documentation method used as the primary means of communicating information about the Internet. Some RFCs are designated by the IAB as Internet standards.

ring   Connection of two or more stations in a logically circular topology. Information is passed sequentially between active stations. Token Ring, FDDI, and CDDI are based on this topology.

ring topology   Network topology that consists of a series of repeating devices connected to one another by unidirectional transmission links to form a single closed loop. Each station on the network connects to the network at a repeater.

RIP (Routing Information Protocol)   A routing protocol for TCP/IP networks. The most common routing protocol in private networks. RIP uses hop count as a routing metric.

RMON (Remote monitor)   A set of SNMP standards used to collect statistical network information. RMON is divided into groups, with each additional group providing more statistical information.

ROM (read-only memory)   Nonvolatile memory that can be read, but not written, by the computer.

routed protocol   Protocol that carries user data so it can be routed by a router. A router must be able to interpret the logical internetwork as specified by that routed protocol. Examples of routed protocols include AppleTalk, DECNet, and IP.

router   Network layer device that uses one or more metrics to determine the optimal path along which network traffic should be forwarded. Routers forward packets from one network to another based on network layer information.

routing   Process of finding a path to a destination host.

routing metric   Method by which a routing algorithm determines preferability of one route over another. This information is stored in routing tables. Metrics may include bandwidth, communication cost, delay, hop count, load, MTU, path cost, and reliability, depending on the routing protocol. Sometimes referred to simply as a metric.

routing protocol   Protocol that accomplishes routing through the implementation of a specific routing algorithm. Examples of routing protocols include IGRP, OSPF, and RIP.

routing table   Table stored in a router or some other internetworking device that keeps track of routes to particular network destinations and metrics associated with those routes.

routing update   Message sent from a router to indicate network reachability and associated cost information. Routing updates are typically sent at regular intervals or after a change in network topology. Compare with **flash update**.

RSRB (remote source-route bridging)   Equivalent to an SRB over WAN links.

RTMP (Router Table Maintenance Protocol)   The protocol used by AppleTalk devices to communicate routing information. Structurally similar to RIP.

runts   Ethernet frames that are smaller than 64 bytes.

SAP (service access point)   1. Field defined by the IEEE 802.2 specification that is part of an address specification. Thus, the destination address plus the destination SAP (DSAP) define the recipient of a packet. The same applies to the source SAP (SSAP). 2. Service Advertising Protocol. IPX protocol that provides a means of informing network routers and servers of the location of available network resources and services.

SAS (single attachment station)   Device attached to the primary ring of an FDDI ring. Also known as a Class B station. *See also* **DAS.**

segment   1. Section of a network that is bounded by bridges, routers, or switches. 2. In a LAN using a bus topology, a segment is a continuous electrical circuit that is often connected to other such segments with repeaters. 3. Term used in the TCP specification to describe a single Transport layer unit of information.

serial transmission   Method of data transmission in which the bits of a data character are transmitted sequentially over a single channel.

session   1. Related set of communications transactions between two network devices. 2. In SNA, a logical connection that enables two NAUs to communicate.

Session layer   Layer 5 of the OSI reference model. This layer establishes, manages, and terminates sessions between applications and manages data exchange between Presentation layer entities. Corresponds to the data flow control layer of the SNA model. *See also* **Application layer; Data Link layer; Network layer; OSI reference model; Physical layer; Presentation layer; Transport layer.**

sliding window flow control   Method of flow control in which a receiver gives a transmitter permission to transmit data until a window is full. When the window is full, the transmitter must stop transmitting until the receiver acknowledges some of the data, or advertises a larger window. TCP, other transport protocols, and several Data Link layer protocols use this method of flow control.

SLIP (Serial Line Internet Protocol)   Uses a variation of TCP/IP to make point-to-point serial connections. Succeeded by PPP.

SNAP (Subnetwork Access Protocol) Internet protocol that operates between a network entity in the subnetwork and a network entity in the end system. SNAP specifies a standard method of encapsulating IP datagrams and ARP messages on IEEE networks.

SNMP (Simple Network Management Protocol) Network management protocol used almost exclusively in TCP/IP networks. SNMP provides a means to monitor and control network devices, and to manage configurations, statistics collection, performance, and security.

SNMP manager Software used to manage network devices via SNMP. Often includes graphical representation of the network and individual devices, and the ability to set and respond to SNMP traps.

SNMP trap A threshold of some sort which, when reached, causes the SNMP managed device to notify the SNMP manager. This allows for immediate notification, instead of having to wait for the SNMP manager to poll again.

socket Software structure operating as a communications endpoint within a network device.

SONET (Synchronous Optical Network) High-speed fault-tolerant synchronous network specification developed by Bellcore and designed to run on optical fiber.

source address Address of a network device that is sending data.

spanning tree Loop-free subset of a network topology. *See also* Spanning-Tree Protocol.

Spanning-Tree Protocol Developed to eliminate loops in the network. The Spanning-Tree Protocol ensures a loop-free path by placing redundant bridge ports in "blocking mode," preventing the forwarding of packets through all ports except one.

SPF (shortest path first algorithm)   Routing algorithm that sorts routes by length of path to determine a shortest-path spanning tree. Commonly used in link-state routing algorithms. Sometimes called Dijkstra's algorithm.

SPIDs (Service Profile Identifiers)   These function as addresses for B channels on ISDN BRI circuits. When call information is passed over the D channel, the SPIDs are used to identify which channel is being referred to. SPIDs are usually some variant of the phone number for the channel.

split-horizon   Routing technique in which information about routes is prevented from being advertised out the router interface through which that information was received. Split-horizon is used to prevent routing loops.

SPX (Sequenced Packet Exchange)   Reliable, connection-oriented protocol at the Transport layer that supplements the datagram service provided by IPX. Similar to TCP.

SR/TLB (source-route translational bridging)   Method of bridging that supports source-route bridging, as well as translation between Token Ring and Ethernet frame formats.

SRB (source-route bridging)   Method of bridging in Token Ring networks. In an SRB network, before data is sent to a destination, the entire route to that destination is predetermined by sending "explorer" packets.

SRT (source-route transparent bridging)   IBM's merging of SRB and transparent bridging into one bridging scheme. Packets with source-route information are bridged in SRB fashion, while other traffic is bridged transparently.

standard   Set of rules or procedures that are either widely used or officially specified.

star topology LAN topology in which endpoints on a network are connected to a common central device by point-to-point links. A ring topology that is organized as a star implements a unidirectional closed-loop star, instead of point-to-point links. Compare with **bus topology**, **ring topology**, and **tree topology**.

static route Route that is explicitly configured and entered into the routing table. Static routes generally take precedence over routes chosen by dynamic routing protocols.

subinterface A virtual interface defined as a logical subdivision of a physical interface.

subnet address Portion of an IP address that is specified as the subnetwork by the subnet mask. *See also* **IP address**; **subnet mask**; **subnetwork**.

subnet mask 32-bit address mask used in IP to indicate the bits of an IP address that are being used for the subnet address. Sometimes referred to simply as mask. *See also* **address mask**; **IP address**.

subnetwork 1. In IP networks, a network sharing a particular subnet address. 2. Subnetworks are networks arbitrarily segmented by a network administrator in order to provide a multilevel, hierarchical routing structure while shielding the subnetwork from the addressing complexity of attached networks. Sometimes called a subnet.

SVC (switched virtual circuit) Virtual circuit that can be established dynamically on demand, and which is torn down after a transmission is complete. SVCs are used when data transmission is sporadic.

switch 1. Network device that filters, forwards, and floods frames based on the destination address of each frame. The switch operates at the Data Link layer of the OSI model. 2. General term applied to an electronic or mechanical device that allows a connection to be established as necessary and terminated when there is no longer a session to support.

T1   Digital WAN carrier facility. T1 transmits DS-1-formatted data at 1.544 Mbps through the telephone-switching network, using AMI or B8ZS encoding. Compare with **E1**. *See also* **AMI**; **B8ZS**.

TCP (Transmission Control Protocol)   Connection-oriented Transport layer protocol that provides reliable full-duplex data transmission. TCP is part of the TCP/IP protocol stack.

TCP/IP (Transmission Control Protocol/Internet Protocol) Common name for the suite of protocols developed by the United States Department of Defense in the 1970s to support the construction of worldwide internetworks. TCP and IP are the two best-known protocols in the suite.

TDR (time-domain reflectometer)   A TDR test is used to measure the length of a cable, or the distance to a break. This is accomplished by sending a signal down a wire, and measuring how long it takes for an echo of the signal to bounce back.

TEI (Terminal Endpoint Identifier)   Field in the LAPD address that identifies a device on an ISDN interface.

Telnet   Standard terminal emulation protocol in the TCP/IP protocol stack. With Telnet, users can log in to remote systems and use resources as if they were connected to a local system.

TFTP (Trivial File Transfer Protocol)   Simplified version of FTP that allows files to be transferred from one computer to another over a network.

three-way handshake   The three required packets to set up a TCP connection. It consists of a SYN packet, acknowledged by a SYN+ACK packet, which is finally acknowledged by an ACK packet. During this handshake, sequence numbers are exchanged.

throughput   Rate of information arriving at, and possibly passing through, a particular point in a network system.

timeout   Event that occurs when one network device expects to hear from another network device within a specified period of time, but does not. A timeout usually results in a retransmission of information or the termination of the session between the two devices.

token   Frame that contains only control information. Possession of the token allows a network device to transmit data onto the network. *See also* **token passing**.

token passing   Method by which network devices access the physical medium based on possession of a small frame called a token. Compare this method to **circuit switching** and **contention**.

Token Ring   Token-passing LAN developed and supported by IBM. Token Ring runs at 4 or 16 Mbps over a ring topology. Similar to IEEE 802.5. *See also* **IEEE 802.5**; **ring topology**; **token passing**.

TokenTalk   Apple Computer's data-link product that allows an AppleTalk network to be connected by Token Ring cables.

transparent bridging   Bridging scheme used in Ethernet and IEEE 802.3 networks. Allows bridges to pass frames along one hop at a time, based on tables that associate end nodes with bridge ports. Bridges are transparent to network end nodes.

Transport layer   Layer 4 of the OSI reference model. This layer is responsible for reliable network communication between end nodes. The Transport layer provides mechanisms for the establishment, maintenance, and termination of virtual circuits, transport fault detection and recovery, and information flow control.

tree topology   A LAN topology that resembles a bus topology. Tree networks can contain branches with multiple nodes. In a tree topology, transmissions from a station propagate the length of the physical medium, and are received by all other stations.

twisted-pair   Transmission medium consisting of two insulated wires arranged in a regular spiral pattern. The wires can be shielded or unshielded. Twisted-pair is common in telephony applications and is increasingly common in data networks.

UDP (User Datagram Protocol)   Connectionless Transport layer protocol in the TCP/IP protocol stack. UDP is a simple protocol that exchanges datagrams without acknowledgments or guaranteed delivery, requiring that error processing and retransmission be handled by other protocols. UDP is defined in RFC 768.

unicast   Regular IP packet sent from a single host to a single host.

UTP (unshielded twisted-pair)   Four-pair wire medium used in a variety of networks. UTP does not require the fixed spacing between connections that is necessary with coaxial-type connections.

virtual circuit (VC)   Logical circuit created to ensure reliable communication between two network devices. A virtual circuit is defined by a VPI/VCI pair, and can be either permanent or switched. Virtual circuits are used in Frame Relay and X.25. In ATM, a virtual circuit is called a virtual channel.

VLAN (virtual LAN)   Group of devices on one or more LANs that are configured (using management software) so that they can communicate as if they were attached to the same wire, when in fact they are located on a number of different LAN segments. Because VLANs are based on logical instead of physical connections, they are extremely flexible.

VLSM (Variable-length Subnet Masking)   Ability to specify a different length subnet mask for the same network number at different locations in the network. VLSM can help optimize available address space.

VTY (Virtual Terminal)   VTYs work like physical terminal ports on routers so they can be managed across a network, usually via Telnet.

WAN (wide area network)   Data communications network that serves users across a broad geographic area and often uses transmission devices provided by common carriers. Frame Relay, SMDS, and X.25 are examples of WANs. Compare with **LAN** and **MAN**.

wildcard mask   32-bit quantity used in conjunction with an IP address to determine which bits in an IP address should be matched and ignored when comparing that address with another IP address. A wildcard mask is specified when defining access list statements.

X.121   ITU-T standard describing an addressing scheme used in X.25 networks. X.121 addresses are sometimes called IDNs (International Data Numbers).

X.21   ITU-T standard for serial communications over synchronous digital lines. The X.21 protocol is used primarily in Europe and Japan.

X.25   ITU-T standard that defines how connections between DTE and DCE are maintained for remote terminal access and computer communications in public data networks. X.25 specifies LAPB, a Data Link layer protocol, and PLP, a network layer protocol. Frame Relay has largely superseded X.25.

ZIP broadcast storm   Occurs when an AppleTalk route advertisement without a corresponding zone triggers the network with a flood of Zone Information Protocol requests.

zone   In AppleTalk, a logical group of network devices.

Zone Information Protocol (ZIP)   A protocol used in AppleTalk to communicate information about AppleTalk zone names and cable ranges.

Zone Information Table (ZIT)   A table of zone name to cable range mappings in AppleTalk. These tables are maintained in each AppleTalk router.

INDEX

Note: Page numbers for illustrations and tables are in italics.

Q

R

Custom Corporate Network Training

Train on Cutting Edge Technology   We can bring the best in skill-based training to your facility to create a real-world hands-on training experience. Global Knowledge has invested millions of dollars in network hardware and software to train our students on the same equipment they will work with on the job. Our relationships with vendors allow us to incorporate the latest equipment and platforms into your on-site labs.

Maximize Your Training Budget   Global Knowledge provides experienced instructors, comprehensive course materials, and all the networking equipment needed to deliver high quality training. You provide the students; we provide the knowledge.

Avoid Travel Expenses   On-site courses allow you to schedule technical training at your convenience, saving time, expense, and the opportunity cost of travel away from the workplace.

Discuss Confidential Topics   Private on-site training permits the open discussion of sensitive issues such as security, access, and network design. We can work with your existing network's proprietary files while demonstrating the latest technologies.

Customize Course Content   Global Knowledge can tailor your courses to include the technologies and the topics which have the greatest impact on your business. We can complement your internal training efforts or provide a total solution to your training needs.

Corporate Pass   The Corporate Pass Discount Program rewards our best network training customers with preferred pricing on public courses, discounts on multimedia training packages, and an array of career planning services.

Global Knowledge Training Lifecycle   Supporting the Dynamic and Specialized Training Requirements of Information Technology Professionals

- Define Profile
- Assess Skills
- Design Training
- Deliver Training
- Test Knowledge
- Update Profile
- Use New Skills

College Credit Recommendation Program   The American Council on Education's CREDIT program recommends 53 Global Knowledge courses for college credit. Now our network training can help you earn your college degree while you learn the technical skills needed for your job. When you attend an ACE-certified Global Knowledge course and pass the associated exam, you earn college credit recommendations for that course. Global Knowledge can establish a transcript record for you with ACE, which you can use to gain credit at a college or as a written record of your professional training that you can attach to your resume.

Registration Information

COURSE FEE: The fee covers course tuition, refreshments, and all course materials. Any parking expenses that may be incurred are not included. Payment or government training form must be received six business days prior to the course date. We will also accept Visa/ MasterCard and American Express. For non-U.S. credit card users, charges will be in U.S. funds and will be converted by your credit card company. Checks drawn on Canadian banks in Canadian funds are acceptable.

COURSE SCHEDULE: Registration is at 8:00 a.m. on the first day. The program begins at 8:30 a.m. and concludes at 4:30 p.m. each day.

CANCELLATION POLICY: Cancellation and full refund will be allowed if written cancellation is received in our office at least six business days prior to the course start date. Registrants who do not attend the course or do not cancel more than six business days in advance are responsible for the full registration fee; you may transfer to a later date provided the course fee has been paid in full. Substitutions may be made at any time. If Global Knowledge must cancel a course for any reason, liability is limited to the registration fee only.

GLOBAL KNOWLEDGE: Global Knowledge programs are developed and presented by industry professionals with "real-world" experience. Designed to help professionals meet today's interconnectivity and interoperability challenges, most of our programs feature hands-on labs that incorporate state-of-the-art communication components and equipment.

ON-SITE TEAM TRAINING: Bring Global Knowledge's powerful training programs to your company. At Global Knowledge, we will custom design courses to meet your specific network requirements. Call 1 (919) 461-8686 for more information.

YOUR GUARANTEE: Global Knowledge believes its courses offer the best possible training in this field. If during the first day you are not satisfied and wish to withdraw from the course, simply notify the instructor, return all course materials, and receive a 100% refund.

In the US:

CALL: 1 (888) 762-4442

FAX: 1 (919) 469-7070

VISIT OUR WEBSITE:

www.globalknowledge.com

MAIL CHECK AND THIS FORM TO:

Global Knowledge

Suite 200

114 Edinburgh South

P.O. Box 1187

Cary, NC 27512

In Canada:

CALL: 1 (800) 465-2226

FAX: 1 (613) 567-3899

VISIT OUR WEBSITE:

www.globalknowledge.com.ca

MAIL CHECK AND THIS FORM TO:

Global Knowledge

Suite 1601

393 University Ave.

Toronto, ON M5G 1E6

REGISTRATION INFORMATION:

Course title _____

Course location _____   Course date _____

Name/title _____   Company _____

Name/title _____   Company _____

Name/title _____   Company _____

Address _____ Telephone _____ Fax _____

City _____ State/Province _____ Zip/Postal Code _____

Credit card _____ Card # _____ Expiration date _____

Signature _____

LICENSE AGREEMENT

Prepare for Exam 640-404: CCNP Cisco LAN Switch Configuration using the most effective Test-Prep CD-ROM available!

ON THE CD-ROM YOU'LL FIND:

- The *CCNP Cisco LAN Switch Configuration (Exam 640-404)* TEST YOURSELF Personal Testing Center Software, which includes more than 250 challenging practice questions with detailed answers – see facing page.

- Complete electronic version of study guide with hyperlinked table of contents – easy to search and convenient for online studying.